COMEDY: *Meaning and Form*

COMEDY
Meaning and Form

Edited with an Introduction by

Robert W. Corrigan

NEW YORK UNIVERSITY

 **CHANDLER PUBLISHING COMPANY**
An Intext Publisher · Scranton, Pennsylvania 18515

International Standard Book No. 0-8102-0070-8
Copyright © 1965 by Chandler Publishing Company
Library of Congress Catalog Card No. 65-17452
Printed in the United States of America

I-U-RI

For Eric Bentley, who continues to lead us.

Contents

A Note on Organization ix

INTRODUCTION 1
  Robert W. Corrigan *Comedy and the Comic Spirit* . . 1

I. THE SPIRIT OF COMEDY 13
  Christopher Fry *Comedy* 15
  Wylie Sypher *The Meanings of Comedy* 18
  W. H. Auden *Notes on the Comic* 61
  George Santayana *The Comic Mask* and *Carnival* . . . 73
  Nathan A. Scott, Jr. *The Bias of Comedy and
    the Narrow Escape into Faith* 81

II. THE FORM OF COMEDY 117
  Susanne Langer *The Comic Rhythm* 119
  Northrop Frye *The Mythos of Spring: Comedy* . . . 141
  Benjamin Lehmann *Comedy and Laughter* 163

III. THE CHARACTERISTICS OF COMEDY 179
  L. C. Knights *Notes on Comedy* 181
  Harold H. Watts *The Sense of Regain: A Theory of Comedy* 192
  L. J. Potts *The Subject Matter of Comedy* 198
  Arthur Koestler *Comedy* 214

IV. THE NATURE OF COMEDY 217
  Al Capp *The Comedy of Charlie Chaplin* 219
  J. L. Styan *Types of Comedy* 230
  Richard Duprey *Whatever Happened to Comedy?* . . . 243

V. THE PSYCHOLOGY OF COMEDY 251
  Sigmund Freud *Jokes and the Comic* 253

Ludwig Jekels *On the Psychology of Comedy* 263
Martin Grotjahn *Beyond Laughter: A Summing Up* . . 270

VI. ON FARCE AND SATIRE 277
Eric Bentley *Farce* 279
Vsevolod Meyerhold *Farce* 304
Robert C. Stephenson *Farce as Method* 317
R. C. Elliott *The Satirist and Society* 327
Al Capp *"It's Hideously True"* 343

VII. THE CRITICISM OF COMEDY 351
Robert W. Corrigan *Aristophanic Comedy: The Conscience
of a Conservative* 353
C. L. Barber *The Saturnalian Pattern in
Shakespeare's Comedy* 363
Gustave Lanson *Molière and Farce* 378
L. C. Knights *Restoration Comedy: The Reality
and the Myth* 397
Reed Whittemore *Shaw's Abstract Clarity* 415
Ruby Cohn *A Comic Complex and a Complex Comic* . . 427

VIII. FROM THE CLASSICS OF COMIC THEORY . . 441
Molière PREFACE TO *Tartuffe* 443
Charles Baudelaire *On the Essence of Laughter* . . . 448
George Meredith FROM *An Essay on Comedy* 466
Henri Bergson FROM *Laughter* 471

SELECTED BIBLIOGRAPHY 478

A Note on Organization

The eight sections into which I have divided this book probably do not need much explaining. Part I deals with the spirit of comedy, which I discuss in "Comedy and the Comic Spirit." In Parts II through IV I have included essays which are primarily concerned with the nature and form of comedy. While I do not believe that comedy has a fixed form, the essays in Part II do discuss several basic formal patterns which generally apply to most comedy written before the twentieth century, and they can also be helpful to us in our attempts to understand the comedies of today insofar as they describe what the modern writer of comedy is rebelling against. Section V is, regretably, too small. A whole book of essays could be devoted to the question "Why do we laugh?" My only consolation is that even if such a book existed, we probably would not be much closer to a definitive answer to this sticky question. Section VI is a cause for both joy and despair. Like its counterpart, melodrama, farce has been woefully neglected by modern critics. Erroneously, we seem to be above farce. Only the giant among our present-day critics, Eric Bentley, has dealt with the subject, and his essay (based on his earlier one, "The Psychology of Farce") is the only full-dress attempt to deal with the subject in any adequate way. It is sad that the pickings are so slim. I am delighted to be able to use both of Mr. Capp's essays, and particularly "It's Hideously True." I believe it to be one of the "buried" (in *Life* magazine) classics of modern criticism, and I know of few pieces that reveal so much about the nature of satire and its relationship to political freedom. This essay, written at the height of the late Senator McCarthy's power, is both a challenge and a warning which we can still take seriously today. The rationale of Section VII is fairly obvious. I have tried to select relatively recent essays which discuss the comedy of six of the great masters of the comic. Finally, in Section VIII, I have included excerpts from four of the classics of comic theory. With one important exception, there is nothing new in this. Most of this material is readily available elsewhere; however, I have included it for those teachers who may, quite legitimately, want to relate the modern essays to the earlier thinking on comedy.

Finally, I should like to acknowledge the help of those who did so much to make this book possible. As always, the permission editors of the various publishers with whom I have corresponded have been most cooperative, and I particularly want to thank Helen Schwabe of Doubleday who has been so consistently gracious. I also want to thank Wylie Sypher, Lionel Knights, Al Capp, Robert Stephenson, Ruby Cohn, and Harold Watts for their willingness to let me use their work. I have acknowledged my debt to and admiration for Eric Bentley elsewhere.

R. W. C.

COMEDY: *Meaning and Form*

INTRODUCTION

Comedy and the Comic Spirit

ROBERT W. CORRIGAN

A few years ago in a seminar on comedy I asked (I am sure because of my own frustration at being unable to solve so many of comedy's baffling problems) the students in the class for a definition of comedy in one hundred words or less. After what seemed an interminable silence—we were all a little embarrassed by the directness of my question—a young man reached into his pocket and pulled out a crumpled newspaper clipping and passsed it up to me, mumbling something to the effect that "this is it!" I read it; it was not a definition but it was a wholly valid example:

MAN'S CORK LEG CHEATS DEATH
Keeps Him Afloat After Leap Into River

A carpenter's cork leg kept him afloat and prevented him from taking his life by jumping into the Mississippi river from a Canal St. ferry, Fourth District police reported Monday.

Taken to Charity hospital after his rescue was Jacob Lewis, Negro, 52, 2517 Annette. Suffering from a possible skull fracture and internal injuries, he was placed in a psychiatric ward for examination.

Police said that after his release from the hospital he would be booked for disturbing the peace by attempting to commit suicide.

The incident occurred about 11:25 p.m. Sunday while the ferry, M. P. Crescent was tied up on the Algiers side of the river.

Police quoted a ferry passenger as saying he saw the man leap from a rest room window into the water. When the call was sounded, two employes, James McCaleb, 43, 709 Wilks Lane, and Edward Johnson, 54, 2113 Whitney, Algiers, both Negroes, lowered a boat and rescued Lewis.

He was brought into the boat about 100 yards from the ferry after he refused to grab life preservers the men threw him.

Ferry employes said he told them he had no desire to live. His attempt on
his life might have succeeded if his cork leg had not kept him afloat, police
said. (*New Orleans Times-Picayune*)

We cannot help but laugh at this grotesque report of a thwarted suicide, and yet in its own grim way it does reiterate the commonplace
that comedy and laughter are serious business.

Strangely enough, while comedy's intriguing complexities have always been of special interest to philosophers—and more recently psychologists—they seldom have been dealt with in any extensive or
systematic way by the critics and theorists of the drama. But this state
of affairs seems to be changing. In a time when our next tomorrow
must always be in question, comedy's tenacious greed for life, its instinct
for self-preservation, and its attempts to mediate the pressures of our
daily life seem to qualify it as the most appropriate mode for the
drama of the mid-twentieth century. Realizing these facts, the critic's
vision has begun to expand: not merely is he interested in the
comic elements of a particular play (or group of plays), he is beginning now to investigate the whole of comedy's wide world.

Coming relatively late in the critical game, the new criticism of comedy tends to be freer and more adventurous in spirit than that of the
other forms, and especially that of tragedy. There are no authorities to
get in the way; none of the age-old assumptions to overcome; few
widely held prejudices to discard; and no attractive, but false, critical
positions to mislead us. As this volume testifies, this attitude has resulted in a rapidly growing body of critical work on comedy which is
as exciting as it is penetrating, and which convinces without being
dogmatic.

But in spite of all this activity we must enter the realm of comedy
with caution. "Beware" must be the watchword, because countless pit-
falls must be avoided, one being the risk of missing the subject altogether. (To deal with tragedy, by comparison, is relatively simple.)
Nor should we forget the lesson to be learned from the first recorded
attempt to take comedy seriously. Recall the prophecy of Plato's
Symposium: It is early morning and Socrates is still rambling on. He
finally begins talking about comedy and proposes his theory that
tragedy and comedy spring from the same roots. "To this they were
constrained to assent, being drowsy, and not quite following the argument. And first of all Aristophanes dropped off to sleep." "Such was
the charm," as Henry Myers has pointed out, "of the first theory of
comedy! We leave the *Symposium* with an unforgettable picture of

an eminent philosopher putting an eminent comic poet to sleep with a lecture on the comic spirit."

With this image fresh in our minds, we move on. A second warning: In our investigation of the general nature of comedy we must resist falling victim to what I have called the "formalistic fallacy" in the study of dramatic genres. This is a kind of thinking about drama based on the assumption that there are certain formal and structural characteristics which all comedy of all ages must share in common. But where in the history of drama will one find such formal consistency? Certainly not in classical Greek or Roman drama; nor in English stage comedy of the Elizabethan, Restoration, or eighteenth century periods; nor, for that matter, in the so-called "black" comedy of our own age. While it is true that there seem to be some characteristics of comedy which can be called "universal"—the presence of lovers, the defeat of an imposter figure and his subsequent assimilation into the restored social fabric, an inverted Oedipal pattern in which the son triumphs over the father, and the presence of violence without its consequences—these finally have thematic rather than structural significance. The structure of each play is unique, and even within the work of a given playwright (as opposed to a theatre machinist) there is an evolution of form which makes it impossible to consider his work in terms of consistent structural patterns.

The constant in comedy is the comic view of life or the comic spirit: the sense that no matter how many times man is knocked down he somehow manages to pull himself up and keep on going. Thus, while tragedy is a celebration of man's capacity to aspire and suffer, comedy celebrates his capacity to endure. Eric Bentley put it another way in his magnificent book, *The Life of the Drama:* "In tragedy, but by no means comedy, the self-preservation instinct is overruled. . . . The comic sense tries to cope with the daily, hourly, inescapable difficulty of being. For if everyday life has an undercurrent or cross-current of the tragic, the main current is material for comedy." And Christopher Fry describes how these two currents flow together to form the mainstream of life when he writes in the opening essay of this book:

Laughter did not come by chance, but how or why it came is beyond comprehension, unless we think of it as a kind of perception. The human animal, beginning to feel his spiritual inches, broke in onto an unfamiliar tension of life, where laughter became inevitable. But how? Could he, in his first unlaughing condition, have contrived a comic view of life and then developed the strange rib-shaking response? Or is it not more likely that when he was able to grasp the tragic nature of time he was of a stature to sense its comic nature also; and, by the experience of tragedy and the intuition of comedy, to make his difficult way? The difference between tragedy and comedy is the difference between experience and intuition. In the experience we strive against every condition of our animal life: against death, against the frustration of ambition, against the instability of human love. In the intuition we trust the arduous eccentricities we're born to, and see the oddness of a creature who has never got acclimatized to being created.

Although identifying the continuing spirit of comedy is essential, it does not help us very much when it comes to explaining why particular plays which we are accustomed to calling comedies are comic. It is at this point that we enter the realm of contradiction. For, while it is true, as Dr. Johnson once observed that "comedy has been particularly unpropitious to definers," we do nonetheless know that it exists and is readily identifiable. We laugh at Volpone even when his situation is desperate, and we are moved to tears by Charlie Chaplin at the end of *City Lights* in spite of the ludicrousness of some of the early scenes. Even in those plays where the laughable and the painful are inextricably combined—for example, the Falstaff plays or Peter Brook's "Beckettized" production of *King Lear*—audiences have no difficulty following the right threads in the design. In short, the problems of comedy are seldom artistic; playwrights know how to write plays which their audiences will recognize as comic. The big question is: How do we know?

Invariably, every discussion of comedy begins with (or eventually reaches) at least a passing reference to tragedy. The reverse is seldom true: in most essays on tragedy, comedy is never mentioned. This is more than a quirk in the history of dramatic criticism. Indeed, this phenomenon might just provide us with an important clue in our search for an answer to "How do we know?" In this regard, an apparent exception to the rule is illuminating. In the beginning of the fifth chapter of *The Poetics,* Aristotle defines comedy as follows:

Comedy is an artistic imitation of men of an inferior moral bent; faulty, however, not in any or every way, but only in so far as their shortcomings are ludicrous; for the Ludicrous is a species or part, not all, of the Ugly. It may be described as that kind of shortcoming and deformity which does not strike us as painful, and causes no harm to others; a ready example is afforded by the comic mask, which is ludicrous, being ugly and distorted, without any suggestion of pain.

The two key ideas in this definition are *the Ludicrous* and *the absence of pain;* and although it is clear from what follows that Aristotle is more concerned with their tragic contrasts—*the serious* and *the pain-*

ful—he does establish two fundamental boundaries of the comic. Let us examine them briefly.

In making this distinction between the ludicrous and the serious Aristotle was not denying the potential seriousness of comedy, rather, much like Plato, he was postulating the idea that comedy—as well as tragedy—derives from positive attitudes toward value. For something to be serious we must assign to it serious value, and this can occur only when there exists a larger system of values which we accept as valid and of which the specific value is a part. Thus, while Aristotle describes the ludicrous as a species of the ugly which has no painful effects, it is impossible to set the limits of the ludicrous until the serious has first been defined and accepted. A thing cannot be ugly or immoral until we have first agreed upon what is beautiful and moral. This explains why it is we can discuss tragedy (which deals directly with the serious) without reference to comedy, but when talking about comedy, why we must always refer to the standards of seriousness which give it its essential definition. (This also explains something I shall touch upon later in this essay: why it is that when commonly accepted standards of value disintegrate—as they have in our own time—the clear-cut distinctions between tragedy and comedy break-down as well, with the result that the dominant form of drama is one in which the serious and the ludicrous have merged to the point that they are nearly inseparable.)

Thus, for all of its positive characteristics, comedy is negative in its definition. An audience will refuse to react positively (in this case, laugh) to any presentation in a ludicrous manner of what they believe to be the true, the good, or the beautiful. We laugh, for example, at the absent-minded professor, not because of his learning, but because his absent-mindedness is not consistent with his erudition. If in an episode of *Li'l Abner,* Al Capp has Senator Jack S. Phogbound fall off the platform in the middle of a speech most of us would think of it as a comic event. (If we were interested at all; indifference is the deadly foe of all comedy.) If, on the other hand, the same thing were to happen to Sir Winston Churchill, we would not, although it is conceivable that a member of the extreme left wing might think such an event were funny. But if he did so, it would be because such a person did not accept those values which Sir Winston embodies as good, and therefore he is an appropriate subject for ridicule. In the same way, we can never be induced to laugh at the beautiful *as* beautiful. A beautiful woman is not funny; a beautiful woman who opens her mouth and speaks in a high, squeaking voice is very funny, because she fails to measure up to the standard which her appearance had previously established. Such a standard may not always be a logically defensible one—more often than not it isn't—but it holds in the theatre so long as the audience takes it to be so. Such is also the case with the beautiful but dumb blonde. The dumbness is an analog to the squeaking voice, though there is no logical, necessary relationship between beauty and intelligence. It is merely that we somehow expect it.

However, our laughter in these instances cannot be explained in the simple terms of incongruity. For incongruity, no matter how it is conceived—expectation and consequence, tension and elasticity, reality and illusion—does not, as many theorists have maintained, necessarily evoke a comic response, nor is it unique to the comic form. Incongruity is a technique which has been effectively used in all dramatic forms— serious and comic. It is capable of producing dire emotions as well as side-splitting laughter. The coming of Birnam Wood to Dunsinane, for instance, is unquestionably incongruous, but no one in the play or the audience thinks it is funny. The same is true of Richard III's seduction of Lady Anne. Indeed, as Aristotle pointed out in Chapter XIV of *The Poetics,* to show a terrible act committed by a character from whom we expect love (hence, an incongruous act) is the most effective way of producing a tragic effect. In fact, I believe a good case could be made for the idea that incongruity is the cause of horror in the theatre as well as laughter. What is operative in the ludicrous is not a question of mere incongruity, but a perceptible falling short of an already agreed upon standard of seriousness which we have set for the object, or which is set by the object for itself.

One boundary of the comic's realm, then, is that line where the ludicrous and the serious meet. We turn now to its other boundary. In his essay on farce (see page 279), Eric Bentley characterizes that form as one in which violence can operate without fear of consequence. He goes on to show how the violence of farce becomes the basic ore of comedy. This observation is significant, but it needs enlarging. One essential difference between comedy and farce is that in the former there are definite consequences (one reason why we say comedy *is* of greater consequence than farce). But these consequences have had all of the elements of pain and permanent defeat removed. Thus it is that the pratfall is the symbol of the comic, and this symbol can be carried to its outermost limits by saying that in comedy death is never taken seriously or even considered as a serious threat. Aristotle perceived, correctly, that while the ludicrous (whether it take the form of the grotesque, of exaggeration, or of physical deformity) was the proper subject matter for comedy, manifestations of the ludicrous must be rendered painless before they can become comic. The writhings of the cartoon character who has just received a blow on the head, the violent events in some of Molière's plays, or the mayhem committed on and by slapstick clowns remains funny only so long as it is quite clear that no real pain is involved. One reason why the violence of slapstick is so effective in films (one thinks of the pies and boppings of the Three Stooges or the Ritz Brothers) is that it is next to impossible to fear for the characters since the actors have no physical reality. On the stage, if a fight—even one intended to be funny—appears to be an actual fight, the audience may well begin to fear for the actors, that is, take seriously the possibility of pain. This very phenomenon is in fact used as a dramatic device by Leoncavallo in the last scene of *I Pagliacci*. So far as the audience on the stage is concerned, the threats to the heroine are only simulated, and this audience laughs. We, who know the true nature of the events and realize that if Canio should get his hands on Nedda she would be slain immediately, not only fail to find the situation funny but also feel fear for the girl. Indeed, our feelings are heightened by the lack of awareness on the part of those people who are close enough to save the doomed Nedda. Thus it is that whenever a serious deed or event is allowed to enter the field of comedy (as frequently happens) the serious effect must, in some way, be cut off. Such is the case in Jonson's *Volpone* in which the possibility of the rape is never seriously considered because of the nature of the circumstances in which the scene occurs; or in *The Merchant of Venice* in which the presence of Portia as the judge assures us that the potentially dreadful bond will never be paid.

From these examples we may draw our second conclusion: comedy operates in that middle zone between the serious and the absurd which Aristotle called the Ludicrous. It is an area which excludes nobility of character, painful consequences, and the consummation of any events which are likely to offend our moral sensibilities.

Another false, but widely held, assumption about comedy is that there are certain themes, situations, or character types which are the special province of comedy, or are at least thought to be especially compatible to the comic muse. But if we examine the history of drama, we discover that we must reject the assumption. In this regard, I am particularly indebted to Richmond Lattimore, who clarifies this problem once and for all in his fine book, *The Poetry of Greek Tragedy*. He shows that *Oedipus Rex* is an example of the story of "the lost one found." As such it is, like *The Importance of Being Earnest,* a "success" story, a story type which traditionally has been particularly well-suited to comedy. There is no doubt that *Oedipus Rex* is a success story, but no one would ever call it a comedy.

All of the materials available to the dramatist, whether they be from his own experience, from history, or from the accrued traditions of the drama itself are, in fact, neutral. It is only by the playwright's shaping of them that they take on meaning—a meaning which may be tragic, comic, melodramatic, farcical, or what have you. Not to understand this fact is to blur the crucial distinctions which exist between art and life. In life, the meaning we assign to any situation will be the product of personal determinants. But our response to an event which occurs in a play will be the product of the causes built into that play by the playwright. In both cases it is the view and the value assigned to it which will determine whether we consider a situation as serious or comic or remain completely indifferent to it. For example, the "battle of the sexes" is usually mentioned as a typical comic plot. And while it is true that the struggle for power in the home has provided a comic impetus for many plays, beginning with *Lysistrata* right up to the latest Broadway comedy hit, this same struggle is also at the heart of such eminently serious works as *Macbeth* and Strindberg's *The Father*. Or again, a girl surrounded by a host of suitors has been used as the basic predicament of countless comic plots, but surely this is the situation of Penelope, Nina Leeds, and even (in a perverted way) of Hedda Gabler as well. Nor will it do for us to claim for comedy the generation of action out of ignorance or wrong reason, since *Oedipus Rex, King Lear,* and *Othello* come to mind as readily as *As You Like It, The Would-Be Gentleman,* and *The School for Scandal.* In short, for every comic use that has been made of a given situation, one can find examples of a serious use made of the same situation. And the reverse of this is equally true. In each case the deciding factor is the way in which the artist has operated upon his materials so they will assume a shape that will be either comic or serious. In so doing he will also shape the audience's response to his creation.

Why, then, it might be asked, do we sometimes laugh at works—such as nineteenth-century melodramas—which were intended to have a serious effect, but now clearly no longer do? Do such plays, unlike cheese, become milder with age? If, as we have said, the ultimate effect of a play is dependent upon values assigned to it by the audience, then one of the chief functions of the artist is to provide those signs which will lead the audience to draw the proper conclusions about the play's meaning. These signs are usually of two kinds: nat-

ural signs which all men know and recognize (weeping as a sign of
pain or grief), and conventional signs which are commonly agreed
upon for a given time and place (a black arm band as a sign of
mourning). Often, signs of this latter kind have been used by dramatists to signify moral significance. Thus, when a black moustache is
used to signify an evil man, it is quite clear that this significance is
valid only so long as the audience assigns the value on the basis of
such a sign. When, for whatever reason, the sign is no longer accepted,
and when no other natural signs are present in the work, the inference from sign to value is impossible, and the sign ceases to have
meaning. Further, when it is obvious that a work was intended to be
taken seriously, but the basis for such valuation has lost its meaning,
the work becomes absurd, and therefore laughable. This change does
not mean that the play has become a comedy; it is simply that the
work has fallen short of that level of seriousness which it has set for
itself, and has consequently become, *de facto,* an object of ridicule.

I could go on discussing the many aspects of comedy, but this is,
after all, the purpose of the essays which follow. There is, however,
one other broad area of misunderstanding which I should like to
clarify at least a little bit before the reader enters comedy's labyrin-
thine world. One of the most striking characteristics of the modern
drama is the way in which the age-old distinctions between the tragic
and the comic (the serious and the ludicrous, the painful and the
painless) have been obliterated. This has not been a process of com-
mingling as so many critics have, I believe, erroneously asserted. The
combining of the tragic and the comic in a single play is nearly as old
as the drama itself—I can trace it back at least to Sophocles. But
what is happening today is something quite different. So much so,
that it is questionable whether we should even use the terms comedy
and tragedy any longer.

As I said earlier in this introduction, both tragedy and comedy
depend upon generally accepted standards of values. Such norms make
it possible to establish those hierarchies of seriousness upon which the
drama has been traditionally based. However, because in our time
Nietzsche shouted, "God is dead!" there are no generally accepted
values, no universally valid systems, no publicly meaningful hierarchies. Without them all experience becomes equally serious or equally
ludicrous. Or, as Ionesco said, "It all comes to the same thing anyway;
comic and tragic are merely two aspects of the same situation, and I
have now reached the stage when I find it hard to distinguish one
from the other."

The first playwright to reflect this changed perception in the theatre was Chekhov.[1] Critics are continually telling us that Chekhov is funny, and furthermore we know that both *The Sea Gull* and *The Cherry Orchard* were called comedies by their author, and that he conceived of none of his plays as tragedies. But Chekhov's plays are so unlike most of the comedies of the past that we are not sure we should trust even the author's calling them comedies. Perhaps a better way of understanding what is meant when we describe Chekhov as a comic writer is to recall that he was writing a drama that was to show "life as it is." Another way of putting Chekhov's phrase, "life as it is" is expressed in Santayana's statement, "Everything in Nature is lyrical in its ideal essence, tragic in its fate, and comic in its existence." This provides a very important insight into the nature of Chekhovian comedy (not to mention the form and tone of his plays), for his characters respond to all three of Santayana's levels with an especial intensity. They are comedians by necessity, smitten with a tragic sense of life, and lyrically in love with the ideal in a world poorly equipped to satisfy such aspirations.

The essential quality of the "is-ness" of life is its absurdity, its futility. Some would argue that this is tragic, perhaps the most tragic condition of all, but as Dorothy Sayers has wisely pointed out: "The whole tragedy of futility is that it never succeeds in achieving tragedy. In its blackest moments it is inevitably doomed to the comic gesture." But make no mistake, this is a special kind of comedy, a grotesque kind of comedy, which makes us laugh with a lump in our throats. This is so because for all of its awareness of the absurdity of experience, it is also extremely conscious of the suffering, struggle, and failure of experience. Both the complexity of this condition and the difficulty that the playwright has in giving it dramatic form is beautifully described by Christopher Fry in his already mentioned essay.

I know that when I set about writing a comedy the idea presents itself to me first of all as tragedy. The characters press on to the theme with all their divisions and perplexities heavy about them; they are already entered for the race to doom, and good and evil are an infernal tangle skinning the fingers that try to unravel them. If the characters were not qualified for tragedy there would be no comedy, and to some extent I have to cross the one before I can light the other. In a century less flayed and quivering we might reach it more directly, but not now unless every word we write is going to mock us.

---

[1] The remarks on Chekhov which follow are in large measure similar to what I have already written on this subject in my introduction to *Six Plays of Chekhov*.

In the past fifty years the Chekhovian form has come to dominate much of the theatre. We see it in the plays of such different writers as Beckett, Ionesco, Pinter, and Albee, all of whom use what were once considered comic techniques to serve serious aims. Their belief that life is a grand guignol, but with less sense—that to live is only to make the comic gesture, or what Pirandello called the comic grimace—employs the ludicrousness of comedy to show that life is itself absurd. It is a view of life and drama which employs the comic to make its point, a point that is comic only in the sense that Baudelaire found life comic. In the work of all these playwrights the lines of the comic mask have become those of the tragic; in them we find that the relationship of means to ends is a paradox. Whereas in the comedy of earlier times, comic means were used to comic ends, in the modern theatre comic means are employed to serious ends. The comic has become a transparency through which we see to the serious. Comedy is unquestionably the proper mirror of our times; but it is also true that it reveals our life to us as "through a glass darkly."

Part One

THE SPIRIT OF COMEDY

Christopher Fry

COMEDY

Wylie Sypher

THE MEANINGS OF COMEDY

W. H. Auden

NOTES ON THE COMIC

George Santayana

THE COMIC MASK *AND* CARNIVAL

Nathan A. Scott, Jr.

THE BIAS OF COMEDY AND THE NARROW ESCAPE INTO FAITH

Comedy

CHRISTOPHER FRY *

A friend once told me that when he was under the influence of ether he dreamed he was turning over the pages of a great book, in which he knew he would find, on the last page, the meaning of life. The pages of the book were alternately tragic and comic, and he turned page after page, his excitement growing, not only because he was approaching the answer but because he couldn't know, until he arrived, on which side of the book the final page would be. At last it came: the universe opened up to him in a hundred words: and they were uproariously funny. He came back to consciousness crying with laughter, remembering everything. He opened his lips to speak. It was then that the great and comic answer plunged back out of his reach.

If I had to draw a picture of the person of Comedy it is so I should like to draw it: the tears of laughter running down the face, one hand still lying on the tragic page which so nearly contained the answer, the lips about to frame the great revelation, only to find it had gone as disconcertingly as a chair twitched away when we went to sit down. Comedy is an escape, not from truth but from despair: a narrow escape into faith. It believes in a universal cause for delight, even though knowledge of the cause is always twitched away from under us, which leaves us to rest on our own buoyancy. In tragedy every moment is eternity; in comedy eternity is a moment. In tragedy we suffer pain; in comedy pain is a fool, suffered gladly.

Charles Williams once said to me—indeed it was the last thing he said to me: he died not long after: and it was shouted from the tail-board of a moving bus, over the heads of pedestrians and bicyclists outside the Midland Station, Oxford—"When we're dead we shall have the sensation of having enjoyed life altogether, whatever has

---

* Christopher Fry, "Comedy," *Vogue* (January), 1951.

happened to us." The distance between us widened, and he leaned out into the space so that his voice should reach me: "Even if we've been murdered, what a pleasure to have been capable of it!"; and, having spoken the words for comedy, away he went like the revelation which almost came out of the ether.

He was not at all saying that everything is for the best in the best of all possible worlds. He was saying—or so it seems to me—that there is an angle of experience where the dark is distilled into light: either here or hereafter, in or out of time: where our tragic fate finds itself with perfect pitch, and goes straight to the key which creation was composed in. And comedy senses and reaches out to this experience. It says, in effect, that, groaning as we may be, we move in the figure of a dance, and, so moving, we trace the outline of the mystery.

Laughter did not come by chance, but how or why it came is beyond comprehension, unless we think of it as a kind of perception. The human animal, beginning to feel his spiritual inches, broke in on to an unfamiliar tension of life, where laughter became inevitable. But how? Could he, in his first unlaughing condition, have contrived a comic view of life and then developed the strange rib-shaking response? Or is it not more likely that when he was able to grasp the tragic nature of time he was of a stature to sense its comic nature also; and, by the experience of tragedy and the intuition of comedy, to make his difficult way? The difference between tragedy and comedy is the difference between experience and intuition. In the experience we strive against every condition of our animal life: against death, against the frustration of ambition, against the instability of human love. In the intuition we trust the arduous eccentricities we're born to, and see the oddness of a creature who has never got acclimatized to being created. Laughter inclines me to know that man is essential spirit; his body, with its functions and accidents and frustrations, is endlessly quaint and remarkable to him; and though comedy accepts our position in time, it barely accepts our posture in space.

The bridge by which we cross from tragedy to comedy and back again is precarious and narrow. We find ourselves in one or the other by the turn of a thought; a turn such as we make when we turn from speaking to listening. I know that when I set about writing a comedy the idea presents itself to me first of all as tragedy. The characters press on to the theme with all their divisions and perplexities heavy about them; they are already entered for the race to doom, and good and evil are an infernal tangle skinning the fingers that try to unravel them. If the characters were not qualified for tragedy there would be no comedy, and to some extent I have to cross the one before I can light on the other. In a century less flayed and quivering we might reach it more directly; but not now, unless every word we write is going to mock us. A bridge has to be crossed, a thought has to be turned. Somehow the characters have to unmortify themselves: to affirm life and assimilate death and preserve in joy. Their hearts must be as determined as the phoenix; what burns must also light and renew: not by a vulnerable optimism but by a hard-won maturity of delight, by the intuition of comedy, an active patience declaring the solvency of good. The Book of Job is the great reservoir of comedy. "But there is a spirit in man . . . Fair weather cometh out of the north . . . The blessing of him that was ready to perish came upon me: And I caused the widow's heart to sing for joy."

I have come, you may think, to the verge of saying that comedy is greater than tragedy. On the verge I stand and go no further. Tragedy's experience hammers against the mystery to make a breach which would admit the whole triumphant answer. Intuition has no such potential. But there are times in the state of man when comedy has a special worth, and the present is one of them: a time when the loudest faith has been faith in a trampling materialism, when literature has been thought unrealistic which did not mark and remark our poverty and doom. Joy (of a kind) has been all on the devil's side, and one of the necessities of our time is to redeem it. If not, we are in poor sort to meet the circumstances, the circumstances being the contention of death with life, which is to say evil with good, which is to say desolation with delight. Laughter may seem to be only like an exhalation of air, but out of that air we came; in the beginning we inhaled it; it is a truth, not a fantasy, a truth voluble of good which comedy stoutly maintains.

The Meanings of Comedy*

WYLIE SYPHER

I. Our New Sense of the Comic

Doubtless Meredith and Bergson were alike wearied by the "heavy moralizings" of the nineteenth century, with its "terrific tonnage," and thus sought relief in comedy of manners. For both really confine their idea of comedy within the range of comedy of manners; and they have given us our finest, most sensitive theory of that form. Comedy, says Bergson, is a game—a game that imitates life. And in writing the introduction to *The Egoist,* Meredith thinks of this game as dealing with human nature in the drawing room "where we have no dust of the struggling outer world, no mire, no violent crashes." The after-taste of laughter may be bitter, Bergson grants, but comedy is itself only "a slight revolt on the surface of social life." Its gaiety happens like froth along a beach, for comedy looks at man from the outside: "It will go no farther."

For us, today, comedy goes a great deal farther—as it did for the ancients with their cruel sense of the comic. Indeed, to appreciate Bergson and Meredith we must see them both in a new perspective, now that we have lived amid the "dust and crashes" of the twentieth century and have learned how the direst calamities that befall man seem to prove that human life at its depths is inherently absurd. The comic and the tragic views of life no longer exclude each other. Perhaps the most important discovery in modern criticism is the perception that comedy and tragedy are somehow akin, or that comedy can tell us many things about our situation even tragedy cannot. At the heart of the nineteenth century Dostoevsky discovered this, and Søren Kierkegaard spoke as a modern man when he wrote that the comic

---

* Wylie Sypher, "The Meanings of Comedy," in *Comedy,* Wylie Sypher, ed. (Doubleday & Company, 1956), pp. 193–258.

involuntary impulses; they make "psychological gestures." Surrealism surprises us with the *imprévu,* the unexpected psychic gesture controlled by the Id.

Thus the comic gesture reaches down toward the Unconscious, that dim world usually assigned to tragedy, the midnight terrain where Macbeth met the witches. The joke and the dream incongruously distort the logic of our rational life. The joke and the dream are "interruptions" in the pattern of our consciousness. So also, possibly, is any truly creative work of art a form of "interruption" of our normal patterns or designs of seeing and speaking, which are mere formulas written on the surface layer of the mind. Underneath this surface layer is the pattern-free (non-Gestalt) activity of the unconscious, undisciplined self, which cannot be expressed by the forms consciousness imposes on our vision and thought. The deepest "meanings" of art therefore arise wherever there is an interplay between the patterns of surface-perception and the pressures of depth-perception. Then the stated meanings will fringe off into unstated and unstatable meanings of great power, felt dimly but compellingly. Behind the trim scaffolding of artistic "form" and logic there whispers, for a moment, the wild voice of the unconscious self—using the disturbed language of the dream and the jest, as well as the language of tragedy. This uncivilized but knowing self Nietzsche once called Dionysian, the self that feels archaic pleasure and archaic pain. The substratum of the world of art, Nietzsche says, is "the terrible wisdom of Silenus," and Silenus is the satyr-god of comedy leading the ecstatic "chorus of natural beings who as it were live ineradicably behind every civilization." The confused statements of the dream and the joke are intolerable to the daylight, sane, Apollonian self.

No doubt the tragic experience reaches deeply down into the "interruptions" of conscious life, conjuring up our grim disinherited selves and expressing the "formless" intimations of archaic fear and archaic struggle. But in an artist like Dostoevsky the comic experience can reach as deeply down, perhaps because the comic artist begins by accepting the absurd, "the improbable," in human existence. Therefore he has less resistance than the tragic artist to representing what seems incoherent and inexplicable, and thus lowers the threshold of artistic perception. After all, comedy, not tragedy, admits the disorderly into the realm of art; the grotesque depends upon an irrational focus. Ours is a century of disorder and irrationalism.

Is it any wonder that along with our wars, our machines, and our neuroses we should find new meanings in comedy, or that comedy should represent our plight better than tragedy? For tragedy needs

the "noble," and nowadays we seldom can assign any usable meaning
to "nobility." The comic now is more relevant, or at least more
accessible, than the tragic. As Mephisto explains to God, one cannot
understand man unless one is able to laugh: "For man must strive,
and striving, he must err."

Man has been defined as a social animal, a tool-making animal, a
speaking animal, a thinking animal, a religious animal. He is also a
laughing animal (Malraux takes the "archaic smile" in sculpture as
a sign man has become aware of his soul). Yet this definition of man
is the obscurest of all, for we do not really know what laughter is, or
what causes it. Though he calls his essay "Laughter," Bergson never
plumbs this problem. We have never agreed about the motives, mechanism, or even the temper of laughter. Usually the Greeks laughed
to express a disdain roused by seeing someone's mischance, deformity,
or ugliness. One of the least agreeable scenes in classical literature is
the cruel, casual slaying of wretched Dolon, a Trojan spy caught
skulking one night by Diomedes and Ulysses near the Greek camp;
after tormenting Dolon with a hint he can save his life, the gleeful
Ulysses, smiling no doubt an archaic smile, watches Diomedes strike
off the head of their captive, "green with fear." There is also scan-
dalous Homeric mirth among the Olympians themselves when lame
Hephaistos calls the gods together to ridicule his wife Aphrodite, lying
trapped with brazen Ares, god of war. To be laughed at by the
ancients was to be defiled.

Malice, however, is only one of the many obscure motives for
laughing, which has been explained as a release from restraint, a
response to what is incongruous or improper, or a sign of ambivalence—
our hysteric effort to adjust our repulsion from, and our attraction
to, a situation. Certainly laughter is a symptom of bewilderment or
surprise. Sometimes it is said that a laugh detonates whenever there
is a sudden rupture between thinking and feeling.[2] The rupture
occurs the instant a situation is seen in another light. The shock of
taking another point of view causes, in Bergson's words, a momentary
"anesthesia of the heart."

During the Middle Ages people seem to have laughed at the grotesque as when, for instance, Chrétien de Troyes brings among the
dainty knights and ladies of his romance *Yvain* a rustic lout whose
"ears were big and mossy, just like an elephant's," or when Dante's
gargoylelike demons caper through the lower circles of hell making
obscene noises. In pious legends like "The Tumbler of Our Lady"

---

[2] This theory of laughter as being due to a "bisociation" of sensibility is discussed at length in Arthur Koestler: *Insight and Outlook,* 1949.

medieval laughter is charitable, becoming almost tender in anecdotes about Friar Juniper, that tattered soul who in meekness and humility played seesaw with children.

Renaissance laughter was complex. Sometimes it was like Cellini's, swaggering with contempt—*sprezzatura.* When Machiavelli laughs he almost sneers, notably in his play *Mandragola,* showing how a stupid old husband is cuckolded. We can fancy that his Prince would laugh somewhat like a Borgia. Then there is Erasmus' satire, quiet and blighting; less boisterous than Rabelais' monstrous glee. Ben Jonson's plays ridicule the classic-bourgeois "types" (as Bergson would call them) who, like Rabelais' mammoths, are laughable because they have an excess of one "humor" in their disposition or "complexion." Shakespeare's theatre is filled with medically "humorous" persons like Falstaff, who raise a laugh at once brutal, loving, and wise. The laughter in Cervantes' *Quixote* is gentler and more thoughtful, and not so corrosive as Hamlet's wit, which is tinged with Robert Burton's melancholy.

Hamlet's "disturbed" laughter was very "modern," as was also the strained, joyless grimace of Thomas Hobbes, who explained laughter as a sense of "sudden glory" arising from our feeling of superiority whenever we see ourselves triumphantly secure while others stumble. Hobbes brings in the note of "biological" laughter, for he takes life to be a struggle for power waged naturally in a brutish combat "where every man is enemy to every man." Some three hundred years later Anthony M. Ludovici rephrased Hobbes's theory in Darwinian form by supposing that a laugh is man's way of showing his fangs.[3] And man needs, like any animal, to show his fangs only when he is threatened; we laugh in self-defense and bare our teeth to recruit our sinking spirits or to ease our aching sense of inferiority or danger. Laughter is a tactic for survival, a mark of "superior adaptation" among gregarious animals. The weak and the savage both laugh. Ludovici agrees with Nietzsche that man laughs only because he can suffer excruciatingly; and his direst, most inward sickness is the thwarting of his will.

On this latter theme we can play every variation of modern comedy with all its satanic ironies and romantic dreamwork. The "genial" romantics of the early nineteenth century assumed, with Charles Lamb, that laughter is an overflow of sympathy, an amiable feeling of identity with what is disreputably human, a relish for the whimsical, the odd, the private blunder. Carlyle (of all people!) cheerfully supposed that the man who smiles is affectionate. But there were the diabolic

---

[3] Anthony M. Ludovici: *The Secret of Laughter,* 1932.

romantics, too, driven by the Will to Power or consumed by their own poisons, and they laughed menacingly, frantically. Baudelaire's laugh, heard in the dark bohemian world of Paris—the Paris which drove men desperate and betrayed their ideals—is "a nervous convulsion, and involuntary spasm," a proof of man's fallen state.[4] The feverish laugh of Baudelaire's hero sears his lips and twists his vitals; it is a sign of infinite nobility and infinite pain. Man laughed only after the Exile, when he knew sin and suffering; the comical is a mark of man's revolt, boredom, and aspiration. "The laugh is satanic; it is likewise deeply human." It is the bitter voice of nineteenth-century disillusion. Schopenhauer was the first to define the romantic irony in this desolate laugh of the "underground man": laughter "is simply the sudden perception of incongruity" between our ideals and the actualities before us. Byron jested "And if I laugh at any mortal thing/'Tis that I may not weep."

The mirth of the disenchanted and frustrated idealist, frenzied by his sense of the impassable distance between what might be and what is, reaches its shrillest pitch in Nietzsche, the scorpion-philosopher, exempt from every middle-class code, whose revolt is, unlike Bergson's comedy of "slight revolt on the surface of social life," savage. Nietzsche is able to transvalue all social values by pain, disgust, fury. This sickly laughter of the last romantics is the most confused and destructive mirth Western man has ever allowed himself. It has all the pessimism which Bergson chose not to consider. Rimbaud's laugh is a symptom of anguish and a glimpse into the abyss of the self. It is a terrifying scorn, a shameless expense of lust, an eruption of the pleasure-principle in a world where pleasure is denied. Nietzsche's laughter is a discharge far more "possessed" than the Freudian sexual release.

So Bergson's analysis of laughter is incomplete, which may explain why he thinks comedy works only from "the outside." Comedy may, in fact, not bring laughter at all; and certain tragedies may make us laugh hysterically. It was Shelley who found the comedy in *King Lear* to be "universal, ideal, and sublime." Ben Jonson himself noted "Nor is the moving of laughter always the end of comedy." When Coleridge lectured on *Hamlet* and *Lear* he pointed out that terror is closely joined with what is ludicrous, since "The laugh is rendered by nature itself the language of extremes, even as tears are." Thus

---

[4] Probably the most important discussion of "satanic" laughter is Baudelaire's brief essay "On the Essence of Laughter, and In General, On the Comic in the Plastic Arts," which appeared as early as 1855 and was reprinted in *Aesthetic Curiosities*. [See in this volume p. 448.]

Hamlet "will be found to touch on the verge of the ludicrous," because "laughter is equally the expression of extreme anguish and horror as of joy." The grimace of mirth resembles the grimace of suffering; comic and tragic masks have the same distortion. Today we know that a comic action sometimes yields tragic values.[5] In Balzac's *human* comedy (*Comédie humaine*) we meet Old Goriot and Cousin Pons, those heroes of misery.

If we have no satisfactory definition of laughter, neither do we have any satisfactory definition of comedy. Indeed, most of the theories of laughter and comedy fail precisely because they oversimplify a situation and an art more complicated than the tragic situation and art. Comedy seems to be a more pervasive human condition than tragedy. Often we are, or have been, or could be, Quixotes or Micawbers or Malvolios, Benedicks or Tartuffes. Seldom are we Macbeths or Othellos. Tragedy, not comedy, limits its field of operation and is a more closely regulated form of response to the ambiguities and dilemmas of humanity. The comic action touches experience at more points than tragic action. We can hardly hope that our various definitions of comedy will be more compatible than our definitions of laughter; yet each of the many definitions has its use in revealing the meanings of comedy. Bergson's alone will not suffice, or Meredith's either; and they both will mean more when seen against the full spectrum of comic values.

Ordinarily we refer to "high" and "low" comedy; but we cannot speak of "low" tragedy. All tragedy ought to be "high." There are, of course, various orders of tragic action, such as *drame* and "heroic tragedy"; however, as tragedy falls away from its "high" plane it tends to become something else than tragedy. Tragedy is indeed "an achievement peculiarly Greek"—and needs a special view of man's relation to the world.[6] But comedy thrives everywhere and fearlessly runs the gamut of effects from "high" to "low" without diminishing its force or surrendering its values or even jeopardizing them. Once Mme. de Staël said: "Tragedies (if we set aside some of the masterpieces) require less knowledge of the human heart than comedies." What a strange opinion! Yet which of Shakespeare's plays really shows a more profound knowledge of the hearts of fathers and children: *Lear,* or *Henry IV,* 1 and 2, and *Henry V?* Is not the crisis luridly overstated in *Lear* and met with greater insight in the figures of Henry

---

[5] According to L. C. Knights "comedy is essentially a serious activity" ("Notes on Comedy" in *Determinations,* ed. F. R. Leavis, 1934). [See in this volume p. 181.]

[6] As Edith Hamilton says in *The Greek Way.*

IV, Hal, Hotspur, and Falstaff? Can we honestly claim that Shakespeare reveals more about life in the tragedy of Lear than in the
conflicts between Henry and his wild son? Are not many of the problems raised in the great tragedies solved in the great comedies?

Mme. de Staël continues: "The imagination without much difficulty
can represent what often appears—the features of sorrow. Tragic
characters take on a certain similarity that blurs the finer distinctions
between them, and the design of a heroic action determines in advance the course they must take." (Whereas Bergson claims it is
comedy that deals with types.) Surely the comic action is more unpredictable, and delight is an emotion quite as individual as grief,
remorse, or guilt.

Further, and illogically, "low" comedy is as legitimate as "high."
In fact, the lower the range, the more authentic the comedy may be,
as we know when we behold the Wife of Bath, that slack daughter
of Eve, or Falstaff, that ruffian always on the point of untrussing. At
the bottom of the comic scale—where the human becomes nearly
indistinguishable from the animal and where the vibration of laughter
is longest and loudest—is the "dirty" joke or the "dirty" gesture. At
this depth comedy unerringly finds the lowest common denominator
of human response, the reducing-agent that sends us reeling back
from our proprieties to the realm of old Pan. The unquenchable
vitality of man gushes up from the lower strata of Rabelais' comedy,
inhabited by potbellied monsters who tumultuously do as they wish
in a world built entirely with the apparatus of a gargantuan peda-
gogy. There we drop the mask which we have composed into the
features of our decent, cautious selves. Rabelais strips man of his
breeches; he is the moral sans-culotte. Psychologists tell us that any
group of men and women, no matter how "refined," will, sooner or
later, laugh at a "dirty" joke, the question being not whether they
will laugh but when, or at precisely what "dirty" joke; that is, under
exactly what co-efficient of stress a code of "decency" breaks apart
and allows the human being to fall steeply down to the recognition
of his inalienable flesh.

Yet laughter at the obscenest jest forever divides man from animal,
because the animal is never self-conscious about any fleshly act whatever; whereas man is not man without being somehow uneasy about
the "nastiness" of his body. One of the deepest paradoxes in comedy
thus reveals itself in obscenity, which is a threshold over which man
enters into the human condition; it is a comic equivalent to the religious state of original sin or of tragic "error," and man may as justly
be thought human because of his sense of what is "dirty" as because

of his sense of what is "evil," "sinful," or fearful. This elemental self-awareness—this consciousness of shame at one's flesh—sets one of the lowest margins for civilization; and, conversely, a hypersensitivity to what is "obscene" is a mark of a decadent society. The paradox in comic filth was madly intensified in the satire of Jonathan Swift, that puritan pornographer, who wrote in his notebook that "A nice man is a man of nasty ideas." Swift forces comic obscenity to its extremes in Gulliver's disgust at the Yahoos; his fastidiousness is insane when Gulliver is frightened by the red-haried female Yahoo who stands gazing and howling on the bank, inflamed with desire to embrace his naked body.

As we move "up" the scale of comic action, the mechanisms become more complex but no more "comic." [7] Physical mishaps, pratfalls, and loud collisions are the crudest products of Bergson's comic "automatism." It is hard to distinguish these pleasures from our glee at physical deformity; and here we detect the cruelty inherent in comedy, which may perhaps be another form of the cruelty inherent in tragic disaster. Essentially our enjoyment of physical mishap or deformity springs from our surprise and delight that man's motions are often absurd, his energies often misdirected. This is the coarsest, most naïve, comedy of manners. Another sort of mechanical comedy is the farce—mistaken identities, coincidences, mistimings—which can be a very complicated engine of plot devices. In this range of comedy the characters need only be puppets moved from the outside, as events require. There is the right key to the wrong door, or the wrong key to the right door; and it does not matter very much who is inside, provided it is the unexpected figure. In these comic vehicles fate takes the guise of happy or unhappy chance, which is, of course, only a tidy arrangement of improbable possibilities. On this sort of artificial framework comedy displays some of its most glittering designs.

Or comedy can be a mechanism of language, the repartee that sharply levels drama and life to a sheen of verbal wit. Congreve's cool, negligent persons like Fainall are beings who have a *verbal* existence, of extremely delicate taste, and able to refine all their pleasures to raillery: "I'd no more play with a man that slighted his ill fortune than I'd make love to a woman who undervalued the loss of her reputation." The transparent Mrs. Fainall lives and moves in the same dry atmosphere and speaks with the same brittle tongue: "While I only hated my husband, I could bear to see him; but since I have

---

[7] The "scale" of comic effects is arranged in Alan Reynolds Thompson: *The Anatomy of Drama*, 1942, Chapter VI. I have modified Thompson's scale in certain ways.

despised him, he's too offensive." Such comedy of manners does not
hesitate to sacrifice humanity to dialogue. Or rather, the dialogue
itself may be a fragile mechanism of wit to elevate the comedy to
"intellectual" heights. Shakespeare's intricate wit in *Love's Labour's
Lost,* with its "flowers of fancy, the jerks of invention," demands of
us an agility that makes the brain spin. The play is a thin fabric of
banter dazzling us with preciosity, its quick venue of phrase—"snip,
snap, and home." At its gilded moments this comedy feeds upon
dainties, delights to drink ink, to eat paper, to replenish the spirit
with joy, to come to honorable terms with a code of manners, and
to leave trudging far behind those who are sensible only in the duller
parts.

But it is more than a parterre of devices: it is a drama played
by those odd, lovable Shakespearean creatures for whom Bergson
seems to have so little feeling—they are "characters" in the British
sense of the word. Berowne and Don Armado are among them, and
they inhabit the higher domain of comedy where we meet Fielding's
Squire Western, Chaucer's Monk, Cervantes' Quixote, Sterne's Uncle
Toby, and Dickens' Sam Weller. Such persons cannot exist in the
dry seclusion of farce. They require the mellow neighborhood of a
comedy of humors which gathers into its action spirits of strong and
perverse disposition and convincing weight. These characters thrive at
more genial latitudes than Ben Jonson allowed them in his comedy
of humors, which was too harshly satiric. English literature is, as
Taine said, the native province of these unruly creatures whose life
blood pulses richly, whose features are odd, and whose opinions,
gestures, vices, and habits control the mechanism of the plot in which
they happen to be cast. Indeed, such dispositions may temper the
whole climate in which events happen and constantly threaten to
wreck the tight logic of a fiction. Mercutio and Benedick are incorrigible fellows of this sort. We never take seriously the action in
which they have a role; but we take them seriously. They live for
us as Falstaff lives; for Falstaff is more than a sack of guts. He
moves the whole play from within; he is a temperamental as well as
an anatomical grotesque.

These "characters" realized in depth stand at the threshold of
"high" comedy, which is really a transformation of comedy of manners. Whenever a society becomes self-conscious about its opinions,
codes, or etiquette, comedy of manners may serve as a sort of philosophic engine called "comedy of ideas." Frail as they are, and known
best in their moments of raillery, Millamant and Mirabell raise Congreve's *Way of the World* to a bolder order of comedy of manners:

"Let us," says Millamant to Mirabell, "be as strange as if we had been married a great while, and as well bred as if we were not married at all." The edge of this comedy is sharpened by sanity as well as verbal wit, and, as Meredith clearly saw, Molière magnified comedy of manners to the dimensions of a criticism of life. Our most provoking social critic is Shaw, although Pirandello soars farther into a crystalline sphere of ideas. The world of Aristophanes could have been shaped only in the sophisticated theatre of an Athens that had begun to examine its own conventions. Aristophanes is like Erasmus or Gide, who serve as the intellectual conscience of a nervous and self-scrutinizing society where all is not now so well as it might be or has been or seems to be.

At the radiant peak of "high" comedy—a peak we can easily sight from Meredith's essay—laughter is qualified by tolerance, and criticism is modulated by a sympathy that comes only from wisdom. Just a few writers of comedy have gained this unflinching but generous perspective on life, which is a victory over our absurdities but a victory won at a cost of humility, and won in a spirit of charity and enlightenment. Besides Shakespeare in, perhaps, *The Tempest,* one might name Cervantes and Henry James and Jane Austen, or Thomas Mann in his *Magic Mountain,* when pliable, diseased Clavdia yields carelessly to the stricken Hans Castorp in a scene where the grimness of human life, its folly and its error, are seen clearly and with a perverse tenderness: *"Petit bourgeois!"* she says to him—*"Joli bourgeois à la petite tache humide."* For they both know that the body, love, and death are all three the same thing, and that the flesh is sickness and desire, and life only a fever in matter. This is how "high" comedy chastens men without despair, without rancor, as if human blunders were seen from a godlike distance, and also from within the blundering self. The deep humiliation and reassurance in Don Quixote's madness and recovery, with his resignation, detachment, and self-awareness, are all confirmed by the experience of Shakespeare's Benedick—to whom Meredith appealed. After proving himself as foolish as the rest of the world, Benedick comes to a vision of the human condition: "For man is a giddy thing, and this is my conclusion." Benedick speaks without bitterness, bias, or pride; and has learned, like Hans Castorp, to accept the insufficiency of man without being damaged.

So the range of comedy is more embracing than the range of tragedy; and if tragedy occurs at some middle point in ethical life where failure is weighed against man's nobility of spirit, comedy ventures out into the farther extremes of experience in both directions, toward

the bestial or "obscene," and at the other end of the spectrum toward
the insane heroics of Nietzsche or the vision of Prospero, who sees sin
as the last mistake of all our many mistakes, dispelled before our
clearer reason whenever hate seems more absurd than charity.

We may prefer one theory of comedy to another; but we shall find
it hard to get along without the other. In *Winter's Tale,* Autolycus
meditates on his lot: "I am courted now with a *double occasion.*"
The phrase is useful, for comedy is built upon double occasions,
double premises, double values. "Nothing human is alien to me," says
the character in Terence. Nothing human is alien to comedy. It is
an equivocal art. If we now have trouble isolating comedy from
tragedy, this is not because comedy and tragedy are identical, but
rather because comedy often intersects the orbit of tragic action without losing its autonomy. Instead, comedy in its own right, boldly and
illogically, lays claim to some of the values that traditionally are
assigned to tragedy alone. Think, for example, of Henry James's
"Beast In the Jungle," which really is comedy of manners suddenly
consumed in the flame of Marcher's grief that he has lost May forever through his own selfishness. Here is comedy seen ruthlessly "from
within" as Bergson did not allow. Marcher is a fool—but a sinister
fool, an egoist far more barbaric than Meredith's sleek Sir Willoughby
Patterne. And James's London, a society of genteel manners and frail
nerves, is a scene where savage eyes glare behind the social simper.

II. The Ancient Rites of Comedy

In fact, to interpret the complications and contradictions in comedy,
we must look far backward toward Aristotle and the Greeks; for the
meanings in comedy are tribally old, and Bergson and Meredith refine almost beyond recognition the primitive violence of comedy, which,
curiously, reappears again in James, Kafka, and "us moderns."

The notion of an affinity between tragedy and comedy would not
be strange to the Greeks: not to Socrates, we know, because of what
happens in *The Symposium,* a very dramatic dialogue where Plato
brings together in debate the comedian Aristophanes, the tragedian
Agathon, and along with them the goat-faced Socrates, the philosophic clown, a figure who stands near the center of all the larger
problems of comedy. In the course of this night-long dialogue Socrates
is described by Alcibiades as looking "exactly like the masks of Silenus." He turns to Socrates and asks: "You will not deny that your
face is like that of a satyr? And there is a resemblance in other
points too. For example, you are a bully." Yet Socrates makes the
notorious Alcibiades ashamed of his misdeeds. Alcibiades complains,

"Mankind are nothing to him; all his life is spent in mocking and flouting at them." This Socrates, resembling a caricature of a man, is the person who alone is able to make the dissolute Athenians care for their souls; his words "amaze and possess the soul of every man." Plato reports that by daybreak only Aristophanes and Agathon are still awake to hear Socrates insisting that anyone who can write tragedy can also write comedy because the craft (*techne*) of writing comedy is the same as the craft of writing tragedy.

Surely Socrates, comedian and martyr, mocker and moralist, was the proper one to hold this notion, which has gained new implication now that the social anthropologists have discovered what Aristotle already knew—namely, that comedy is a primal rite; a rite transformed to art. As F. M. Cornford puts it, comedy is "a scene of sacrifice and a feast." [8] Aristotle intimated as much in the *Poetics* by stating that at first both tragedy and comedy were improvisations, the one rising from the Dithyramb, the other from phallic songs "still used as ritual in many of our cities." These improvisations having evolved in different ways, each found its "natural form," the comic writer presenting men as "worse than they are," the tragic writer as "better," and the comic being a version of the Ludicrous— which in turn is a variety of the Ugly without being painful or destructive. Comedy, he adds, has no history—that is, it passed unnoticed for a long time, although it had definite "forms" (*schemata*) even in the early poets. Aristotle thinks that tragedy gained its "magnitude" after it passed its "satyric" phase and took on a "stately manner" at a "late phase" of its history. Thereafter tragedy imitated "noble actions" of "noble personages," whereas comedy dealt with the "meaner sorts of actions among the ignoble." He also says that comedy turned from an early use of "invective" to a "dramatizing of the ridiculous." In early satyric dramas, poetry was adapted to dancing.

However cryptic Aristotle's comment may be, it is clear that he traces the origins of drama to some sort of fertility rite—Dionysiac or phallic—the primitive "sacrifice and feast" mentioned by Cornford. It is now accepted that art is born of rites and that the comic and tragic masks are themselves archetypal symbols for characters in a

---

[8] Behind my whole discussion of this rite and my whole account of the inconsistent theories necessary to explain comedy is Francis M. Cornford: *The Origin of Attic Comedy*, 1914. Cornford's interpretation seems to me to offer our only means of understanding the incompatibles in comedy without laying ourselves open to a charge of willful illogicality. These incompatibles in comedy are also dealt with effectively in Johan Huizinga: *Homo Ludens* and in Élie Aubouin: *Technique et psychologie du comique*. See also Northrop Frye: "The Argument of Comedy" in *English Institute Essays, 1948.*

34 THE SPIRIT OF COMEDY

tribal "semantics of ritual." Behind tragedy and comedy is a pre-historic death-and-resurrection ceremonial, the rite of killing the old year (the aged king) and bringing in the new season (the resurrection or initiation of the adolescent king). Associated with killing the old king and devouring his sacrificial body was the ancient rite of purging the tribe by expelling a scapegoat on whose head were heaped the sins of the past year. Frazer describes what happened during this "public expulsion of evils" at a season when there was an "oblation of first fruits":

. . . the time of year when the ceremony takes place usually coincides with some well-marked change of season. . . . this public and periodic expulsion of devils is commonly preceded or followed by a period of general license, during which the ordinary restraints of society are thrown aside, and all offences, short of the gravest, are allowed to pass unpunished. (*Golden Bough*)

At this public purging or catharsis the scapegoat was often the divine man or animal, in the guise of victim, to whom were transferred the sins and misfortunes of the worshipers. Eventually the divine character of the scapegoat was forgotten; as Frazer notes, he became an ordinary victim, a wretch who was a condemned criminal perhaps, actually as well as ritually guilty. This ancient death-and-resurrection rite, then, seems to have had a double meaning: the killing of the god or king to save him and the tribe from the sterility of age, and the expulsion of evils (or devils) amid rejoicing of a people who were redeemed by the sacrifice of a hero-victim.

From this rudimentary sacrifice-and-feast evolved comic and tragic poetry, using a "canonical" plot formula older than either art, an elemental folk drama from which derived in obscure ways the "action" (myth) of the Athenian theatre. In its typical form the archaic fertility ceremony—involving the death or sacrifice of a hero-god (the old year), the rebirth of a hero-god (the new year), and a purging of evil by driving out a scapegoat (who may be either god or devil, hero or villain)—requires a contest or *agon* between the old and new kings, a slaying of a god or king, a feast and a marriage to commemorate the initiation, reincarnation, or resurrection of the slain god, and a final triumphal procession or *komos,* with songs of joy. Behind the marriage ceremonial probably lies the myth of the primal union between the earth-mother and the heaven-father. Following this revelation of the mysteries of life, the new hero-king is proclaimed and elevated: there is an "apotheosis," epiphany, or manifestation of the young hero-god (a theophany).

The rites may take the guise of an initiation or testing of the strength of the hero or his fertility, perhaps in the form of a "questioning" or catechism, after which there comes to him a "discovery" or "recognition"—an *anagnorisis* or new knowledge. Or else the sacrifice may be interrupted by an unwelcome intruder (an *alazon*) who views the secret rites; he is a profaner of the mysteries, an alien. This character must be put to flight or else confounded in a "struggle" that may also occur in the form of a catechism, to which he does not know the proper answers. In either case there is a debate, a dialectic contest, which is preserved in Aristophanes' *Clouds,* for instance, as an argument between "Right Logic" and "Wrong Logic." Thus again the comic action is double, since it is both a rational debate and a phallic orgy. Logic and passion appear together in the primal comic formula.

In Cornford's opinion the dramatic form known as tragedy eventually suppressed the sexual magic in this canonical plot, leaving only the portrayal of the suffering and death of the hero, king, or god. Comedy, however, kept in the foreground the erotic action, together with the disorderly rejoicing at the rebirth or resurrection of the god-hero who survives his *agon.* In this sense comedy preserves the archaic "double occasion" of the plot formula, the dual and wholly incompatible meanings of sacrifice and feast, cruelty and festival, logic and license. So much we may read into Aristotle's remark that comedy was, like tragedy, originally an improvisation, its "action" being a procession of the devotees of Phales carrying the emblem of the god, that profane and sacred symbol, the ithyphallus, the *penis erectus.* After pausing at the place of sacrifice to pray to Dionysus they continued their procession to the burden of phallic songs.

If this indeed be the origin of comedy we can guess why Aristotle said that "tragedy advanced by slow degrees, and having passed through many changes, found its natural form and then stopped evolving." Unlike comedy, tragedy is a "closed" form of art, with a single, fixed, and contained meaning (by contrast to the disorderly relaxed meanings in comedy). Tragedy demands a law of necessity or destiny, and a finality that can be gained only by stressing a logic of "plot" or "unified action" with a beginning, middle, and end. Within the confines of this action the hero is given to sacrifice or death. That is, tragedy performs the sacrificial rite without the festival—which means that it is a less complex, less ambiguous form of drama than comedy. Retaining its double action of penance and revel, comedy remains an "improvisation" with a loose structure and a precarious logic that can tolerate every kind of "improbability."

The coherent plot is vital to tragic theatre (Aristotle says that plot is the very soul of tragedy); and a tragic action needs to convey a sense of destiny, inevitability, and foreordination. The tragic poet often implies there are unchanging moral laws behind the falling thunderbolt. The fate of a tragic hero needs to be made "intelligible" as the comic hero's fate does not; or at least tragic fate has the force of "necessity" even if it is not "intelligible." Somehow tragedy shows what "must" happen, even while there comes a shock of un-surmised disaster. As Aristotle said, in tragedy, coincidence must have an air of probability. Then too, tragedy subordinates "character" to the design of the plot; for the purpose of tragedy, says Aristotle, is not to depict "character," but, rather, to show "men in action," so that the "character" of a tragic hero reveals itself in a deed which expresses his moral disposition. Comedy, on the contrary, can freely yield its action to surprise, chance, and all the changes in fortune that fall outside the necessities of tragic myth, and can present "character" for its own sake.

Following what Aristotle implied, Cornford is able to say that if tragedy requires plot first of all, comedy is rooted so firmly in "character" its plot seems derivative, auxiliary, perhaps incidental. Unlike tragedy, comedy does not have to guard itself by any logic of inevitability, or by academic rules. Comedy makes artistic all the unlikely possibilities that tragic probability must reject. It keeps more of the primitive aspect of *play* than does tragedy.

From the anthropologist's view the tragic action, however inspiring and however perfect in artistic form, runs through only one arc of the full cycle of drama; for the entire ceremonial cycle is birth: struggle: death: resurrection. The tragic arc is only birth: struggle: death. Consequently the range of comedy is wider than the tragic range—perhaps more fearless—and comic action can risk a different sort of purgation and triumph.[9] If we believe that drama retains any of the mythical values of the old fertility rite, then the comic cycle is the only fulfilled and redemptive action, and, strange to think, the death and rebirth of the god belong more fittingly to the comic than to the tragic theatre. Is this the reason why it is difficult for tragic art to deal with Christian themes like the Crucifixion and the Resurrection? Should we say that the drama of the struggle, death, and rising—Gethsemane, Calvary, and Easter—actually belongs in the comic rather than the tragic domain? The figure of Christ as god-man is surely the archetypal hero-victim. He is mocked, reviled, crowned with thorns—a scapegoat King.

---

[9] Gertrude Rachel Levy in *The Gate of Horn* (1948), p. 319 ff., stresses this interpretation; but, again, my primary debt is to Cornford.

If the authentic comic action is a sacrifice and a feast, debate and passion, it is by the same token a Saturnalia, an orgy, an assertion of the unruliness of the flesh and its vitality. Comedy is essentially a Carrying Away of Death, a triumph over mortality by some absurd faith in rebirth, restoration, and salvation. Originally, of course, these carnival rites were red with the blood of victims. The archaic seasonal revel brought together the incompatibles of death and life. No logic can explain this magic victory over Winter, Sin, and the Devil. But the comedian can perform the rites of Dionysus and his frenzied gestures initiate us into the secrets of the savage and mystic power of life. Comedy is sacred and secular.

Thus it happens that from the earliest time the comic ritual has been presided over by a Lord of Misrule, and the improvisations of comedy have the aspect of a Feast of Unreason, a Revel of Fools— a *Sottie*. Comedy is a release, a taking off the masks we have put on to deal with others who have put on decent masks to deal with us. The Church herself knew how salutary is this comic rite of unmask-ing, for near the season of Lent the monks used to appoint one of their number to be Lord of Unreason and chant the liturgy of Folly, during which an Ass was worshiped and the mass parodied in a ceremony no less religious, in its profane way, than the Dionysian and Saturnalian revels of Greece and Rome.[10] During these *ludi inhonesti* the monks at vespers gave the staff of office to a Lord of Misrule while they chanted *"deposuit potentes de sede, et exultavit humiles."* In performing the mock mass the celebrants brayed the responses. The first Herod of the mystery plays may have been *Rex Stultorum,* and we know that medieval drama never excluded the comic from its religious ritual. Those in the thrall of carnival come out, for a moment, from behind the façade of their "serious" selves, the façade required by their vocation. When they emerge from this façade, they gain a new perspective upon their official selves and thus, when they again retire behind their usual *personae,* they are more conscious of the duplicity of their existence. That is why Freud thought of the comic as an "unmasking," a mechanism that allows, whether we watch or play it, a "free discharge" of impulses we daily have to repress. The carnival is an hour when we are permitted to recover our "lost infantile laughter" and to rejoice again with the pleasure of a child. It redeems us from our "professional" life.

Aristotle said that tragedy works a purgation or "catharsis" and carries off harmful passions by means of an allowed public cleansing

---

[10] This parody is described in A. P. Rossiter: *English Drama from Early Times to the Elizabethans,* 1950.

of the self, enabling us to face with poise the calamities of life.
Tragedy has been called "mithridatic" because the tragic action,
inoculating us with large doses of pity and fear, inures the self to
the perils we all face. Comedy is no less mithridatic in its effects on
the self, and has its own catharsis. Freud said that nonsense is a
toxic agent acting like some "poison" now and again required by
the economy of the soul. Under the spell of this intoxication we re-
claim for an instant our "old liberties," and after discharging our
inhibited impulses in folly we regain the sanity that is worn away
by the everyday gestures. We have a compulsion to be moral and
decent, but we also resent the obligations we have accepted. The
irreverence of the carnival disburdens us of our resentment and purges
our ambivalence so that we can return to our duties as honest men.
Like tragedy, comedy is homeopathic. It cures folly by folly.

The tragic law works a transformation: from sin and suffering
come calm of mind and resistance to disaster, to fears that weaken
us. The transformations in comedy are equally miraculous: from
license and parody and unmasking—or putting on another mask—
come renewed sanity and responsibility, a confidence that we have
looked at things from a lower angle and therefore know what is in-
corruptible. In Shakespeare's play the madness of midsummer night
is necessary to purge doting and inconstant lovers. After the fierce
vexation of their dreams comes the bright Athenian dawn, with secure
judgment. As Hippolyta says:

> And all their minds transfigured so together,
> More witnesseth than fancy's images,
> And grows to something of great constancy;
> But howsoever, strange and admirable.

The comic perspective can be reached only by making game of
"serious" life. The comic rites are necessarily impious, for comedy is
sacrilege as well as release. That is one reason why comedy is intolerable to the sober moralist Rousseau, who gravely protests that the
women of Geneva will be corrupted by going to the theatre to see
how Molière satirizes virtuous men like Alceste. Plato has the same
puritan timidity, despising the art that stirs up "the rebellious principle" in men, "especially at a public festival when a promiscuous
crowd is assembled in a theatre" where passions are roused and fed.
Plato's high-minded snobbism, like Rousseau's petty-bourgeois "seriousness," is brought to bear chiefly against tragedy; yet both have
an abiding fear of the carnival, which has the power "of harming
even the good" by its contagious impieties. Plato warns his Guardians

of the ideal State not to be given to laughter, for "violent laughter tends to provoke an equally violent reaction." He especially fears buffooneries or any "impulse to play the clown"—"and by encouraging its impudence at the theatre you may be unconsciously carried away into playing the comedian in your private life." But Freud saw what this impudence means, for the comic action is a mode of "representation through the opposite," and man must periodically befoul the holy and reduce himself to folly. We find ourselves reflected in the comedian, who satisfies our need for impieties.

Nietzsche believed that we discover truth in the excesses of a Dionysiac orgy, which is ecstasy as well as pain. This orgy takes place in the theatre he calls "epidemic" because it sweeps the individual into the tide of a mass emotion. In *The Birth of Tragedy* Nietzsche says that Greek drama was played at a point of conflict between our Apollonian and our Dionysian selves. The Apollonian self is reason (*logos*), while the unruly Dionysiac self finds its voice in song (*melos*)—the song of the chorus. Who are the chorus, singing before the actors (who stand apart to speak their dialogue)? They are the satyr-selves, the natural beings madly giving out cries of joy and sorrow that arise from the vast cosmic night of primordial existence. "Is it possible," Nietzsche asks, "that madness is not necessarily a symptom of degeneration, of decline, of a decadent culture? Perhaps this is a question for alienists—there are neuroses of *health?*" Nietzsche finds the substratum of both comedy and tragedy in the old satyr-self: "Our deepest insights must—and should—appear as follies, and under certain circumstances as crimes." So Zarathustra rejoices in the Ass-Festival: "A little valiant nonsense, some divine service and ass-festival, some old joyful Zarathustra-fool, some blusterer to blow your souls bright." When he sings the wild songs of Bacchus, man loses his personal identity, his "differentiation," and ceases to be a thinker. He becomes the Dionysiac hero, the archetypal Reveller. In the epidemic theatre there is a metamorphosis, for civilized man finds again his archaic being among the throng.

The Dionysiac theatre consecrates truth by outbursts of laughter. Comedy desecrates what it seeks to sanctify. The orgiastic cleansing of the self and the tribe is ritually performed in Shakespeare's *Henry IV*, 1 and 2, which is a Feast of Unreason ceremonially held in the taverns of Eastcheap, with Falstaff presiding as Lord of Misrule. The Lancastrian king Henry IV, Bolingbroke, has under the guise of just causes usurped the throne and slain the anointed king, Richard II. After this stroke of power politics Henry has ventured to put on the mask of repute and piety; but behind this decent royal *persona* is the

"shadow" self of the old unscrupulous Bolingbroke, and he confesses
to Hal:

> . . . God knows, my son,
> By what by-paths and indirect crookt ways
> I met this crown; and I myself know well
> How troublesome it sat upon my head . . .

Henry cannot wear the royal garments easily because he has come to
his throne by the unholy cunning of the opportunist. Richard's blood
will not out, and like a tragic guilt it stains the grace of Henry's
rule. Yet Bolingbroke cannot drop the mask. So Hal's heritage is
tainted, and the Lancastrian line must be purged. This false righteousness can be washed away only by rites acted hilariously on
Gadshill, where Hal connives at another, baser thievery that is detected—
a parody of his father's practice. In the depths of bohemia, amid
whores, parasites, and cowards, a realm where Falstaff is king and
priest, young Hal is initiated into the company of Fools and Rogues.
Falstaff asks the ruthless question: "What is honor?" The Lancas-
trians must answer before they are legitimate kings. With all the
lewdness of the comedian Falstaff reduces to absurdity the lineage
of Bolingbroke when he jests at the parentage of young Harry and
knows him to be his father's son only by a villainous hanging lip,
which proclaims him honestly begot. In this pit of degradation Hal
cleanses himself and his line from the policy of his ancestors, and
by coming out from behind the façade of Lancastrian pompousness
he proves that he is, indeed legitimately, the heir apparent. By stoop-
ing to Doll Tearsheet, Harry makes himself eligible to woo Kate of
France. Falstaff is at once devil and priest, coward and hero, tempter
and scapegoat, and essentially the satyr who lives ineradicably behind
the façade of every culture. Without his ribaldry, his drunken wisdom, Britain cannot be redeemed.

III. The Guises of the Comic Hero

Hence the range of comic action is far wider than Bergson supposed when he remarked that the comic is something mechanical
encrusted on what is living and that the comic hero is dehumanized
because he makes only gestures, automatic motions, which look ridiculous when they are "interrupted." Bergson, perhaps following Stendhal's
notion that we remain untouched by the plight of the comic figure,
saw him from only one angle, treating him as if he were a toy manikin
which, wound up, is geared to execute the same motion wherever
he is put. Bergson's comic hero is only a caricature of a man. Yet

Don Quixote, even while making mechanical gestures, enters the realm of *human* action as a figure like Tartuffe cannot. In Dickens and Dostoevsky, too, the characters are geared to make a few stormy gestures, but are not merely comic machines like Tartuffe and Harpagon, who by contrast merely gesticulate. Chaucer's Wife of Bath is another creature capable of only a few responses who is, nevertheless, more than an automaton.

Above all other comic heroes, perhaps, Falstaff is a grotesque who has by no means disqualified himself from being a man; in fact, he has a kind of massive "probability" and authentic selfhood-in-depth. Behind his great belly there is an ample personality, and his gesticulations, mechanical as they seem, are comparable to the moral "action" of a tragic hero. Nor is Falstaff isolated from us like Tartuffe, even when his cowardly motions are "interrupted" as he is caught red-handed at Gadshill or on the field at Shrewsbury. Exactly when Falstaff is driven into the tightest corner—when like Tartuffe he is "caught" firmly in the mechanical trap of comedy—he asks his most troublesome questions: What is honor? What is so much like a counterfeit man as a dead hero? Tartuffe does not have this ingenuity, this power to come to grips with us at close quarters. Falstaff is never so dangerous as when he is at bay—which proves that he has an existence of his own apart from the intrigue in which he has a role. Some of Dostoevsky's grotesque people who have obsessive notions also have this power to challenge us as we stand outside the comic arena and watch them from a position of presumed safety. The sickly hero of *Notes from the Underworld* faces us with some very awkward problems which a character so absurd and artificial has no right to raise. Furthermore, at the basest level of his "low" comedy Falstaff ventures to address himself directly to us, making us doubt Bergson's opinion that only "high" comedy is close to life. Indeed, Falstaff shows how narrow the margin sometimes is between high and low comedy, for he was doubtless born a comic machine of a very low order—the *miles gloriosus*—yet as if by a leap he traverses the whole distance between "low" and "high" and is able to dwell disturbingly among us in his own libertine way.

The truth is that the comic hero has a complexity of character Bergson and Meredith did not suspect. Falstaff and Hal are both comedians who take part in the ancient ritual of feast and sacrifice, orgy and debate. In the oldest comedy there was a struggle, or *agon,* with the Imposter (or *alazon*) who looked with defiling eye upon the sacred rites that must not be seen. The alazon was put to flight after a contest with either the young king or with a character known as the *eiron,* "the ironical man." The alazon is a boaster who claims, traditionally, more than a share of the agonist's victory. It was the duty of the eiron, who often professed ignorance, to reduce the alazon, to bring him to confusion. Sometimes the king himself assumed the character of the eiron—"the ironical buffoon"—to deflate the boaster or "unwelcome intruder" who appeared to know more than he actually did. Thus somewhere at the heart of old comedy—ritual comedy— was a combat of the king-eiron against the imposter-intruder-alazon.

This ancient struggle was still being waged in Aristotle's *Ethics* (II, 7; IV, 7, 8) in the contrast beween the boaster (alazon) and the self-depreciator (eiron); and midway between these two characters is the "straightforward" man who neither exaggerates nor understates. Here, as in old comedy, the alazon is the alter ego of the eiron. The two extremes appear together.

Aristotle mentions Socrates as the "mock-modest" character who understates things; and, in fact, Socrates is a kind of alter ego to Falstaff, the boaster-buffoon. The double nature of the comic hero is symbolized in these two: Falstaff and Socrates. They are of opposite disposition, yet not so unlike as we might think. The essential character of the eiron is incarnate in Socrates, who was "ignorant" and who also had the disposition of the "buffoon" or "fool," the features of the comic spirit itself, the coarse, ugly mask of the satyr or clown. The Socratic method is a tactic of winning victory by professing ignorance, by merely asking questions of the "impostors," the so-called "wise" men of Athens. Irony "defeats the enemy on his own ground," for in the course of the comic debate the supposed wisdom of the alazon is reduced to absurdity, and the alazon himself becomes a clown. Thus Socrates, without risking any dogmatic answers, corrects the folly of those sophists who claimed to know the truth, or who were ignorant enough to presume there is no truth. So the ironical man by his shrewd humility ("lying low beneath the gods and saying nothing") proves to be wiser than the wisdom of the world. Irony has been called one of the faces of shame. Yet we must remember that Falstaff the buffoon and impostor used the same sort of interrogation Socrates the ironist used. He asks the same sort of questions: What is honor? Socrates asked: What is justice?

Socrates, like Falstaff, is both ironist and buffoon; he is the questioner using a philosophic buffoonery to seek the truth. In *The Republic* Thrasymachus speaks of Socrates' "shamming ignorance" in his "imbecile way." Socrates is a sort of supersophist who inquires or doubts, and thus again resembles Falstaff. He has a double or triple character, for he is, as Falstaff was, both victor and victim—a

victim, eventually, of the unthinking Athenians who refused to have
their creed unsettled. He was finally condemned to drink the hem-
lock because he asked too many impious questions. And Falstaff is
rejected by King Hal. The eiron himself, with the rude face of the
satyr, is at last, like the king in the fertility rite, sacrificed by the
tribe. Socrates is a kind of alazon too, since he did claim to have
his "wisdom," given him by his daemon, a still small voice he held
sacred. When he is condemned to death by the court he stubbornly
insists that if they kill him they will injure themselves far more than
they injure him, for they will not find another like him, a gadfly
given to the city by God. This is a considerable claim. He adds,
"I know but little, and I do not suppose that I know. But I do know
that injustice and disobedience to a better, whether God or man, is
evil and dishonorable." Here we need to recall that Aristotle classified
comic characters as being of three kinds: buffoon, ironist, and impostor. Socrates is all three—and so is Falstaff.

Thus is revealed the deep ambiguity in the comic hero: the Impostor, the enemy of God, is not only the alter ego of the ironist;
he is, in Cornford's phrase, the double of the very god himself. The
god must be slain and devoured; therefore the guilt feeling of the
tribe arising from sacrificing their god-king is transferred to the figure
of the alazon, the antagonist and profaner who serves as scapegoat
for the injury done the god during the fertility ceremony. The impostor profanes the rites; then he is beaten and driven out. So the
tribe rationalizes its sin by persecuting the One Who Dares To Look.
Cornford says: "The reviling and expulsion of the Antagonist-
Impostor is the darker counterpart of the *Kômos,* which brings in the
new God, victorious over him in the *Agon.*" The god who is savior
must be hated and slain. He has a double nature: he who is ven-
erated, he who is reviled. Before the resurrection there is the crowning
with thorns. The alazon is one of the disguises worn by the god-hero
before he is sacrificed; he is also, by the same token, the "antagonistic"
self that must be disowned before the worshiper is "possessed" by the
god. Hence the ambivalence toward the comic hero.

Or the alazon-eiron may be simply the agent of God, like Goethe's
Mephisto, who explains how he is "the spirit that endlessly denies"
but is also "part of a power that would alone work evil, but engenders good." The Impostor, Profaner, or Devil is a "darkness that
is part of light." Evil is inherent in Good, and to reach salvation
man must pass through a "negation of negation." Therefore Faust
finds himself bound to the impudent spirit who is only his darker
self. Faust exclaims: "Why must I be fettered to this infamous com-

panion who battens upon mischief and delights in ruin?" He does
not yet know that the one who goads him—the Tempter—is a deputy
of God. And the eiron, who can put on the features of the buffoon
and scapegoat, is, in his other self, a mocker, blasphemer, and Of-
fender. He embodies, again, the side of the god that must be rebelled
against before the god can be worshiped. God must be hated before
he can be loved, denied before he is believed. The comedian plays
the role of Doubting Thomas. He is at once a stone rejected by the
builder, and the cornerstone of the temple. Comedy is destructive
and creative. So Falstaff, like Socrates, has a double nature and a
double fate: eiron and alazon, tempter and clown, hero and knave,
the great god Pan and also Pharmakos—he who is expelled with
communal sins heaped on his head.

   Falstaff is a central image in comedy. Symbolically he is the Fool;
and the province of the Fool is the whole wide circuit of life and
death, laughter and tears, wisdom and ignorance.[11] The fool is comic
man. He is no mechanical figure. His gestures have daemonic power,
and he carries his scepter by right of ancient rule. We fear him as
god; we laugh at him as clown. All the ambiguities and ambiva-
lences of comic action pivot on this archetypal hero of many guises.
The fool wears motley—the particolor of human nature—and quickly
changes one mask for another, putting on indifferently and recklessly
the shifting features of man, playing with gusto more roles than are
suitable to the tragic hero. The fool at last proves to be the clown;
and the clown is He Who Gets Slapped—and "is none the worse
for his slapping." He is resilient with a vitality lacking to the tragic
hero, who must accept his misfortune and his responsibility with a
stoic face, with a steadier logic than the absurd logic of comedy.

   In general one may distinguish two orders of fool, natural and
artificial. The natural fool is the archaic victim who diverts the wrath
of the gods from the anointed figure of the king. He is the alter ego
of the Successful Man, who needs to exempt himself from the jealousy and ill will of the Olympians and who therefore provides himself with someone insolent or ignorant, whom the gods smite. The
fool is vicarious Sufferer. He is reviled, beaten, and stricken; but he
has the privilege of vilifying the Prosperous Man; he is free to hum-
ble the Exalted by mockery. The fool saves the hero from the awful
sin of pride (hubris). He is the Ugly One who by slandering, guards
the king, or even the priest, from the evil eye. He may be dwarfed

---

[11] In discussing the nature of the Fool and his many roles, I have relied
heavily on Enid Welsford: The Fool, 1935, as well as on Kris: Psychoanalytic
Explorations in Art, 1952, and J. A. K. Thomson: Irony, 1927.

and deformed; he may be an idiot. But the idiot has the wisdom of innocence and the naïveté of the child.

To this order of natural fools belongs Friar Juniper, the holy clown of the Franciscan order, whose antics were a token of grace, who had great power against the Devil and went about in ragged cowl, greatly comforted when the people called him blockhead. In his mind the fool bears the stigmata of holiness. Dostoevsky's saintly prostitutes like Sonia, or his "idiots" like Muishkin and Alyosha, have a close kinship with the natural fool. Kafka's heroes—those anonymous abused innocents known only as K—are natural fools who behold their own affliction with wide, credulous eyes. Everything strikes K with wonder and surprise, since he is the amateur in living who cannot be sophisticated by custom, who never learns his way around. For him life is always astonishment, effort, and uncertainty.

At his most contemptible the artificial fool may be the parasite of the old Greco-Roman comedies, a servile instrument in the hands of wealth and power. These fools use the oily manners of Rosencrantz and Guildenstern, or Osric, that yeasty, superserviceable knave spacious only in the possession of dirt.

But the fool can also be the seer, the prophet, the "possessed," since the madness of the fool is oracular, sibylline, delphic. He may be the voice crying in the wilderness, an Evangelist or Baptist, or an Imbecile-Prince like Muishkin, whose friends tell him he will always be a child, and who has revelations: "The recognition of God as our Father, and of God's joy in men as His own children, which is the chief idea of Christ." The fool may be the godly Dolt like the medieval Tumbler of Our Lady, or the poetic Seer like Rimbaud. He may, like Touchstone, look askance at life with a cool reluctance to commit himself. Sometimes his intuition is tragic, like the naïve cynicism of Lear's Fool, who sees the folly of playing Machiavellian games in a world rent by tempest. In the Sermon on the Mount, Jesus tells us with the voice of Innocence that we must accept the ridiculous as the basis of morality: "Blessed are the meek, for they shall inherit the earth."

The comedian is indeed a "revolutionary simpleton." No modern has claimed this more emphatically than Kierkegaard, who saw how the religious man must first of all be a comedian: "The religious individual has as such made the discovery of the comical in largest measure." Kierkegaard's religious man is not necessarily the comic poet or actor, but he is the one who has seen that our deepest experiences come to us in the form of contradictions. Therefore he is afflicted with the "higher madness" that is the comedy of faith, a passionate belief in the absurd. The knight of faith knows that the pathetic is inherent in the comic, that suffering is a mark of blessedness: "And hence it comes about that one is tempted both to weep and to laugh when the humorist speaks." Kierkegaard restates in another key the theme of Nietzsche's existential comedy: that one who suffers "by virtue of his suffering *knows more* than the shrewdest and wisest can ever know." Like a modern saint Nietzsche writes: "Suffering makes noble: it separates."

Thus in almost all his roles the fool is set apart, dedicated, alienated, if not outcast, beaten, slain. Being isolated, he serves as a "center of indifference," from which position the rest of us may, if we will, look through his eyes and appraise the meaning of our daily life. Archimedes is said to have promised "Give me a place to stand, and I will move the earth." In art, in ethics, in religion the fool finds a place to stand, for he is the detached spectator who has been placed, or has placed himself, outside accepted codes. From this point "outside"—this extrapolated fulcrum—he takes his leverage on the rest of us, and from his point of vantage can exclaim with Puck, the comic avenger, "Lord, what fools these mortals be."

There is something malign in Puck's spirit; he is scornful and delights in confusion. When this scorn is fierce enough we have the comic spirit of Swift, who frightens us out of laughter into dismay, if not despair. Just as Kierkegaard discovers the extreme absurdities of faith by extrapolating the attitude of the humorist, so Jonathan Swift leads us to the verge of a gulf of hopelessness by extrapolating the mischievous attitude of Puck. His Majesty of Brobdingnag tells Gulliver, after deliberation, "I can not but conclude the bulk of your natives to be the most pernicious race of little odious vermin that nature ever suffered to crawl upon the surface of the earth." The most galling of all comic figures are Swift's loathsome Yahoomen who reduce us all to intolerable shame.

There is something Puckish, also, in Hamlet's spirit, taunting and curious as it is. Amid the rottenness of Denmark the Prince serves as a philosophic and temperamental fool, a center of "indifference." He stands apart from gross revelry under his own melancholy cloud; and from his distance he is able to perceive more things than philosophy can dream; for the dust of great Alexander may stop a bunghole, and however thick my lady paints, she comes to a foul grave, the noisome state of Yorick, who is eaten by the same worms that feed upon Polonius, that duller fool. Hamlet is humorist and sufferer existing alone with his disdainful soul. He allows himself every incaution, and with midsummer lunacy puts an antic disposition on. Some of

Hamlet's motives are devilish—Mephistophelian; his vocation is pica-resque, to ask impudent questions and lead us along the narrow ledge where the immoralist walks, making us quarter our thoughts with an obsessive guile. Hamlet, Mephisto, Byron, Stendhal, Nietzsche, and Gide are heroes who belong in a comic theatre where man is goaded and teased, led down the dimmest passes of sin, to see what is learned by evil.

When he appears as tempter, the fool—the comic hero who stands "outside"—must put on the mask. He disguises himself as clown or devil, wearing as need arises the garb of buffoon, ironist, madman. He must lead us, finally, to the witches' kitchen and the Walpurgis Night; or to the wilderness where we meet our "shadow" selves face to face, although we have disowned these selves in our public life. There in the wilderness or on the Brocken the god in us is confronted by the Adversary, our "other" self, who lays before us illusions of pomp, knowledge, and pleasure. In tempting us the Ad-versary must have the features of innocence, must charm us with mannerly good will, gaiety, finesse, and high spirits. He may seem as honest as Iago, whose motiveless malignity wears the bland mask of friendship. Iago is the Socratic interrogator who destroys us with our own ideals; yet he is an illusion: "I am not what I am," he says. This Adversary may speak folly or profanity; or jest insanely, as did Nietzsche, who tempted the whole respectable middle class with his madness. His Satyr-Heroes have recognized Dionysus as god and they "*revert* to the innocence of the beast-of-prey conscience, like jubilant monsters, who perhaps come from a ghostly bout of murder, arson, rape, and torture with bravado and moral equanimity, as though merely some wild student's prank had been played."

The rebel, the immoralist, the free and licensed self in this terrible comedy of the future has passed "beyond" and looks back from a new and daring perspective upon the morality of the herd, which is hollow. Nietzsche's comic hero is the Despiser, the Blond Beast; or else he is the Great Sick Man overcome by his disgust, his nausea as he examines, from his point "outside," the premises of a morality we have never examined. To feel the spell of this Tempter we must take the awful risk of entering into a "boundary-situation" where nothing is taken for granted and where all our values must be found anew without help from "the others." Here we walk alone upon the margin of Reason. The Adversary goes with us to this highest preci-pice of comedy, the edge of the abyss where we glance with Nietzsche into Chaos. There we must stand on the brink of Nonsense and Absurdity and not be dizzy. If we do not fall, or plunge, we may be saved. Only by taking this risk can we put Satan behind us. Only thus can the Rebel learn what is Good. The comic Feast of Unreason is a test and a discovery, and our season spent mumming with the Lord of Misrule can show what will redeem us. The Adversary must be expelled. The Tempter must perish. That is, we must sacrifice him to save ourselves.

Young Hamlet, late from Wittenberg, stands alone on the brink of this abyss, sees himself as a ridiculous fellow crawling between heaven and earth with more sins at his beck than he has time to act. So he puts on the antic disposition of the fool. And if a sense of contradiction and absurdity is a cause of comedy, then Hamlet is a profoundly comic character. He encounters what Kierkegaard calls either/or choices, the extremes that cannot be mediated but only transcended. That is, the comic hero and the saint accept the irreconcilables in man's existence. Both find themselves face to face with the Inexplicable and the Absurd. When, for example, as Kierkegaard points out, Abraham holds the knife above Isaac and at the command of God is about to slay his son, he places himself outside and beyond all moral norms and is either, quite simply, a murderer or a believer. He stands alone in a situation that allows no middle term whatever. He meets an extreme peril that cannot be related to "virtue" or any human ethic. His dilemma can only be transcended by a "perspective from infinity"—looking at it from the infinite distance of faith, a perspective so far extrapolated beyond ethics that it extends from "eternity." Then Abraham is rescued from the irreconcilables in his crisis.

The comic hero finds himself in situations like Abraham's because comedy begins from the absurd and the inexplicable and, like faith, tolerates the miraculous. Dostoevsky, as usual, begins with the Unaccountable when old man Karamazov lies with Stinking Lizaveta and begets Smerdyakov, who is as truly his son as the saintly Alyosha. In the same way Miranda in *The Tempest* knows that good wombs have borne bad sons: Antonio is proof. Prospero accepts these incompatibles in reality, then transcends them by his "perspective from infinity," for at the farthest reaches of his magical vision life is like some dream that seems to come and fade. Precisely because he is face to face with the Inexplicable the comic hero is eligible for "rescue," like Don Quixote, who is mad to the degree of pouring curds over his poor head but who dies, like a saint, in a state of grace.

Often the comic hero is rescued because Improvisation and Uncertainty are the premises of comic action, and the goddess Fortuna presides over great tracts of the comic scene. But the law of Inevitability or Necessity bears heavily on the tragic hero, who is not eligible for rescue because in tragedy man must somehow take responsibility for the flaws in the nature of things or at least pay a penalty for them. To be sure, the tragic hero meets the Inexplicable—by what logic does Oedipus happen to confront his father on the road to Thebes and kill him in a narrow pass? Behind tragedy, too, is a riddle of the Sphinx, the warning of oracles only hoarsely spoken. In any case the tragic poet feels some compulsion to look backwards across the gulf of disaster and help us understand why the hero met his doom. Or he must fortify us against the Inexplicable and reassure us that Justice is not wrecked by it; whereas the comic artist can accept absurdities as the open premises of his account of life and not be troubled by them. The comedian practices an art of exaggeration, or overstatement.

The tragic hero, however, must heed some "golden mean" between extremes; he does not dare *play* with life as the comic hero does. The tragic hero meets either/or dilemmas but must pay some penalty for not being able to conciliate incompatibles. His only refuge from despair is a stoic endurance between those incompatibles; he must somehow prove himself adequate to the disasters he suffers. The tragic poet cannot, like the comic artist or the religious hero, look at man's struggle from infinite distances and revise its human weight or its penalties. Tragedy is a form of ethical heroism, suggesting that "man is the measure," even between desperate choices.

The tragic hero, noble and magnified, can be of awesome stature. The comic hero refuses to wear the trappings of moral or civil grandeur, usually preferring motley, or the agility of the clown. He is none the less man, and Hamlet more than once rouses our suspicion that the tragic hero is eligible for comic roles: or is it the other way round, that Hamlet is a comic hero who generates tragic values? The Prince touches his deepest meanings when he has on his antic humor. Then he needs no grandeur to hide his weakness, which is laughably naked.

Under the auspices of Fortuna comedy allows a play of character impossible in tragedy, which requires a hero "greater and better than most men" but capable of "error." As Aristotle says, the tragic hero cannot be either "depraved" or simply a victim of "bad luck." Comedy, however, delights to deal with those who are victims of bad luck, along with those who are "depraved" or "vicious"—by means of the grotesque. By disfiguring the hated person in caricature, comedy is able to elevate hatred to art. Swift evidently saw man as depraved and vicious, and projected his hatred into the grotesques called Ya-

hoos. At the severest phase of grotesque we can behold the unnatural
figures of King Lear and his daughters, who seem to have reduced
life to horrors from which tragedy turns away. The crazy Lear wails:

> When we are born, we cry that we are come
> To this great stage of fools.

In this savage play men seem to be puppets (but not automatons).

Cornford tells us why comedy can utilize the grotesque. In Greece
and Rome comedy was gradually transmuted from religious Mystery
to theatrical Mime. So when comedy lost its appearance of being
what originally and essentially it was, a fertility celebration, the characters tended to become grotesques, and the comedian continued
using many of the stock masks tragedy had discarded. The original
chorus of celebrant animal-figures gave a name to some of Aristophanes' comedies like *The Birds* and *The Wasps*. The old goat-chorus
and satyr-masks invaded the final comic unit of the tetralogy. The
Impostor, particularly, became a stylized, stereotyped figure, like the
Vice in medieval plays with his lath dagger and his sortie from
Hell-Mouth. In this way the comic personality did indeed become
dehumanized when it was a vehicle for making certain gestures—
the automatic gestures of Punch and Pierrot. Are not these lively
creatures the ancestors of Tartuffe and other caricatures? They are
born of Mime and live the repetitive existence of Bergson's manikins,
oscillating between life and art. Yet we must once more remind ourselves that Falstaff born of a "mask," generates a personality and
temperament more human than his gestures entitle him to.

IV. The Social Meanings of Comedy

The tradition of Mime, Mask, and Caricature, then, explains why
Bergson thought, with Stendhal, that comedy requires a certain rigidity
in the comic personage, an *insociabilité* in the hero and a degree of
insensibilité in the spectator. But Falstaff breaks down this insensi-
bility and offers us a sort of release and purgation Pierrot cannot.
Falstaff proves what Freud suspected: that comedy is a process of
safeguarding pleasure against the denials of reason, which is wary of
pleasure. Man cannot live by reason alone or forever under the rod
of moral obligation, the admonition of the superego. In the person of
Falstaff the superego "takes a holiday." The comedian is the self
behaving as prodigal and bohemian. From its earliest days comedy is
an essential pleasure mechanism valuable to the spectator and the
society in which he lives. Comedy is a momentary and publicly useful
resistance to authority and an escape from its pressures; and its mech-

provocateur. In Gide and Goya and Swift the tenor of comedy is uncompromising, irreverent.

In her own quiet way Jane Austen devastates our compromises and complacencies—especially male complacency. It is said one can read her novels and never guess that France was red with terror or that British troops were dying at Waterloo. She leaves all that turmoil to the "romantics." Meanwhile Miss Austen placidly undermines the bastions of middle-class propriety. Her irreverence is calm, but she knows better than the "romantics" that one must not compromise one's honesty. She is not the less dangerous because she operates inconspicuously. There she resembles Henry James, who lays bare in his overbred prose the shameless vulgarity of the *haute bourgeoisie.* We must not be deceived, either, about Miss Austen's cool disposition, which seems defensive, wary of being taken in. She is using the caution native to those comic artists who contrive to protect themselves against scorn while they are making us scorn others. Her contempt is polite.

This is comedy near its "highest," which, Bergson and Meredith agree, is a game played in social life. In *Two Sources of Morality and Religion* Bergson described two orders of society, the one unchanging, mechanical stratified, conservative, and "closed"; the other mobile, organic, fluid, and "open." A colony of insects is a "closed" order, alert for danger, attack, defense. It is a society with Spartan efficiency and, ability to survive. The members of a closed society care nothing for humanity but live untroubled by dreams or doubts. The open society has a different morality because it is sensitive to the fringe of intuition, "vague and evanescent," that envelops every clear idea. Those living in an open society are self-aware, responsive to the nuance, the not-wholly-formulated. The open society gives play to individuality, true selfhood. Stendhal's hero Julien Sorel belongs in an open society but is trapped within the confines of a closed caste system. So his adventures become a picaresque comedy played at the expense of the insensitive people about him and of his own malaise.

To expand Bergson's idea a little, we may say that the "lower" the comedy, the more it needs a "closed" social order, and the "higher" the comedy, the more the situation is "open" socially and morally. The mechanics of Shakespeare's *Comedy of Errors* are possible in a situation firmly "closed," where events exactly balance each other in a series of neatly arranged coincidences. The moral rigidity in this world is suggested by the Duke's mechanical, paralyzing ethic which causes him to say to Aegeon: "For we may pity, though not pardon, thee."

The situation in *Twelfth Night* seems to be more "open" but really is not. Behind the delicate manners in Illyria is a tightly closed social order, as the aspiring Malvolio finds, to his distress and our delight. The fellow is a bounder; his eye is fixed hard on Olivia; he is the butler who woos his mistress. The man is a yellow-stockinged fool; and he is a fool first of all because he wishes to leap the barriers, which are far too high. At all costs Malvolio must not climb. Obviously Malvolio is an ass—obviously. Yet no more so than Sir Andrew Aguecheek, at whom we laugh, but not malignly as we do at Malvolio. Sir Andrew has a prerogative of asininity in virtue of his birth. He is a natural, not a bounder. Hard-mindedly we identify our scapegoat, Malvolio parading cross-gartered, even if we do not choose to see him for what, socially, he is: the Impostor who must be expelled with a vengeance. Sir Andrew cannot be devalued by the sneer alone, because he is guarded by his rank. But Malvolio the popinjay rouses our archaic wrath at the Pretender—who is, in this event, our own social alter ego to be publicly tormented, disclaimed, icily denied. Comedy of manners often releases the cruelty in a closed society; and the stiff ranks in this society put us in unnatural positions.

At the height of comedy the whole situation "opens" in many directions. *Love's Labour's Lost* begins as if it were to be a "closed" comedy like *Twelfth Night,* for the scene is the fastidious Academe in Navarre where some precious fools are pledging themselves to an ascetic life for three years, depriving themselves of sleep, food, and love. Berowne alone protests, in the name of "grace." Then one by one the lordly fantasticoes fall in love with very frail women and break their vows, yielding to the flesh. These wits bring themselves face to face with human realities. But before they can readjust, the King of France dies, and they all find themselves standing at the mouth of the grave, where they must pause. The entire company disperses with a curiously somber and hesitant benediction: "You that way, we this way." The play shows how the movement of high comedy is expanding, scattering itself from situation to situation always farther abroad, opening toward other possibilities, holding all in suspense.[16] Berowne is one of those who, with Benedick and Mercutio and Hamlet, cannot be at home in a closed plot, a closed society, a closed ethic.

Shakespeare's most "open" comedy—nearly mystic in Bergson's sense—is *The Tempest,* where all the machinery of plot is suspended in evanescent meanings that are almost musical. This play disperses

---

[16] The point is made by Paul Goodman: *The Structure of Literature,* 1954, p. 89 ff.

into unknown modes of being, where even Caliban can seek for grace. The act of forgiveness is the moral pole of this comedy, and under the spell of Prospero's sea-change we are able to look as if from afar, backward upon the wrongs done in the dark abysm of the past. Evil is there, in Antonio and Sebastian, in Stephano and Trinculo and Caliban; but at these moral latitudes we can see even the vicious Antonio as if he were only a troubling recollection. Amid devouring shows and strange noises human nature is transfigured. Prospero's magic is the godlike charity of understanding, thus enduring, all. Using the tolerance of high comedy, and its confidence, Prospero speaks gently to those who tried to kill him. In this larger perspective sin seems to be the last delusion of man's mind, an error that is absurd. Prospero's vision of life is not tragic because sin is seen from distances that exempt man from disastrous penalties. All miracles are performed at this height of comedy, which brings us into a shifting, open world that continuingly transforms itself without being emptied of the cruelest actualities. Antonio is eager to murder with his three inches of obedient steel; yet these failings in men cannot damage the illusion that is truth. The vile Antonio cannot destroy what is good. Tragic danger is here cancelled by a feat of moral insight. The drama of Prospero's isle, the farthest reach of comedy, is an insubstantial pageant. It is also a triumphant revision of life, a politics of illusion.

Bergson must have seen life as Prospero did, since he described this politics of illusion in *Two Sources of Morality and Religion:*

The open society is the society which is deemed in principle to embrace all humanity. A dream dreamt, now and again, by chosen souls, it embodies on every occasion something of itself in creations, each of which, through a more or less far-reaching transformation of man, conquers difficulties hitherto unconquerable.

Prospero's charity is the imaginative fulfillment of an ethic such as Bergson mentions. There is nothing in actuality to justify his mercy, his confidence, or his vision; yet these master the failings of nature and work a change in man. Comedy is, indeed, like a dream, as even Bergson perhaps did not suspect. In saying that life is rounded with a sleep, Prospero is but repeating the words spoken by Theseus, king of a realm where there were midsummer-night dreams; for when Theseus saw the silly interlude rudely played by the mechanicals in honor of him and Hippolyta he explained: "The best in this kind are but shadows, and the worst are no worse if imagination amend them." Theseus saw that the drama was there, even if it was badly played; and he was grateful to the wretched players, who gained their triumph not on their poor stage but in Theseus' fancy.

The high comic vision of life is humane, an achievement of man as a social being. Meredith addressed himself to "our united social intelligence, which is the Comic Spirit." He suspected that comedy is "the ultimate civilizer." If Prospero's comedy is transcendentally "open," Meredith's social comedy remains a worldy discipline with, nevertheless, full moral overtones. In all civilized societies, Meredith insists, the comic spirit must hover overhead, its lips drawn in a slim, hungry smile, wary and tense, thoughtfully eager to see the absurdities of polite men and women. Kierkegaard might have been describing Meredith's faun when he said the "comic spirit is not wild or vehement, its laughter is not shrill." For Kierkegaard, too, the highest comedy, like the highest pathos, rarely attracts attention by making great shows. Only the "lower forms of the comical do show themselves by something extrinsic. The highest in life does not make a showing, because it belongs to the last sphere of inwardness." No society is in good health without laughing at itself quietly and privately; no character is sound without self-scrutiny, without turning inward to see where it may have overreached itself. The perception of the self as comic touches the quick; and honest self-inspection must bring a sense of the comical. This kind of awareness is an initiation into the civilized condition; it lightens the burden of selfishness, cools the heat of the ego, makes us impressionable by others.

So the comic spirit keeps us pure in mind by requiring that we regard ourselves skeptically. Indeed this spirit is an agent of that civilizing activity Matthew Arnold called "criticism," which is essential to "culture." It is an activity necessary to middle-class society, where we gravitate easily toward that dead center of self-satisfaction, the Philistine. Arnold tells us why criticism brings salvation, and why culture *is* criticism:

And thus culture begets a dissatisfaction, which is of the highest possible value in stemming the common tide of men's thoughts in a wealthy and industrial community, and which saves the future, as one may hope, from being vulgarized, even if it cannot save the present. (*Culture and Anarchy*)

Shakespeare's plays, says Meredith, are saturated with the golden light of comedy—the comedy that is redemptive as tragedy cannot be. Consider what happens in *Much Ado About Nothing* when Benedick makes the startling comic discovery that he himself, together with the other mistaken people in the play, is a fool. Here is a moral perception that competes with tragic "recognition." The irony of

Benedick's "recognition" is searching, for he has boasted, all along, that he cannot find it in his heart to love any of Eve's daughters, least of all Beatrice. And Beatrice, for her part, has avowed she will never be fitted with a husband until God makes men of some other metal than earth. Both these characters are too deep of draught to sail in the shoal waters of sentimentality, and both have bravely laid a course of their own far outside the matchmaking that goes easily on in Messina. Each is a mocker, or eiron; but in being so, each becomes the boaster (alazon) betrayed into the valiant pose that they are exempt from love. Then they both walk, wide-eyed, like "proud" Oedipus, into the trap they have laid for themselves. There they see themselves as they are. When Benedick hears himself called hard-hearted he suffers the bewilderment of comic discovery and knows that his pose as mocker is no longer tenable. So he turns his scornful eye inward upon his own vanity: if Beatrice is sick for love of his ribald self he must give up his misogyny and get him a wife. He yields himself, absurdly, to Beatrice, saying "Happy are they that hear their detractions and can put them to mending." At the extreme of his own shame Benedick is compelled to see himself as he sees others, together along a low horizon. Thus occur the comic purgation, the comic resignation to the human lot, the comic humbling of the proud, the comic ennobling after an act of blindness. Those who play a comic role, like Benedick or Berowne or Meredith's Sir Willoughby Patterne, wrongheadedly are liable to achieve their own defeat and afterwards must hide their scars. The comic and the tragic heroes alike "learn through suffering," albeit suffering in comedy takes the form of humiliation, disappointment, or chagrin, instead of death.

There is a comic road to wisdom, as well as a tragic road. There is a comic as well as a tragic control of life. And the comic control may be more usable, more relevant to the human condition in all its normalcy and confusion, its many unreconciled directions. Comedy as well as tragedy can tell us that the vanity of the world is foolishness before the gods. Comedy dares seek truth in the slums of Eastcheap or the crazy landscape Don Quixote wanders across or on the enchanted Prospero isle. By mild inward laughter it tries to keep us sane in the drawing room, among decent men and women. It tells us that man is a giddy thing, yet does not despair of men. Comedy gives us recognitions healing as the recognitions of tragic art. They are sometimes revelations and come in the moonlit forest of a summer night; then Bottom, with his ass head, is transformed to a Seer, a Visionary, and Bottom's Dream is apocalyptic. For Bottom, the poor weaver, reports: "I have had a dream; past the wit of man to say

what dream it was. Man is but an ass if he go about to expound
this dream." After this midnight dream everything is seen from a new
distance; as Hermia says:

> Methinks I see these things with parted eye
> When every thing seems double.

Tragedy needs a more single vision than comedy, for the comic perception comes only when we take a double view—that is, a human
view—of ourselves, a perspective by incongruity. Then we take part
in the ancient rite that is a Debate and a Carnival, a Sacrifice and
a Feast.

Notes on the Comic*

W. H. AUDEN

*If a man wants to set up as an innkeeper and he does not succeed,
it is not comic. If, on the contrary, a girl asks to be allowed to set up
as a prostitute and she fails, which sometimes happens, it is comic.*
—SØREN KIERKEGAARD

*A man's character may be inferred from nothing so surely as from
the jest he takes in bad part.*—G. C. LICHTENBERG

General Definition

A contradiction in the relation of the individual or the personal to
the universal or the impersonal which does not involve the spectator
or hearer in suffering or pity, which in practice means that it must
not involve the actor in real suffering.

A situation in which the actor really suffers can only be found
comic by children who see only the situation and are unaware of the
suffering, as when a child laughs at a hunchback, or by human swine.

A few years ago, there was a rage in New York for telling "Horror
Jokes." For example:

A mother (to her blind daughter): Now, dear, shut your eyes and count
twenty. Then open them, and you'll find that you can see.
Daughter (after counting twenty): But, Mummy, I still can't see.
Mother: April fool!

This has the same relation to the comic as blasphemy has to belief
in God, that is to say, it implies a knowledge of what is truly comic.

We sometimes make a witty remark about someone which is also

---

* W. H. Auden, "Notes on the Comic," in *The Dyer's Hand* (Random
House, 1952), pp. 371–385.

cruel, but we make it behind his back, not to his face, and we hope
that nobody will repeat it to him.

When we really hate someone, we cannot find him comic; there are
no genuinely funny stories about Hitler.

A sense of humor develops in a society to the degree that its members are simultaneously conscious of being each a unique person and
of being all in common subjection to unalterable laws.

Primitive cultures have little sense of humor; firstly, because their
sense of human individuality is weak—the tribe is the real unit—and,
secondly, because, as animists or polytheists, they have little notion of
necessity. To them, events do not occur because they must, but because some god or spirit chooses to make them happen. They recognize a contradiction between the individual and the universal only
when it is a tragic contradiction involving exceptional suffering.

In our own society, addicted gamblers who make a religion out of
chance are invariably humorless.

Among those whom I like or admire, I can find no common denominator, but among those whom I love, I can: all of them make
me laugh.

Some Types of Comic Contradiction

1) The operation of physical laws upon inorganic objects associated
with a human being in such a way that it is they who appear to be
acting from personal volition and their owner who appears to be the
passive thing.

Example: A man is walking in a storm protected by an umbrella when a
sudden gust of wind blows it inside out. This is comic for two reasons:

a) An umbrella is a mechanism designed by man to function in a particular manner, and its existence and effectiveness as a protection depend upon
man's understanding of physical laws. An umbrella turning inside out is funnier than a hat blowing off because an umbrella is made to be opened, to
change its shape when its owner wills. It now continues to change its shape,
in obedience to the same laws, but against his will.

b) The activating agent, the wind, is invisible, so the cause of the umbrella turning inside out appears to lie in the umbrella itself. It is not particularly funny if a tile falls and makes a hole in the umbrella, because the cause
is visibly natural.

When a film is run backwards, reversing the historical succession
of events, the flow of volition is likewise reversed and proceeds from
the object to the subject. What was originally the action of a man
taking off his coat becomes the action of a coat putting itself on a man.

The same contradiction is the basis of most of the comic effects of the clown. In appearance he is the clumsy man whom inanimate objects conspire against to torment; this in itself is funny to watch, but our profounder amusement is derived from our knowledge that this is only an appearance, that, in reality, the accuracy with which the objects trip him up or hit him on the head is caused by the clown's own skill.

2) A clash between the laws of the inorganic which has no *telos,* and the behavior of living creatures who have one.

Example: A man walking down the street, with his mind concentrated upon the purpose of his journey, fails to notice a banana skin, slips and falls down. Under the obsession of his goal—it may be a goal of thought—he forgets his subjection to the law of gravity. His goal need not necessarily be a unique and personal one; he may simply be looking for a public lavatory. All that matters is that he should be ignoring the present for the sake of the future. A child learning to walk, or an adult picking his way carefully over an icy surface, are not funny if they fall down, because they are conscious of the present.

Comic Situations in the Relationship Between the Sexes

As a natural creature a human being is born either male or female and endowed with an impersonal tendency to reproduce the human species by mating with any member of the opposite sex who is neither immature nor senile. In this tendency the individuality of any given male or female is subordinate to its general reproductive function. (*Male and female created He them . . . Be fruitful and multiply.*)

As a historical person, every man and woman is a unique individual, capable of entering into a unique relation of love with another person. As a person, the relationship takes precedence over any function it may also have. (*It is not good for man to be alone.*)

The ideal of marriage is a relationship in which both these elements are synthesized; husband and wife are simultaneously involved in relations of physical love and the love of personal friendship.

The synthesis might be easier to achieve if the two elements remained distinct, if the physical, that is, remained as impersonal as it is among the animals, and the personal relation was completely unerotic.

In fact, however, we never experience sexual desire as a blind need which is indifferent to its sexual object; our personal history and our culture introduce a selective element so that, even on the most physical level, some types are more desirable than others. Our sexual desire, as such, is impersonal in that it lacks all consideration for the person who is our type, but personal in that our type is our personal taste, not a blind need.

This contradiction is fertile ground for self-deception. It allows us to persuade ourselves that we value the person of another, when, in fact, we only value her (or him) as a sexual object, and it allows us to endow her with an imaginary personality which has little or no relation to the real one.

From the personal point of view, on the other hand, sexual desire, because of its impersonal and unchanging character, is a comic contradiction. The relation between every pair of lovers is unique, but in bed they can only do what all mammals do.

Comic Travesties

Twelfth Night. The pattern of relationships is as follows:

1) Viola (Caesario) is wholly in the truth. She knows who she is, she knows that the Duke is a man for whom she feels personal love, and her passionate image of him corresponds to the reality.

2) The Duke is in the truth in one thing; he knows that he feels a personal affection for Caesario (Viola). This is made easier for him by his boylike appearance—did he look like a mature man, he would fall into a class, the class of potential rivals in love. The fact that he feels personal affection for the illusory Caesario guarantees the authenticity of his love for the real Viola as a person, since it cannot be an illusion provoked by sexual desire.

His relation to Olivia, on the other hand, is erotic-fantastic in one of two ways, and probably in both: either his image of her does not correspond to her real nature or, if it does correspond, it is fantastic in relation to himself; the kind of wife he really desires is not what he imagines. The fact that, though she makes it clear that she does not return his passion, he still continues to pursue her and by devious strategies, demonstrates that he lacks respect for her as a person.

3) Olivia has an erotic-fantastic image of Caesario (Viola). Since she is able to transfer her image successfully to Caesario's double, Sebastian, and marry him, we must assume that the image of the kind of husband she desires is real in relation to herself and only accidentally fantastic because Caesario happens to be, not a man, but a woman in disguise.

4) The illusion of Antonio and Sebastian is not concerned with the erotic relationship, but with the problem of body-soul identity. It is a general law that a human face is the creation of its owner's past and that, since two persons cannot have the same past, no two

faces are alike. Identical twins are the exception to this rule. Viola and Sebastian are twins, but not identical twins, for one is female and the other male; dress them both, however, in male or female clothing, and they appear to be identical twins.

It is impossible to produce *Twelfth Night* today in an ordinary theatre since feminine roles are no longer played, as they were in Shakespeare's time, by boys. It is essential to the play that, when Viola appears dressed as a boy, the illusion should be perfect; if it is obvious to the audience that Caesario is really a girl, the play becomes a farce, and a farce in bad taste, for any serious emotion is impossible in a farce, and some of the characters in *Twelfth Night* have serious emotions. A boy whose voice has not yet broken can, when dressed as a girl, produce a perfect illusion of a girl; a young woman, dressed as a boy, can never produce a convincing illusion of a boy.

Der Rosenkavalier and Charley's Aunt. To Baron Lerchenau, the seduction of young chambermaids has become a habit, i.e., what was once a combination of desire and personal choice has become almost an automatic reflex. A costume suggests to him the magic word *chambermaid,* and the word issues the command *Seduce her.* The baron, however, is not quite a farce character; he knows the difference between a pretty girl and an ugly one. The mezzo-soprano who plays Octavian should be good-looking enough to give the illusion of a good-looking young man, when dressed as one. In the third act, when she is dressed as what she really is, a girl, she will be pretty, but her acting the role of a chambermaid must be farcical, and give the impression of a bad actor impersonating a girl, so that only a man as obsessed by habit as the Baron could fail to notice it.

Charley's Aunt is pure farce. The fortune-hunting uncle is not a slave of habit; he really desires to marry a rich widow, but her riches are all he desires; he is totally uninterested in sex or in individuals. He has been told that he is going to meet a rich widow, he sees widow's weeds and this is sufficient to set him in motion. To the audience, therefore, it must be obvious that she is neither female nor elderly, but a young undergraduate pretending, with little success, to be both.

The Lover and the Citizen

Marriage is not only a relation between two individuals; it is also a social institution, involving social emotions concerned with class status and prestige among one's fellows. This is not in itself comic;

it only becomes comic if social emotion is the only motive for a marriage, so that the essential motives for marriage, sexual intercourse, procreation and personal affection, are lacking. A familiar comic situation is that of *Don Pasquale*. A rich old man plans to marry a young girl against her will, for she is in love with a young man of her own age; the old man at first looks like succeeding, but in the end he is foiled. For this to be comic, the audience must be convinced that Don Pasquale does not really feel either desire or affection for Norina, that his sole motive is a social one, to be able to boast to other old men that he can win a young wife when they cannot. He wants the prestige of parading her and making others envy him. If he really feels either desire or affection, then he will really suffer when his designs are foiled, and the situation will be either pathetic or satiric. In *Pickwick Papers,* the same situation occurs, only this time it is the female sex which has the social motive. Widow after widow pursues Weller, the widower, not because she wants to be married to him in particular, but because she wants the social status of being a married woman.

The Law of the City and the Law of Justice

Example: Falstaff's speech on Honour (*Henry IV,* Part I, Act V, Scene II.)

If the warrior ethic of honor, courage and personal loyalty were believed by an Elizabethan or a modern audience to be the perfect embodiment of justice, the speech would not be sympathetically comic, but a satirical device by which Falstaff was held up to ridicule as a coward. If, on the other hand, the warrior ethic were totally unjust, if there were no occasions on which it was a true expression of moral duty, the speech would be, not comic, but a serious piece of pacifist propaganda. The speech has a sympathetically comic effect for two reasons, the circumstances under which it is uttered, and the character of the speaker.

Were the situation one in which the future of the whole community is at stake, as on the field of Agincourt, the speech would strike an unsympathetic note, but the situation is one of civil war, a struggle for power among the feudal nobility in which the claims of both sides to be the legitimate rulers are fairly equal—Henry IV was once a rebel who deposed his King—and a struggle in which their feudal dependents are compelled to take part and risk their lives without having a real stake in the outcome. Irrespective of the speaker, the speech is a comic criticism of the feudal ethic as typified by Hotspur. Courage is a personal virtue, but military glory for military glory's sake can be a social evil; unreasonable and unjust wars create the paradox that the personal vice of cowardice can become a public virtue.

That it should be Falstaff who utters the speech increases its comic effect. Falstaff has a fantastic conception of himself as a daredevil who plays highwayman, which, if it were true, would require exceptional physical courage. He tries to keep up this illusion, but is always breaking down because of his moral courage which keeps forcing him to admit that he is afraid. Further, though he lacks courage, he exemplifies the other side of the warrior ethic, personal loyalty, as contrasted with Prince Hal's Machiavellian manipulation of others. When Falstaff is rejected by the man to whom he has pledged his whole devotion, his death may truly be called a death for the sake of his wounded honor.

The Banal

The human person is a unique singular, analogous to all other persons, but identical with none. Banality is an illusion of identity for, when people describe their experiences in clichés, it is impossible to distinguish the experience of one from the experience of another.

The cliché user is comic because the illusion of being identical with others is created by his own choice. He is the megalomaniac in reverse. Both have fantastic conceptions of themselves but, whereas the megalomaniac thinks of himself as being somebody else—God, Napoleon, Shakespeare—the banal man thinks of himself as being everybody else, that is to say, nobody in particular.

VERBAL HUMOR

Verbal humor involves a violation in a particular instance of one of the following general principles of language.

1) Language is a means of denoting things or thoughts by sounds. It is a law of language that any given verbal sound always means the same thing and only that thing.

2) Words are man-made things which men use, not persons with a will and consciousness of their own. Whether they make sense or nonsense depends upon whether the speaker uses them correctly or incorrectly.

3) Any two or more objects or events which language seeks to describe are members, either of separate classes, or of the same class, or of overlapping classes. If they belong to separate classes, they must be described in different terms, and if they belong to the same class

they must be described in the same terms. If, however, their classes
overlap, either class can be described metaphorically in terms which
describe the other exactly, e.g., it is equally possible to say—the
plough swims through the soil—and—the ship ploughs through the
waves.

4) In origin all language is concerete or metaphorical. In order
to use language to express abstractions, we have to ignore its original
concrete and metaphorical meanings.

The first law is violated by the pun, the exceptional case in which
one verbal sound has two meanings.

> When I am dead I hope it may be said:
> His sins were scarlet, but his books were read.

For the pun to be comic, the two meanings must both make sense
in the context. If all books were bound in black, the couplet would
not be funny.

Words which rhyme, that is to say, words which denote different
things but are partially similar in sound, are not necessarily comic.
To be comic, the two things they denote must either be so incongruous with each other that one cannot imagine a real situation in
which a speaker would need to bring them together, or so irrelevant
to each other, that they could only become associated by pure chance.
The effect of a comic rhyme is as if the words, on the basis of
their auditory friendship, had taken charge of the situation, as if,
instead of an event requiring words to describe it, words had the
power to create an event. Reading the lines

> There was an Old Man of Whitehaven
> Who danced a quadrille with a raven

one cannot help noticing upon reflection that, had the old gentleman
lived in Ceylon, he would have had to dance with a swan; alterna-
tively, had his dancing partner been a mouse, he might have had to
reside in Christ Church, Oxford.

The comic rhyme involves both the first two laws of language;
the spoonerism only the second. *Example:* a lecturing geologist introduces a lantern slide with the words: "And here, gentlemen, we
see a fine example of erotic blacks."

So far as the speaker is concerned he has used the language incorrectly, yet what he says makes verbal sense of a kind. Unlike the pun,
however, where both meanings are relevant, in the spoonerism the
accidental meaning is nonsense in the context. Thus, while the comic
nature of the pun should be immediately apparent to the hearer, it

should take time before he realizes what the speaker of the spoonerism intended to say. A pun is witty and intended; a spoonerism, like
a comic rhyme, is comic and should appear to be involuntary. As with
the clown, the speaker appears to be the slave of language, but in
reality is its master.

Just as there are people who are really clumsy so there are incompetent poets who are the slaves of the only rhymes they know; the
kind of poet caricatured by Shakespeare in the play of *Pyramus and
Thisbe:*

> Those lily lips,
> This cherry nose,
> These yellow cowslip cheeks,
> Are gone, are gone,
> Lovers make moan;
> His eyes were green as leeks.
> O Sisters Three,
> Come, come to me
> With hands as pale as milk;
> Lay them in gore,
> Since you have shore
> With shears his thread of silk.

In this case we laugh at the rustic poet, not with him.

One of the most fruitful of witty devices is a violation of the third
law, namely, to treat members of overlapping classes as if they were
members of the same class. For example, during a period of riots and
social unrest when the mob had set fire to hayricks all over the country Sidney Smith wrote to his friend, Mrs. Meynell:

What do you think of all these burnings? and have you heard of the new
sort of burnings? Ladies' maids have taken to setting their mistresses on fire.
Two dowagers were burned last week, and large rewards are offered. They
are inventing little fire-engines for the toilet table, worked with lavender
water.

The fourth law, which distinguishes between the occasions when
speech is used to describe concrete things and those in which it is
used for abstract purposes, provides an opportunity for wit, as in
Wilde's epigram:

Twenty years of romance make a woman look like a ruin, and twenty years
of marriage make her look like a public building.

Ruin has become a "dead" metaphor, that is to say, a word which
normally can be used as an abstraction, but public building is still a
concrete description.

Literary Parody, and Visual Caricature

Literary parody presupposes a) that every authentic writer has a unique perspective on life and b) that his literary style accurately expresses that perspective. The trick of the parodist is to take the unique style of the author, *how* he expresses his unique vision, and make it express utter banalities; *what* the parody expresses could be said by anyone. The effect is of a reversal in the relation between the author and his style. Instead of the style being the creation of the man, the man becomes the puppet of the style. It is only possible to caricature an author one admires because, in the case of an author one dislikes, his own work will seem a better parody than one could hope to write oneself.

> *Example:*
>> As we get older we do not get any younger.
>> Seasons return, and to-day I am fifty-five,
>> And this time last year I was fifty-four,
>> And this time next year I shall be sixty-two.
>> And I cannot say I should like (to speak for myself)
>> To see my time over again—if you can call it time:
>> Fidgeting uneasily under a draughty stair,
>> Or counting sleepless nights in the crowded tube.
>>   (HENRY REED, *Chard Whitlow.*)

Every face is a present witness to the fact that its owner has a past behind him which might have been otherwise, and a future ahead of him in which some possibilities are more probable than others. To "read" a face means to guess what it might have been and what it still may become. Children, for whom most future possibilities are equally probable, the dead for whom all possibilities have been reduced to zero, and animals who have only one possibility to realize and realize it completely, do not have faces which can be read, but wear inscrutable masks. A caricature of a face admits that its owner has had a past, but denies that he has a future. He has created his features up to a certain point, but now they have taken charge of him so that he can never change; he has become a single possibility completely realized. That is why, when we go to the zoo, the faces of the animals remind one of caricatures of human beings. A caricature doesn't need to be read; it has no future.

We enjoy caricatures of our friends because we do not want to think of their changing, above all, of their dying; we enjoy caricatures of our enemies because we do not want to consider the possibility of their having a change of heart so that we would have to forgive them.

Flyting

Flyting seems to have vanished as a studied literary art and only to survive in the impromptu exchanges of truckdrivers and cabdrivers. The comic effect arises from the contradiction between the insulting nature of what is said which appears to indicate a passionate relation of hostility and aggression, and the calculated skill of verbal invention which indicates that the protagonists are not thinking about each other but about language and their pleasure in employing it inventively. A man who is really passionately angry is speechless and can only express his anger by physical violence. Playful anger is intrinsically comic because, of all emotions, anger is the least compatible with play.

Satire

The object of satire is a person who, though in possession of his moral faculties, transgresses the moral law beyond the normal call of temptation. The lunatic cannot be an object of satire, since he is not morally responsible for his actions, and the wicked man cannot be an object because, while morally responsible, he lacks the normal faculty of conscience. The commonest object of satire is the rogue. The rogue transgresses the moral law at the expense of others, but he is only able to do this because of the vices of his victims; they share in his guilt. The wicked man transgresses the moral law at the expense of others, but his victims are innocent. Thus a black marketeer in sugar can be satirized because the existence of such a black market depends upon the greed of others for sugar, which is a pleasure but not a necessity; a black marketeer in penicillin cannot be satirized because, for the sick, it is a necessity and, if they cannot pay his prices, they will die.

After the rogue, the commonest object of satire is the monomaniac. Most men desire money and are not always too scrupulous in the means by which they obtain it, but this does not make them objects of satire, because their desire is tempered by a number of competing interests. A miser is satirizable because his desire overrides all desires which normal selfishness feels, such as sex or physical comfort.

The Satirical Strategy

There is not only a moral human norm, but also a normal way of transgressing it. At the moment of yielding to temptation, the normal human being has to exercise self-deception and rationalization, for in order to yield he requires the illusion of acting with a good conscience: after he has committed the immoral act, when desire is satisfied, the normal human being realizes the nature of his act and feels guilty. He who is incapable of realizing the nature of his act is mad, and he who, both before, while, and after committing it, is exactly conscious of what he is doing yet feels no guilt, is wicked.

The commonest satirical devices therefore, are two: 1) To present the object of satire *as if* he or she were mad and unaware of what he is doing.

> Now Night descending, the proud scene was o'er,
> But lived in Settle's numbers, one day more. (POPE.)

The writing of poetry which, even in the case of the worst of poets, is a personal and voluntary act, is presented as if it were as impersonal and necessary as the revolution of the earth, and the value of the poems so produced which, even in a bad poet, varies, is presented as invariable and therefore subject to a quantitative measurement like dead matter.

The satiric effect presupposes that the reader knows that in real life Settle was not a certifiable lunatic, for lunacy overwhelms a man against his will: Settle is, as it were, a self-made lunatic.

2) To present the object of satire as if he or she were wicked and completely conscious of what he is doing without feeling any guilt.

> Although, dear Lord, I am a sinner,
> I have done no major crime;
> Now I'll come to Evening Service
> Whensoever I have time.
> So, Lord, reserve for me a crown,
> And do not let my shares go down. (JOHN BETJEMAN.)

Again, the satiric effect depends upon our knowing that in real life the lady is not wicked, that, if she were really as truthful with herself as she is presented, she could not go to Church.

Satire flourishes in a homogeneous society where satirist and audience share the same views as to how normal people can be expected to behave, and in times of relative stability and contentment, for satire cannot deal with serious evil and suffering. In an age like our own, it cannot flourish except in intimate circles as an expression of private feuds: in public life the evils and sufferings are so serious that satire seems trivial and the only possible kind of attack is prophetic denunciation.

The Comic Mask *and* Carnival*

GEORGE SANTAYANA

THE COMIC MASK

The clown is the primitive comedian. Sometimes in the exuberance of animal life a spirit of riot and frolic comes over a man; he leaps, he dances, he tumbles head over heels, he grins, shouts, or leers, possibly he pretends to go to pieces suddenly, and blubbers like a child. A moment later he may look up wreathed in smiles, and hugely pleased about nothing. All this he does hysterically, without any reason, by a sort of mad inspiration and irresistible impulse. He may easily, however, turn his absolute histrionic impulse, his pure fooling, into mimicry of anything or anybody that at the moment happens to impress his senses; he will crow like a cock, simper like a young lady, or reel like a drunkard. Such mimicry is virtual mockery, because the actor is able to revert from those assumed attitudes to his natural self; whilst his models, as he thinks, have no natural self save that imitable attitude, and can never disown it; so that the clown feels himself immensely superior, in his rôle of universal satirist, to all actual men, and belabours and rails at them unmercifully. He sees everything in caricature, because he sees the surface only, with the lucid innocence of a child; and all these grotesque personages stimulate him, not to moral sympathy, nor to any consideration of their fate, but rather to boisterous sallies, as the rush of a crowd, or the hue and cry of a hunt, or the contortions of a jumping-jack might stimulate him. He is not at all amused intellectually; he is not ren-

---

* George Santayana, "The Comic Mask" and "Carnival," *in Soliloquies in England and Later Soliloquies* (Charles Scribner's Sons, 1922), pp. 135–144.

dered wiser or tenderer by knowing the predicaments into which people inevitably fall; he is merely excited, flushed, and challenged by an absurd spectacle. Of course this rush and suasion of mere existence must never fail on the stage, nor in any art; it is to the drama what the hypnotizing stone block is to the statue, or shouts and rhythmic breathing to the bard; but such primary magical influences may be qualified by reflection, and then rational and semi-tragic unities will supervene. When this happens the histrionic impulse creates the idyl or the tragic chorus; henceforth the muse of reflection follows in the train of Dionysus, and the revel or the rude farce passes into humane comedy.

Paganism was full of scruples and superstitions in matters of behaviour or of *cultus,* since the *cultus* too was regarded as a business or a magic craft; but in expression, in reflection, paganism was frank and even shameless; it felt itself inspired, and revered this inspiration. It saw nothing impious in inventing or recasting a myth about no matter how sacred a subject. Its inspiration, however, soon fell into classic moulds, because the primary impulses of nature, though intermittent, are monotonous and clearly defined, as are the gestures of love and of anger. A man who is unaffectedly himself turns out to be uncommonly like other people. Simple sincerity will continually rediscover the old right ways of thinking and speaking, and will be perfectly conventional without suspecting it. This classic iteration comes of nature, it is not the consequence of any revision or censorship imposed by reason. Reason, not being responsible for any of the facts or passions that enter into human life, has no interest in maintaining them as they are; any novelty, even the most revolutionary, would merely afford reason a fresh occasion for demanding a fresh harmony. But the Old Adam is conservative; he repeats himself mechanically in every child who cries and loves sweets and is imitative and jealous. Reason, with its tragic discoveries and restraints, is a far more precarious and personal possession than the trite animal experience and the ancestral grimaces on which it supervenes; and automatically even the philosopher continues to cut his old comic capers, as if no such thing as reason existed. The wiseacres too are comic, and their mask is one of the most harmlessly amusing in the human museum; for reason, taken psychologically, is an old inherited passion like any other, the passion for consistency and order; and it is just as prone as the other passions to overstep the modesty of nature and to regard its own aims as alone important. But this is ridiculous; because importance springs from the stress of nature, from the cry of life, not from reason and its pale prescriptions. Reason cannot stand alone; brute habit and blind play are at the bottom of art and morals, and unless irrational impulses and fancies are kept alive, the life of reason collapses for sheer emptiness. What tragedy could there be, or what sublime harmonies rising out of tragedy, if there were not spontaneous passions to create the issue, no wild voices to be reduced to harmony? Moralists have habitually aimed at suppression, wisely perhaps at first, when they were preaching to men of spirit; but why continue to harp on propriety and unselfishness and labour, when we are little but labour-machines already, and have hardly any self or any passions left to indulge? Perhaps the time has come to suspend those exhortations, and to encourage us to be sometimes a little lively, and see if we can invent something worth saying or doing. We should then be living in the spirit of comedy, and the world would grow young. Every occasion would don its comic mask, and make its bold grimace at the world for a moment. We should be constantly original without effort and without shame, somewhat as we are in dreams, and consistent only in sincerity; and we should gloriously emphasize all the poses we fell into, without seeking to prolong them.

Objections to the comic mask—to the irresponsible, complete, extreme expression of each moment—cut at the roots of all expression. Pursue this path, and at once you do away with gesture: we must not point, we must not pout, we must not cry, we must not laugh aloud; we must not only avoid attracting attention, but our attention must not be obviously attracted; it is silly to gaze, says the nursery-governess, and rude to stare. Presently words, too, will be reduced to a telegraphic code. A man in his own country will talk like the laconic tourist abroad; his whole vocabulary will be *Où? Combien? All right! Dear me!* Conversation in the quiet home will dispense even with these phrases; nothing will be required but a few pragmatic grunts and signals for action. Where the spirit of comedy has departed, company becomes constraint, reserve eats up the spirit, and people fall into a penurious melancholy in their scruple to be always exact, sane, and reasonable, never to mourn, never to glow, never to betray a passion or a weakness, nor venture to utter a thought they might not wish to harbour for ever.

Yet irony pursues these enemies of comedy, and for fear of wearing a mask for a moment they are hypocrites all their lives. Their very reserve becomes a pose, a convention imposed externally, and their mincing speech turns to cant. Sometimes this evasion of impulse sentiment fosters a poignant sentimentality beneath. The comedy goes on silently behind the scenes, until perhaps it gets the upper hand

and becomes positive madness; or else it breaks out in some shy, indirect fashion, as among Americans with their perpetual joking. Where
there is no habitual art and no moral liberty, the instinct for direct
expression is atrophied for want of exercise; and then slang and a
humorous perversity of phrase or manner act as safety-valves to
sanity; and you manage to express yourself in spite of the censor by
saying something grotesquely different from what you mean. That is
a long way round to sincerity, and an ugly one. What, on the contrary, could be more splendidly sincere than the impulse to play in
real life, to rise on the rising wave of every feeling and let it burst,
if it will, into the foam of exaggeration? Life is not a means, the
mind is not a slave nor a photograph: it has a right to enact a
pose, to assume a *panache,* and to create what prodigious allegories
it will for the mere sport and glory of it. Nor is this art of innocent
make-believe forbidden in the Decalogue, although Bible-reading
Anglo-Saxondom might seem to think so. On the contrary, the Bible
and the Decalogue are themselves instances of it. To embroider upon
experience is not to bear false witness against one's neighbour, but
to bear true witness to oneself. Fancy is playful and may be misleading to those who try to take it for literal fact; but literalness is
impossible in any utterance of spirit, and if it were possible it would
be deadly. Why should we quarrel with human nature, with metaphor,
with myth, with impersonation? The foolishness of the simple is delightful; only the foolishness of the wise is exasperating.

CARNIVAL

In this world we must either institute conventional forms of expression or else pretend that we have nothing to express; the choice
lies between a mask and a fig-leaf. Art and discipline render seemly
what would be unseemly without them, but hypocrisy hides it osten-
tatiously under something irrelevant, and the fig-leaf is only a more
ignominious mask. For the moment it is certainly easier to suppress
the wild impulses of our nature than to manifest them fitly, at the
right times and with the proper fugitive emphasis; yet in the long
run suppression does not solve the problem, and meantime those
maimed expressions which are allowed are infected with a secret
misery and falseness. It is the charm and safety of virtue that it is
more natural than vice, but many moralists do their best to deprive
it of this advantage. They seem to think it would lose its value if
they lost their office. Their precepts, as distinguished from the spontaneous appreciations of men, are framed in the interests of utility, and
are curiously out of sympathy with the soul. Precept divides the moral

world materially into right and wrong things; but nothing concrete is right or wrong intrinsically, and every object or event has both good and bad effects in the context of nature. Every passion, like life as a whole, has its feet in one moral climate and its head in another. Existence itself is not a good, but only an opportunity. Christians thank God for their creation, preservation, and all the blessings of this life, but life is the condition and source of all evil, and the Indians thank Brahma or Buddha for lifting them out of it. What metaphysical psychologists call Will is the great original sin, the unaccountable and irrational interest which the spirit takes, when it is incarnate, in one thing happening rather than another; yet this mad interest is the condition of generosity and of every virtue. Love is a red devil at one end of its spectrum and an ultraviolet angel at the other end.

Nor is this amphibious moral quality limited to the passions; all facts and objects in nature can take on opposite moral tints. When abstracted from our own presence and interests, everything that can be found or imagined is reduced to a mere essence, an ideal theme picked out of the infinite, something harmless, marvellous, and pure, like a musical rhythm or geometrical design. The whole world then becomes a labyrinth of forms and motions, a castle in the clouds built without labour and dissolved without tears. The moment the animal will reawakes, however, these same things acquire a new dimension; they become substantial, not to be created without effort nor rent without resistance; at the same time they become objects of desire and fear; we are so engrossed in existence that every phenomenon becomes questionable and ominous, and not so much a free gift and manifestation of its own nature as a piece of good or bad news. We are no longer surprised, as a free spirit would be, at the extraordinary interest we take in things turning out one way rather than another. We are caught in the meshes of time and place and care; and as the things we have set our heart on, whatever they may be, must pass away in the end, either suddenly or by a gentle transformation, we cannot take a long view without finding life sad, and all things tragic. This aspect of vanity and self-annihilation, which existence wears when we consider its destiny, is not to be denied or explained away, as is sometimes attempted in cowardly and mincing philosophies. It is a true aspect of existence in one relation and on a certain view; but to take this long view of existence, and look down the avenues of time from the station and with the emotions of some particular moment, is by no means inevitable, nor is it a fair and sympathetic way of viewing existence. Things when they are actual do

not lie in that sort of sentimental perspective, but each is centred
in itself; and in this intrinsic aspect existence is nothing tragic or
sad, but rather something joyful, hearty, and merry. A buoyant and
full-blooded soul has quick senses and miscellaneous sympathies: it
changes with the changing world; and when not too much starved
or thwarted by circumstances, it finds all things vivid and comic. Life
is free play fundamentally and would like to be free play altogether.
In youth anything is pleasant to see or to do, so long as it is spontaneous, and if the conjunction of these things is ridiculous, so much
the better: to be ridiculous is part of the fun.

Existence involves changes and happenings and is comic inherently,
like a pun that begins with one meaning and ends with another. Incongruity is a consequence of change; and this incongruity becomes
especially conspicuous when, as in the flux of nature, change is going
on at different rates in different strands of being, so that not only
does each thing surprise itself by what it becomes, but it is continually astonished and disconcerted by what other things have turned
into without its leave. The mishaps, the expedients, the merry solutions of comedy, in which everybody acknowledges himself beaten
and deceived, yet is the happier for the unexpected posture of affairs,
belong to the very texture of temporal being; and if people repine
at these mishaps, or rebel against these solutions, it is only because
their souls are less plastic and volatile than the general flux of nature.
The individual grows old and lags behind; he remembers his old pain
and resents it when the world is already on a new tack. In the
jumble of existence there must be many a knock and many a grief;
people living at cross purposes cannot be free from malice, and they
must needs be fooled by their pretentious passions. But there is no
need of taking these evils tragically. At bottom they are gratuitous,
and might have been avoided if people had not pledged their hearts
to things beyond their control and had not entrenched themselves in
their illusions. At a sufficient remove every drama seems pathological
and makes much ado about what to other people is nothing. We are
interested in those vicissitudes, which we might have undergone if
placed under the given circumstances; but we are happy to have escaped them. Thus the universe changes its hues like the chameleon,
not at random but in a fashion which moral optics can determine,
as it appears in one perspective or another; for everything in nature
is lyrical in its ideal essence, tragic in its fate, and comic in its
existence.

Existence is indeed distinguishable from the platonic essences that
are embodied in it precisely by being a conjunction of things mutually

irrelevant, a chapter of accidents, a medley improvised here and now for no reason, to the exclusion of the myriad other farces which, so far as their ideal structure is concerned, might have been performed just as well. This world is contingency and absurdity incarnate, the oddest of possibilities masquerading momentarily as a fact. Custom blinds persons who are not naturally speculative to the egregious character of the actual, because custom assimilates their expectations to the march of existing things and deadens their power to imagine anything different. But wherever the routine of a barbaric life is broken by the least acquaintance with larger ways, the arbitrariness of the actual begins to be discovered. The traveller will first learn that his native language is not the only one, nor the best possible, nor itself constant; then, perhaps, he will understand that the same is true of his home, religion, and government. The naturalist will begin by marvelling at the forms and habits of the lower animals, while continuing to attribute his own to their obvious propriety; later the heavens and the earth, and all physical laws, will strike him as paradoxically arranged and unintelligible; and ultimately the very elements of existence—time, change, matter, habit, life cooped in bodies—will reveal themselves to him in their extreme oddity, so that, unless he has unusual humility and respect for fact, he will probably declare all these actual things to be impossible and therefore unreal. The most profound philosophers accordingly deny that any of those things exist which we find existing, and maintain that the only reality is changeless, infinite, and indistinguishable into parts; and I call them the most profound philosophers in spite of this obvious folly of theirs, because they are led into it by the force of intense reflection, which discloses to them that what exists is unintelligible and has no reason for existing; and since their moral and religious prejudices do not allow them to say that to be irrational and unintelligible is the character proper to existence, they are driven to the alternative of saying that existence is illusion and that the only reality is something beneath or above existence. That real existence should be radically comic never occurs to these solemn sages; they are without one ray of humour and are persuaded that the universe too must be without one. Yet there is a capital joke in their own systems, which prove that nothing exists so strenuously, that existence laughs aloud in their vociferations and drowns the argument. Their conviction is the very ghost which it rises to exorcise; yet the conviction and the exorcism remain impressive, because they bear witness to the essential strangeness of existence to the spirit. Like the Ghost in *Hamlet* this apparition, this unthinkable fact, is terribly disturbing and emphatic; it

cries to us in a hollow voice, "Swear!" and when in an agony of
concern and affection we endeavour to follow it, " 'Tis here! 'Tis here!
'Tis gone!" Certainly existence can bewitch us; it can compel us to
cry as well as to laugh; it can hurt, and that is its chief claim to
respect. Its cruelty, however, is as casual as its enchantments; it is
not cruel on purpose but only rough, like thoughtless boys. Coarseness—and existence is hopelessly coarse—is not an evil unless we demand refinement. A giggling lass that peeps at us through her fingers
is well enough in her sphere, but we should not have begun by
calling her Dulcinea. Dulcinea is a pure essence, and dwells only
in that realm. Existence should be met on its own terms; we may
dance a round with it, and perhaps steal a kiss; but it tempts only
to flout us, not being dedicated to any constant love. As if to acknowledge how groundless existence is, everything that arises instantly backs
away, bowing its excuses, and saying, "My mistake!" It suffers from
a sort of original sin or congenital tendency to cease from being. This
is what Heraclitus called *Dikê,* or just punishment; because, as
Mephistopheles long afterwards added, *alles was entsteht ist wert dass
es zugrunde geht*—whatsoever arises deserves to perish; not of course
because what arises is not often a charming creation, but because it
has no prerogative to exist not shared by every Cinderella-like essence
that lies eternally neglected in that limbo to which all things intrinsically belong—the limbo of unheard melodies and uncreated
worlds. For anything to emerge from that twilight region is inexplicable and comic, like the popping up of Jack-in-the-box; and the shock
will amuse us, if our wits are as nimble as nature and as quick as
time. We too exist; and existence is a joy to the sportive side of our
nature, itself akin to a shower of sparks and a patter of irrevocable
adventures. What indeed could be more exhilarating than such a
rout, if only we are not too exacting, and do not demand of it
irrelevant perfections? The art of life is to keep step with the celestial
orchestra that beats the measure of our career, and gives the cue for
our exits and our entrances. Why should we willingly miss anything,
or precipitate anything, or be angry with folly, or in despair at any
misadventure? In this world there should be none but gentle tears,
and fluttering tip-toe loves. It is a great Carnival, and amongst these
lights and shadows of comedy, these roses and vices of the playhouse,
there is no abiding.

The Bias of Comedy and the Narrow Escape into Faith*

NATHAN A. SCOTT, JR.

THE NAME AND NATURE OF OUR PERIOD STYLE

In one of his brilliant *Partisan Review* essays back in the 'forties, Clement Greenberg attempted to define "our period style" in the visual arts, the style that is fundamentally characteristic of all the painting and sculpture and decoration and design of our time and that furnishes the basic norm which underlies all the shifts and changes that have occurred in twentieth-century vision and taste. And, in a similar vein, the student of modern literature will be led to search, in this area too, for that which constitutes "our period style." What is the modality of vision and belief, or of disbelief, of affirmation or of denial, of faith or of scepticism, that furnishes the literature that we recognize to be "ours" with its essential spiritual structure? In what particular accents and stresses do we discern that special style or signature that proves itself upon our own sensibilities to be a true expression of the age? This is a major question that must face contemporary criticism whenever it attempts to move beyond the trees to get a view of the forest and of the general terrain.

And we have, I think, lived long enough with the literature of the age of Joyce and Kafka to be certain that, in so far as it proceeds from any *mal du siècle,* this is a debility that is itself rooted in that same ontological crisis which Nietzsche made a kind of scandal by his announcement in 1882 of "the death of God." It is true, of course, that ultimate explanations of this sort may, in their very ultimacy,

* Nathan A. Scott, Jr., "The Bias of Comedy and the Narrow Escape into Faith," *The Christian Scholar,* Vol. XLIV (Spring, 1961), pp. 9–39.

appear to sweep the critic away from all the interesting particularities of literary actuality and into the nebulousness of the metaphysical ether. But the fact of the matter is that even the most cautious notaries in contemporary criticism are increasingly recognizing that the truly significant particularities that characterize modern literature all speak in various ways of tragic losses, and of losses ultimately rooted in the loss of God. This surely is a part of what Richard Chase must have in mind when he remarks that "the greatest writers of the first half of the twentieth century lived in a high, tense world of strenuous and difficult metaphysics . . . and religious feeling." [1]

We have, however, been recently reminded by R. W. B. Lewis that we live today under the immediate pressure not of the generation of Joyce and Kafka but of Moravia and Camus and Silone and that these are writers who have foregone the metaphysical radicalism of the classic modern generation for a quieter kind of humanism, a humanism which commits them not to the practice of the presence (or absence) of God but to the practice of the presence of man. [2] Now I have no doubt but that Mr. Lewis is right in contending that the *avant-garde* tradition of this century has already thus begun to periodize itself and that the dominant vision of those writers who have followed the great pioneers has this essentially anthropocentric focus. But, on the other hand, it is also to be asserted that the effort to redeem the time by sacramentalizing the relation between man and man is, by the generation of Camus and Silone, conceived to be the one remaining way of shoring up the human enterprise in this late, bad time of our abandonment. "In the sacred history of man on earth," says Silone, "it is still, alas, Good Friday." And in the greatest testament of his career Camus declared that "only two possible worlds can exist for the human mind: the sacred (or, to speak in Christian terms, the world of grace) and the world of rebellion. The disappearance of one is equivalent to the appearance of the other. . . . [And today] we live in an unsacrosanct moment in history. . . . [So] rebellion is one of the essential dimensions of man. It is our historic reality." And many similar testimonies could be drawn from the work of such writers of the present time as Samuel Beckett and Friedrich Duerrenmatt and Jean Genet and Alberto Moravia and Tennessee Williams.

So the "cosmic homelessness" and the strenuous metaphysics of the

---

[1] Richard Chase, *The Democratic Vista* (Garden City: Doubleday Anchor Books, 1958), p. 16.

[2] *Vide* R. W. B. Lewis, *The Picaresque Saint* (Philadelphia: J. B. Lippincott Co., 1959), Chapter I.

generation of Joyce and Kafka, though perhaps they assert themselves today less stridently than at an earlier time, have yet not been put aside, and their basic premise continues to be the unquestioned axiom of the modern imagination—that what we ultimately face is a Silence, an Absence, a threatening Emptiness at the center. The grime and grit and seediness that we encounter in so many of Graham Greene's novels; the glum, dispirited ennui and acedia of Moravia's Roman world; the nasty, viscous disintegration of the phenomena of daily life in Sartre's *La Nausée;* or, among younger writers even, the arid, cheerless, chromium world of Norman Mailer's *The Deer Park* and the dingy bleakness of the landscape that we sometimes meet in the fiction of Britain's "young rebels" (reminiscent of the early Orwell) and the curiously abstract violence of Kerouac's *On the Road*—these are among the characteristic and most frequently encountered qualities of recent literature. Our dominant metaphors are still metaphors of dearth and deprivation, and the world that is explored and rendered in contemporary fiction is very often, like that which is presented by the earlier literature of this century, a world that has been evacuated of radical significance. Beckett and Moravia and Alain Robbe-Grillet and Natalie Sarraute and Norman Mailer are writers, in other words, who live under a spiritual dispensation that is essentially the same that is classically emblematized by such modern texts as *Hugh Selwyn Mauberley* and *The Waste Land* and *The Magic Mountain* and *The Castle* and *The Sun Also Rises.* Which is to say that "our period style," despite the numerous elaborations of it that are added by each successive decade of this century, continues, in its deepest aspects, to be that which was forged by Dostoievski and Conrad and Hardy and Kafka and Hemingway, by those in whom was born the characteristically modern vision of a world with nothing at the center.

So when Melville, at a central point in *Moby Dick,* remarks that "though in many of its aspects this visible world seems formed in love, the invisible spheres were formed in fright," he seems almost, with a remarkable prescience, to be anticipating what was to become a tacit assumption in the twentieth century. For many of our writers— the Elias Canetti of *Auto da Fé,* the Malcolm Lowry of *Under the Volcano,* the Camus of *L'Étranger,* the Penn Warren of *Brother to Dragons*—have made us feel that the world for them was very nearly a kind of nightmare, and Joyce does indeed seem to have been their spokesman when he declared: "History is a nightmare from which I am trying to awake"—or, as Henry James phrased it in his last years, "a nightmare from which there is no waking save by sleep." And it is not surprising that James should have called his last novel *The Ivory Tower*, for, when the earth has become "merely a planet in the company of planets," [3] when it is no longer "the center of divine attention," [4] when human thought is no longer steadied by any Incarnational principle, when Meaning and Reality are sundered, and when poetic art seems fated to be only a desperate

> raid on the inarticulate
> With shabby equipment always deteriorating,
> In the general mess of imprecision of feeling,
> Undisciplines squads of emotion. . . .[5]

—when this is the writer's situation, then he will indeed seek out some barely tolerable *tour d'ivoire:* or else, being given a kind of courage by his very despair, he will simply plunge into the whirling vortex of the world's disorder and make a kind of Absolute out of the sheer absurdity of existence itself. And, for all of James's greatness, it is the fact that he more nearly inclines to the former than to the latter course which establishes the distance at which he stands from what we recognize as the characteristic style and stance of the modern imagination. For, as Hannah Arendt has remarked in *The Origins of Totalitarianism,* "to yield to the mere process of disintegration has become [for the modern intelligence] an irresistible temptation, not only because it has assumed the spurious grandeur of 'historical necessity' but also because everything outside it has begun to appear lifeless, bloodless, meaningless, and unreal." [6] And, in the things of the imagination, it is this fascination with the Abyss which is perhaps the chief characteristic of our time.

In much of the great literature of our period, then, the world is perceived as opaque, as undependable and strange. The English critic J. Isaacs says: "The topography of Hell and its interior decoration is a very great concern of the modern dramatist and the modern novelist." [7] And it is, indeed, in terms of the image of man amidst the dilapidation and ruins of modern existence that Hell is conceived in Pound's *Hugh Selwyn Mauberley* and Eliot's *The Waste Land,*

---

[3] Erich Heller, *The Hazard of Modern Poetry* (Cambridge: Bowes and Bowes, 1953), p. 13.

[4] *Ibid.,* p. 17.

[5] T. S. Eliot, "East Coker," *Four Quartets* (New York: Harcourt, Brace and Co., 1943), pp. 16–17.

[6] Hannah Arendt, *The Origins of Totalitarianism* (New York: Harcourt, Brace and Co., 1951), p. viii.

[7] J. Isaacs, *An Assessment of Twentieth-Century Literature* (London: Secker & Warburg, 1951), p. 59.

in Ford's *The Good Soldier* and Fitzgerald's *The Great Gatsby,* in Faulkner's *Sanctuary* and Nathanael West's *The Day of the Locust,* in Cocteau's *The Infernal Machine* and Sartre's *No Exit.* Time itself even is very often experienced as a kind of captivity to what is deficient and oppressive: one might say perhaps that the soteriology of modern fiction often involves either some attempt to obliterate time in the interests of a mystical simultaneity (as in the most characteristic novels of Virginia Woolf) or some stratagem of rebellion, as in the novels of Camus. Which is to say that even in our most secularized literature there is a central core of eschatological passion or at least, as Lionel Trilling puts it, a certain "resistance to history," a "secret hope . . . that . . . man's life in history shall come to an end." [8] What Henri-Charles Puech says of the Salvation that was envisaged in the ancient texts of primitive Gnosticism does, in fact, describe with a most startling exactness the controlling vision in many of the most representative literary expressions of the modern sensibility: it was, he says, a Salvation which "takes place in time, but the act on which it is founded is intrinsically atemporal. It is an interior and individual illumination, a revelation of oneself to oneself, a sudden, gratuitous act which is accomplished by a predestined individual and which presupposes no previous condition or preparation in time." [9] And it is precisely such an extreme impatience as this with our life in time that lies behind those emotions of apathy and nausea, of vertigo and anguish, of terror and despair, that make up the staple in the literature that has become for the modern imagination a kind of scripture.

Nor is it at all gratuitous to recall in this context the witness of ancient Gnosticism, for here it is that we get a kind of elaboration into metaphysical system of many of the formative attitudes in the literature of our period. The disquiet, the sense of insecurity, the metaphysical radicalism that the French associate with what they call *littérature problématique*—these attitudes which we meet in the books of Hardy and Kafka and Camus and Beckett are all based, at bottom, upon a fundamental mistrust of the created orders of finitude, upon a suspicion either that they are not stout enough to withstand the invading pressures of the Abyss or that they are not reliable enough to be "a glass of vision" into ultimate reality. And it is

---

[8] Lionel Trilling, *The Liberal Imagination* (New York: The Viking Press, 1950), p. 195.

[9] Henri-Charles Puech, "Gnosis and Time," *Man and Time* (Papers from the *Eranos Yearbooks* for 1949 and 1951), ed. by Joseph Campbell (New York: Pantheon Books, 1957), p. 76.

just this breakdown and resignation of courage in the presence of the limited, concrete actualities of historical existence—it is just this that constitutes what was the essential heresy of Basilides and Valentinus and Marcion and those others who brought into being that dissident movement of the second century which we call Gnosticism. These ancient heresiarchs and *gnostikoi* postulated an absolute seclusion of that which is Radically Significant from all the provisional and proximate meanings of historical experience, and they conceived the world of finite existence to be a delusive and fraudulent imposture. Theirs, in other words, was a God unknowable by nature (*naturaliter ignotus*) and utterly incommensurable with the created order, and man's involvement in time and history was, therefore, felt by them to be a crushing burden and the ultimate disaster from which he was to be rescued. Professor Puech summarizes their sense of things in this wise:

Present life with its infinite sufferings is not true Life. Still more, time, whose instants engender and destroy one another, in which each moment arises only to be engulfed in the next moment, in which all things appear, disappear, and reappear in a twinkling, without order, without aim or cessation or end—time contains within it a rhythm of death beneath an appearance of life.[10]

So, far from being any kind of *paidagogia* whereby man is formed and educated by God into an adequate maturity, time itself for these *pneumatikoi* was anguish, and they understood the human situation to be one of abandonment in a treacherous and indifferent world.

Now it is this same profound scepticism about the possibility of any commerce between the two spheres of time and eternity which distinguishes our own "period style" and which makes it a variant of an ancient heresy. But, says the poet of "Burnt Norton," "Only through time time is conquered" [11]—by which, presumably, he means that it is only by moving deeply into the exigent realities of our human condition that there is any good chance of that condition being reconstituted in ways that are more promising and hopeful. And, in searching for that stratagem of the literary imagination that is most likely to assist us in "redeeming the time," it may well be that, instead of relying on some yet to be developed mutation within the terms of modern Gnosticism, we ought rather to explore the resources of another kind of radicalism altogether—namely, the radicalism of Comedy.

---

[10] *Ibid.*, pp. 65–66.
[11] T. S. Eliot, "Burnt Norton," *op. cit.*, p. 5.

ARISTOTLE ON COMEDY

And no sooner have we turned to the problem of comedy than we are given what may be still another measure of the imbalance of the modern mind toward the various Gnostic and proto-Gnostic forms of tragedy, for, apart from Bergson's essay on *Laughter,* there is no indispensable treatise by any modern theorist on the comic imagination. We have George Meredith's *Essay on Comedy,* which has something of the dusty status of a school classic, and, in many ways, it is a genuinely useful guide; but, in the special attention that it gives to those "volleys of silvery laughter" that will be provoked by the vanities and pretensions of men in society, it limits itself rather closely to comedy of manners. And there are also other less well known formulations of more recent date by James Feibleman and Albert Cook and Northrop Frye and Arthur Koestler. But even the recent literature of the subject has no very high interest, and it is neither rich nor various. So an approach to the subject at the present time will inevitably entail some bit of reconnoitering in order to discover a preliminary point of purchase, and it may not be, therefore, improper simply to return to the very beginning of the tradition and to inaugurate the inquiry by considering the cues that may be found in Aristotle.

It will not, of course, be forgotten that the central subject of the *Poetics* is tragedy; but it has long been thought that Aristotle also, at some time or other in the course of his career, produced a treatise on comedy, his interest in the subject being clearly attested to by several passages in the *Poetics.* And since, in the XVIIIth Chapter of Book III of the *Rhetoric,* he speaks of having already classified "Jests" in the *Poetics,* many scholars (Bywater among them), taking this to be a reference to a discussion of comedy, have even concluded that this material which does not appear in the existing *Poetics* must have made up the second part of a work of which the extant *Poetics* constituted Book I. But, however this particular issue be disposed of, judging from internal evidence within the *Poetics* itself, it would seem by no means implausible to suppose that he did produce an analysis of comedy that, in its comprehensiveness and systematic rigor, was comparable to his analysis of the forms of tragedy; and, for reasons which need not be gone into here, it also seems likely that much of his generalization in this area was based on the Old Comedy of Aristophanes.

Now the basic consistencies of the *Poetics* suggest that Aristotle regarded all forms of literary art as subject to the executive principle of *mimesis,* and he doubtless made as much a point of this in whatever treatise he devoted to comedy as he does in his discussion of tragedy. The poet, he insisted, imitates human beings in action, men and women who are doing something—and personages who are to be differentiated from one another in terms of their moral qualities: they are either better or worse than we are. Indeed, it is just at this point that Aristotle does explicitly distinguish in the extant *Poetics* between comedy and tragedy, for, as he says at the close of Chapter II, "Comedy aims at representing men as worse, Tragedy as better than in actual life": or, as he says more systematically at the beginning of the Vth Chapter, "Comedy is . . . an imitation of persons inferior—not, however, in the full sense of the word bad, the Ludicrous being merely a subdivision of the ugly. It consists in some defect or ugliness which is not painful or destructive." And this defect, presumably, consists in one or in some combination of the vices enumerated in the *Nicomachaean Ethics,* such as vulgarity or buffoonery or foolhardiness.

So much, then, for the object of the comic poet's imitation, in Aristotle's probable understanding of the matter: it is an action which is ludicrous or mirthful, the action being rendered in the several media of language and rhythm and harmony. But what is the end of comedy: what function does it perform? If Aristotle's way of dealing with the problem of tragedy is at all to be taken as indicative of the way in which he wanted to deal with drama generally, it would seem that he very probably conceived it to be the function of comedy (like all the various forms of mimetic art) to conduce to a special sort of pleasure. And, in the XIth Chapter of Book I of the *Rhetoric,* he tells us what he means by "pleasure": it is, he says, "a movement by which the soul as a whole is consciously brought into its normal state of being."

Now tragedy has, of course, its distinctive way of bringing the soul into its "normal state of being"—that is, of rendering it efficient for the conduct of the affairs of life. For, since the presence in the self to any excessive degree of the emotions of pity and fear would render it incompetent, tragedy arouses these emotions in order that they may be worked off and expelled, or purged: tragic pleasure, in other words, is an affair of the *katharsis* of the tragic emotions: it is something essentially medical and therapeutic.

And, similarly, it seems reasonable to suppose, Aristotle very probably also conceived the ultimate effect of comedy to involve a special sort of pleasure, a pleasure partaking of a comic *katharsis.* Of this there is no indubitable proof, but it seems to be at least a good guess. We cannot, of course, at this point rely too heavily upon the

Tractatus Coislinianus, and yet its testimony is significant. This document bears the name by which it is generally referred to because it is a part of the De Coislin Collection in the Bibliothèque Nationale in Paris. It is a manuscript of the tenth century A.D. whose contents date apparently from about the first century B.C., and, though it is only a brief fragment, it is, apart from the *Poetics* and Plato's *Philebus,* the only other important vestige of a theory of comedy that we have coming down to us in the Greek tradition. And what is significant is that it very definitely embraces a theory of comic *katharsis;* indeed, it says: "Comedy is an imitation of an action that is ludicrous and imperfect . . . through pleasure and laughter effecting the purgation of the like emotions." Now this is patently a gloss on Aristotle; but, whether or not it truly reflects the position that he actually held, it at least seems to be a plausible guess. For Aristotle believed that comedy properly deals with the ludicrous and arouses in the spectator the sense of the ridiculous. "But," as John Crowe Ransom has observed, "this sense is analogous to pity and terror, in that it unfits a man for this duty: for there is implied in the citizen, if he goes about finding everything ridiculous, the belief that he is witnessing an irrational universe." [12] So it seems likely that Aristotle concluded that, just as there must be *katharsis* in tragedy, so too must the comic drama issue in a genuinely cathartic experience in which potentially disabling emotions are harmlessly discharged.

Here, then, are what were probably the main elements of Aristotle's conception of comedy, and, when taken all together, they amount to an exact transposition of his definition of tragedy: formally phrased, it would go like this: "Comedy, then, is an organically complete imitation of an action which is ludicrous; in language embellished with each kind of artistic ornament, the several kinds being found in separate parts of the play; in the form of action, not of narrative; with incidents arousing pleasure and laughter, wherewith to accomplish its katharsis of such emotions."

THE TRAGIC RHYTHM

So now, despite the unhelpful tenuity of modern criticism, we have at last, through Aristotle, a way into our subject. And, though the conception of things that we derive from him may require a very considerable recasting, it does, if only in providing us with something to resist or to negate, enable us to begin to draw a circle of definition about the fundamental issues. And, indeed, perhaps our very first

---

[12] John Crowe Ransom, *The World's Body* (New York: Charles Scribner's Sons, 1938), p. 189.

response to Aristotle ought to be a demurrer. "Comedy," he tells us, "aims at representing men as worse, Tragedy as better than in actual life." But is this really so? It is true, of course, that tragedy and comedy represent men differently, but is the difference quite of the sort which Aristotle suggests?

Let us approach the matter in this way. We may say, I think, that true tragedy has always thrust us into those acute situations of crisis in which (as Kierkegaard puts it) man's "unhappy consciousness" of the contradictions of human existence impels him to perform an act of radical self-transcendence. He is led to ask himself what it means to be a man, what it means to be rather than not-to-be, and how dependable is the essentially human thing in himself. And when a man thus becomes a problem to himself, it is because, in some critical moment, life, in its fundamental axiological structure, has appeared to be at cross-purposes with itself, ultimately and irremediably. What he discovers is that that which he believes to be most valid and authentic in himself is somehow radically contradicted or threatened by the objective order of things that constitutes the theatre of the human enterprise. So he begins to wonder how he can "choose" himself or if perhaps, in a universe in which man as such is fundamentally defective, his having already "chosen" himself is not the cause of his present embarrassments. But, in this "boundary-situation," the tragic man is not simply a passive agonizer: he is committed to a course of action, and this is why it is proper to refer, as we do, to the great tragedies in literature as "tragic actions," for in them the central figure is one who not only suffers but who actively resists whatever it is that would destroy his dignity and bring to naught his highest purposes. What we see, in Richard Sewall's summary of the matter, is "man at the limits of his sovereignty—Job on the ash-heap, Prometheus on the crag, Œdipus in his moment of self-discovery, Lear on the heath, Ahab on his lonely quarter-deck." [13] And here, "with all the protective covering stripped off," [14] the hero, facing into the utter insecurity of his situation, is led to muster all his resources in one great effort to transcend the fundamental limitations of his creaturehood. It is not, in other words, as Aristotle says, that he is better than we are: it is rather that he is, as Henry Myers puts it, more of an extremist than most of us are. "To reach his goal, whatever it may be, he is always willing to sacrifice everything else, including his life. Œdipus will press the search for the

---

[13] Richard B. Sewall, *The Vision of Tragedy* (New Haven: Yale University Press, 1959), p. 5.
[14] *Ibid.*

unknown murderer, although he is warned of the consequences; Hamlet
will prove the King's guilt and attempt to execute perfect justice,
whatever the cost may be to his mother, to Laertes, to Ophelia, and
to himself; Ibsen's Solness will climb the tower he has built, at the
risk of falling into the quarry; Ahab will kill Moby Dick or die in
the attempt." [15] It is precisely with this kind of intensity that the
protagonists of the great tragic actions live in the world, and it is not,
therefore, surprising that they, most of them, die early and never
enjoy the felicity of a long and complete life. For they soon exhaust
themselves in the effort to gain release from the restrictions that are
a consequence of their finitude: this is an essential part of what we
are to include in the "tragic rhythm of action" [16]—which is the
rhythm that man's life has when it is lived at the difficult and perilous limits of the human condition.

THE RHYTHM OF COMEDY IN THE ADVENTURES OF THE CLOWN

But, now, the systole and diastole of the "comic rhythm of action"
are something altogether different, and the best way of measuring
the difference is to consider the personage who has always been the
presiding genius of comedy—namely, the clown. And the particular
clown whom I want to recall is Charlie Chaplin, whose art places
him, I believe, among the few great comic geniuses of the modern
period. It is not, however, the Chaplin image of the late films—of
Monsieur Verdoux, or *Limelight,* or even of *The Great Dictator*—
that I have in mind, but rather it is the Tramp of the early and
middle films, of *The Kid* and *The Gold Rush* and *City Lights:* I
am thinking of the little downtrodden but urbane and chivalrous
man, in the big baggy trousers and the wrinkled, out-of-size shoes,
with the expression of amazement and alarm written into the innocence of his face, for this is the Chaplin who has provided us
with an image more memorable than anything else in the history of
the cinema, of the lonely and unprotected individual clinging to his
humanity amidst the horrible impersonality and dehumanization of
the modern world. And this is what Charlie Chaplin's Tramp represented: he was the little man, the *homunculus,* who, amidst the
dreary facelessness of men completely involved in the rituals of a
money culture, insisted on behaving as though his fellow human
beings were still human. And he was, of course, as a result, a scandal,

---

[15] Henry Alonzo Myers, *Tragedy: A View of Life* (Ithaca: Cornell University
Press, 1956), p. 45.
[16] *Vide* Francis Fergusson, *The Idea of a Theatre* (Princeton: Princeton University Press, 1949), Chapter I.

an utterly absurd little scandal. But he was never regarded as a serious threat, for the society's dedication to its own materialism was so complete that it never really took the trouble to consider his eccentricity for the profoundly subversive thing it was: in film after film he was simply regarded by the sober fools with whom he collided as a charming, though utterly irrelevant, little scapegrace.

Yet, erratic and unpredictable as the Tramp's behavior was, he was never ridiculous. One wants instead to say that he was *touching*, for everything that he did was so utterly human, even his pranks and his mischief. And when one sees these old films occasionally today on the screens of little art-cinema houses, one feels that here is a man, that here is a richly particularized and wonderfully eccentric human being living out his life—a little hobo whose every gesture somehow manages to redeem the human image by revealing how beautifully mysterious it would be were it unencumbered by the mechanical reflexes which it has learned in an unpropitious time. When, in *The Kid*, he dreams that all men are angels, when he topples over the bannisters in *His Favorite Pastime*, when he shares his last sausage with a bulldog in *The Champion*, when he sets out to walk to the horizon in *The Tramp*, we feel that here is the real human thing itself—clothed not in the unearthly magnificence of tragic heroism but in the awkward innocence of essential humanity.

The film that I have particularly in mind is *City Lights*, a movie in which the tramp strikes up a relation with a rich man on a drunken spree who, taking a fancy to Charlie, domiciles him in his great mansion. But then, when his host recovers his sobriety, he is so repelled by the little man that he flings him out of the house. And the fun of the movie arises out of the alternations that ensue between inebriate acceptance and sober rejection and that continue to the utter bafflement of Charlie. Now, in the allegory of the film, the rich man is a representative of that bourgeois mentality which is completely captive to the materialistic ethic of "the skin game." When he is half seas over, he cannot resist the charming gaiety and insouciance of the little fellow who regards material affluence as too ephemeral and as requiring altogether too much trouble to make it worth scrambling after, and one suspects that he embraces Charlie in his drunkenness because the lackadaisical little tramp is in some way his own deeper self which he has submerged and repressed and for which he yearns. But in his moments of sobriety he rejects Charlie, expels him from his house—and, again, one suspects that he does so because the tramp, with his languid, smiling irony, engenders in him the remembrance of the fact that to be a man and to be a great material success are not one and the same thing, and this is a fact which he has not the courage to face. So he drives the clown out of his life, since Charlie evokes memories with which he has not the spiritual resources to deal.[17]

Now here we come upon what is perhaps the basic function of the comic man, and it is, I believe, simply to be a kind of icon of the human actuality. It is not, as Aristotle suggests, that the tragic man is *better* than we are: no, what differentiates him from the rest of us is that he is more of an extremist than most of us are; and, in the resistance that he offers against that which he feels ultimately to threaten the human enterprise, he is, as he seeks to transcend the limitations that attach to our creatureliness, always in danger of forgetting that he is not an angel and only a man. Whereas the comic man is not, as Aristotle suggests, *worse* than we are: indeed, on the contrary, it is his function simply to be an example of the contingent, imperfect, earth-bound creature that in truth we all really are, and it is also his function to awaken in us a lively recognition of what in fact our true status is. He asks us not to be afraid to acknowledge that we are only human and that our residence is not in the heavens. And he asks us to examine critically all the spurious stratagems that we employ to evade a frank acceptance of our finitude, whether they be those of bourgeois worldliness or of philosophical and religious mysticism. What the comic man cannot abide is the man who will not consent to be simply a man, who cannot tolerate the thought of himself as an incomplete and conditioned creature of a particular time and a particular space.

The great difference, in other words, between the tragic man and the comic man is something that arises out of their different ways of dealing with the burden of human finitude. For the tragic man it is a profound embarrassment and perhaps even a curse, for he would be pure intellect or pure will or pure something-or-other, and nothing wounds him more deeply than to be reminded that his life is a conditioned thing and that there is nothing absolute at all in the human stuff out of which he is made. But the comic man is unembarrassed by even the grossest expressions of his creatureliness: though the world may not be all dandy, he has no sense of being under any cruel condemnation; nor does he have any sense of desperate entrapment within a caged prison. He can say, without ironic bitterness, "I'm only human," in full recognition of the fact that the making of this admission is itself the condition of his life being tolerable and of his

---

[17] *Vide* Parker Tyler, *Magic and Myth of the Movies* (New York: Henry Holt and Co., 1947), pp. 36–38.

being able to address to God an appropriate *Confiteor*. He does not insist upon life's conforming to his own special requirements but consents to take it on the terms of its own created actuality, and the art of comedy is devoted to an exhibition of his deep involvement in the world: so it shirks nothing—none of the irrelevant absurdities, none of the vexatious inconveniences, that are the lot of such finite creatures as ourselves.

COMEDY AND THE "WHOLE TRUTH"

There is an incisive little essay of Aldous Huxley's called "Tragedy and the Whole Truth" that begins by recalling that famous Twelfth Book of Homer's *Odyssey*, in which Odysseus and his men, in the course of their journey back to Ithaca, encounter the monster Scylla and the whirlpool Charybdis. And in this Twelfth Book, as Odysseus tells his story, he relives that dreadful day and sadly remembers the poor, hapless souls whom Scylla devoured. He sees them being lifted, struggling, into the air: he hears their screams and the despairing cries for help. He recalls how he and the other survivors could only look helplessly on the awful struggle, and he adds that it was the most pitiable sight he ever saw in all his "explorings of the passes of the sea." But, then, as Mr. Huxley reminds us, once the danger that night had been passed, Odysseus and his men went ashore to prepare their dinner on the Sicilian beach—and prepared it, as Homer says, "expertly." And the whole episode is concluded by the poet's telling us that "when they had satisfied their thirst and hunger, they thought of their dear companions and wept, and in the midst of their tears sleep came gently upon them."

Now this, Mr. Huxley tells us, is "the truth, the whole truth and nothing but the truth." "In any other poem but the *Odyssey*, what," he asks,

would the survivors have done? They would, of course, have wept, even as Homer made them weep. But would they previously have cooked their supper, and cooked it, what's more, in a masterly fashion? Would they previously have drunk and eaten to satiety? And after weeping, or actually while weeping, would they have dropped quietly off to sleep? No, they most certainly would not have done any of these things. They would simply have wept, lamenting their own misfortune and the horrible fate of their companions, and the canto would have ended tragically on their tears.

Homer, however, preferred to tell the Whole Truth. He knew that even the most cruelly bereaved must eat; that hunger is stronger than sorrow and that its satisfaction takes precedence even of tears. He knew that experts continue to act expertly and to find satisfaction in their accomplishment, even when friends have just been eaten, even when the accomplishment is only cooking the supper. He knew that, when the belly is full (and only when the belly is full) men can afford to grieve, and that sorrow after supper is almost a luxury. And finally he knew that, even as hunger takes precedence of grief, so fatigue, supervening, cuts short its career and drowns it in a sleep all the sweeter for bringing forgetfulness of bereavement. In a word, Homer refused to treat the theme tragically. He preferred to tell the Whole Truth.[18]

Now Mr. Huxley does not go on to say that the Whole Truth is the truth of comedy, but this is a line that he might very well have taken. And, indeed, if I may propose at this point another amendment of the Aristotelian formulation, I should say that the art of comedy is not an art that is dedicated to the ludicrous, but is rather an art that is dedicated to the telling of the Whole Truth: this is what it is that comedy "imitates"—not the ludicrous, but the Whole Truth. And surely Mr. Huxley is luminously right in finding Homer to be a poet of the Whole Truth, for here was one who knew that, however grief-stricken men may be by the loss of dearly beloved companions, they will remember to weep only after they have satisfied their hunger and that they will then forget their tears in slumber. The point, in other words, that the *Odyssey* is making is that men are not pure sensibility, that they also have bodies which must be fed and which, when overcome by fatigue, must relax in sleep. And this is, in a way, the point that comedy is always making, that we are not pure, disembodied essences, that indeed we are not pure anything-at-all, but that we are men and that our health and happiness are contingent upon our facing into the fact that we are finite and conditioned and therefore subject to all sorts of absurdities and interruptions and inconveniences and embarrassments—and weaknesses. This is, we might say, the courage that the comic imagination requires of us.

ANTITYPES OF THE COMIC IMAGINATION

But turn now from this poet of ancient Hellas to such a modern novelist as Virginia Woolf, and immediately we have before us a splendid example in the literature of our own time of what the comic writer is most emphatically not like.

To recall Mrs. Woolf's achievement in the novel is, of course, at some point or other in the course of one's reflections, to be put in mind of her much-quoted essay of 1919 called "Modern Fiction," for it was in this early statement that she summarized the aims to

---

[18] Aldous Huxley, "Tragedy and the Whole Truth," in *A Book of English Essays,* selected by W. E. Williams (Harmondsworth, Middlesex: Penguin Books, 1948), pp. 265–266.

which the whole of her subsequent career as an artist was devoted. Here she was attempting to set forth the reasons for her dissatisfaction with the realism of the generation of Galsworthy and Wells and Bennett, whose books, however many of the journeyman virtues of the professional novelist they might occasionally reflect, did not, she felt, plunge beneath the merest surface of life. The spirit of this manifesto shows itself in the following passage: she says:

Examine for a moment an ordinary mind on an ordinary day. The mind receives a myriad of impressions—trivial, fantastic, evanescent, or engraved with the sharpness of steel. From all sides they come, an incessant shower of innumerable atoms; and as they fall, as they shape themselves into the life of Monday or Tuesday, the accent falls differently from of old; the moment of importance came not here but there; so that, if a writer were a free man and not a slave, if he could write what he chose, not what he must, if he could base his work upon his own feeling and not upon convention, there would be no plot, no comedy, no tragedy, no love interest or catastrophe in the accepted style, and perhaps not a single button sewn on as the Bond Street tailors would have it. Life is not a series of gig lamps symmetrically arranged; but a luminous halo, a semitransparent envelope surrounding us from the beginning of consciousness to the end. Is it not the task of the novelist to convey this varying, this unknown and uncircumscribed spirit, whatever aberration or complexity it may display, with as little mixture of the alien and external as possible? [19]

"Let us record," said Mrs. Woolf, "the atoms as they fall upon the mind in the order in which they fall, let us trace the pattern, however disconnected and incoherent in appearance, which each sight or incident scores upon the consciousness." [20] And this was precisely what she undertook to do. As she said in an essay written five years later under the title *Mr. Bennett and Mrs. Brown,* she felt that the Wellses and the Bennetts and the Galsworthys had "laid an enormous stress upon the fabric of things." They, in their old-fashioned naturalism, were preoccupied with the literalities and the surfaces of life: so she proposed that they be called "materialists." Were they, for example, travelling in the same compartment from Richmond to Waterloo with a frayed, timid, little old lady named Mrs. Brown, Wells, she suggested, in his account of the trip, "would instantly project upon the windowpane a vision of a better, breezier, jollier, happier, more adventurous and gallant world, where these musty railway carriages and fusty old women do not exist." Galsworthy,

---

[19] Virginia Woolf, "Modern Fiction," *The Common Reader* (New York: Harcourt, Brace and Co., 1925), pp. 212-213.
[20] *Ibid.*, p. 213.

"burning with indignation, stuffed with information, arraigning civilization, . . . would only see in Mrs. Brown a pot broken on the wheel and thrown into the corner." And Bennett would proceed to make meticulously accurate notations on the appointments of the carriage and on the details of Mrs. Brown's attire and appearance— on everything, indeed, except whatever it is that constitutes Mrs. Brown's human identity. And so it was, Mrs. Woolf was contending, with the Edwardians generally: their vision was superficial: they entirely neglected Mrs. Brown. "In order to complete them," she said, "it seems necessary to do something—to join a society, or, more desperately, to write a cheque." [21] But Mrs. Brown, she was insisting, is the proper focus and subject of literature, and had you asked her who Mrs. Brown was, she would, one imagines, have referred you back to her earlier statement of 1919 and said that Mrs. Brown is just, quite simply, "the atoms as they fall upon the mind in the order in which they fall."

Now this was the reality that Mrs. Woolf—like Joyce and other writers who were to follow them—wanted to get into her books. So it is no wonder that she could say, "When I write I am merely a sensibility." And thus it is also no wonder that, as one of her critics who intends to be complimentary has said, her "characters . . . are not characters," but are, "like her incidents and her intuitions . . . unfinished, spreading as the ripples of a lake spread in the sunlight." [22]

Though her first novel, *The Voyage Out,* is by far exceeded in importance by some of her later books, it is, nevertheless, a good case in point and beautifully illustrates the method and the manner. The central character is Rachel Vinrace, whose twenty-four years of life in Richmond have, by her father and two maidenly aunts, been sheltered from everything that might have deepened and sophisticated her moral sensibilities. But now, on her father's boat, the *Euphrosyne,* she is going to the Villa San Gervasio in Santa Marina for a South American holiday with her uncle and aunt, Professor and Mrs. Ambrose, and Helen Ambrose intends to take her education in hand. This purpose is somewhat forwarded by the boarding of Mr. and Mrs. Richard Dalloway, when the steamer drops anchor in the mouth of the Tagus, for Dalloway—"a rather dull, kindly, plausible" gentleman recently a Member of Parliament—soon begins a flirtation with Rachel. But when he kisses her one stormy afternoon, amidst

---

[21] Virginia Woolf, "Mr. Bennett and Mrs. Brown," in *The Hogarth Essays* (Garden City: Doubleday, Doran & Co., 1928), p. 14.

[22] Bernard Blackstone, *Virginia Woolf: A Commentary* (London: The Hogarth Press, 1949), p. 10.

the lurchings of the ship, she trembles: "a chill of body and mind" creeps over her, and she is struck by the insignificance of the event. Then, at the Villa San Gervasio, she meets young Terence Hewet, who is writing a novel about "Silence, or the Things People don't Say," because he wants his characters to be "more abstract than people who live as we do." After a time, the two become engaged, but nothing is to come of it, for, in a few weeks, Rachel contracts a severe headache one day after a picnic-expedition, takes to her bed with a fever, and in a short time is dead. But, in the brief period that these two young people have together, we are often in their company on afternoon strolls through the hot forests of the place, and, one day, as they are out together, they come upon two young people who are also living at the hotel, Susan Warrington and Arthur Venning: "They lay in each other's arms and had no notion that they were observed."

"Here's shade," began Hewet, when Rachel suddenly stopped dead. They saw a man and woman lying on the ground beneath them, rolling slightly this way and that as the embrace tightened and slackened. The man then sat upright and the woman, who now appeared to be Susan Warrington, lay back upon the ground, with her eyes shut and an absorbed look upon her face, as though she were not altogether conscious. Nor could you tell from her expression whether she was happy, or had suffered something. When Arthur again turned to her, butting her as a lamb butts a ewe, Hewet and Rachel retreated without a word. Hewet felt uncomfortably shy.

"I don't like that," said Rachel after a moment.

And Hewet says: "It's so enormously important, you see. Their lives are now changed for ever." To which Rachel agrees, saying that she could almost burst into tears. And Terence says, after a moment's consideration, "Yes, there's something horribly pathetic about it, I agree." And on still another occasion Rachel, with an inspired breath-lessness, says to Hewet: "Does it ever seem to you, Terence, that the world is composed entirely of vast blocks of matter and that we're nothing but patches of light?" Or, again, we are told that one day "They stood together in front of the looking-glass, and with a brush tried to make themselves look as if they had been feeling nothing all the morning, neither pain nor happiness. But it chilled them to see themselves in the glass, for instead of being vast and indivisible they were really very small and separate, the size of the glass leaving a large space for the reflection of other things."

Now this is the tone of the book, and it is not surprising that one of Mrs. Woolf's admirers should have found it "vague and universal," for everything is fleeting deliquescence and vague, shadowy mistiness:

indeed, many of the characters themselves, amidst the hallucinatory flashes of significance that punctuate the story, are often wondering what it all comes to. And the "vagueness" and the "universality" of *The Voyage Out* were to become even more emphatically characteristic of Mrs. Woolf's performance in the later books, in *Jacob's Room* and *To the Lighthouse* and *Mrs. Dalloway.* She was bent on dissolving the substantialities of character and event into that "luminous halo" which, in her understanding of the novelist's art, was the great thing to be striven for. And finally, as the famous "delicacy" and "sensitivity" operate on experience, we begin to feel, amidst the tenuous and fragile little epiphanies, that the hegemony of the objective world has been completely broken and that we are flapping about in a void.

Indeed, what is most impressive in Mrs. Woolf's most characteristic novels—particularly in *Mrs. Dalloway, To the Lighthouse,* and *The Waves*—is the profound distaste for and the deep fear of the conditioned and limited world that is actually the scene of human life. Hers is an intelligence—and in this she is like so many of the artists of our time—which has neither the courage nor the patience to temporize with the concrete, substantial stuff that constitutes the occasion and the circumstance of man's actual career in time. It is an intelligence that cannot dive into the thick, coarse realities of the human condition, for these are not realities that are regarded as leading anywhere or as associable with what is Radically Significant in life. There is no deep faith or confidence in the realm of human finitude and in the possibility of its being "a glass of vision" into the ultimate. So an effort is made to flee into the safe and impregnable citadel of pure consciousness, and this is surely what accounts for the vulgarity that we may sometimes feel in the very refinement and delicacy and exquisiteness of sensibility that Mrs. Woolf's most ardent admirers like so much to praise. That is to say, we find vulgarity in the delicacy and the elegant sensitiveness, because it is all so bloodless and so far removed from the elemental things of human life. There is so much impatience with the clumsy grossness of the human creature and with the rough, ragged edges of life—and there is so much in the daily round of human living that Mrs. Woolf will not deign to bring within her orbit that, at last, paradoxically, we feel (as D. H. Lawrence might put it) that a kind of dirt is being done on life. She will never allow us to wallow about in the rucky mire of our humanness, and no one in her books ever howls or moans or really laughs over the human fate. And there is no passion because the characters in her novels have all been abstracted by her preciousness into fragile, gossamer-like "states of mind": it seems that only in this way could the human thing for her become just barely tolerable.

But the recoil into "sensibility" is but one of many detours away from the human actuality to be encountered in modern literature, and principal among these others is the recoil into "disgust" which is archetypally expressed in Jean-Paul Sartre's novel of 1938, *La Nausée*. The hero, Antoine Roquentin, is a young intellectual who takes up residence in the provincial town of Bouville-sur-Mer to finish a biography of an obscure eighteenth-century nobleman, the Marquis de Rollebon. And the novel which is written in the form of his journal is devoted to the record that he keeps of his experience during the period of his sojourn in this place. As he lives alone in his squalid roominghouse and works amidst the dreariness of the town's public library, Roquentin's spirits are soon depressed to the point of utter distraction by the drabness and monotony of life in this little coastal village, and, after a time, his restlessness making sustained scholarly labor impossible, his thinking becomes solely a matter of introspection and self-analysis. What is borne in upon him ever more deeply in the vacant, joyless days that ensue is his own isolation and the unshakeable indifference of the world to the human spirit. So intense does this vision of things become till he is stricken by first one and then another attack of sheer physical wretchedness: he is positively sickened by the amorphous factuality of the phenomenal world, by the obscene stubbornness with which things persist in re-taining a *thereness* that seems to have no link with his own existence and that seems, therefore, to that extent to oppose his own inward being. Indeed, his inner exacerbation becomes so acute that even the most commonplace objects in his environment at last prove capable of throwing him into a spasm of retching or into utter gloom—a pebble on the beach, a glass of beer, his own face in a mirror, the knob of a door. The whole of existence becomes for him simply one vast, obscene, bulging pile of junk, and his fundamental sensations come to be those of nausea and disgust. It is the very arbitrariness with which events occur and things exist that fills him with distress, for it deepens his sense of the contingency and finitude of his own being. Everything seems to be fragmentary and disheveled and messy— and the obscenity of it all makes him twitch with fury.

There is only one thing that lights up the gray tedium of his days: it is to hear a gramophone record of a Negro songstress singing the jazz melody "Some of These Days." And at the end of the novel, after having given up his research and completed preparations for his departure, as he sits in a dingy little *café* listening to the song and its saxophone accompaniment for the last time, what he has really wanted all his life suddenly dawns on him: it has been, as he says, "to chase existence out of me, empty the moments of their fat, wring them out, dry them, purify myself, harden myself, so as to give out finally the clean, precise note of a saxophone."

Now it is clear that the thing that fills Roquentin with horror is simply the sheer untidiness of existence: what he is oppressed by is the messiness of things, the bedragglement of the world; and his imagination is fixed upon images of *le visqueux,* because it is the opaqueness of things that reveals to him how ultimate is the ontological discontinuity between himself as a discrete, finite creature and everything else that exists. Every object and every event that he experiences seem, in the sheer arbitrariness and contingency of their reality, to imply that the kind of metaphysical order that he craves is an impossibility. So his sense of justice is outraged, and, in his consuming disgust, he desires to be disembodied into the purity of sound made by a blues-saxophonist: he would live the incorporeal life of the angels, being no longer a man but a mere breath of music.

Now this deep shudder of Sartre's hero before the phenomenal world presents us with an excellent example of the response that is made to existence by the antitype of the comic man. What Antoine Roquentin reveals, in the violence of his distaste for the created order, is precisely that profound distrust of creation which the testimony of the comedian always calls into question, at least in effect, if not by intention. For his is a mind that, characteristically, wallows in the thickness and the density of the concrete world of human experience, in all of its smells and sounds and sights and tactilities. The comedian is not, characteristically, an aviator: he does not journey away from this familiar world of earth: he refuses the experiment of angelism: he will not forget that we are made out of dust, and, when his wrath is aroused, as it sometimes is, it is not because man is bound to the things of earth but rather because man sometimes foolishly supposes that he can simply fly away from them.

THE LESSON OF COMEDY

This is, indeed, always the lesson of Comedy, that we are creatures whose nature it is to form an earthly City and who become ridiculous when we commit ourselves to some abortive venture beyond the precincts within which alone we can hope to win some proper understanding of our true human stature. It is not, of course, the purpose of the comedian to enforce a simple Sunday-School lesson: all he wants to do is to give his suffrage to the Whole Truth and, as Susanne Langer says, to "reincarnate for our perception, the motion and rhythm of [our] living" [23] in the world. "Real comedy," says Mrs. Langer, "sets up in the audience a sense of general exhilaration, because it presents the very image of 'livingness' " [24]— because, we might add, it tells us what Homer tells us in the Twelfth Book of the *Odyssey,* what Shakespeare tells us through Jack Falstaff when he takes us into Eastcheap or onto Gadshill, or what Charlie Chaplin tells us in *City Lights.* But this means, of course, that, when men decide that they are pure mind or pure will or pure sensibility, it is natural for the comic imagination to take on a critical, and even a polemical, aspect. It is appropriate, for example, that the Socrates of *The Clouds* who, in his contempt of the common world of human experience and in his consuming passion for the clear and distinct idea, lives ridiculously suspended in a basket high up in the air—it is appropriate that this man should, by Aristophanes, be brought down from his basket, that he should not be allowed to get away with this pretense that he lives above the relativities of history, and that he should be made to confront some of the elemental facts of life. Or, again, we feel the justice of comedy to be operative in Molière's *Le Misanthrope,* when the outrageous pharisaism of Alceste has, finally, the effect of relegating him to an essentially private universe between which and the actual world there ceases to be any connection at all. And had an Antoine Roquentin entered the orbit of so superb a modern comedian as Joyce Cary, he would have been reminded that he is not really a pure breath of music but that he is a man who eats and sleeps and defecates and catches colds in winter when he leaves off his long drawers, and that he had better remember these undignified facts if he wants to retain any dignity as a man.

The major purpose of the comedian, in other words, is to remind us of how deeply rooted we are in all the tangible things of this world, and he is not, like Shelley or the author of *To the Lighthouse,* a poet of an "unbodied joy." The motions of comedy do, to be sure, finally lead toward joy, but it is a joy that we win only after we have consented once again to journey through this familiar, actual world of earth which is our home and, in doing so, have had our faith in its stability and permanence restored. The joy of comedy is a great joy, but it is a joy which can sometimes come only after a

---

[23] Susanne K. Langer, *Feeling and Form: A Theory of Art* (New York: Charles Scribner's Sons, 1953), p. 344. [See in this anthology p. 135.]

[24] *Ibid.,* p. 348. [See, as above, p. 138.]

humiliation—the humiliation that the arrogant millionaire suffers
when, as he walks down the street, with his mind concentrated on
his dignity and importance, he slips on the banana peeling that he
failed to notice and is thus reminded that he is, after all, only a
man and is as much subject to the law of gravitation as is the rest
of humankind. The event may not at first bring joy to the man
himself, if the capacity in him for self-transcendence has been so
long unused that he cannot immediately regard with wry amusement
the spectacle that he creates before the gaping schoolchildren. But,
even if he is not the comic hero but rather merely the comic butt
of the event, we who are also looking on grasp the meaning of what
has occurred, and it brings us joy because it reminds us again how
inescapable our humanity is, how established and permanent and
indestructible it really is. To be sure, the man's backside is bruised
as a result of the fall—yet what is really hurt in him is his pride.
The truly human thing in him is not bruised: indeed, it is the lesson
of comedy that this does somehow manage, again and again, to remain intact: it is true that it is often challenged, and men themselves
do sometimes become ashamed of it and tamper with it and even
reject it, but this stuff that is constitutive of what is human in them
does, nevertheless, remain intact—and its reassertion of itself ·is the
central moment of comedy.

This, then, is *the comic way:* it is a way that descends into the
mundane, conditioned world of the human creature, moving confidently into all the diverse corners of man's habitation. And the
difference between this way and the tragic way is not that the one
leads into suffering and agony and that the other leads into rollicking
mirth and jollity, for the men and women of comedy sometimes
suffer too: indeed, one of the most heartrending moments in all of
Shakespearean drama is that in which (*Henry IV,* part II, V, 5)
Falstaff, having heard Prince Hal declare: "I know thee not, old
man. . . . ," turns to Justice Shallow and says: "Master Shallow,
I owe you a thousand pound"; and, in this moment, his anguish
is hardly less than that of the Lear who moans: "How sharper than
a serpent's tooth it is / To have a thankless child!" But the agonies
of the comic protagonist never have the kind of chemical purity
that belongs to the sufferings of the tragic hero: the comic man,
when he becomes involved in real difficulty, is no more pure suffering
than he is pure anything-else: Odysseus and his men, when they
finally stumbled upon the Sicilian beach that night, first ate their
supper before weeping for their lost comrades, and then, being exhausted, their tears ceased to flow, and they fell off to sleep.

So the art of comedy reminds us, however far we may venture into the strange corridors of the world or however high we may climb the treacherous mountains of the mind, that we are of the earth, earthy—that we are creatures whose finitude is ineluctable. In one of Kafka's Parables, he says:

[Man] is a free and secure citizen of the world, for he is fettered to a chain which is long enough to give him the freedom of all earthly space, and yet only so long that nothing can drag him past the frontiers of the world. But simultaneously he is a free and secure citizen of Heaven as well, for he is also fettered by a similarly designed heavenly chain. So that if he heads, say, for the earth, his heavenly collar throttles him, and if he heads for Heaven, his earthly one does the same.[25]

And though it may be the office of tragedy to be the heavenly collar that throttles us when we head for earth, it is certainly the office of comedy to be the collar that throttles us when we make up our minds to expatriate ourselves from the conditioned realm of historical existence. For what comedy never gives up insisting upon is that we are not angels and that we belong, therefore, not to any unhistorical heaven of pure essences but to the moving, restless, dynamic world of time and space.

Now this brings me to the point of at last tentatively proposing a definition of the comic, and it will be a gloss on the definition which W. H. Auden offered a few years ago in his "Notes on the Comic," in which he said that it is "a contradiction in the relation of the individual or personal to the universal or impersonal which does not involve the spectator in suffering or pity." [26] I should, however, prefer to put the matter a little differently and to say that the comic is a contradiction in the relation of the human individual to the created orders of existence which arises out of an over-specialization of some instinct or faculty of the self, or out of an inordinate inclination of the self in some special direction, to the neglect of the other avenues through which it ought also to gain expression. And it is this predilection of the self to identify itself too completely with some special interest or project (cf. Aristophanes' Socrates or Jonson's Volpone or Molière's Tartuffe or Sterne's Walter Shandy or Shaw's Professor Higgins)—it is this by which the self is blinded to the integral character of its humanity and thus thrown out of gear with the fundamental norms and orders of human existence. But, in

---

[25] Franz Kafka, Parables (New York: Schocken Books, 1947), p. 27.
[26] W. H. Auden, "Notes on the Comic," Thought, Vol. XXVII, No. 104 (Spring, 1952), p. 57. [See in this anthology p. 61.]

the comic action, this contradiction in the individual's relation to the created orders of life "does not involve the spectator in suffering or pity," for he is not led to identify himself with the protagonist who does, indeed, become, in the course of the action, the butt of his laughter.

But, now, this definition of the comic is not yet complicated enough, for it suggests what is not quite the case—namely, that the comic protagonist is always the butt of laughter, and of laughter that is untempered with love or sympathy. This is, of course, very often the case, but it is not always the case, and it is most certainly not true of the figure who has centrally to be taken into account in any theory of comedy—namely, Sir John Falstaff. This "swoll'n parcel of dropsies," this "huge bombard of sack," this "stuff'd cloakbag of guts," is—let us admit it—a rogue and a cheat, a braggart and a sensualist. Yet he is the most lovable rogue in all of literature. He is old and fat and broken-winded, and yet there is in him a kind of fresh, prelapsarian innocence that makes us think of him always as youthful and even boyish. And like many of the boys in our own American tradition, from Mark Twain's Huck Finn to J. D. Salinger's Holden Caulfield, Falstaff is a great liar—who lies, however, like Huck and Holden, in order to protect himself against the conventional dishonesty of other men. He has moved throughout the world, has bumped into all kinds of people, suffered all sorts of hard knocks, and pinched ladies' buttocks in every corner of England: yet there is in him no fatigue, no world-weariness, and he retains a remarkable zest and enthusiasm for the human adventure. And, above all else, he has a great capacity for living intensely in the present moment: one might say that he is the original existentialist hero, if one means by "existentialist hero" not the fastidious and disgusted man of Sartre's *La Nausée* but rather the man who is *engagé,* who is intensely committed to the present moment and the present task: indeed, in this sense, Falstaff is perhaps the original prototype of the existentialist man. And this may be why he is so impatient with the restraints of conventional moral codes and laws, for, however relevant they may be to the general circumstances of life, he finds them to be always ineffective and irrelevant to the immediate occasion, in all of its uniqueness and contingency. Yet, despite the outrageous improvisation in morality that it entails, it is this passionate commitment to the present moment and to the concrete reality that makes Falstaff so wonderfully and richly human.

Sir John's great scenes are, of course, in the two parts of *Henry IV* rather than in *The Merry Wives of Windsor,* and it is no wonder that here his role becomes finally that of victim. For these are plays whose whole drama is stirred into being by the anarchy that has overtaken the English realm; and since, in the world of Shakespearean experience, civil anarchy, of whatever sort, is most "unnatural," the drama of the two parts of *Henry IV* must, therefore, move towards the recovery of order in the body politic. Prince Hal is the one who is destined to be the agent whereby order will be restored; and since he finds in plump Jack a symbol of everything that would endanger or subvert decorum and order, he drives him off. And this is, to be sure, precisely what Falstaff does stand for: in the boldness and enterprise and vivacity and wit of this fat old rascal we have the most brilliant image that the literary tradition affords of that zest and spontaneity and independence in the human creature that would make him an intractable nuisance for every order that would define itself in such exclusively political terms as to prevent its making any room for a man to move about in and stretch himself. One might even say perhaps that his rejection by Hal is the evidence that Shakespeare provides of his human authenticity. So, despite all his faults, we have finally to face the fact that there is greatness in Sir John. He has vices, it is true, but, as Mark Van Doren says, "they have not the sound of vices. None of them is an end in itself—that is their secret. . . . He does not live to drink or steal or lie or foin o'nights. He even does not live in order that he may be the cause of wit in other men." [27] He simply lives for the joy of the adventure itself—and we must say, I think, to the glory of God. There is in him nothing of the protestant (and the "p" is small): he has no quarrel with life: he is not a romantic: he is engaged in no cosmic debate: he is content simply to be a man. And though he is not a very virtuous, not a very good man, though he is a rascal and a scalawag, he *is* a man, always and intensely human—and this, I take it, is why he is the great saint of Western comedy. We laugh at old Jack, but we also admire him and love him; and, when we laugh at him, it is simply because he is so different from the rest of us—different because he is so deeply rooted in the human condition that he restores our confidence in its resilience, in its essential stoutness and vitality. Which is simply to say that he is the archetypal instance of the comic *hero*.

And thus I am now brought to the point of being able to widen my definition of comedy to the extent of providing for two types of protagonist. That is to say, he may, on the one hand, like Volpone or Tartuffe or Dostoievski's "Underground" man, be one who is the

---

[27] Mark Van Doren, *Shakespeare* (Garden City: Doubleday Anchor Books, 1953), p. 114.

target of a fundamentally unsympathetic laughter because of his deviation from the natural human norm. Or, on the other hand, like Don Quixote or Falstaff or Joyce Cary's Gulley Jimson, he may be a figure of heroic proportions whom we laugh at and yet admire. And it is the presence in a given action of the one or the other type which determines the character of the resulting *katharsis.*

The comic *katharsis* does, I think, essentially involve such a restoration of our confidence in the realm of finitude as enables us to see the daily occasions of our earth-bound career as being not irrelevant inconveniences but as possible roads into what is ultimately significant in life. But this restoration of our confidence in the conditioned realities of historical existence may be managed by the comedian in either of two ways, depending on which of the two types of comic protagonist he has placed at the center of his action. If his central personage is one whose eccentricity arises out of some wilfully maintained imbalance of character which is not of the sort that excites pity or fear, our awareness of the validity of the human norm from which he has deviated will be renewed and deepened, as he shows himself to have been rendered incompetent by this eccentricity. And I take it that the Socrates of Aristophanes' *The Clouds* is an example of this kind of comic figure. But if, on the other hand, the protagonist is, like Falstaff, a man whose eccentricity is a consequence not of his deviateness but of the very depth of his rootedness in the stuff of our common humanity, then the experience of *katharsis* is something that grows out of the joy that we take in the discovery of how stout and gamy the human thing really is. And this is, of course, the discovery that the comic *hero* enables us to make, for he is, as Mrs. Langer says,

the indomitable living creature fending for itself, tumbling and stumbling . . . from one situation into another, getting into scrape after scrape and getting out again, with or without a thrashing. He is the personified *élan vital;* his chance adventures and misadventures, without much plot, though often with bizarre complications, his absurd expectations and disappointments, in fact his whole improvised existence has the rhythm of primitive . . . life coping with a world that is forever taking new uncalculated turns, frustrating, but exciting. He is . . . now triumphant, now worsted and rueful, but in his ruefulness and dismay he is funny, because his energy is really unimpaired and each failure prepares the situation for a new fantastic move.[28]

This is the comic man *par excellence,* and this is the "rhythm of action" that, in its greatest moments, his life exemplifies.

---

[28] Susanne K. Langer, *op. cit.,* p. 342. [In this anthology p. 133, 134.]

THE COMIC IMAGINATION AND THE CHRISTIAN SENSE OF REALITY

Now it seems to me that the great sympathy which the Christian imagination may feel for the testimony of the comedian is in large part a consequence of the extent to which it is governed by the same gross materialism in which comedy itself is so deeply rooted. And this is a characteristic of Christianity that, among its recent interpreters, the late Archbishop Temple most liked to remark: indeed, one of the most striking sentences in his Gifford Lectures asserts that "one ground for the hope of Christianity that it may make good its claim to be the true faith lies in the fact that it is the most avowedly materialist of all the great religions." [29] And I take it that, when Dr. Temple spoke of the materialistic character of Christianity, he meant that the Christian belief in the Creation and the Incarnation makes for a kind of profound respect for nature and time and history which is not easily to be found elsewhere in the history of religion. Which means that the Christian imagination is enabled to rejoice in the quiddities and hecceities of existence in a way that accords very closely with the path that is taken by the comic vision.

And that which first guarantees the Christian's confidence in the realm of the finite is his belief in the doctrine of Creation. This is not, of course, a doctrine that purports to be a scientifically accurate account of a dateable beginning of the cosmic process. It is, rather, a mytho-religious way of asserting that, though man and his world are in all respects enmeshed in relativity and contingency, they are neither illusory nor evil nor a mere concretion of some universal World Spirit. To say, as the Bible does, that God created the world out of nothing is, of course, to assert that He is the sole Ground and Source of everything that exists, and it is to assert the utter dependence of the world upon Him; but it is also, against all the various forms of Idealism and Gnosticism, to emphasize the genuine reality of finite existence: for it was *made* by God. And though this world of ours has been injured by man's sin, it is, despite its distinctness from God, *essentially* good, because it proceeds from Him and exists by His design. Nor can the doctrine of Creation be reconciled to any form of Pantheism, for in effect it denies both that the world is identical with God and that it is in some way an emanation of the "World Soul"; it says that "every creature in [the world] possesses a true self which, however much perfected . . . , is never swallowed up or lost in God. Therefore, all God's creatures are images of Him in the same

---

[29] William Temple, *Nature, Man and God* (New York: The Macmillan Co., 1934), p. 478.

way, and to the same limited extent, as a work of art is an image
of its maker—his, yet in a manner distinct from him." [30]

The crucial Biblical word here is a very simple word: it falls at the
very beginning of the story, in the great first chapter of the Book of
Genesis—"And God saw everything that he had made, and behold,
it was very good." And upon what is implicit in this single sentence
rests the whole Biblical interpretation of life and history, for that is a
view of things which is fundamentally premissed upon the assumption
that the world of finite and contingent existence is not essentially
defective simply by reason of its finiteness. Indeed, when the Christian
faith has been true to itself, it has never quite forgotten that its genius
in large part consists in its understanding that the finitude and par-
ticularization of created existence are not in themselves evil, since they
are a part of God's plan for the world.

There are, of course, many passages in Biblical literature that dwell
upon the absoluteness of the discrepancy between the Creator and the
created world. "All flesh is grass and all the godliness thereof is as the
flower of the field; The grass withereth, the flower fadeth: . . . but
the word of our God shall stand forever." "Thou, Lord, in the beginning hast laid the foundation of the earth; and the heavens are the
work of thy hands: They shall perish; but Thou remainest; and they
all shall wax old as doth a garment; and as a vesture shalt thou fold
them up, and they shall be changed: but Thou art the same, and thy
years shall not fail." "Behold, the nations are as a drop of a bucket,
and are counted as the small dust of the balance: . . . all nations
before him are as nothing; and they are counted to him less than
nothing." And one could go on to cite many other such passages which
point to the incommensurability between the created world and its
Creator. But what is significant is that this kind of testimony never
has it as its purpose to suggest that the transiency and fragmentariness are in themselves evil. On the contrary: as Reinhold Niebuhr
remarks at one point in his Gifford Lectures, "The fragmentary character of human life is not regarded as evil in Biblical faith because
it is seen from the perspective of a centre of life and meaning in which
each fragment is related to the plan of the whole, to the will of
God. The evil arises when the fragment seeks by its own wisdom to
comprehend the whole or attempts by its own power to realize it." [31]

There is, in other words, in the Biblical doctrine of Creation a kind

---

[30] Dorothy L. Sayers, *Further Papers on Dante* (New York: Harper and
Brothers, 1957), p. 187.

[31] Reinhold Niebuhr, *The Nature and Destiny of Man,* Vol. I (New York:
Charles Scribner's Sons, 1943), p. 168.

of sober realism and sanity that prompts the Hebraic imagination simply to accept the insufficiency and the incompleteness of human life
as a part of God's design. And when, in Biblical literature, the transiency
and finiteness of human existence are dwelt upon, they are stressed
only in contrast to and as proof of the glory and majesty of God, and
there is no suggestion that this discrepancy bears any moral connota-
tion: what is robustly affirmed, on the contrary, is that the created
world is good, because it is the work of God.

The finiteness of the human condition is, of course, never minimized;
our human nature remains creatural, even in the highest reaches of
its freedom and self-transcendence, and we never cease to be involved
in the relativities of historical existence. But always in Christian history, when the full implications of the doctrine of Creation have been
understood, the Biblical insights into the essential goodness of finite
existence have been preserved. "And God saw everything that he had
made, and behold, it was very good."

But now perhaps even the more crucial doctrine for the Christian
estimate of the essential character of finitude is the doctrine of the
Incarnation—whereby it is declared that the glory of God Himself
dwelt in our mortal flesh and became manifest to the eyes of men.
Even the distinguished Protestant theologian Karl Barth, who is
closely associated with the contemporary reaction against the "Jesus of
history" movement of nineteenth-century Liberalism, insists in his
Kirchliche Dogmatik that the central passage of the New Testament
is John 1:14, "The word became flesh and dwelt among us." And the
Christian community has, from time immemorial, perceived that what
is of the essence of the Gospel is a divine act of Condescension to our
low estate—whereby, as the Nicene Creed puts it, "God the Father
Almighty, Maker of heaven and earth, ... for us men and for our
salvation came down from heaven, And was incarnate by the Holy
Ghost of the Virgin Mary, And was made man. . . ." This is unquestionably the heart of the Gospel and the central miracle of Christian experience.

Now when, in its worship, the Church recites these words, its intention is to assert that, "in the fullness of time," God did really become
man without ceasing to be God. It does not merely assert that, through
the life of Jesus the carpenter of Galilee, we may come to discern
what God is like: it says, rather, that Jesus Christ *is* God Himself
incarnate. We have not, in other words, in Christ to do merely with a
religious genius or hero of some sort: nor are we dealing, in the New
Testament, with a God who, like the gods of pagan Greece, merely
disguised Himself as a man. On the contrary: as Langmead Casserley
so robustly puts it:

His was a real babyhood and youth, a real growth in mind and stature, a desperately human hunger, an exquisitely human pain, an agonizingly human death. In His thirty years of incarnate existence, God was touched and harrowed by all that is most menacing in the lot of man—physical pain, economic insecurity, subtle temptation, a tragic death foreseen and awaited, the frustration of noble purposes, intellectual misunderstanding, the wearisome, disillusioning absence of sympathy, slander, unpopularity, injustice, persecution, rejected love. All that most easily overcomes the spirit of man He faced without defeat, all that is most prone to embitter and distort the human character He absorbed without bitterness or spiritual loss, smiled kindly through the endless frustrations which so often cynicize and disillusion romantic and idealistic men, loved unwearyingly through the rejection of love with a love which not even hatred could remould in its own image, confronted temptation with an invincible perfection of character and purpose against which the hitherto victorious powers of evil were powerless, and finally placed in the hands of death a life so intense and concentrated on its destiny that death's age-old mastery over life was revealed as a broken thing.[32]

Now it is the Christian faith that a tremendous thing occurred in this astonishing series of events, that in the altogether unique segment of history that is constituted by our Lord's earthly career we were, in effect, "delivered from the woe of being alive." [33] And I take it that this is in part what Paul Tillich means when he speaks, as he so often does, of Christ as "the center" of history, the center round which the entire human story arranges itself. For, in the event of Jesus Christ, the whole of human existence, contaminated though it had been by the poisons of sin, was made valid and put right again, when God himself entered the sphere of our life and brought grace and truth into our very midst.

Emil Brunner is, of course, altogether right in contending, as he does in his little book *The Divine-Human Encounter,* that the ultimate significance of the Incarnation is misunderstood if it is supposed that Jesus Christ came merely to come: no, says Dr. Brunner, He "did not come merely to come, but He came to redeem. To be sure, only the Incarnate Lord—very God, very man—can be the Redeemer. But the Bible guides us to ponder less the secret of the Person of Jesus than the mystery of His work." [34] And I do not myself want to suggest here that the full significance of the doctrine of the

---

[32] J. V. Langmead Casserley, *No Faith of My Own* (New York: Longmans, Green and Co., 1952), pp. 35–36.

[33] Denis de Rougemont, *Passion and Society,* trans. by Montgomery Belgion (London: Faber and Faber Ltd., 1940), p. 81.

[34] Emil Brunner, *The Divine-Human Encounter* (Philadelphia: The Westminster Press, 1943), p. 142.

Incarnation is properly construed in terms merely of the *Person* of Christ or in terms of how it illumines the true relation of the finite and the infinite. But, at the same time, I am eager to avoid the imbalance that so much of Protestant theology often represents today, of interpreting the Incarnation in such a way that, as the Lutheran theologian Joseph Sittler has noticed, it receives "only that light which can be reflected backward upon it from Calvary. While, to be sure, these events cannot be separated without the impoverishment of the majesty of the history of redemption, it is nevertheless proper to suggest," says Dr. Sittler, "that our theological tendency to declare them only in their concerted meaning *at the point of fusion* tends to disqualify us to listen to the ontological-revelational overtones of the Incarnation." [35] And surely it is not to do violence to the true import of Biblical faith to insist that God's having condescended to "tabernacle amongst us," to assume a human body, a human mind, a human soul, and to submit Himself to all the conditions of our life in the natural order—surely it is not improper to insist that His having deigned to do this has the effect of giving a new value to all the finite vehicles and instrumentalities which He thus employed. And the consequence is that the Christian's fundamental attitude toward existence must always be profoundly affirmative: its particularity and fragmentariness can never be, for him, the offense that they are to more fastidious men: nor can he ever in any way impugn the validity of the natural and the temporal order, since for thirty years this was the home of God Himself.

Now, this, then, is what I take Dr. Temple to have had in mind when he spoke of the "materialism" of Christianity—this attitude, that is, of respect, of esteem, of love even, for the actual, specific, concrete things of this world which belong to the order created by God and which formed an adequate theatre for the drama in which His Son took the leading part. The Christian imagination does not shrink, in other words, from the tangibility, from the gross concreteness, of our life in time, and it is not afraid to face the limited, conditioned nature of human existence. It is, indeed, affirmative—radically affirmative—in its attitude toward nature and time and history. It does not spend its time looking about for an elevator that will whisk it up out of the world into eternity, for it is committed to the world, and it wants the world to come to itself, not to run away from itself. It believes that God's way of dealing with us is by and through the things and creatures of this world, and that He is Himself to be met not *in*

---

[35] Joseph Sittler, "A Theology for Earth," *The Christian Scholar,* Vol. XXXVII, No. 3 (September, 1954), p. 374.

Himself but in His works and in His gifts. And it believes that in the Incarnation God Himself has affirmed the world, has affirmed the realm of finitude, the realm of nature and of history. So the religion which finds its main fulcrum in the Incarnational event is a faith which does not take us out of this world: it takes us, rather, deeper and deeper into it. Which is to say that, unlike the kind of modern imagination represented by Virginia Woolf, the Christian has no desire to be an angel, but, rather, to the scandalization of all types of idealists and angelists, it does persist in wallowing about in all the temporal, creatural stuff of human life, for it was in this stuff that God Himself became Incarnate.

Now I have been contending that it is the function of comedy to enliven our sense of the human actuality, to put us in touch with the Whole Truth—particularly when, in the pursuit of some false and abstract image of ourselves, we have become embarrassed by the limitations of our creatureliness and undertaken to bring our life in history to an end either by some violently conclusive action or by some disillusioned flight into the realm of pure idea. Forsaking all the meretricious forms of eschatology, comedy moves toward the actual: it asks us to be content with our human limitations and possibilities and to accept our life in this world without the sentimentality either of smugness or of cynicism. And when we wish to be pure discarnate spirit or pure discarnate intellect, the comedian asks us to remember the objective, material conditions of life with which we must make our peace, if we are to retain our sanity and survive. He will not let us forget that we are men, that we are finite and conditioned creatures—not angels. And, in its deeply affirmative attitude toward the created orders of existence, in the profound "materialism" of its outlook, the comic imagination, it seems to me, summarizes an important part of the Christian testimony about the meaning of human life.

COMEDY'S DISTILLATION OF THE DARK INTO LIGHT

Indeed, it is this profoundly affirmative quality in the comic vision which makes the appreciation of it involve in our time so strenuous an effort of the moral imagination. For the kind of vision which has the most direct appeal for us is one which, in offering some radical and extremist conception of ourselves, promises to increase the psyche's temperature. The great heroes of our cultural life, as Mr. Trilling has remarked, are "the tigers of wrath" [36]—the Kafkas and the Sartres and the Becketts; and they are cherished as examples of a charismatic

---

[36] Lionel Trilling, *The Opposing Self* (New York: The Viking Press, 1955), p. 132.

power which we covet for ourselves, of being able to endure the stigmata of our Alienation with such fierceness and valor that the inconveniences and disadvantages of history might be left behind and the
spirit liberated from the conditioned character of our mundane existence. We are, in fact, as a people always on the verge of electing to
bring our life in history to an end. We

> are discontented with the nature rather than with the use of the human
> faculty; deep in our assumption lies the hope and the belief that humanity
> will end its career by developing virtues which will be admirable exactly be-
> cause we cannot now conceive them. The past has been a weary failure, the
> present cannot matter, for it is but a step forward to the final judgment;
> we look to the future when the best of the works of man will seem but the
> futile and slightly disgusting twitchings of primeval creatures. . . .[37]

So the way of comedy which attempts to lead us into that special sort
of truth which Aldous Huxley calls the "Whole Truth"—this is a
way that is one of the most difficult ways which the modern imagination can be asked to take. Yet, if this way be taken, it may be a
preparatio that will permit us once more to be brought to the point
of being able, with both laughter and reverence in our hearts, to say
with the Psalmist, "The earth is the Lord's and the fulness thereof,
the world and those who dwell therein." And this, I suspect, is a
large part of what Christopher Fry means, when he tells us that
"comedy is an escape, not from truth but from despair: a narrow
escape into faith." [38] It is, he suggests, the "angle of experience where
the dark is distilled into light. . . . It says, in effect, that, groaning
as we may be, we move in the figure of a dance, and, so moving,
we trace the outline of the mystery." [39]

Fr. William Lynch tells us that "it would be unfair to tragedy to
think that it is only to the tragic that comedy is addressing itself as
semantic challenger, vocabulary against vocabulary." [40] And Mr. Fry
says that he is always on "the verge of saying that comedy is greater
than tragedy." But, he says, "On the verge I stand and go no further." [41]
Nor have I wanted to put comedy into the kind of competition with
tragedy that would necessitate our opting for one against the other:
so to pose the issues would, of course, entail an impossibly narrow

---

[37] Lionel Trilling, *E. M. Forster* (New York: New Directions, 1943), p. 22.
[38] Christopher Fry, "Comedy," *The Tulane Drama Review*, Vol. IV, No. 3
(March, 1960), p. 77. [See in this anthology p. 15.]
[39] *Ibid.* [p. 16.]
[40] William F. Lynch. s.j., *Christ and Apollo* (New York: Sheed and Ward,
1960), p. 95.
[41] Christopher Fry, *op. cit.,* p. 78. [p. 17.]

kind of scholasticism, since "we find ourselves in [comedy] or [tragedy] by the turn of a thought"[42] and since, as Mr. Fry has reminded us, the man who is unqualified for tragedy is also unqualified for comedy. But I have wanted to suggest that comedy affords the Christian student of modern literature a high and promising ground from within literature itself for a radical critique of the various "Gnosticized" forms of tragedy that constitute "our period style." And, obversely, I have also wanted to suggest something of the kind of constructive theological insight (heretical as this may be within the forums of post-Arnoldian criticism) that the literary imagination itself, in its comic phase, proposes to the Christian intelligence—that, as Fr. Lynch puts it (and in all this he has been, as his readers will recognize, my fundamental guide):

a thing need not step out of the human to be all things, and to achieve the liberty of the children of God. The mud in man, the lowermost point in the subway, is nothing to be ashamed of. It can produce . . . the face of God. . . . To recall this, to recall this incredible relation between mud and God, is, in its own distant, adumbrating way, the function of comedy.[43]

---

[42] *Ibid.* [p. 16.]
[43] William F. Lynch, s.j., *op. cit.,* p. 109.

Part Two

THE FORM OF COMEDY

Susanne Langer
THE COMIC RHYTHM

Northrop Frye
THE MYTHOS OF SPRING: COMEDY

Benjamin Lehmann
COMEDY AND LAUGHTER

The Comic Rhythm*

Of all the arts, the most exposed to non-artistic interpretation and criticism are prose fiction and the drama. As the novel has suffered from being treated as a psycho-biographical document, drama has suffered from moralism. In the theater, most people—and especially the most competent spectators—feel that the vision of destiny is the essence of the work, the thing that unfolds before their eyes. In critical retrospect they forget that this visibly growing future, this destiny to which the persons in the play are committed, is the artistic form the poet set out to make, and that the value of the play lies in this creation. As critics, they treat the form as a device for conveying a social and moral content; almost all drama analysis and comment is concerned with the moral struggle involved in the action, the justice of the outcome, the "case" of society against the tragic hero or the comic villain, and the moral significance of the various characters.

It is true that tragedy usually—perhaps even always—presents a moral struggle, and that comedy very commonly castigates foibles and vices. But neither a great moral issue, nor folly inviting embarrassment and laughter, in itself furnishes an artistic principle; neither ethics nor common sense produces any image of organic form. Drama, however, always exhibits such form; it does so by creating the semblance of a history, and composing its elements into a rhythmic single structure. The moral content is thematic material, which, like everything that enters into a work of art, has to serve to make the primary illusion and articulate the pattern of "felt life" the artist intends.

"The tragic theme" and "the comic theme"—guilt and expiation, vanity and exposure—are not the essence of drama, not even the de-

---

* Susanne Langer, "The Comic Rhythm," in *Feeling and Form* (Charles Scribner's Sons, 1953), pp. 326–350. [Footnotes have been renumbered.]

terminants of its major forms, tragedy and comedy; they are means of dramatic construction, and as such they are, of course, not indispensable, however widespread their use. But they are to European drama what the representation of objects is to painting: sources of the Great Tradition. Morality, the concept of deed and desert, or "what is coming to the doer," is as obvious a subject for the art of creating a virtual future as the depiction of objects is for the art of creating virtual space. The reason for the existence of these two major themes, and for their particular respective contents, will be apparent as soon as we consider the nature of the two great forms, comic drama and tragic.

It is commonly assumed that comedy and tragedy have the same fundamental form, but differ in point of view—in the attitude the poet and his interpreters take, and the spectators are invited to take, toward the action.[1] But the difference really goes deeper than surface treatment (i.e., relative levity or pathos). It is structural and radical. Drama abstracts from reality the fundamental forms of consciousness: the first reflection of natural activity in sensation, awareness, and expectation, which belongs to all higher creatures and might be called, therefore, the pure sense of life; and beyond that, the reflection of an activity which is at once more elaborate, and more integrated, having a beginning, efflorescence, and end—the personal sense of life, or self-realization. The latter probably belongs only to human beings, and to them in varying measure.

The pure sense of life is the underlying feeling of comedy, developed in countless different ways. To give a general phenomenon one name is not to make all its manifestations one thing, but only to bring them conceptually under one head. Art does not generalize and classify; art sets forth the individuality of forms which discourse, being essentially general, has to suppress. The sense of life is always new, infinitely complex, therefore infinitely variable in its possible expressions. This sense, or "enjoyment" as Alexander would call it,[2] is the realization in direct feeling of what sets organic nature apart from inorganic: self-preservation, self-restoration, functional tendency, purpose. Life is teleological, the rest of nature is, apparently,

---

[1] Cf., for instance, the letters of Athene Seyler and Stephen Haggard, published under the title: *The Craft of Comedy*. Miss Seyler writes: ". . . comedy is simply a point of view. It is a comment on life from outside, an observation on human nature. . . . Comedy seems to be the standing outside a character or situation and pointing out one's delight in certain aspects of it. For this reason it demands the cooperation of . . . the audience and is in essence the same as recounting a good story over the dining-table." (p. 9.)

[2] S. Alexander, *Space, Time and Deity*. See Vol. I, p. 12.

mechanical; to maintain the pattern of vitality in a non-living universe is the most elementary instinctual purpose. An organism tends to keep its equilibrium amid the bombardment of aimless forces that beset it, to regain equilibrium when it has been disturbed, and to pursue a sequence of actions dictated by the need of keeping all its interdependent parts constantly renewed, their structure intact. Only organisms have needs; lifeless objects whirl or slide or tumble about, are shattered and scattered, struck together, piled up, without showing any impulse to return to some pre-eminent condition and function. But living things strive to persist in a particular chemical balance, to maintain a particular temperature, to repeat particular functions, and to develop along particular lines, achieving a growth that seems to be preformed in their earliest, rudimentary, protoplasmic structure.

That is the basic biological pattern which all living things share: the round of conditioned and conditioning organic processes that produces the life rhythm. When this rhythm is disturbed, all activities in the total complex are modified by the break; the organism as a whole is out of balance. But, within a wide range of conditions, it struggles to retrieve its original dynamic form by overcoming and removing the obstacle, or if this proves impossible, it develops a slight variation of its typical form and activity and carries on life with a new balance of functions—in other words, it adapts itself to the situation. A tree, for instance, that is bereft of the sunshine it needs by the encroachment of other trees, tends to grow tall and thin until it can spread its own branches in the light. A fish that has most of its tail bitten off partly overcomes the disturbance of its locomotion patterns by growing new tissue, replacing some of the tail, and partly adapts to its new condition by modifying the normal uses of its fins, swimming effectively without trying to correct the list of its whole body in the water, as it did at first.

But the impulse to survive is not spent only in defense and accommodation; it appears also in the varying power of organisms to seize on opportunities. Consider how chimney swifts, which used to nest in crevasses among rocks, have exploited the products of human architecture, and how unfailingly mice find the warmth and other delights of our kitchens. All creatures live by opportunities, in a world fraught with disasters. That is the biological pattern in most general terms.

This pattern, moreover, does not develop sporadically in midst of mechanical systems; when or where it began on the earth we do not know, but in the present phase of this planet's constitution there appears to be no "spontaneous generation." It takes life to produce further life. Every organism, therefore, is historically linked with other organisms. A single cell may die, or it may divide and lose its identity in the reorganization of what was formerly its protoplasm round two nuclei instead of one. Its existence as one maturing cell is a phase in a continuum of biological process that varies its rhythm at definite points of growth, starting over with multiplied instances of the immature form. Every individual in this progression that dies (i.e. meets with disaster) instead of dividing is an offshoot from the continuous process, an end, but not a break in the communal biography.

There are species of such elementary life that are diffused in air and water, and some that cohere in visible colonies; above all, there are genetically related organic structures that tend to interact, modify each other, vary in special ways, and together—often by hundreds, thousands, millions together—produce a single higher organism. In such higher organisms, propagation no longer occurs by binary fission, and consequently the individual is not a passing phase in an endless metabolic process; death, which is an accident in amoeboid existence, becomes the lot of every individual—no accident, but a phase of the life pattern itself. The only "immortal" portion of such a complex organism is a class of cells which, during its lifetime, forms new individuals.

In relatively low forms of individualized life, for instance the cryptogams, new specimens may spring entirely from one parent, so that the entire ancestry of an organism forms a single line. But the main evolutionary trend has been toward a more complex form of heredity: two cells of complementary structure, and from different individuals, fuse and grow into a common offspring. This elaborate process entails the division of the race into two sexes, and radically affects the needs and instincts of its members. For the jellyfish, the desire for continuity is enough; it seeks food and avoids destructive influence. Its rhythm is the endless metabolic cycle of cellular growth, punctuated by fissions and rearrangements, but ageless except for the stages of each passing individuation, and in principle deathless. The higher organisms, however, that do not give themselves up by division into new units of life, are all doomed to die; death is inherent in a form of life that achieves complete individuation. The only vestige in them of the endless protoplasmic life passing through organism after organism is their production of the "immortal" cells, ova or spermatozoa; this small fraction of them still enjoys the longer life of the stock.

The sex impulse, which presumably belongs only to bisexual creatures (whatever equivalents it may have in other procreative processes), is closely intertwined with the life impulse; in a mature organism it is part and parcel of the whole vital impetus. But it is a specialized part, because the activities that maintain the individual's life are varied and adaptable to many circumstances, but procreation requires specific actions. This specialization is reflected in the emotional life of all the higher animals; sexual excitement is the most intense and at the same time the most elaborately patterned experience, having its own rhythm that engages the whole creature, its rise and crisis and cadence, in a much higher degree than any other emotive response. Consequently the whole development of feeling, sensibility, and temperament is wont to radiate from that source of vital consciousness, sexual action and passion.

Mankind has its rhythm of animal existence, too—the strain of maintaining a vital balance amid the alien and impartial chances of the world, complicated and heightened by passional desires. The pure sense of life springs from that basic rhythm, and varies from the composed well-being of sleep to the intensity of spasm, rage, or ecstasy. But the process of living is incomparably more complex for human beings than for even the highest animals; man's world is, above all, intricate and puzzling. The powers of language and imagination have set it utterly apart from that of other creatures. In human society an individual is not, like a member of a herd or a hive, exposed only to others that visibly or tangibly surround him, but is consciously bound to people who are absent, perhaps far away, at the moment. Even the dead may still play into his life. His awareness of events is far greater than the scope of his physical perceptions. Symbolic construction has made this vastly involved and extended world: and mental adroitness is his chief asset for exploiting it. The pattern of his vital feeling, therefore, reflects his deep emotional relation to those symbolic structures that are his realities, and his instinctual life modified in almost every way by thought—a brainy opportunism in face of an essentially dreadful universe.

This human life-feeling is the essence of comedy. It is at once religious and ribald, knowing and defiant, social and freakishly individual. The illusion of life which the comic poet creates is the oncoming future fraught with dangers and opportunities, that is, with physical or social events occurring by chance and building up the coincidences with which individuals cope according to their lights. This ineluctable future—ineluctable because its countless factors are beyond human knowledge and control—is Fortune. Destiny in the guise of Fortune is the fabric of comedy; it is developed by comic action, which is the upset and recovery of the protagonist's equilibrium, his contest with the world and his triumph by wit, luck, personal power, or even humorous, or ironical, or philosophical acceptance of mischance. Whatever the theme—serious and lyrical as in *The Tempest,* coarse slapstick as in the *Schwänke* of Hans Sachs, or clever and polite social satire—the immediate sense of life is the underlying feeling of comedy, and dictates its rhythmically structured unity, that is to say its organic form.

Comedy is an art form that arises naturally wherever people are gathered to celebrate life, in spring festivals, triumphs, birthdays, weddings, or initiations. For it expresses the elementary strains and resolutions of animate nature, the animal drives that persist even in human nature, the delight man takes in his special mental gifts that make him the lord of creation; it is an image of human vitality holding its own in the world amid the surprises of unplanned coincidence. The most obvious occasions for the performance of comedies are thanks or challenges to fortune. What justifies the term "Comedy" is not that the ancient ritual procession, the Comus, honoring the god of that name, was the source of this great art form—for comedy has arisen in many parts of the world, where the Greek god with his particular worship was unknown—but that the Comus was a fertility rite, and the god it celebrated a fertility god, a symbol of perpetual rebirth, eternal life.

Tragedy has a different basic feeling, and therefore a different form; that is why it has also quite different thematic material, and why character development, great moral conflicts, and sacrifice are its usual actions. *It is also what makes tragedy sad,* as the rhythm of sheer vitality makes comedy happy. To understand this fundamental difference, we must turn once more to the biological reflections above, and carry them a little further.

In the higher forms of life, an organism is not split up into other organisms so as to let its career as an individual properly end without death and decay; each separate body, on the higher levels, having completed its growth, and normally having reproduced, becomes decadent and finally dies. Its life has a definite beginning, ascent, turning point, descent, and close (barring accidental destruction of life, such as simple cells may also suffer); and the close is inevitably death. Animals—even highly developed ones—instinctively seek to avoid death when they are suddenly confronted with it, and presumably do not realize its coming if and when they die naturally. But human beings, because of their semantically enlarged horizon, are aware of individual history as a passage from birth to death. Human life, therefore, has a different subjective pattern from animal existence; as "felt life" (to borrow Henry James' phrase once more) it has a different dimension. Youth, maturity, and age are not merely states in which a creature may happen to be, but are stages through which persons must pass. Life is a voyage, and at the end of it is death.

The power to conceive of life as a single span enables one also to think of its conduct as a single undertaking, and of a person as a unified and developed being, a personality. Youth, then, is all potentiality, not only for physical growth and procreation, but also for mental and moral growth. Bodily development is largely unconscious and involuntary, and the instincts that aid it are bent simply upon maintaining the vital rhythms from moment to moment, evading destruction, letting the organism grow in its highly specialized fashion. Its maturation, procreative drive, then a fairly long period of "holding its own" without further increase, and finally the gradual loss of impetus and elasticity—these processes form one organic evolution and dissolution. The extraordinary activity of man's brain, however, does not automatically parallel his biological career. It outruns the order of animal interests, sometimes confusing his instincts, sometimes exaggerating them (as simple sexual passion, for instance, is heightened by imagination into romantic passion and eternal devotion), and gives his life a new pattern dominated by his foreknowledge of death. Instead of simply passing through the natural succession of his individualized existence, he ponders its uniqueness, its brevity and limitations, the life impulses that make it, and the fact that in the end the organic unity will be broken, the self will disintegrate and be no more.

There are many ways of accepting death; the commonest one is to deny its finality, to imagine a continued existence "beyond" it—by resurrection, reincarnation, or departure of the soul from the body, and usually from the familiar world, to a deathless existence in hades, nirvana, heaven or hell. But no matter how people contrive to become reconciled to their mortality, it puts its stamp on their conception of life: since the instinctive struggle to go on living is bound to meet defeat in the end, they look for *as much life as possible* between birth and death—for adventure, variety and intensity of experience, and the sense of growth that increase of personality and social status can give long after physical growth has stopped. The known limitation of life gives form to it and makes it appear not merely as a process, but as a career. This career of the individual is variously conceived as a "calling," the attainment of an ideal, the soul's pilgrimage, "life's ordeal," or self-realization. The last of these designations is, perhaps, the most illuminating in the present context, because it contains the notion of a limited potential personality given at birth and "realized," or systematically developed, in the course of the subject's total activity. His career, then, appears to be preformed in him; his successive adventures in the world are so many challenges to fulfill his individual destiny.

Destiny viewed in this way, as a future shaped essentially in advance and only incidentally by chance happenings, is Fate; and Fate is the "virtual future" created in tragedy. The "tragic rhythm of action," as Professor Fergusson calls it, is the rhythm of man's life at its highest powers in the limits of his unique, death-bound career. Tragedy is the image of Fate, as comedy is of Fortune. Their basic structures are different; comedy is essentially contingent, episodic, and ethnic; it expresses the continuous balance of sheer vitality that belongs to society and is exemplified briefly in each individual; tragedy is a fulfillment, and its form therefore is closed, final and passional. Tragedy is a mature art form, that has not arisen in all parts of the world, not even in all great civilizations. Its conception requires a sense of individuality which some religions and some cultures—even high cultures—do not generate.

But that is a matter for later discussion, in connection with the tragic theater as such. At present I wish only to point out the radical nature of the difference between the two types of drama, comedy and tragedy; a difference which is, however, not one of opposites—the two forms are perfectly capable of various combinations, incorporating elements of one in the other. The matrix of the work is always either tragic or comic; but within its frame the two often interplay.

Where tragedy is generally known and accepted, comedy usually does not reach its highest development. The serious mood is reserved for the tragic stage. Yet comedy may be serious; there is heroic drama, romantic drama, political drama, all in the comic pattern, yet entirely serious; the "history" is usually exalted comedy. It presents an incident in the undying life of a society that meets good and evil fortunes on countless occasions but never concludes its quest. After the story comes more life, more destiny prepared by the world and the race. So far as the story goes, the protagonists "live happily ever after"—on earth or in heaven. That fairy-tale formula is tacitly understood at the close of a comedy. It is implicit in the episodic structure.

Dante called his great poem a comedy, though it is entirely serious—visionary, religious, and sometimes terrible. The name *Divina Commedia,* which later generations attached to it, fits it, even if not too literally since it is not actually a drama as the title suggests.[3]

---

[3] Professor Fergusson and Mr. T. S. Eliot both treat *The Divine Comedy* as an example of genuine drama. The former even speaks of "the drama of Sophocles and Shakespeare, the *Divina Commedia* of Dante—in which the idea of a theater has been briefly realized." (*The Idea of a Theater,* p. 227.) But between drama and dramatic narrative there is a world of difference. If everything these two eminent critics say of great drama holds also for Dante's poem, this does not mean that the poem is a drama, but that the critics have reached a generalization applying to more than drama.

Something analogous to the comedy pattern, together with the tones of high seriousness that European poets have generally struck only in tragedy, yields a work that invites the paradoxical name.

Paradoxical, however, only to our ears, because our religious feeling is essentially tragic, inspired by the contemplation of death. In Asia the designation "Divine Comedy" would fit numberless plays; especially in India triumphant gods, divine lovers united after various trials (as in the perennially popular romance of Rama and Sita), are the favorite themes of a theater that knows no "tragic rhythm." The classical Sanskrit drama was heroic comedy—high poetry, noble action, themes almost always taken from the myths—a serious, religiously conceived drama, yet in the "comic" pattern, which is not a complete organic development reaching a foregone, inevitable conclusion, but is episodic, restoring a lost balance, and implying a new future.[4] The reason for this consistently "comic" image of life in India is obvious enough: both Hindu and Buddhist regard life as an episode in the much longer career of the soul which has to accomplish many incarnations before it reaches its goal, nirvana. Its struggles in the world do not exhaust it; in fact they are scarcely worth recording except in entertainment theater, "comedy" in our sense—satire, farce, and dialogue. The characters whose fortunes are seriously interesting are the eternal gods; and for them there is no death, no limit of potentialities, hence no fate to be fulfilled. There is only the balanced rhythm of sentience and emotion, upholding itself amid the changes of material nature.

The personages in the nataka (the Sanskrit heroic drama) do not undergo any character development; they are good or evil, as the case may be, in the last act as they were in the first. This is essentially a comedy trait. Because the comic rhythm is that of vital continuity, the protagonists do not change in the course of the play, as they normally do in tragedy. In the latter there is development, in the former developments. The comic hero plays against obstacles presented either by nature (which includes mythical monsters such as dragons, and also "forces," personified like the "Night Queen," or impersonal like floods, fires, and pests), or by society; that is, his fight is with obstacles and enemies, which his strength, wisdom, virtue, or other assets let him overcome.[5] It is a fight with the uncongenial world, which he shapes to his own fortunes. Where the basic feeling of

---

[4] Cf. Sylvain Lévi, *Le théâtre indien,* p. 32: "The heroic comedy (nataka) is the consummate type of Indian drama; all dramatic elements can find their place in it."

[5] In Chinese drama, even exalted heroes often conquer their enemies by ruse rather than by valor; see Zucker, *The Chinese Theater,* especially p. 82.

dramatic art always has the comic rhythm, comedy enjoys a much fuller development than it does where tragedy usurps its highest honors. In the great cultures of Asia it has run through all moods, from the lightest to the most solemn, and through all forms—the one-act skit, the farce, the comedy of manners, even to dramas of Wagnerian proportions.

In the European tradition the heroic comedy has had a sporadic existence; the Spanish *Comedia* was perhaps its only popular and extended development.[6] Where it reaches something like the exalted character of the nataka, our comedy has generally been taken for tragedy, simply because of its dignity, or "sublimity," which we associate only with tragedy. Corneille and Racine considered their dramas tragedies, yet the rhythm of tragedy—the growth and full realization of a personality—is not in them; the Fate their personages meet is really misfortune, and they meet it heroically. This sad yet non-tragic character of the French classical drama has been noted by several critics. C. V. Deane, for instance, in his book, *Dramatic Theory and the Rhymed Heroic Play,* says of Corneille: "In his tragedies the incidents are so disposed as to bring out to the full the conflict between an overmastering will and the forces of Fate, but the interest centres in the dauntless endurance of the individual, and there is little attempt to envisage or suggest the universal moral problem inherent in the nature of Tragedy, nor do his chief characters submit to ordinary morality; each is a law unto himself by virtue of his particular kind of heroism." [7] Earlier in the book he had already remarked on the fact that the creation of human personalities was not the aim of these playwrights; [8] and in a comment on Otway's translation of Racine's *Bérénice* he really exposed—perhaps without realizing it himself—the true nature of their tragedies, for he said that Otway was able "to reproduce the spirit of the original," though he was not scrupulously true to the French text. "Even Otway, however, adapts rather than translates," he observed, "and the tilt toward the happy ending in his version betrays an acquiescence in the stereotyped poetic justice which the English playwrights (appreciably influenced by Cor-

---

[6] Brander Matthews describes the *Comedia* as "often not a comedy at all in our English understanding of the term, but rather a play of intrigue, peopled with hot-blooded heroes. . . ." (Introduction to Lope De Vega Carpio's *The New Art of Writing Plays.*)

[7] *Dramatic Theory and the Rhymed Heroic Play,* p. 33.

[8] *Ibid.,* p. 14: "It is true that during the course of its history the heroic play seldom succeeded in creating characters which were credible as human beings; this, however, was really foreign to its purpose."

neille's practice) deemed inseparable from the interplay of heroism and honor." (p. 19.)

How could a translator-editor bring a tragic play to a happy ending and still "reproduce the spirit of the original"? Only by virtue of the non-tragic structure, the fundamentally comic movement of the piece. These stately Gallic classics are really heroic comedies. They are classed as tragedies because of their sublime tone, which is associated, in our European tradition, with tragic action,[9] but (as Sylvain Lévi pointed out) [10] they are really similar in spirit and form to the nataka. Corneille's and Racine's heroic characters are godlike in their rationality; like the divine beings of Kalidasa and Bhavabhuti, they undergo no real *agon*, no great moral struggle or conflict of passions. Their morality (however extraordinary) is perfect, their principles clear and coherent, and the action derives from the changes of fortune that they meet. Fortune can bring sad or happy occasions, and a different course of events need not violate "the spirit of the original." But there is no question of how the heroes will meet circumstances; they will meet them rationally; reason, the highest virtue of the human soul, will be victorious. This reason does not grow, through inner struggles against passional obstacles, from an original spark to full enlightenment, as "the tragic rhythm of action" would demand, but is perfect from the outset.[11]

---

[9] The strength of this association is so great that some critics actually treat "sublimity" as the necessary and sufficient condition for tragedy. Racine himself said: "It is enough that its action be great, its actors heroic, that the passions be excited in it; and that the whole give the experience of majestic sadness in which the whole pleasure of tragedy resides." (Quoted by Fergusson, *op. cit.,* p. 43.)

The same criteria are evidently applied by Professor Zucker when he writes: "Tragedy is not found in the Chinese drama. The plays abound in sad situations, but there is none that by its nobility or sublimity would deserve to be called tragic." (*Op. cit.,* p. 37.) Jack Chen, on the other hand, in his book *The Chinese Theater,* says that during the Ching dynasty "Historical tragedy was greatly in vogue. *The Bloodstained Fan* dealing with the last days of the Mings and *The Palace of Eternal Life . . .* are perennially popular even today." (p. 20.) The last-named play, which deals with the death of Lady Yang, is certainly a genuine tragedy.

[10] See *Le théâtre indien,* p. 425.

[11] Cf. Fergusson's analysis of *Bérénice:* "The scenes of dialogue correspond to the agons; but the polite exchange between Arsace and Antiochus, in the first act, is far from the terrible conflict between Oedipus and Tiresias, wherein the moral beings of the antagonists are at stake. . . . [In *Bérénice*] the moral being is unmistakable and impossible to lose while the stage life continues at all . . . the very possibility of the interchange depends upon the authority of reason, which secures the moral being in any contingency. . . . But if the moral being is *ex hypothesi* secure, . . . there cannot be a pathos in the Sophoclean sense at all." (*Op. cit.,* p. 52.)

Romantic drama such as Schiller's *Wilhelm Tell* illustrates the
same principle. It is another species of serious heroic comedy. Tell
appears as an exemplary personage in the beginning of the play, as
citizen, husband, father, friend and patriot; when an extreme political
and social crisis develops, he rises to the occasion, overcomes the
enemy, frees his country, and returns to the peace, dignity and harmonious joy of his home. The balance of life is restored. As a personage he is impressive; as a personality he is very simple. He has
the standard emotions—righteous indignation, paternal love, patriotic
fervor, pride, anxiety, etc.—under their obvious conditions. Nothing
in the action requires him to be more than a man of high courage,
independent spirit, and such other virtues as the mountaineers of
Switzerland boasted, to oppose the arrogance and vanity of foreign
oppressors. But this ideal male he was from the start, and the Gessler
episode merely gives him opportunity to show his indomitable skill
and daring.

Such are the serious products of comic art; they are also its rarer
examples. The natural vein of comedy is humorous—so much so that
"comic" has become synonymous with "funny." Because the word
"comic" is here used in a somewhat technical sense (contrasting "the
comic rhythm" with "the tragic rhythm"), it may be well to say
"comical" where the popular sense is intended. There are all degrees
of humor in comedy, from the quick repartee that elicits a smile by
its cleverness without being intrinsically funny at all, to the absurdity
that sets young and old, simple or sophisticate, shouting with merriment. Humor has its place in all the arts, but in comic drama it
has its home. Comedy may be frivolous, farcical, ribald, ludicrous to
any degree, and still be true art. Laughter springs from its very
structure.

There is a close relation between humor and the "sense of life,"
and several people have tried to analyze it in order to find the basis
of that characteristically human function, laughter; the chief weakness in their attempts has been, I think, that they have all started
with the question: What sort of thing makes us laugh? Certainly
laughter is often evoked by ideas, cognitions, fancies; it accompanies
specific emotions such as disdain, and sometimes the feeling of pleasure; but we also laugh when we are tickled (which may not be
pleasurable at all), and in hysterics. Those predominantly physiological
causes bear no direct relation to humor; neither, for that matter, do
some kinds of pleasure. Humor is one of the causes of laughter.

Marcel Pagnol, who published his theory of laughter in a little
book entitled *Notes sur le rire,* remarks that his predecessors—he

names particularly Bergson, Fabre, and Mélinand—all sought the source of laughter in funny things or situations, i.e. in nature, whereas it really lies in the subject who laughs. Laughter always—without exception—betokens a sudden sense of superiority. "Laughter is a song of triumph," he says. "It expresses the laugher's sudden discovery of his own momentary superiority over the person he laughs at." This, he maintains, "explains all bursts of laughter in all times and all countries," and lets us dispense with all classifications of laughter by different kinds or causes: "One cannot classify or arrange in categories the radii of a circle." [12]

Yet he proceeds directly to divide laughter into "positive" and "negative" kinds, according to its social or antisocial inspiration. This indicates that we are still dealing with *ludicrous situations,* though these situations always involve the person to whom they are ludicrous, so it may be said that "the source of the comical is in the laughter." [13] The situation, moreover, is something the subject must discover, that is, laughter requires a conceptual element; on that M. Pagnol agrees with Bergson, Mélinand, and Fabre. Whether, according to Bergson's much-debated view, we see living beings following the law of mechanism, or see absurdity in midst of plausibility as Mélinand says, or, as Fabre has it, create a confusion only to dispel it suddenly, we feel our own superiority in detecting the irrational element; more particularly, we feel superior to those who perform mechanical actions, introduce absurdities, or make confusions. Therefore M. Pagnol claims that his definition of the laughable applies to all these supposedly typical situations.

It probably does; but it is still too narrow. *What is laughable* does not explain the nature of laughter, any more than what is rational explains the nature of reason. The ultimate source of laughter is physiological, and the various situations in which it arises are simply its normal or abnormal stimuli.

Laughter, or the tendency to laugh (the reaction may stop short of the actual respiratory spasm, and affect only the facial muscles, or even meet with complete inhibition) seems to arise from a surge of vital feeling. This surge may be quite small, just so it be sudden enough to be felt distinctly; but it may also be great, and not particularly swift, and reach a marked climax, at which point we laugh or smile with joy. Laughter is not a simple overt act, as the single word

---

[12] *Notes sur le rire,* p. 41. His argumentation is, unfortunately, not as good as his ideas, and finally leads him to include the song of the nightingale and the rooster's crow as forms of laughter.

[13] *Ibid.,* p. 17.

suggests; it is the spectacular end of a complex process. As speech is the culmination of a mental activity, laughter is a culmination of feeling—the crest of a wave of felt vitality.

A sudden sense of superiority entails such a "lift" of vital feeling. But the "lift" may occur without self-flattery, too; we need not be making fun of anyone. A baby will laugh uproariously at a toy that is made to appear suddenly, again and again, over the edge of the crib or the back of a chair. It would take artful interpretation to demonstrate that this fulfillment of his tense expectation makes him feel superior. Superior to whom? The doll? A baby of eight or nine months is not socialized enough yet to think: "There, I knew you were coming!" and believe that the doll couldn't fool him. Such self-applause requires language, and enough experience to estimate probabilities. The baby laughs because his wish is gratified; not because he believes the doll obeyed his wishing, but simply because the suspense is broken, and his energies are released. The sudden pleasure raises his general feeling tone, so he laughs.

In so-called "gallows humor"—the harsh laugh in distress—the "lift" of vital feeling is simply a flash of self-assertion. Something similar probably causes the mirthless laughter of hysterics: in the disorganized response of a hysterical person, the sense of vitality breaks through fear and depression spasmodically, so that it causes explosive laughter, sometimes alternating with sobs and tears.

Laughter is, indeed, a more elementary thing than humor. We often laugh without finding any person, object, or situation funny. People laugh for joy in active sport, in dancing, in greeting friends; in returning a smile, one acknowledges another person's worth instead of flaunting one's own superiority and finding him funny.

But all these causes of laughter or its reduced form, smiling, which operate directly on us, belong to actual life. In comedy the spectator's laugh has only one legitimate source: his appreciation of humor in the piece. He does not laugh with the characters, not even at them, but at their acts—at their situations, their doings, their expressions, often at their dismay. M. Pagnol holds that we laugh at the characters directly, and regards that as a corroboration of his theory: our pleasure in the comic theater lies in watching people to whom we feel superior.[14]

There is, however, one serious defect in that view, namely that it supposes the spectator to be aware of himself as a being in the same "world" as the characters. To compare them, even subconsciously, to himself he must give up his psychical Distance and feel himself

---

[14] *Ibid.*, p. 92. There is further discussion of this problem at the end of the present chapter [selection].

copresent with them, as one reads an anecdotal news item as something apart from one's own life but still in the actual world, and is moved to say: "How could she do such a thing! Imagine being so foolish!" If he experiences such a reaction in the theater, it is something quite aside from his perception of the play as a poetic fabrication; he has lost, for the moment, his Distance, and feels himself inside the picture.

Humor, then, would be a by-product of comedy, not a structural element in it. And if laughter were elicited thus by the way, it should not make any difference to the value of the work where it occurred; a stage accident, a bad actor who made every amateur actor in the audience feel superior, should serve as well as any clever line or funny situation in the play to amuse the audience. We do, in fact, laugh at such failures; but we do not praise the comedy for that entertainment. In a good play the "laughs" are poetic elements. Its humor as well as its pathos belongs to the virtual life, and the delight we take in it is delight in something created for our perception, not a direct stimulus to our own feelings. It is true that the comical figures are often buffoons, simpletons, clowns; but such characters are almost always sympathetic, and although they are knocked around and abused, they are indestructible, and eternally self-confident and good-humored.

The buffoon is, in fact, an important comic personage, especially in folk theater. He is essentially a folk character that has persisted through the more sophisticated and literary stages of comedy as Harlequin, Pierrot, the Persian Karaguez, the Elizabethan jester or fool, the *Vidusaka* of Sanscrit drama; but in the humbler theatrical forms that entertained the poor and especially the peasantry everywhere before the movies came, the buffoon had a more vigorous existence as Hans Wurst, as Punch of the puppet show, the clown of pantomime, the Turkish Karagöz (borrowed from Persian tradition) who belongs only to the shadow play.[15] These anciently popular personages show what the buffoon really is: the indomitable living creature fending for itself, tumbling and stumbling (as the clown physically illustrates) from one situation into another, getting into scrape after scrape and getting out again, with or without a thrashing. He is the personified *élan vital;* his chance adventures and misadventures, without much plot, though often with bizarre complications, his absurd expectations and disappointments, in fact his whole improvised existence has the rhythm of primitive, savage, if not animalian life, coping with a world that is forever taking new uncalculated turns,

---

[15] See N. N. Martinovitch, *The Turkish Theater, passim.*

frustrating, but exciting. He is neither a good man nor a bad one, but is genuinely amoral,—now triumphant, now worsted and rueful, but in his ruefulness and dismay he is funny, because his energy is really unimpaired and each failure prepares the situation for a new fantastic move.[16] The most forthright of these infantilists is the English Punch, who carries out every impulse by force and speed of action—chastises his wife, throws his child out of the window, beats the policeman, and finally spears the devil and carries him out triumphantly on a pitchfork. Punch is not a real buffoon, he is too successful; his appeal is probably a subjective one, to people's repressed desires for general vengeance, revolt, and destruction. He is psychologically interesting, but really a degenerated and stereotyped figure, and as such he has little artistic value because he has no further poetic progeny. What has caused his persistence in a single, mainly vulgar, and not particularly witty role, I do not know, nor is this the place to investigate it; but when he first appeared in England as Punchinello, borrowed from the Italian marionettes, he was still the pure comic protagonist. According to a statement of R. M. Wheeler in the *Encyclopaedia Britannica,* which we may, presumably, take as authority, "The older Punchinello was far less restricted in his actions and circumstances than his modern successor. He fought with allegorical figures representing want and weariness as well as with his wife and the police, was on intimate terms with the patriarchs and the seven champions of Christendom, sat on the lap of the Queen of Sheba, had kings and dukes for his companions, and cheated the Inquisition as well as the common hangman."

The high company this original Punch keeps is quite in accordance with the dignified settings in which he makes his appearance. From the same article we learn that the earliest recorded appearances of Punch in England were in a puppet play of the Creation of the World, and in another representing the Deluge. To the modern, solemn religious mind, scriptural stories may seem a strange context for such a secular character, and perhaps this apparent incongruity has led to the widespread belief that the clown in modern comedy derives from the devil of mediaeval miracle plays.[17] The devil is, of course, quite at home in sacred realms. It is not impossible that this relation between devil and fool (in his various forms as clown, jester, freak) really holds; yet if it does, that identifies the devil with the flesh, and sin with lust. Such a conception brings the spirit of life

---

[16] Falstaff is a perfect example of the buffoon raised to a human "character" in comedy.

[17] See the article "Clown" (unsigned) in the *Encyclopaedia Britannica.*

and the father of all evil, which are usually poles apart, very close together. For there is no denying that the Fool is a red-blooded fellow; he is, in fact, close to the animal world; in French tradition he wears a cockcomb on his cap, and Punchinello's nose is probably the residue of a beak. He is all motion, whim, and impulse—the "libido" itself.

But he is probably older than the Christian devil, and does not need any connection with that worthy to let him into religious precincts. He has always been close to the gods. If we view him as the representative of mankind in its struggle with the world, it is clear at once why his antics and impertinences are often an integral part of religious rites—why, for instance, the clowning orders in Pueblo society were held in high honor: [18] the clown is Life, he is the Will, he is the Brain, and by the same token he is nature's fool. From the primitive exuberant religions that celebrate fertility and growth he tends ever to come into the ascetic cults, and tumble and juggle in all innocence before the Virgin.

In comedy the stock figure of the buffoon is an obvious device for building up the comic rhythm, i.e. the image of Fortune. But in the development of the art he does not remain the central figure that he was in the folk theater; the lilt and balance of life which he introduced, once it has been grasped, is rendered in more subtle poetic inventions involving plausible characters, and an *intrigue* (as the French call it) that makes for a coherent, over-all, dramatic action. Sometimes he remains as a jester, servant, or other subsidiary character whose comments, silly or witty or shrewd, serve to point the essentially comic pattern of the action, where the verisimilitude and complexity of the stage-life threaten to obscure its basic form. Those points are normally "laughs"; and that brings us to the aesthetic problem of the joke in comedy.

Because comedy abstracts, and reincarnates for our perception, the motion and rhythm of living, it enhances our vital feeling, much as the presentation of space in painting enhances our awareness of visual space. The virtual life on the stage is not diffuse and only half felt, as actual life usually is: virtual life, always moving visibly into the future, is intensified, speeded up, exaggerated; the exhibition of vitality rises to a breaking point, to mirth and laughter. We laugh in the theater at small incidents and drolleries which would hardly rate a chuckle off-stage. It is not for such psychological reasons that we go there to be amused, nor are we bound by rules of politeness to hide

---

[18] On the secret societies of clowns, see F. H. Cushing, *Zuni Creation Myths* (Report of the Bureau of American Ethnology, 1892), concerning the order of "Koyemshi" ("Mudheads").

our hilarity, but these trifles at which we laugh are really funnier *where they occur* than they would be elsewhere; they are employed in the play, not merely brought in casually. They occur where the tension of dialogue or other action reaches a high point. As thought breaks into speech—as the wave breaks into form—vitality breaks into humor.

Humor is the brilliance of drama, a sudden heightening of the vital rhythm. A good comedy, therefore, builds up to every laugh; a performance that has been filled up with jokes at the indiscretion of the comedian or of his writer may draw a long series of laughs, yet leave the spectator without any clear impression of a very funny play. The laughs, moreover, are likely to be of a peculiar sameness, almost perfunctory, the formal recognition of a timely "gag."

The amoral character of the comic protagonist goes through the whole range of what may be called the comedy of laughter. Even the most civilized products of this art—plays that George Meredith would honor with the name of "comedy," because they provoke "thoughtful laughter"—do not present moral distinctions and issues, but only the ways of wisdom and of folly. Aristophanes, Menander, Molière—practically the only authors this most exacting of critics admitted as truly comic poets—are not moralists, yet they do not flaunt or deprecate morality; they have, literally, "no use" for moral principles—that is, they do not use them. Meredith, like practically all his contemporaries, labored under the belief that poetry must teach society lessons, and that comedy was valuable for what it revealed concerning the social order.[19] He tried hard to hold its exposé of foibles and vindication of common sense to an ethical standard, yet in his very efforts to justify its amoral personages he only admitted their amoral nature, and their simple relish for life, as when he said: "The heroines of comedy are like women of the world, not necessarily heartless from being clear-sighted. . . . Comedy is an exhibition of their battle with men, and that of men with them. . . ."

---

[19] His well-known little work is called *An Essay on Comedy, and the Uses of the Comic Spirit.* These uses are entirely non-artistic. Praising the virtues of "good sense" (which is whatever has survival value in the eyes of society), he says: "The French have a school of stately comedy to which they can fly for renovation whenever they have fallen away from it; and their having such a school is the main reason why, as John Stuart Mill pointed out, they know men and women more accurately than we do." (pp. 13–14.) And a few pages later: "The *Femmes Savantes* is a capital instance of the uses of comedy in teaching the world to understand what ails it. The French had felt the burden of this new nonsense [the fad of academic learning, new after the fad of excessive nicety and precision in speech, that had marked the *Precieuses*] ; but they had to see the comedy several times before they were consoled in their suffering by seeing the cause of it exposed." (pp. 19–20.)

There it is, in a nutshell: the contest of men and women—the most universal contest, humanized, in fact civilized, yet still the primitive joyful challenge, the self-preservation and self-assertion whose progress is the comic rhythm.

This rhythm is capable of the most diverse presentations. That is why the art of comedy grows, in every culture, from casual beginnings—miming, clowning, sometimes erotic dancing—to some special and distinctive dramatic art, and sometimes to many forms of it within one culture, yet never seems to repeat its works. It may produce a tradition of dignified drama, springing from solemn ritual, even funereal, its emotional movement too slow to culminate in humor at any point; then other means have to be found to lend it glamor and intensity. The purest heroic comedy is likely to have no humorous passages at all, but to employ the jester only in an ornamental way reminiscent of tragedy, and in fact to use many techniques of tragedy. It may even seem to transcend the amoral comic pattern by presenting virtuous heroes and heroines. But their virtue is a formal affair, a social asset; as Deane remarked of the French classic heroes,[20] they do not submit to ordinary morality; their morality is "heroism," which is essentially strength, will, and endurance in face of the world. Neither have the divinities of oriental drama any "ordinary morality"; they are perfect in virtue when they slay and when they spare, their goodness is glory, and their will is law. They are Superman, the Hero, and the basic pattern of their conquest over enemies whose only wickedness is resistance, is the amoral life pattern of fencing with the devil—man against death.

Humor, then, is not the essence of comedy, but only one of its most useful and natural elements. It is also its most problematical element, because it elicits from the spectators what appears to be a direct emotional response to persons on the stage, in no wise different from their response to actual people: amusement, laughter.

The phenomenon of laughter in the theater brings into sharp focus the whole question of the distinction between emotion symbolically presented, and emotion directly stimulated; it is, indeed, a *pons asinorum* of the theory that this distinction is radical, because it presents us with what is probably the most difficult example. The audience's laugh at a good play is, of course, self-expressive, and betokens a "lift" of vital feeling in each laughing person. Yet it has a different character from laughter in conversation, or in the street when the wind carries off a hat with the "hair-do" attached, or in the "laugh house" at an amusement park where the willing victims meet

---

[20] Cf. *supra*, p. 336.

distorting mirrors and things that say "boo." All these laughs of daily
life are direct responses to separate stimuli; they may be as sporadic
as the jokes bandied in a lively company, or may be strung along
purposely like the expected and yet unforeseen events in the "laugh
house," yet they remain so many personal encounters that seem funny
only if one is in the mood for them. Sometimes we reject witticisms
and are bored with tricks and clowning.

It is different in the theater: the play possesses us and breaks our
mood. It does not change it, but simply abrogates it. Even if we come
in a jovial mood, this does not notably increase our appreciation of
humor in the play; for the humor in a good comedy does not strike
us directly. What strikes us directly is the dramatic illusion, the stage
action as it evolves; and the joke, instead of being as funny as our
personal response would make it, seems as funny as its occurrence
in the total action makes it. A very mild joke in just the right place
may score a big laugh. The action culminates in a witticism, an absurdity, a surprise; the spectators laugh. But after their outburst there
is not the letdown that follows an ordinary laugh, because the play
moves on without the breathing spell we usually give our own thought
and feeling after a joke. The action carries over from one laugh to
another, sometimes fairly far spaced; people are laughing *at the play,*
not at a string of jokes.

Humor in comedy (as, indeed, in all humorous art) belongs to the
work, not to our actual surroundings; and if it is borrowed from the
actual world, its appearance in the work is what really makes it funny.
Political or topical allusions in a play amuse us because they are
used, not because they refer to something intrinsically very comical.
This device of playing with things from actual life is so sure to bring
laughs that the average comic writer and improvising comedian over-
does it to the point of artistic ruin; hence the constant flood of "shows"
that have immense popularity but no dramatic core, so they do not
outlive the hour of their passing allusions.

Real comedy sets up in the audience a sense of general exhilaration,
because it presents the very image of "livingness" and the perception
of it is exciting. Whatever the story may be, it takes the form of a
temporary triumph over the surrounding world, complicated, and thus
stretched out, by an involved succession of coincidences. This illusion
of life, the stage-life, has a rhythm of feeling which is not transmitted
to us by separate successive stimulations, but rather by our perception
of its entire *Gestalt*—a whole world moving into its own future. The
"livingness" of the human world is abstracted, composed, and presented to us; with it the high points of the composition that are

illuminated by humor. They belong to the life we see, and our laugh belongs to the theatrical exhilaration, which is universally human and impersonal. It is not what the joke happens to mean to us that measures our laughter, but what the joke does in the play.

For this reason we tend to laugh at things in the theater that we might not find funny in actuality. The technique of comedy often has to clear the way for its humor by forestalling any backsliding into "the world of anxious interest and selfish solicitude." It does this by various devices—absurd coincidences, stereotyped expressions of feeling (like the clown's wails of dismay), a quickened pace of action, and other unrealistic effects which serve to emphasize the comic structure. As Professor Fergusson said, "when we understand a comic convention we see the play with godlike omniscience. . . . When Scaramouche gets a beating, we do not feel the blows, but the idea of a beating, at that moment, strikes us as funny. If the beating is too realistic, if it breaks the light rhythm of thought, the fun is gone, and the comedy destroyed." [21]

That "light rhythm of thought" is the rhythm of life; and the reason it is "light" is that all creatures love life, and the symbolization of its impetus and flow makes us really aware of it. The conflict with the world whereby a living being maintains its own complex organic unity is a delightful encounter; the world is as promising and alluring as it is dangerous and opposed. The feeling of comedy is a feeling of heightened vitality, challenged wit and will, engaged in the great game with Chance. The real antagonist is the World. Since the personal antagonist in the play is really that great challenger, he is rarely a complete villain; he is interesting, entertaining, his defeat is a hilarious success but not his destruction. There is no permanent defeat and permanent human triumph except in tragedy; for nature must go on if life goes on, and the world that presents all obstacles also supplies the zest of life. In comedy, therefore, there is a general trivialization of the human battle. Its dangers are not real disasters, but embarrassment and loss of face. That is why comedy is "light" compared to tragedy, which exhibits an exactly opposite tendency to general exaggeration of issues and personalities.

The same impulse that drove people, even in prehistoric times, to enact fertility rites and celebrate all phases of their biological existence, sustains their eternal interest in comedy. It is in the nature of comedy to be erotic, risqué, and sensuous if not sensual, impious, and even wicked. This assures it a spontaneous emotional interest, yet a danger-

---

[21] *Op. cit.*, pp. 178–179.

ous one: for it is easy and tempting to command an audience by direct stimulation of feeling and fantasy, not by artistic power. But where the formulation of feeling is really achieved, it probably reflects the whole development of mankind and man's world, for feeling is the intaglio image of reality. The sense of precariousness that is the typical tension of light comedy was undoubtedly developed in the eternal struggle with chance that every farmer knows only too well— with weather, blights, beasts, birds and beetles. The embarrassments, perplexities and mounting panic which characterize that favorite genre, comedy of manners, may still reflect the toils of ritual and taboo that complicated the caveman's existence. Even the element of aggressiveness in comic action serves to develop a fundamental trait of the comic rhythm—the deep cruelty of it, as all life feeds on life. There is no biological truth that feeling does not reflect, and that good comedy, therefore, will not be prone to reveal.

But the fact that the rhythm of comedy is the basic rhythm of life does not mean that biological existence is the "deeper meaning" of all its themes, and that to understand the play is to interpret all the characters as symbols and the story as a parable, a disguised rite of spring or fertility magic, performed four hundred and fifty times on Broadway. The stock characters are probably symbolic both in origin and in appeal. There are such independently symbolic factors, or residues of them, in all the arts,[22] but their value for art lies in the degree to which their significance can be "swallowed" by the single symbol, the art work. Not the derivation of personages and situations, but of the rhythm of "felt life" that the poet puts upon them, seems to me to be of artistic importance: the essential comic feeling, which is the sentient aspect of organic unity, growth, and self-preservation.

---

[22] E.g., the symbolization of the zodiac in some sacred architecture, of our bodily orientation in the picture plane, or of walking measure, a primitive measure of actual time, in music. But a study of such non-artistic symbolic functions would require a monograph.

The Mythos of Spring: Comedy*

NORTHROP FRYE

Dramatic comedy, from which fictional comedy is mainly descended, has been remarkably tenacious of its structural principles and character types. Bernard Shaw remarked that a comic dramatist could get a reputation for daring originality by stealing his method from Molière and his characters from Dickens: if we were to read Menander and Aristophanes for Molière and Dickens the statement would be hardly less true, at least as a general principle. The earliest extant European comedy, Aristophanes' *The Acharnians,* contains the *miles gloriosus* or military braggart who is still going strong in Chaplin's *Great Dictator;* the Joxer Daly of O'Casey's *Juno and the Paycock* has the same character and dramatic function as the parasites of twenty-five hundred years ago, and the audiences of vaudeville, comic strips, and television programs still laugh at the jokes that were declared to be outworn at the opening of *The Frogs.*

The plot structure of Greek New Comedy, as transmitted by Plautus and Terence, in itself less a form than a formula, has become the basis for most comedy, especially in its more highly conventionalized dramatic form, down to our own day. It will be most convenient to work out the theory of comic construction from drama, using illustrations from fiction only incidentally. What normally happens is that a young man wants a young woman, that his desire is resisted by some opposition, usually paternal, and that near the end of the play some twist in the plot enables the hero to have his will. In this simple pattern there are several complex elements. In the first place, the movement of comedy is usually a movement from one kind of society to another. At the beginning of the play the obstructing char-

---

* Northrop Frye, "The Mythos of Spring: Comedy," in *The Anatomy of Criticism* (Princeton University Press, 1957), pp. 163–186.

acters are in charge of the play's society, and the audience recognizes
that they are usurpers. At the end of the play the device in the plot
that brings hero and heroine together causes a new society to crystallize
around the hero, and the moment when this crystallization occurs is
the point of resolution in the action, the comic discovery, *anagnorisis*
or *cognitio*.

The appearance of this new society is frequently signalized by some
kind of party or festive ritual, which either appears at the end of the
play or is assumed to take place immediately afterward. Weddings are
most common, and sometimes so many of them occur, as in the
quadruple wedding at the end of *As You Like It,* that they suggest
also the wholesale pairing off that takes place in a dance, which is
another common conclusion, and the normal one for the masque. The
banquet at the end of *The Taming of the Shrew* has an ancestry
that goes back to Greek Middle Comedy; in Plautus the audience is
sometimes jocosely invited to an imaginary banquet afterwards; Old
Comedy, like the modern Christmas pantomime, was more generous,
and occasionally threw bits of food to the audience. As the final
society reached by comedy is the one that the audience has recognized
all along to be the proper and desirable state of affairs, an act of
communion with the audience is in order. Tragic actors expect to be
applauded as well as comic ones, but nevertheless the word "plaudite"
at the end of a Roman comedy, the invitation to the audience to
form part of the comic society, would seem rather out of place at
the end of a tragedy. The resolution of comedy comes, so to speak,
from the audience's side of the stage; in a tragedy it comes from some
mysterious world on the opposite side. In the movie, where darkness
permits a more erotically oriented audience, the plot usually moves
toward an act which, like death in Greek tragedy, takes place offstage,
and is symbolized by a closing embrace.

The obstacles to the hero's desire, then, form the action of the
comedy, and the overcoming of them the comic resolution. The obstacles are usually parental, hence comedy often turns on a clash between a son's and a father's will. Thus the comic dramatist as a rule
writes for the younger men in his audience, and the older members
of almost any society are apt to feel that comedy has something subversive about it. This is certainly one element in the social persecution
of drama, which is not peculiar to Puritans or even Christians, as
Terence in pagan Rome met much the same kind of social opposition
that Ben Jonson did. There is one scene in Plautus where a son and
father are making love to the same courtesan, and the son asks his
father pointedly if he really does love mother. One has to see this

scene against the background of Roman family life to understand its importance as psychological release. Even in Shakespeare there are startling outbreaks of baiting older men, and in contemporary movies the triumph of youth is so relentless that the moviemakers find some difficulty in getting anyone over the age of seventeen into their audiences.

The opponent to the hero's wishes, when not the father, is generally someone who partakes of the father's closer relation to established society: that is, a rival with less youth and more money. In Plautus and Terence he is usually either the pimp who owns the girl, or a wandering soldier with a supply of ready cash. The fury with which these characters are baited and exploded from the stage shows that they are father-surrogates, and even if they were not, they would still be usurpers, and their claim to possess the girl must be shown up as somehow fraudulent. They are, in short, impostors, and the extent to which they have real power implies some criticism of the society that allows them their power. In Plautus and Terence this criticism seldom goes beyond the immorality of brothels and professional harlots, but in Renaissance dramatists, including Jonson, there is some sharp observation of the rising power of money and the sort of ruling class it is building up.

The tendency of comedy is to include as many people as possible in its final society: the blocking characters are more often reconciled or converted than simply repudiated. Comedy often includes a scapegoat ritual of expulsion which gets rid of some irreconcilable character, but exposure and disgrace make for pathos, or even tragedy. *The Merchant of Venice* seems almost an experiment in coming as close as possible to upsetting the comic balance. If the dramatic role of Shylock is ever so slightly exaggerated, as it generally is when the leading actor of the company takes the part, it is upset, and the play becomes the tragedy of the Jew of Venice with a comic epilogue. *Volpone* ends with a great bustle of sentences to penal servitude and the galleys, and one feels that the deliverance of society hardly needs so much hard labor; but then *Volpone* is exceptional in being a kind of comic imitation of a tragedy, with the point of Volpone's hybris carefully marked.

The principle of conversion becomes clearer with characters whose chief function is the amusing of the audience. The original *miles gloriosus* in Plautus is a son of Jove and Venus who has killed an elephant with his fist and seven thousand men in one day's fighting. In other words, he is trying to put on a good show: the exuberance of his boasting helps to put the play over. The convention says that

the braggart must be exposed, ridiculed, swindled, and beaten. But
why should a professional dramatist, of all people, want so to harry
a character who is putting on a good show—*his* show at that? When
we find Falstaff invited to the final feast in *The Merry Wives,* Caliban
reprieved, attempts made to mollify Malvolio, and Angelo and
Parolles allowed to live down their disgrace, we are seeing a fundamental principle of comedy at work. The tendency of the comic society
to include rather than exclude is the reason for the traditional importance of the parasite, who has no business to be at the final festival
but is nevertheless there. The word "grace," with all its Renaissance
overtones from the graceful courtier of Castiglione to the gracious
God of Christianity, is a most important thematic word in Shakespearean comedy.

The action of comedy in moving from one social center to another
is not unlike the action of a lawsuit, in which plaintiff and defendant
construct different versions of the same situation, one finally being
judged as real and the other as illusory. This resemblance of the
rhetoric of comedy to the rhetoric of jurisprudence has been recognized
from earliest times. A little pamphlet called the *Tractatus Coislinianus,*
closely related to Aristotle's *Poetics,* which sets down all the essential
facts about comedy in about a page and a half, divides the *dianoia*
of comedy into two parts, opinion (*pistis*) and proof (*gnosis*). These
correspond roughly to the usurping and the desirable societies respec-
tively. Proofs (i.e., the means of bringing about the happier society)
are subdivided into oaths, compacts, witnesses, ordeals (or tortures),
and laws—in other words the five forms of material proof in law
cases listed in the *Rhetoric.* We notice how often the action of a
Shakespearean comedy begins with some absurd, cruel, or irrational
law: the law of killing Syracusans in the *Comedy of Errors,* the law
of compulsory marriage in *A Midsummer Night's Dream,* the law that
confirms Shylock's bond, the attempts of Angelo to legislate people into
righteousness, and the like, which the action of the comedy then
evades or breaks. Compacts are as a rule the conspiracies formed
by the hero's society; witnesses, such as overhearers of conversations
or people with special knowledge (like the hero's old nurse with her
retentive memory for birthmarks), are the commonest devices for
bringing about the comic discovery. Ordeals (*basanoi*) are usually
tests or touchstones of the hero's character: the Greek word also
means touchstones, and seems to be echoed in Shakespeare's Bassanio
whose ordeal it is to make a judgement on the worth of metals.

There are two ways of developing the form of comedy: one is to
throw the main emphasis on the blocking characters; the other is to

throw it forward on the scenes of discovery and reconciliation. One is the general tendency of comic irony, satire, realism, and studies of manners; the other is the tendency of Shakespearean and other types of romantic comedy. In the comedy of manners the main ethical interest falls as a rule on the blocking characters. The technical hero and heroine are not often very interesting people: the *adulescentes* of Plautus and Terence are all alike, as hard to tell apart in the dark as Demetrius and Lysander, who may be parodies of them. Generally the hero's character has the neutrality that enables him to represent a wish-fulfilment. It is very different with the miserly or ferocious parent, the boastful or foppish rival, or the other characters who stand in the way of the action. In Molière we have a simple but fully tested formula in which the ethical interest is focussed on a single blocking character, a heavy father, a miser, a misanthrope, a hypocrite, or a hypochondriac. These are the figures that we remember, and the plays are usually named after them, but we can seldom remember all the Valentins and Angeliques who wriggle out of their clutches. In *The Merry Wives* the technical hero, a man named Fenton, has only a bit part, and this play has picked up a hint or two from Plautus's *Casina,* where the hero and heroine are not even brought on the stage at all. Fictional comedy, especially Dickens, often follows the same practice of grouping its interesting characters around a somewhat dullish pair of technical leads. Even Tom Jones, though far more fully realized, is still deliberately associated, as his commonplace name indicates, with the conventional and typical.

Comedy usually moves toward a happy ending, and the normal response of the audience to a happy ending is "this should be," which sounds like a moral judgement. So it is, except that it is not moral in the restricted sense, but social. Its opposite is not the villainous but the absurd, and comedy finds the virtues of Malvolio as absurd as the vices of Angelo. Molière's misanthrope, being committed to sincerity, which is a virtue, is morally in a strong position, but the audience soon realizes that his friend Philinte, who is ready to lie quite cheerfully in order to enable other people to preserve their self-respect, is the more genuinely sincere of the two. It is of course quite possible to have a moral comedy, but the result is often the kind of melodrama that we have described as comedy without humor, and which achieves its happy ending with a self-righteous tone that most comedy avoids. It is hardly possible to imagine a drama without conflict, and it is hardly possible to imagine a conflict without some kind of enmity. But just as love, including sexual love, is a very different

thing from lust, so enmity is a very different thing from hatred. In
tragedy, of course, enmity almost always includes hatred; comedy is
different, and one feels that the social judgement against the absurd
is closer to the comic norm than the moral judgement against the
wicked.

The question then arises of what makes the blocking character
absurd. Ben Jonson explained this by his theory of the "humor,"
the character dominated by what Pope calls a ruling passion. The
humor's dramatic function is to express a state of what might be
called ritual bondage. He is obsessed by his humor, and his function
in the play is primarily to repeat his obsession. A sick man is not a
humor, but a hypochondriac is, because, *qua* hypochondriac, he can
never admit to good health, and can never do anything inconsistent
with the role that he has prescribed for himself. A miser can do and
say nothing that is not connected with the hiding of gold or saving
of money. In *The Silent Woman,* Jonson's nearest approach to
Molière's type of construction, the whole action recedes from the
humor of Morose, whose determination to eliminate noise from his
life produces so loquacious a comic action.

The principle of the humor is the principle that unincremental
repetition, the literary imitation of ritual bondage, is funny. In a
tragedy—*Oedipus Tyrannus* is the stock example—repetition leads
logically to catastrophe. Repetition overdone or not going anywhere
belongs to comedy, for laughter is partly a reflex, and like other reflexes
it can be conditioned by a simple repeated pattern. In Synge's *Riders
to the Sea* a mother, after losing her husband and five sons at sea,
finally loses her last son, and the result is a very beautiful and moving
play. But if it had been a full-length tragedy plodding glumly through
the seven drownings one after another, the audience would have been
helpless with unsympathetic laughter long before it was over. The
principle of repetition as the basis of humor both in Jonson's sense
and in ours is well known to the creators of comic strips, in which a
character is established as a parasite, a glutton (often confined to one
dish), or a shrew, and who begins to be funny after the point has
been made every day for several months. Continuous comic radio
programs, too, are much more amusing to habitués than to neophytes.
The girth of Falstaff and the hallucinations of Quixote are based
on much the same comic laws. Mr. E. M. Forster speaks with disdain
of Dickens's Mrs. Micawber, who never says anything except that she
will never desert Mr. Micawber: a strong contrast is marked here
between the refined writer too finicky for popular formulas, and the
major one who exploits them ruthlessly.

The humor in comedy is usually someone with a good deal of social prestige and power, who is able to force much of the play's society into line with his obsession. Thus the humor is intimately connected with the theme of the absurd or irrational law that the action of comedy moves toward breaking. It is significant that the central character of our earliest humor comedy, *The Wasps,* is obsessed by law cases: Shylock, too, unites a craving for the law with the humor of revenge. Often the absurd law appears as a whim of a bemused tyrant whose will is law, like Leontes or the humorous Duke Frederick in Shakespeare, who makes some arbitrary decision or rash promise: here law is replaced by "oath," also mentioned in the *Tractatus.* Or it may take the form of a sham Utopia, a society of ritual bondage constructed by an act of humorous or pedantic will, like the academic retreat in *Love's Labor's Lost.* This theme is also as old as Aristophanes, whose parodies of Platonic social schemes in *The Birds* and *Ecclesiazusae* deal with it.

The society emerging at the conclusion of comedy represents, by contrast, a kind of moral norm, or pragmatically free society. Its ideals are seldom defined or formulated: definition and formulation belong to the humors, who want predictable activity. We are simply given to understand that the newly-married couple will live happily ever after, or that at any rate they will get along in a relatively unhumorous and clear-sighted manner. That is one reason why the character of the successful hero is so often left undeveloped: his real life begins at the end of the play, and we have to believe him to be potentially a more interesting character than he appears to be. In Terence's *Adelphoi,* Demea, a harsh father, is contrasted with his brother Micio, who is indulgent. Micio being more liberal, he leads the way to the comic resolution, and converts Demea, but then Demea points out the indolence inspiring a good deal of Micio's liberality, and releases him from a complementary humorous bondage.

Thus the movement from *pistis* to *gnosis,* from a society controlled by habit, ritual bondage, arbitrary law and the older characters to a society controlled by youth and pragmatic freedom is fundamentally, as the Greek words suggest, a movement from illusion to reality. Illusion is whatever is fixed or definable, and reality is best understood as its negation: whatever reality is, it's not *that.* Hence the importance of the theme of creating and dispelling illusion in comedy: the illusions caused by disguise, obsession, hypocrisy, or unknown parentage.

The comic ending is generally manipulated by a twist in the plot. In Roman comedy the heroine, who is usually a slave or courtesan,

turns out to be the daughter of somebody respectable, so that the
hero can marry her without loss of face. The *cognitio* in comedy,
in which the characters find out who their relatives are, and who is
left of the opposite sex not a relative, and hence available for marriage, is one of the features of comedy that have never changed much:
The Confidential Clerk indicates that it still holds the attention of
dramatists. There is a brilliant parody of a *cognitio* at the end of
Major Barbara (the fact that the hero of this play is a professor of
Greek perhaps indicates an unusual affinity to the conventions of
Euripides and Menander), where Undershaft is enabled to break
the rule that he cannot appoint his son-in-law as successor by the fact
that the son-in-law's own father married his deceased wife's sister in
Australia, so that the son-in-law is his own first cousin as well as
himself. It sounds complicated, but the plots of comedy often are
complicated because there is something inherently absurd about complications. As the main character interest in comedy is so often focussed
on the defeated characters, comedy regularly illustrates a victory of
arbitrary plot over consistency of character. Thus, in striking contrast
to tragedy, there can hardly be such a thing as inevitable comedy,
as far as the action of the individual play is concerned. That is, we
may know that the convention of comedy will make some kind of
happy ending inevitable, but still for each play the dramatist must
produce a distinctive "gimmick" or "weenie," to use two disrespectful
Hollywood synonyms for *anagnorisis*. Happy endings do not impress
us as true, but as desirable, and they are brought about by manipulation. The watcher of death and tragedy has nothing to do but
sit and wait for the inevitable end; but something gets born at the
end of comedy, and the watcher of birth is a member of a busy society.

The manipulation of plot does not always involve metamorphosis
of character, but there is no violation of comic decorum when it
does. Unlikely conversions, miraculous transformations, and providen-
tial assistance are inseparable from comedy. Further, whatever emerges
is supposed to be there for good: if the curmudgeon becomes lovable,
we understand that he will not immediately relapse again into his
ritual habit. Civilizations which stress the desirable rather than the
real, and the religious as opposed to the scientific perspective, think
of drama almost entirely in terms of comedy. In the classical drama
of India, we are told, the tragic ending was regarded as bad taste,
much as the manipulated endings of comedy are regarded as bad
taste by novelists interested in ironic realism.

The total *mythos* of comedy, only a small part of which is ordinarily presented, has regularly what in music is called a ternary form:

the hero's society rebels against the society of the *senex* and triumphs, but the hero's society is a Saturnalia, a reversal of social standards which recalls a golden age in the past before the main action of the play begins. Thus we have a stable and harmonious order disrupted by folly, obsession, forgetfulness, "pride and prejudice," or events not understood by the characters themselves, and then restored. Often there is a benevolent grandfather, so to speak, who overrules the action set up by the blocking humor and so links the first and third parts. An example is Mr. Burchell, the disguised uncle of the wicked squire, in *The Vicar of Wakefield*. A very long play, such as the Indian *Sakuntala,* may present all three phases; a very intricate one, such as many of Menander's evidently were, may indicate their outlines. But of course very often the first phase is not given at all: the audience simply understands an ideal state of affairs which it knows to be better than what is revealed in the play, and which it recognizes as like that to which the action leads. This ternary action is, ritually, like a contest of summer and winter in which winter occupies the middle action; psychologically, it is like the removal of a neurosis or blocking point and the restoring of an unbroken current of energy and memory. The Jonsonian masque, with the antimasque in the middle, gives a highly conventionalized or "abstract" version of it.

We pass now to the typical characters of comedy. In drama, characterization depends on function; what a character is follows from what he has to do in the play. Dramatic function in its turn depends on the structure of the play; the character has certain things to do because the play has such and such a shape. The structure of the play in its turn depends on the category of the play; if it is a comedy, its structure will require a comic resolution and a prevailing comic mood. Hence when we speak of typical characters, we are not trying to reduce lifelike characters to stock types, though we certainly are suggesting that the sentimental notion of an antithesis between the lifelike character and the stock type is a vulgar error. All lifelike characters, whether in drama or fiction, owe their consistency to the appropriateness of the stock type which belongs to their dramatic function. That stock type is not the character but it is as necessary to the character as a skeleton is to the actor who plays it.

With regard to the characterization of comedy, the *Tractatus* lists three types of comic characters: the *alazons* or impostors, the *eirons* or self-deprecators, and· the buffoons (*bomolochoi*). This list is closely related to a passage in the *Ethics* which contrasts the first two, and then goes on to contrast the buffoon with a character whom Aristotle

calls *agroikos* or churlish, literally rustic. We may reasonably accept
the churl as a fourth character type, and so we have two opposed
pairs. The contest of *eiron* and *alazon* forms the basis of the comic
action, and the buffoon and the churl polarize the comic mood.

We have previously dealt with the terms *eiron* and *alazon*. The
humorous blocking characters of comedy are nearly always impostors,
though it is more frequently a lack of self-knowledge than simple
hypocrisy that characterizes them. The multitudes of comic scenes in
which one character complacently soliloquizes while another makes
sarcastic asides to the audience show the contest of *eiron* and *alazon*
in its purest form, and show too that the audience is sympathetic to
the *eiron* side. Central to the *alazon* group is the *senex iratus* or
heavy father, who with his rages and threats, his obsessions and his
gullibility, seems closely related to some of the demonic characters of
romance, such as Polyphemus. Occasionally a character may have the
dramatic function of such a figure without his characteristics: an
example is Squire Allworthy in *Tom Jones,* who as far as the plot is
concerned behaves almost as stupidly as Squire Western. Of heavy-
father surrogates, the *miles gloriosus* has been mentioned: his popularity is largely due to the fact that he is a man of words rather
than deeds, and is consequently far more useful to a practising
dramatist than any tight-lipped hero could ever be. The pedant, in
Renaissance comedy often a student of the occult sciences, the fop or
coxcomb, and similar humors, require no comment. The female *alazon*
is rare: Katharina the shrew represents to some extent a female *miles
gloriosus,* and the *précieuse ridicule* a female pedant, but the "menace"
or siren who gets in the way of the true heroine is more often found
as a sinister figure of melodrama or romance than as a ridiculous
figure in comedy.

The *eiron* figures need a little more attention. Central to this
group is the hero, who is an *eiron* figure because, as explained, the
dramatist tends to play him down and make him rather neutral and
unformed in character. Next in importance is the heroine, also often
played down: in Old Comedy, when a girl accompanies a male hero
in his triumph, she is generally a stage prop, a *muta persona* not
previously introduced. A more difficult form of *cognitio* is achieved
when the heroine disguises herself or through some other device brings
about the comic resolution, so that the person whom the hero is seeking turns out to be the person who has sought him. The fondness
of Shakespeare for this "she stoops to conquer" theme needs only to
be mentioned here, as it belongs more naturally to the *mythos* of
romance.

Another central *eiron* figure is the type entrusted with hatching the schemes which bring about the hero's victory. This character in Roman comedy is almost always a tricky slave (*dolosus servus*), and in Renaissance comedy he becomes the scheming valet who is so frequent in Continental plays, and in Spanish drama is called the *gracioso*. Modern audiences are most familiar with him in Figaro and in the Leporello of *Don Giovanni*. Through such intermediate nineteenth-century figures as Micawber and the Touchwood of Scott's *St. Ronan's Well,* who, like the gracioso, have buffoon affiliations, he evolves into the amateur detective of modern fiction. The Jeeves of P. G. Wodehouse is a more direct descendant. Female confidantes of the same general family are often brought in to oil the machinery of the well-made play. Elizabethan comedy had another type of trickster, represented by the Matthew Merrygreek of *Ralph Roister Doister,* who is generally said to be developed from the vice or iniquity of the morality plays: as usual, the analogy is sound enough, whatever historians decide about origins. The vice, to give him that name, is very useful to a comic dramatist because he acts from pure love of mischief, and can set a comic action going with the minimum of motivation. The vice may be as light-hearted as Puck or as malignant as Don John in *Much Ado,* but as a rule the vice's activity is, in spite of his name, benevolent. One of the tricky slaves in Plautus, in a soliloquy, boasts that he is the *architectus* of the comic action: such a character carries out the will of the author to reach a happy ending. He is in fact the spirit of comedy, and the two clearest examples of the type in Shakespeare, Puck and Ariel, are both spiritual beings. The tricky slave often has his own freedom in mind as the reward of his exertions: Ariel's longing for release is in the same tradition.

The role of the vice includes a great deal of disguising, and the type may often be recognized by disguise. A good example is the Brainworm of Jonson's *Every Man in His Humour,* who calls the action of the play the day of his metamorphoses. Similarly Ariel has to surmount the difficult stage direction of "Enter invisible." The vice is combined with the hero whenever the latter is a cheeky, improvident young man who hatches his own schemes and cheats his rich father or uncle into giving him his patrimony along with the girl.

Another *eiron* type has not been much noticed. This is a character, generally an older man, who begins the action of the play by withdrawing from it, and ends the play by returning. He is often a father with the motive of seeing what his son will do. The action of *Every Man in His Humour* is set going in this way by Knowell Senior. The disappearance and return of Lovewit, the owner of the house which is the scene of *The Alchemist,* has the same dramatic function, though the characterization is different. The clearest Shakespearean example is the Duke in *Measure for Measure,* but Shakespeare is more addicted to the type than might appear at first glance. In Shakespeare the vice is rarely the real *architectus:* Puck and Ariel both act under orders from an older man, if one may call Oberon a man for the moment. In *The Tempest* Shakespeare returns to a comic action established by Aristophanes, in which an older man, instead of retiring from the action, builds it up on the stage. When the heroine takes the vice role in Shakespeare, she is often significantly related to her father, even when the father is not in the play at all, like the father of Helena, who gives her his medical knowledge, or the father of Portia, who arranges the scheme of the caskets. A more conventionally treated example of the same benevolent Prospero figure turned up recently in the psychiatrist of *The Cocktail Party,* and one may compare the mysterious alchemist who is the father of the heroine of *The Lady's Not for Burning.* The formula is not confined to comedy: Polonius, who shows so many of the disadvantages of a literary education, attempts the role of a retreating paternal *eiron* three times, once too often. *Hamlet* and *King Lear* contain subplots which are ironic versions of stock comic themes, Gloucester's story being the regular comedy theme of the gullible *senex* swindled by a clever and unprincipled son.

We pass now to the buffoon types, those whose function it is to increase the mood of festivity rather than to contribute to the plot. Renaissance comedy, unlike Roman comedy, had a great variety of such characters, professional fools, clowns, pages, singers, and incidental characters with established comic habits like malapropism or foreign accents. The oldest buffoon of this incidental nature is the parasite, who may be given something to do, as Jonson gives Mosca the role of a vice in *Volpone,* but who, *qua* parasite, does nothing but entertain the audience by talking about his appetite. He derives chiefly from Greek Middle Comedy, which appears to have been very full of food, and where he was, not unnaturally, closely associated with another established buffoon type, the cook, a conventional figure who breaks into comedies to bustle and order about and make long speeches about the mysteries of cooking. In the role of cook the buffoon or entertainer appears, not simply as a gratuitous addition like the parasite, but as something more like a master of ceremonies, a center for the comic mood. There is no cook in Shakespeare, though there is a superb description of one in the *Comedy of Errors,* but a similar role is often attached to a jovial and loquacious host, like the "mad host" of *The Merry Wives* or the Simon Eyre of *The Shoe-makers Holiday*. In Middleton's *A Trick to Catch the Old One* the mad host type is combined with the vice. In Falstaff and Sir Toby Belch we can see the affinities of the buffoon or entertainer type both with the parasite and with the master of revels. If we study this entertainer or host role carefully we shall soon realize that it is a development of what in Aristophanic comedy is represented by the chorus, and which in its turn goes back to the *komos* or revel from which comedy is said to be descended.

Finally, there is a fourth group to which we have assigned the word *agroikos,* and which usually means either churlish or rustic, depending on the context. This type may also be extended to cover the Elizabethan gull and what in vaudeville used to be called the straight man, the solemn or inarticulate character who allows the humor to bounce off him, so to speak. We find churls in the miserly, snobbish, or priggish characters whose role is that of the refuser of festivity, the killjoy who tries to stop the fun, or, like Malvolio, locks up the food and drink instead of dispensing it. The melancholy Jaques of *As You Like It,* who walks out on the final festivities, is closely related. In the sulky and self-centered Bertam of *All's Well* there is a most unusual and ingenious combination of this type with the hero. More often, however, the churl belongs to the *alazon* group, all miserly old men in comedies, including Shylock, being churls. In *The Tempest* Caliban has much the same relation to the churlish type that Ariel has to the vice or tricky slave. But often, where the mood is more light-hearted, we may translate *agroikos* simply by rustic, as with the innumerable country squires and similar characters who provide amusement in the urban setting of drama. Such types do not refuse the mood of festivity, but they mark the extent of its range. In a pastoral comedy the idealized virtues of rural life may be represented by a simple man who speaks for the pastoral ideal, like Corin in *As You Like It.* Corin has the same *agroikos* role as the "rube" or "hayseed" of more citified comedies, but the moral attitude to the role is reversed. Again we notice the principle that dramatic structure is a permanent and moral attitude a variable factor in literature.

In a very ironic comedy a different type of character may play the role of the refuser of festivity. The more ironic the comedy, the more absurd the society, and an absurd society may be condemned by, or at least contrasted with, a character that we may call the plain dealer, an outspoken advocate of a kind of moral norm who has the sympathy of the audience. Wycherley's Manly, though he provides the name for the type, is not a particularly good example of it: a much

better one is the Cléante of *Tartuffe*. Such a character is appropriate
when the tone is ironic enough to get the audience confused about
its sense of the social norm: he corresponds roughly to the chorus in
a tragedy, which is there for a similar reason. When the tone deepens
from the ironic to the bitter, the plain dealer may become a mal-
content or railer, who may be morally superior to his society, as he is
to some extent in Marston's play of that name, but who may also be
too motivated by envy to be much more than another aspect of his
society's evil, like Thersites, or to some extent Apemantus.

In tragedy, pity and fear, the emotions of moral attraction and
repulsion, are raised and cast out. Comedy seems to make a more
functional use of the social, even the moral judgement, than tragedy,
yet comedy seems to raise the corresponding emotions, which are sympathy and ridicule, and cast them out in the same way. Comedy
ranges from the most savage irony to the most dreamy wish-fulfilment
romance, but its structural patterns and characterization are much
the same throughout its range. This principle of the uniformity of
comic structure through a variety of attitudes is clear in Aristophanes.
Aristophanes is the most personal of writers, and his opinions on
every subject are written all over his plays. We know that he wanted
peace with Sparta and that he hated Cleon, so when his comedy
depicts the attaining of peace and the defeat of Cleon we know that
he approved and wanted his audience to approve. But in *Ecclesiazusae*
a band of women in disguise railroad a communistic scheme through
the Assembly which is a horrid parody of a Platonic republic, and
proceed to inaugurate its sexual communism with some astonishing
improvements. Presumably Aristophanes did not altogether endorse
this, yet the comedy follows the same pattern and the same resolution.
In *The Birds* the Peisthetairos who defies Zeus and blocks out Olympus
with his Cloud-Cuckoo-Land is accorded the same triumph that is
given to the Trygaios of the *Peace* who flies to heaven and brings a
golden age back to Athens.

Let us look now at a variety of comic structures between the extremes of irony and romance. As comedy blends into irony and satire
at one end and into romance at the other, if there are different
phases or types of comic structure, some of them will be closely parallel
to some of the types of irony and of romance. A somewhat forbidding
piece of symmetry turns up in our argument at this point, which
seems to have some literary analogy to the circle of fifths in music. I
recognize six phases of each *mythos,* three being parallel to the phases
of a neighboring *mythos.* The first three phases of comedy are parallel
to the first three phases of irony and satire, and the second three to

the second three of romance. The distinction between an ironic comedy and a comic satire, or between a romantic comedy and a comic
romance, is tenuous, but not quite a distinction without a difference.

The first or most ironic phase of comedy is, naturally, the one in
which a humorous society triumphs or remains undefeated. A good
example of a comedy of this type is *The Alchemist,* in which the returning *eiron* Lovewit joins the rascals, and the plain dealer Surly
is made a fool of. In *The Beggar's Opera* there is a similar twist
to the ending: the (projected) author feels that the hanging of the
hero is a comic ending, but is informed by the manager that the
audience's sense of comic decorum demands a reprieve, whatever
Macheath's moral status. This phase of comedy presents what Renaissance critics called *speculum consuetudinis,* the way of the world,
cosi fan tutte. A more intense irony is achieved when the humorous
society simply disintegrates without anything taking its place, as in
Heartbreak House and frequently in Chekhov.

We notice in ironic comedy that the demonic world is never far
away. The rages of the *senex iratus* in Roman comedy are directed
mainly at the tricky slave, who is threatened with the mill, with being
flogged to death, with crucifixion, with having his head dipped in tar
and set on fire, and the like, all penalties that could be and were
exacted from slaves in life. An epilogue in Plautus informs us that
the slave-actor who has blown up in his lines will now be flogged;
in one of the Menander fragments a slave is tied up and burned
with a torch on the stage. One sometimes gets the impression that
the audience of Plautus and Terence would have guffawed uproariously all through the Passion. We may ascribe this to the brutality
of a slave society, but then we remember that boiling oil and burying
alive ("such a *stuffy* death") turn up in *The Mikado.* Two lively
comedies of the modern stage are *The Cocktail Party* and *The Lady's
Not for Burning,* but the cross appears in the background of the one
and the stake in the background of the other. Shylock's knife and
Angelo's gallows appear in Shakespeare: in *Measure for . Measure*
every male character is at one time or another threatened with death.
The action of comedy moves toward a deliverance from something
which, if absurd, is by no means invariably harmless. We notice too
how frequently a comic dramatist tries to bring his action as close to
a catastrophic overthrow of the hero as he can get it, and then reverses
the action as quickly as possible. The evading or breaking of a cruel
law is often a very narrow squeeze. The intervention of the king at
the end of *Tartuffe* is deliberately arbitrary: there is nothing in the
action of the play itself to prevent Tartuffe's triumph. Tom Jones in

the final book, accused of murder, incest, debt, and double-dealing, cast off by friends, guardian, and sweetheart, is a woeful figure indeed before all these turn into illusions. Any reader can think of many comedies in which the fear of death, sometimes a hideous death, hangs over the central character to the end, and is dispelled so quickly that one has almost the sense of awakening from nightmare.

Sometimes the redeeming agent actually is divine, like Diana in *Pericles;* in *Tartuffe* it is the king, who is conceived as a part of the audience and the incarnation of its will. An extraordinary number of comic stories, both in drama and fiction, seem to approach a potentially tragic crisis near the end, a feature that I may call the "point of ritual death"—a clumsy expression that I would gladly surrender for a better one. It is a feature not often noticed by critics, but when it is present it is as unmistakably present as a stretto in a fugue, which it somewhat resembles. In Smollett's *Humphry Clinker* (I select this because no one will suspect Smollett of deliberate mythopoeia but only of following convention, at least as far as his plot is concerned), the main characters are nearly drowned in an accident with an upset carriage; they are then taken to a nearby house to dry off, and a *cognitio* takes place, in the course of which their family relationships are regrouped, secrets of birth brought to light, and names changed. Similar points of ritual death may be marked in almost any story that imprisons the hero or gives the heroine a nearly mortal illness before an eventually happy ending.

Sometimes the point of ritual death is vestigial, not an element in the plot but a mere change of tone. Everyone will have noted in comic actions, even in very trivial movies and magazine stories, a point near the end at which the tone suddenly becomes serious, sentimental, or ominous of potential catastrophe. In Aldous Huxley's *Chrome Yellow,* the hero Denis comes to a point of self-evaluation in which suicide nearly suggests itself: in most of Huxley's later books some violent action, generally suicidal, occurs at the corresponding point. In *Mrs. Dalloway* the actual suicide of Septimus becomes a point of ritual death for the heroine in the middle of her party. There are also some interesting Shakespearean variations of the device: a clown, for instance, will make a speech near the end in which the buffoon's mask suddenly falls off and we look straight into the face of a beaten and ridiculed slave. Examples are the speech of Dromio of Ephesus beginning "I am an ass indeed" in the *Comedy of Errors,* and the speech of the Clown in *All's Well* beginning "I am a woodland fellow."

The second phase of comedy, in its simplest form, is a comedy in which the hero does not transform a humorous society but simply escapes or runs away from it, leaving its structure as it was before. A more complex irony in this phase is achieved when a society is constructed by or around a hero, but proves not sufficiently real or strong to impose itself. In this situation the hero is usually himself at least partly a comic humor or mental runaway, and we have either a hero's illusion thwarted by a superior reality or a clash of two illusions. This is the quixotic phase of comedy, a difficult phase for drama, though *The Wild Duck* is a fairly pure example of it, and in drama it usually appears as a subordinate theme of another phase. Thus in *The Alchemist* Sir Epicure Mammon's dream of what he will do with the philosopher's stone is, like Quixote's, a gigantic dream, and makes him an ironic parody of Faustus (who is mentioned in the play), in the same way that Quixote is an ironic parody of Amadis and Lancelot. When the tone is more light-hearted, the comic resolution may be strong enough to sweep over all quixotic illusions. In *Huckleberry Finn* the main theme is one of the oldest in comedy, the freeing of a slave, and the *cognitio* tells us that Jim had already been set free before his escape was bungled by Tom Sawyer's pedantries. Because of its unrivalled opportunities for double-edged irony, this phase is a favorite of Henry James: perhaps his most searching study of it is *The Sacred Fount*, where the hero is an ironic parody of a Prospero figure creating another society out of the one in front of him.

The third phase of comedy is the normal one that we have been discussing, in which a *senex iratus* or other humor gives way to a young man's desires. The sense of the comic norm is so strong that when Shakespeare, by way of experiment, tried to reverse the pattern in *All's Well,* in having two older people force Bertram to marry Helena, the result has been an unpopular "problem" play, with a suggestion of something sinister about it. We have noted that the *cognitio* of comedy is much concerned with straightening out the details of the new society, with distinguishing brides from sisters and parents from foster-parents. The fact that the son and father are so often in conflict means that they are frequently rivals for the same girl, and the psychological alliance of the hero's bride and the mother is often expressed or implied. The occasional "naughtiness" of comedy, as in the Restoration period, has much to do, not only with marital infidelity, but with a kind of comic Oedipus situation in which the hero replaces his father as a lover. In Congreve's *Love for Love* there are two Oedipus themes in counterpoint: the hero cheats his father out of the heroine, and his best friend violates the wife of an impotent old man who is the heroine's guardian. A theme which would be recognized in real life as a form of infantile regression, the hero pretending to be impotent in order to gain admission to the women's quarters, is employed in Wycherley's *Country Wife*, where it is taken from Terence's *Eunuchus*.

The possibilities of incestuous combinations form one of the minor themes of comedy. The repellent older woman offered to Figaro in marriage turns out to be his mother, and the fear of violating a mother also occurs in *Tom Jones*. When in *Ghosts* and *Little Eyolf* Ibsen employed the old chestnut about the object of the hero's affections being his sister (a theme as old as Menander), his startled hearers took it for a portent of social revolution. In Shakespeare the recurring and somewhat mysterious father-daughter relationship already alluded to appears in its incestuous form at the beginning of *Pericles*, where it forms the demonic antithesis of the hero's union with his wife and daughter at the end. The presiding genius of comedy is Eros, and Eros has to adapt himself to the moral facts of society: Oedipus and incest themes indicate that erotic attachments have in their undisplaced or mythical origin a much greater versatility.

Ambivalent attitudes naturally result, and ambivalence is apparently the main reason for the curious feature of doubled characters which runs all through the history of comedy. In Roman comedy there is often a pair of young men, and consequently a pair of young women, of which one is often related to one of the men and exogamous to the other. The doubling of the *senex* figure sometimes gives us a heavy father for both the hero and the heroine, as in *The Winter's Tale*, sometimes a heavy father and benevolent uncle, as in Terence's *Adelphoi* and in *Tartuffe*, and so on. The action of comedy, like the action of the Christian Bible, moves from law to liberty. In the law there is an element of ritual bondage which is abolished, and an element of habit or convention which is fulfilled. The intolerable qualities of the *senex* represent the former and compromise with him the latter in the evolution of the comic *nomos*.

With the fourth phase of comedy we begin to move out of the world of experience into the ideal world of innocence and romance. We said that normally the happier society established at the end of the comedy is left undefined, in contrast to the ritual bondage of the humors. But it is also possible for a comedy to present its action on two social planes, of which one is preferred and consequently in some measure idealized. At the beginning of Plato's *Republic* we have a sharp contest between the *alazon* Thrasymachus and the ironic Socrates. The dialogue could have stopped there, as several of Plato's dialogues do, with a negative victory over a humor and the kind of society he suggests. But in the *Republic* the rest of the company, including Thrasymachus, follow Socrates inside Socrates's head, so to speak, and contemplate there the pattern of the just state. In Aristophanes the comic action is often ironic, but in *The Acharnians* we have a comedy in which a hero with the significant name of Dicaeopolis (righteous city or citizen) makes a private peace with Sparta, celebrates the peaceful festival of Dionysos with his family, and sets up the pattern of a temperate social order on the stage, where it remains throughout the play, cranks, bigots, sharpers, and scoundrels all being beaten away from it. One of the typical comic actions is at least as clearly portrayed in our earliest comedy as it has ever been since.

Shakespeare's type of romantic comedy follows a tradition established by Peele and developed by Greene and Lyly, which has affinities with the medieval tradition of the seasonal ritual-play. We may call it the drama of the green world, its plot being assimilated to the ritual theme of the triumph of life and love over the waste land. In *The Two Gentlemen of Verona* the hero Valentine becomes captain of a band of outlaws in a forest, and all the other characters are gathered into this forest and become converted. Thus the action of the comedy begins in a world represented as a normal world, moves into the green world, goes into a metamorphosis there in which the comic resolution is achieved, and returns to the normal world. The forest in this play is the embryonic form of the fairy world of *A Midsummer Night's Dream,* the Forest of Arden in *As You Like It,* Windsor Forest in *The Merry Wives,* and the pastoral world of the mythical sea-coasted Bohemia in *The Winter's Tale.* In all these comedies there is the same rhythmic movement from normal world to green world and back again. In *The Merchant of Venice* the second world takes the form of Portia's mysterious house in Belmont, with its magic caskets and the wonderful cosmological harmonies that proceed from it in the fifth act. We notice too that this second world is absent from the more ironic comedies *All's Well* and *Measure for Measure.*

The green world charges the comedies with the symbolism of the victory of summer over winter, as is explicit in *Love's Labor's Lost,* where the comic contest takes the form of the medieval debate of winter and spring at the end. In *The Merry Wives* there is an elaborate ritual of the defeat of winter known to folklorists as "carrying out Death," of which Falstaff is the victim; and Falstaff must have felt that, after being thrown into the water, dressed up as a witch and beaten out of a house with curses, and finally supplied with a beast's head and singed with candles, he had done about all that could reasonably be asked of any fertility spirit.

In the rituals and myths the earth that produces the rebirth is generally a female figure, and the death and revival, or disappearance and withdrawal, of human figures in romantic comedy generally involves the heroine. The fact that the heroine often brings about the comic resolution by disguising herself as a boy is familiar enough. The treatment of Hero in *Much Ado,* of Helena in *All's Well,* of Thaisa in *Pericles,* of Fidele in *Cymbeline,* of Hermione in *The Winter's Tale,* show the repetition of a device in which progressively less care is taken of plausibility and in which in consequence the mythical outline of a Proserpine figure becomes progressively clearer. These are Shakespearean examples of the comic theme of ritual assault on a central female figure, a theme which stretches from Menander to contemporary soap operas. Many of Menander's plays have titles which are feminine participles indicating the particular indignity the heroine suffers in them, and the working formula of the soap opera is said to be to "put the heroine behind the eight-ball and keep her there." Treatments of the theme may be as light-hearted as *The Rape of the Lock* or as doggedly persistent as *Pamela.* However, the theme of rebirth is not invariably feminine in context: the rejuvenation of the *senex* in Aristophanes' *The Knights,* and a similar theme in *All's Well* based on the folklore motif of the healing of the impotent king, come readily to mind.

The green world has analogies, not only to the fertile world of ritual, but to the dream world that we create out of our own desires. This dream world collides with the stumbling and blinded follies of the world of experience, of Theseus' Athens with its idiotic marriage law, of Duke Frederick and his melancholy tyranny, of Leontes and his mad jealousy, of the Court Party with their plots and intrigues, and yet proves strong enough to impose the form of desire on it. Thus Shakespearean comedy illustrates, as clearly as any *mythos* we have, the archetypal function of literature in visualizing the world of desire, not as an escape from "reality," but as the genuine form of the world that human life tries to imitate.

In the fifth phase of comedy, some of the themes of which we have already anticipated, we move into a world that is still more romantic, less Utopian and more Arcadian, less festive and more pensive, where the comic ending is less a matter of the way the plot turns out than of the perspective of the audience. When we compare the Shakespearean fourth-phase comedies with the late fifth-phase "romances," we notice how much more serious an action is appropriate to the latter: they do not avoid tragedies but contain them. The action seems to be not only a movement from a "winter's tale" to spring, but from a lower world of confusion to an upper world of order. The closing scene of *The Winter's Tale* makes us think, not simply of a cyclical movement from tragedy and absence to happiness and return, but of bodily metamorphosis and a transformation from one kind of life to another. The materials of the *cognitio* of *Pericles* or *The Winter's Tale* are so stock that they would be "hooted at like an old tale," yet they seem both far-fetched and inevitably right, outraging reality and at the same time introducing us to a world of childlike innocence which has always made more sense than reality.

In this phase the reader or audience feels raised above the action, in the situation of which Christopher Sly is an ironic parody. The plotting of Cleon and Dionyza in *Pericles,* or of the Court Party in *The Tempest,* we look down on as generic or typical human behavior: the action, or at least the tragic implication of the action, is presented as though it were a play within a play that we can see in all dimensions at once. We see the action, in short, from the point of view of a higher and better ordered world. And as the forest in Shakespeare is the usual symbol for the dream world in conflict with and imposing its form on experience, so the usual symbol for the lower or chaotic world is the sea, from which the cast, or an important past of it, is saved. The group of "sea" comedies includes *A Comedy of Errors, Twelfth Night, Pericles,* and *The Tempest. A Comedy of Errors,* though based on a Plautine original, is much closer to the world of Apuleius than to that of Plautus in its imagery, and the main action, moving from shipwreck and separation to reunion in a temple in Ephesus, is repeated in the much later play of *Pericles.* And just as the second world is absent from the two "problem" comedies, so in two of the "sea" group, *Twelfth Night* and *The Tempest,* the entire action takes place in the second world. In *Measure for Measure* the Duke disappears from the action and returns at the end; *The Tempest* seems to present the same type of action inside out, as the entire cast follows Prospero into his retreat, and is shaped into a new social order there.

These five phases of comedy may be seen as a sequence of stages in the life of a redeemed society. Purely ironic comedy exhibits this society in its infancy, swaddled and smothered by the society it should replace. Quixotic comedy exhibits it in adolescence, still too ignorant of the ways of the world to impose itself. In the third phase it comes to maturity and triumphs; in the fourth it is already mature and established. In the fifth it is part of a settled order which has been there from the beginning, an order which takes on an increasingly religious cast and seems to be drawing away from human experience altogether. At this point the undisplaced *commedia,* the vision of Dante's *Paradiso,* moves out of our circle of *mythoi* into the apocalyptic or abstract mythical world above it. At this point we realize that the crudest of Plautine comedy-formulas has much the same *structure* as the central Christian myth itself, with its divine son appeasing the wrath of a father and redeeming what is at once a society and a bride.

At this point too comedy proper enters its final or sixth phase, the phase of the collapse and disintegration of the comic society. In this phase the social units of comedy become small and esoteric, or even confined to a single individual. Secret and sheltered places, forests in moonlight, secluded valleys, and happy islands become more prominent, as does the *penseroso* mood of romance, the love of the occult and the marvellous, the sense of individual detachment from routine existence. In this kind of comedy we have finally left the world of wit and the awakened critical intelligence for the opposite pole, an oracular solemnity which, if we surrender uncritically to it, will provide a delightful *frisson.* This is the world of ghost stories, thrillers, and Gothic romances, and, on a more sophisticated level, the kind of imaginative withdrawal portrayed in Huysmans' *À Rebours.* The somberness of Des Esseintes' surroundings has nothing to do with tragedy: Des Esseintes is a dilettante trying to amuse himself. The comic society has run the full course from infancy to death, and in its last phase myths closely connected psychologically with a return to the womb are appropriate.

Comedy and Laughter*

BENJAMIN LEHMANN

The student of literature, reviewing what has been written about comedy, may well be dismayed. For what has been written about the subject is, except for incidental insights, not about comedy. It is about satire. There are indeed studies of individual comedies, of comic devices, of a single writer's practices, and of comedy in a period or in a tradition. But these also more or less involve themselves, without due distinction of terms, with satire. And with an incidental exception or two when a general view of comedy is undertaken, attention is fixed upon the ludicrous, the absurd, the ridiculous. Laughter is said to be provoked by these human manifestations. The laughter, it is said, is corrective; we are invited to believe that the chief end of comedy is to reform manners and dispositions. Laughter itself has been inquired into; its bases in physiology, in psychology, and in group reaction have been explored, not without illumination. The illumination falls, however, not on comedy; it is shed on satire and on the comic, those fragments of action and utterance which beget the flash laugh. It does not fall on the work of literary art all consent to call comedy, whether for audiences in a theater or for readers by a fireside.

Yet the literary mode called comedy is an ancient one, and in our time of remarkable vitality. Epic, we often hear, is no longer possible; lyric, we are told, is now for a special audience; of tragedy, it is said, the essentials no longer exist in our world view. Comedy prospers. We may set aside as childish the notion that the age seeks merely to be amused; it seeks recreation, an honorable seeking which the arts are intended to foster. In design and color, in tone and implication, comedy seems now even more than in other times to meet a need, to

* Benjamin Lehmann, "Comedy and Laughter," in *University of California Publications. English Studies,* Vol. 10 (University of California Press, 1954), pp. 81–101.

correspond to a primary and universal intuition of life and the world. Is it not possible to examine the comedies, to discover that intuition of life and the world which so persistently captivates the human spirit? The incongruities and all the rest of which the critics speak are in the service of a vision of reality the average man takes daily for granted and delights to see illustrated and affirmed. In the service of that vision are also the mistaken identities, disguises, the eaves-dropping, the non-sequiturs, the famous mechanical incrustation of vitality; even the wisecrack and the pratfall, for which the average man invented words.

At the outset, we must observe that though we laugh at actions and utterances in comedy, we do not laugh at the comedy as a whole. For the comedy as a whole is a serious work, making an affirmation about life that chimes with our intuitive sense of how things are and with our deep human desire to have the necessary and agreeable prevail and our even deeper human desire to arrest before our minds a condition of things pleasant in itself and completely free from the threat of time and of disruption. For time brings the after-math, in which the seeds of disruptive forces will sprout, in which decay will set in, and the whole process of making the necessary and agreeable secure will have to start over. That golden lads and girls must like chimney sweepers come to dust is not the stuff of comedy; it is a comment from beyond comedy's world on that world, and so appalling that its truth must be obscured by a pun. Never in comedy are we without love, and almost never without lovers. Comedy fixes the lads and girls forever in their brilliant moment; it usually con-trives to close our minds to what lies ahead. This is not from any desire to deny life all its stages. We know it would be no true bliss that was bliss always, and that this enchanting hour is itself possible because of the not entirely comfortable growth that preceded it. Ambivalently perhaps, but certainly, though we desire for these lovers and for ourselves all the stages of life, it is yet pleasant, it agrees with the feeling we have of valuable things, to put a period here where the mates are free of all save their own inner commitment. That commitment is of course one in which we have a vicarious re-freshment of old innocence, or, if we are very young, a veiled prevision of an hour when innocence will be lost. But it is more than that. It reassures us about life and its continuation—the more so, that these lovers are so young, so beautiful or so charming, if also so compelled. We do not laugh at all this. We are delighted; we are content. The folk have a phrase for it: all the world loves a lover, they say.

But the folk have another phrase: the course of true love never runs smooth, they also say. If this saying is large enough to include postmarital trials, that is as it should be, for comedy, in putting a period at mating, does not deny the aftermath; it simply ignores it for these lovers. The course of true love that does not run smooth is in comedy the preceding course. In that phase, there are difficulties. They arise at many points and from many causes in human nature and human circumstance: social prejudice, finances, an older generation that has forgotten its youth, even conflicts within the lovers that for a while thwart their profound instinctive sense that they can, in the mysterious way of things, complete one another. Against that prevision of completeness nothing can prevail: not poverty, not social barriers, not advice, not even upon occasion a glimpsing foresight that life may be one long bickering. The elements, within and around lovers, which stand in the way of their fulfilling themselves and their biological function, are in comedy usually treated with sympathetic derision. It is folly to oppose this compulsion to mate, and what opposes properly falls under a derisive light.

The forces that oppose lovers, however, are themselves constituted in the nature of things. All these exasperating parents, these crotchety uncles and spinster aunts with lapdogs and money, these competing lovers, jealous, irresponsible, full of devious plans, these group attitudes regarding social status, race, religion, culture—these too have come into existence as inevitably as the lovers' promptings. The manners and the morals of the group, and the members of the group themselves, are manifestations of the freedom of all things to be what they are, to improve such opportunities as exist for realizing the never ceasing activity of becoming what further they may become. Consequently in the world of comedy the greatest diversity of being and of morals is deployed, and it is granted that those who seek to frustrate our lovers have a right to be what they are. Yet since not all possibilities of being can happily exist together, some must be sacrificed, some must be defeated. Social homogeneity, or true unity, cannot be always maintained; there is bound to be schism. But the sacrificed will be gently discarded, after being duly wrapped in derision, away from our complete sympathy; and the mutually opposed parties will fuse once more in a firm social unity.

The vision of comedy, then, keeps its eye on lovers, its foresight upon their prosperous mating and on implied procreation. And it consents heartily that the world they live in shall be populated by a richly diverse humanity, some for and some against the desired consummation, provided only all these illustrate the variety of the possibilities of being, generous or crabbed, fulfilled or thwarted, and provided further that the crabbed and the thwarted exhibit to us within their limits the best realization of their meager possibilities and, when necessary, yield duly to clear the way for fuller, better-natured possibilities. The vision of comedy fixes its eye on separateness, on diversity, even on oppositions, but it insists at last on togetherness for lovers and on the restored social fabric, on solidarity for the group. From its world are excluded insurmountable barriers, unassimilable evils, and suffering that strikes at the core or is irremediable. In that world all is tipped toward life, abundance, health, energy, companionship, respect, and admiration. Song, music, dance, feasting belong in it. Whatever within the range of vision is otherwise will be minimized by laughter, though it is understood it cannot be abolished from the world, and that all will end happily for human beings, not merely for human minds.

Historically, what is called comedy grew out of carnival, and the secrets of carnival are masquerade, fellow feeling, and such immersion in being that the sense of impermanence vanishes. Originally the carnival was dedicated to the continuity of life; in its beginnings comedy was involved with the fertility of the species, and with that animality which puritans might condemn but could only advertise. That nothing lasts, that we may as well be ourselves, that when we are ourselves the mask is thrown off and primal forces emerge in us, these ancient intuitions in the circumstances of carnival call out gaiety and joyousness. The sense of human isolation is dissolved by the communal activity and the sense of impermanence is annihilated by the promised projection of life. The participants seem to say, we are not only solidly here in this company, but in time to come there will also be others. Birth, maturity, mating—though these are not the ecclesiastical sacraments, for life they are sacramental, and they are ceremonially so recognized in all religions. Comedy, from this point of view, is seen, once again, to deal with mating and marriage, with maturity which is their condition, and birth which is their consequence.

Seeing things as they are, however, involves more than a clear gaze at the agents of the life-stream. Though these agents are rarely left out of the picture, and though they are sometimes exhibited in a more advanced phase, shown for example as married and readjusting with the passing years and the changing natures, often they constitute a contrapuntal design in a picture of the diversely populated world, or a reassuring frame for the picture of that world. If from Menander to our own day we can follow the tradition the folk has summarized in the sayings that all the world loves a lover and that the course of true love never runs smooth, we can also from Aristophanes to Shaw follow another tradition. In it derision, verging on half-affectionate raillery, is played upon human instances and patterns of behavior that appear to prevent free fulfillment of any kind whatsoever. Long ago Wilamovitz made clear that Aristophanic comedy was not intended to improve the morals of the audience, and Werner Jaeger has in recent years and in a larger context taken the same position. What an unbiased reading of the comedies of Aristophanes shows us is that, except when—as in his invective against Cleon—he is a bitter satirist, he stands for freedom. The freedom he stands for is sometimes the freedom of the immediate past, but it is always the freedom of man to be and to become what it lies in him to be and to become, unhampered by the community, by the mob, by law, by too much or too little money, by the newfangled and the restricting old-fashioned. "Freedom to *be*" is the motto, freedom from disorder, lust, cruelty, war. The image is Cloud-Cuckoo-Land where all the hampering forces are abolished, where not only lovers but every man is free and winged, subject only to those self-deceptions which are harmless because they are in the nature of things and laughable because they are harmless. Cloud-Cuckoo-Land comes through into our day in such plays as *Harvey, Arsenic and Old Lace,* and in the Wonderland of Alice. It is not love of lovers but love of humanity's best and most various possibilities which is the spirit of this comedy. Such comedy realizes the insight of certain Pythagoreans and of Plato that civilization should foster the fulfillment of the real individual both in himself and in his natural affiliations. The freedom desired is beyond any conceived in political and economic utopias and would of course be impossible under political or economic despotism. Under despotism, deviation from the prescribed would be the object of unmitigated ridicule and invective, what we call satire. It is in democracy that comedy particularly prospers, for true democracy and true comedy are of an immense hospitality and have respect for all men. That Molière, for example, lived under a sort of despotism does not alter the case. An era is not despotic about everything: about the forms Molière chiefly explored and exhibited, his era was not despotic; when he moved into the areas of supposed unalterable truth he was forced to recast his work. Straight satire, in fact, is itself despotic; it assumes the absolute validity of the satirist's values and is intolerant; it judges without misgiving; it does more than condemn, it excludes. Aristophanes and Molière, thus, show themselves despotic in behalf of freedom when they are primarily satirists.

At its truest, comedy of the Aristophanic kind is devoted to the free maturing of diverse and even of eccentric possibilities. Like the comedy of lovers, this is a serious affirmation of life, delightedly asserted, joyously accepted, and oftenest with laughter. The fullest comedy, at all events, intuitively rendering unity in diversity, now and in time to come, views the world simultaneously in both the Aristophanic and the Menanderian modes. When it does not, the boy-gets-girl fable will seem trite and perhaps trivial, for it will lack reference, relation, affiliation. It will be what we call romance. In romance life has ceased to be a forest; it has become a park. The underbrush has been cleaned out, the windfalls and the deadfalls have been cleaned up, and nature's way of enriching herself by her own decay is lost to us. On the other hand, without the lovers the satiric practice which derides the old-established morals in the hope of destroying them will seem, if not heartless, at least without a sufficient symbol of dedication; and all observations of human nature will seem too intellectual not because there is too much intellect in the observation but because it is observation without love of life. Phenomenal mental energy, expressed in notable wit, may conceal this truth, as it sometimes does in Aristophanes and in Shaw and in Ben Jonson.

By glancing now at individual works, we can perhaps at once test the validity of the general position here set forth and take note of some of the special ways in which comedy employs congenial attitudes and convenient devices, of what may be called the practice of comedy, as distinguished from comic vision. We can also by proceeding in this way suggest the complexity which is characteristic of a wholly achieved work of literary art in this genre, the more readily if we include among our instances some works which though deficient as works of art have proved persuasive for large audiences.

Between the mating young and the old lies family life and the commitments of the social group. In *Abie's Irish Rose*, financial considerations and the blood feud between Jew and non-Jew, presented in stereotypes, are treated as barriers. The Rabbi and the Priest are of a most sweet broadmindedness, conditioned no doubt by the professional sense of sacramental marriage and by a professional belief that it is better to marry than to burn, learned from St. Paul who is of the race of the Rabbi and of the church of the Priest. The lovers are young moderns who have to bring their own intelligences to bear in order to support their natural promptings against their conditioned reluctances about miscegenation. The capitulation of both their fathers when they become grandfathers—in the presence of twins—is both touching and laughable: we have in that future

generation not only a boy and a girl, but it may be a Jew and a
Catholic. All this, and also the acceptance of roast pork—which enlarges the range of festive feeding—and of Christmas, which com-
memorates the birthday of a glorious figure of the race of one family
and the religion of the other. In the most popular of modern comedies,
fusion and unity are achieved without neglect of the life-stream and
with persuasive setting aside of commitments. Yet it is shallow stuff,
true only in a single plane, the possibilities not realized. In *Ah, Wilderness,* we are not taken so far into the future, but we go deeper.
Reciprocally in the world of the family Miller, everyone is loved not
alone for himself but for his idiosyncracies. In regard to the adolescent,
that means "keeping up," since adolescents spawn new idiosyncracies
in a day: the man you say good night to is not the child you
greeted at breakfast; he may well for the time being have grown unbearable. But it is not otherwise with grown-ups when they have let
liquor have its way, and if as with Sid Davis this is a recurrent
phenomenon, it frustrates love and life. Yet the family before us is
so firmly on its feet, the group so inwardly attuned by time and custom, that this frustration is ameliorated; it becomes, almost, a nostalgia for something once had and lost rather than for something
dreamed of and never had. And at the close, in young Richard, the
dream—on the piazza, until the moon sets—is a forecast upon that
fate which nature has decreed for all who live, though some miss it.
Not, however, before we have seen that young Richard has an inkling that it has been so before his time, and incidentally that those
old people, his parents, were young once. He learns not to forget that
way back then the moon was the same—"and everything." Everything—the freshness, the discovery, the magic, the love. The threatened
break of the texture of family life is avoided, and there is a creating
future.

Comic vision sometimes presents us these characteristic matters not
in a city milieu but in the country, among those nearer the earth,
where the procreative is in the daily visible round. In *Tobacco Road,*
Jeeter is a hungry man, haunted by a kind of negative feasting, but
his greatest hunger is to till the soil, to plant a crop and, when it
appears for a short time that they may be given seed for a crop, even
the selfish and rebellious Dude helps to burn off the fields. Framed by
an illusory sense of Earth's harvest, the drive to beget runs wild, coming to little as civilization counts, but never coming to nothing. Pearl
was clearly meant to beget her kind and, escaping, doubtless will do
so. Ellie May, harelipped and urgent, goes to cook for Lov and, who
can doubt, to bear him children, out of wedlock probably. Dude is a

born father, though he may postpone the time. It is a world without conventions; so far as it has any mores, they are in the service of life. Millions have been delighted to see it so. In *They Knew What They Wanted,* upon the land thriftily husbanded, Tony, who loves eating, drinking, all the good physical things, who has affection for children and for men and women in general, accepts a child for his child. That his stand-in as father is his hired man, that the circumstances from his point of view appear to violate all the loyalties, releases a berserk fury in him, when he is informed of the facts. However, with his country-bred sense of such things, he is easily calmed, and the child and mother fall in with all the festive elements that make his life. That the hired man goes his way is in nature, too, for paternity is accidental and, in nature, not generally responsible. That in *Tobacco Road* the impoverished picture rendered for us provokes more laughter than one might expect of an audience setting so great store by "more things for more people" at a play in which a superannuated mother is killed by one of those "things" would surprise us if we did not realize that, when we laugh, we are affirming ancient truths about humanity. That we laugh at all before the intensities of *They Knew What They Wanted* would surprise us, too, if it were not intimated to us by the title that this is a comedy of fulfillment.

In Restoration comedy, the tone and the practice are both largely those of satire, that is, derision of pretense, of sterility, of form without matter, of what is not directed lifeward. Nonetheless, by its gusto, its tolerant consent that it shall seem in the nature of its creatures so to pervert nature, and by its recognition that conflicts are resolved in marriages and in reconciliations among the married, satire is given comic values. Our general impression is that life in its essential force cannot be annihilated even by these manners that are satirized. In the finest of Restoration comedies, indeed, we are presented with two people in whom natural promptings served by brilliant gifts attain their true destiny by manipulating the trivialities and irrelevances of upper-class life. In *The Way of the World* mating is central, and marriage, though basely illustrated by others, is richly conceived by the lovers. Mirabell converts the looseness of his philandering ways into premarital experience and Millamant transmutes her coquetry, so that these two at last stand as peerless examples of human beings using their environment for their love. Early in the play Mirabell says of Lady Wishfort that she lets "posterity shift for itself, she'll breed no more." Throughout, it reverberates to our sense that this society is in every way sterile, but it is steadily made clear that for our lovers it is and will be fruitful. In a passage of shining wittiness, they speak of the children they will have, of pregnancy, and of domestic routine. Millamant acts to preserve her wealth as the condition of a good life for children and parents. This is a recognition that their life is to be lived in their accustomed world. But it is not to be lived in the accustomed way. The glitter that surrounds them is bedizenment; it does not come from life within, warm and bright, from life tended, kept fresh. In the last of their swift interchanges, they see in the inevitable repetitions of conjugal life an opportunity. They will give themselves "over and over again." Thus, whereas in *The Country Wife* the ignorant naturalness of Margery accents the satire of a sophisticated unnatural society, in *The Way of the World* that society is exhibited to reveal how those duly endowed may live life truly. In nothing are these brilliant lovers so brilliant as in the attainment of that triumph which is ideally possible to all.

From *They Knew What They Wanted,* where the subject is "played straight," without derision, to *The Way of the World,* where derision is neatly balanced by approvals, in these instances no pain is irremediable. That, we ventured, is the condition of comic vision. Yet there are works in which this condition is barely met, and others in which it is aimed at but missed. In *Pride and Prejudice,* a wonderful skill just prevents Mr. Bennet from being the object of our pity. Had he not the sanctuary of his library, delight in the gentle taunt, happy communication with his daughter Elizabeth, his predicament would strike us as painful. As it is, his story encloses the matchmaking that is the chief matter, and gives the book an extra dimension. The daughters of Mr. and Mrs. Bennet are ready for marriage, or in the case of Lydia for a mate. Pursuit of a husband or a mate is exhibited in great variety. Beset by caste snobberies and by personal snobberies, the girls may not be able to marry according to the promptings of their natures, and that will be bad; but if they should succeed in doing so,—well, look at what happened to father. Mr. Bennet had married Mrs. Bennet for herself alone; she had a negligible fortune, she had negligible intelligence, but she had what was required to enmesh her man. She thereupon bore him five daughters, trying for the son who would lift the entail. Now, with luck, the girls will be off his hands, and one day Mr. Bennet will live in an empty house with Mrs. Bennet, until he dies and leaves Mrs. Bennet a propertyless nuisance in the house of a son-in-law. Yet while he lives there will be his daughter Elizabeth to correspond with, to visit; there will be seclusion with books; there will be the gibes at Mrs. Bennet for safety valve. At least two of the daughters will marry fortunes. Life is not quite sweet; it has more flavor than that; it is bittersweet. Jane Austen, then, just prevents our pain.

Whether Shakespeare did so in *Twelfth Night* is debatable, a matter of how we read the play, or how it is directed. It is a question of the intonation of Olivia's final speeches, of the compassion and warmth she shows toward a tried though illuded retainer. If the derision of Malvolio is reserved to Sir Toby Belch and Sir Andrew Aguecheek and Maria, comedy is safe; if it is Shakespeare deriding a puritan, our pain is past remedy. For Malvolio is also himself, showing a quite human aspiration, however inappropriate. And in any case it is clear that he will be continued in Olivia's household, where we might well have seen him, earlier, under other circumstances, competent, apt, a careful steward, dignified and even decorative as the house of a great lady requires. Shylock takes us, in our day, out of the world comedy appears to prescribe for itself. Even if he were not deprived of his loved property and if his Jessica were not hedged away from him, he is clearly no kinsman of Solomon Levy in *Abie's Irish Rose,* and he can therefore not bear that the flesh of his flesh shall feast on pork and submit to wedding outside the snyagogue. For him, whom we see last in the courtroom, there is no resumption of anything at all. He stands alone before the bar of justice, he leaves alone. His house, bereft of daughter and of wealth, is no home. Since for our day he is too grounded in his humanity to be a derided figure of greed, he is painful. Not all the delectable goings on at Portia's villa on the Brenta can reassure us, after he goes. With Falstaff, as we last see him, it is different. The King may not know the old man. The best of fellows, and of audience, is lost, but Falstaff will make the best of what is left.

> . . . go with me to dinner.
> Come, Lieutenant Pistol; come, Bardolph. I shall
> be sent for soon at night.

The group is not intact, but it is still a group; there will be festivity, and—who knows?—later an account, pure fabrication and wonderfully acted, of being introduced into King Henry's chamber by palace backways and of having caroused with a prince who for an hour threw off affairs of state. Banishment of them all to the Fleet till their conversation appear more wise and modest to the world is only for an interval, we feel. The pain is just not too much, because the life in Falstaff is just enough and because he is not deprived of what to him is indispensable—fellowship.

Comic practice, we said, views with half-affectionate derision the unfruitful, the incomplete, and the contrived, when they seek to frustrate vitality and fulfillment, and, when they merely exist in the neighborhood, presents such to us as examples of the rich variety in the human scene. Though comic vision is devoted to spontaneous and fulfilling expression, it knows that fulfillment is not always possible. Then comic practice shows us how the wise keep their heads down. Shandean comedy exhibits the disparity between the dreams that are enclosed in such words as love, war and glory, reason, and the world of fact. Love and war, in *Tristram Shandy,* are exhibited not in their glamorous phases but in their tawdry aftermaths as demonstrations of that inevitable coming to earth of which Yorick warns us. Reason, which in man is thought so ennobling, is reduced by a battery of non-sequiturs endlessly replenished from the associative faculty. The manifestation of the life-force itself sets the pattern of non-sequitur, for Tristram is the son in the flesh of a woman who cannot catch an implication and a man who tortures all reality to fit hypothesis—Tristram who has a genius for implication and who had the intuition to find that the reality of the world is what it is, that if you keep expanding a hypothesis to fit the facts you presently have no hypothesis at all, moral or intellectual or scientific: you have only nature. The Shandean way is to disclose nature's secret and bid us go along with it. The secret is that, as man imagines possibilities, nothing is complete or enduring, and our dreams are inordinate. Yorick and all the jesters have told us so; thus they safeguard the human, preserve it from pain. They say, when aspiration is incommensurate with reality, it is wise in human beings to cut aspiration back. There is no absolute freedom of being.

At least not in this world. In *Man and Superman* it is only in another world—in a dream hell—that John Tanner masquerading as Don Juan can assert without desperation that it is the role of mind to steer nature, not to drift with her. In that other world of dream, he leaves hell to find his way to heaven where he may fulfill "Life's incessant aspiration to higher organization, wider, deeper, intenser self-consciousness, and clearer self-understanding," where only human perfection will be worth dying for. But he does not get to heaven. He wakes up. And waking he takes the sober view that he has been dreaming damnably. And so he has. For he now confronts once more the world where Life's incessant determination that there shall be more life grips him, in the interest of a household and a family. In *Man and Superman,* in a little imagined universe diversely enough populated, man's highest and most articulate aspiration is brought to earth. Man's greatest freedom, as woman's too, is only to be one-

self, so far as one may. Jack Tanner ends asking Anne a curious pair
of questions: "What have you grasped in me? Is there a father's
heart as well as a mother's?" In his half-century exploitation of a form
that combines the Platonic dialogue with the operatic fable, Shaw
sought to help man be a free, a winged creature by showing how
desirable it is to abolish ignorance, disease, poverty, war and—some
would say—marriage. But the abolition of marriage would not get to
the heart of the matter. Men and women would still be biological
entities. Tanner gives up.

So men view the world, Laurence Sterne by intuition and Shaw
by intelligence, but all men somehow or other, it appears. Unphrased
intuition or that wordless understanding we call common sense creates
the enormous audience for Dickens' Pickwickian world. That world is
as profuse an array of the possibilities of being as can be imagined,
and it extends from the *Pickwick Papers* to the last of the novels,
through all of which it refreshes itself, no matter how melodramatic
the story. For author, for reader, and for the creatures themselves
it is infused with the faith that life in all its infinite variety is made
livable through the constant, vigilant application of the generous, the
humane impulses that arise in most people most of the time, and is
made secure by troops of children. Even in the presence of depriva-
tions that forbid laughter, the ancient ingenuity of pure being—its
exuberance and resilience—calls for delight, and the lower classes
from which Dickens' imagination always reluctantly turned afford
us a greater sense of richness and variety, because in the lower classes
"good form" has made fewer prescriptions and nature is freer to
exhibit her fertility.

It is such a vision of the richness and variety in nature, rather
than the necessity to complicate an action, that brings the lower classes
into Shakespeare's comic world. It is of course at its freest within
the Forest, in the Dream, or on the Magic Island. That comic world
as it is rendered in his earlier comedies is exactly as we should expect
it from an imagination that was almost without party or class bias.
The activities of lovers prosper and are utterly delightful. The de-
sirability of progeny is implicit in their good looks, their charm, their
power to rejoice. The socal fabric, however rent by usurpation, or
illusions pursued, or foolhardy commitments, is restored. The more
so, because those who cannot partake of the golden last state of
things give their approval. In that world who would not sing or listen
to music? Who would not dance or look on at dancing? Who would
not sit down heartily to feast or serve the feast?

Yet from the earliest Shakespearean comedies, there is also a troubled note. Winter as well as spring sounds at the close of *Love's Labour's Lost;* in *A Midsummer Night's Dream* the wonderful spoofing covers but does not conceal the sadness of Pyramus' and Thisbe's fate; in *Much Ado* brother John's punishment is merely postponed till tomorrow; Jacques is alone, Feste is alone, finally. And from *Troilus and Cressida* through *The Winter's Tale* there is enough of the pain of the world to make us doubt the well-being possible to mortals. The bitter is often not overbalanced by the sweet, until in *The Tempest* the golden state of things is once more raised before us. And then not by an affirmative love of life operating directly. In *The Tempest* only magic can procure the condition of delight, joy, and peace. From *Troilus and Cressida* to *The Winter's Tale,* Shakespeare, though he continues to employ the devices of comic practice, appears to be reaching for a form that several centuries later came to be called the problem play. For the problem play exhibits those human predicaments out of which we cannot escape by death and an accompanying sense of enlarged understanding, as in tragedy, or by mating and thinking well of life in limited areas because so much of it is clearly a positive good, humanity being what it is. Such plays do not invite us to immerse ourselves in life, nor do they spark in us impulses to transcend life in ultimate ways.

Molière appears sometimes to have been caught by the same aspect of things. In *The Misanthrope* society is brilliantly satirized in the interest of something which is not satirized but approved—the love of a man and a woman. Philinte could sacrifice his life and soul for the hand of Eliante, he says. But for Célimène Alceste will not sacrifice even his opinions, at least not yet, though Philinte's final speech suggests they may bring him around. Molière's animus has counterpoised against the artificiality of society an unnaturalness in Alceste which we do not see brought back to nature. Yet he is clearly under Célimène's spell, and the example of the other pair of lovers shows us how these things should be. In *Tartuffe,* too—in Molière's final version—the interplay of a great hypocrite and a greater fool is mercilessly satirized in the interest of preserved property and a sweet union of lovers. As in *The Miser,* as also often in Ben Jonson— *Volpone,* for example—so also in *Tartuffe* the obstacles to decency, to good human promptings bulk too large; they present a problem which no marriages of the innocent, no social fabric renewed can overcome. When Philinte compares rogues to vultures, the unjust to mischievous apes, and the selfish to fury-lashed wolves, he misunderstands the nature of men and animals alike; and it is not clear that Molière in a troubled hour is not failing in the same way. At all events, these plays exhibit the limits rather than the powers of humanity, they fix our attention on human destructiveness rather than creativeness, without consolation, on the perversion of the promptings rather than on their expression. They are not, then, true comedies, for in them the practices of comedy are brought to bear upon insoluble human problems which are not susceptible to comic vision. Elsewhere, Molière for the most part avoided such painful cases. The preservation of property for those who will know how to enjoy it, the evenhanded revelation of fidelity and infidelity, the just exhibition of ignorance and comprehension, the unsealing of blind eyes, the sound country-bred sense of servants—in play after play all flow into one channel. Through the symbol of mating lovers or of lovers reunited they become an affirmation of life as it is, and are presented with a witty poetry that arises directly from the affirmation. Laughter is provoked by the witty utterance and the witty situation in Molière always, but we cannot say that *The Miser* and *Tartuffe* reassure us, or that in the presence of *The Misanthrope* our joy is unqualified.

Of course, the reassurance which comedy gives us may be less than total, and it may be involved with the tragic, or with those phenomena which we call problems. For example, midway in *Madame Bovary,* itself a tragic work, Flaubert remarks:

Never had Madame Bovary been so beautiful as at this period; she had that indefinable beauty that comes from joy, from enthusiasm, from success, and that is only the harmony of temperament with circumstances. Her desires, her sorrows, the experience of pleasure, and her ever-young illusions had, as manure, rain, winds and the sun make flowers grow, gradually developed her; she had at length blossomed in all the plentitude of her nature.

At the moment Emma Bovary herself is a figure comedy could delight in. She is, however, not a figure of comedy because, that she might become what she then was, the social fabric had to be broken beyond repair. In *High Noon* the hero and heroine are figures of comedy, suspended between social obligation and their own promptings to fulfillment; but the people of the town in the emergency, huddled in their church and their saloon, withhold their hand from the community good. Hence, we have at best comedy in a minor key, for, though all these townfolk are behaving characteristically and the threats to personal fulfillment and to the continuing of life are removed, the lovers are alone. They will have to find their social fabric elsewhere. The failure of solidarity is symbolized by the empty streets, is accented by the uneasy huddles at altar and at bar, and counterpointed by the couples seen in rooms here and there. In *Come*

Back, Little Sheba the matter of comedy is barely asserted, as contrast, by the young girl married at the end and by the doubly anonymous men from Alcoholics Anonymous entering the picture. The story is a tragic instance of biological necessity betrayed by biological necessity itself, and the husband and wife though restored to one another are bitterly without affiliation, for his parents are dead and hers are alienated; they are without friends, and will be without children. In these instances, from novel and from motion picture, there is a remarkable absence of the festive and the convivial, which increases our sense that no matter what laughter is provoked from moment to moment all is not well with life. A way of life has been attained, reasonable no doubt but not what reason would approve in an ideal world or what our intuition of nature yearns for. We are confronted with a problem, with which two people have learned to live in reconciliation.

Reason is a function much spoken of in connection with comedy. Sometimes it is made the heart of the matter. In that case we observe a snobbery of the self-valuing intelligence; more often we are in the presence of a failure to understand the role reason plays in human affairs. Reason, when it shows to a degree at which it may be separately designated, sees the many diverse claims made upon our imagination, our loyalties, our sympathies, our energy, or our time. It may sometimes appear to make a choice among these diverse claims. But reason is not really free. Were it not tied to the needs of the body and the demand of events, it would still be the creature of the nervous system, at the very least enslaved by accustomed ways of being reasonable. To be natural, which we are by virtue of being alive, and to be rational is to be confronted from hour to hour not so much by choice, as by the necessity for adapting, for making the best of it, as we say, even perhaps for throwing reason out. Reason is not the instrument of comic vision. It is part of the material upon which comic vision gazes.

Here we have the overarching incongruity, which all other incongruities are lighted by. There are many others. Under the most fortunate circumstances it is incongruous that mind should see clearly and sometimes soar but the body should feed and sleep; that the human spirit should feel perennial and the matter of which spirit is a function should be changing always; that the state of being whose nature it is to pledge itself eternally should be so fragilely grounded, so briefly possible; and it is incongruous that the freedom lovers find to commit themselves should at once deprive them of their freedoms. Since nothing remains as it is, it is inconsistent to take satisfaction in an arrived-at solidarity, for it too will be destroyed and succeeded by another, different, whether better or worse. The freedom Aristophanes desired would be procured at the cost of freedom to other entities to be themselves. All other incongruities arise from these, and illustrate these, actually or typically or symbolically.

Comedy did not invent incongruity, it discovered it. Long before psychiatry formulated analogous concepts, comedy discovered the masque, the disguise, mistaken identity. Comedy found them what we call laughable, but on the deeper level felt them as symbolic expression. It recognized in non-sequiturs the verbal symbol of those minor derangements in the sequence of events which are always present when we view reality with preconceptions. It found in wit—the surprising juxtaposition, implied or expressed and happily phrased—the verbal suggestion of the infinite possibilities of being and of connection. In those unillusioned judgments made with love, what we call humor, it found the manner of consent to all possible being and all possible connection. In puns, which begin with one meaning and end with another, it found the verbal means of rendering those random collisions of phenomena which both do, and do not, make sense. And each of these, perceived, may make us laugh; but their doing so is incidental to another effect which is a delight too deep for laughter, a joy too pervasive for laughter. That effect is a felt affirmation about life which chimes with our intuitive sense of how things are and with our deep human desire to be re-created by seeing true humanness prevail, against the frightening altitudes of aspiration, against the set mechanism of the habitual and conventional, against the threat of corruption and of time.

Part Three

THE CHARACTERISTICS
OF COMEDY

L. C. Knights

NOTES ON COMEDY

Harold H. Watts

THE SENSE OF REGAIN:
A THEORY OF COMEDY

L. J. Potts

THE SUBJECT MATTER OF COMEDY

Arthur Koestler

COMEDY

Notes on Comedy*

L. C. KNIGHTS

I

Labour-saving devices are common in criticism. Like the goods ad-
vertised in women's journals they do the work, or appear to do it,
leaving the mind free for the more narcotic forms of enjoyment. Generalizations and formulae are devices of this kind. It is as easy and
unprofitable to discuss the "essence" of the tragic and the comic
modes as it is to conduct investigations in aesthetics which end with
the discovery of Significant Form.

Comedy has provided a happy hunting-ground for the generalizers.
It is almost impossible to read a particular comedy without the interference of critical presuppositions derived from one or other of those
who have sought to define comedy in the abstract. In the first place,
we all know that comedy makes us laugh. "Tragedy and comedy bear
the same relation to one another as earnestness and mirth. Both these
states of mind bear the stamp of our common nature but earnestness
belongs more to the moral, and mirth to the sensual side. . . . The
essence of the comic is mirth." Put in this form, the error is sufficiently
obvious, but it lurks behind most of our generalizations about the
nature of the comic and the function of comedy. Meredith's hyper-
gelasts are enemies of the comic spirit, but his ideal audience all
laugh, in their polite drawing-room way. "The test of true Comedy,"
he says, "is that it shall awaken thoughtful laughter."

Once an invariable connexion between comedy and laughter is assumed we are not likely to make any observations that will be useful
as criticism. We have only to find the formula that will explain laugh-

* L. C. Knights, "Notes on Comedy," in *The Importance of Scrutiny,* Eric
Bentley, ed. (New York University Press, 1964).

ter and we know the "secret" of Jonson and Rabelais, Chaucer and Fielding, Jane Austen and Joyce. "Men have been wise in very different modes; but they have always laughed the same way." So if we are looking for a simple explanation we can refer to "a sudden glory," "incongruity," "the mechanical encrusted on the living," "tendency wit," or any of the other half-dozen solutions of the problem of laughter, none of which, however, will help us to become better, because more responsive, readers of Molière. There is evidence, on the other hand, that reading capacity is diminished by reliance upon any one of them. But it is time to clear away this particular obstruction. A neglected passage of *Timber* reads: "Nor is the moving of laughter always the end of Comedy. . . . This is truly leaping from the Stage to the Tumbrell again, reducing all wit to the original Dungcart." Comedy is essentially a serious activity.

After this particularly vulgar error the most common is that comedy is a Social Corrective, comic laughter a medicine administered to society to cure its aberrations from the norm of Good Sense. Meredith's celebrated essay, in which this theory is embedded, has been a misfortune for criticism. It has won eminence as a classic without even the merit of containing a sharply defined falsehood. The style is that of an inaugural lecture in a school of *belles-lettres*. The idle pose is betrayed by the key-words—"high fellowship," "the smile finely tempered," "unrivalled politeness," "a citizen of the selecter world"— and the theory emerges obscurely from the affected prose. "The comic poet is in the narrow field, or enclosed square, of the society he depicts"—a commonplace as true of any representational art as it is of comedy—"and he addresses the still narrower enclosure of men's intellects"—the implication is false; there is emotion in Jonson and Molière—"with reference to the operation of the social world upon their characters." With the aid of what has gone before we can make out the meaning. Comedy is "the firstborn of common-sense." "It springs to vindicate reason, common-sense, rightness and justice," and this Sir Galahad of the arts springs to attack whenever men "wax out of proportion, overblown, affected, pretentious, bombastical, hypocritical, pedantic; whenever it sees them self-deceived or hood-winked, given to run riot in idolatries . . . planning shortsightedly, plotting dementedly." There is nothing that can be said of such a theory except that it is of no use whatever in elucidating particular comedies and in forming precise judgments. But it has the ill effect of providing the illusion that we know all this is necessary about a comedy when we know very little. "The Comic Idea enclosed in a comedy makes it more generally perceptible and portable, which is an advantage." Exactly; there is no need to distinguish between the comedy of *Tom Jones* and *The Secret Agent* when we have this Comic Idea to carry around with us.

In Meredith's essay we hear much of "the mind hovering above congregated men and women" and we learn that the author was in love with Millamant, but if we look for particular judgements we find: "the comic of Jonson is a scholar's excogitation of the comic. . . . Shakespeare is a well-spring of characters which are saturated with the comic spirit . . . they are of this world, but they are of the world enlarged to our embrace by imagination, and by great poetic imagination. They are, as it were, . . . creatures of the woods and wilds . . . Jaques, Falstaff and his regiment, the varied troop of Clowns, Malvolio, Sir Hugh Evans and Fluellen—marvellous Welshmen!—Benedick and Beatrice, Dogberry and the rest, are subjects of a special study in the poetically comic." None of which helps us at all in understanding *Volpone* or *Henry IV*. We are not surprised when we find: "O for a breath of Aristophanes, Rabelais, Voltaire, Cervantes, Fielding, Molière!" as though these diverse writers had the same literary problems or solved them in the same way.

Profitless generalizations are more frequent in criticism of comedy than in criticism of other forms of literature. Since we continue to speak of the Comic Spirit after we have ceased to speak of the spirit of tragedy or the essence of the epic, that bogus entity may be held responsible. "It has the sage's brows, and the sunny malice of a faun lurks at the corners of the half-closed lips drawn in an idle wariness of half tension."

Meredith's essay serves as a warning that essays on comedy are necessarily barren exercises. The point is brought home if we consider how profitless it would be to compare one of Blake's *Songs of Experience* with a poem of Hopkins as Manifestations of the Lyric Impulse. As in all criticism the only generalizations which may be useful are those, usually short, based on sensitive experience of literature, containing, as it were, the distilled essence of experience, capable of unfolding their meaning in particular application, and those which suggest how the mind works in certain classes of experience. Of the latter kind one of the most fruitful occurs on page 209 of I. A. Richards's *Principles of Literary Criticism:* "Besides the experiences which result from the building up of connected attitudes, there are those produced by the breaking down of some attitude which is a clog and a bar to other activities." The breaking down of undesirable attitudes is normally part of the total response to a comedy. But to say this is to admit that all the work remains to be done in each particular case. We have to determine exactly how this breaking down is effected, exactly what attitude is broken down, and what takes its place.

Apply Dr. Richards's remark, with the necessary qualifications in each case, to *Volpone* and *Le Misanthrope,* and it is apparent how divergent the effects and methods of comedy may be. Jonson is concerned to create the mood which is the object of contemplation. He works by selection, distortion, and concentration so that the attitude created by the interaction of Volpone, Corvino, Corbaccio, and the rest finally, as it were, blows itself up by internal pressure. The method is cumulative.

> Good morning to the day; and next, my gold!
> Open the shrine, that I may see my saint.
> Hail the world's soul, and mine!

The exaggeration reaches a climax in the attempted seduction of Celia:

> See here, a rope of pearl; and each more orient
> Than the brave Aegyptian queen caroused:
> Dissolve and drink them. See, a carbuncle,
> May put out both the eyes of our St. Mark;
> A diamond would have bought Lollia Paulina,
> When she came in like star-light, hid with jewels.

The world thus created, already undermined by the obscene songs and antics of the Dwarf, the Eunuch, and the Hermaphrodite, is demolished by the plots and counterplots of the final scenes. But the catastrophe is not mechanical: it represents on the plane of action the dissolution that is inherent in the swelling speeches of Volpone and Mosca:

> I fear I shall begin to grow in love
> With my dear self, and my most prosperous parts,
> They do so spring and burgeon; I can feel
> A whimsy in my blood: I know not how,
> Success hath made me wanton.

In *Volpone* the cathartic effect is relevant solely to the conditions of the play. Molière, on the other hand, is more directly satiric, drawing more directly upon the actual world for the attitudes which he refines and demolishes. The play is a pattern of varied satiric effects. How it works may be best discovered by comparing it with a direct satire such as the *Epistle to Arbuthnot*. The pitch and tempo of Pope's poem vary, but the tone is fairly consistent. In *Le Misanthrope,* on the other hand, the tone varies not only from character to character, but also within the limits of a single speech, of a few lines; and the speed with which the point of view shifts and the tone changes sets free the activity which breaks down the impeding attitudes. This is to confine our attention merely to one aspect of the play, but no criticism can be relevant which does not consider the peculiar mental agility required to follow the changes of this kind. Unlike *Volpone* the effects are repetitive (in kind, they are obviously not all the same) and a close examination of the tone and intention of each line in the first scene is the best way of discovering how the play as a whole should be read. Even to discover the points at which the author might be identified with the speaker is instructive.

It is obvious that the Social Corrective theory not only precludes discussion of a comedy in terms of the effects we have described, but prevents those who accept it from even realizing that such discussion is possible. Its inadequacy should be no less plain even if we admit, for the moment, that the function of comedy is "critical." Malvolio, Sir Tunbelly Clumsy, Squire Western, may be considered simply as failures judged by some social norm, but in many comedies the "criticism" is directed not only at the man who fails to live up to standard but also at the standard by which his failure is judged. In Shirley's *Love in a Maze* Sir Gervase Simple, reproached that he is dumb in the presence of his mistress, replies, "I cannot help it: I was a gentleman, thou knowest, but t'other day. I have yet but a few compliments: within a while I shall get more impudence, and then have at her." Here the object of criticism is not only the simpleton who has no court manners, but also the courtiers, acquaintance with whom he hopes will fill him with unmannerly boldness. The method of two-edged satire is of particular importance in a consideration of literature in relation to the social environment. Chapman's *The Widow's Tears* may serve as an example. Part of the play is concerned with a wife who, after expressing her horror of second marriages, yields to the first stranger who makes love to her on the, supposed, death of her husband, the stranger being her husband in disguise. The critics have seen here a satire on the frailty of woman, speaking of the "almost brutal cynicism" of the play. But the satire is directed not only at such frailty but at the contemporary attitude towards widowhood. "He that hath her," said Overbury of a remarried widow, "is but lord of a filthy purchase," and a minor moralist writes with approval of widows who have lived alone as they ought: "Their rooms bore the habit of mourning; funeral lamps were ever burning; no musical strain to delight the ear, no object of state to surprise the eye. True sorrow had there his mansion; nor could they affect any

other discourse than what to their husbands' actions held most relation." The effect of the play is to cast doubts on the reasonableness
of such an attitude. The speech in praise of the horn at the end of
All Fools may be considered in relation to seventeenth-century marriage customs and cuckoldry. But the method is relevant when we
are discussing plays, etc., as social documents rather than as literature independent of temporary conditions for their effect.

"Social Satire" is too vague and general to be of any use for the
purpose of criticism. It needs to be defined in each instance in terms
of the mental processes involved. The greatness of any comedy can only
be determined by the inclusiveness, the coherence and stability of the
resultant attitude; to define its method is the work of detailed and
particular analysis, and abstract theories of comedy can at best only
amuse. An examination of *Henry IV* will help to make this plain.

II

Henry IV does not fit easily into any of the critical schemata,
though "incongruity" has served the critics in good stead. But, at any
rate, since the time of Morgann, Falstaff has received a degree of
sympathetic attention (how we love the fat rascal!) that distorts
Shakespeare's intention in writing the two plays. We regard them as a
sandwich—so much dry bread to be bitten through before we come to
the meaty Falstaff, although we try to believe that "the heroic and
serious part is not inferior to the comic and farcical." Actually each
play is a unity, sub-plot and main plot co-operating to express the
vision which is projected into the form of the play. And this vision,
like that of all the great writers of comedy, is pre-eminently serious. It
is symptomatic that Hazlitt, defending Shakespeare's tragedies against
the comedies, said, "He was greatest in what was greatest; and his
forte was not trifling."

The first speech of the King deserves careful attention. The brittle
verse suggests the precarious poise of the usurper:

> So shaken as we are, so wan with care,
> Find we a time for frighted peace to pant,
> And breathe short-winded accents of new broils
> To be commenced in stronds afar remote.

The violence of the negative which follows suggests its opposite:

> No more the thirsty entrance of this soil
> Shall daub her lips with her own children's blood:
> No more shall trenching war channel her fields,
> Nor bruise her flowerets with the armed hoofs
> Of hostile paces.

"Thirsty" contains the implication that the earth is eager for more blood; and when the prophecy of peace ends with the lisping line, "Shall now, in mutual well-beseeming ranks," we do not need a previous knowledge of the plot or of history to realize that Henry is actually describing what is to come. The account of the proposed crusade is satiric:

> But this our purpose is a twelvemonth old, . . .
> Therefore we meet not now.

Throughout we are never allowed to forget that Henry is a usurper. We are given four separate accounts of how he gained the throne— by Hotspur again (I, III, 160–186), by Henry himself (III, II, 39–84), by Hotspur again (IV, III, 52–92), and by Worcester (V, I, 32–71). He gained it by "murd'rous subornation," by hypocrisy, his "seeming brow of justice," by "violation of all faith and troth." Words expressing underhand dealing occur even in the King's account to his son:

> And then I stole all courtesy from Heaven,
> And dress'd myself in such humility
> That I did pluck allegiance from men's hearts.

There is irony in the couplet that concludes the play:

> And since this business *so fair* is done,
> Let us not leave till all *our own* be won.

The rebels, of course, are no better. The hilarious scene in which the plot is hatched (I, III, 187–302) does not engage much sympathy for the plotters, who later squabble over the expected booty like any long-staff sixpenny strikers. Their cause does not bear prying into by "the eye of reason" (IV, I, 69–72), and Worcester, for his own purposes, conceals "the liberal kind offer of the King" (V, II, 1–25). But this is relatively unimportant; there is no need to take sides and "like Hotspur somewhat better than the Prince because he is unfortunate." The satire is general, directed against statecraft and warfare. Hotspur is the chief representative of chivalry, and we have only to read his speeches to understand Shakespeare's attitude towards "honour"; there is no need to turn to Falstaff's famous soliloquy. The description of the Mortimer-Glendower fight has just that degree of exaggeration which is necessary for not-too-obvious burlesque, though, oddly enough, it has been used to show that Hotspur "has the imagination of a poet." But if the image of the Severn—

> Who then, affrighted with their bloody looks,
> Ran fearfully among the trembling reeds,
> And hid his crisp head in the hollow bank—

is not sufficient indication, the rhyme announces the burlesque intention:

> He did confound the best part of an hour
> In changing hardiment with great Glendower.

There is the same exaggeration in later speeches of Worcester and Hotspur; Hotspur's "huffing part"—"by Heaven methinks it were an easy leap"—did not need Beaumont's satire. In the battle scene the heroics of "Now, Esperance! Percy! and set on," the chivalric embrace and flourish of trumpets are immediately followed by the exposure of a military dodge for the preservation of the King's life. "The King hath many marching in his coats."—"Another King! They grow like Hydra's heads."

The reverberations of the sub-plot also help to determine our attitude towards the main action. The conspiracy of the Percys is sandwiched between the preparation for the Gadshill plot and counterplot and its execution. Poins has "lost much honour" that he did not see the "action" of the Prince with the drawers. When we see the court we remember Falstaff's joint-stool throne and his account of Henry's hanging lip. Hotspur's pride in himself and his associates ("Is there not my father, my uncle and myself?") is parodied by Gadshill: "I am joined with no foot land-rakers, no long-staff sixpenny strikers . . . but with nobility and tranquility, burgomasters and great oneyers." The nobles, like the roarers, prey on the commonwealth, "for they ride up and down on her and make her their boots."

The Falstaff attitude is therefore in solution, as it were, throughout the play, even when he is not on the stage; but it takes explicit form in the person and speeches of Sir John. We see a heroic legend in process of growth in the account of his fight with the men in buckram. The satire in the description of his ragged regiment is pointed by a special emphasis on military terms—"soldiers," "captain," "lieutenant," "ancients, corporals . . . gentlemen of companies." His realism easily reduces honour to "a mere scutcheon." Prince Henry's duel with Hotspur is accompanied by the mockery of the Douglas-Falstaff fight, which ends with the dead and the counterfeit dead lying side by side. If we can rid ourselves of our realistic illusions and their accompanying moral qualms we realize how appropriate it is that Falstaff should rise to stab Hotspur's body and carry him off as his luggage on his back.

The satire on warfare, the Falstaff attitude, implies an axis of reference, which is of course found in the gross and vigorous life of the body. We find throughout the play a peculiar insistence on imagery deriving from the body, on descriptions of death in its more gruesome forms, on stabbing, cutting, bruising, and the like. We expect to find references to blood and death in a play dealing with civil war, but such references in *Henry IV* are far more pervasive than in a war play such as *Henry V*. In the first scene we hear of the earth "daubing her lips with her own children's blood." War is "trenching"; it "channels" the fields and "bruises" the flowers. "The edge of war" is "like an ill-sheathed knife" which "cuts his master." Civil war is an "intestinal shock," and battles are "butchery." We learn that the defeated Scots lay "balk'd in their own blood," and that "beastly shameless transformation" was done by the Welsh upon the corpses of Mortimer's soldiers. Later Hotspur mentions the smell of "a slovenly unhandsome corpse," and we hear of Mortimer's "mouthed wounds." So throughout the play. The dead Blunt lies "grinning, Hotspur's face is "mangled," and Falstaff lies by him "in blood." Falstaff's "honour" soliloquy insists on surgery, on broken legs and arms.

To all this Falstaff, a walking symbol, is of course opposed. "To shed my dear blood drop by drop i' the dust" for the sake of honour appears an imbecile ambition. Falstaff will "fight no longer than he sees reason." His philosophy is summed up when he has escaped Douglas by counterfeiting death: "S'blood! 'twas time to counterfeit, or that hot termagant Scot had paid me scot and lot too. Counterfeit? I lie, I am no counterfeit: to die is to be a counterfeit; for he is but the counterfeit of a man who hath not the life of a man; but to counterfeit dying, when a man thereby liveth, is to be no counterfeit, but the true and perfect image of life indeed." The same thought is implicit in the honour soliloquy.

Once the play is read as a whole, the satire on war and policy is apparent. It is useful to compare the first part of *Henry IV* with *King John* in estimating the development of Shakespeare's dramatic power. *King John* turns on a single pivotal point—the Bastard's speech on commodity, but the whole of the later play is impregnated with satire which crystalizes in Falstaff. Now, satire implies a standard, and in *Henry IV* the validity of the standard itself is questioned; hence the peculiar coherence and universality of the play. "Honour" and "statecraft" are set in opposition to the natural life of the body, but the chief body of the play is, explicitly, "a bolting-hutch of beastliness."— "A pox on this gout! or a gout on this pox, I should say." Other speeches reinforce the age-and-disease theme which, it has not been observed, is a significant part of the Falstaff theme. Hotspur pictures the earth as an "old beldam"

> pinch'd and vex'd
> By the imprisoning of unruly wind
> Within her womb.

Again, he says:

> The time of life is short;
> To spend that shortness basely were too long,
> If life did ride upon a dial's point,
> Still ending at the arrival of an hour.

The last two lines imply that no "if" is necessary; life does "ride upon a dial's point," and Hotspur's final speech takes up the theme of transitoriness:

> But thought's the slave of life, and life time's fool:
> And time, that takes survey of all the world,
> Must have a stop.

There is no need to emphasize the disease aspect of Falstaff (Bardolph's bad liver is not merely funny). He "owes God a death." He and his regiment are "mortal men." It is important to realize, however, that when Falstaff feigns death he is meant to appear actually as dead in the eyes of the audience; at least the idea of death is meant to be emphasized in connexion with the Falstaff-idea at this point. No answer is required to the Prince's rhetorical question,

> What! old acquaintance! could not all this flesh
> Keep in a little life? Poor Jack, farewell!

The stability of our attitude after a successful reading of the first part of *Henry IV* is due to the fact that the breaking-down process referred to above is not simple but complex; one set of impulses is released for the expression of the Falstaff-outlook; but a set of opposite complementary impulses is also brought into play, producing an effect analogous to that caused by the presence of comedy in *King Lear* [1] (compare the use of irony in *Madame Bovary*). *Lear* is secure against ironical assault because of the irony it contains; *Henry IV* will bear the most serious ethical scrutiny because in it the "serious" is a fundamental part of the "comic" effect of the play. (The second part of *Henry IV* is no less interesting. No one has yet pointed out that drunkenness, lechery, and senile depravity [in II, iv, for example] are *not* treated by Shakespeare with "good-natured tolerance." Shakespeare's attitude toward his characters in 2 *Henry IV* at times approaches the attitude of Mr. Eliot towards Doris, Wauchope, etc., in *Sweeney Agonistes*. Northumberland's monody on death [I, i] needs to be studied in order to understand the tone of the play.)

This summary treatment of a play which demands further elucida-

---

[1] See the admirable essay on "Lear and the Comedy of the Grotesque" in *The Wheel of Fire*, by G. Wilson Knight.

tion on the lines suggested is, I think, sufficient to illustrate the main points of the notes on comedy which precede it. No theory of comedy can explain the play; no theory of comedy will help us to read it more adequately. Only a morbid pedantry would be blind to the function of laughter in comedy, but concentration upon laughter leads to a double error: the dilettante critic falls before the hallucination of the Comic Spirit, the more scientifically minded persuade themselves that the jokes collected by Bergson and Freud have something to do with the practice of literary criticism.

The Sense of Regain:
A Theory of Comedy*

HAROLD H. WATTS

Aristotle is silent. Discussions of the nature of comedy lack the peak
which dominates all journeys exploring the nature of tragedy. Such
journeys can be measured by the distance which lies between them
and the sacred mountain; speculations about comedy cannot be. An
effort to trace the psychological effects of comedy is—one may as well
confess—chiefly a product of one age. When one writes about comedy—indeed, when one *writes* comedy—he should know that he can
no more than touch or assess current risibilities. The comic dramatist,
at least, does not dream of making bold claims for his work. The
teller of the *grants douleurs* of Tristan and Iseut might boast that
their grief speaks to unknown times. Indeed, modesty may not be
one of the chief virtues; and it is certainly not the virtue of the
tragic poet. But modesty of a particular kind dominates the mind of
a man who writes comedy, and this even though his play be as gross
and immodest as the symbol of Priapus.

II

A sort of modesty, then, is the *vade mecum* of the comic playwright.
He may or may not be aware of its presence; but so long as he
writes comedy, it guides him. It does not hold him from bold judgment of the vices and follies of his time; it lets him speak boldly in
the forum. But it keeps him in the forum; that is the clue to this
sort of modesty. The comic writer may not leave the market-place; to

---

* Harold H. Watts, "The Sense of Regain: A Theory of Comedy," *University of Kansas City Review,* Vol. xiii, No. 1 (Autumn, 1946), pp. 19–23.

ascend the hill, to address Capitoline Jove in eternal accents is not
not permitted him. His modesty constrains him from making assertions
that the tragic poet *must* make if, indeed, he is to be a tragic poet.
The tragic poet supposes that he sees truly and profoundly as concerns the will of the gods, human greatness and vileness, and the ties
that link man with man. The tragic poet reports little or nothing of
how people dress and amuse themselves, how they make their living,
and how they consult one soothsayer after another. Not his concern
is man's stubborn refusal to understand his fellows—and, for that
matter, his even more stubborn timidity which keeps him from pushing
to bloody extremes the results of his misunderstanding. These things
lie in the province of the comic writer.

Again, as the tragic writer tells of the love of Tristan and Iseut, he
should (we feel) keep at a minimum his accounts of tapestries and
table-manners. This same feeling is at work in the production we
give to an old tragic drama. We suppress antiquarian clutter; we aim
at a style of acting that is simple and eternal. All this indicates our
belief that enjoyment of great tragedy ought to be natural and immediate—and that, if we do not, the fault is ours and not the tragic
poet's. It is some imperfection of our own that holds us back from
the complete identification that the dead poet confidently expected.

It is true that we may also fail to come to grips with the comedy
of another age, Goldoni's or Marivaux's or Sheridan's. But here we
do not feel ashamed. Why *this* failure does not trouble us, we perhaps
may not formulate; but we admit our incapacity cheerfully. Scrutiny
suggests that the "fault" lies in the very nature of comedy itself. It
is a by-product of that modesty which kept the comic writer strolling
in the public square and which forbade him to have traffic with
holy places, be they temples or churches, synagogues or chapels. Usually, we are content to say that an old comedy is too quaint; it is
our right to be ignorant of the sedan-chairs and the pomades of
another time. But perhaps we do not see that these objects, which
once cluttered the foreground of men's minds, are a sign-manual, the
expression of the particular modesty which pervades all comedy. This
modesty is likely to inhibit profound insight; it certainly encourages
reportage.

This barrier of facts observed at a particular moment in a particular
street or chamber bars the way to the reader of an old comedy.
Sometimes it will seem that the old play is *all* reportage and our
reading of it bootless. This we distinctly feel in reading certain comic
scenes of Shakespeare, even though we have realized that comedy, of
its very nature, permits scenes that are no more than a tissue of re-

portage. In fact, the opposite is non-existent: comic scenes devoid of reportage. For we cannot imagine Maria and Sir Toby Belch and Malvolio sitting at any other board than one of Jacobean oak; we cannot fancy Lady Teazle hiding behind a screen covered with anything else than scenic paper. In short, to enjoy old comedy, we must in the first place cultivate antiquarian enthusiasm: the sort of emotion that impels us to exclaim with amusement, when we are at a museum, "Did they actually ride in such carriages!"

Only this acquired taste will get us over the initial barricade thrown up by the modesty of the old comic writer. Even if he had had foresight, he could not have freed himself of these imperfections, this excess of reporting. Had he tried, he would have moved away from the public area; he would have ceased to write comedy.

From this, it is plain that the only comedy for which we can have spontaneous enthusiasm is the comedy of our own day. Comedy never intends to speak across the years; it is a dramatic representation addressed to *us*. We frequent certain places of business and amusement, we read certain books, and (unlike our forbears) we pronounce *tea* to rhyme with *bee*. A comedy must be written in a certain year of grace; as Maugham has observed, it cannot hope to have a natural, easy existence for more than ten or twenty years.

These observed circumstances point to the psychological values of comedy, which are in sharp contrast to the better known ones of tragedy. Further, the truth of any assertion one makes about comedy can be verified only in the comedy of our own period, of our own market-place. Other comedy can offer but halting evidence. We can *suspect* that comedy had, in another age, certain psychological functions; we cannot declare.

III

Comedy of our own day—comedy which does not demand spade-work, comedy to which we can give a response naive and true—gives us two immediate pleasures: (1) that of recognition; and (2) that of applying a limited scale of human truth. These separate pleasures are found together; they produce, almost, a single effect—they call forth what one may call a sense of regain. What this sense is we cannot justly state until we study in isolation each pleasure that stimulates it.

Recognition is the pleasure given us by certain objects and ideas which we find in the comedy of our own period. They are the very ideas and objects which will challenge the antiquary and discourage the student of time to come. But their griefs do not concern us. We only feel (rather than know) that, in today's comedy, the characters must lead the kind of lives we lead, or at least the kind of lives led by certain of our acquaintance. The characters must follow a modern schedule of living, depending on the appliances and catch-words we depend on. They must make their living—and their often silly economies—as we make ours. They must be guilty of the same false emphasis that our neighbors make today and that we (alas, for our folly!) made yesterday. We go to the theatre determined to encounter the mental and material bric-a-brac of our stretch of time.

From this it should be plain—the list of items asserts it—that this process of recognition is not the same as the process of identification (complete or partial) which tragedy demands. If we "recognize" with anything but calm or lively pleasure, the dramatist has ceased to be comic, has stepped into the shadow of a nearby temple. For recognition is always made with a crucial reservation: Here is something that is a part of my experience, *but not an immediate part*. Even when we recognize ourselves in a comedy, it is ourselves as we were some years since, not as we now are. (Tragedy, of course, directs our gaze to our present moral nature.) Thus, a collection of peccadilloes that *were* ours moves us no more deeply than the sight of our faces in an old picture or the sound of our voices on a recording machine. Even as we acknowledge the likeness, we privately repudiate it: the real, essential ego has escaped the comic arrow. The egos that do not escape really rough handling (hence our delight) are those of our dear friends and relatives. Their folly we have always suspected, and now the dramatist has put it in a revealing light. That the dramatist's models do not see what has happened to them adds the final, ironical spice to the act of recognition.

IV

In actuality, this pleasure intertwines with the other delight which a comic dramatist gives: that of exercising an extremely limited scale of values, of saying glibly, "How true to human nature!" This pleasure, admittedly, still lurks for us, behind the reportage of old comedies. But it exists immediate and delicious in a comedy of our own age. Our reaction is so "natural," so keen in our joy at having certain of our values affirmed, that we are blind as to what has really taken place. In the first place, the dramatist has, by surprise and contrast, forced the "natural" exclamation from us; further, his ingenuity conceals from us that no comedy is true to human nature as we seriously know it. It is true to human nature only as we (with the dramatist for cicerone) know it from our walks in public places. It has nothing to say of that nature when it is really most human; that is, private, retired, tragic. It is the trick of comedy to confirm all our superficial judgments; it must make us ignore those which we regard as profound and eternal.

Our superficial judgments, we see when we inspect them—a scrutiny the comic dramatist discourages—are those which we hold in common with our fellows, with those who are of like background and education. In the sixteenth century, it was a belief in the humors and their power to shape folly. In the eighteenth century, it was belief in good sense and its power to avert folly. We of the twentieth share, perhaps, a belief in complete relativity and its power maliciously to illuminate all firm adherences, whether to outworn traditions or to new dogma. Such held beliefs enable us to live at peace with our neighbors and, quite often, in ignorance of what we as individuals are. When we participate in comedy, we are spared asking how much we decline from, how much we overshoot the normal beliefs of our age. Comedy fully enjoyed reiterates that these beliefs are the only ones worth pursuing; comedy indicates deftly the folly of men who ponder a measure of vice and virtue different from the pat discriminations which stabilize affairs of state, of the counting-house, and (even) of the heart. Malvolio may be own cousin to Hamlet, but since he figures in a comedy, we join Maria and Sir Toby in reassuring laughter.[1] Likewise, we are glad to see that Lydia Languish decides that the nameless stirrings in her breast are indeed vapors. And we are grateful to a playwright like Mr. Maugham who assures us that efforts to discover and comply with laws of behavior are no more than "stuffy"; for we have moments when we suspect that all life is not just a flux, jolly and formless.

Tragedy, more or less great, does the opposite of confirming us in a conventional set of values. It gives us Hamlet for Malvolio, a Chekhov woman for Lydia Languish, and—or so Mr. O'Neill supposes—Nina Leeds for a Maugham heroine. And these are gifts that the human spirit can only at its peril reject, since all of them—well or less well—point to that within us which rejects the values that have forum-currency. Tragic figures affect us entirely otherwise than do comic. They stir us to thought which is inconvenient in the marketplace (and in the comedy) of any age. The true relation of man to the gods (or God), the duty of man to himself, the validity of all concepts of good and evil—these are the stuff of tragedy, and they are the stuff of that life of our own which is secret and often—thanks to comedy and our participation in it—most ignored. We are

---

[1] This after *reportage* is penetrated, to be sure.

content to recognize, we are glad to cry a facile *Hail* to truth of a sort. We are eager to find an abiding place in the type of universe the comic dramatist provides for us. It is a universe compact of familiar objects and painless ideas. To reside there is to be cradled, to forego mental and spiritual growth in favor of a lively jounce.

V

But too often we, like the greatest comic dramatists, slip unwillingly into tragedy. With them and with the professedly tragic writers, we wander toward the sacred hill which rises above trade and gaiety. Yet, since we are quite limited beings—not tragic poets—we must retreat from the precipices where one stands to talk to the gods. It is the comic writer who shows us how to retreat, who recalls us "to ourselves," as the saying goes. To our relief, he offers us recognition and a commonplace set of values. He provides a mediocre kind of sanity in place of the destructive truth which tragedy and the secret parts of our own nature contain. He stirs in us, for evil or for good, a sense of regain. The familiar objects reproduced, the current platitudes buttressed—it is these that give us a sense of regaining what the more cowardly part of our natures had feared might be gone forever. It is, to be accurate, a repossession of objects that some part of our being should say farewell to without a sigh.

But few of us are ready to say farewell without a sigh. We do not desire to turn to a deep, consistently tragic view of man's life. When this view threatens to dominate our minds, then do we welcome the power of comedy to stir in us a sense of return, of a restored "sense of balance." We are willing to overlook the fact that balancing involves cancellation. We do not care what we strike out; simply we pant to walk in the public place again, to be repatriated in the world of mediocrity from which tragedy and our own self-knowledge have drawn us away.

In tragedy (and in religion) we come to see man's character as it is. In the facile and compromising world of comedy we learn how to be content with man's nature as it seems to be. One must note that the person who wills to live in no other world has confessed that for him no other attitude is possible. Perhaps, however, there persist in him impulses maimed and unfruitful. One need not be an enemy of comedy to observe that for such a lack the brightness and unimplemented scepticism of modern comedy is no anodyne.

The Subject Matter of Comedy*

L. J. POTTS

I

. I began this book by saying that comedy depends on the eye of the beholder, not on the character of the object he has in view; that nothing in nature is categorically comic—whether it is so or not depends on what you make of it. It would seem to follow that anything or everything is suitable subject matter for comedy. From a strictly philosophical point of view, that is so. But comedy is a tradition as well as an idea; and to the writer and reader of comedy the selection of subject matter and setting is as important as abstract notions about art, if not more so. Of course, in making his selection, the writer will be influenced consciously or unconsciously by the ideal character of his art, or at least by his opinions about it.

He is trying to present a social point of view; to measure human conduct against a norm rather than an ideal. He is, or should be, actuated always by a sense of proportion. What he depicts—his subject matter—may therefore be defined as the abnormal. He may include some normal characters in his work, to serve as a kind of yard-stick; but for the most part he will leave his public to deduce his norm from the way he depicts the clash and contrast of varied abnormalities. In any case, far the greater part of his matter must inevitably be abnormal.

This indicates another difference between tragedy and comedy. It has been argued convincingly that the characters and even the events in a tragedy must be normal if we are to feel the full tragic effect. But can the character and behaviour of Macbeth, for example, be called normal? A clear distinction must be drawn between the *normal*

---

* L. J. Potts, "The Subject Matter of Comedy," in *Comedy* (Hutchinson's University Library, London, 1950), pp. 45–63.

and the *usual*. Tragedy of course deals with unusual situations and
consequently with unusual states of mind; but we should always feel
that the situation is one in which we might have been placed, and
that in similar circumstances we should, or at least very probably
might, have felt as the characters of the tragedy do. We should be
able to identify ourselves with them for the time being. The problem
for the tragic writer is to bridge the gap between the terrible and
the normal: to show us, for example, a murderer like Macbeth or a
madman like Lear, who yet retain the deepest and sanest human
feelings. He does this, not by stressing normality, but by making us
feel it as an undertone in the situation: by speeches like Macbeth's

> If thou couldst, doctor, cast
> The water of my land, find her disease,
> And purge it to a sound and pristine health,
> I would applaud thee to the very echo,
> That should applaud again;

or Lear's

> Poor naked wretches, wheresoe'er you are
> That bide the pelting of this pitiless storm,
> How shall your houseless heads and unfed sides,
> Your loop'd and window'd raggedness, defend you
> From seasons such as these?

It may be said that whereas tragedy deals with the unusual but
normal, comedy deals with the abnormal but not unusual. The abnormality of comic characters is not absolute; we should feel that
they are capable of behaving normally if they would. But it is the
main concern of the comic writer to discriminate between what is
normal and abnormal in human behaviour; he is detached from his
subject matter in a sense in which other artists are not. He needs
not merely a strong feeling for normality, but also a clear notion of
it. It is therefore necessary for him to be in some measure a moral
philosopher; for the norm is a philosophical concept. The usual, or
average, is not; it can be calculated statistically from observed facts.
But normality, like the cognate concepts of health and sanity, is not
a fact, nor a complex of facts, nor even a simplification of facts; it
is an idea, and exists only in the mind that has brought itself to
bear on all the relevant facts. There is not one norm of human
behaviour, but many: some of them widely divergent and even contradictory. Jane Austen's norm differs drastically in some respects
from Chaucer's or Fielding's. But all comic writers must have a norm
in view. To detect eccentricity you must have a centre: that is to

say a consistent, if not consciously worked out, standard of character and conduct.

From these considerations it might be deduced that the world of comedy would be a realistically depicted world peopled by eccentric characters. This formula fits some comic writers: Fielding and Jane Austen in particular. It was also the formula laid down by Ben Jonson and in the main followed by him. But as a general definition it is too narrow, and also radically misleading. Meredith puts his finger on the error contained in it, in the passage I have quoted on page 16: comedy *may be taken for* a slavish reflex of real life, *until its features are closely studied.* There is always an element of caricature in comedy, the caricature being so designed as to stress the eccentricity of the individual. Everyone, however nearly normal, has his foibles, however slight. But this, perhaps, is obvious.

A more serious objection to this formula is that comedy is not necessarily at all realistic in technique. None of Shakespeare's comedies are: even *Measure for Measure,* which is often classed as a realistic play, is strange and remote—suffused in "the light that never was on sea or land". The Fable (as used by Aesop, for example) is one of the earliest and most efficient vehicles for comedy, and it is quite unrealistic. Even allegory, which is more unrealistic still, adapts itself well and easily to comic purposes: the vice in the late medieval morality plays was a comic figure, and probably the literary ancestor of Shakespeare's Falstaff. Even in so tedious an allegory as the *Roman de la Rose* the character of Fals-Semblant is fully developed comedy; it provided Chaucer with the outline of the character of his Pardoner. Chaucer himself took his first exercises in comedy in *The House of Fame* and *The Parliament of Fowls* (an allegory and a fable). I have already called attention to the technique of the Bottom-Titania scene in *A Midsummer Night's Dream,* which is unrealistic and close to allegory. The best plays of the first great European comic writer, Aristophanes, are all fantasies, although the central character in an Aristophanic comedy is usually a realistically conceived middle-aged and middle-class Athenian citizen. There is a similar blend of realism and fantasy in the greatest of all European comedies, *Don Quixote;* and there is comedy, both realistic and unrealistic, in Bunyan's *Pilgrim's Progress,* the general structure of which is allegorical.

Even this cursory survey shows that comedy demands the utmost latitude in its choice of setting and in the form of its subject matter; and that its bias is away from rather than towards, a close imitation, or as Meredith puts it, a slavish reflexion, of real life.

II

In the prologue to *Every Man in his Humour,* Ben Jonson professed to "sport with human follies, not with crimes"; and perhaps there is little more to be said about the subject matter of comedy. According to the gentler Congreve, natural folly (being incurable) is not a fit subject for comedy; it is unseemly to mock at it; he therefore took affectation for the theme of his masterpiece, *The Way of the World.* This seems on the whole to have been Shakespeare's practice also. It is a more attractive, and perhaps profounder, notion than Jonson's (though, by the way, affectation was one of the main follies Jonson ridiculed). But Congreve's scruples limit comedy rather too drastically. Even in *The Way of the World* one has to strain the definition of affectation to the utmost if it is to cover the criminal folly of Mrs Marwood and the criminal cunning of Fainall; though if duplicity may be regarded as a crude form of affectation the formula will work. There are advantages in Jonson's wider formula. He himself certainly did not regard folly as either natural or incurable. And if the stress is laid on folly, rather than wickedness on the one hand or misfortune on the other, it follows that the comic situation is involuntary but avoidable, whereas the tragic hero deliberately (if blindly) presses on to an inevitable doom. This is very generally true.

But Jonson's formula does not tell us very much. For one thing, folly can be tragic without being actually criminal, as in Lear, and perhaps also some of Shakespeare's other heroes. Further, both Jonson and Congreve seem to assume that comic situations arise solely from flaws in character. This is not so. They can arise between quite healthy people (like Higgins and Eliza in *Pygmalion*) as the result of natural or accidental misunderstanding; though unless they are to be merely farcical, character must play a part in them. The situation need not be caused by character, but it must reveal character. Perhaps the subject matter of comedy might be defined as "curable or manageable faults or maladjustments". The disturbances with which comedy deals are not always curable; but if they cannot be cured, then their ill-effects are strictly circumscribed; they do not ultimately cause widespread damage to the society in which they occur, and when they are finally isolated in the lives of one or two people, they do not prevent even those people from finding a *modus vivendi.* The situation in Molière's *Misanthrope* is of that kind. On the other hand, where the disturbance leads to or results from the widespread maladjustments of a whole group of people, it must be such as to work itself out to a cure. That would describe the situation in *Tom Jones.*

Is comedy then essentially trivial? In one sense, yes.

> "Great things are done when men and mountains meet;
> This is not done by jostling in the street".

These two lines of Blake's are good symbols for tragedy and comedy. But what happens as we jostle against each other in our homes and businesses and villages and towns is perhaps by accumulation more important than the "great things" in determining human happiness and unhappiness, and even in determining the way of the world.

It is not therefore surprising that easily the favourite topic of comedy is sex. In no other department of life is there more "jostling". And nowhere else can we *all* be said to be eccentric; but here we can. All women appear abnormal to all men, and all men to all women; and rightly, for sex carries with it specialisation and so a departure from the *common* human pattern. This departure is accentuated in civilised life. There is a wide gap between the impulses that precede and accompany human mating, and the codes of manners and sentiment between men and women that prevail from time to time. Such widely different works as Chaucer's *Troilus and Criseyde,* Fielding's *Tom Jones,* and Mr. Shaw's *Candida,* all make comedy out of the clash between sentiment and behaviour, the ideal and the real. It is this inconsistency in almost all civilisations and almost all people that makes the comic writers choose sex for one of their main themes, and also makes comedy the best, perhaps the only really humane, attitude to sex. For comedy denies neither the romance and delicacy that has in some odd way become a second nature in civilised men and women, nor the primitive chase, enticement, conquest, and yielding that we share with other animals.

And lastly the mere fact that no other human relationship is so natural as this one; that the survival of the race depends on it; and that it is the commonest disturbing influence to which human nature and social life are subject—this ensures that it should be the most persistent theme of comedy.

And so, in fact, it is: in Chaucer and Shakespeare, in Restoration Comedy, in Fielding and Sterne, Sheridan and Goldsmith, Jane Austen and Mr. Bernard Shaw.

But, alas, comedy has given the most widespread and bitter offence by its attitude to sex. It seems that whatever the comic writer does some one will complain loudly. Jane Austen writes within the strictest bounds of propriety; so she is charged with prudishness. She has her "centre" from which to judge what is or is not socially normal; and from it she utterly condemns all licence between men and women.

Moreover, as an artist, she "quits such odious subjects as soon as she can". I do not think that even the fanatics of literary criticism insist that she ought to *approve* of licentiousness; but they do complain that she leaves the unruly workings of passion out of her books. It may be replied to this complaint that she is under no obligation to depict erotic passion; but that if it could be proved that she ignores it or pretends that it does not exist, she might be charged with prudishness. It cannot be proved; and the contrary can be proved. It is the impact of Lydia's seduction on *Pride and Prejudice* that shocks the characters of the story out of their unreally trivial life. In *Mansfield Park* loose conduct is analysed (though not depicted) in some detail in the characters of Henry and Mary Crawford, who are condemned not for the strength of their passions, but for shallowness and lack of sensibility. The main theme of *Persuasion* is the danger of allowing one's feelings to be swayed overmuch by prudence and the worldly advice of one's seniors. And let those who think that Jane Austen handles sex timidly, read this passage from *Sanditon:*

Sir Edward's great object in life was to be seductive. With such personal advantages as he knew himself to possess, and such talents as he did also give himself credit for, he regarded it as his duty. He felt that he was formed to be a dangerous man—quite in the line of the Lovelaces. The very name of Sir Edward, he thought, carried some degree of fascination with it. To be generally gallant and assiduous about the fair, to make fine speeches to every pretty girl, was but the inferior part of the character he had to play. Miss Heywood, or any other young woman with any pretensions to beauty, he was entitled (according to his own views of Society) to approach with high compliment and rhapsody on the slightest acquaintance; but it was Clara alone on whom he had serious designs; it was Clara whom he meant to seduce. Her seduction was quite determined on. Her situation in every way called for it. She was his rival in Lady Denham's favour, she was young, lovely and dependent. He had very early seen the necessity of the case, and had now been long trying with cautious assiduity, to make an impression on her heart, and to undermine her principles. Clara saw through him, and had not the least intention of being seduced; but she bore with him patiently enough to confirm the sort of attachment which her personal charms had raised. A greater degree of discouragement, indeed, would not have affected Sir Edward. He was armed against the highest pitch of disdain or aversion. If she could not be won by affection, he must carry her off. He knew his business. Already had he had many musings on the subject. If he *were* constrained so to act, he must naturally wish to strike out something new, to exceed those who had gone before him; and he felt a strong curiosity to ascertain whether the neighbourhood of Tombuctoo might not afford some solitary house adapted for Clara's reception; but the expense, alas! of measures in that masterly style was ill-suited to his purse, and prudence obliged him to prefer the quietest sort of ruin and disgrace for the object of his affections to the more renowned.

It is not however by squeamishness that comedy most often gives offence, but by licentiousness or obscenity. The two charges are usually confused or combined, but they are really quite different; it is one thing to advocate lax conduct, and quite a different thing to display in the open matters over which politeness draws a veil. The former concerns morality; the latter good taste. Let us therefore treat the first as a moral question and the second as an aesthetic question.

In its historical beginnings comedy was a species of authorised licence. That does not mean that it was an attack on morality, good manners, or social discipline; in fact, Aristophanes (the only dramatist of this phase whose works have survived in bulk) had and expressed strict views about conduct, and in the *Frogs* he takes Euripides to task for laxity of principle about many matters, including sex. Aristophanes is far from primitive in his dramatic art, indeed he was the very last writer of the Attic Old Comedy; but his plays belong to the licentious class. What this means is that the comedy was a safety-valve or outlet for disorderly passions, including erotic passions; and by treating them in an unserious spirit it rendered them less dangerous socially. How far this has remained a deliberate purpose of comic writers is very doubtful. It seems to have been in Fielding's mind when he wrote *Tom Jones;* Tom's frequent falls from grace are upon the whole treated as a joke, for two reasons. Fielding does not wish to approve of them, but at the same time he wishes to insist that natural faults are curable, and far less serious than cold-blooded selfish dishonesty, as exemplified in Tom's foil, Blifil. I think almost any scene in *Tom Jones* makes Fielding's attitude clear; this passage from Chapter 10 of the Fifth Book will do as well as any:

Jones retired from the company in which we have seen him engaged, into the fields, where he intended to cool himself by a walk in the open air before he attended Mr Allworthy. There, whilst he renewed those meditations on his dear Sophia which the dangerous illness of his friend and benefactor had for some time interrupted, an accident happened, which with sorrow we relate, and with sorrow, doubtless, will it be read; however, that historic truth to which we profess so inviolable an attachment obliges us to communicate it to posterity.

It was now a pleasant evening in the latter end of June, when our hero was walking in a most delicious grove, where the gentle breezes fanning the leaves, together with the sweet trilling of a murmuring stream, and the melodious notes of nightingales, formed all together the most enchanting harmony. In this scene, so sweetly accommodated to love, he meditated on his dear Sophia. While his wanton fancy roved unbounded over all her beauties, and his lively imagination painted the charming maid in various ravishing forms, his warm heart melted with tenderness, and at length, throwing himself on the ground by the side of a gently murmuring brook, he broke forth into the following ejaculation:

"O Sophia, would Heaven give thee to my arms, how blest would be my condition! Curst be that fortune which sets a distance between us! Was I but possessed of thee, one only suit of rags thy whole estate, is there a man on earth whom I would envy? How contemptible would the brightest Circassian beauty, drest in all the jewels of the Indies, appear to my eyes! But why do I mention another woman? Could I think my eyes capable of looking at any other with tenderness, these hands should tear them from my head. No, my Sophia, if cruel fortune separates us for ever, my soul shall doat on thee alone. The chastest constancy will I ever preserve to thy image. Though I should never have possession of thy charming person, still shalt thou alone have possession of my thoughts, my love, my soul. Oh! my fond heart is so wrapt in that tender bosom, that the brightest beauties would for me have no charms, nor would a hermit be colder in their embraces. Sophia, Sophia alone, shall be mine. What raptures are in the name! I will engrave it on every tree."

At these words he started up, and beheld—not his Sophia—no, nor a Circassian maid richly and elegantly attired for the grand signior's seraglio. No; without a gown, in a shift that was somewhat of the coarsest and none of the cleanest, bedewed likewise with some odoriferous effluvia, the produce of the day's labour, with a pitchfork in her hand, Molly Seagrim approached. Our hero had his penknife in his hand, which he had drawn for the beforementioned purpose of carving on the bark; when the girl, coming near him, cried out with a smile, "You don't intend to kill me, squire, I hope?" "Why should you think I would kill you?" answered Jones. "Nay," replied she, "after your cruel usage of me when I saw you last, killing me would, perhaps, be too great kindness for me to expect."

Here ensued a parley, which, as I do not think myself obliged to relate, I small omit. It is sufficient that it lasted a full quarter of an hour, at the conclusion of which they retired into the thickest part of the grove.

But in other writers, such as Chaucer, there seems no such motive, or if it is present it is very slight. The "swiving" of the Miller's wife and daughter in the *Reeve's Tale* is described with the most light-hearted high spirits; for the girl it was perhaps a piece of pleasure and kindness that had rarely come her way in a home presided over by such unpleasant parents (Chaucer may not have meant to imply this, but he certainly implies that she enjoyed her night with the young man); for the parents it was a comic punishment of their self-importance and of the miller's dishonesty. In *Troilus and Criseyde,* the detailed description of Criseyde's seduction, and particularly Pandarus's part in it, serves a different purpose. Partly it brings out a contrast between the characters of Pandarus and Criseyde on the one hand and Troilus on the other; and partly it reveals the divided impulses in Troilus himself, for the main theme of the poem is the inconsistency of feeling and motive in which he is involved (like all decent and natural young lovers) between plain physical desire and respect for the feelings and interests of the woman. The convention of courtly love was one of those codes of sentiment for civilising sex of which I have spoken; it is not to be despised, nor does Chaucer despise it; the despairs and scruples of Troilus are by no means unnatural and have their counterpart even in enlightened (or cynical) ages like the present. But love is desire as well as sentiment; Chaucer's Troilus was a flesh-and-blood young man, not a mere collection of ideals; he wanted to possess Criseyde and he was human enough to enjoy possessing her. The truth to life of this great love story demanded that every side of Criseyde's seduction should be fully revealed. Yet although Chaucer included *Troilus and Criseyde* among the sinful works of which he repented in his famous retraction at the end of the *Canterbury Tales,* it is not in the least an immoral work. The love-affair comes to grief because of faults in all the three main characters; but chiefly because Pandarus, by his well-meaning but unprincipled interference, degraded it into a mere fornication.

But there are comic works that are more reasonably accused of advocating licence. All our Restoration comedies, from Etherege to Farquhar, take seduction for granted as a normal form of sport, which indeed upon the whole it was for Charles II and his courtiers. The mere fact that they take it *for granted* partially acquits them of advocating it; and Wycherley, who has the worst reputation of them all, was obviously unhappy about its results and implications— so much so that *The Country Wife,* in which he accepts it and exploits its comic possibilities without reserve, is a far healthier and therefore more moral play than *The Plain Dealer,* in which he is both fiercely satirical and morbidly sentimental. *The Country Wife,* indeed, has a moral, and a sound one: that the husband who mistrusts his wife and tries to keep her from other men will merely stimulate her desires and teach her to deceive him, however ill-equipped she is with natural cunning. This is in accord with the rationalism of the period. The comic dramatists of the late Seventeenth Century treat sex as an opportunity for pleasure but a potential source of trouble; and their norm of conduct is to get a fair share of the pleasure with the least possible distress to all concerned. For the most part their men and women are of the same class, and treat each other as equals; and in one respect their morality compares favourably with the average Victorian morality, for they have roughly the same standards for men as for women. The Victorian code (both legal and social) was that whereas a wife should forgive her husband's infidelity if he asked her to, a husband was under no obligation to forgive his wife's. In the Seventeenth Century, divorce could only be obtained by an *ad hoc* Act of Parliament; it was therefore very rare, and perhaps for that very reason there was greater mutual tolerance among civilised people though of course they were often very unhappy, as is made clear by Halifax's *Advice to a Daughter*. And there were husbands who literally locked their wives up, though public opinion censured that kind of behaviour. A cynic might say that there was an obvious reason for the censure: that every man was interested in having his neighbour's wife at large and accessible. But the cynicism would not be altogether justified; cynicism seldom is. The Restoration wits, however little respect they had for the Seventh Commandment, were upon the whole humane towards women and respected them as equals. There were among them notorious rakes, such as Rochester; but the general feeling was against the extremes of debauchery. That is at any rate the standpoint of Etherege, Congreve and Vanbrugh. Wycherley's Horner is not a typical Restoration gentleman; he is a comic rogue, comparable on a different plane to Shakespeare's Autolycus or Ben Jonson's Volpone; his function is to expose the other characters and keep the plot in motion.

But for the moralist to condemn any comedy because of its subject matter is an error of judgment. It is not the business of comedy to inculcate moral doctrine. Its business is to satisfy a healthy human desire; the desire to understand the behaviour of men and women towards one another in social life, and to judge them according to their own pretensions and standards. So far as it does this well and truly it makes for righteousness. We may, and probably most of us do, dissent from the moral standards of Etherege or Wycherley, at least in part; but unless our morality is of the kind that needs wrapping up in cotton wool, we need not be protected against their plays. I will go further than this: even assuming that the moral standards of Restoration Comedy are utterly bad, we ought to be able to enjoy the comedies themselves, and to do so will strengthen rather than weaken our moral fibre, provided always that we have grown out of the cotton wool stage. All we are justified in asking of the comic writer is that his standards should be consistent; not that they should be right. The whole question is part of a wider quarrel between moralists and artists. But let me make it clear that I am not on the side of the artist *against* the moralist; I believe myself to be on the side of morality *and* art, as Milton was in *Areopagitica* and Shelley in his *Defence of Poetry*.

With the other charge, of obscenity, as it is much less serious, I will be very brief. There are people who object to many comedies, and particularly all Restoration comedies on the ground that they are indecent. It is difficult, and perhaps futile, to argue about questions of taste such as this. We can only state our own tastes and plead for some tolerance on both sides of the question. Sex is a nuisance; we all sometimes wish we could dispense with it. But there it is; and just as the poets have paid tribute to its noblest and most beautiful manifestations and also reviled it for cruelties and humiliations, so let the comic writers enjoy it as the greatest of eternal jokes. But let them do it with a certain discretion of speech. I cannot see the objection to innuendo. It offends some people, who feel it to be cowardly; if we are to have filth, they say, let us have frank filth. But this use of the word filth is equivocal; and it is begging the question to equate coarseness with frankness. In literature and drama, surely the crude and limited vocabulary of the navy and that of the clinical lecture-room are equally out of place—and they are the only two perfectly plain vocabularies available for use in this connexion. It is true that the point of an innuendo can be missed, if one is not on the look-out; but on this, of all subjects, it is proper to make jokes with a certain finesse.

The most daring and notorious joke in Restoration Comedy occurs in Act IV, Scene 3 of *The Country Wife,* where Wycherley comes as near as possible to depicting "the lineaments of gratified" (and ungratified) "desire" by a very clever innuendo.

Re-enter Lady Fidget with a piece of china in her hand, and Horner following.

LADY FIDGET (*to Mrs Squeamish*) . . . I have been toiling and moiling, for the prettiest piece of china, my dear.

HORNER   Nay, she has been too hard for me, do what I could.

MRS SQUEAMISH   Oh lord, I'll have some china too. Good Mr Horner, don't think to give other people china, and me none; come in with me too.

HORNER   Upon my honour, I have none left now.

MRS SQUEAMISH Nay, nay, I have known you deny your china before now, but you shan't put me off so, come—

HORNER This lady had the last there.

LADY FIDGET Yes, indeed, Madam, to my certain knowledge, he has no more left.

MRS SQUEAMISH O, but it may be he may have some you could not find.

LADY FIDGET What, d'ye think if he had had any left, I would not have had it too? for we women of quality never think we have china enough.

HORNER Do not take it ill I cannot make china for you all; but I will have a roll-wagon for you too, another time.

MRS SQUEAMISH Thank you, dear toad.

The disguise is purely verbal and scenic; there can be no doubt of what the characters are talking about. The question, and it is merely a question of taste, is whether it should be talked about so openly on the stage. The answer will depend mainly on whether the situation is comic, or only coarse; and comic it certainly is in this scene. But any one who is squeamish had better not go to see *The Country Wife* without first reading it.

III

Comedy depicts men and women in society. Meredith stresses this point; and it leads him to the questionable conclusion that the setting of comedy should be urban and that Shakespeare's characters, being "creatures of the woods and wilds" are "subjects of a special study in the poetically comic". It is true that Shakespeare's comedy is unique, because of his apparent inability to write with his imagination at less than full stretch: he was *incapable* of realism. But it is not clear, without better reasons than Meredith gives, that pure comedy cannot be staged in a fairy-tale setting as successfully as in Paris or London. Meredith seems to have been misled by the special narrow use of the word society in the Victorian and Edwardian periods, and indeed to have been obsessed by the idea of Society with a capital S: a select class of wealthy and leisured persons, speaking an artificial language of their own and spending all their time and energy in entertaining themselves and one another. Certainly that kind of society provides a good setting for comedy; but to *limit* comedy to it is simply to fly in the face of the facts.

Characters like Bottom were too close to nature for Meredith's strict notion of comedy; and Titania, a "creature of the woods and wilds", was quite outside his pale. But no particular class of person or environment is in itself either comic or un-comic; it is the imagination of the writer or spectator that makes them so. Meredith's argument is parallel to the orthodox renascence convention of dramatic propriety, according to which a king or a statesman should not be made ridiculous or contemptible. Dr Johnson met this pedantry with a common sense if not completely conclusive rejoinder:

Shakespeare always makes nature predominate over accident; and if he preserves the essential character, is not very careful of distinctions superinduced and adventitious. His story requires Romans or Kings, but he thinks only on men. He knew that Rome, like any other city, had men of all dispositions; and wanting a buffoon he went into the Senate-house for that which the Senate-house would certainly have afforded him. He was inclined to shew an usurper and a murderer not only odious but despicable, he therefore added drunkenness to his other qualities, knowing that kings love wine like other men, and that wine exerts its natural power upon kings. These are the petty cavils of petty minds; a poet overlooks the casual distinctions of country and condition, as a painter, satisfied with the figure, neglects the drapery.

As for Meredith's thesis, it is probably true that man in his urban environment lends himself more readily to comedy; and certainly true that comedy is essentially concerned with men and not with fairies. But all art is in greater or less degree symbolic: as Johnson said, imitations convince not because they are mistaken for realities, but because they bring realities to mind. Surely even in the strictest sense, rustics can be comic, and not only rustics but animals and even vegetables; and not only things in nature, but purely imaginary creatures like Titania. In transporting Bottom into fairy-land Shakespeare knew very well what he was doing, and was well within his rights as a comic dramatist. The situation of course is unrealistic and dreamlike; but any one who has himself dreamed will know how much richer in comedy the world of dreams is than the circumspect world of every-day working reality.

Society in the proper sense—or at least in the sense in which the word defines the setting of comedy—stands for an idea rather than a particular set of persons. It stands for coherence; for a common body of opinions and standards and a disposition to co-operate. It can be contracted to a very small class living together in a small area; it can be extended to the whole of humanity or even beyond the limits of the human species. Its extent will depend partly on the power of statesmen, philosophers, and artists to impose unity on apparently heterogeneous material; partly on the social conditions of the time and place in which they are living; partly on the purpose they have in view. To the mind of Shakespeare and his fellow-Elizabethans the universe was more homogeneous than it is to us; for our moral ideas lag behind the lessons of modern physics and economics. Shakespeare did not therefore need to restrict his setting at all. The distinctions between man, beast, and spirit, which our minds can only surmount by a change of gear and often a very violent one, did not trouble him; Prospero, Ariel, and Caliban are all members of one society. For Chaucer it was the same. His range was somewhat narrower; but that was because his imagination, powerful and adventurous though it was, had not quite the range of Shakespeare's, not because the medieval world was in any except the strictly material sense narrower than the Elizabethan. Chaucer's comic world contains Chantecleer, and the Eagle in the *House of Fame;* January and May in the *Merchant's Tale* (the story is an allegory, though a very realistic one); the Prioress and the Wife of Bath; Troilus, Criseyde, and Pandarus. It is a world at least as varied, if not quite so cosmic, as Shakespeare's.

But about the beginning of the Seventeenth Century the outlook of the educated Englishman changed; not in a single generation, but with the rapidity of a revolution. Men's eyes turned towards the material world in which they lived; and in this movement towards materialistic rationalism Ben Jonson was the central literary figure, as he was also the founder of modern comedy. There were to be no more fairies in comedy. Into the merits of the controversy about realism I will not go here. One can only be thankful that Jonson was in the field a few years later than Shakespeare, and not a few years earlier. But probably the reaction was both inevitable and salutary. Fletcher's realistic comedies are altogether superior to *The Faithful Shepherdess* and the romantic tragedies and tragi-comedies that earned him from Dryden the disparaging description, "a limb of Shakespeare". Be this as it may, Jonson narrowed the field to particular time and place. But his own comedy was still very wide in range. Society for him was still at least as wide as human nature, though his imagination was only at its ease in the underworld of London. The test his characters have to submit to—the standard they have to satisfy—is a hard but crude one. They have to survive in the world of *Bartholomew Fair.*

Later writers, lacking the large ideal vision of Shakespeare and Chaucer, and the robust digestion of Jonson, have discovered an excellent convention which is somethimes called the Comic Microcosm. They take for the setting of their comedy a "little world," a strictly limited society with fairly homogeneous traditions, standards, and habits. In such a world, where the rules of the game of life are the same for everybody, where all know the rules and accept them in theory at least, it is easy to measure men and women against each other fairly, and to pick out the good and the bad mixers, at the same time depicting even in the good mixers those faults of temperament and foibles of the intellect that cause both the graver irritations and the pleasant smaller frictions provocative of nothing worse than a smile. The first very clear example of the Comic Microcosm in our literature is the world of Restoration comedy. Perhaps Etherge, the earliest of the Restoration comic dramatists, deserves the credit of discovering it; but he did not invent it, he saw it around him. How closely he followed in his plays the pattern of a real little world in which he lived may be seen from his letters. I have said something of the standards of this society, and it only remains to repeat that for the purpose of comedy (as outlined in the third sentence of this paragraph) it does not matter so much that they should be morally sound as that they should be consistent, clearly understood, and generally accepted within the society.

The world of Restoration comedy, small and never very important historically, soon melted away. In the Eighteenth Century English civilisation broke up into innumerable units centered in the home. This decentralisation gave birth to *The Spectator;* and Addison created around Sir Roger de Coverley a kind of domestic comedy new to English literature, unless it had been foreshadowed by the country seat of Mr Justice Shallow in Shakespeare's *Henry IV*. In a nation alive with vigorous and self-centred homes the domestic world offers an obvious microcosm to the comic writer. In the early days of our literature, Chaucer had used it for many of his best Canterbury Tales. In Eighteenth Century England domestic comedy revived. By a charming irony it was a homeless Irish wanderer, Goldsmith, who wrote the best of all our domestic plays, *She Stoops to Conquer;* I wish I could rank his even more domestic novel *The Vicar of Wakefield* as highly, but it is too unequal, ill-constructed, and heterogeneous to be quite successful as a comedy or anything else. I suppose the most *remarkable* of all domestic microcosms is Shandy Hall, the setting of one of the greatest and most sustained flights of comic imagination in our literature. But a single home is rather small to allow comedy to display its full powers; *Tristram Shandy* is a tour-de-force, and Sterne himself is rather too much of a virtuoso—even an exhibitionist—to keep consistently within the bounds of comedy. Jane Austen saw what was wanted; her "three or four families in a country village" provided the most successful, and famous, of all English comic microcosms.

No later writer has created comedy to equal hers. Trollope's Barsetshire is a convincing little world and offers some high moments of comedy: the death of Mrs Proudie, for instance. Unfortunately it is not a purely *comic* microcosm; Trollope sacrifices too many of his characters to the demons of sensationalism and sentimentality. Meredith's "Society" is too unreal to serve convincingly as a measure of character. Mr Shaw has not chosen to use any consistent convention for his settings; they are varied, and all of them more or less fantastic even when they appear most realistic. Since his comedy is a comedy of ideas its material setting has little importance except for theatrical purposes. He has a sort of intellectual microcosm: the world of self-conscious middle-class ideas which flourished at the end of the Nineteenth Century. One is conscious in his plays of a consistent milieu, in which the mental habits of his characters can be accurately measured against each other. Lastly, James Joyce's Dublin is a little world within which he achieved a masterpiece; but *Ulysses* is more than a comedy, it is what he intended it to be, an epic.

Comedy*

ARTHUR KOESTLER

Most of the devices employed in comedy have already been analysed in previous chapters. It was once usual to classify comedies into those relying on the comic of situations, manners, and character; and though all such classifications are of small value, they may serve as an approximate guide.

In his discussion of the comic of situations, Bergson came nearest to the essence of the comic itself: "A situation is always comic," he writes, "if it participates simultaneously in two series of events which are absolutely independent of each other, and if it can be interpreted in two quite different meanings." One is tempted to cry "Fire!" but a couple of pages further on Bergson has dropped the clue and gone back to his metaphysical hobby; the interference of two independent series in a given situation is merely a further example of the "mechanisation of life."

In fact the interference of series in its many variations—coincidence, mistaken identity, and so forth—is the clearest example of bisociated contexts. Any attempt at enumerating the various patterns of the comic of situations (disguise, confusion of time and occasion, and so on) would be tedious and repetitive. Similarly the main techniques of the comedy of manners have been discussed under the headings of Satire, Irony, and Caricature, and need no further elaboration. Our concluding remarks concern the comic of *character*.

A good history of literature could be written which would use as leitmotif the gradually growing realization of the complexities of character, its internal contradictions, its simultaneous existence on several planes. There are ups and downs on his curve according to

---

* Arthur Koestler, "Comedy," in *Insight and Outlook* (The Macmillan Company, 1949), pp. 102–104.

the rise and fall of civilizations, but if we could draw the average curve, it would probably show that, as far as literature can be said to "progress," it progresses in the direction of growing insight into the complexities of the human condition. Masterpieces are produced in each peak period, but they are relative peaks on a steadily mounting tide and can only be appreciated by an attitude of (not necessarily deliberate or conscious) regression to an earlier level. Hence the impossibility of copying their method and approach, even if we are taught to regard them as immortal models of perfection; they are perfect only relative to their own level of complexity.

This development can easily be demonstrated in the progress from the comic "type" to the comic "character." The type is a caricature in which exaggeration and simplification of one feature are carried almost to the point of abstraction—the miser, the glutton, the misanthropist, the cuckold, and so forth. The mechanism of the comic resulting from this technique has been analysed before, and needs no further comment. Equally obvious is the marked increase of complexity in the characters of modern comedy—in Tchekhov, Wilde, Shaw, or even Sacha Guitry.

A parallel development, and directly dependent on the first, is the gradual displacement of character features and of the situations deriving from them, from the comic towards the tragic end of the spectrum. Timidity, adolescent gaucherie, clumsiness in athletic games have moved from the sphere of the ludicrous to that of the psychological novel and self-pitying autobiography. Cuckoldry is no longer comic; the classic triangle has migrated from the vaudeville stage to the waiting room of the psychoanalyst. Harpagon's pedantry and meanness are aspects of his anal-erotic fixation; the bearded Jew is recognized as a scapegoat for irrational aggression; obesity and thinness, the deformities of body or mind are objects of sympathy. The turning point can be clearly seen where Shakespeare's figures change from comic into tragic characters: Shylock, the clown in Lear, Caliban, Falstaff at the end of *Henry V*. Growing insight into the complexities of human character, including one's own, has as its inevitable consequence sympathy and identification with the weaknesses and foibles of others. Hence the modern comedy has increasingly to rely for its effects on a change from caricature to witticism, from the comic of situations to brilliant dialogue. But while individual aggression is in steady retreat and leads to the decline of the types of comic based on it, collective social aggressiveness against institutions, between classes and nations increases, and so, in consequence, does social satire on the stage, in novels, and cartoons. The old character types, the miser and cuckold, are replaced by social types: Blimp, the fox-hunting squire, the long-haired aesthete. With the crumbling of sex taboos, the sexy joke becomes increasingly sophisticated and implicit, sometimes almost a riddle, as in Peter Arno's cartoons. The general increase in education and sophistication furthers the tendency towards the dry, allusive wisecrack and the apparent nonsense joke. Charlie Chaplin marked the end of an era of social sentimentality towards the Little Man, the timid and downtrodden; the Marx Brothers are a mixture of buffoonery in a crazy, disintegrating world, with a kind of surrealistic logic—the twisted laws and curved spaces of the non-Euclidean geometries.

Part Four

THE NATURE OF COMEDY

Al Capp
THE COMEDY OF CHARLIE CHAPLIN

J. L. Styan
TYPES OF COMEDY

Richard Duprey
WHATEVER HAPPENED TO COMEDY?

The Comedy of Charlie Chaplin*

AL CAPP

I

It is the ambition of every newspaper cartoonist to get published in something that won't be used to wrap fish in the next morning, and so, the other day, I was writing a book. It was a book about comedy. I came to the part about Charlie Chaplin, remembered some of his gags, and wrote about them. Then, when I read what I had written, I stopped, because I was afraid my memory had been playing tricks on me. Was he that good? I had to know. After some nagging, United Artists arranged a screening for me of the only Chaplin film then available in its New York office. It was *City Lights*. It hadn't been out of the can in years.

In the projection room were about a dozen people: United Artists publicity men and executives (whose idea of escape from the drabness of *their* lives is to not go to the movies), two girls, and a Wife. The girls were a couple of cute secretaries who wandered into the projection room to wait wearily, because they had dates with the executives, and the Wife had suddenly turned up, I rather think, because the excuse of her executive husband that he had to stay late at the office because some cartoonist with influence wanted to see a twenty-year-old movie sounded to her like the kind of lie he might whip up to cover up the fact that he had a date with one of the secretaries.

Nobody in that projection room really wanted to be there except me, and I was pretty uncertain myself. Here I was taking the chance that a second look, after all those years, might prove that Chaplin wasn't such a hell of an artist after all.

---

* Al Capp, "The Comedy of Charlie Chaplin," *The Atlantic Monthly*, Vol. 185, No. 2 (February, 1950).

Then, at the opening shot, everybody began to laugh. And for an hour and a half we all roared and howled and bellowed with delight, until the final scene. This is when the blind girl, no longer blind, realizes that the miserable little tramp to whom she is giving a quarter is the dream knight of her blindness; and when the tramp realizes that the masquerade is over and that she knows him as the ludicrous, flea-bitten thing he is, and when his heart is both over-flowing with joy that she can see, and breaking with sadness that she can see *him*.

So shattering was the tragedy of those last few minutes that, when the lights went on, none of us in that projection room dared look at the others. While we'd laughed, we had been delighted to laugh openly and in concert, but suddenly (although all through the master-piece are forebodings of its final tragedy) our hearts had been touched, and we were embarrassed for our tears, and ashamed to look one another in the face. Because in each face was the thing that men are most ashamed for other men to see, and that is self-pity.

Terrible disasters had happened to Chaplin all through the film—and the more terrible they were, the harder we laughed. For we were laughing at him. And then, because he is the most understanding and exquisite of artists, Chaplin's final tragedy became somehow our tragedy. He entered into us. We felt then all he felt, and the pity in us was no longer pity for a thing apart, because that comes out laughter; it was pity for a thing that great art had made a part of ourselves, and we were all embarrassed—each for the others as well as himself—when the lights went on.

Well, I had taken a second look, and I'd found that I was right the first time, only not right enough.

All comedy is based on man's delight in man's inhumanity to man. I know that is so, because I have made forty million people laugh more or less every day for sixteen years, and this has been the basis of all the comedy I have created. I think it is the basis of all comedy.

But I had forgotten, until I saw Chaplin again, that comedy can become sublime when it makes men sorrow at man's inhumanity to man by making men pity themselves.

When the history of art in our time is written, and when the ideological passions of our time are laughable curios, the great artist that our time has produced will be recognized as Charlie Chaplin.

Just as Shakespeare's *Hamlet* was, at first, regarded as a good job done by a well-known entertainer who had done other good jobs; and was applauded, forgotten, and then looked at again by another generation (whose added respect this entertainer had earned by now being dead), and only then discovered to be a job so very good, indeed, that it was better than any other job ever done—so will Chaplin's *City Lights* take its place among those works of art that men cherish and revere and use as proof that they are not animals, but have in them a touch of divinity, since one of their kind created this.

City Lights was released in 1929. It was a great success, it made a lot of money, everyone saw it—and then it was forgotten. Because, after all, it was merely a movie, and we all know that a work of art can endure only if it is done on canvas or printed on a page, because those are the traditional, respectable materials of art, and a can of film is not.

II

For anyone whose profession is to be visual comedy, it is as necessary to study the work of Charlie Chaplin as it is for the engineer to study mathematics. It is a crime that our libraries and schools don't have permanent examples of his work, as they do of the work of Michelangelo and Mozart. They should be available to students not only of visual comedy but of fine arts, sociology, history, ballet, drama and composition, as are all masterworks.

In the Chaplin films you will find thousands of miraculously funny gags (and no matter how much they've been copied, his originals have still a pure, bright freshness). You will find scores of unique characters, each warmly funny because, no matter how wildly they're drawn, they're based on real, instantly recognizable types. You'll find a treasure-trove of hilarious and intricate comedy situations—you'll find everything that comedy is made of. But the most important thing you'll find is this: that for all his dazzling succession of gags, characters, and situations, Charlie Chaplin told again and again, with infinite variation, one story—the story of man's inhumanity to man. And that is a very funny story.

You say you remember the Chaplin pictures and they were all about pie-throwing, cop-being-chased-by, and the horribly efficient machines that fed miserable helpless factory workers automatically, so they wouldn't have to stop using their hands to work? Well, analyze any Chaplin picture, any Chaplin gag. For instance, an old classic called *The Pilgrim*.

The title itself is a comment on the cruel foolishness of a familiar kind of American thinking. With us that word "Pilgrim" has come to exude a certain rich, ripe, aristocratic air. To be descended from "the Pilgrims" means you are, somehow, a better, a realer, a little more than merely 100 per cent American. It means to some people (and you'll find 'em in Congress and on committees to "protect" and "preserve" their own idea of "real" Americanism) that they have a right to be stuffy and irritated about the coming to this country of the ragtag and refuse of Europe and Asia. Some Americans feel that, because they are descended from the Pilgrims, they are our aristocracy, and hence have a right to yammer and complain about other pilgrims.

So Chaplin, who told in his picture the story of a boatload of frightened, starving, sniveling, dirty, depressed D.P.'s of twenty years ago, called the most miserable of 'em all—the character he played—"The Pilgrim" to remind us gently that those who rant and rave against the coming to America of today's D.P.'s are the children of precisely the same kind of D.P.'s of another day. The title itself is a reminder to man that his inhumanity to his fellow man is one of the most ridiculous things about him.

One of the first scenes of this comedy classic is a delicious example of Chaplin's carrying of man's inhumanity to man to its ultimate absurdity—namely, the inhumanity of men *other* men have been inhuman *to*.

The refugees travel steerage of course. They are given one meal a day; one bowl of slops. But not quite one bowl, because at mealtime, while there are *two* rows of refugees seated, facing each other across the table, there is only *one* row of bowls. Which row of refugees gets a chance at the slops depends on which way the boat rolls, because, while the poor starving wretches must remain seated where they are, drooling and clutching their spoons, the slop bowls slither from one side to the other with the crazy rhythm of the boat.

And for twenty years, audiences have been laughing their heads off at this scene.

Why?

It is because we are eternally delighted at the inhumanity of man to man.

First, at the colossal evil of the shipowners who have devised such a simple and satanic scheme to degrade and cheat their most helpless guests. And second, at the crookedness of the helpless themselves, as they, in turn, devise little ways to cheat each other out of a morsel of slops here, a morsel there.

And the fact that countless audiences of normal, decent human beings have screamed with happy, carefree laughter at this almost unbearably heart-rending scene is a further and highly helpful example of real man's inhumanity to cinema man.

III

Next to Death, man's greatest fear is Hunger. Yet Chaplin has made us laugh at *his* hunger. In *The Tramp* we first see him a starving bum, looking hungrily into the window of a cheap restaurant, watching a fat man being served a huge steak. The starving, fascinated bum drools.

Now right here is where everybody in the audience begins to grin. Chaplin's starvation gives us a nice, warm feeling. We feel nice and warm because, unlike that poor soul, we know *we're* going to eat after the show. His misery emphasizes our security. And thinking of our security makes us feel good, so we grin. Not starving is a nice thing. And nice things make us grin.

On with the story. The fat man cuts the steak with a flourish and lifts a juicy morsel to his mouth. The fascinated bum unconsciously mimics every move. He's lost in a dream world of steak. The fat man tentatively munches the morsel, the bum munches his dream morsel; he is floating in ecstasy until he sees that the fat man has suddenly stopped munching and is looking indignant. The bum instantly stops munching too, and he looks indignant, although *he* doesn't know what the hell they're both so indignant about. The fat man roars to the waiter that his steak is too rare, and orders him to take it back. The fat man is the second most furious person in the scene. The first most furious is the bum. You see, he was having a wonderful time with that dream steak until the fat man ordered it taken away. The fat man will get his real steak back. The bum won't ever again get his dream steak. His dream has been shattered. And we sit there, watching this pitiful scene, and roar with laughter.

We didn't laugh because we were heartless wretches. We laughed because we are normal human beings, full of self-doubt, full of vague feelings of inferiority, full of a desperate need to be reassured. Somehow that whole scene made us feel superior. First, no matter how badly off any one of us was, we were all in better shape than that bum. The fact that we'd had enough spare cash to buy a ticket to that movie made us superior to him. That was the first thing that made us feel good. Next, we saw him starving. That wasn't going to happen to us—another reason for feeling superior, better off at least than one person.

As the scene continued, it gave us a feeling of emotional and intellectual superiority. That was when the bum, so immersed in the sight of the fat man cutting the steak, began to imagine that *he* had a steak. He had been happy munching his dream steak. He had become wildly, luxuriously lost in his dream. He didn't know that he was, inevitably, due for a terrible shock when he realized that the steak wasn't real. But we did. We were way ahead of him. We had the inside dope and we delightedly anticipated his hideous disappointment when he found out something *we'd* known all along. We laughed because we were smarter than he was. We laughed because we were pleased with this tiny reassurance of our own superiority.

A millionaire passes in a limousine. He looks at a silver dollar dubiously—he bites it. It bends slightly. He grimaces. It's a counterfeit. He throws it out into the gutter. The bum finds it. Delirious with joy, he rushes into the tough restaurant and, drunk with power, orders a plate of beans.

And the people laugh.

Why?

Because we're smarter than he is and that makes us feel good. We know plenty that he doesn't know. He thinks he's rich. We know he isn't. He thinks he's going to have a fine time. We know better.

The bum devours his first plate of beans and orders another. All the time, he lovingly fingers his silver dollar, he polishes it on his sleeve, he kisses it. He trusts that silver dollar—it gives him confidence, security, dignity; it gives him a place in the world. It even gives him the right to be nasty to the ape-waiter, whose fatness he had been admiring just a moment ago, before the silver dollar.

Now the ape-waiter pretends to admire *him!* The silver dollar has changed everything. The waiter hopes to get the change from it as a tip.

We laugh because we know the bum is going to get a beating from the waiter when he finds out, and although we're sorry for the bum, we're going to enjoy the beating.

Well, Chaplin finds out before the waiter does. While the ape is off to bring him his third plate of beans, he drops the silver dollar. It doesn't ring true. It makes a dull, lead-like thud. Sweating, he bites it. It bends, horribly. It's a phony. The world comes crashing down around the bum's head.

We laugh—we smell blood.

The waiter brings his third plate of beans and indicates that his working day is up. He'd like Chaplin to hurry through this, pay for it, tip him, and let him go home. Chaplin miserably giggles that of course he'll hurry. He wouldn't dream of keeping him waiting. He indicates that he too is a man of affairs, and can't afford to linger over a mere plate of beans. His assurances are elaborate and verbose, and take up a lot of time. That's what the poor wretch wants to do—take up a lot of time before the inescapable revelation comes and he is beaten to a pulp.

We laugh at Chaplin's pitiful, transparent lies. He hopes to avert the massacre, but we know he can't. Sitting there in the theater, we are all gods on Olympus, watching an inferior being trying to escape the destiny we, in our omniscience, know must be his. Gosh, we feel good, even the most miserable of us.

As the waiter cuts off Chaplin's long-winded explanation of how fast he'll eat the beans, and tells him to get on with it, the fat man (the one who likes his steak well done) is whizzed by the table, being beaten to a bloody pulp by a dozen ape-waiters. Chaplin's own ape-waiter explains this: "He was," he tells him, "a nickel short."

The audience screams with joy.

The poor bum knows now that, if he ever finishes that plate of beans, his fate will be a thousandfold bloodier. Studiously averting the waiter's impatient eye, he makes an elaborate and pitiful ceremony of each bean. First he carefully selects one, after much thought (a lovely bit, because no two things look more alike, or taste more alike, or have less individual personality, than beans from the same plate). Having thoughtfully selected from the thousand the one bean which at that moment seemed most to suit his mood, he doesn't eat it. He peels it. He slices it. He seasons each half of each bean. He tastes one half, puts it back, tastes the other. He thinks about the taste, as a gourmet would ponder over rare wines.

And we laugh because we know how futile it all is—we know how sick he feels inside, how terrified he is, how hopeless he is—and so, naturally, we feel great.

Chaplin, more than any other comic of our time, understood his fellow man's pitiful and cruel mixture of insecurity and inhumanity.

A few years ago, Chaplin was shown around a great automobile factory. Its owners were mighty proud of their new gadgets. They were proud because their new gadgets were time-saving. Chaplin was horrified because they were also man-killing.

The superiority of gadget to man, the slavery of man to gadget, was to him a hilarious perversion of the only sane reason *for* the gadget—namely, to make man's life easier.

So Chaplin made a picture called *Modern Times.* In it he played a harassed little worker in a gigantic factory. Because this worker had become part of the gadget he operated, he had become utterly dehumanized. He moved jerkily, in complete coordination with the time-saving gadget, instead of gracefully and inefficiently like one of those time-wasting human beings; he ate when the gadget fed him and not

simply when he was hungry, like a sloppy and unreliable man; he
didn't waste time thinking—the gadget worked perfectly, so *that* wasn't
necessary. There was one thing, however, that the gadget couldn't do—
it couldn't go to the toilet for him.

This was very humiliating to his boss, and it worried that good
man considerably—but in the toilet he had another gadget. When
Chaplin had been there long enough (according to scientific sched-
ules, time-charts, and Gallup polls), a vast face of his boss appeared
on a screen above the bowl and told him to stop fooling around and
get the hell back to work.

Well, people howled at *Modern Times,* and industry howled *to*
Chaplin. It was un-American, said they, to make people laugh at the
inhumanity of gadget to man. Gadgets, they claimed, were a blessing
to man. It had been okay for the comic to make people laugh at a
vaguely inhuman Society that generally kicked 'em around, but it was
unfair, and unsporting really, to make people laugh at a specific
system of dignified industrial "efficiency" that robbed them of their
dignity as human beings.

IV

In practicing the art of love, men endure their most terrible confusions, miseries, and disasters. No matter how great and certain a
man may have become in every other area of his life, in courtship
(trying to convince a certain sweet someone that you are the sweetest
someone ever produced by a certain other sex) all men are unsure,
fumbling, and feel rotten most of the time.

No confused, despondent lover ever saw a Chaplin picture who
didn't come away feeling considerably cheered up. Cheered up because,
no matter how inept in his love-making he had been, he had seen
someone even more inept; no matter that the fair object of his affections had been unresponsive, the girl Chaplin courted had been down-
right contemptuous. Chaplin understood that the surest way to delight
a world of lovers who suffered because they weren't loved enough was
to show them a lover who wasn't loved at all.

There was always a beautiful girl in the Chaplin pictures. And the
only reason she had anything to do with Chaplin was that nobody
else wanted her because of some terrible handicap—terrible to everyone except Chaplin, who was grateful for any attention from any
girl, no matter what was wrong with her, just as long as she was
recognizably a girl and recognizably alive. The instant, however, the
girl was all right again, she would inevitably abandon Chaplin.

The utter defeat of Chaplin as a lover made our own unsatisfactory romances seem much less humiliating. Nothing that ever happened to any of us could possibly be as disappointing as what always happened to him.

At least, if we had been spurned by a Beloved, there was something left. Hope. Hope that another, less ambitiously selected or more wisely courted, Beloved would accept us. *We* had a chance. Not Chaplin. Nobody wanted him. Nobody ever would.

We laughed at Chaplin's romances because no matter how often we had been licked, we could get started again and it *might* come out good; and because, on the other hand (and a comforting thing it was for us to realize), no matter *how* often he started again, it couldn't come out anything but bad, because he was licked before he started.

We knew that once the lame girl who looked fondly up at him from her wheelchair could walk, she'd walk away from him. We knew that the starving dance-hall blowzer who had agreed to come to his little cabin for dinner would forget him and that date the minute anyone in the saloon offered to feed her there, because what she was interested in wasn't romance—it was fast chow. We knew that the blind girl was sweet to him only because she couldn't see him, and that the instant she could, she'd laugh her pretty head off at him.

We felt fine watching Chaplin's courtships because he gave us a couple of things that make men feel fine. Omniscience; *we* knew something the poor little bum didn't know—that he didn't have a chance. We knew something that would have crushed his hopeful heart if he were as wise as his art had made us; we knew his desperate, eager efforts were all in vain. We knew that no girl would ever want him, and that emphasized the fact that some girl would or did want us, and that gave us the other thing that makes men feel fine, security.

In my own work—this is a footnote—I have tried to make cheerier a world of disappointed lovers. No lover is ever anything but disappointed, since the greatest of all disappointments is the final triumphant possession of the love one has dreamt of having. It's never as wonderful as your dreams of it, because there are no limits to wonderfulness in dreaming. I try to make a disappointed lover feel better by having "Li'l Abner" never know what to do about a succession of eager, luscious girls who throw their juicy selves at him. "Li'l Abner" doesn't know what to do, and so he does nothing. And that makes every male who reads "Li'l Abner" feel fine. Because *he* would know what to do. No matter how fumbling or stupid he has been, compared with "Li'l Abner" he's Don Juan. It makes him feel fine to be Don Juan. So he feels fine about "Li'l Abner."

The more secure a man feels, the more ready he is to laugh. So Chaplin—the instant he appeared—gave us all a feeling of security. Certainly none of us, no matter how badly off we were, were as badly off as this bundle of rags.

Let's go back to the picture I began with, *City Lights*. In it Chaplin, homeless, penniless, nervous about cops, meets a very rich man. We know that he has millions, not because he wears a silk hat and white tie well, but because he wears them badly and sloppily. This guy is so rich that he is contemptuous of attire that would overawe a less rich man. Also he is very drunk. He is so drunk that he does not cringe from Chaplin in distaste. He embraces Chaplin. He tells the little bum that he loves him and is going to show him a good time. Chaplin is deliriously happy and so we laugh at him.

We know that the rich man, once he sobers up, will loathe the pitiful little bum. We know that Chaplin's security isn't going to last, and ours to a degree is. Chaplin is at the mercy of a rich drunk's whim. If things go badly—that is, if the drunk sobers up—Chaplin will have nothing. We are better off than somebody. We are such a hell of a lot better off than he is that he has made us feel secure and protected and we laugh.

Arm in arm, the slobbering millionaire and the little bum wander off in search of food and fun. After a night of wild, expensive revelry, arm in arm they lurch back to the millionaire's town house. The butler, a man of aristocratic impulses although a servant, wants to beat up the tramp and toss him back into the gutter. But the millionaire still loves him. The bum is his li'l pal. He is to be given everything in the house.

Chaplin takes on airs and graces. He orders the butler around. He snaps his fingers in his face. The butler grinds his teeth and waits. He knows that his master will be sober in the morning. He knows that in the morning his master will see the bum as clearly as he does. He knows that the bum will get his, and we know it, but the bum doesn't.

The millionaire wakes up. He is terribly sober. He sees the bum sleeping next to him. He calls the butler in and asks who it is. Brutally aroused, the bewildered bum pleads with the millionaire to remember their everlasting, to-the-death friendship of only a few short hours before. The millionaire looks at him coldly, uncomprehendingly, and with distaste. He orders the butler to throw him out.

Disillusioned and embittered, the little bum resumes his miserable existence. Months pass. One night a figure in top hat and tails lurches out of a gaudy café and throws his arms around him. It is the millionaire again. Again he is plastered, and again he loves the little bum, with a passion that knows no bounds. He weeps that their friendship is everlasting, that he will fight for him to the death, that everything he has is his, and he wants to give him a big party. At first the little bum is suspicious. He has been fooled before. But as the millionaire continues to slobber over him, that old look of love and trust comes back into the bum's eyes. And this is where we laugh loudest. The little bum is such a sucker. We would know enough, even the dumbest of us, never again to trust that man. But Chaplin isn't smart. He isn't even as smart as we are. We feel fine.

And that's what a comedian is for, isn't he? To make people feel fine?

Types of Comedy*

J. L. STYAN

The recognized theories of comedy do not help us any the more to understand the characteristic drama of the twentieth century. Ideas about the comic have never been expressed as abundantly as those about tragedy, both because the seriousness of comedy has not been as evident to writers as its more impressive high-toned counterpart, and because the ways and intentions of comedy may be more tiresome to explain. Up to the beginning of this century, comedy suffered a hardening in its arteries and its critics had grown further and further away from the practice on the stage. Certainly, no theorist seemed capable of putting forward an explanation sufficiently all-embracing, and the philosophical and the psychological approaches have both been wanting.

The diagnosis of comedy presents many difficulties. Laughter, a recurring and therefore an evidently important ingredient, seems to arise from a great variety of sources: we laugh at other people's bad luck, or at relief from embarrassment, or at a little flattery, or even when we do not want to laugh. We laugh heartily, or smile gently, or at some comedy we may not laugh at all. There are so many uses to which laughter can be put, from the promotion of a cold vindictive sarcasm to that of the empty gaiety of knock-about. There is considerable discrepancy between the things we find comic in life and those contrived on the stage: a man falling on his face in the street may be an object of pathos, but on the stage an object of derision. There is confusion between the techniques of comedy designed to raise laughter and the use to which the laughter is put: why should an anticlimax make us happy, or a clown make us sad?

---

* J. L. Styan, "Types of Comedy," in *The Dark Comedy* (Cambridge University Press, 1962), pp. 42–58. [The footnotes in this selection have been renumbered.]

There are too many 'types' of the comic, and we plague ourselves by trying to sort comedy from burlesque, satire and farce, notwithstanding that in Shakespearian comedy elements of each seem to be present, and the points where they overlap are none too clearly defined. We are often at a loss to assess a total impression: even where in Molière the play's parts have been largely sweet and farcical, the whole when swallowed can leave a bitter taste in the mouth.

We find that when a joke is dissected, it abruptly ceases to be funny, which is disconcerting to say the least. It is also notorious that a 'sense of humour' is an unreliable quality, and what will seem laughable to an English audience will not necessarily seem so to a Scottish. As a psychologist has written, 'If members of a social group observe that their own objects of laughter do not produce laughter in another social group they are inclined to express this fact by saying that the second group has "no sense of humour" '.[1] From the world of the theatre we might add that what will seem laughable on Monday may be damned on Tuesday. It is, moreover, a nuisance that what is comic to one age is not to another: Shylock was a butt for the Elizabethans, but not for the Victorians; Richard III was played for comedy by Irving, but for pathos by Olivier. Fashions in laughter change too readily, and we are in some doubt today whether to laugh at or sympathize with a Falstaff or a Tartuffe or a Sir Peter Teazle. Furthermore, should we begin by studying crowd psychology or the particular successes of a particular writer? And if we are to set our standards by one author, who shall it be?—Aristophanes, Shakespeare, Molière, Shaw?

For Hazlitt [2] the essence of the laughable was 'the incongruous', a distinction between 'what things are and what they ought to be'. This happily enough explains what we may call 'satirical' laughter, the laughter by which the spectator refuses to acknowledge the propriety of the fop and the coquette in Restoration comedy, when he recognizes the affectation in their gesture and speech, or by which he knows to ridicule the seriousness with which the characters in *The Importance of Being Earnest* pursue their absurd ends. But Hazlitt lets fall a damning admission: 'It is perhaps the fault of Shakespeare's comic muse that it is too good-natured and magnanimous. We sympathize with his characters more often than we laugh at them.' It is a *fault*!

---

[1] R. H. Thouless, *General and Social Psychology* (London, 2nd ed., 1937), p. 209.

[2] Hazlitt, Introduction to *The English Comic Writers* (1818).

For Meredith [3] 'the test of true Comedy is that it shall awaken thoughtful laughter', but he too can only comfortably explain the *raison d'être* of the 'high' comedy of intellect: 'The laughter of Comedy is impersonal and of unrivalled politeness. . . . It laughs through the mind, for the mind directs it.' And though in another place he suggests, attempting to distinguish between comedy and humour, 'The stroke of the great humourist is world-wide, with lights of Tragedy in his laughter', he will not admit that this quality can also appear in the greatest forms of comedy. Shakespeare is again the stumbling-block: because Shakespeare paints 'humanity' rather than 'manners', he does not begin to explain Shakespeare's eye for the comic. 'Jaques, Falstaff and his regiment, the varied troop of Clowns, Malvolio, Sir Hugh Evans and Fluellen—marvellous Welshmen!—Benedick and Beatrice, Dogberry, and the rest, are subjects of a special study in the poetically comic.' So we move on to safer ground with Molière, some of whose success he can account for.

After Meredith has named this glittering variety of the ostensibly comic, should he not have tried to understand them? Neither Hazlitt nor Meredith can explain the warm comic success of these and others like Rosalind and Touchstone and Quince and Bottom and that great host of Shakespeare's comic creation which reflects so closely the 'English' sense of humour. Moreover, they cannot help us to sense the nature of the achievement in plays like *The Wild Duck, The Cherry Orchard, Major Barbara* and *Waiting for Godot*, ambiguous plays of the modern theatre which challenge our laughter, as we shall see.

Bergson [4] with every good intention turned to example after example to establish his precepts, but concerned himself too much with first causes and with the detail of technique rather than the odd results produced in the theatre. He further remained rather parochial in drawing too much on the kind of comedy which has so admirably set the standard for the French comic stage, that of Molière. It is noticeable that his examples are drawn chiefly from the farces and farcical moments of Molière and Labiche (author of such plays as *Le Voyage de M. Perrichon* and *Un Chapeau de paille d'Italie*) or the comical-absurd of such works as *Don Quixote*. He diagnoses comedy as arising from the incongruity of 'something mechanical encrusted on the living': 'the attitudes, gestures, and movements of the human

---

[3] Meredith, 'On the Idea of Comedy and of the Uses of the Comic Spirit', a lecture delivered in 1877.

[4] Bergson, *Laughter, an Essay on the Meaning of the Comic*, trans. C. Brereton and F. Rothwell (London, 1921), first French ed. 1889.

body are laughable in exact proportion as that body reminds us of a mere machine'. He thus cites as laughable the forms and movements of the puppet, and in the same way Molière's Sganarelle and his kind. Sganarelle, *The Doctor in Spite of Himself,* is enjoying his new-found power as a man of medicine, when he is accused by Géronte of reversing the position of the heart and the liver:

GÉRONTE ... the heart should be on the left side, and the liver on the right.

SGANARELLE Yes, it used to be so, but we have changed all that.

Likewise, Dr Bahis of *Love's the Best Doctor,* provides an excellent example of professional automatism when he advises that 'It's better [for a patient] to die through following the rules than to recover through violating them'. This argument of course helps us to explain the fun in much of Molière, and the comedy of snobbery in Lady Bracknell, and how in Fry's *The Lady's Not For Burning* Tyson's pomposity as mayor is belied by his having a frightful cold in the head. It explains all manner of caricature in character and action on the stage. It explains the prohibition of much emotionality from the comic theatre. It does not explain the force of its *presence,* and emotion is often present to great purpose in comedy. Bergson declares rigidly 'laughter is incompatible with emotion', when we know well enough from experience, if not from countless moments on the comic stage, that we *do* have the faculty of laughing and feeling at one and the same time. It must exclude Shakespeare once again, and, what is more, it cannot approach our true sense of Molière's greatest achievement, *The Misanthrope.* Bergson's laughter is a 'social corrective', as Meredith's was an 'agent of civilization', but it trades on the debased and degraded in human nature and cannot respond to the warmth of comic humanity which remains after the eccentricities have been skimmed off.

The argument was not quite over. Freud [5] arbitrarily narrowed his field to include only what he pleased to call 'wit', and satisfactorily explains to us, after much belabouring, that wit serves as an escape from authority just as nonsense serves as an escape from critical reason (with occasional help from alcohol). Having said this at great length, he has said little that we did not know already. Others have since taken up the challenge, and J. B. Priestley's essay on humour [6] was a hopeful advance on his predecessors. Where Freud started from

---

[5] Freud, *Wit and its Relation to the Unconscious,* trans. Brill (London, un-dated, ?1906).

[6] J. B. Priestley, *English Humour* (London, 1929).

minimal instances, with little wish to move into the wider world of comedy, Priestley saw all the limitations and difficulties and perhaps would embrace too much. He would admit Shakespeare into the ranks, and goes some way to explaining his humour as the product of the close observation of human character and behaviour in its incongruities.

Among all the hints offered by these writers, certain recurring elements in the comic stand out. A sense of incongruity, with a resulting release of tension, is felt within the mind. Whether by the laughter of success or of failure, whether arising from the recognition of a friend or a tune, or from Santayana's 'little triumph' of the mind when it receives an illumination, whether by the laughter that follows upon bathos or upon the loss of a lady's dignity when her hat is blown off by the wind, some bulwark of our natural resistance, little or big, is broken down, and a weapon of unquestionable power is in the hands of the one who can effect this artificially. The comedian is suddenly free to pour his shafts through the gap, rebuffing us with mockery or drawing us with tears. Whatever the technique he employs he has his audience captive.

On the other hand, that a comedy *should* make you laugh is not admissible as an argument: incongruity is not necessarily laughable. There are too many plays, patently not tragedies, which clearly evoke no laughter, or little that is perceived as laughter; too many fine plays end in questions and by sobering us, from *Troilus and Cressida* and *The Misanthrope* to the comedies of Pirandello. The interested reader should look into that excellent discussion initiated by L. J. Potts in a more recent essay on our subject. [7] Where it does arise laughter can be a means to a greater end than itself, creating the conditions for the dramatic achievement of other things. The values of the comic attitude appear only when we measure the *uses* to which it is put. Nor should we deceive ourselves into thinking that its uses are not infinitely variable. The evidence suggests that the conventions of the comic stage readily admit an admixture of seemingly extraneous elements like the tragic and the pathetic, whereas tragedy has its fabric dangerously stretched to admit the comic or the farcical. What then are the traditional uses of comedy?

Broad comedy had contrived the release of laughter for partly satirical purposes by a relatively uncomplicated incongruity. Just as we laugh at the clown who sacrifices his self-respect by wearing trousers that are excessively too big for him, or at Charlie Chaplin for his exaggerated delight in a 'house' whose wall afterwards collapses when

---

[7] L. J. Potts, *Comedy* (London, 1948), esp. pp. 18–22.

he leans on it, so we laugh at Harpagon, grotesque in his avarice, faced with the costly processes of being in love; or we laugh at the newly honoured Lord Foppington's airs and graces as he incongruously rehearses his part for the evening's *levée* while still in his nightgown: 'Well, 'tis an unspeakable pleasure to be a man of quality—Strike me dumb—My Lord—Your lordship—My Lord Foppington. . . .' Of course, it is the situation which the dramatist may complicate, and the wink at the audience can be very much more subtle when, say, Lady Bracknell finally succumbs to hard cash in lieu of the desirable attributes of an elegant lineage, or when Volpone the fox out-foxes himself. The bookworm is funnier and more like a bookworm on a dance-floor than in a library, the flirt funnier and more of a flirt in a library than on a dance-floor.

Even at the level of the near-farcical, where the merely physical sensationalism of the laugh is uppermost in the playwright's mind, such drama can sometimes justify itself morally by being acutely pointed in its object of derision. The contrivance of derisive laughter by the exaggeration of some affectation of human behaviour is a time-honoured method used since the days of Aristophanes. Thus the learned Meton of *The Birds* arrives in Cloudcuckooland to 'subdivide the air into square acres':

METON Observe:
The conformation of the air, considered as
a total entity, is that of a conical damper.
Very well. At the apex of this cone we apply
the ruler, bracketing in the dividers to allow
for the congruent curve. Q.E.D. . . .

But his notions are not received as gratefully as he expected:

PISTHETAIROS . . . we've passed a law
that charlatans shall be whipped in the public square.

METON Oh. Then I'd better be going.

PISTHETAIROS   You're almost too late.
Here's a sample, God help you!   (*Knocks him down.*)

METON   My head! My head! [8]

One would not of course think that there were a majority of learned mathematicians in the Greek audience to make the satirical and corrective point of this very far-reaching. Nor would Molière have expected to find too many hypochondriacs like Argan in the court of Louis XIV. These comedies can nevertheless give us, perhaps inciden-

---

[8] Aristophanes, *The Birds*, version by D. Fitts (London, 1958).

tally, many tiny and momentary insights into human nature through the agency of puppets like Meton and Argan. We all share a little of Meton's desire to make order of fantasy, to stiffen what should be flexible. Even if we would not confess to being, each of us, a little of the hypochondriac with a natural fear for our health, we must feel just a touch of fellow-feeling for Argan when M. Purgon the doctor wreaks his rage like this:

M. PURGON I foretell that within four days you'll be in an incurable condition.

ARGAN Oh mercy!

M. PURGON You'll fall into a state of bradypepsia.

ARGAN M. Purgon!

M. PURGON From bradypepsia into dyspepsia.

ARGAN M. Purgon!

M. PURGON From dyspepsia into apepsia.

ARGAN M. Purgon!

M. PURGON From apepsia into diarrhoea and lientery.

ARGAN M. Purgon!

M. PURGON From lientery into dysentery.

ARGAN M. Purgon!

M. PURGON From dysentery into dropsy.

ARGAN M. Purgon!

M. PURGON And from dropsy to autopsy that your own folly will have brought you to.

ARGAN Oh my God! I'm dying.[9]

Here character, situation and dialogue are 'artificial' and the playing demands a special degree of stylized speech and movement, all apparently earnest in manner. The characters' behaviour tends to puppetry, and the situations, though still recognizable, may be outrageous: the ways of the actors are deliberately shown at some 'distance' from normal behaviour in order that the spectator can freely laugh across the gap at what he believes different from his own. The classical methods of comedy, whether broad and low, romantic and pastoral, or high and mannered, have always been anti-naturalistic. A stage extravagant in word and deed permitted those excesses which

---

[9] Molière, *The Imaginary Invalid,* in *The Misanthrope and Other Plays,* trans. J. Wood (London, 1959).

still compel us to deride certain characters and their attitude to life.
To talk of 'stylization' equally to cover *As You Like It, Volpone, The
Way of the World, The School for Scandal, The Importance of Being
Earnest* and *Man and Superman* is perhaps an impertinence, but in
each of these plays the dramatist invented a world to different degrees
fantastic the better to compare our own. Artificial characters in an
artificial situation gained him more freedom and more force for his
dramatic effects. It is only after we have laughed spontaneously that
we perhaps perceive that the laugh has rebounded upon us, and
that the artificiality was all a snare. In the same way a simple verbal
witticism can leave some permanent mark upon us—if it includes
some quality of illuminating humour too.

Thus the best comedy teases and troubles an audience; it *can* be
painful. Comic method can serve to create an imaginative but dis-
passionate attitude; to create the conditions for thinking; to free the
dramatist in his attempt to tap certain rational resources of mind
in his audience. Derisory laughter may be used for this and it may
arise from this; it may not. Clearly it must do so in mannered comedy
like Shaw's *Arms and the Man* or *Heartbreak House,* where we are
encouraged for the most part to keep our critical distance from the
central characters Raina and Ellie the better to recognize their whole
significance. It may do so in surrealistic comedy like Samuel Beckett's
Waiting for Godot, where the slapstick convention of the play deceives
us most of the time into thinking that we are not looking at ourselves.
It probably will not do so in *King Lear,* where an ironic joke from
the Fool, laughable out of its context, is the more caustic in context
because we feel our sympathies are too directly its butt. The urgent
fact remains that, whether we laugh or not, the 'comic' attitude may
be present in any genre of play. The best jokes are not only compatible
with the most solemn intention, but are likely to be the best jokes for
that reason.

As the gap narrows so that what remains incongruous is still funny,
but too close to the bone to laugh at, then we move swiftly across
the frontier into the realms of the tragic. We have seen that plays with
large measures of sympathy felt through the laughter, like Shakespeare's romantic comedies, were inconvenient to the theorists. Similarly, plays which came near to closing the gap between the normality
of the audience and the abnormality of the stage, plays like *Measure
for Measure* or *The Misanthrope,* have been regarded as on the suspect fringe of the comic tradition, unwelcome exceptions to the rule.
The presence of the comic eye in the midst of tragedy, as in *King
Lear* or *Hamlet,* was put down to the licence of genius. Now, in the

work of Chekhov, Pirandello and Anouilh, and many others, it is the rule and not the exception to mingle the laughter and the tears; large numbers of plays today merely *use* the mechanism of laughter without granting its expected release of tension.

For our overall understanding of the comic in drama today, we should turn, not to Hazlitt and Meredith, nor to Bergson and Freud, but to Pirandello, whose essay *L'Umorismo* offers the key to the comedy of our own times. In this he suggests a brilliant example, which demonstrates among other things how flexible and serviceable for serious purposes is the comic attitude once the dramatist can evoke it. Imagine, he says, an elderly lady: we are immediately predisposed to be sympathetic. But she is overdressed, her face painted, her hair dyed like a girl's: we find this comic and we are ready to laugh. Yet suppose she is aware of the figure she is cutting, and is behaving in this way in order to hold the affections of her husband: we are sobered. The old lady seems pathetic again, and the laugh is 'on us'. The comic may be no laughing matter.[10]

Pirandello in 1908 was feeling for those qualities demanded by the modern stage in acknowledging with some finality the flexible nature of the theatre as a medium. Through it an audience could, and should, be drawn, repelled and drawn again, the 'gap' closed, opened and closed again. Since the comic view has always been instinctively felt to be an indispensable, if not quite respectable, prophylactic in drama as in life, so the methods of broad and artificial comedy were devised to make the comic view presentable. Now Pirandello insists that the comic view is a powerful and essential element in the effective control of an audience and an immensely serviceable corrective for its image of the play in the process of its formation. The fidelity of the drama to truth of feeling, and its accuracy of understanding in its handling of life on the stage, may depend upon the command the author has of the comic view and the keenness of his comic eye. How the comic may make of the drama a world living and flexible, and yet one unnaturally confined within the strict bounds of the stage, is also our concern in this study.

A simple short example for analysis is chosen to demonstrate the way impressions flow from actor to spectator with the kind of ironies most typical of the drama of recent times. In *The Rose Tattoo*, Tennessee Williams is catching at the incongruities of life by overtly setting them on the stage in their barefaced opposition. The scene is the home of Serafina delle Rose, who lives in a Sicilian colony on the

---

[10] Pirandello, *L'Umorismo*, 2nd ed. (Florence, 1920), p. 179.

coast between New Orleans and Mobile. The cottage is presented as a sectional 'frame', set in the semi-tropical vegetation of the place and in 'extremely romantic' lighting; this method of stage-setting is one that Williams has practised carefully both in order that we should retain a sense of environment throughout the play by actually seeing it, and that we should feel some initial detachment from the persons of the play. The characters are to be both typical and particular: we are to spy on them without joining them, and Serafina is to be 'a strange beast in a cage'.

Against the romantic setting and lighting we see the odd details of the living-room, introducing both Serafina and the incongruities of feeling that are to ensue. Serafina takes in sewing, and in a room cluttered with 'at least seven' dressmaker's dummies 'in various shapes and attitudes', as the author's production notes tell us, we see

an interior that is as colourful *as a booth at a carnival*. There are many religious articles and pictures *of ruby and gilt,* the *brass* cage of a *gaudy* parrot, a large bowl of *goldfish,* cutglass decanters and vases, *rose-patterned* wallpaper and a *rose-coloured* carpet. . . . There is a small shrine against the wall between the rooms, consisting of a prie-dieu and a little statue of the Madonna in a *starry blue* robe and a *gold* crown. Before this burns always a vigil light in its *ruby* glass cup. [The italics are mine.]

This is the passionate but limited world of the heroine of the play, bold in its contradictions. Williams significantly adds the comment, 'Our purpose is to show these gaudy, childlike mysteries with sentiment and humour in equal measure, without ridicule'.

Serafina, fiercely in love with her truck-driver husband, learns in the course of the play that not only has he been killed, but that he was, in spite of her love, unfaithful to her. She has regarded her marriage with the same kind of reverence that she reserved for the Madonna, and now her worship of her dead Rosario is turned to bitter grief, in its expression a kind of blasphemy. This little tragedy is presented to us against the incongruous details of her ordinary life, which includes the chase of a symbolic goat around the house by Serafina dressed in high-heeled slippers and a tight silk skirt, frequent screaming matches with the neighbours and their children, and the grotesque intrusion of the two prostitutes, Flora, 'tall and angular', and Bessie, 'rather stubby'. It is these who reveal the husband's infidelity against a background noise of a Souza march indifferently played by the band of her daughter's high school. Every ironic impression is a signal to the audience to revalue its estimate of Serafina's importance. Curiously she grows more weighty the more her simple dignity is under-

mined, and the strength of the ironic method Williams uses carries
the play through many of the crudities of the theme's heated overstatement.

In the second act, the man who is to replace the magnificent Rosario
arrives: 'He is short in stature, has a massively sculptural torso and
bluish-black curls. His face and manner are clownish; he has a charming awkwardness.' Serafina's first comment upon him when she is alone
sums up the whirling mixture of our own image: 'Madonna Santa!—
My husband's body, with the head of a *clown! (She crosses to the
Madonna.)* O Lady, O Lady! *(She makes an imploring gesture.)*
Speak to me!' But Alvaro Mangiacavallo, for that is indeed his name,
is, we learn, hardly sincere in his feelings for Serafina in the way
that she wants him to be.

The following, finally, is the kind of sequence with which the play
impresses itself upon its audience. The last act begins with both the
widow and the wooer prepared ludicrously for their assignation.
Serafina has put on an intolerably tight girdle, which she has only
just managed 'with much grunting' to strip off again before the arrival
of her lover. Alvaro has soaked rose oil in his hair and has had a
rose tattooed upon his chest, reminder of the dead Rosario, and the
better to appeal, as he thinks, to Serafina's sensibilities. Now—horror!
—a contraceptive drops from his trousers' pocket—their ludicrous passions thus merging into the repulsive.

SERAFINA . . . You think you got a good thing, a thing that is cheap!

ALVARO You make a mistake, Baronessa! *(He comes in and drops to his
knees beside her, pressing his cheek to her flank. He speaks rhapsodically.)*
So soft is a lady! So, so, so, so, so *soft*—is a lady!

SERAFINA Andate via, sporcaccione, andate a casa! Lasciatemi! Lasciatemi
stare!
*(She springs up and runs into the parlour. He pursues. The chase is gro-
tesquely violent and comic. A floor lamp is overturned. She seizes the
chocolate box and threatens to slam it into his face if he continues towards
her. He drops to his knees, crouched way over, and pounds the floor with
his fists, sobbing.)*

ALVARO Everything in my life turns out like this!

SERAFINA Git up, git up, git up!—you village idiot's grandson! There is
people watching you through that window, the—strega next door. . . .

So Alvaro is humiliated, though not as much as Serafina herself.

If we examine the impressions passed to us by the actors within
this short space of time, we may begin to feel something of the

way modern dark comedy operates. First, any sympathy we felt for Serafina in her grief is taken up and strengthened by her new agony, much as she had brought it upon herself. Her implication that she is not a 'thing' to be bought so cheaply, spoken with all the ferocious dignity of her Sicilian birth, is entirely as we would have her speak. To this extent we are self-composed, a relaxed audience, and Alvaro's abasement in his half-drunken state, with Serafina's spitting and lashing abuse of him, comforts us in our need to raise the widow as someone worthy of our commiseration. She has been outraged enough already.

But at this point in the play, Serafina's own baser instincts begin to emerge, though she cannot this time begin to elevate her new relationship to the holy level of her intimacy with her late husband. In all her self-righteous fury, she is already unbending a little, and in her 'Lasciatemi stare', 'let me be', we hear the old note re-enter her voice. We feel some of her willing pity for this fool who presumes to take the place of Rosario. And in her one ironic gesture of *running* from him, inviting his pursuit, our composure is shattered by a contradictory impression, and our image of the play once again turns turtle. Instead of growing to a nobility, Serafina, with the incongruous rose in her hair, shrinks to be another clown with Alvaro: 'The chase is grotesquely violent and comic.' She fights with the box of chocolates he had brought her, he drops to the floor sobbing like a frustrated child: 'Everything in my life turns out like this!' We might say that here an incipient tragic convention has become a comic one by inversion.

This is the way that Serafina's romantic obsession is punctured. We know her humiliation more than she knows it herself, since we have the complete situation in view and the whole counterpoint of the action violently registered in our minds. And it seems even Serafina has some sense of objective appearances, feeling her indignity, when she draws attention to the 'witch' next door: 'There is people watching you.' As she says this she knows the eyes are on herself.

This is a play about human illusions, about a simple woman who believes too much in herself; it is about her sin of pride. It is not about the man Mangiacavallo, who has few illusions and no pride. He is introduced into the action, this man with the head of a clown, simply as an agent of destruction, not so much to destroy Serafina as to destroy our image of human worth. But, oddly, the heroine in her simplicity and in spite of her littleness and nakedness, is given by this author an ineluctable stature by her very weaknesses, warmly comprehensive and curiously close to us. The summation of the individual ironies of the play's action is the huge particular irony of the total image the play leaves with us. We do not now deal in tragedies, nor in comedies, nor indeed in the nondescript 'tragicomedy'. There flourish—what?—dramas of 'mood'. These are not necessarily plays calling up a peculiar atmosphere, but plays which attempt to control the exceptionally disparate audiences of modern times by teasing the mind and the emotion this way and that, making the one deceive, encourage and contradict the other. . . .

Whatever Happened to Comedy?*

RICHARD DUPREY

When your world becomes black and blue and you retreat into the corners of your life, feeling for all the world like the monkey in the schoolyard rhyme who chased his tail around the flagpole, there is nothing like a little comedy to prove to you that things might be considerably worse. As you roar at the lady who sat on the coconut-cream pie or at the discomfiture of Sganerelle or at Malvolio's humiliation at the hands of Sir Toby, there is a certain release of your own torrent of troubles onto the heads of these hapless ones. Just as the tragic figure assumes our burden in the rhythm of the tragedy with its sacrificial inevitability, the comic butt takes another human burden upon himself as he executes the comic pratfall.

For all the jollity of the comic form, however, comedy is one of the most truly serious things in this world and in its surgical "pessimism" lies most of its value and much of its appeal. While noble tragedy with its so-called cathartic action on the emotions cleanses one, so they tell us, of fear and pity, comedy, with an appeal to the mind rather than to the heart, shows us the stupidity of our earthly ways. In the failings of the common man we see more than a faint glimmer of our own imperfection. Dealing as it does with the folly of mankind, the comedy lays bare man's foolishness, ferocity, frivolousness, and the phoniness of so many of his human institutions. As a social corrective it helps us to see our own faults, both as individuals and in groups, and it provides us with a sort of "misery loves com-

---

* Richard Duprey, "Whatever Happened to Comedy?" in *Just off the Aisle* (Newman Press, 1962), pp. 149–156.

pany" refreshment as we see other men struck down with the slapstick. We sit smiling from the relative safety of our theatre seat.

There is a need for laughter in this macabre age, but in the words
of G. K. Chesterton, ". . . in a world where everything is ridiculous,
nothing can be ridiculed. You cannot unmask a mask; when it is
admittedly hollow as a mask. You cannot turn a thing upside down,
if there is no theory about its being right side up. If life is really so
formless that you cannot make head nor tail of it, you cannot pull
its tail; and you certainly cannot make it stand on its head." (*Eight
Great Comedies,* Mentor Books.)

Perhaps this is the problem of our theatre that is vastly more
critical than our contemporary failure to write Aristotelian tragedy. We
haven't been able to write comedy—something vastly more necessary
to society's well-being. There have been an increasing number of
theories heard lately concerning the demise of great comedy in our
theatre. Since the last George S. Kaufman comedy left the boards a
few years back, American stage humor has been restricted to the sex
farces of George Axelrod, the specialized humor of Thurber, the
work of an occasional European wit (usually too ironical for sentimental Americans), or the grand, but again specialized work of those
who create revues for the Yiddish stage.

Now and then we find flashes of comic brilliance in plays that are
not essentially comic, as for example, in Paddy Chayefsky's *The Tenth
Man,* but for the most part, great comedy has disappeared from our
stage and no one seems to know why.

Great comedy is the result of keen observation of the world. The
comic writer, a sharp and perceptive man who stands on the sidelines
and views the staggering gyrations of mankind, records in his detached
and facile manner the errors of humanity. He sees all the silly, pre-
posterous, utterly absurd things that his fellow man does. He takes note
of the countless deviations from the norm in the lives of his col-
leagues in flesh. Not, in truth, feeling anything for them but a careful
objectivity, he dispassionately compares them with what they ought to
be. The writer who pictures a fat-bottomed friar solemnly peddling
an English bicycle, who depicts an irate political leader paddling a
baby's behind rather than kissing its cherubic face, or who visualizes
for his readers the glorious absurdity of a garbage man in white tie
and tails, is observing the violation of a standard—the shattering of
an expected pattern of human action.

Today, our human society is a fragmented thing. Dwelling in an
age of self-centeredness, our eyes are turned inward and every man
has attempted to make of himself a social and ideological island.

Though we conform blindly to hollow mores and obsolete social usages, we cry out for individual interpretation of nearly everything
else, and even those of us who follow a faith, who subscribe to a
set philosophy, or who vote consistently with one political party, hear
ourselves—our own voices—speaking out from time to time in terms
of relative truth. Rather than right reason we are guided by sentiment
and often our religious orientation, our philosophy of life, our political
affiliations, become a matter of "team spirit" or mass psychology
rather than a matter of earnest conviction. With the playwright Luigi
Pirandello, father of a whole school of artistic relativists, we say,
"Right you are, if you think you are!"

Our forefathers in theocratic Greece, in medieval Europe, in Elizabethan England, knew how to laugh, for they had before them in
the ideals and attitudes of their societies a requisite for true comedy.
With a sense of order, a knowledge of the nature of things—a knowledge that all society shared—they could see clearly the incongruity of
man's deviations from the norms and natural laws of a sensible universe. Human nature was a known thing, subject to the laws of God
and the "ground rules" of his creation.

Today, every man sets himself up as a prophet, subject to his own
rules of behavior. Fortunately there is some semblance of respect for
law and order persisting, though there are indications that the evident
breakdown of the family and the softening of paternal authority in our
society, even this regard is beginning to fade. If there are no generally
held social norms, then there can be no great comedy. The break
from the norm has no meaning unless there is a commonly held norm
from which to break. This is the axiom of both human culture and
the historical patterns of art. It is also common sense.

Another factor that holds our theatre back from the heights of
comic fulfillment is the element of fear. Man is too frightened today
with all the world's unrest really to laugh with heartiness. One must
remain rather unemotional about something to enjoy real laughter at
its expense. When a loved one, your father, let's say, falls flat on his
face in a mud puddle after having meticulously prepared himself for
a fancy dress ball, our laughter fades when we realize who it is and
that he may have hurt himself. Even the comedian, like Chaplin, or
more recently, Jackie Gleason, who sees fit to flirt with pathos, must
hide his real humanity behind certain stereotyped symbols like the
strange walk, the Hitlerian moustache, and the trademark bowler, in
order to keep us from experiencing an excess of emotional identification which would immediately banish mirth from the scene.

With the ever present fear of contemporary life gnawing at us,

it is difficult to become detached enough even for the initial guffaw. The great problems of the century are too grim for our laughter.
With the absurdity of these cruel times, the chortle of amusement
sounds too much like "the death rattle," and so our prophets of
the absurd, Camus, Sartre, Duerenmatt and all the rest, see absurdity
from the position of "engagement" rather than that of comic detachment. Thus comedy dies as we allow our small fears to mushroom
into great ones.

For example, no one is writing quality comedy about the spectre
of atomic war, the race problem, the withering of the family, and the
threat of economic and ideological takeover by the Soviet Union. We
are far too worried about these things and we have allowed too many
of them—these troubles we exist with from day to day—to progress
to the brink of disaster. The Romans, in the decadent autumnal days
of their Empire, did not write comedy about the threat of barbarian
invasion and how ill-equipped they were to face so frightening an
eventuality. Instead they chatted about sex and social usages in their
theatres. They did not direct the comic barrage to point up their
weaknesses in the hope of transmuting them into strengths. They
were a people who had fallen in love with their own infirmities. And
so Rome fell!

Like the Romans, we follow suit: We produce our tedious sex jokes;
our little joshings of earnestness and sincerity wherever and whenever
we find them, and now and then, on the threshold of panic, we
write grim sociological tracts about the dangers of mass "genocide-
by-the-bomb" or other things equally cheery—serious warnings which
do little to relieve the tension of the times or to rectify its problems.

The laughter of comedy is a social corrective. Many a grievous
problem has been laughed away, for evil, based as it is on pride, cannot bear the stings of society's laughter. The comedies of Aristophanes
and Molière, to cite but two of the greatest, lashed out at the evils
of their day. Aristophanes tried with some measure of success (though
who can measure the results of this sort of thing) to discredit the
Sophists and some of the political demagogues of Athens. Molière
sought to expose the charlatans of the then fraudulent medical profession, the hypocrisy of some of the churchmen at court, the *poseurs*
and *dilettanti* of his society. They were not thanked for making these
exposures, and they give evidence to the fact that the comic artist—
one who would satirize the foibles of the world—must be made of
heroic stuff. His targets are not only moving ones but they often fire
back and usually their ammunition is physical or social punishment
rather than a mere barrage of wit. Most of the great comic artists

in the theatre—Gogol, Synge, Cervantes, Gay and others—were slandered and villified, if not subjected to worse treatment. Who is there now with the solid, generally accepted ideology *and* the courage to strike down the frauds and cheats of today?

With stringent libel laws and the extreme sensitivity of the great medias of publishing and the electronic media, it is all but impossible to stand up and expose the evils of society in anything but the most general way, for fear of treading on the toes of some influential fool. Only noted public bogeys like Señor Castro and Tovarich Khrushchev are legitimate goats. If we start striking too close to home with our comic brickbats, someone screams "foul" and the world starts battening down the hatches against us.

Our theatre today does laugh, but its laughter could better be characterized as a snicker than an honest roar of delight. It ridicules the staunchly honest, the intellectual, the chaste, and the peaceful. In the professional playscript, a girl who wants to stay chaste, the man who wishes to stay faithful to his wife, one who seeks knowledge for its own sweet sake, and one who bids for peace, are the butts and gulls of audience laughter. Of course we know that humor always had a talent for iconoclastic attack. The rich, the learned, the powerful, those who appear virtuous, have always provided targets for laughter down through the centuries. The Romans managed to attack the gods and the medieval Christian had many a good laugh at one saint or another. However, there is a *malaise* in our contemporary theatre in which good becomes the butt and evil the heroic quality *almost always,* as they are exposed to a shifting and, in a sense, ghostly standard of morality.

It's a sorry state of affairs with no immediate solution in view. It makes one think upon certain ominous historical parallels and precedents. The person who loses the ability to laugh at himself and the society which loses sight of its own foibles and failings are both riding for a fall. "Pride goeth before the fall," we are told. May we someday find our way back to a theatre that can laugh and say, "What fools we mortals be!"

Though we have lost the real comic sense—that of Aristophanes and Molière—the ability to detect absurdity has not been totally lost today. Though it has clearly passed out of the comic realm where it can inspire true laughter, there is a force somehow comic that can precipitate action from absurdity—from the serious contemplation of human irrationality.

Writers like the late Albert Camus and the remarkable Swiss novelist-playwright Friedrich Duerenmatt have manifested that they possess a clear vision of the world's absurdity—its deviation from its very own standards of humanity. Camus, rendering loathsome portraits of man's behavior toward his fellow man, shows a clear vision and a perceptive analysis of the horror that a lack of love or, at bottom, respect, can wreak. Duerenmatt with crystal-clear conception sees through a crawling mass of rationalization to the selfishness of what we humans too often call justice—self-interest. There is no question that these men perceive a standard and write with that standard in mind.

Their problem, like that of many other sincerely engaged writers of our times who revile the world in their writing, is the very vehemence with which they write. They become so enmeshed—so passionately involved—in the emotion of disgust that they often lead their audiences to the brink of hopelessness and despair. Does the work of Camus make us want to go out and rectify things or does it force us back to the lonely barricade of desperation? In the play *Caligula,* are the issues clear enough for us to know what to fight or are we so choked with his catalogue of moral horrors that our intellect refuses to act? We could wish that Camus had aimed his works deliberately at the comic effect rather than attempting tragedy, for the tradition of tragedy precludes action. Who walks away from Oedipus wanting to cure anything? Rather, one walks off saying, "Oedipus, despite his sin—despite the fact that he is but corrupt flesh—has won, through his pain, a moral victory and has saved his people. All is well with the world." By the passion of his *agon* he has saved us and we have been cleansed by his victory.

In comedy, the problem is quite different. We seek to cure the sores and boils that have formed on the susceptible flesh of history. This can be accomplished only by a *controlled* and *reasoned* disgust: a disgust that doesn't release the intellect from the problem of witnessing man and his actions in the theatre; a disgust that *involves* and yet does not excuse one from responsibility; a disgust of such a nature that it leaves room for hope and engenders a feeling within us that the wrongs can be and ultimately must be righted.

Bertolt Brecht, the strange genius of East Germany's *Berlinner Ensemble,* found the recipe for this therapeutic drama, this dark-masked comedy where absurdity is shown, where we are prompted to make corrections in the direction of our lives and our ideals. We see in his plays a world where man must sell himself in order to live—where he must not hesitate to drain his fellow man in order to sustain life. In the case of Brecht, the comic dynamism is put to use in the service of Marx—in the pursuit of the revolutionary paradise of economic, social, and political "pie in the sky." Brecht would essay to point out inconsistencies in our moral code based on our failure to conform and then send us from the theatre to revolt against our ideals, fashioning new ones more conformable to present expectations. For instance, in the concluding passages of *The Good Woman of Setzuan* the prescription is "bigger, better gods or none." To be sure, Brecht is stacking the cards against us, but he has at least found a way to use humor significantly. He gives us the technical plan for a theatre to serve as a social scourge.

Perhaps today there is something to be called "the black mask of comedy." It may be that in our times we can find a certain new dramatic dimension which can serve as a social corrective—a leaven to bring forth this reasoned disgust of which we speak so as to precipitate meaningful and effective action.

It is indeed no accident that the ancient mask of "Arlecchino" is one of comedy's traditional symbols. It is a black, ugly thing, patched with grotesque hair, and staring out at life with an exacting, bestial intelligence. Comedy itself is a basically pessimistic thing which shows us man, not as he ought to be, but as he is—calced over with the lewd scales of vice and wrapped in the hypocrisy of his fallen nature. In the work of Boccaccio, in that of Rabelais, that of Chaucer, Swift, Gogol, and Cervantes we see an image of the same poor foolish man that was driven naked from Paradise, his flaccid haunches lashed raw by the angel with the flaming sword.

Part Five

THE PSYCHOLOGY OF COMEDY

Sigmund Freud

JOKES AND THE COMIC

Ludwig Jekels

ON THE PSYCHOLOGY OF COMEDY

Martin Grotjahn

BEYOND LAUGHTER: A SUMMING UP

Jokes and the Comic*

SIGMUND FREUD

It is only with misgivings that I venture to approach the problem of the comic itself. It would be presumptuous to expect that my efforts would be able to make any decisive contribution to its solution when the works of a great number of eminent thinkers have failed to produce a wholly satisfactory explanation. My intention is in fact no more than to pursue the lines of thought that have proved valuable with jokes a short distance further into the sphere of the comic.

The comic arises in the first instance as an unintended discovery derived from human social relations. It is found in people—in their movements, forms, actions and traits of character, originally in all probability only in their physical characteristics but later in their mental ones as well or, as the case may be, in the expression of those characteristics. By means of a very common sort of personification, animals become comic too, and inanimate objects. At the same time, the comic is capable of being detached from people, in so far as we recognize the conditions under which a person seems comic. In this way the comic of situation comes about, and this recognition affords the possibility of making a person comic at one's will by putting him in situations in which his actions are subject to these comic conditions. The discovery that one has it in one's power to make someone else comic opens the way to an undreamt-of yield of comic pleasure and is the origin of a highly developed technique. One can make *oneself* comic, too, as easily as other people. The methods that serve to make people comic are: putting them in a comic situation, mimicry, disguise, unmasking, caricature, parody, travesty, and so on. It is

* Sigmund Freud, "Jokes and the Comic," in *Jokes and Their Relation to the Unconscious,* James Strachey, ed. and tr. (W. W. Norton, 1960), pp. 188–221. [Footnotes have been renumbered; editor's minor footnotes were deleted.]

obvious that these techniques can be used to serve hostile and aggressive purposes. One can make a person comic in order to make him become contemptible, to deprive him of his claim to dignity and authority. But even if such an intention habitually underlies making people comic, this need not be the meaning of what is comic spontaneously.

This irregular survey of the occurrences of the comic will already show us that a very extensive field of origin is to be ascribed to it and that such specialized conditions as we found, for instance, in the naïve are not to be expected in it. In order to get on the track of the determining condition that is valid for the comic, the most important thing is the choice of an introductory case. We shall choose the comic of movement, because we recollect that the most primitive kind of stage performance—the pantomime—uses that method for making us laugh. The answer to the question of why we laugh at the clown's movements is that they seem to us extravagant and inexpedient. We are laughing at an expenditure that is too large. Let us look now for the determining condition outside the comic that is artificially constructed—where it can be found unintended. A child's movements do not seem to us comic, although he kicks and jumps about. On the other hand, it *is* comic when a child who is learning to write follows the movements of his pen with his tongue stuck out; in these associated motions we see an unnecessary expenditure of movement which we should spare ourselves if we were carrying out the same activity. Similarly, other such associated motions, or merely exaggerated expressive movements, seem to us comic in adults too. Pure examples of this species of the comic are to be seen, for instance, in the movements of someone playing skittles who, after he has released the ball, follows its course as though he could still continue to direct it. Thus, too, all grimaces are comic which exaggerate the normal expression of the emotions, even if they are produced involuntarily as in sufferers from St. Vitus's dance (chorea). And in the same way, the passionate movements of a modern conductor seem comic to any unmusical person who cannot understand their necessity. Indeed, it is from this comic of movement that the comic of bodily shapes and facial features branches off; for these are regarded as though they were the outcome of an exaggerated or pointless movement. Staring eyes, a hooked nose hanging down to the mouth, ears sticking out, a hump-back—all such things probably only produce a comic effect in so far as movements are imagined which would be necessary to bring about these features; and here the nose, the ears and other parts of the body are imagined as more movable than they are in reality. There is no doubt that it is comic if someone can "waggle his ears", and it would certainly be still more comic if he could move his nose up and down. A good deal of the comic effect produced on us by animals comes from our perceiving in them movements such as these which we cannot imitate ourselves.

But how is it that we laugh when we have recognized that some other person's movements are exaggerated and inexpedient? By making a comparison, I believe, between the movement I observe in the other person and the one that I should have carried out myself in his place. The two things compared must of course be judged by the same standard, and this standard is my expenditure of innervation, which is linked to my idea of the movement in both of the two cases. . . .

Thus a uniform explanation is provided of the fact that a person appears comic to us if, in comparison with ourselves, he makes too great an expenditure on his bodily functions and too little on his mental ones; and it cannot be denied that in both these cases our laughter expresses a pleasurable sense of the superiority which we feel in relation to him. If the relation in the two cases is reversed—if the other person's physical expenditure is found to be less than ours or his mental expenditure greater—then we no longer laugh, we are filled with astonishment and admiration.[1] . . .

Mankind have not been content to enjoy the comic where they have come upon it in their experience; they have also sought to bring it about intentionally, and we can learn more about the nature of the comic if we study the means which serve to *make* things comic. First and foremost, it is possible to produce the comic in relation to oneself in order to amuse other people—for instance, by making oneself out clumsy or stupid. In that way one produces a comic effect exactly as though one really were these things, by fulfilling the condition of the comparison which leads to the difference in expenditure. But one does not in this way make oneself ridiculous or contemptible, but may in some circumstances even achieve admiration. The feeling of superiority does not arise in the other person if he knows that one has only been pretending; and this affords fresh evidence of the fundamental independence of the comic from the feeling of superiority.

As regards making *other people* comic, the principal means is to put them in situations in which a person becomes comic as a result

---

[1] The contradictoriness with which the determining conditions of the comic are pervaded—the fact that sometimes an excess and sometimes an insufficiency seems to be the source of comic pleasure—has contributed no little to the confusion of the problem. Cf. Lipps (1898, 47).

of human dependence on external events, particularly on social factors, without regard to the personal characteristics of the individual concerned—that is to say, by employing the comic of situation. This putting of someone in a comic situation may be a *real* one (a practical joke)—by sticking out a leg so that someone trips over it as though he were clumsy, by making him seem stupid by exploiting his credulity, or trying to convince him of something nonsensical, and so on—or it may be simulated by speech or play. The aggressiveness, to which making a person comic usually ministers, is much assisted by the fact that the comic pleasure is independent of the reality of the comic situation, so that everyone is in fact exposed, without any defence, to being made comic.

But there are yet other means of making things comic which deserve special consideration and also indicate in part fresh sources of comic pleasure. Among these, for instance, is *mimicry,* which gives quite extraordinary pleasure to the hearer and makes its object comic even if it is still far from the exaggeration of a caricature. It is much easier to find a reason for the comic effect of *caricature* than for that of mere mimicry. Caricature, parody and travesty (as well as their practical counterpart, unmasking) are directed against people and objects which lay claim to authority and respect, which are in some sense 'sublime'.[2] They are procedures for *Herabsetzung,* as the apt German expression has it. What is sublime is something large in the figurative, psychical sense; and I should like to suggest, or rather to repeat my suggestion, that, like what is somatically large, it is represented by an increased expenditure. It requires little observation to establish that when I speak of something sublime I innervate my speech in a different way, I make different facial expressions, and I try to bring the whole way in which I hold myself into harmony with the dignity of what I am having an idea of. I impose a solemn restraint upon myself—not very different from what I should adopt if I were to enter the presence of an exalted personality, a monarch, or a prince of science. I shall hardly be wrong in assuming that this different innervation in my ideational mimetics corresponds to an increased expenditure. The third instance of an increased expenditure of this kind is no doubt to be found when I proceed in abstract trains of thought instead of in the habitual concrete and plastic ones.

---

[2] 'Degradation' [in English in the original]. Bain (1865, 248) writes: 'The occasion of the Ludicrous is the Degradation of some person or interest, possessing dignity, in circumstances that excite no other strong emotion.' [The English word 'degradation' has accordingly been used in all that follows as a translation of '*Herabsetzung*'.]

When, therefore, the procedures that I have discussed for the degradation of the sublime allow me to have an idea of it as though it were something commonplace, in whose presence I need not pull myself together but may, to use the military formula, 'stand easy', I am being spared the increased expenditure of the solemn restraint; and the comparison between this new ideational method (instigated by empathy) and the previously habitual one, which is simultaneously trying to establish itself—this comparison once again creates the difference in expenditure which can be discharged by laughter.

Caricature, as is well known, brings about degradation by emphasizing in the general impression given by the exalted object a single trait which is comic in itself but was bound to be overlooked so long as it was only perceivable in the general picture. By isolating this, a comic effect can be attained which extends in our memory over the whole object. This is subject to the condition that the actual presence of the exalted object himself does not keep us in a reverential attitude. If a comic trait of this kind that has been overlooked is lacking in reality, a caricature will unhesitatingly create it by exaggerating one that is not comic in itself; and the fact that the effect of the caricature is not essentially diminished by this falsification of reality is once again an indication of the origin of comic pleasure.

Parody and *travesty* achieve the degradation of something exalted in another way: by destroying the unity that exists between people's characters as we know them and their speeches and actions, by replacing either the exalted figures or their utterances by inferior ones. They are distinguished from caricature in this, but not in the mechanism of their production of comic pleasure. The same mechanism is also used for *unmasking,* which only applies where someone has seized dignity and authority by a deception and these have to be taken from him in reality. We have already met with a few examples of the comic effect of unmasking in jokes—for instance, in the story of the aristocratic lady who, at the first onset of her labour-pains, exclaimed 'Ah! mon Dieu!' but whom the doctor would not assist till she cried out 'Aa-ee, aa-ee!' Having come to know the characteristics of the comic, we can no longer dispute that this anecdote is in fact an example of comic unmasking and has no justifiable claim to be called a joke. It only recalls jokes by its setting and by the technical method of 'representation by something very small' [loc.cit.]—in this case the patient's cry, which is found sufficient to establish the indication for treatment. It nevertheless remains true that our linguistic sense, if we call on it for a decision, raises no objection to our calling a story like this a joke. We may explain this by reflecting that linguistic usage is not based on the scientific insight into the nature of jokes that we have arrived at in this laborious investigation. Since one of the functions of jokes is to make hidden sources of comic pleasure accessible once more, any device that brings to light something that is not manifestly comic may, by a loose analogy, be termed a joke. This applies preferably, however, to unmasking as well as to other methods of making people comic.[3]

Under the heading of 'unmasking' we may also include a procedure for making things comic with which we are already acquainted—the method of degrading the dignity of individuals by directing attention to the frailties which they share with all humanity, but in particular the dependence of their mental functions on bodily needs. The unmasking is equivalent here to an admonition: such and such a person, who is admired as a demigod, is after all only human like you and me. Here, too, are to be placed the efforts at laying bare the monotonous psychical automatism that lies behind the wealth and apparent freedom of psychical functions. We came across examples of 'unmasking' of this kind in the marriage-broker jokes, and felt a doubt at the time whether these anecdotes have a right to be counted as jokes. We are now able to decide with greater certainty that the anecdote of the echo who reinforced all the assertions of the marriage-broker and finally confirmed his admission that the bride had a hump with the exclamation 'And *what* a hump!'—that this anecdote is essentially a *comic* story, an example of the unmasking of a psychical automatism. Here, however, the comic story is only serving as a façade. For anyone who will attend to the hidden meaning of the marriage-broker anecdotes, the whole thing remains an admirably staged joke; anyone who does not penetrate so far is left with a comic story. The same thing applies to the other joke, about the marriage-broker who, in order to answer an objection, ended by confessing the truth with a cry of "But I ask you, who would lend such people anything?" Here again we have a comic unmasking as the façade for a joke, though in this instance the characteristic of a joke is much more unmistakable, since the marriage-broker's remark is at the same time a representation by the opposite. In trying to prove that the people are rich he at the same time proves that they are *not* rich, but very poor. Here a joke and the comic are combined, and teach us that the same remark can be both things at once. . . .

---

[3] 'Thus every conscious and ingenious evocation of the comic (whether the comic of contemplation or of situation) is in general described as a joke. We, of course, cannot here make use of this concept of the joke either.' (Lipps, 1898, 78.)

Every theory of the comic is objected to by its critics on the score that its definition overlooks what is essential to the comic: 'The comic is based on a contrast between ideas.' 'Yes, in so far as the contrast has a comic and not some other effect.' 'The feeling of the comic arises from the disappointment of an expectation.' 'Yes, unless the disappointment is in fact a distressing one.' No doubt the objections are justified; but we shall be over-estimating them if we conclude from them that the essential feature of the comic has hitherto escaped detection. What impairs the universal validity of these definitions are conditions which are indispensable for the generating of comic pleasure; but we do not need to look for the essence of the comic in them. In any case, it will only become easy for us to dismiss the objections and throw light on the contradictions to the definitions of the comic if we suppose that the origin of comic pleasure lies in a comparison of the difference between two expenditures. Comic pleasure and the effect by which it is known—laughter—can only come about if this difference is unutilizable and capable of discharge. We obtain no pleasurable effect but at most a transient sense of pleasure in which the characteristic of being comic does not emerge, if the difference is put to another use as soon as it is recognized. Just as special contrivances have to be adopted in the case of jokes in order to prevent the use elsewhere of the expenditure that is recognized as superfluous, so, too, comic pleasure can only appear in circumstances that guarantee this same condition. For this reason occasions on which these differences in expenditure occur in our ideational life are uncommonly numerous, but the occasions on which the comic emerges from those differences are relatively quite rare.

Two observations force themselves on anyone who studies even cursorily the conditions for the generation of the comic from difference in expenditure. First, there are cases in which the comic appears habitually and as though by force of necessity, and on the contrary others in which it seems entirely dependent on the circumstances and on the standpoint of the observer. But secondly, unusually large differences very often break through unfavourable conditions, so that the comic feeling emerges in spite of them. In connection with the first of these points it would be possible to set up two classes—the inevitably comic and the occasionally comic—though one must be prepared from the first to renounce the notion of finding the inevitability of the comic in the first class free from exceptions. It would be tempting to enquire into the determining conditions for the two classes.

The conditions, some of which have been brought together as the 'isolation' of the comic situation, apply essentially to the second class. A closer analysis elicits the following facts:

(*a*) The most favourable condition for the production of comic pleasure is a generally cheerful mood in which one is 'inclined to laugh'. In a toxic mood of cheerfulness almost everything seems comic, probably by comparison with the expenditure in a normal state. Indeed, jokes, the comic and all similar methods of getting pleasure from mental activity are no more than ways of regaining this cheerful mood—this euphoria—from a single point of approach, when it is not present as a general disposition of the psyche.

(*b*) A similarly favourable effect is produced by an *expectation* of the comic, by being attuned to comic pleasure. For this reason, if an intention to make something comic is communicated to one by someone else, differences of such a low degree are sufficient that they would probably be overlooked if they occurred in one's experience unintentionally. Anyone who starts out to read a comic book or goes to the theatre to see a farce owes to this intention his ability to laugh at things which would scarcely have provided him with a case of the comic in his ordinary life. In the last resort it is in the recollection of having laughed and in the expectation of laughing that he laughs when he sees the comic actor come on to the stage, before the latter can have made any attempt at making him laugh. For that reason, too, one admits feeling ashamed afterwards over what one has been able to laugh at at the play.

(*c*) Unfavourable conditions for the comic arise from the kind of mental activity with which a particular person is occupied at the moment. Imaginative or intellectual work that pursues serious aims interferes with the capacity of the cathexes for discharge—cathexes which the work requires for its displacements—so that only unexpectedly large differences in expenditure are able to break through to comic pleasure. What are quite specially unfavourable for the comic are all kinds of intellectual processes which are sufficiently remote from what is perceptual to bring ideational mimetics to a stop. There is no place whatever left for the comic in abstract reflection except when that mode of thought is suddenly interrupted.

(*d*) The opportunity for the release of comic pleasure disappears, too, if the attention is focused precisely on the comparison from which the comic may emerge. In such circumstances what would otherwise have the most certain comic effect loses its comic force. A movement or a function cannot be comic for a person whose interest is directed to comparing it with a standard which he has clearly before his mind. Thus the examiner does not find the nonsense comic which the candidate produces in his ignorance; he is annoyed by it, while the candidate's fellow students, who are far more interested in what luck he will have than in how much he knows, laugh heartily at the same nonsense. A gymnastic or dancing instructor seldom has an eye for the comic in his pupils' movements; and a clergyman entirely overlooks the comic in the human weaknesses which the writer of comedies can bring to light so effectively. The comic process will not bear being hypercathected by attention; it must be able to take its course quite unobserved—in this respect, incidentally, just like jokes. It would, however, contradict the nomenclature of the 'processes of consciousness' of which I made use, with good reason, in my *Interpretation of Dreams* if one sought to speak of the comic process as a necessarily unconscious one. It forms part, rather, of the preconscious; and such processes, which run their course in the preconscious but lack the cathexis of attention with which consciousness is linked, may aptly be given the name of 'automatic'. The process of comparing expenditures must remain automatic if it is to produce comic pleasure.

(*e*) The comic is greatly interfered with if the situation from which it ought to develop gives rise at the same time to a release of strong affect. A discharge of the operative difference is as a rule out of the question in such a case. The affects, disposition and attitude of the individual in each particular case make it understandable that the comic emerges and vanishes according to the standpoint of each particular person, and that an absolute comic exists only in exceptional instances. The contingency or relativity of the comic is therefore far greater than that of a joke, which never happens of its own accord but is invariably *made,* and in which the conditions under which it can find acceptance can be observed at the time at which it is constructed. The generation of affect is the most intense of all the conditions that interfere with the comic and its importance in this respect has been nowhere overlooked.[4] For this reason it has been said that the comic feeling comes easiest in more or less indifferent cases where the feelings and interests are not strongly involved. Yet precisely in cases where there is a release of affect one can observe a particularly strong difference in expenditure bring about the automatism of release. When Colonel Butler[5] answers Octavio's warnings by exclaiming 'with a bitter laugh': '*Thanks* from the House of

---

[4] 'It is easy for you to laugh; it means nothing more to you.'

[5] [In Schiller's tragedy *Wallensteins Tod* (II, 6). Colonel Butler, a veteran Irish soldier in the Imperial army during the Thirty Years War, believes that he has been snubbed by the Emperor and is preparing to desert to his enemies. Octavio Piccolomini, his superior officer, begs him to reconsider the position and reminds him of the thanks which Austria owes him for his forty years' loyalty, and to this Butler replies in the words quoted above.]

Austria!' his embitterment does not prevent his laughing. The laugh applies to his memory of the disappointment he believes he has suffered; and on the other hand the magnitude of the disappointment cannot be portrayed more impressively by the dramatist than by his showing it capable of forcing a laugh in the midst of the storm of feelings that have been released. I am inclined to think that this explanation would apply to every case in which laughter occurs in circumstances other than pleasurable ones and accompanied by intensely distressing or strained emotions.

(*f*) If we add to this that the generating of comic pleasure can be encouraged by any other pleasurable accompanying circumstance as though by some sort of contagious effect (working in the same kind of way as the fore-pleasure principle with tendentious jokes), we shall have mentioned enough of the conditions governing comic pleasure for our purposes, though certainly not all of them. We can then see that these conditions, as well as the inconstancy and contingency of the comic effect, cannot be explained so easily by any other hypothesis than that of the derivation of comic pleasure from the discharge of a difference which, under the most varying circumstances, is liable to be used in ways other than discharge.

On the Psychology of Comedy*

LUDWIG JEKELS

We are indebted to psycho-analysis for much valuable insight into the psychology of tragedy. Not only has psycho-analysis made us recognise that the "tragic guilt" of the hero, postulated by aesthetics, actually stems from the repressed Oedipus-wishes of the dramatist but it has also drawn our attention to the interrelation of dramatist and audience; that is, to the fact of a common guilt as the decisive psychological factor which, on the one hand, enables the dramatist to create his work and, on the other, produces the Aristotelian catharsis, or "purging of the passions." Freud,[1] in particular, established the psychological traces of the primal crime in classical tragedy and following in his tracks, Winterstein [2] has recently subjected the origins of tragedy to intensive study and radically clarified them.

By contrast, how little has psycho-analysis bothered about comedy! So far it has hardly attracted any interest worth mentioning: at most it was granted a modest domicile in that basement of research, the footnote, there to be dealt with in a cursory manner.

And yet it seems to me that comedy well deserves serious and detailed investigation, and not only because it contains the problem of the comic, which is admittedly one of the most difficult and complicated in psychology; a problem, in fact, which even Freud [3] approached "not without some trepidation," although he was able later to clarify it greatly. As this rough outline will help to show, the psycho-analytical investigation of comedy can bring to light much that may claim our fullest interest.

---

[1] Freud, *Totem and Taboo.*

[2] Alfred Winterstein, *Der Ursprung der Tragödie.*

[3] Freud, *Jokes and Their Relation to the Unconscious.*

* Ludwig Jekels, "On the Psychology of Comedy," in *Selected Papers of Ludwig Jekels,* I. Jarosy, tr. (International Universities Press).

My analysis of several classical comedies led to the surprising result that I found them characterised by a mechanism of inversion: *the feeling of guilt which, in tragedy, rests upon the son, appears in comedy displaced on the father; it is the father who is guilty.*

This fact was probably already noticed by Diderot; at the same time it seems to have elicited an effective disagreement on his part, for in his *Discours sur la poésie dramatique* he writes: "It seems to me that Terence succumbed, on one occasion, to this fault. His 'Heautontimorumenos' ('The Self-Tormentor'), is a father who grieves over the violent decision to which he has driven his son by excessive strictness; he therefore punishes himself by miserably depriving himself of food and clothing, shunning all company, dismissing his servants and tilling the soil with his own hands. One may justly remark that such a father does not exist. The largest town would hardly be able to furnish an example of such strange sorrow in a hundred years."

We shall attempt to substantiate our thesis, though only in outline, with the help of other examples. The jumbling together of works belonging to very different cultures, and to epochs which are frequently millennia apart, may be explained by the fact that we are guided by, and seek to establish, one particular point of view and so, for the time being, consciously neglect all others.

The *Merchant of Venice,* until fairly recently, was regarded by Shakespearean scholars as one of the most debatable works of the poet—not only as concerns its basic theme, but as regards its dramatic genre. On the basis of our theory, which postulates that, in comedy, the father-figure must be represented as weighed down by guilt, we must regard this work as comedy, for the father's guilt is almost expressly indicated. Antonio, who is so dangerously threatened by Shylock, is certainly a father-figure. That this psycho-analytical assumption is well-founded, is shown by the fact that he derives from the Messer Ansaldo of the text which Shakespeare used as his source (Fiorentino's *Pecorone*); that Messer Ansaldo who appears as a "fatherly friend" in the story is a man full of love, of infinite patience and ready to make great sacrifices for his adopted son. The poet, however, allows Antonio to become "guilty" in the first act of the play:

> Therefore go forth;
> Try what my credit can in Venice do:
> That shall be rack'd, even to the uttermost,

and to give Shylock his bond.

It need hardly occasion surprise if we here regard a money-debt as a mere substitute for moral guilt. The extremely close connection between the two, which, so far as I know, Müller-Braunschweig[4] first demonstrated among psycho-analysts, Nietzsche had already emphasized in his *Genealogy of Morals*.[5] The intimate connection between these two groups of ideas, as well as their substitutive relation, is unquestionable. The very ancient provision of monetary fines in criminal law, and the fact that not only German, but also many other languages (among them French and Polish) use the same word to denote both a material debt and moral guilt, provides eloquent testimony to the truth of this view. And, last but not least, the substitution of the idea of a money debt for that of moral guilt is hardly surprising to the psycho-analyst, who frequently observes this substitutive relation in the dreams and resistances of his patients.

The same expression of this motif is also found in that finest of German comedies, Lessing's *Minna von Barnhelm*.

The complications of the plot, it will be recalled, are based on events which occur before the play opens: Major van Tellheim, entrusted to collect a levy from a hostile Diet, in order to avoid resorting to harsh measures, himself advances the money to the King against a note of credit issued by the said Diet. But when he requires its repayment once peace is concluded, his demand is rejected and, suspected of accepting enemy bribes, he is compelled to submit to a judicial enquiry. This he regards not only as a heavy blow to his honour, but as an insurmountable obstacle to his marriage with Minna, who loves him and whom he loves.

Again we can only reduce this coherent and richly elaborated story to the bald formula that it is the father (the King) who is guilty. This is confirmed not only by the fact that the ensuing entanglements are resolved by the King's personal intervention and payment of his debt, but even the minor scenes of the comedy, as those in which the valet Just and Werner appear, are permeated with Tellheim's resistance: "I will not be your debtor." In spite of excellent rationalisations, one can hardly regard this constant resistance as indicating anything but the son's complete rejection of all guilt, the more completely and demonstratively to stress the father's.

With this interpretation we have, however, penetrated straight to the root of that guilt which is levelled against the father: the King stands in the way of Tellheim's love and marriage!

That this, in fact, is the play's latent basic trend is shown by the

---

[4] Dr. Karl Müller-Braunschweig: *Psychoanalytische Gesichtspunkte zur Psychogenese der Moral, insbesondere des moralischen Aktes.* Imago VII (1921).

[5] Chapter 4: ". . . that the cardinal moral idea of 'guilt' originates from the very material idea of 'debt.' "

following circumstance, as I have already pointed out in my study of *Macbeth;* [6] namely, that in dramatic works the basic motif is presented twice; in a way that is nearer consciousness, and then in a remoter manner; i.e. in a fairly direct as well as a veiled form. This phenomenon can be observed with such regularity that even the converse—every motif that occurs twice in a drama is its basic theme—now seems to me, after considerable re-examination, entirely valid.

Now *Minna von Barnhelm* does actually contain such a second, considerably less veiled hint of the father as obstacle between the lovers. It is the passage where, somewhat mysteriously, Minna informs the obdurate Tellheim that she is persecuted by her uncle and guardian Count Bruchsall, who has disinherited her for not wishing to accept a husband of his choosing. Hardly has the Count made Tellheim's acquaintance however, when the latter addresses him as "my father" and the Count, in turn, calls him "son."

The reproach "Father—disturber of love," which establishes the father's guilt, is the latent content of most comedies of the kind discussed.

This motif is brought out extremely clearly in Molière's *L'Avare,* where neither the father-son relationship nor their sexual rivalry is in any way masked. Here Harpagon steps between his son and the latter's bride, because he himself desires to marry her.

But the same motif also appears in *Tartuffe,* if one regards the hypocrite as a mere derivative of the father Orgon who, thereby, becomes the son's rival for the mother's affections.

In Terence's *Phormio*—one of the finest of classical comedies—the father, who is opposed to the love-choice of his son (Phaedria), is similarly made amenable to the son's will by the unmasking of his sexual misbehaviour. The play significantly closes with the father's words: "But where is Phaedria, who must be our judge?" [7]

The following comedies betray, in their manifest content, nothing of those "family" relationships which, in the plays just discussed, stood out so clearly; their basic psychological situation is, nevertheless, the same.

In Plautus's justly famed *Miles Gloriosus* for instance, the bombastic, vain fool, Pyrgopolinikes, is placed in a double relationship: as father towards the young Athenian Pleusikles, whose sweetheart he carries off, and as son towards the jovial Ephesian Periplekomenos, whose supposed wife, in the intrigues of the plot, he attempts to seduce away from him.

---

[6] Cf.: "The Riddle of Shakespeare's *Macbeth*" and "The Problem of the Duplicated Expression of Psychic Themes."

[7] *The Plays of Terence,* trans. William Ritchie (London, 1927).

In conclusion we may cite Kleist's *Der zerbrochene Krug,* which is no less illustrative of our thesis. Its theme is an investigation into whether the father (Judge Adam) or the son (Ruprecht) is responsible for a nocturnal burglary, and the "breaking of Eve's pitcher!"

In complete accordance with our thesis, the verdict "guilty" is passed on the father.

* * *

The significance of these conclusions will be elucidated by a passage from Bergson's *Laughter.*[8] He believes that the essence of the comic consists in the mechanisation of life, an effect which can be obtained by the process of *inversion* as well as by two other processes, *repetition* and *reciprocal interference of series.* He states: "Picture to yourself certain characters in a certain situation; if you reverse the situation and invert the rôles, you obtain a comic scene . . . There is no necessity, however, for both the identical scenes to be played before us. We may be shown only one, provided the other is really in our minds . . . The plot of the villain who is the victim of his own villainy, or the cheat cheated, forms the stock-in-trade of a good many plays. We find this even in primitive farce . . . In modern literature we meet with hundreds of variations on the theme of the robber robbed. In every case the root idea involves an inversion of rôles, and a situation which recoils on the head of its author."

"Here we apparently find the confirmation of a law, some illustrations of which we have already pointed out. When a comic scene has been reproduced a number of times, it reaches the stage of being a classical type or model. It becomes amusing in itself, quite apart from the causes which render it amusing. Henceforth, new scenes, which are not comic *de jure,* may become amusing *de facto,* on account of their partial resemblance to this model. They call up in our mind a more or less confused image which we know to be comical. They range themselves in a category representing an officially recognised type of the comic. The scene of the 'robber robbed' belongs to this class. It casts over a host of other scenes a reflection of the comic element it contains. In the end it renders comic any mishap that befalls one through one's own fault, no matter what the fault or mishap may be—nay, an allusion to this mishap, a single word that recalls it, is sufficient."

It is probably unnecessary to stress that we claim this central significance of the "model scene" for the element we have singled out.

* * *

---

[8] Henri Bergson, *Laughter. An Essay on the Meaning of the Comic,* trans. C. Brereton and F. Rothwell (London, 1911), pp. 94–96.

In this passage a penetrating philosopher has approached remarkably near our own position and has even increased the area within which we assumed the factor we discovered in comedy, and its allied manifestations, to hold valid. As regards the riddle which comedy presents, little however has been gained towards solving it.

It can be taken for granted that the writer of comedies possesses the same creative impulses, and is subject to the same psychological laws, as those long known to be valid—especially through the excellent work of Sachs [9] for the writer of tragedies; this applies especially to the imperative urge to effect the discharge of his repressed complexes, which the dramatist is able to satisfy by, as it were, distributing his feeling of guilt among the many.

On the other hand, the analyses of the comedies cited, summary though these be, leaves little doubt that the material employed is identical with that employed by the writer of tragedies: in both cases the Oedipus situation is involved.

It may be due to this identity that, in so many plays, their nature remains unclear long after the action begins to unfold, so that for a time the final result may equally be comedy as tragedy: it is only a delayed swift turning-point which finally decides us as to its genre.

But how does it happen that from such identical psychological pre-suppositions, such completely, even diametrically opposite effects, result; that from a similar foundation, tragic guilt and expiation arise in one case, and effervescent high spirits in the other?

We believe that we possess the key to this riddle in the factor we have isolated in our analyses: namely, displaced guilt.

In the last resort, this infantile phantasy of the father as the disturber of love is nothing but a projection of the son's own guilty wish to disturb the love of the parents. *By displacing this phantasy on the father, by endowing him with this specifically filial attitude, it becomes clear that the father is divested of his paternal attributes, and thus is removed as a father and degraded into a son.*

This displacement proceeds from the same psychological motives as the "unmasking" generally employed in so many comedies, of which we cited *Tartuffe, Der zerbrochene Krug,* and *Phormio;* which motives are summed up by Freud in the formula "You, too, are only a human being like myself." Like the unmasking, this phantasy is employed in comedy in order to degrade the father, to degrade him to a son, or to the level ordinarily appropriate to the son. This turning-the-father-into-a-son, this inverted world, *"le monde renversé,"*

---

[9] Hanns Sachs, *Gemeinsame Tagträume.*

as Bergson puts it, represents the very core of his *"inversion,"* the innermost purpose of the displacement of guilt.

Only the fact that the father is given the status of a mere son explains why, in comedy (from classical comedy to the contemporary bedroom farce), it is generally the father who is beaten in the trial of strength. For the same reason, returning to our examples, Harpagon must lose the game and, thereby, the love-object, and the King in *Minna von Barnhelm* must not only clear obstacles away, but even far exceed the necessary meed of reparation.

Only this reduction of the father to a son can explain how writers of comedies can unleash so wide a range of aggression (scorn, derision, etc.) against the father, and allow, for instance, Antonio in the *Merchant of Venice,* and even more obviously Bramabras, taken by surprise in his love-suit, to stand in such open danger of being castrated. Only by such a reduction can we understand the call to the pardoned man: " 'Twill soon be finished with your fatherhood!"

This doing away with the father and his dissolution in the son, this withdrawal of the super-ego and its merging in the ego, are all in complete psychological conformity with the phenomena of mania.

In each case we find the ego, which has liberated itself from the tyrant, uninhibitedly venting its humour, wit, and every sort of comic manifestation in a very ecstasy of freedom.

We shall resist the temptation to discuss the psychological relation, now very apparent, between tragedy and melancholic depression—a connection already hinted at in the words of the Byzantine Suidas: *"ê chrê tragôdein pantas ê melagcholan,"* [10] and shall limit ourselves to the statement that comedy represents an aesthetic correlate of mania.

---

[10] I am indebted to Winterstein for drawing my attention to this passage.

Beyond Laughter:
A Summing Up*

MARTIN GROTJAHN

A happy life is not necessarily all fun and laughter or amusing or entertaining. The happiness of a person, of a period of time, or of a culture cannot be measured by the length and strength of laughter. Happiness is a function of creativity. The analytic study of laughter is a study of creative communication between the unconscious and the conscious, leading to the experience of happiness in fulfilling one's potentialities. This is man's challenge, his destiny, and the meaning of human life.

We started our task historically in these pages. When Sigmund Freud discovered the unconscious meaning of dreams and when he told his friends about it, they laughed. Freud became interested in the unconscious reason for this merriment of his students and started to investigate the similarities between dreams and jokes. Five years after the publication of his history-making book, "The Interpretation of Dreams," he published his work on jokes and their relation to the unconscious (1905).

Freud's thesis is simple and straightforward: Laughter occurs when repressing energy is freed from its static function of keeping something forbidden under repression and away from consciousness. A witticism starts with an aggressive tendency or intent—an insultlike, shocking thought. This has to be repressed and disappears into the unconscious like a train into a mountain tunnel. The wit work begins there in the darkness of the unconscious, like the dream work; it disguises

---

* Martin Grotjahn, "Beyond Laughter: A Summing Up," in *Beyond Laughter* (McGraw-Hill, 1957), pp. 255–264.

the latent aggressive thought skillfully. It combines the disguised aggression with playful pleasure, repressed since childhood and waiting for a chance to be satisfied. After this wit work is accomplished, the witticism reappears at the other end of the tunnel and sees the daylight of consciousness and conscience again. By now it has become acceptable, and the energy originally activated to keep the hostility under repression is freed into laughter. The repressed energy is no longer needed; the shock of freedom of thought and freedom from repression is enjoyed and leads to laughter.

Because of the double-edged character of wit, its disguise must be tested by telling the joke. The reaction of the third person (the teller and the victim of the joke are the first two) shows the success or failure of the wit work. The disguise must go far enough to avoid guilt; it must not go so far that the thrill of aggression is lost. The quality of the witticism is judged only according to the skill of the disguise, not according to the content. If the disguise is unsuccessful, pleasure will change to displeasure, embarrassment, shame, and guilt about aggressive and infantile indulgence in a childhood pleasure.

While wit saves energy by releasing repression of an aggressive thought, the enjoyment of the comic liberates energy from an intended motor outlet, according to Freud. In humor, especially in Freud's favorite "gallows" humor, energy is saved from the repressing emotion: I do not need to pity the condemned criminal because he is strong, he can take it, he does not need my pity. He is stronger than his fate and possibly stronger than reality.

We then considered the humorist as a personality type. We found him to be related to the masochist and to the melancholic. He behaves as if he knows the misery of this world but resolutely proceeds to disregard it. He remains aware of this valley of tears but behaves as if it is still the Garden of Eden. He proceeds not by denying the existence of misery but by pretending to be victorious over it. He illustrates for us the hope for the victory of infantile narcissism over all experience. His victory is only partial and temporary; what he may gain in inner strength and kindness, he will lose in the world of reality and adjustment. He may be free but not necessarily happy or well adjusted to his environment.

The wit as a person is closely related to the sadist. Under the disguise of brilliance, charm, and entertainment the wit—and we do not mean only the practical joker—is a sadist at heart. He is sharp, quick, alert, cold, aggressive, and hostile. He is inclined to murder his victims in thought; if he inhibits himself and if he does not succeed in transforming his brain child into a joke, he may develop a migraine attack instead.

The sense of humor develops in stages and gradually during a lifetime. Every step is connected with mastery of a new anxiety, and each conflict mastered at the different developmental stages is marked by a growth of the sense of humor. So people are inordinately proud of it—often even those who have no sense of humor at all. It is the mark of distinction, of having achieved strength and maturity.

The smile is older than laughter and appears when the human infant is only a few days old. It characterizes the baby as genuinely human. It signifies the intimate contact between human mother and human infant. The human mother is more a mother than any animal mother, and the human infant is more and longer an infant than any animal baby. (Regretfully, we pointed out that the human male is not necessarily more masculine than his opposite number from the animal kingdom. This is a sad fact, and the consequences are not yet settled.) With the mother smiling at the child in her arms and the child looking up into the mother's face and smiling back, human communication was born and facial expression originated.

In the development of mankind a similar chain reaction was started when man assumed the upright posture; this freed the hand for reaching and holding, and the human mouth was free to talk, to smile, and to laugh, no longer being needed to hold things, like the mouth of a dog. When man developed intelligence, he progressed from the sign to the symbol and the word, leading to the great human triumph of verbal speech over the language of the body. The human brain is the most fetal and infantile brain of all animals, looking, with its grotesquely enlarged forebrain, like a prematurely born fetus of one of the lower animals. To be youthful, to be unfinished, means to be human. Being the oldest of all animals, man is simultaneously the youngest of them all. Only he understands the symbol in word and thought and may react with laughter.

Physical, instinctual, and biologic development was replaced in man's evolution by his greatest achievement: culture. The start of cultural development is symbolized in the Sphinx, the union of man and beast, combining animal spirits and human intelligence. The Sphinx, who is so significantly placed by Sophocles at the beginning of the Oedipus trilogy, seems to ask in her riddle: Who loves the one he is not allowed to love? In this way the Sphinx declares that at the beginning of cultural development stands the incest taboo and the repression of man's love for his mother. This repression separates man's instinctual life from that of the animal, where any cub growing sexually mature is just another competitor, free to woo his mother. In contrast to all other animals, only the human animal must not approach his mother for purposes of procreation.

The child does not begin to laugh until it has mastered or almost mastered the movements of the body. Flatus is the forerunner of the belly laugh. The child's understanding of jokes and witticisms begins when the language of the body is replaced by the mastery of speech. The Little Moron jokes are a horrible example of this period, as the pun is a later residue of it. In the third phase—not always reached by everybody—the enjoyment of humor occurs as a sign of emotional maturity and mastery. The humorist finally recreates in himself the good, kind, tolerant mother who has to smile at the misery of her unruly and guilty child whom she more or less willingly forgives.

When Freud discovered the unconscious during his great creative period, he found also in the Oedipus situation the genuine meaning of all great human tragedy: the infatuation with the mother, the taboo of incest, the rebellion of the son against the tyrannical father, the guilt and the punishment by castration for the crime in thought or action, conscious or unconscious. The Oedipus situation is the gravestone on the lost paradise of our childhood and at the same time the cornerstone of all culture as we know it. After the repression of the sexual longing for the mother, cultural development took the place of physical and instinctual or biologic progress.

The psychodynamics of the comedy can be understood as a kind of reversed Oedipus situation in which the son does not rebel against the father but the son's typical attitudes of childhood longing are projected upon the father. The son plays the role of the victorious father with sexual freedom and achievement, while the father is cast in the role of the frustrated onlooker. The reversed Oedipus situation is repeated in every man's life when the younger generation grows up and slowly infiltrates and replaces the older generation in work and in life. The clown is the comic figure representing the impotent and ridiculed father. He also represents the sadness of things and finally comes to stand for death in the person of the tragic truly great clown. This is the point where tragedy and comedy finally meet and symbolize human life.

As the spirit of irreverence is necessary for laughter, it is not easy to use the symbol of the mother for the purpose of ridicule. There are no female clowns; the Red-hot Mama, the burlesque queen, and the comedienne have to be specially censored in order to conceal the return of the repressed longing for the mother in new disguise. The symbol of the mother who understands the desires of her son is greatly treasured by the Oedipus in all of us who try courageously to grow up as long as we live. The mother figure may show with the smile of Mona Lisa that she understands the desires of her son and secretly accepts them. She gives hope to Oedipus. To seduce is a mother's destiny. When the son finally reaches her embrace it is the embrace of death, for the grave is, symbolically speaking, similar to the cradle.

The Oedipus drama, the essence of tragedy and comedy, helps the audience to work through their difficulties in the mastery of cultural discontent and collective repression. Problems as the child experiences them before he feels the full impact of the Oedipus situation do not belong on the stage of the legitimate theater but in the circus arena. While we, at least within ourselves, participate in the performance on the stage, we are only onlookers at the "Greatest Show on Earth." Physical mastery, terror and nightmares, problems of bisexuality and of ambivalence, of time, space, and balance, of animal instincts and beauty are illustrated in the show, but no real conflicts are worked out. In the circus the child is participating only with his eyes, while on the stage of the theater the adult is actually working-through his residual Oedipus conflict. The strange institution of amusement parks and fun fairs with their mechanized fairylands illustrates similar dynamics.

Dreams at night and in the light of day, fantasies and fairy tales— all art leads us to islands of true freedom where we do not need to submit to cruel reality, to renunciation and repression. Following the creative artist into the artistic experience, we work on our unconscious conflicts. This makes us stronger, more mature, and better able to live in the world of reality and civilization after our experience in the realm of esthetics. Mere entertainment does not offer this kind of analytic working-through. Psychoanalysis aims at a similar working-through, but on a different level and with different methods. Where the artist works in the esthetic dimension, the psychoanalyst tries to reach the level of scientific interpretation, integration, and insight.

A peculiarly distorted childhood curiosity explains our interest in the mystery story. There was a time when we were all mystery fans, when we were all Peeping Toms and would almost risk our lives to see and hear and learn what happened on the hidden stage of the parental bedroom. The primal scene appears to the child like a bloody, cruel, wild, and lustful performance, with the mother as the victim, the father as the rapist or murderer, the child as the clever little detective who connects the clues and explains it all to the stupid Dr. Watson. The police, of course, protect the vested interests of the parental authorities and do not help in discovering the mystery of crime and sex. Actually the facts of life are obvious. In the mystery story, the facts of the crime can be deduced from obvious clues by anyone who wants to see. Clues are all around us, and so is murder and crime and lust—if we only are allowed or allow ourselves to see. The mystery fan is a Peeping Tom who looks desperately and persistently through the wrong keyhole.

The contemporary Oedipus may appear in cowboy boots and enliven our movie and television screen. The difference between art creation and the trashy sentimentality of so much shallow entertainment is related to the lifting and working-through of repressions in art and analysis.

Laughter is taken as a sign of strength, freedom, health, beauty, youth, and happiness. It may appear in dreams and even in psychoanalysis. A patient may bring a favorite joke, which can then be used like a dream or a recollection or a stream of free associations to gain insight. Uncontrollable laughter, however, can be a sign of hysteria as well as a sign of intoxication or encephalitis or brain tumor. Inappropriate laughter is a significant sign of deterioration. It may herald the danger of an approaching psychosis.

The importance and meaning of Ferdinand the Bull and Mickey Mouse, together with Alice in Wonderland, illustrated our need for free and episodic regression—or communication with our unconscious, as in sleep and dream—in order to gain strength for this reality we live in. We need such anxiety-free communication with our unconscious to keep our imagination and intuition alive; to create freely; to form our life. With such rebirth, experienced without guilt, fear, or anxiety, performed with grace and with ease, with a smile and with laughter, we become essentially—and incurably—human.

Part Six

ON FARCE AND SATIRE

***

Eric Bentley

FARCE

Vsevolod Meyerhold

FARCE

Robert C. Stephenson

FARCE AS METHOD

R. C. Elliott

THE SATIRIST AND SOCIETY

Al Capp

"IT'S HIDEOUSLY TRUE"

Farce*

ERIC BENTLEY

VIOLENCE

I have been speaking about the violence in, and of, melodrama. Farce is perhaps even more notorious for its love of violent images. And since the violence of farce and melodrama is not excluded from comedy and tragedy, it will be well to ask the question: What about violence in art? What does it signify? What does it do to us? Here is the classic statement on the subject:

When we listen to some hero [in Homer or] on the tragic stage moaning over his sorrows in a long tirade, or to a chorus beating their breasts as they chant a lament, you know how the best of us enjoy giving ourselves up to follow the performance with eager sympathy. . . . Few I believe are capable of reflecting that to enter into another's feelings must have an effect on our own: the emotions of pity our sympathy has strengthened will not be easy to restrain when we are suffering ourselves. . . . Does not the same principle apply to humor as well as to pathos? You are doing the same thing if, in listening at a comic performance or in ordinary life to buffooneries which you would be ashamed to indulge in yourself, you thoroughly enjoy them instead of being disgusted with their ribaldry. There is in you an impulse to play the clown, which you have held in restraint from a reasonable fear of being set down a buffoon; but now you have given it rein, and by encouraging its impudence at the theatre you may be unconsciously carried away into playing the comedian in your private life. Similar effects are produced by poetic representation of love and anger and all those desires and feelings of pleasure and pain which accompany our every action. It waters the growth of passions which should be allowed to wither away and sets them up in control, although the goodness and happiness of our lives depend on their being held in subjection.

---

* Eric Bentley, "Farce," in *The Life of the Drama* (Atheneum, 1964), pp. 219–256.

Thus Plato in the tenth book of *The Republic*. The question has come up again and again down the centuries, not least in our own age, the age of the most extensive, as well as the most atrocious, violence that the world has ever known. In such an age, it is naturally a matter of concern to the humane that the reading matter of the mass of men (and one should now include the "viewing" matter) has no tendency to wean them from violence but, on the contrary, tends to inure them to it. And one of the glaring moral contradictions of our cultural scene is that protests are made against the presentation of healthy sensuality in good art by people who quietly accept outrageous cruelty in bad art. All this being so, it is not surprising to find a warm-hearted physician like Dr. Fredric Wertham coming out, in his book *Seduction of the Innocent,* against the violence in our so-called "comic books." And I for one had not realized how ugly and nasty-minded these books are until I read Dr. Wertham's text and examined the illustrations. Comic books are bad art, and bad humanity, and therefore meager and possibly noxious food for the minds of the young—or old.

This much could probably be accepted by any humane person, but Dr. Wertham will not rest his case there. On at least one page he indicates that artistic merit is, as it were, no excuse: the cruelties of Grimm's fairy tales are to be condemned along with those of the "comic books." Here surely we have caught the good doctor regretting that art is serious, for if art did not treat violence, it could not go to the heart of things. Without violence, there would be nothing in the world but goodness, and literature is not mainly about goodness: it is mainly about badness. When, on another page, Dr. Wertham complains of sympathy being thrown to bad characters, we realize that he is placing himself squarely in that Puritan tradition which is hostile to art as such, and whose father is Plato—or part of Plato: the part that would have thrown the poets out of his ideal republic.

The Platonists in this argument disregard the distinction between fact and fantasy. Suppose you saw one man force the head of another through the glass of a street lamp so that the latter will be gassed by the fumes. It sounds like some Nazi atrocity, and Plato would no doubt be indignant at the notion of re-enacting the incident in a work of art. Nonetheless it *was* re-enacted in Charlie Chaplin's film *Easy Street,* and in all the years no one has protested. We have all very much enjoyed seeing Mack Swain gassed and Charlie triumphant. And in general—though what we consciously remember from the Chaplin films may be Chaplin's incomparable delicacy, they are for the most part taken up with violent pursuit and violent combat. Here fantasy multiplies movements and blows by a thousand. The villain is a giant whose strength passes the limits of nature. He can bend lamp posts with his bare hands. Since the "little man's" revenges have to be more than proportionate to the provocation (as with Brecht's Pirate Jenny), he can drop a cast-iron stove on the villain's head and ram that head inside a street lamp with the gas turned on.

Another symptom of cruelty is the abstractness of the violence. Prongs of a rake in the backside are received as pin pricks. Bullets seem to pass right through people, sledge-hammer blows to produce only momentary irritation. The speeding up of movement contributes to the abstract effect. So, even more, does the silence proper to the screen of those days, many of the effects being lost when a sound track is superimposed. The cops shoot, but there is no noise. Heavy objects fall, but there is no crash. Gruesome infighting has the air of shadowboxing. All of which signifies that, in farce, as in drama, one is permitted the outrage but spared the consequence. Chaplin's delicacy of style is actually part of the pattern: he parades an air of nonchalance when acting in a manner that, in real life, would land him in Bellevue or Sing Sing.

Though Plato has shown us the importance of thought, and modern psychology has exhibited the power of fantasy, we cannot allow ourselves to be jockeyed into regarding the distinction between thought and act, fantasy and fact, as a sort of minor detail. The person who confuses the two sets of categories is not eccentric, he is insane. Conversely, it is possible for a thinker and fantasist to bank heavily on the sanity of his audience; and this is what Charlie Chaplin or any other farceur emphatically does.

Certainly, teachers and parents have to cope with the fact that in some situations children do not make a clear distinction between fantasy and reality. But they must understand that these situations do not include all the violence in drama and other fiction. Think of the tremendous violence in fairy tales, and ask yourself how many small children have actually tried to duplicate it in real life. Grimm's fairy tales do not seem to justify Dr. Wertham's fears.

For people who can distinguish between fantasy and reality certain indulgences are possible in fantasy which should not be permitted in "real life." Most notably: they can indulge in reckless violence. That extraordinary passage in *The Republic* was answered by Aristotle, though perhaps not intentionally and certainly not at length. His answer is to be found in the famous phrase about tragedy in *The*

Poetics: "through pity and fear effecting the proper catharsis of these emotions." True, there is a permanent debate about the meaning of the word "catharsis," but all the debaters could agree, I think, on that solid part of the meaning that is relevant here, namely: Aristotle is rejecting the notion that tragedy might reduce us to a quivering jelly of pity and fear, and is formulating an exactly contrary conclusion: tragedy is not only an excitement but a release from excitement. It will not burst the boiler with its steam because it is precisely the safety valve. It is the exactly contrary character of Aristotle's view to Plato's that most powerfully suggests that it might be a deliberate reply. And it is this character that makes it perhaps somewhat polemical, and hard to go all the way with. One feels that the cathartic theory exaggerates. Surely not all this happens to one's emotional system during a performance of *Hamlet?* But the theory can hardly be rejected in substance unless one wishes to side with Plato, Bishop Bossuet, Dr. Wertham, and the Motion Picture Production Code.

Gilbert Murray has suggested that the idea of catharsis is easier to apply to comedy than to tragedy—easier in the sense that we agree to it more easily. There is already a certain consensus of opinion that some of our psychic violence—what our grandparents called excess animal spirits—can be worked off in laughter. It is generally agreed that a good laugh does us good, and that it does us good as a sort of emotional "work-out."

Impropriety is of the essence. As Murray put it: "Comedy . . . must . . . not be spoilt by any tiresome temperance or prudential considerations of the morrow." And again: "The anarchist and the polygamist, close-prisoned and chained in ordinary life, enjoy their release in comedy." Murray thought of comedy as continuous with orgies and fertility rites. Perhaps his doctrine implies the same error as that of the Platonists: a disregard of the difference between doing and imagining. The image of an orgy that we may get in a work of art should not be equated with the acting out of an orgy in real life; and comedy gives only a faded image of an orgy at that. Still, since the rise of Christianity, even the image of an orgy is a little more than many people bargain for. And there has been war between comedy and established religion down through the ages. The Motion Picture Production Code is but its latest embodiment. We mustn't laugh at a priest, it implies, or religion is in danger.

SCOFFING AT MARRIAGE

Above all we must not laugh at the family and its source, the institution of marriage. If crime comics are rampant among the underprivileged young, equally rampant among the overprivileged middle-aged is a literature whose patron saint is Tartuffe. In one of those family magazines that are so moralistic as to be morally nauseating, I came across an article entitled "Don't Let Them Scoff at Marriage" in which the moral crisis of our times was confidently attributed to jokes against marriage. "The gross libel on marriage is the notion," the author wrote, "that the chase, the allure, is the goal. Marriage is seen as a dull aftermath." As a psychologist the writer should have known that even gross libels aren't made without provocation. Or if they are, they don't last for centuries and appeal to the whole human race. Obviously the human race finds more interesting what this man calls a gross libel than what he presents as the truth.

It is true, however, that the joke against marriage could be abolished if the family were the unmixed blessing that many of our contemporaries take it for. The chief of the division of Social Medicine at an important American hospital writes as follows:

The family is central to the development of humanity not only for the perpetuation of the race but because the proper psychological development of an individual can only occur within the warm circle of the nuclear family. Social and psychological studies indicate quite clearly that a strong family structure helps to develop and maintain a personality free of dangerous (to self and society) characteristics.

And the author draws the conclusion that sexual deviation and juvenile delinquency can be prevented by closer, warmer family relations. "The family that prays together stays together." "Where family life stops delinquency starts."

No doubt there is some truth in all this. Unhappily there is truth in a precisely opposite proposition. The close, warm family is also the seedbed of neurosis, vice, and crime. About the same time as this article appeared, a newspaper picture caught my eye. It showed a beaming public-relations executive with his good-looking wife and three attractive children. They seemed a model American family in a model American home and one could imagine the picture passing in triumph around the public-relations office. The caption underneath, however, reported that the mildest and most candid-looking of the boys had just killed the mother and sister and told the police that he had planned to kill the rest of the family as well. It would be comforting to think that such a shocking event could be declared irrelevant to the experience of normal folk. But it isn't, because normal folk share his wishes though they do not carry them out. An art like farce embodies such wishes: wishes to damage the family, to desecrate the household gods.

And tragedy is no different in this respect. The Greeks, who invented it, did not do so before they had created the patriarchal family and an ideology to fit it. They seem to have found the supreme virtue in the pious and loyal relation of husband to wife, of child to parent, of sibling to sibling. The subject of tragedy, over and over again, was the violation of such piety. Now what would be the worst conceivable violation of both the marital and filial pieties? Why, the double crime of Oedipus.

An entry in *The Oxford Companion to the Theatre* reads:

The word *farce* is applied to a full-length play dealing with some absurd situation hingeing generally on extra-marital relations—hence the term *bedroom farce*. . . .

The phrase "some absurd situation hingeing . . . on extra-marital relations" suggests various tragic plots, that of *Othello,* for example. But what "situation hingeing . . . on extra-marital relations" is not full of absurdities and therefore potentially melodramatic or farcical, tragic or comic, according to the temperament, state of mind, and view of life of the witness? Outrage to family piety is certainly at the heart of farce as we know it—"hence," as our companionable book says, "the term *bedroom farce.*"

It is, of course, Freud who has taught us to find such impieties in tragedy. And one of his early followers, Ludwig Jekels, applied the idea of the Oedipus complex to comedy. If tragedy, he says, shows the son paying for his rebellion against the father, comedy shows the son victorious, the father discomfited. Father and son compete for the possession of the mother, and the son wins. The element of disguise by which this naked fantasy is clothed consists very often in the son's being presented as just some young man who happens along. But many of the disguises for the theme are more elaborate. It seems to me that the modern "triangle" drama might be regarded as one of them: husband, wife, and lover being the disguise for father, mother, and son. If this were so, then the answer to the question why modern playwrights have been obsessed with adultery is that they have *not* been obsessed with adultery: they have been obsessed with incest. In Bernard Shaw's *Candida,* Morell, Candida, and Marchbanks would be the mask of a father, mother, and son. (I do not cite the evidence from Bernard Shaw's life that the three characters were indeed father [or foster-father], mother, and son [himself] to the author. That is a matter of origin. More relevant here is the possibility that Morell, Candida, and Marchbanks would still be *a* father, mother, and son for the unconscious of spectators even if we knew nothing of

Shaw's life.) Such is the conversion to late nineteenth-century problem drama of the Oedipus story. In another early Shaw play, *Mrs. Warren's Profession*, the incest theme shows through, as it already had in two of the most famous plays of Shaw's playwright-father, Henrik Ibsen: namely, *Ghosts* and *Rosmersholm*. Yet for contemporaries all three of these plays seemed to be about current social problems exclusively (white slavery, hereditary syphilis, advanced ideas, etc.). For them, the incest theme remained under a veil, and when one notes what that veil was, one may begin to see social realism in a different light. By which I do not mean that the "social" content is always mere camouflage for psychological motifs but only that it can serve as such camouflage vis à vis a given public. The plays I have named are better understood today when audiences recognize the Oedipal theme at once and so take the plays to be what they are: "social" and "psychological" at the same time.

COMIC CATHARSIS

Gilbert Murray has spoken of the "close similarity between Aristotle and Freud," and actually Freud carried the idea of Catharsis further than any Aristotelian commentator had ever dreamt of. In the eighteen-nineties the new therapy escaped being named cathartic instead of psycho-analtyic only by a hair's breadth. For Freud, jokes are fundamentally cathartic: a release, not a stimulant. This is why Freud, unlike our magazine moralists, would "let them scoff at marriage." (He would also know he could never stop them.) It is a sort of open secret, Freud says in his book on jokes, that "marriage is hardly an arrangement to satisfy the sexual demands of the husband," also that this secret is half-kept, half-told, in a million male jokes against marriage. I would add that the supreme form of the marriage joke takes a couple of hours to tell and has a cast of three characters known as *le mari, la femme, et l'amant*—"hence the term *bedroom farce.*" Just as Restoration Comedy was provoked by the Puritans and is forever dedicated to their memory, the farce of adultery throughout our Protestant-bourgeois epoch has been provoked by faithful husbands and will only end when they become unfaithful on principle.

Farce in general offers a special opportunity: shielded by delicious darkness and seated in warm security, we enjoy the privilege of being totally passive while on stage our most treasured unmentionable wishes are fulfilled before our eyes by the most violently active human beings that ever sprang from the human imagination. In that application of the formula which is bedroom farce, we savor the adventure of adultery, ingeniously exaggerated in the highest degree, and all without taking the responsibility or suffering the guilt. Our wives may be with us leading the laughter.

Why do we laugh at jokes? The point of a joke can be explained, but the explanation is not funny. The intellectual content is not the essence. What counts is the experience which we call "getting" the joke or "seeing the point." This experience is a kind of shock, but, whereas shocks in general are unpleasant, this one opens a sluicegate somewhere and brings a sudden spurt or gush of pleasure. Nor is the pleasure of the laugh continuous with the mild amusement that precedes it. A joke is a purling stream most of the way, then suddenly from one of its pools rises up a veritable geyser.

The phenomenon seems less mysterious if we see it as limited to grown human beings, and grown human beings as full of anxiety and guilt. Neither supermen nor babies have a sense of humor. They don't need one. Men and women do because they have inhibited many of their strongest wishes.

How does the sense of humor go to work? Its aim is to gratify some of the forbidden wishes. But what is repressed is repressed. We cannot get at it. Our anxiety and guilt are taking care of that. Only, there are tricks for eluding anxiety and guilt, and the commonest, the least artificial, is the sense of humor. The mildly amusing preliminaries of a joke allay our fears, lower our resistance. The gratification of the forbidden wish is then slipped upon us as a surprise. Before our guilt and anxiety have time to go into action, the forbidden pleasure has been had. A source of pleasure far deeper than those directly available has been tapped. Inhibitions are momentarily lifted, repressed thoughts are admitted into consciousness, and we experience that feeling of power and pleasure, generally called elation. Here is one of the few forms of joy that are readily available. Hence the immense contribution of humor to the survival of the species.

Hence also a paradox. Through the funny, we tap infantile sources of pleasure, we become infants again, finding the intensest satisfaction in the smallest things, the highest ecstasy in the lowest thoughts. And yet infants themselves are without humor. But the paradox is no contradiction, for at bottom no experiences could be further apart than is the momentary return to childhood from the experience of being a child. The actual innocence of infancy is never regained but as far as pleasure is concerned there is an increment in sheer nostalgia. No little girl can love little-girlhood as Lewis Carroll did. No infant shares the grownup's enjoyment in returning, or seeming to return, to infancy. Humor has a great deal to do with the distance between the infancy returned to and the point from which the return journey is undertaken. In fact the premise that children have no sense of humor, useful at the outset, needs qualification at a later stage of the investigation. Children *develop* a sense of humor as they move away from primal innocence. They have only to hear a few of the "songs of experience," which are songs of setback, disappointment, and disillusion, and the wholehearted cheerfulness of a baby's smile can give place on the face of a three-year-old to the aggressive smirk or the twisted half-smile of defeat. "Innocence" is whole and single. With "experience" come division and duality—without which there is no humor, no wit, no farce, and no comedy.

Jokes and the Theatre

One of the key insights of both Bergson and Freud is that to make jokes is to create a theatre. Bergson says that any witticism, if articulated at all, articulates itself in scenes—which are an inchoate comedy. Freud points out that it takes, not one or two, but three to make a joke. These are the jokester, the butt of the joke, and the listener. The trio is familiar in the form of comedian, straight man, and audience. This trio of vaudeville suggests in turn the ironist, the impostor, and the audience of the traditional comic theatre.

To say that the jokester needs a butt is only to say that he needs a joke. Does he need even a joke as much as he needs a listener? Let each of us ask himself why, at a given moment, he wishes to tell a joke. It cannot be because one wishes to be amused by it, since jokes are not amusing the second time around, and one cannot tell a joke one has not already heard. (I exclude from consideration any superman who can invent his jokes as he goes along. He is irrelevant here because the subject I am now approaching is the comedian, who certainly does not write his lines as he goes along.) Anyhow, if one's need was to *hear* the joke one could tell it to oneself. It is inescapable that the need is not for the joke at all: it is for the audience.

Anyone who has known comedians off stage can testify, I think, that they are often men with a need of applause and appreciation that goes beyond even that of other actors. And there is a reason why men with this need—whether they are gifted humorists or not—should seek out the comedian's profession. Only the joke gets from its audience a reaction whose tenor is unmistakable and enthusiastic: laughter. The tragic actor gets no such indication, at the end of his "To be or not to be" speech, that it went over well. He will be pleased if there was silence in the house; even so he may wonder if everyone had gone to sleep. He may wonder whether his feeling that it went well is an illusion. But there is no such thing, as Ramon Fernandez puts it, as an illusion that an audience is laughing. So their laughter is peculiarly attractive to a person who needs an audience reaction every minute or two and needs to be sure that it is highly favorable. On the night when the audience does not laugh, the clown goes out and shoots himself. At least he might as well, since the one thing he has lived for is not forthcoming.

I have suggested that the comedian is the man whose need of applause is the most insistent and mistrustful. An alternative interpretation is that the comedian is the most gifted of compulsive talkers. Every cocktail party entertains many people who will not stop talking so long as they have an audience. The jokester is such a compulsive talker, it could be, who gets away with it because his talk is amusing. The burst of laughter that greets each story is a diploma stating that he has succeeded in not boring his audience. He may now be tempted to tell his stories to larger and larger groups. If he ends up on a stage talking to people he has never met, he is a professional comedian.

That what purport to be studies of comedy often turn out to be only studies of laughter is to be regretted, yet the circumstance faithfully reflects the mentality of the comedian. His wish is to capture and hold captive his audience, and he knows his wish fulfilled only when the audience laughs. Hence, though laughter may be no proper emblem for comedy, it does set the seal on jokes. For this reason entertainment merchants may be forgiven a certain hysteria on the subject, and we should receive more in sorrow than in anger the news that the television people are measuring the duration and volume of laughs with laugh meters.

If philosophers can reduce comic art to laughter, then surely the entrepreneurs can reduce laughter to the noise it makes. But in both cases, the real topic is narrowed down too much. The student of laughter should study the whole curve of which the burst of noise is but the final inch. Before people will burst out laughing they have to be prepared to burst out laughing. The only sure preparation is a particular state of expectation and sensitivity that amounts to a kind of euphoria. It can be more important than the joke itself. A stage of excitement can be reached at which people will laugh at anything. The performer may have to ask himself what they will *not* laugh at if he is to forestall chaos. He has to watch that the girls don't get the giggles and the ladies the hysterics.

In all this, the theatre stands with the art of telling jokes, not with the art of writing books. We read in solitude; and we think it remarkable if once in a while we laugh out loud. At that it is a single burst of laughter, a self-conscious, if loud, single bark. The rest of the family is sure one did it to attract attention, and asks what's so funny. And very likely one did. But when Cousin Seamus tells us his Irish jokes, we can really let go, and in ten minutes we are as "high" as any whiskey could make us. Such is the psychology of the comedian in the theatre.

In this respect, as in others, the art of farce is but joking turned theatrical—joking fully articulated as theatrical characters and scenes. It is correct to say that its aim is laughter, but this is to say no simple thing. Laughter may signify this or that, and in any case has to be most carefully prepared. Also modulated. Future students of the subject would do well to drop the individual joke and the reasons why it is funny and turn to the question: just how funny is it in particular contexts? It will be found that sometimes it is hardly funny at all, and that other times it is very funny indeed. It is a matter of how the audience was led to the point where the laugh should break out and the fun be proved.

I have been speaking of one burst of laughter with one preparation, and even in so small an event there is plenty to observe. But any farce that lasts more than a minute or two has to make the audience laugh out loud a considerable number of times. This cannot be done by just stringing along the jokes one after the other. The general elation is so much more potent than any particular punch line that one may begin to wonder: what *is* a joke? As I have said, if one succeeds very well with a first joke, the audience may get into a state of mind where anything seems funny. All one needs is a new turn of events, and a new shriek of laughter will greet it. But this state of mind will not last very long unaided. And it may not be wise to try to sustain it indefinitely lest the result be sheer exhaustion. He who organizes a whole evening of "merriment" must indeed be an organizer. Nothing could be more fatal than to stake all on making a good beginning and then to let events take their course. Which is something any good vaudeville producer always knew; and it is something every author of a farce must have in mind—or, better, in his bones.

A sidelight is provided by something Sir John Gielgud once said about producing *The Importance of Being Earnest*. It was to the effect that the director must learn to prevent the audience from laughing in too many places. Those who saw Sir John's production of the play will know what he meant. The comic temperature was raised so high, the elation of the audience was so intense, that the performance at many points could hardly continue. Wilde had written dialogue so witty that any line whatever could be the signal for renewed shrieks and whoops. The breakup of the performance—even in shrieks of merriment—is no desirable aim. What the actors had to do was the opposite of "milking" every line for the fun in it. It was to throw away a lot of the fun of individual lines for the sake of more important fun. The aim of Sir John's strategy was not merely the avoidance of riot. It was the fullest enjoyment of the occasion. Spectators are babies, and have no idea what they will like. If one lets them, they will laugh so hard that later on they can only have the hysterics or the sulks. They have to be prevented from doing violence to their own nervous systems. Laughter cannot be regular and sustained. It cannot begin *pianissimo* and then get gradually louder *ad infinitum*. Nor can it maintain the same intensity steadily like a factory siren. It is tied to our very limited respiratory and vocal system, not to mention our psychology.

If a laugh meter could measure the merit of a show, then the ideal show would be one that elicited a single uninterrupted peal of laughter which lasted from eight thirty till eleven o'clock. It would therefore consist of a play which not only could not proceed but could not begin. Actually, there is no ratio between enjoyment and the duration of audible laughter. But too little laughter is better than too much. If no comedy, however great, could make people laugh all the time, there could be a great comedy that never made them laugh at all.

How often, incidentally, does one really listen to laughter? It is quite an ugly sound. How often has one looked at people while they do it? It is not a pretty sight. And how little laughter there is on stage in a good theatre! The place for laughter is the auditorium. Perhaps one reason is that in the auditorium one does not have to see it. One sees the actors. They laugh seldom, and chiefly for negative effects. Only the other day I opened a magazine and came upon a most expressive laugh on the face of an actor. The caption told me that it was Gustav Gruendgens—as Mephistopheles.

Sweet and Bitter Springs

Freud distinguishes two kinds of jokes, one which is innocent and harmless, and one which has a purpose, a tendency, an end in view. He distinguishes in turn two kinds of purpose: to destroy and to expose—to smash and to strip. Destructive jokes fall under such headings as sarcasm, scandal, and satire, denuding jokes under such headings as obscenity, bawdry, ribaldry.

I think the only startling thing about this classification is that it places obscenity side by side with satire. If we agree, we may take another step by observing that there is destructive force also in the joke that exposes. It is hostile either to the thing exposed or to the audience watching the exposure or both. Modifying Freud's formulation, I conclude that both the satiric and the obscene come under the heading of aggression.

We have, then, aggressive jokes and nonaggressive jokes. Everyone, in fact, assumes no less, and quite widespread in our middle-class culture is a preference for the nonaggressive joke. Are we not a Christian civilization? I myself was brought up on a little hymn that went:

> Teach us delight in simple things
> And mirth that has no bitter springs.

It seemed a reasonable enough demand to make, especially since, at the time, I was not aware that mirth *ever* had bitter springs. I certainly did not know that the author of that very hymn was a man of inordinate pugnacity. (It is by Kipling.)

Some people want their jokes pleasant and harmless, and some people want their farces pleasant and harmless. Indeed it is common to interpret farce as precisely the pleasant treatment of what would otherwise have been an unpleasant subject. Here is the great theatre critic of nineteenth-century France—Sarcey—discussing the greatest farceur of nineteenth-century France:

I had often complained that they bored us constantly with this question of adultery, which nowadays is the subject of three quarters of the plays. Why, I asked, take pleasure in painting its dark and sad sides, enlarging on the dreadful consequences which it brings with it in reality? Our fathers took the thing more lightheartedly in the theatre and even called adultery by a name which awoke in the mind only ideas of the ridiculous and a sprightly lightheartedness. . . . Chance brought it about that I met Labiche. "I was very struck," he said to me, "with your observations on adultery and on what could derive from it . . . for farce . . . I agree . . ." I had almost forgotten this conversation when I saw the title posted outside the Palais Royal. . . . It was my play: it was adultery treated lightheartedly. . . .

Anglo-Saxon opinion has been against admitting such subjects as adultery into the nonserious drama at all, and yet there is one English critic who, before Sarcey, had carried Sarcey's argument yet further. This is Charles Lamb in his once-famous essay on Restoration Comedy. In substance, though this is not his vocabulary, he argues that the subject matter of Restoration comedy becomes palatable if we regard the finished product as farce rather than satire. For this is to judge leniently as in play, not harshly as one would have to in real life.

I could never connect those sports of a witty fancy in any shape with any result to be drawn from them to imitation in real life. They are a world of themselves almost as much as fairy land. . . . The Fainalls and the Mirabells, the Dorimants and the Lady Touchwoods, in their own sphere, do not offend my moral sense. . . . They break through no laws, or conscientious restraints. They know of none. They have got out of Christendom into the land—what shall I call it?—of cuckoldry—the Utopia of gallantry, where pleasure is duty, and the manners perfect freedom. It is altogether a speculative scene of things, which has no reference whatever to the world that is.

Now both Sarcey and Lamb are saying things that are undeniably true. If adultery in the drama is becoming a solemn bore, then certainly it would be fun to try the farceur's approach. If parents are becoming solemn bores in suggesting that a Restoration comedy might have an inordinate and immoral influence on their daughters, then certainly it is good to remind them of the distinction between art and life, fiction and fact. But the real question is the significance of the gaiety Sarcey speaks of, and of what Lamb calls the sports of a witty fancy, his Utopia of gallantry, his land of cuckoldry. Both critics assume that they have closed the discussion once they have invoked the twin spirits of gaiety and fantasy. Yet that is where the real discussion begins, and that is where Freud takes it up in his monograph on jokes. Granting that jokes exist which are "innocent," Freud goes on to say that it is only the tendentious ones, the jokes with a purpose, which can make people burst out laughing. The innocent jokes don't pack that much of a punch. We do not feel them so keenly. Our need for them is not so great. We crave stronger meat. We want satire. We want ribaldry. Our receiving apparatus is not so sensitive to them. We want to attack and to expose.

To say that only the joke with a purpose can actually arouse laughter is tantamount to saying that only this type of joking is of much use in the theatre of Farce. And it seems to me that if farces are examined they will be found to contain very little "harmless" joking and very much that is "tendentious." Without aggression farce cannot function. The effects we call "farcical" dissolve and disappear.

What happens in farces? In one of Noel Coward's, a man slaps his mother-in-law's face and she falls in a swoon. Farce is the only form of art in which such an incident could normally occur.

No one ever denied that W. C. Fields' films were aggressive. Audiences became so conscious of the aggressions that they started staying away from Fields' pictures. In Charlie Chaplin's case, they said they liked him because he was less violent. He *seemed* less violent because he put the violence in the other characters. The violence was done *to*

him, not *by* him, and masochistic farce always seems more gentleman-
like than sadistic. But the Tramp of Chaplin is not exclusively masochistic. He is also a sadist. One remembers what happens in *The Kid*
when Charlie finds himself literally holding the baby. By all means, he
is going to become a charming and sentimental foster-father, but as
he sits there with his feet in the gutter he notices an open drain, and
he has almost thrown the baby down it before sentiment comes again
into its own. It is by touches like that—and never by sentiment alone—
that Chaplin has shown himself a great comic.

> Teach us delight in complex things:
> Mirth has both sweet and bitter springs.

THE DIALECTIC OF FARCE

To the simple all things are simple. Yet farce *can* seem a simple
thing, not only to the simple-minded but even to those who recognize
its depth. Farce is simple, on this view, because it goes right "at"
things. You knock your mother-in-law down, and no beating about
the bush. One can wonder, certainly, if this is not the absolutely direct,
unmediated vision, without that duality of mask and face, symbol and
object, which characterizes the rest of dramatic literature.

A second way in which farce may seem simple is in its acceptance
of the everyday appearances and of everyday interpretations of those
appearances. It does not present the empurpled and enlarged images
of melodrama. No, farce can use the ordinary unenlarged environment and ordinary down-at-heel men of the street. The trouble is that
farce is simple in both these ways at once, thereby failing to be simple at all. Farce brings together the direct and wild fantasies and
the everyday and drab realities. The interplay between the two is the
very essence of this art—the farcical dialectic.

If behind the gaiety of farce lurks a certain gravity, it is equally
true that behind the gravity lurks a great deal of gaiety. Farce can
certainly present a grave appearance. Those unsmiling actors again!—
or rather the unsmiling down-at-heel roles which farce offers them.
Here is a point of decisive importance in performance. The amateur
actor misses it, and tries to act the gaiety. The professional knows
he must act the gravity and trust that the author has injected gaiety
into his plot and dialogue.

Actually, to press the analysis a step further, the surface of farce
is grave and gay at the same time. The gay antics of Harlequin are
conducted with poker-faced gravity. Both the gaiety and the gravity
are visible and are part of the style. If we go on to speak of a

contrast in farce between mask and face, symbol and thing symbolized, appearance and reality, this will not be a contrast in styles but a contrast between either the gravity or the gaiety on the surface and whatever lies beneath. What do the gravity and gaiety have in common? Orderliness and mildness. What lies beneath the surface, on the other hand, is disorderly and violent. It is a double dialectic. On the surface, the contrast of gay and grave, then, secondly, the contrast of surface and beneath-the-surface. The second is a larger and even more dynamic contrast.

What farce does with this larger contrast is best seen by comparison with what comedy does. Comedy makes much of appearances: it specializes, indeed, in the *keeping up* of appearances. Unmasking in comedy will characteristically be the unmasking of a single character in a climactic scene—like that of Tartuffe. In farce, unmasking occurs all along. The favorite action of the farceur is to shatter the appearances, his favorite effect being the shock to the audience of his doing so. Bring on stage a farcical comic like Harpo Marx, and all appearances are in jeopardy. For him, all coverings exist to be stripped off, all breakables to be broken. It would be a mistake to bring him into a drawing-room comedy: he would dismantle the drawing room.

If what farce offers is the interaction of violence and something else, it follows that violence by itself is not the essence of farce. The violence of Chaplin is dramatized by a context of great gentleness. The violence of Harpo Marx is offset by something equally important to his roles: his perfectly serious performances on that most delicate of instruments, the harp.

A common mistake is to think that Charlie's and Harpo's effects are softened by the gentleness and delicacy, as if the aim were to reach a compromise between violence and sobriety. But compromises are for life, not art. The purpose of this gentleness and delicacy is to heighten, not lower, the effect of the violence, and vice versa. Dramatic art in general is an art of extremes, and farce is, as it were, an extreme case of the extreme. Farce characteristically promotes and exploits the widest possible contrasts between tone and content, surface and substance, and the minute one of the two elements in the dialectic is not present in its extreme or pure form, there is likely to be a weakening of the drama. This could be exemplified by Noel Coward's little play in which, while an extreme lightness of tone is achieved, punches are pulled (more or less literally) where a straight left to the jaw was just what was needed. In farce, we say: "I'll murder you with my bare hands," playfully, or with that mixture of the grave and gay which defines the tone as farcical, but in a degree we also have to mean it: by some flicker, at least, in word or act, it must become evident that murderous wishes exist in this world—and at this moment. If they exist in Noel Coward, he was too genteel to let his public know it. In our theatre, talents such as his drift away from farce without encountering real comedy, landing in that worst of both worlds, the sentimental "light comedy" of the West End and Broadway.

If it is dangerous to attempt a compromise between the two conflicting opposites of a dialectic, it is disastrous to accept one and forget the other. Sheer aggression is just oppressive, as many motion-picture cartoons illustrate. Sheer flippancy is just boring, as most "light comedy" illustrates. The dialectical relation is one of active conflict and development. A dialogue has to be established between the aggression and the flippancy, between hostility and lightness of heart.

MISCHIEF AS FATE

Every form of drama has its rendezvous with madness. If drama shows extreme situations, *the* extreme situation for human beings— short of death—is the point where our sanity gives out. In a very famous scene Ibsen has shown this point reached on stage; and Racine's *Andromache* had ended in much the same way as Ibsen's *Ghosts*.

Our colloquial use and abuse of words is always full of meaning, and what we mean when we say of some non-theatrical phenomenon, "It's a farce," or "It's absolutely farcical," throws light back on the theatrical phenomenon. We mean: farce is absurd; but not only that, farce is a veritable structure of absurdities. Here the operative word is *structure,* for normally we think of absurdities as amorphous. It is only in such a syndrome as paranoia that we find reason in the madness: the absurdities which we would be inclined to call stupid are connected in a way we cannot but consider the reverse of stupid. There is an ingenious and complex set of interrelationships.

I was speaking in the previous chapter of the long arm of coincidence in melodrama. It is an arm that does not get any shorter in farce. In both cases there is an acknowledgment of absurdity—and in both cases, a counterclaim to a kind of sense. A paranoiac finds a structure in coincidences, which is to say that to him they are not coincidences. The playwright incorporates coincidences in a structure, which is to say that they will not be coincidences to his audience. The melodramatist creates a sense of fatality, and, in the light of that sense, apparent coincidence reveals itself as part of a baleful pattern.

And do not imagine, as William Archer did, that the tragic writer is any different. Think, rather, how the Oedipus of Sophocles has spent a lifetime just happening to be at the wrong place at the wrong time and meeting the wrong person there. Farce differs from the other genres in that its use of coincidence is accepted. People have such a low opinion of farce that they don't mind admitting it uses such a low device.

What do the coincidences of farce amount to? Not surely to a sense of fate, and yet certainly to a sense of something that *might* be called fate if only the word has less melancholy associations. In farce chance ceases to seem chance, and mischief has method in its madness. One final effect of farce is that mischief, fun, misrule seem an equivalent of fate, a force not ourselves making, neither for righteousness nor for catastrophe, but for aggression without risk.

Perhaps every type of dramatic action has to have its inevitability, including the types, such as the comic types, that seem dedicated to the opposite. The heaping up of crazy coincidences in farce creates a world in which the happily fortuitous is inevitable. And so, in a Feydeau play, the careful plan for the husband to be absent when the lover arrives is a gilt-edged guarantee that he will turn up.

What is usually said about surprises in farcical plots has to be qualified. On the surface of our minds we are surprised; but somewhere deeper down we knew all along. The convention itself creates certain expectations without which we would not have paid the price of admission. The expectation may go back before the first scene of the play to the rubric "A Farce" in the program or before that to the name "Feydeau" in the advertisements.

I have suggested that the characteristic melodramatic situations and plots derive directly from more or less paranoid fantasies—generally the fantasy of innocence surrounded by malevolence. Pity and fear are certainly aroused and possibly "abreacted"—worked through and worked off. If there is an equivalent in farce and comedy for pity and fear in melodrama and tragedy, it is sympathy and contempt. As pity is the weaker side of melodrama, sympathy is the weaker side of farce. It usually amounts to little more than mild fellow feeling with the hero and heroine. Charlie Chaplin, as an exception, was able to make more of it because he was not a juvenile lead but a character man. The character he chose—that of the Tramp—was such as to make the audience's sympathy play a very large part in the proceedings.

Innocence is probably as important to farce as to melodrama. We are as firmly identified with it. The difference is that whereas in melodrama we recoil from the enemy in fear, in farce we retaliate. If melodrama generally depends for its power on the degree of fear it can arouse, farce depends on the degree of aggression. "The comedian," says Sidney Tarachow, "is a hostile sharpshooter loudly proclaiming his own innocence." In this respect, the writer of farces is a comedian. The hostility, like the terror of melodramas, is so unqualified by any sense of justice or truth, that it creates forms that resemble sick fantasies. The closed structure of the Well Made Play as used by Georges Feydeau suggests a closed mental system, a world of its own lit by its own lurid and unnatural sun. If we were not laughing so hard, we would find such worlds terrifying. Their workings are as perilous as acrobatics. One touch, we feel, and the whole thing might go spinning into space. A Feydeau play has points in common with a highly elaborated and crazy delusion.

The masters of French farce in the nineteenth century used incredibly elaborate plots, and it is often said of their plays that they are "all plot." Here we have another aspect of the madness of farce. Human life in this art form is horribly attenuated. Life is a kind of universal milling around, a rushing from bedroom to bedroom driven by demons more dreadful than sensuality. The kind of farce which is said to be "all plot" is often much more than ingenious, it is maniacal. When one saw the actors of the Montreal *Théâtre du nouveau monde* giving positively spastic movements to Molière's farce characters, one said to oneself: after all there is something spastic about farce generally. Dryden says: "The persons and actions of a farce are all unnatural and their manners false."

Much more is involved in the movement of the story than we commonly realize. Why, for example, do directors of farce always call for tempo, tempo, tempo? It is not just because they admire business efficiency, nor is there anything to the common belief of theatre people that *fast* is always better than *slow*. It is a question of the speeding up of human behavior so that it becomes less than human. Bergson might say this was one of the ways in which human behavior becomes funny by resembling the working of high-speed machines. The speeding up of movement in the typical silent-movie farces had a definite psychological and moral effect, namely, of making actions seem abstract and automatic when in life they would be concrete and subject to free will. It is a conception that bristles with menace.

Conversely, to think of a good farcical pattern of action is to think of a good pretext for rapid movement. The chase was the pride and glory of the Keystone Cops. The plot of *An Italian Straw Hat* is one long pretext for flight and pursuit. So is the plot of that homely English imitation of French farce, *Charley's Aunt*.

IN THE IMAGE OF THE APE

The farceur is a heretic: he does not believe that man was made in God's image. What are the principal images of men in farce and what do they amount to?

If one tells the story of some farces, one will start talking of young lovers, but if instead of telling the story, one looks at what has remained in one's memory from a farce, one will not find young lovers there but two other characters: the knave and the fool. One will then find that the plot itself hinges less on what the young lovers do than on what the knave does. The knave in farce is the equivalent of the villain in melodrama. "Passions spin the plot." If the passion that spins the melodramatic plot is sheer wickedness, the passion that spins the farcical plot is that younger brother of wickedness, the spirit of mischief. Shakespeare's Puck could be the knave of a farce. He is not deep or purposive enough to be a villain. He is a trouble-maker by accident and even by nature but not always by design and never with intent to do serious damage. He is a prankster—like Harlequin.

If mischief becomes a sort of comic equivalent of fate, it is usually through the Puck, the Harlequin, the Brighella, the Scapin, the Figaro that it does so. In its simpler forms, the idea of a prankster is desperately primitive, and even in Shakespeare the pranks hover on the brink of the abysmally unfunny. (What, for example, is so fascinating about the gulling of Malvolio in *Twelfth Night?* If we didn't know the name of the author, we would dismiss it as tiresome.) On the other hand, modern names and interesting ideas should not hide from us the fact that, for example, Signor Laudisi in Pirandello's *Right You Are* is the same old prankster in sophisticated disguise.

If knaves are more influential, fools are more numerous. How many fools are there to each knave of one's acquaintance? The Romans seem to have thought the normal ratio is three to one. Their Atellan Farces had four type characters: the Blockhead, the Braggart, the Silly Old Man, and the Trickster. Only the last is a knave. The others are three different kinds of fool: the moron, defeated before he starts; the braggart, defeating himself as he goes along; and the man who has recently become a fool through senility and can remember the gay days when he was a knave and heard the chimes at midnight.

It is perhaps wrong to speak of knaves and fools separately, for what has most value to farce and comedy is their interrelationship. F. M. Cornford has shown that one of the oldest relationships in the comic drama is that between the ironical man and the impostor. These are the comedian and the straight man, one a knave, the other a fool, the fun resulting from the interaction between the two. If we say that the farcical image of man is the image of a human couple, that couple will not be the *jeune premier* and the *ingénue* but the knave and the fool, the ironist and the impostor, Sir Toby Belch and Sir Andrew Aguecheek, Jack Tanner and Octavius Robinson.

To this polarity, add a paradox. In the last analysis the knave, too, is a fool. Farce and comedy are forever demonstrating that the knave's ingenuities get him nowhere. The cleverness which seems to be capability proves in the end a rhetorical or gymnastic flourish.

The farceur does not show man as a little lower than the angels but as hardly higher than the apes. He shows us man in the mass, in the rough, in the raw, in anything but fine individual flower. If Mr. Auden is right in saying that "art can have but one subject; man as a conscious unique person," then farce is not an art. The *Oxford Companion* seems to regret that the characters of farce are stupid. But they are deliberate monuments to stupidity, disturbing reminders that God has lavished stupidity on the human race with His own unrivaled prodigality.

I have mentioned some points, and they are many, where farce and tragedy meet, but here we find them at the poles. Pascal called man a thinking reed. The metaphor embraces two characteristics: intellect and weakness. If farce shows man to be deficient in intellect, it does not show him deficient in strength or reluctant to use it. Man, says farce, may or may not be one of the more intelligent animals, he is certainly an animal, and not one of the least violent either. He may dedicate what little intelligence he possesses precisely to violence, to plotting violence, or to dreaming violence. (Mona Lisa's smile might mean that she was plotting murder, but is more likely to signify that she was dreaming murders she would never plot.)

"A Mad World, My Masters!" A play with a cast of fools tells us that it is a world of fools we live in. If that is not a tragic image, it is not, on the other hand, an image which the tragic poets would find beneath them. I take from what is perhaps the greatest of tragedies these words:

> When we are born we cry that we are come
> To this great stage of fools.

What wisdom can there be without a poignant sense of wisdom's opposite, which is folly?

THE QUINTESSENCE OF THEATRE

When we talk of Charlie Chaplin are we talking of acting or the thing acted? Nearly all discussions of him pass imperceptibly from the

one topic to the other, and this is as it should be. Meyerhold said:
"The idea of the actor's art, based on the worship of the mask, gesture, and movement is inseparably linked with the idea of farce."

If melodrama is the quintessence of drama, farce is the quintessence
of theatre. Melodrama is written. A moving image of the world is
provided by a writer. Farce is acted. The writer's contribution seems
not only absorbed but translated. Melodrama belongs to the words and
to the spectacle; the actor must be able to speak and make a handsome or monstrous part of the tableau. Farce concentrates itself in
the actor's body, and dialogue in farce is, so to speak, the activity of
the vocal cords and the cerebral cortex. Consider the figures in Jacques
Callot's engravings, *Dances of Naples* (*Balli di Sfessania*). One cannot imagine them performing melodramas. They have always been
considered the very incarnation of *commedia dell'arte;* and obviously
they are the incarnation of farce. One cannot imagine melodrama being improvised. The improvised drama was pre-eminently farce. In its
pride it would call itself *commedia*. But we do not hear of *tragedia
dell'arte*. And so I am reversing Meyerhold's dictum and saying: the
idea of farce is inseparably linked with the idea of the actor's art,
the *arte of commedia dell'arte*.[1] The theatre of farce is the theatre of
the human body but of that body in a state as far from the natural
as the voice of Chaliapin is from my voice or yours. It is a theatre
in which, though the marionettes are men, the men are supermario-
nettes. It is the theatre of the surrealist body.

The entertainments of the *commedia dell'arte* were Atellan Farces
raised to a higher power. The fools are no longer limited to three
kinds, nor the knaves to one. There is a complete human menagerie.

The celebrated types of the *commedia* have deeper roots than
social manners or even society itself. In Callot's *Dances* the animal
origin of the characters is clear. It has been suggested that Callot may
not be giving an accurate portrait of the *commedia*, but it is likely
that any deviation came from knowledge and intuition as to what the
commedia in essence was. Aristophanes' birds represent a sophisticated
use of animal fable, which could not have been sophisticated from the
beginning. The characters of comedy come in time to stand for the
human in the most restricted sense, the human cut off from Nature.
But originally they represented human nature as part of Nature-in-
general, human life as part of all life. Conversely, external nature was
not external: the general forces of life were to be found in the human

---

[1] Following Allardyce Nicoll (in his *The World of Harlequin,* Cambridge
University Press, 1963, p. 26), I am assuming that the traditional interpretation of the word *"arte"* as "the acting profession" is incorrect. But that interpretation presents no threat to my thesis about farce.

figures. If on the tragic side, gods merge with heroes, on the comic side the knaves and fools merge with the lower orders of spirits, as they are still doing in Shakespeare's *Midsummer Night's Dream* and *The Tempest*.

The *commedia dell'arte* petered out in the eighteenth century. The nearest thing we can see to it today is a type of theatre that is not influenced by it: the so-called Peking Opera. But there is a vestige of the *commedia* in the theatre of Eduardo de Filippo in Naples, and there have been convincing attempts to reconstruct entertainments in *commedia* style by the Piccolo Teatro di Milano.

Charlie Chaplin's silent comedies are not merely vehicles for the greatest comedian of the twentieth century, they are masterpieces of farce. And there are dozens of them. No one at the time realized what they were worth, and only, I believe, the Cinemathèque in Paris has made a systematic attempt to preserve them. Even now, if these works are spoken of as art, it is the art of film that is meant. The idea of a masterpiece *of farce* seems an unacceptable proposition, perhaps even to Mr. Chaplin himself, who in later life has aimed at forms with higher standing—not with uniformly happy results.

That the era of great farce in the motion picture runs from about 1912 to about 1927 seems to many a result of mechanical accident. The motion picture camera had just been invented, the sound track had not yet been combined with it: farce was happily suited to the silent screen. It is true that certain aspects of farce could be developed on the screen far beyond the possibilities of the stage. The screen could obviously do much more with the traditional chase and pursuit. Trick photography opened up new territory for zany behavior. Even pantomime changed. The old mimes delighted to work with imaginary props. Part of their art was to do without the actual objects. On the screen, objects—from the automobile to the alarm clock— became a vast new subject matter for farce and gave us what was in many ways a new kind of farce.

But the flowering of an art form could never be mainly the result of a mechanical invention. It happened that the invention was made toward the end of an era of great farce, one of the few. "In our day," said Nietzsche in 1870, "only the farce and the ballet may be said to thrive." He was right, but no one seems to know it. To the extent that the history of Victorian theatre and drama is taught at all in the schools, the word has been that before Shaw and Wilde there were only some shadowy and austere figures like Bulwer Lytton and Tom Robertson. That is misleading because the real glory of the Victorian stage lay in the farce, the extravaganza, and the comic opera. The great names are Gilbert and Sullivan, and the young Pinero.

As for France, there is the same contrast between what one is told and the actual situation. One is told of the serious thesis drama of the younger Dumas and Augier, drama that has seemed dated since around 1900. But there is French theatre of 1860 that is still fresh today, notably the operettas of Offenbach and the farces of Labiche. In the wake of these two geniuses of light theatre came Georges Feydeau, possibly the greatest writer of farce of any country at any time. He has not had worthy successors. The era of modern farce ended with his death in 1921—which was almost exactly the time when Chaplin began to give farce up.

Chaplin's farces, then, mark not the beginning of an era, but the end of one. The movie-makers did not follow in his footsteps. And though the farcical bits were the best parts of the later Chaplin pictures, they were only parts—of satire, of tragicomedy, of drama of ideas.

There is a special niche for the pictures that the Marx Brothers made in the thirties and for those of W. C. Fields in the same period and a little later. But whereas the early Chaplin films had been a pure triumph, both the Marx Brothers and Fields had an uphill battle to fight with the times. The age of phony seriousness was upon us. There was too much aggression in Chaplin, in Fields, in the Marx Brothers for the age of Rodgers and Hammerstein, Norman Vincent Peale, and Dwight D. Eisenhower.

"THE BREATH OF IMAGINARY FREEDOM"

While defining melodrama as savage and infantile, I have sought also to defend it as an amusing and thrilling emanation of a natural self which we do well not to disown. And I follow Aristotle, rather than Plato, on the question of violence in art, concluding that melodrama, far from tending to make Hitlers of us, affords us, insofar as it has any effect at all, a healthy release, a modest catharsis. Much the same can be said of farce, except that the principal motor of farce is not the impulse to flee (or Fear), but the impulse to attack (or Hostility). In music, says Nietzsche, the passions enjoy themselves. If in melodrama fear enjoys itself, in farce hostility enjoys itself.

A generation ago people used to talk against the idea of art as escape—they had in mind escape from social problems. Melodrama and farce are both arts of escape and what they are running away from is not only social problems but all other forms of moral responsibility. They are running away from the conscience and all its creations, as at the orgies that the classical scholars have sometimes talked about. Charles Lamb called Restoration Comedies "those Saturnalia of two or three brief hours," and again we can apply Lamb's words to farce:

I am glad for a season to take an airing beyond the diocese of the strict conscience—not to live always in the precincts of the law-courts—but now and then, for a dreamwhile or so, to imagine a world with no meddling restrictions. . . . I wear my shackles more contentedly for having respired the breath of imaginary freedom.

"Not to live always in the precincts of the law-courts." To escape the law courts, to escape the tyranny of society and public opinion, to escape also the law courts of the mind and the tyranny of the judge within each breast, the inner conscience—this sounds like an admirable prescription for the pursuit of pleasure. Then why and how do these law courts and these tyrannies get into dramatic literature? Is plain pleasure not the aim of literature? Or is there another and higher pleasure to be found "in the precincts of the law-courts," both kinds of law courts?

Farce*

VSEVOLOD MEYERHOLD

"Mystery in the Russian Theatre" is the title given by Benois to one of his "Letters on Art." [1] One might think that in this article he is discussing a production of one of Aleksei Remizov's plays written in the style of a medieval mystery play. Or, perhaps, Scriabin has already realized one of his dreams, and Benois is hastening to announce to the public the greatest event on the Russian stage—the appearance of a new theatrical form reviewing the mystic rites of ancient Greek culture.

It seems that neither Remizov nor Scriabin has written a mystery; according to Benois the Moscow Art Theatre has produced a mystery with its performance of *The Brothers Karamazov*. But just what characteristics of the medieval mystery plays could be found in the performance of *The Brothers Karamazov?* Perhaps here the purified ancient Greek mysteries were combined with the visual edification of the medieval mystery play?

In Dostoevsky's novel the traits of purification and edification are present, but they are contained in the ingenious structure of thesis and antithesis: God and the devil. These two inseparable elements of the novel are to be found in Zossima and the Karamazovs, the symbol of divinity and the symbol of the devil.

On the stage, the center of gravity in the development of the plot is shifted to Dimitri. In transforming Dostoevsky's novel into a play, the intricate interrelationships of Zossima, Aliosha, and Ivan have been lost. *The Brothers Karamazov* becomes simply the dramatized plot of the novel, or more accurately—several chapters from the novel. Such

---

[1] A. N. Benois, well-known painter, art critic, and art historian, wrote regularly his "Letters on Art" for the newspaper *Rech*. (Trans.)

* Vsevolod Meyerhold, "Farce," Nora Beeson, tr., *Tulane Drama Review*, Vol. 4, No. 1 (September, 1959), pp. 139–149.

a transformation is not only a sacrilege against Dostoevsky, but also against the idea of the authentic mystery play (if the directors wanted to make this production into a mystery play).

If one is to expect a "mystery" from the Russian theatre, who but Remizov or Scriabin would write it? But the question is, has the time arrived? And here is another question: Is the theatre ready for a "mystery"?

Scriabin in his first symphony sang a hymn to art as religion. In his third symphony he revealed the force of the liberated spirit. And in his *Poem of Ecstacy* [2] man is seized with joy at the realization that he has passed the thorny path, and that the hour of creation has arrived. In each of these works Scriabin gathered valuable material which might be used for a majestic ritual called a "mystery," where music, dance, light, and the intoxicating scent of wild flowers combine into a single work.[3] Realizing how miraculously fast Scriabin has passed from his first symphony to his *Prometheus,* one can say with assurance that he is ready to present a "mystery" to the public. But if *Prometheus* has not united the contemporary audience into a single community, will Scriabin want to present a "mystery"? Not without reason does the author of *Prometheus* long for the banks of the Ganges. He has not yet found an audience for a "mystery." He has not yet gathered around himself the initiated and faithful.

I am convinced that until the writers of contemporary mysteries break their ties with the theatre and leave the theatre entirely, the mystery play will only hinder the theatre, and the theatre the mystery.

Andrei Bely is right. Analyzing the contemporary symbolical theatre he comes to the following conclusion: "Let the theatre remain the theatre, and the mystery remain the mystery." He clearly sees the danger in mixing these two opposing types of performance. And recognizing that a rebirth of the real mystery play is impossible in our age of religious inertia, Andrei Bely hopes "that the traditional theatre will be revived on its own modest merits."

The revival of the traditional theatre is hindered by the public itself which has formed an alliance with the so-called dramatists— those playwrights who transform literature for reading into literature for the theatre. In the public's mind there is already enough confusion about the theatre. And Benois, by calling the performance of *The Brothers Karamazov* a mystery, creates only greater confusion.

Certain lines in Benois' article give the key, if not to what he meant by a mystery, then at least to an understanding of his relation-

---

[2] Scriabin's fourth symphony. (Trans.)
[3] At his death in 1915 Scriabin left such a *Mystery* uncompleted. (Trans.)

ship to the theatre. Benois writes: "And so I repeat that the Moscow Art Theatre, as well as Dimitri, is incapable of lying." And further on: "The Comédie Française has found success, and so may Reinhardt and Meyerhold, in illusion and 'cabotinage'; this is foreign to the Art Theatre."

Benois gives a negative meaning to the word "cabotinage." He thinks the people concerned with reforming the contemporary stage deceive the public by inventing some fiction about a regenerated theatre. Only the Moscow Art Theatre, Benois thinks, "is incapable of lying." He considers "cabotinage" an evil in the theatre. To those "incapable of lying" (the directors of the Art Theatre) illusion and "cabotinage" are foreign.

However, what is the theatre without "cabotinage," and what is this "cabotinage" which Benois hates? Cabotin was a wandering comedian. He was a relative of the mimes, *histriones,* jugglers. Cabotin possessed a miracle-working acting technique. Cabotin was the upholder of the tradition of the authentic acting art. With his assistance the western theatre (the seventeenth-century Spanish and Italian theatre) attained its greatness. Benois is delighted with the renaissance of the mystery play on the Russian stage, but writes scornfully about "cabotinage"; whereas even mysteries sought the assistance of the "cabotins." The "cabotin" appeared wherever performances were given, and the producers of mystery plays expected him to help with all the difficult tasks of a mystery. From the history of the French theatre we know that an interpreter in a mystery play found it impossible to solve his problems without the aid of a juggler. At the time of Philip le Beau a farce about the improper pranks of Renard, the Fox, suddenly appeared among religious plays. And who could play this farce except the "cabotin"? With the gradual development of processional mystery plays new subjects appeared which demanded more and more technique from the actors. Only the "cabotin" could solve the most complicated problems of a mystery play. So we can see that "cabotinage" was not alien to the mystery plays, and that the "cabotin" played an important role in their development,

As the mystery play gradually included the popular elements of miming it was forced to leave the church; first the pulpit, then the porch and graveyard, and finally it passed into the market place. Wherever the mystery play tried to make an alliance with the theatre, it had to rely on miming elements, and as soon as it became allied to the actor's art, it ceased to be a mystery play.

Probably it is always true that—no "cabotin," no theatre; and vice versa—as soon as the theatre rejects the fundamental laws of theatricality, then it feels capable of existing without "cabotins."

For Benois, evidently, the mysteries can help save the Russian theatre from decline, but "cabotinage" only harms the theatre. I think the reverse is true: the mystery play, which Benois describes, is harmful to the theatre, and "cabotinage" might save it. In order to rescue the Russian stage from becoming a slave to literature it is necessary to return to the stage the cult of "cabotinage."

But how can this be done?

First of all, I think, one must study and revive those former theatres in which the cult of "cabotinage" reigned.

Our playwrights are totally ignorant of the laws of the authentic theatre. Instead of the old vaudeville [4] of the nineteenth-century Russian theatre, we have brilliant dialectics, *pièces à thèse,* realistic plays, and plays of mood.

The novelist is reducing the number of descriptive passages and, for the liveliness of the story, increasing the characters' dialogue, until he finally invites his reader to pass from the library into the auditorium. Does the novelist need the services of the "cabotin"? Of course not. The readers themselves can come onto the stage, assume parts, and read aloud to the audience the dialogue of their favorite novelist. This is called "a harmoniously performed play." A name is quickly given to the reader-transformed-into-actor, and a new term, "an intelligent actor," is coined. The same dead silence reigns in the auditorium as in the library. The public is dozing. Such immobility and solemnity is appropriate only in a library.

To transform the novelist who is writing for the stage into a playwright, he should be compelled to write a few pantomimes. A good "antidote" to the superfluity of words! But the playwright need not fear that he will have no opportunity to speak. He will be allowed to give words to the actor, but only after the scenario has been written. When will the following law be added to the commandments of the theatre—*words in the theatre are only a design on the canvas of motion?*

---

[4] I am referring to the old vaudeville not because it must be brought back to the theatre at all cost, but because I consider this form to be an example linked not with literary, but with theatrical traditions on the one hand, and with popular taste on the other. One must remember that vaudeville came to us from France, and we know that French vaudeville was created in the following manner (see Fournel, *Spectacles popul et artistes des rues,* pp. 320–21): "An improvisational, popular theatre performed for a long time near the Porte St. Jacques; the people came in crowds to hear the gay songs, and to watch three merry performers. All three had come from Normandie; all three were apprentices in the baker's guild, had come to Paris to try their fortune, and had brought to the capital the bawdy and clever popular Normandie songs and verses which consequently introduced vaudeville to France. Everyone knew and loved them, and their names—Gaultier Garguille, Turlupin, and Gros Guillaume—will forever be remembered in the history of French humor." So we see that vaudeville arose from popular songs and humor.

Somewhere I read that the "drama in reading is mainly dialogue, controversy, intense dialectic. Drama on stage is mainly action, intense struggle. Here words are only overtones of action, so to speak. They must involuntarily burst from the actor who is caught by the elemental motion of the dramatic conflict."

The organizers of medieval mystery ceremonies recognized perfectly well the magic power of the pantomime. The most touching scenes in the French mystery plays of the late fourteenth and the early fifteenth centuries were always dumb shows. The movements of the actors explained the subject matter of the show much better than profuse discourses in verse or prose.[5] It is instructive to note that as soon as the mystery play passed from the dry rhetoric of religious ceremonies to a new form of action filled with emotional elements (first to the miracle play, then to the morality, and finally to the farce)—then immediately pantomime and the juggler appeared on stage.

Pantomime shuts the mouth of the rhetorician whose place is on the rostrum and not in the theatre; and the actor proclaims the self-sufficiency of the acting craft—the expressiveness of gesture and bodily movement. The juggler demands for himself a mask, plenty of rags for a bright costume, plenty of balloons, feathers, and bells, plenty of everything that lends brilliance and noise to the performance.

Although the organizers of religious performances were pious, they nevertheless presented three nude girls as sirens at the festivities for the entry of Louis XI; at the entry of Queen Isabelle of Bavaria, in the midst of a religious setting, the good burghers enacted the great battle of King Richard against Saladin and the Saracens; at the entry of Queen Ann of Bavaria, an actor appeared addressing the crowd with a prologue in verse. Each of these examples shows the important role played by "cabotinage" in the spectacles. Processions, battles, prologues, parades, even mystery plays could not forgo these elements of true theatricality.

---

[5] An episode from another period recalls the meaning and power of pantomime: "According to the words of a Roman writer, in Nero's reign a foreign ruler was attending a pantomime performance in which a famous actor performed the twelve labors of Hercules with such expressiveness and clarity that the foreign ruler understood everything without any explanation. He was so surprised, that he begged Nero to give him this actor as a present. Nero was very much astonished at this request, but then the guest explained that next to his kingdom lived a wild tribe whose language no one could understand. The savages, likewise, could not comprehend what their neighbors wanted from them. With pantomime this remarkable actor could make the savages understand what was wanted from them, and they undoubtedly could grasp his meaning well." *Tantsy, ikh istoriia i razvitie s drevnykh vremen do nashikh dnei* (Dances, their History and Development from Ancient Times to Our Days), St. Petersburg, 1902, p. 15, Po Viuile.

The beginning of the theatre must be sought in just such periods of highly developed "cabotinage." It would be a mistake to think that the theatre in the Hospital of the Holy Trinity,[6] for example, originated from mystery plays. No. It originated among the street mimes at the festive entries of kings.

At present most stage directors are turning to pantomimes and prefer this kind of theatre to spoken drama. This is not mere chance, nor is it just a matter of taste. Nor are the directors trying to cultivate this genre because a very special charm is hidden in the pantomimes. In reconstructing the theatre of former times, the modern director finds it necessary to begin with pantomimes because in staging these wordless plays the primary force of the theatre is revealed to the actors—the power of masks, gestures, movements, and plot.

Mask, gesture, movement, and the plot are ignored completely by the modern actor. He has lost all connection with the tradition of the great masters of the acting art. The modern actor has been transformed into an "intelligent reader." "The play will be read in costume and make-up" could be written on our programs. The new actor plays without mask and juggling technique. The mask is replaced by make-up which has to reproduce accurately the features of the face as it is in real life. The modern actor does not need the juggler's technique because he never "acts" but only "lives" on the stage. He does not understand "acting," the theatre's magic work, because an imitator is not capable of improvisation based on technique.

The cult of "cabotinage," which I am sure will come back with the restoration of the traditional theatre, will help the modern actor understand the fundamental laws of theatricality.

The restorers of old scenarios, deriving their knowledge from forgotten theories of scenography, from old theatrical chronicles and iconography, are attempting to make the actor believe in the strength and importance of acting.

Just as the novelist interested in a certain style reconstructs the past from old chronicles which he embellishes with his own fantasy, so the actor from material gathered for him, can recreate the craft of the forgotten comedians.

Enthusiastic over the simplicity, the refined nobility, and the great artistry of the old yet eternally new acting methods practiced by the *histriones, mimi, atellani, scurrae, jaculatores,* and *ministrelli,* the actor of the future can and must (if he wants to remain an actor) coor-

---

6 Les Confrères de la Passion of The Community of the Holy Trinity, in sixteenth-century Paris, moved indoors and gave performances on a platform stage. (Trans.)

dinate his emotions and his craftsmanship within the traditional framework of the theatre.

Whenever the revival of old styles is mentioned, one always hears
how boring it is for the modern playwright to be forced to compete
with the old-fashioned Cervantes *intermedia,* Tirso de Molina dramas,
or Carlo Gozzi tales. If the modern playwright does not want to follow
the traditions of the old theatre, if, for a time, he leaves the theatre
which seeks its regeneration from the past, then the modern theatre
will be benefited. The actor who is bored with practicing his trade in
defunct plays will soon want not only to act, but even to compose
for himself. In this way the Theatre of Improvisation finally makes
its appearance. If, however, the playwright wants to help the actor,
the dramatist's role will be confined to the seemingly simple, but in
reality very intricate, role of inventing the scenarios and the prologues
which present to the public the outline of what the actor is going
to perform. I hope the playwright will not be humiliated by such a
role. Did Carlo Gozzi lose anything when, after giving a scenario to
the Sacci Company, he permitted the actors to improvise monologues
and dialogues?

I am asked: Why is it so necessary for the theatre to have all
these prologues, parades and the like? Isn't a single scenario sufficient?

The prologue and the parade that follows, as well as the concluding address to the audience so favored by the Italians and Spaniards of the eighteenth century and the French vaudevillists—all these
elements of the traditional theatre compelled the spectator to regard
the performance as nothing but play. Whenever the actor had enticed
the spectator too deeply into the land of fiction, the actor, as quickly
as possible, by some unexpected remark or a long aside, reminded the
audience that everything presented was only "a play."

While Remizov and Scriabin are waiting for their place in the new
theatres, while their mysteries are awaiting the initiated, the theatre
which restores the juggler will wage a desperate fight with realistic
and dialectical dramas, with *pièces à thèse,* and plays of mood. The
new Theatre of Masks will learn from the Spaniards and Italians of
the seventeenth century how to build its repertory on the laws of the
farce where amusement comes before instruction, and movement is
valued more highly than words. Not without reason was pantomime
the favorite dramatic expression of the "Clercs de la Basoche." [7]

Schlegel maintained that in ancient Greece pantomime attained an

---

[7] The Clercs de la Basoche, in the middle of the fifteenth century in Paris
were a guild of legal scribes famous for their performance of satirical farces.
(Trans.)

incredible perfection. And M. K. added that 'pantomime could develop and be brought to perfection only by a people who so successfully practiced the plastic arts, and only a country whose many statues
imparted grace to all things." [8]

Will not a constant preoccupation with the art of pantomime bring
us to these wonders of grace even though we do not have the sky
and the sun of ancient Attica?

II

There are two kinds of puppet theatres.

The director of one wants his puppets to resemble the human being
in all its features and peculiarities, just as the heathen wants his idol
to nod its head, and the toymaker wants his doll to make sounds
resembling the human voice. In his desire to reproduce reality, the
director continues to perfect his puppets until he realizes that there
is a simpler solution to this complex problem, namely, to transform
them into a man.

The other director sees that the audience in his theatre is amused
not only by the witty plays performed by his puppets, but probably
more by the puppets' movements which, however much they try to
imitate life, never entirely resemble what the audience sees in life.

When I watch the performance of modern actors, it is always clear
to me that I see before my eyes the perfected puppet theatre of the
first of these two directors—the one where man has replaced the
puppet. Here man equals the puppet in its efforts to imitate life. The
human being has been called upon to replace the puppet because in
copying reality the human being can be more successful than the
puppet.

The other director, who also tried to make his puppet resemble a
living person, noticed quickly that when he began to improve his
puppet's mechanism, it lost some of its charm. It even seemed to him
that the whole nature of the puppet opposed this barbarous alteration.
This director realized in time that there are limits to a transformation which, if exceeded, will inevitably lead to the replacement of the
puppet by man.

But is it possible to part company with the puppet which has succeeded in creating such an enchanting world in the theatre with expressive gestures governed by a special, bewitching technique and with
an angularity of movement that cannot be compared to anything else?

I have described two puppet theatres in order to force the actor

---

[8] *Opyt istorii teatra* (An Experiment in the History of the Theatre) Moscow, 1849, p. 126.

into a thoughtful mood: should he replace the puppet and continue in a subservient role which gives no freedom to his own personal creativity, or should he fashion a theatre such as the puppet could defend, refusing to submit to the director's attempts to transform his nature? The puppet did not want to be an exact image of man because the world the puppet reflects is a wonderful imaginary world, and the character it reflects is an imaginary character, and the stage it moves on is like a sounding board along which lie the strings of its skill. The puppet's stage is as it is not because of the puppet's nature, but because of its will, and its will is not to imitate but to create.

When the puppet cries, its hand holds the handkerchief but does not touch its eyes; when the puppet kills, it pierces its opponent so gently that the tip of the sword does not touch his chest; and when the puppet slaps someone, the color does not fade from his cheek; and the puppet lovers embrace with such reserve that the spectator, observing their caresses from a considerable distance, does not ask his neighbor how these embraces end.

But when a human being appears on stage, why does he blindly subject himself to a director who wants to turn him into a puppet of the naturalistic school? The human does not wish to present *his art* on the stage. The contemporary actor refuses to understand that the comedian-mime is supposed to lead the audience into the land of imagination, and on his way entertain with his technical brilliance.

The invented gesture, suitable only in the theatre, the stylized movement, conceivable only in the theatre, the artificiality of stage elocution—all this is being criticized by the public as well as the critics because the idea of "theatricality" has not yet been divorced from the acting of the so-called "actors of mood."

The "actor of inner mood" wants to depend only on his own state of mind. He does not want his will to command his technique. He is proud of bringing to the stage the brilliance of his improvisation, and naïve enough to believe that his improvisation has something in common with the improvisation of the old Italian comedy. He does not know that the *commedia dell'arte* performers cultivated their improvisations only on the basis of a refined technique. He resolutely denies all technique. "Technique hinders the freedom of the creative act"—is how this actor speaks. Only the moment of unconscious creativity based on emotion has any value to him. If there is such a moment, then there is success; without it—no success.

But does an actor's intellect really hinder the display of emotion? It was a living man who acted and danced around the altar of Dionysus; his emotions were aroused; the altar fire raised his feelings

to ecstacy. However, the ritual dedicated to the god of wine has pre-
established meters and rhythms, and certain prescribed methods of
movement and gesture. Here the actor's reasoning did not obstruct
his temperament. The dancing Greek, although obliged to observe a
whole series of traditional rules, could nevertheless introduce into his
dance many innovations.

Not only does the contemporary actor lack all rules of the comedian's art (for art is only that which is governed by laws; according
to Voltaire "dancing is an art because it is governed by rules"), but
he also has created a frightful chaos in his art. As if this were not
enough, he considers it his duty to bring chaos into the other spheres
of art. If he wants to enter the field of music, he invents recitation
to music. If he reads poetry from the stage, he pays attention only
to the subject of the poetry, and arranges the logical stresses without
concerning himself in any way with meter and rhythm, caesura and
pauses, or musical intonation.

Modern actors, in their attempt at reincarnation, set themselves the
problem of destroying their "I" and of producing an illusion of life
on the stage. Why, then, are the names of the actors announced on
the placards? When the Moscow Art Theatre produced Gorky's *Lower
Depths,* instead of an actor a real tramp was brought onto the stage.
The tendency toward reincarnation reached a point where the actor
was relieved of his function altogether. Why was the name of the
actor performing the role of Teterev printed on the posters? Is it possible to call someone an "actor" when he appears on the stage as
he is in real life? Why deceive the public?

The public comes to the theatre to see the art of man, but what
kind of art is it to walk on the stage as one really is? The public
expects fantasy, acting, skill, and instead sees either life or a slavish
imitation of it.

Once having discarded the shelter of one's surroundings, does not
man's art on the stage consist of skillfully selecting a mask and a
decorative costume, and of dazzling the public with the technical
brilliance of either a dancer, or an intriguer (as at a masquerade ball),
or a simpleton of the old Italian comedy, or a juggler?

The mask's magic power becomes apparent after one reads carefully
the forgotten collections of scenarios, those of Flaminio Scala (1613),
for example.

Harlequin, a native of Bergamo, the servant of a stingy doctor, is
forced by his master's avarice to wear a suit of many-colored patches.
Harlequin is the silly fool, the cunning servant who seems always
merry. But look what is hidden under his mask—Harlequin, the mighty

magician, sorcerer, and wizard; Harlequin, the representative of the infernal powers. The mask is capable of hiding more than just these two opposing figures. These two aspects of Harlequin are two poles between which lie infinite varieties. How is this great diversity shown to the spectator? By the mask.

The actor in control of the art of gesture and movement (here lies his strength!) will wear the mask in such a way that the spectator knows clearly who is before his eyes: the silly fool from Bergamo, or the devil. This chameleon quality, hidden under the comedian's fixed mask, provides the theatre with an enchanting play of light and shade. Is it not the mask which aids the spectator to fly into the land of fantasy? The mask makes the spectator see not only one particular Harlequin, but all the Harlequins in his memory. In Harlequin the spectator sees all the people which in any way resemble this image. But is the mask the only source of the theatre's fascination? No.

It is the actor who, with his art of gesture and movement, compels the spectator to be whisked into a fairyland where the blue bird flies, where the beasts talk, and where the loafing, roguish, or infernal Harlequin is transformed into a simpleton who performs wonderful tricks. Harlequin is an acrobat, sometimes a rope walker. His leaps are exceedingly dextrous. His improvised jokes startle the audience by an exaggerated improbability which even the dramatists did not dream of. The actor is a dancer. He can dance the graceful *monferrina* [9] as well as the coarse English jig. The actor can make you cry and a few seconds later laugh. He carries the fat Doctor on his shoulders and jumps around with him as if there were nothing to it. Now he is soft and flexible, now clumsy and awkward. The actor has at his command a thousand different intonations with which he does not imitate specific characters, but which he uses rather to decorate and supplement. He can speak fast, when playing the role of a rogue, or slowly and in a drawl when imitating the pedant. On the stage he can trace geometric figures with his body, or he can leap happily and recklessly as if flying through air.

The face of the actor is covered by a mask, but by his skill he can use it in such ways, and contort his body in such positions that the dead mask becomes alive.

Since the appearance of Isadora Duncan, and even more since Jacques Dalcroze's eurhythmic theory, the modern actor has gradually begun to understand the meaning of gesture and movement. However, a mask still interests him very little. Whenever the subject of masks arises the actor asks: is it possible for the mask and cothurn of the

[9] *La monfrina,* or *monferrina*—a popular Italian dance. (Trans.)

ancient theatre to reappear on the contemporary stage? To the modern actor, the mask is something which once was used to overcome poor acoustical conditions, or was used to emphasize a role in an exaggerated but stereotyped way.

We are still waiting for the time when an actor without a mask will arouse the indignation of the public, as was the case in the reign of Louis XIV, when the dancer Hardel was the first who dared appear without a mask. But at present the modern actor will under no circumstances recognize the mask as a symbol of the theatre—and not only the actor.

I have made the experiment of interpreting the figure of Don Juan according to the principles of the Theatre of Masks.[10] But even such an art critic as Benois did not understand the mask on Don Juan's face.

"Molière loves Don Juan. Don Juan is his hero, and as with all heroes, he is even a little Molière's portrait. To substitute for this hero some satyr type is not only a mistake, but something worse." [11]

This is how Benois regards Molière's Don Juan. He would like to see in Don Juan the image of the "Seville seducer" as portrayed by Tirso de Molina, Byron, and Pushkin.

In his wanderings from one poet to the next, Don Juan preserved the basic features of his character, but he reflected, as a mirror, the diverse natures of his authors, the life of the most divergent countries, and the expression of various social ideals.

Benois forgets completely that Molière was attracted to the character of Don Juan not as a goal, but as a means to an end.

Molière wrote *Don Juan* after *Tartuffe* had aroused a storm of indignation among the clergy and nobility. He was accused of a number of base offenses, and the poet's enemies were anxious to find a worthy punishment for him. He could fight this injustice with his only weapon, the theatre. In order to ridicule the bigotry of the clergy and the hypocrisy of the aristocracy which he hated so intensely, he grasped Don Juan as a drowning man clutches a straw. A number of scenes and separate sentences, though inconsistent with the mood of the action and the characteristics of the protagonist, are introduced by Molière as a revenge on those who had hampered the success of *Tartuffe*. Molière exposes to ridicule and abuse this very "jumping, dancing and grimacing Lovelace" [12] in order to make him a target for the poet's bitter attacks against pride and vanity. And at the same

---

[10] My revival of Molière's *Don Juan* was first given in the Imperial Alexandrinsky Theatre, November 9, 1910.

[11] In the newspaper *Rech,* No. 318, November 19, 1910.

[12] *Ibid.*

time Molière places in the mouth of this frivolous dandy, whom he had just ridiculed, a brilliant characterization of the period's prevailing vices—hypocrisy and bigotry.

One more consideration should not be forgotten. Just at the time when Molière was greatly distressed by the withdrawal of *Tartuffe* from the stage, the poet suffered a family tragedy. "His wife, little capable of appreciating her husband's genius, was unfaithful to him with the most unworthy rivals, falling in love with *salon* gossipers whose noble birth was their only distinction. Even before this, Molière had never missed an opportunity to hurl gibes at the *Marquis ridicules.*" [13] Now he uses the figure Don Juan for new attacks on his rivals.

Molière needed the scene with the peasant girls, not so much for characterizing Don Juan, as for drowning with the intoxicating wine of comic scenes the drama of a man deprived of family happiness by such flippant and egotistical "breakers of women's hearts."

It is only too clear that for Molière Don Juan is a puppet necessary to the author for settling his accounts with his numerous enemies. To Molière Don Juan is a wearer of masks. We see him wearing the masks of licentiousness, contempt for religion, cynicism, and hypocrisy which were worn by the cavaliers of the Sun King's court. He wore the mask of the author-accuser; the nightmarish mask which was stifling the author himself, and the torturing mask which Molière had to wear at court spectacles or before his deceitful wife. Only at the very end of the play does the author give to his puppet the mask reflecting the features of *El Burlador de Sevilla* as he was originally conceived.

The greatest compliment which the director and designer who staged Molière's *Don Juan* could dream of was paid them by Benois when he called the performance a "dressed-up farce." The Theatre of Masks is always a farce, and the idea of the actor's art, based on a worship of mask, gesture, and movement, is indissolubly linked with the idea of the farce. The farce is eternal. If its principles are for a time expelled from the walls of the theatre, we nevertheless know that they are firmly engraved in the lines of the manuscripts left by the theatre's greatest writers.

---

[13] *Artist,* No. 9, 1890.

Farce as Method*

ROBERT C. STEPHENSON

To get at the nature of farce we go back to beginnings, in either time or structure. Russian folk drama from the seventeenth into the twentieth century, for example, recapitulates much of what we know or infer about rude origins. Here, as Berkov [1] remarks, necessity creates and fixes a manner. Out-of-door performance calls for exaggerated tones, sweeping gestures, loud singing and furious dancing, features which persist when public square and puppet stage, but not ground-lings, are left behind. An impudent tone, imposed by the turbulent crowd, provokes performers into the picaresque asides, the jibes and the cheeky stepping out of role which, all the way down from remote beginnings in Attica to *Hellzapoppin* in New York, have raised their roars of laughter. Brutally enlarged, this is the way of folk game and folk tale, and should remind us, once for all, of the indissoluble bond by which farce is tied to folklore in general; and of what it owes to the point of view and the aesthetics of the folk. [2]

It is sufficient, though, to return to vernacular sources from which the line runs unbroken: the *commedia dell'arte;* the repertory of the fourteenth- and fifteenth-century Joyous Brotherhoods in France; and the primitive Spanish drama from Juan del Encina's eclogues in 1492 through the *pasos* of mid-sixteenth-century Lope de Rueda. In these we hope, perhaps, to find the form of farce, not yet pulled out of shape by the gravity of other patterns. If so, our hope is disappointed.

---

[1] *Russkaia Narodnaia Drama* [The Russian Folkdrama—an anthology with notes, a glossary and an introductory essay], edited by P. N. Berkov (Moscow, 1953).

[2] The brilliant phrase "the aesthetics of the folk" likewise comes from Berkov (p. 14).

* Robert C. Stephenson, "Farce as Method," *Tulane Drama Review,* Vol. 5, No. 2 (1961), pp. 85–93.

Early farce covered the range of the comic theatre; it *was* that theatre. Until comedy as such appeared, there was no cognate form against
which to measure farce as such. With the appearance of the new
frame of reference, the problem ought to be simplified: whatever residue of form remains when comedy is removed should be the form of
farce. The difficulty is that nothing of the sort does remain. As in the
moment of original creation, when light was brought into being,
comedy took shape out of the formless. Farce, in other words, was
inchoate *vis comica* in search of a body. When that body emerged,
the form-giving principle turned out to be characterization, continuous
revelation or growth of character through shades of difference. The
essence of this is in gradualness, uninterruptedness, features repugnant
to short-spanned, paratactic farce.

Farces did, and do, have forms, in the plural. But these are borrowed, not inherent. Consider some typical examples. The most famous of medieval farces, *Maître Pathelin,* uses—very satisfactorily, it
is true—the pattern of the cumulative folk tale. The *Farce du Cuvier,*
in which, while his wife is drowning in a washtub, the henpecked
husband, with slow deliberation, consults his list of household duties
and finds nothing there about helping wives out of tubs, is a single
stroke of character-drawing, full of tension but without development
or action. Sometimes, as in Juan del Encina's second carnival eclogue,
which shows us four shepherds over their bread and cheese, the
farce aims solely at physical gusto, devoid of comic elements, and the
laughter it provokes arises from identification of dialect or from the
stirring of animal sympathy.[3] Shepherd and lady may bring two orders of speech together in ludicrous contrast, as in Lucas Fernández'
Cuasi Comedia; or fanfaronade may sound the funnier for being contrasted with rustic speech, as in the same author's *Farsa del Soldado.*
The farce may be a scholastic debate, funny for the level on which
it is couched, as in Diego Sánchez de Badajoz' piece about the
carpenter and the blacksmith arguing, over the wood and nails of the
Cross, as to which is the more ancient and honorable Christian.

At this stage we notice a subsisting response. The worthies just mentioned spoke for their guilds; each of them had his supporters, for
whom his sallies, however feeble, sufficed to raise a loyal laugh. Each
was correspondingly grotesque to the other claque. They were funny in
themselves, by virtue of being; they were funny as labels. In this fact
there is something that nearly supports a definition, by distinguishing

---

[3] This eclogue, incidentally, includes such a passage about the defeat of
Carnival by Lent as anticipates the nature of the Spanish *loa.*

the elementary response from the sophisticated one.[4] To the folk in the audience a schoolteacher's speech, for example, is funny not because it is pedantic but simply because it is his. On the lowest possible level this is the *mot de caractère*: identification affords comic pleasure; to talk like oneself is automatically funny if one is a stock character, which largely explains such characters (the Negro, the simpleton, the doctor, the soldier, the braggart, the glutton, and so on). These, like the stovepipe hat, are funny in advance, in understandable colloquial memories of everyday experience, and there, likewise, have the effect of labels or even of masks. They achieve this effect by being outsiders seen from the outside, as an odd fact corroborates: in folk drama the doctor, but never the village quack, is an object of ridicule;[5] in folk drama, with its satirical outer view of things, the gentleman is that inscrutable and therefore funny fellow who pays a hundred rubles for an ox and a horse but only a couple of glasses of vodka for a man. The audience, bringing characters along in comical (or fearful) recollection, laughs in a special, a *folk*[6] way: without exposition, the ready-madeness of stock characters permits immediate *participation*, in the sense in which the classic audience participated through foreknowledge of the myth.

But to return to the range of forms. Sometimes, as in the anonymous *Entremés de los refranes*, farce is only a cento of proverbs; or, in the likewise anonymous *Entremés de los dos habladores*, it has nothing but garrulity for theme, a subject that relates it to the Farce of the Man that Married a Dumb Wife as we know this from Rabelais' mention of it and Anatole France's reconstruction. The farce may be a practical joke, as in the second *paso* of Lope de Rueda; or, in his first *paso*, gluttonous talk ending in a bit of muscular impudence when the simpleton Alameda slaps an imaginary spider on his master's face (a detail which reappears as the eighteenth-century Russian interlude of "The Fly"); or it may actually be a little playlet like, again, Lope de Rueda's third *paso*, that of the doctor, the cuckold, the faithless wife, and her pretended cousin. It is more likely, though, to be another such practical joke as his fourth *paso*, where a student hides in bed to escape the traveler whom he has invited to dinner, only to have the tables turned on him when his roommate yanks the covers off. Turning the tables, a favorite device with farce writers,

---

[4] Berkov, p. 19, notices this difference.

[5] Berkov, p. 15, supplies this significant fact.

[6] To a degree, if only by an act of group imagination, we all, except for the dramatic critics, perhaps, become members of the folk when we are in the audience.

may seem to be a characteristic pattern. But it, too, is appropriated ready-made and unaltered from anecdote and folk tale. So, likewise, is the fifth *paso,* with its parody of the riddle and with the two rascals that by turns eat a simpleton's lunch basket empty as he sits there open-mouthed and oblivious, listening to their alternate versions of what we would call the Rock Candy Mountain. Again, it may be the schoolboy's trick of proffering something and snatching it away. Here we have action reduced to gesture. This is the pattern of the sixth *paso,* where the simpleton is to carry a sum of money to the right man. Samadel, a trickster, accosts him.

SAMADEL   Ho, there, brother; are you fetching the money?

CEVADON   Is your honor the one who was to receive it?

SAMADEL   I ought to have it in my purse already.

CEVADON   Well, sir, my master told me to give it to you, and for your honor to take it. Fifteen reales.

SAMADEL   That's right, fifteen; hand it over.

CEVADON   Take it. . . . Wait a minute.

SAMADEL   Wait for what?

CEVADON   For what? For the tokens.

SAMADEL   What tokens?

CEVADON   My master said your worship would be wearing a patch over one eye and would drag one leg.

SAMADEL   If that's all, here's a patch.

CEVADON   Go along with you. Is that a patch?

SAMADEL   I say it is.

CEVADON   I say it isn't.

SAMADEL   I say it is, like it or not.

CEVADON   I don't want to like it or not. Por Dios, it's a patch if you say so. But seeing as you had your hat down over your eye, I didn't notice it.

SAMADEL   All right, then. Give me the money.

CEVADON   Here, sir, take it.

SAMADEL   Let's have it.

CEVADON   Wait a minute.

SAMADEL   What's the matter now?

CEVADON   What about dragging one leg?

SAMADEL   Like this?

CEVADON   Take the money, your honor.

SAMADEL   Let's have it.

CEVADON   Wait a minute. [And so on.] [7]

The farce may, finally, no more than act out a fable, like the seventh *paso,* a Spanish version of the milkmaid on her dreaming way to market; or like the Russian folk drama "Mavrukh," it may have no more substance than an echo of a foreign song, in this case "Malbrough s'en v-at-en guerre."

The point of the listing is that the protean farce indifferently assumes the shape of its materials in almost every case; which is a different thing from developing, reshaping those materials as, say, Alarcón reshapes "The Boy and the Wolf" in his *La verdad sospechosa.* It may be argued, though, that later examples developed a *genre* pattern; thus, with Cervantes, the interlude regularly ends in a song and dance, sometimes motivated. Yet such addition, as in nineteenth-century French and Russian vaudeville, is of no help in defining essential structure. It is not specifically *farce* form, rising out of the nature of farce and therefore inevitable. It is general, interchangeable *theatrical* form, borrowed, in this case, from *entr'acte* use of the ballad. Cervantes actually makes little advance, except in the greater length of his pieces. His "La cueva de Salamanca" and "El retablo de las maravillas" do add a trifle of plot-framing to the materials; but the materials come straight, in pattern and use, from folklore; and such equally characteristic interludes of his as "El rufián viudo" and "El juez de los divorcios," like the earlier farce, are fitted to the incidents they contain.

In the eighteenth century, in the hands of Ramón de la Cruz, the farce [8] was still a function of its contents: it was versified, but so was the rest of Spanish drama; otherwise, it was whatever the matter dictated: a stroll through a crowded park; a quarrel among chestnut-vendors; a scene in a tenement house; a feigned illness; an affected salon; mock-heroic buffoonery, as in *Manolo* (another *rufián viudo*); in general, playlets more remarkable for accurate speech than for comic spirit.

We still recognize undeveloped folk pattern in a nineteenth-century Spanish farce like "The Trousers," which are to be shortened for the master to wear them to a banquet, so that everyone officiously takes his turn at snipping a couple of inches off the bottom of them until,

---

[7] Translated from Lope de Rueda, *Teatro* (Madrid, 1924), pp. 249–251.

[8] By this time it is called the *sainete.* I have not discussed the terms, *Plus ça change, plus c'est la même chose.*

by the time they are tried on, they look like a pair of shorts. Perhaps this proves little, but what shall we say of another pair of short trousers, those in Pinero's *The Magistrate?* Here, again, the shape of the play has nothing to do with its being a farce. The shape is that of melodrama, which does possess its germane form. In the most pretentious of nineteenth-century farces, *The Importance of Being Earnest,* it is clearer than ever that farce both stays submissively close to materials and borrows foreign patterns: the content is a protracted pun, the pattern is sentimental comedy.

From this brief list we can draw valid inferences. As Chernyshevski [9] argues, farce sees only surfaces—though not, as he adds, merely material and ugly ones. As other critics insist, farces are, indeed, a low form of comedy—but in the evolutionary sense of the word. Where there is action, this is violent; true, but this action is inessential; more a consequence of mask, marionette, and original public square than of the farcical spirit. In fact, slapstick, stripped of grinning mask, finds its congenial role, today, in gangster plays, where it reveals its natural function, that of adding hysteria to other effects: in melodrama, to suspense; in farce, to laughter. Like the chase that lent excitement to Keystone comedies, it is supererogatory in farce, which may be completely static—as are some of the dialogues of the *skomorokhi,*[10] for example.

It helps to look upon violent action as the gesture that accompanies violent speech. Together they implement the item that withstands scrutiny in definitions of the farce; that is, *brevity.* Not accidentally, as many critics assume, but of their nature, farces are brief. This being true, we might, after all, hazard a definition: farce is the explosion that comes of compressing *vis comica* within narrow limits. Where, conversely, it expands to the dimensions of *The Importance of Being Earnest,* it loses force, and upsets our calculation that within larger bounds it should accomplish something more, even, we absurdly feel, something more serious. Shaw was saying so when he declared that "though extremely funny, [Wilde's play] was essentially hateful." [11]

On first thought it might seem that the brevity in question is a consequence of the materials; derives from corresponding brevity in anecdote, fable, folk tale, and the like. The truth is the reverse: such materials are suitable because the farce requires short subjects. The need for brevity comes, actually, from the essential means: incongru-

[9] Berkov, pp. 11–12.

[10] V. Vsevolodski-Gerngross, *Kratki kurs Istorii Russkogo Teatra* (Moscow, 1936), p. 3.

[11] G. B. Shaw, *Memories of Oscar Wilde,* p. 14. In Frank Harris, *Oscar Wilde* (New York, 1918), 2 vols., Vol. II.

ous juxtapositions; mechanical mystifications; antitheses (of types, accents, dialects, behaviors); staccato successions (in speech, action, scene); arithmetical crescendos (*i.e.,* iterations); exaggerations of all kinds; the *reductio ad absurdum* within simple propositions of behavior; brutal directness; brisk reversals, an effect of the impudent last word, and so on; all of which call for short rhythms and brief limits. It may be said to come, further, from the heartiness with which audiences respond: belly laughs punctuate a scene with unappealable finality.

To employ the means and serve the limits of farce the essential content is dialogue. As action may be dispensed with, so even stock characters, however necessary, are merely devices for getting immediately down to comic speech. The latter is the sufficient stuff—even of the puppet play, as Cervantes' Maese Pedro reminds us; even of the *commedia dell'arte,* as rigidity in the *canevas* and improvising freedom in the lines reminds us once again.

Its quality, instantly recognizable, comes from folk lexicons and levels. It is irreverent, coarse (but rarely obscene), concrete, rudely figurative; in structure it runs to ellipsis, parataxis, and anacoluthon; phonetically, it makes impudent overuse of near-homonyms and metathesis (wherefore the stock characters of the foreigner, the deaf man and, in part, the simpleton, matched against the straight man in what is generally a duel between the literal and the metaphorical, or the derivative and the etymological—a contest paralleling equivoques and deceiving with the truth in higher comedy); among rhetorical devices it chiefly resorts to hyperbole, and an extended oxymoron which, as having gone almost unidentified, requires illustration. From Lope de Rueda to Oscar Wilde and the Marx Brothers, this has been a joyful device, a sure means of punctuating dialogue, at shorter and shorter intervals, with dependable laughter. For example, when Lope's two gluttons are on their way home from a bakeshop, one of them asks, "Have you tasted better eating since your mother bore you?" and the answer, as any farce writer would know, is, "Golly, not since a long time before that." [12] In Wilde it is elaborate but no better:

LADY BRACKNELL I am quite ready to enter your name [into the list of eligible suitors for Gwendolen's hand], should your answers be what a really affectionate mother requires. Do you smoke?

JACK Well, yes, I must admit I smoke.

LADY BRACKNELL I am glad to hear it. A man should always have an occupation of some kind. There are far too many idle men in London as it is.[13]

---

[12] Lope de Rueda, p. 185.
[13] Oscar Wilde, *Works* (New York, 1954), p. 331.

Somewhere in *A Night at the Opera* it finally climbs all the way up the greased pole to the zenith of zanidom.[14] Groucho and Chico are standing alone on the stage, staring at a legal contract, which bewilders them. Groucho looks up doubtfully:

GROUCHO   Did you hear anything?

CHICO   No. . . . Did you say anything?

GROUCHO   No.

CHICO   Maybe that's why I didn't hear anything.

GROUCHO   Maybe that's why I didn't say anything.

To recapitulate; the argument is that: (1) farce, lacking a form of its own, borrows the shape of its material; (2) physical buffoonery, usually accepted as a necessary part of it, is inessential; (3) the essential item in a definition of it is the word *short;* and (4) the essential content is language only.

It follows that farce is less *genre* than tone or method. Even in the style of pantomimists like Cantinflas, Chaplin, Fernandel, and the Marx Brothers we see this. Farce is a figure of theatre as metaphor is a figure of speech or antithesis a figure of rhetoric. Consequently, in tending to lose the status of an independent spectacle, it migrates into longer forms of literary art, where it reappears, organically, in ideal function, as the means of treating minor characters or moments. Here it is the shorthand of comedy, for rapid reporting of the incongruous. In such use it is indispensable to post-romantic novels and dramas. For want of space these cannot handle minor characters as they do major ones; must follow the formula: major characters evolve, minor characters get stated. Where, as in *The Cherry Orchard,* characters are practically all on the same footing, we find them developed farcically. For farce is the ideal way of merely *stating* character; thus, when Mascarille is fetched into a drawing room in his sedan chair, logic could be no more condensed; we laugh, without reflection, but we follow the syllogism: *ordinary* gentlemen are brought to the door in their chairs, but that's not enough for Mascarille, oh, no! [15]

My illustration from Molière reminds us that farce very early began to retreat into crannies of comedy, or, more exactly, continued to scar the body of comedy like an umbilicus, a fabular detail to remind us of how comedy was born. As a matter of fact, two works of Molière's, upon one and the same theme but thirteen years apart,

---

[14] I necessarily quote from memory, but I could hardly forget.

[15] I owe this illustration to my friend Professor Katherine E. Wheatley.

tell the whole story: in the first, *Les precieuses ridicules,* in 1659, farce is independent treatment of a single situation; in the second, *Les femmes savantes,* in 1672, it is secondary method. But this *entr'acte,* this interludicrous use was older still, vastly older than the very term farce (*i.e.,* stuffing). It already has its unmistakable function in *Phormio* and the *Heautontimorumenos;* in other words, with Menander and his Roman followers, where it anticipates the nineteenth-century fortifying of sentiment with laughter. This is the value it has, at its best, in Shakespeare's fools and Lope de Vega's *graciosos.* The latter, in particular, are used to structural purpose: in counterpointing pathos (furnishing relief in the proper sense), they serve as lightning rods to divert laughter from otherwise ridiculous (because excessively sentimental) scenes.

Today, when the disappearance of the independent farce is accelerated by a variety of causes: by the leveling of manners and speech; by the cultivation of minor decencies that goes symptomatically along with the practice of major insanities; by the organized protest of subjects for satire; by the loss of comic courage; by the anti-intellectual hatred of comic laughter; by what one of my friends calls a general lugubriossification of the scene; today, the need, essentially symbolical, for more and more complex patterns, for more and more laminations of meaning and feeling within a work, makes the subordinate, the *methodical,* function of farce a necessity. In such function it is what I call comic shorthand; but it is also the comic relief that we find in Lope de Vega.

Comic relief we must note in concluding is a phrase that critics and dramatists frequently misunderstand. They take it in the medical, or false, instead of the architectural, or true, sense. Perhaps the interlude, designed to control a restive crowd during intermissions, misleads them. Whatever the reason, the notion of a necessary alleviation after preceding serious scenes is absurd. How do we explain Racine under this theory? The true, the musical, explanation appears as early as Juan del Encina, the lyrical old dramatist who, in his *Egloga de Plácida y Vitoriano,* introduces a little scherzo of an interlude *before* the tragic moment. It has a like effect in Ostrovsky's *A 17th-Century Comic Actor,* where it is a comic play within a play but precedes and occasions grim moments.[16] It is even clearer in the gravedigger's scene in *Hamlet.* This serves less as a welcome change from what *precedes* than, technically for all of its macabre extravagance, as an emotional *ritardando* before what *follows;* used so it is *tonal* preparation for

---

[16] *Polnoe Sobranie Sochinenii,* edited by M. I. Pisarev (St. Petersburg, n.d.), 12 vols., Vol. 7, II, v.

lines that the actor, freed for greater effect from circumambient pathos, will utter with heart-rending poignancy. Instead of solacing, it
disarms us. Then, after the rodomontade in the grave itself, come
Hamlet's troubled words,

> Hear you, sir;
> What is the reason that you use me thus?
> I loved you ever: but no matter. . . .[17]

and they strike home.

---

[17] V, i, 311–313.

The Satirist and Society*

R. C. ELLIOTT

It is not for euery one to rellish a true and naturall Satyre. . . .—
JOSEPH HALL, Virgidemiarum, *"A Post-script to the Reader"*

Two cripples, characters in Yeats's play *The King's Threshold* (1904), speak:

SECOND CRIPPLE. If I were the King I wouldn't meddle with him [Senchán, chief poet of Ireland in the seventh century]; there is something queer about a man that makes rhymes. I knew a man that would be making rhymes year in and year out under a thorn at the crossing of three roads, and he was no sooner dead than every thorn-tree from Inchy to Kiltartan withered, and he a ragged man like oursleves.

FIRST CRIPPLE. Those that make rhymes have a power from beyond the world.

The ancient belief that the poet has magical powers is so compelling that it survives in certain distorted ways today. "People speak with justice," says Freud, "of the 'magic of art' and compare artists with magicians. . . ." In early European culture the association led directly into the realms of the forbidden; the artist was regarded as the heritor of the mythical beings whose "creativity" was rebellion and who were punished for their awful audacity: Daedalus, who was imprisoned; Wieland and Hephaestus, both crippled; Prometheus, the great prototype, chained to his rock. For man to create—a statue, a building, a painting, a poem—has always been in some sense to encroach on divine prerogative. Mann's *Dr. Faustus* is a late variation on a perennial theme. Today, writes Ernst Kris, creative personalities still bear part of their ancient heritage, for good and ill. Like their

---

* R. C. Elliott, "The Satirist and Society," in *The Power of Satire* (Princeton University Press, 1960), pp. 257–275. [Footnotes have been renumbered.]

mythical ancestors, they are "to some extent beyond the pale of society, beyond the dictates which normally rule it and hold it together. They enjoy special prerogatives—e.g., the prerogative of greater sexual freedom—but the radius of their lives extends only from Parnassus to bohème; they are the objects of our admiration and the targets of our ambivalence." [1]

The power from beyond the world that the character in Yeats' play speaks of is the power associated with this theme, but the passage has even more direct relevance to our enterprise. Senchán, of whom the cripples speak, is the Senchán of *The Great Visitation to Guaire,* the curious tale we examined above. Yeats here treats him as a symbolic figure: he is The Artist, heroically prepared to die in defense of the ancient right of the poets.[2] In the original tale, however, Senchán was, as we know, a satirist-magician, his power somewhat declined, it is true, as he is mocked by his creator, but "real" enough and inferior only to the power of the saints and the demons. If poets in real life were thought to have such powers, they must as a consequence have stood in a very special relation to their respective societies.

The magician has always and everywhere been the focus of conflict reflecting the double-edged cultural role of magic. On the one hand, says Malinowski, magic "has exercised a profound positive function in organizing enterprise, in inspiring hope and confidence in the individual." It is, he says elsewhere, "one of the means of carrying on the established order [and] is in its turn strengthened by [that order]." [3] Insofar as the magician uses his great powers to enhance the well-being of society—defending it from its enemies, coercing the powers of nature into favorable performance, enriching the inner life of society through ritual performance—he is honored and revered. On the other hand, magic on its dark and fearsome side exerts "disturbing and subversive influences." [4] The very fact that the socially approved practices of the magician are made possible by the exercise of supernatural power implies a complementary danger, for the powers of the magician are not always amenable to social control. In them is potentiality for benefit, but also for danger, both social and personal. The magician is at once prop and threat to the social order; his

----

[1] *Psychoanalytic Explorations in Art,* pp. 78–80.

[2] Yeats says that he "twisted [the tale] about and revised its moral that the poet might have the best of it." *Collected Works* (Stratford-on-Avon, 1908), II, 255.

[3] *Coral Gardens and their Magic,* II, 240; *Argonauts of the Western Pacific,* p. 76.

[4] Malinowski, *Coral Gardens,* II, 240.

relation to society is always colored by the ambivalent emotional attitudes generated by this knowledge.[5]

The situation of the satirist-magician is similar. His satire may contribute to the richness and coherence of his culture by virtue of its being a constitutive element of ritual, as in the Greek Phallic Songs. Or it may be employed in straightforward and warlike defense of his tribe against threat from without. Archilochus cursed the enemy Sapaeans. Arabic satirists were preeminently warriors, their lethal verses their weapons. Irish satire caused the enemy to melt away before it. The satirist may even partake of a partial divinity, as did Archilochus, of whom it was foretold that he would be immortal.[6] In these situations the satirist-magician unquestionably inspires emotions of adulation and respect and awe. But in other, and possibly more characteristic, roles, he becomes the object of hate and fear. Again, Archilochus serves as example. Tributes from classical times to his poetic achievement are nearly rapturous: he is second only to Homer in some pantheons, and he was worshipped after his death; yet the dominant image that has come down through history is that of the implacable foe whose verses, steeped in poison, brought death to Lycambes and his daughter. Similarly, Irish poets were honored and loved in their positive roles, but hated and feared because of their oppressiveness and their power to do harm. Cormac's false etymology of the word for poet reflects well the doubleness of the image. *File* is derived, says Cormac, "from poison (*fi*) in satire and splendour (*li*) in praise."

These attitudes toward poet-magicians are reflected in ancient law. The Roman Twelve Tables, as we have seen, threaten with death anyone who would "chant an evil charm" (*qui malum carmen incantassit*), and Plato's *Laws* recommend extremely severe penalties against similar activity. Old Irish law undertakes zealously to regulate the activity of satirists, making provision for the reward of "good" satire (satire directed, that is, toward socially sanctioned ends), but laying down heavy penalties for "bad" satire, that which wantonly

---

[5] Paul Radin (*The World of Primitive Man* [New York, 1953], pp. 137–50) emphasizes the crucial economic significance of magical practices and institutions in both simple and complex cultures. Old Irish satirist-magicians, according to the tales, often exert their magical powers blatantly in the interests of economic exploitation. Later satirists have behaved similarly; the most notorious example is Pietro Aretino, the scourge of princes, whose satire is said to have caused the death of Antonio Broccardo and who extorted money from nobles by threatening them with his verse. See P. L. Ginguené, *Histoire Littéraire d'Italie* (Paris, 1824), IX. 216.

[6] See *Elegy and Iambus*, ed. Edmonds, II, 93.

injures. Here in the old legal formulas are codified the ambivalent attitudes of a society toward its poet-magicians.

As conscious belief in magic drops away, the role of the satirist
changes: he is no longer a medicine-man, half in society and half
out, as he mediates between his people and higher powers; his mantic
function is preempted by the priest, and interest in his poetic utterance is on aesthetic value rather than on magical potency. Only in
this way can the magic invective of an heroic folk society develop
into literary art. Cassirer's statement, in the final chapter of *Language
and Myth,* is precisely to this point, although he happens here to be
speaking of pictorial art: "The image . . . achieves its purely representative, specifically 'aesthetic' function only as the magic circle with
which mythical consciousness surrounds it is broken, and it is recognized not as a mythicomagical form, but as a particular sort of
formulation." [7] In short, the satirist becomes, instead of a prophet, a
"mere" poet, writing, as he frequently confesses, in an inferior genre.
The distinction is well pointed up by contrasting a statement on the
function of the poet in a heroic society with a comparable statement
of Horace. Carpre, the Irish poet, is asked in one of the sagas what
he will do in battle. "Not hard to say," quoth Carpre. "I will make
a *glám dícind* on them. And I will satirize them and shame them,
so that through the spell of my art they will not resist warriors." The
heroic tone, the magnificent sense of power belong (in Cassirer's
phrase) to a mythically bound society. Horace, in his account to
Augustus of the poet's function, writes: "Though a poor soldier and
slow in the field, the poet is of use to the State, if you grant
that even by small things great ends are helped." [8] However the
characteristic wry understatement discounts the literal meaning, it is
a mighty falling off. But even granting the changed modes of belief
and the relatively inferior status of the poet, it is still possible to
see in the relationship of the satirist to a more sophisticated society
some reflection of the ambiguities we have been considering.

The law continued to pay close heed to the satirist as bans on
magical utterance gave way to bans on libel. From the beginning the
satirical poet has skated on the thin edge of censorship and legal
retribution. Archilochus' poetry was barred from Sparta, according to
Valerius Maximus, on thoroughly modern grounds: because of its indecency and because of the savagery of the poet's "obscenis maledictis"

---

[7] Ernst Cassirer, *Language and Myth,* trans. S. K. Langer (New York,
1946), p. 98.

[8] *The Second Battle of Moytura,* trans. Stokes, RC, xii (1891), pp. 91–93;
Cross and Slover, p. 41; Horace, *Epistles,* ii, 1, ll. 124–125.

against Lycambes and his family.[9] Athens, it is true, allowed its poets almost complete freedom to attack both institutions and individuals. Attempts to censor comedy in general and personal abuse in particular were either abortive or successful for short periods only. Cleon had the young Aristophanes brought before the council on charges of slandering the state, but within a year Aristophanes had his revenge with the performance of the *Knights,* surely one of the most unrestrained assaults on a man in power ever made. But Athens was unique.[10] We know that Horace in his gingerly consciousness of the delicate line he had to draw was justifiably worried over legal retribution. Juvenal's situation was more precarious; his fear of legal sanctions may be taken to account for the extraordinary anticlimax of his first satire in which he announces, after an impassioned outburst, that he will write only of the dead.

In England in 1599 the Archbishop of Canterbury and the Bishop of London issued an order prohibiting the printing of *any* satires thereafter and requiring that works of Hall, Marston, Nashe, and others be burned.[11] Ben Jonson complains that the "apologeticall Dialogue" which he wrote as an Epilogue to *Poetaster* (the Epilogue containing the Archilochean threat) was spoken only once from the stage and was then forbidden by authority. When the play was published in quarto in the same year (1601) the apology was again forbidden; it did not appear in print until the Folio edition of 1616.[12] What seems to be a covert reference to these matters appears in the play itself. Jonson added a scene (III, v) for the Folio. The scene consists entirely of a dialogue between Horace (who stands for Jonson himself) and Trebatius; it is, in fact, a direct, if expansive, translation of Horace's famous *apologia* (*Satires,* II, i). In Horace's poem, we recall, Trebatius warns Horace against writing satire. Horace persists: "whether . . . rich or poor, in Rome, or, if chance so bid, in exile, whatever the colour of my life, write I must" (*quisquis erit vitae scribam color*). Jonson's version is somewhat more pointed; he presents the same alternatives, then:

> What hiew soeuer, my whole state shall beare,
> I will write satyres still, in spight of feare.

---

[9] *Factorum et Dictorum Memorabilium,* Lib. VI, 3, Ext. 1; see the edition of Carolus Kempf (Lipsiae, 1888), p. 291.

[10] See Max Radin, "Freedom of Speech in Ancient Athens," *AJP,* XLVIII (1927), pp. 215 ff.; Victor Ehrenberg, *The People of Aristophanes* (Cambridge, Mass., 1951), pp. 25–26.

[11] The order is reprinted in *A Transcript of the Registers of the Company of Stationers of London,* ed. Edward Arber (London, 1876), III, 316.

[12] *Jonson,* ed. Herford and Simpson, IV, 317, 193.

The greater concreteness of this line probably has autobiographical significance and is specifically related to the prohibition of satire in 1599. It should be added, however, that the censorship was not notably effective, and verse satires continued to be published under some desultory harassment. Still, this episode in Elizabethan literary history provides a forceful reminder of the abiding legal interest in satiric ventures.

The satirist faces comparable problems today. In democratic countries he attacks individuals only at the risk of grave financial loss to himself and his publisher; in totalitarian countries the satirist risks death. No matter how carefully he may choose his target, a shift in governmental policy may undo him completely: what one day seemed worthy the most extreme denunciation may the next day be sacrosanct. It is a harrowing occupational hazard. Under extreme conditions satire against the reigning order is out of the question; so canonical is this rule that political analysts use the amount and character of satire permitted in the Soviet Union as an indication of the relative intensity or relaxation of pressures there at any given time. Isaac Deutscher, for example, interprets the increasing amount of Soviet satire against internal abuses since Stalin's death as a favorable sign.[13]

The relation of satire to the law has had considerable importance in determining the forms satire takes and the methods it uses. When verse satires were banned in Elizabethan England, the poets immediately found a new form in which the satiric impulse might be incorporated. Under the leadership of Ben Jonson and Marston, a new dramatic "kind" was inaugurated: the "comicall satyre," a coinage that Jonson applies to his own *Every Man Out of his Humour, Cynthias Revels,* and *Poetaster.*[14] Professor Campbell shows convincingly that Shakespeare's *Troilus and Cressida* is best thought of as an example of the new form, an offspring, as it were, of satire's perennial conflict with the law.

Such historically demonstrable effects of social pressures on satiric form are impressive, but it seems likely that over the course of history

---

[13] "Russia in Transition," *Dissent,* ii (Winter, 1955), p. 27. Cf. Clifton Daniel's story in the *New York Times* (Jan. 30, 1955), p. 19, on Arkadi Raikin, who gave a popular nightly review in Leningrad in which he satirized "everything from nepotism in the state apparatus to inefficiency in the retail trade network," but not the principles of Communism or the leaders of the party.

[14] This is the thesis of Professor Campbell's *Comicall Satyre.* Miss Mary Claire Randolph arrived independently at a similar conclusion in her unpublished dissertation, "The Neo-Classic Theory of the Formal Verse Satire," University of North Carolina (1939).

the pressures have worked also in more subtle and more pervasive ways. Freud perhaps throws some light here: from the childhood of civilization, he says, society has subjected our impulses of hostility (and our sexual impulses) to progressive restrictions and repressions, just as it restricts similar impulses in us as we grow older as individuals. The hostility remains, of course; but the physical violence that in archaic times might have resulted from it comes to be forbidden by law and is gradually replaced by verbal invectives. Later, even that kind of weapon is rendered inappropriate; as we grow more civilized we realize that to use abusive language is undignified and improper. From prohibitions of this kind, says Freud, developed wit, an effective, if often indirect, agent of hostility.

"Society . . . prevents us from expressing our hostile feelings in action; and hence, as in sexual aggression, there has developed a new technique of invectives, the aim of which is to enlist . . . [society] against our enemy. By belittling and humbling our enemy, by scorning and ridiculing him, we indirectly obtain the pleasure of his defeat by the laughter of the third person [i.e., society]. . . .

"Wit permits us to make our enemy ridiculous through that which we could not utter loudly or consciously on account of existing hindrances. . . ." [15]

Once wit has been brought into the service of the satiric spirit, then all the rhetorical maneuvers by which the literary satirist achieves his end become available: irony, innuendo, burlesque, parody, allegory—all the devices of indirection which help make palatable an originally unacceptable impulse. It is a nice complication, however, that the devices which make satire acceptable to polite society at the same time sharpen its point. "Abuse is not so dangerous," said Dr. Johnson, "when there is no vehicle of wit or delicacy, no subtle conveyance." The conveyances are born out of prohibition.

The Earl of Shaftesbury, writing in the eighteenth century, recognized the "creative" significance of legal and other repressions on the writing of satire. He explains the prevalence of irony, raillery, and writing in disguise as resulting from the weight of censorship. " 'Tis the persecuting spirit has raised the bantering one," he says. "The greater the weight [of constraint] is, the bitterer will be the satire. The higher the slavery, the more exquisite the buffoonery." [16] Shaftesbury's insight requires the qualification made above. Under a massively

---

[15] *Wit and its Relation to the Unconscious*, trans. A. A. Brill (New York, 1916), pp. 148–50.

[16] Anthony Earl of Shaftesbury, *Characteristics*, ed. J. M. Robertson (London, 1900), i, 50–51.

efficient tyranny, satire of the forms, institutions, or personalities of
that tyranny is impossible. But under the more relaxed authoritarian-
ism of an easier-going day, remarkable things could be done. Max
Radin writes of how satirical journals in Germany before the First
World War, even in the face of a severe and rigorously enforced law
against *Majestätsbeleidigung*, vied with each other to see how close
they could come to caricatures of the Kaiser without actually producing them.[17] Kenneth Burke sums up this paradoxical aspect of
satire's relation with the law by suggesting that "the conditions are
'more favorable' to satire under censorship than under liberalism—
for the most inventive satire arises when the artist is seeking simultaneously to take risks and escape punishment for his boldness, and
is never quite certain himself whether he will be acclaimed or punished." [18] Voltaire's whole career is an excellent case in point. Bigots
and tyrants may have turned pale at his name, as Macaulay's hyperbole has it; but Voltaire's life was a long series of niggling subterfuges
to avoid the penalties of the law and to escape the wrath of those
he had angered. The acclaim showered on him was a product of a
kind of illegality, and the praise accorded him had as its concomitant the fear and the hatred which his work inspired. The satirist's
status with respect to society is like that of the magician: it is
necessarily problematic.

We have an excellent opportunity to examine the satirist's claims
for social approval largely by reason of the literary convention which
decrees that he must justify his ungrateful art. From the times of
Horace, Persius, and Juvenal, down to Boileau, Swift, and Pope, and
into our own day with men like Wyndham Lewis, the satirist has felt
compelled to write an *apologia*, whether formal or informal, in verse
or prose. The *apologiae* are remarkably similar in their protestations
(Mr. Lewis dissenting in part); from them we get an ideal image
which the satirist projects of himself and his art. According to the
image the satirist is a public servant fighting the good fight against
vice and folly wherever he meets it; he is honest, brave, protected
by the rectitude of his motives; he attacks only the wicked and then
seldom or never by name; he is, in short, a moral man appalled by
the evil he sees around him, and he is forced by his conscience to
write satire. Juvenal's *facit indignatio versum* is the prototype.[19]

---

[17] "Freedom of Speech in Ancient Athens," *AJP*, XLVIII (1927), p. 226.

[18] *The Philosophy of Literary Form*, pp. 231–232.

[19] The image is not always so solemn. Samuel Butler writes: "A Satyr is
a kinde of Knight Errant that goe's upon Adventures, to Relieve the Distressed
Damsel Virtue, and Redeeme Honor out of Inchanted Castles, And opprest
Truth, and Reason out of the Captivity of Gyants or Magitians." *Characters*,
ed. A. R. Waller (Cambridge, 1908), p. 469.

The satirist claims, with much justification, to be a true conservative. Usually (but not always—there are significant exceptions) he operates within the established framework of society, accepting its norms, appealing to reason (or to what his society accepts as rational) as the standard against which to judge the folly he sees. He is the preserver of tradition, the true tradition from which there has been grievous falling away.

Society, quite naturally, is dubious. On the most obvious level it points to the inevitable discrepancy between the ideal image, projected by rhetorical convention, and what it takes to be the actual fact. Swift, or Pope—so goes the reasoning—was a wicked man; therefore we may dismiss his satire. The *non sequitur* is comforting. But the problem on other levels is more complex. Despite society's doubts about the character of the satirist, there may develop a feeling that in its general application his work has some truth in it—or the feeling that other people may *think* that it has some truth in it. Individuals who recognize characteristics of themselves in the objects of attack cannot afford to acknowledge the identity even privately. So they may reward the satirist as proof of piety, while inwardly they fear him. *"Satyr,"* says Swift in a passage quoted earlier, *"is a sort of* Glass, *wherein Beholders do generally discover every body's Face but their Own; which is the chief Reason for that kind Reception it meets in the World, and that so very few are offended with it."* "Publicly offended," one might add. Publicly the satirist may be honored, but privately he will be feared.

From the beginning satirists have been uneasily explicit about the antagonism they arouse. Each of the three major classical *apologiae* (Horace, II, 1; Persius, I; Juvenal, I) contains a warning from the interlocutor on the animosities stirred up by satire and on the dangers the satirist risks. The dangers are unquestionably real: satirists have always attacked vice and viciousness and stupidity as they exist in the real world, and they have had to face the antagonism that inevitably accompanies such activity. Countless satirists in all lands have been beaten, imprisoned, tortured, even executed as a result of their daring. During James I's reign a Pole named Stercovius wrote a harsh satire on the Scots. King James was furious. In 1609 he had passed an act with the consent of Parliament rigorously forbidding the issuance of "pasquillis, lybellis, rymes, cokalanis, commedies, and siclyk occasionis." Somehow, even though Stercovius was in Poland, James arranged to have him executed. The cost to the British government was six hundred pounds.[20]

---

[20] James Maidment in his ed. of *A Book of Scottish Pasquils,* 1568–1715 (Edinburgh, 1868), pp. ix-xiii, 421.

Even in periods when satire has flourished, opposition to it on moral and pragmatic grounds has been vigorous and outspoken. Gabriel Harvey, for example, writhing under the ridicule of Greene, Nashe, and others, wrote in furious indignation against the outrage of satire: "Inuectiues by fauour haue bene too bolde: and Satyres by vsurpation too-presumptuous: I ouerpasse *Archilochus, Aristophanes, Lucian, Iulian, Aretine,* and that whole venomous and viperous brood, of old & new Raylers: euen *Tully,* and *Horace* otherwhiles ouerreched. . . ." [21] Yet in a bow to his enemies' abuse, Harvey says he will try to amend any defects with which he has justly been charged.

Sir William Temple felt that the popular vein of satire and ridicule (he uses the terms synonymously) was "the Itch of our Age and Clymat" and thoroughly noxious in effect. He cites with at least partial approval the theory of an ingenious Spaniard who held that *Don Quixote,* by subjecting the Spanish romantic attitudes toward love and valor to ridicule, had brought about the ruin of the Spanish monarchy. In England, Temple says, ridicule has "helpt to Corrupt our modern Poesy"; and while he can praise Rabelais and Cervantes, the great masters in this kind of writing, his final attitude is uncompromising: "But let the Execution be what it will, the Design, the Custom, and Example [of satire] are very pernicious to Poetry, and indeed to all Virture and Good Qualities among Men, which must be disheartened by finding how unjustly and undistinguish't they fall under the lash of Raillery, and this Vein of Ridiculing the Good as well as the Ill, the Guilty and the Innocent together." [22]

The most strenuously articulate of all those who have written against satire on whatever grounds was Pierre Bayle, author of the influential *Dictionnaire historique et critique* (Rotterdam, 1697). For Bayle satire was the Art of Poisoning; in hundreds of passages in the *Dictionary* he lashes out at the immorality, the untruthfulness, the cruelty of satire, which, despite its protestations, he says, neither prevents crime nor effects reform. Bayle is clearly fascinated by what horrifies him. In the article on Hipponax he writes: "He was neither the first, nor the only person who have forced people to make away with themselves by their invectives." Then follows a long, long list of historical examples of those who are said to have died as a result of ridicule, vituperation, or reproach. Satire, libel, lampoon, defamation, slander, ridicule—all are one to Bayle, and the satirist no better than a "mad

---

[21] *Fovre Letters and Certeine Sonnets* (1592), ed. G. B. Harrison (London, 1922), p. 15.

[22] "An Essay upon the Ancient and Modern Learning" and "Of Poetry"; see Spingarn's edition of these *Essays,* pp. 41–42, 71–72.

dog," whose motive is to kill: ". . . a satirist who attempts upon the honour of his enemy with libels, would attempt upon their life with sword or poison, if he had the same opportunity." [23]

Bayle's arguments furnished ammunition for dozens of writers in the eighteenth century. Satirists were widely read and publicly applauded, but at the same time the distaste and fear which they inspired are plainly evident in the large body of literature directed against their mode. ". . . whence this Lust to Laugh?" queried William Whitehead lugubriously in his rhymed *Essay on Ridicule* (1743) —a plea for the demise of satire—and answered himself:

> Why, Shaftsb'ry tells us,
> Mirth's the Test of Sense . . .
> Not so, fair Truth. . . .

Many echoed his "Not so." Dr. Johnson had no love for satire. In an allegorical essay in the *Rambler* he wrote that Satire, who was born of an unholy cohabitation of Wit and Malice, carried poisoned arrows which could never be extracted from his victims. Earlier, in a similar allegory, Addison had expressed his disapproval by characterizing satire as a woman with a smile on her face and a dagger concealed under her garment. William Cowper questioned satire's efficacy:

> Yet what can satire, whether grave or gay?
> It may correct a foible, may chastise
> The freaks of fashion, regulate the dress,
> Retrench a sword-blade, or displace a patch;
> But where are its sublimer trophies found?
> What vice has it subdu'd? Whose heart reclaim'd
> By rigour, or whom laugh'd into reform?
> Alas! Leviathan is not so tam'd.[24]

Even Voltaire (who had himself been victimized by libellers) harshly condemned his favorite mode in arguments drawn from Bayle: "If I followed my taste, I would speak of satire only in order to inspire abhorrence and to arm virtue against this dangerous form of writing. Satire is almost always unjust, and that is its least defect. . . . It is a trade, like selling adulterated wine. One must admit that there is

---

[23] *Dictionary*, trans. des Maizeaux, v. 746, 765. See Mary Claire Randolph, "Pierre Bayle's Case against Satire and Satirists," *NQ*, 181 (1941), pp. 310–311.

[24] Johnson, *Rambler*, No. 22; Addison, *Spectator*, No. 63; Cowper, *The Task*, II, ll. 315–322, and cf. "Charity," ll. 491–556.

hardly a trade more unworthy, more cowardly, and more punishable."[25]

By the early nineteenth century the word *satire* had acquired in the popular mind a wide range of generally unpleasant associations. Lady Middleton, in Jane Austen's *Sense and Sensibility* (1811), dislikes Elinor and Marianne Dashwood: ". . . because they were fond of reading, she fancied them satirical: perhaps without exactly knowing what it was to be satirical; but *that* did not signify. It was censure in common use, and easily given." [26] Thackeray's defense of satire in mid-century is totally revealing. He has been deploring the savagery of the caricaturists Gilray and Rowlandson: "We cannot afford to lose Satyr with his pipe and dances and gambols. But we have washed, combed, clothed, and taught the rogue good manners: or rather, let us say, he has learned them himself; for he is of nature soft and kindly, and he has put aside his mad pranks and tipsy habits; and frolicsome always, has become gentle and harmless, smitten into shame by the pure presence of our women and the sweet confiding smiles of our children." [27] Shame, the instrument by which the satirist once killed, and later purported to bring about moral reform, has, in this view, tamed the satirist himself—perhaps a final variation on the satirist-satirized theme. The fear and the hatred have disappeared: but so, clearly, has the satire.

The whole theme of the satirist's ambiguous relation to society is neatly encapsulated, I think, at the end of Juvenal's first satire. The full-blown description of Rome's insanely abandoned ways comes to a climax as Juvenal considers the situation of the poet. No time has ever needed him more, he proclaims: all vice is at its acme, and Juvenal exhorts the poet to spread his sails, to shake out every stitch of canvas. But then the recollection of danger intervenes. Where is the freedom our heroic forefathers had to attack the wicked, to name the evildoer? Anyone who today dared describe Nero's master in debauchery, Tigellinus, would be burned at the stake in the arena. It was not always so: ". . . when Lucilius roars and rages as if with sword in hand, the hearer, whose soul is cold with crime, grows red; he sweats with the secret consciousness of sin. Hence wrath and tears." [28]

---

[25] "Satire" (1749), *Oeuvres complètes* (Paris, 1879), xxiii, 414–417. Cf. his earlier comments on Boileau: "What did his satires accomplish? they raised laughter at the expense of ten or twelve men of letters; they caused two men who had never harmed him to die of shame; they aroused enemies who followed him almost to the grave, and who would have ruined him more than once if he had not had the protection of Louis XIV." "Mémoire sur la satire," *ibid.,* xxiii, 53.

[26] Chap. xxxvi (Oxford World's Classics, 1950), p. 233.

[27] "John Leech's Pictures of Life and Character" (1854), *Works* (New York, 1903), xxv, 484.

[28] i, 149–168, trans. Ramsay.

The image of the satirist projected here is that of a hero; but, "inde ira et lacrimae"—he is a hated hero. The wrath is that of the victim for the satirist; as the context indicates, he may be capable of doing the poet great harm. But the victim also turns red and sweats in his consciousness of guilt. The tears are his as well as the anger. The satire, heroically issued, has aroused wrath and fear; yet it has also performed its moral function. In the phrase "inde ira et lacrimae" is epitomized the purported function of satire and, by implication, the ambiguous situation of the satirist in relation to his contemporaries.

Society has many grounds for its dislike and distrust of satire. No matter what abuses it may expose, no matter what lofty motives the satirist may profess, he has no *right* (so goes the chief moral argument) to take the honor and reputation of other men into his hands or to set himself up as a censor of established institutions or modes of behavior. Further, for all the pain he causes, the satirist never actually brings about reform.[29] These are the objections most often stated. But society has other reasons for dubiety. The pressure of the satirist's art inevitably comes athwart society's efforts to maintain its equilibrium. The satirist usually claims that he does not attack institutions; he attacks perversions of institutions. When, for example, he ridicules a corrupt judge he intends no reflection on the law as such; he is attacking a corruption which has crept into the law. Ben Jonson's Cordatus, the "Moderator" of *Every Man Out of his Humour*, speaks precisely to this point. The innocent will not be injured in this play, he says; to claim injury would be "to affirme, that a man, writing of NERO, should meane all Emperors: or speaking of MACHIAVEL, comprehend all States-men; or in our SORDIDO, all Farmars; and so of the rest: then which, nothing can be vtter'd more malicious, or absurd." [30] In large measure, of course, Cordatus is right. As Northrop Frye says, the satirist attacks primarily neither the man nor the institution; he attacks an evil man who is given gigantic stature and protected by the prestige of the institution. "The cowl might make the monk if it were not for the satirist." [31]

But there is another sense in which Cordatus is wrong, for an at-

---

[29] The sociologist Frederick E. Lumley considers the problem of whether satire accomplishes its purported end. He quotes authors on both sides of the question, then concludes that until "hundreds of testimonies of satire's effectiveness" be collected, "the proposition that satire is an effective instrument of control must be left in the air." *Means of Social Control* (New York, 1925), pp. 251–255.

[30] II, vi, 166–170. See *Jonson,* ed. Herford and Simpson, III, 494–495.

[31] "The Nature of Satire," *University of Toronto Quarterly,* XIV (1944–1945), pp. 79–80. Cf. Dryden's "A satirical poet is the check of the laymen on bad priests." "Preface to the Fables," *Essays,* ed. W. P. Ker (Oxford, 1926), II, 260.

tack by a powerful satirist on a local phenomenon seems to be capable of indefinite extension in the reader's mind into an attack on the whole structure of which that phenomenon is part. Significantly, I think, this imaginative process is magical; it functions by synecdoche, which is one of the foundations of magic. In "mythico-linguistic thought," to use Cassirer's phrase, the part does not merely represent the whole, it *is* the whole; by the magical process of identification the nail paring or the lock of hair from an enemy *is* the enemy, and whoever controls the part has dominion also over the whole. This process is by no means confined to a mythically bound society; as a different order of experience, to be sure, it is the way of the imagination when it is bound, in its own way, by the spell of the creative artist. The judge who has been ridiculed by a powerful satirist comes to stand for—to be—lawyers in general and even the law itself. What starts as local attack ends by calling the whole institution into question. Thus the satirical portraits of Chaucer, who seems to have been thoroughly orthodox in religion, have often been interpreted as evidence of his revolt against the Church; during the Reformation he and Langland were used for purposes doubtless far removed from their intent. Molière proposed in *Tartuffe* to unmask an example of religious hypocrisy. Yet the effect of the play has seemed to many people genuinely subversive, the attack on the hypocrite somehow, insidiously, becoming an attack on religion itself. Two hundred and fifty years after the play was first performed, Brunetière could write that the wound had not closed: ". . . there is no doubt that it was deep; that the hand which made it meant to make it; that therefore it was not only false devotion but also true, which Molière meant to attack. . . ." [32] Brunetière attributes the damage to Molière's evil intentions; in an odd way, if one wants to talk about damage, one is on safer grounds to speak of magic: of synecdoche, of the tainted part becoming through the strange efficacies of art the whole.

The *Tartuffe* dilemma is very ancient; Lucian's dialogue *The Dead Come to Life* turns precisely on it. The question of the dialogue is this: has Lucian's ridicule of individual philosophers (specifically in *Philosophies for Sale*) besmirched Philosophy herself? [33] The problem is treated with the greatest subtlety. Frankness (a transparent alias for Lucian) is hailed up for trial; he is to be accused by Socrates, Plato, Diogenes, and others who are on leave from Hades for a day, and is to be judged by Philosophy. In the course of the trial the

[32] *Brunetière's Essays in French Literature,* trans. D. Nichol Smith (London, 1898), p. 111.
[33] *Lucian,* trans. Harmon, III, 3–81.

following points are established: Philosophy holds that ridicule, far from harming truth, actually enhances it (p. 23); Lucian is found to have ridiculed, not Philosophy, but only impostors and thus to have served truth; and the character of the satirist is established to be that of a "bluff-hater, cheat-hater, liar-hater, vanity-hater," but also that of a "truth-lover, beauty-lover, simplicity-lover," and so on. These latter propensities the satirist has little opportunity to exercise, the world being what it is; but Philosophy consoles him: "the two callings [hating evil and loving good] . . . are but one" (p. 33). Philosophy expresses in a phrase the public rationale of the satirist's activity. Lucian manages his own defense with marvellous skill and impeccable logic; the fact remains, however, that as all readers of Lucian know, Philosophy emerges from his dialogues in very tattered condition indeed.

Swift notoriously found himself in a similar situation with *A Tale of a Tub*. In the "Apology" which he added to the work in 1710, he reverts at least six times to the contention that the *Tale* attacks, not religion and learning, but abuses in religion and learning: *"Religion they tell us ought not to be ridiculed, and they tell us Truth, yet surely the Corruptions in it may; for we are taught by the tritest Maxim in the World, that Religion being the best of Things, its Corruptions are likely to be the worst."* Yet the attack, as Swift's contemporaries saw, could hardly be contained; restricted as the intention may have been, the *Tale* in effect ramified into an attack on religion itself. I believe that Swift was deeply concerned for the welfare of the Established Church as he saw it; but under the impact of his satire one of the great pillars of society rocked a bit. Swift's strength, as Empson puts it, made his instrument too strong for him. His magic, one might say, was his undoing.

The implications are reasonably clear. The satirist, it is true, claims to be conservative, to be using his art to shore up the foundations of the established order; and insofar as one can place satirists politically, I suspect that a large majority are what would be called conservative. Professor Auerbach has emphasized, for example, that in all Molière's plays there is no criticism whatever of the social, political, or economic bases of life. "Molière's criticism is entirely moralistic; that is to say, it accepts the prevailing structure of society, takes for granted its justification, permanence, and general validity, and castigates the excesses occurring within its limits as ridiculous." [34] Yet who could deny the profoundly anarchic thrust of Alceste's sentiments? The play demands that his passionate utterances be given full

---

[34] *Mimesis,* p. 365.

weight in the scale which measures his fanatical sincerity against the social hypocrisy of the Orontes, the Célimènes, the Philintes of his world. It demands that he be taken seriously; and the demand enforces the question: what if he *were* taken seriously? Alceste's commitments and criticisms are moral, as Auerbach says, rather than social or political; but in the area of his interest, and given the power of his utterance, the moral subsumes the social. His ideas are radically disruptive. It is hard to conceive the society that could sustain them.

Such ambiguous results seem almost an inevitable consequence of major satire. Let the conscious intent of the artist be what it will, the local attack cannot be contained: the ironic language eats its way in implication through the most powerful-seeming structures.[35] One final example from Swift. The complexly simple projector of *An Argument against Abolishing Christianity,* the "I" of the piece, argues cogently for the retention of nominal Christianity. To restore "real" Christianity, he says, "would indeed be a wild Project; it would be to dig up Foundations; . . . to break the entire Frame and Constitution of Things; to ruin Trade, extinguish Arts and Sciences, with the Professors of them; in short, to turn our Courts, Exchanges, and Shops into Desarts. . . ." One reads this and one can only say, He is right: the fool speaks truth. Between Swift and the projector, of course, there is a considerable ironic remove, just as there is distance between Swift and some of the meanings set in motion by his creature. We may doubt that Swift the Tory politician, Swift the social man, would have sympathized with breaking the "Frame and Constitution of Things." But here Swift is the artist. The pressure of his art works directly against the ostensibly conservative function which it is said to serve. Instead of shoring up foundations, it tears them down. It is revolutionary.

Society has doubtless been wise, in its old pragmatic way, to suspect the satirist. Whether he is an enchanter wielding the ambiguous power of magic, or whether he is a "mere" poet, his relation to society will necessarily be problematic. He is of society in the sense that his art must be grounded in his experience as social man; but he must also be apart, as he struggles to achieve aesthetic distance. His practice is often sanative, as he proclaims; but it may be revolutionary in ways that society cannot possibly approve, and in ways that may not be clear even to the satirist.

---

[35] See Bishop Warburton's comment: "The Spaniards have lamented, and I believe truly, that Cervantes's just and inimitable ridicule of *knight-errantry* rooted up, with that folly, a great deal of their *real honour.* And it was apparent, that Butler's fine satire on *fanaticism* contributed not a little . . . to bring *sober piety* into disrepute." *Works,* ed. Richard Hurd (London, 1811), I, 155–156. Cf. Northrop Frye, "The Nature of Satire," pp. 82 ff.

"It's Hideously True"*

AL CAPP

You may, unless you had something better to do, have been reading my comic strip *Li'l Abner* this week. If so, you are probably startled to see that my hero is apparently being married to one Daisy Mae Scragg. This time it's the real thing. Yes, after 18 years the poor lout is finally, hopelessly married, and in one of Marryin' Sam's cheapest, most humiliating weddings.

I never intended to do this. My comic-strip characters are not the kind who grow through boyhood and adolescence, get married and raise their own kids. The Yokums of Dogpatch are the same sweet and brainless characters they always were. And the fact that Abner always managed somehow to escape Daisy Mae's warm, eager arms provided me with a story that I could tell whenever I couldn't think of anything better. Frankly I intended to go through life happily and heartlessly betraying you decent, hopeful people who want to see things come out right. I never intended to have Li'l Abner marry Daisy Mae because your pathetic hope that I would was one of the main reasons you 50 million romance lovers read my strip.

For the first few years it was easy to fool you; you didn't know me well then. You followed developments eagerly, trustfully. When I met any of you, I was asked, "When will Li'l Abner marry Daisy Mae?" in a friendly, hopeful tone. Later, as I betrayed your hopes in more and more outrageous ways, your tone became a little bitter. One year I had Daisy Mae marry a tree trunk, thinking that Abner was hiding inside it. Next day, naturally, it turned out that the contents were an old pair of socks, but that Daisy's marriage to them was irrevocably legal. That was a pretty problem. Your tone became threatening. Later on I poisoned her, and Abner consented to marry

* Al Capp, "It's Hideously True," *Life,* Vol. 32, No. 13 (March 13, 1952), pp. 100–108.

her because it was her dying wish (Why not? She would be safely dead in a minute anyway.); but just as you thought the wedding had finally taken place, I let her drink some of Dogpatch's sizzling superfluid, "Kickapoo Joy Juice," which instantly restored her to life, so Abner was no longer bound by his promise. You still asked me when they would *really* marry, but your tone was a little more threatening. Then I let Daisy ecstatically marry a boy who not only turned out to be merely Abner's double but a bigamist too, so even that marriage didn't count. Now your tone was downright mutinous, and your question went something like: "For God's sake, will Abner EVER marry Daisy Mae?" Just the same, I knew you would still keep watching and waiting. This was the kind of suspense I needed to keep you reading my comic strip, so, no matter how impatient or indignant you got, I never intended to let your foolish, romantic dreams come true.

So why did I do it this week? Why, after all these years of tricking you, did I finally trick myself? Well, the real reason isn't as simple as Abner, Daisy or even suspense. To understand why I have done this awful thing you will have to bear with me while I explain how and why I created them in the first place.

When I was in my early 20s and about to start a comic strip, I found myself in a terrible dilemma. The funny comic strip, the kind I wanted to do, was vanishing from the funny page. A frightening new thing had been discovered: namely, that you could sell more papers by worrying people than by amusing them. Comic strips which had no value except that they were comic were beginning to vanish from the funny papers. Rube Goldberg's dazed *Mike and Ike,* Fred Opper's *Happy Hooligan,* who wore a tomato can on his head, Milt Gross's *Count Screwloose,* who regularly escaped from the booby hatch only to return to it because things were more normal there—this beloved procession of clowns, innocents and cheerful imbeciles—slowly faded. In their place came a sobbing, screaming, shooting parade of the new "comic"-strip characters: an orphan who talked like the Republican platform of 1920; a prizefighter who advised children that brains were better than brawn while beating the brains out of his physically inferior opponents; detectives who explored and explained every sordid and sickening byway of crime and then made it all okay by concluding that these attractively blueprinted crimes didn't really pay; and girl reporters who were daily threatened with rape and mutilation.

Don't get me wrong. I was terrified by the emergence of this new kind of comic strip 18 years ago only because I didn't have the special qualities they required—not because they didn't have quality. *Dick Tracy* is a magnificently drawn, exquisitely written shocker comparable, in its own terms, with Poe. But "suspense" strips, though enormously effective, disdain fun and fantasy. Suspense was what editors wanted when I was ready to create my own comic strip—but all I could do was fun and fantasy.

GOOD'UNS AND BAD'UNS

So I tried to draw straight-faced suspense comic strips. I tried to create smart and superior heroes, and submerged them in blood-curdling tragedies, increasing in complexity, hopelessness and horror and thereby creating reader anxiety, nausea and terror—*i.e.,* suspense. But I couldn't do it. I just couldn't believe in them. The suspense strips require one-dimensional characters: good guys and bad guys, and no fooling around with anything in between. I simply couldn't believe in my one-dimensional good guys and bad guys—as I drew them. I discovered good things in the bad guys, and vice versa. So my hero turned out to be big and strong like the suspense-strip heroes, but he also turned out to be stupid, as big, strong heroes sometimes are. His mammy, like mine, and possibly yours, turned out to be a miracle of goodness, but at the same time she was kind of bossy, quite self-righteous and sweetly ridiculous. His girl, although wildly beautiful, is vaguely sloppy and, although infinitely virtuous, pursues him like the most unprincipled seductress.

The good people in my hero's town, possibly like those in your town, often are a pain in the neck. And the bad 'uns, like some bad 'uns in real life, are often more attractive than the good 'uns. The Scragg Boys, Lem and Luke, are fiendish when they are snatching milk from whimpering babies or burning down orphan asylums to get some light to read comic books by (only to realize that they can't read, anyway); but even the most horrified reader can't help being touched by their respectfully asking their pappy's permission to commit all this manslaughter and mayhem. Monsters they certainly are, but they are dutiful children too.

The society people in *Li'l Abner* always have impressive names, but there is always something a little wrong with them too—like Henry Cabbage Cod, Daphne Degradingham, Sir Cecil Cesspool (he's deep), Peabody Fleabody and Basil Bassoon. Dumpington Van Lump seemed a harmless, hospitable kid until it developed that his favorite book was *How to Make Lampshades Out of Your Friends.* Colossal McGenius was so brilliant in giving business advice that he seemed to be justified in charging $1,000 a word for talking to worried tycoons;

but it turned out that his weakness was telling long, involved jokes (at $1,000 a word) about three Bulgarians, whereupon he remembered, much too late, that they were actually three *Persians,* and so he had to start the story all over again. When he finally got to the advice it was great, but by that time the tycoon had gone bankrupt.

When I introduced a mythical country, Lower Slobbovia, I was as technical as the straightest suspense-strip creator, and gave readers a map. The map was perfectly reasonable except that the names of its parts created some distrust and disrespect for the country. The oceans were the Hotlantic and Pitziffic, and there was another body of water called the Gulf of Pincus. The capital, Ceaser Siddy, home of Good King Nogoodnik, was flanked by the twin cities of Tsk-Tsk and Tch-Tch. Its leading citizens had familiar and famous, but somehow embarrassing names like Douglas Snowbanks Jr., Harry S. Rasputintruman and Clark Bagle. Everything in *Li'l Abner* was my effort to be as straight as the straight strips, but colored, however, with my conviction that nothing is ever entirely straight, entirely good, entirely bad, and that everything is a little ridiculous. As in the straight suspense strips, I dutifully created the standard, popular suspense situations, but something forced me to carry them so far that terror became absurdity.

For instance, when the Yokums make gigantic sacrifices for what they are convinced is a noble and beneficial cause, the reader knows they are swindling themselves; even victory will benefit only the enemy. When the Yokums are being heroes they are being not only heroes—they are being damned fools at the same time. When their adversaries are being villainous, they are not only vile, they are also confused and frightened.

Li'l Abner had to come out that way, because that's the way things seem to me. Well, it happened to make a big hit. It was a success because it was something I hadn't thought much about as such. It was a satire. Nobody had done one quite in these terms before. I was delighted that I had. I was exhilarated by the privilege this gave me to kid hell out of everything.

GOOD OLD JACK S.

It was wonderful while it lasted; and I had no reason for marrying Abner off to Daisy Mae. But then something happened that threatens to shackle me and my kind of comic strip. It is what I call the gradual loss of our fifth freedom. Without it, the other four freedoms aren't much fun, because the fifth is the freedom to laugh at each other.

My kind of comic strip finds its fun wherever there is lunacy, and American life is rich in lunacy everywhere you look. I created labor-hating labor leaders, money-foolish financiers, and Senator Jack S. ("Good old Jack S.") Phogbound. When highway billboard advertising threatened to create a coast-to-coast iron curtain between the American motorist and the beautiful American countryside, I got some humorous situations out of that too. Race-hate peddlers gave me some of my juiciest comedy characters, and I had the Yokums tell them what I know is true, that all races are God's children, equally beloved by their Father. For the first 14 years I reveled in the freedom to laugh at America. But now America has changed. The humorist feels the change more, perhaps, than anyone. Now there are things about America we can't kid.

I realized it first when four years ago I created the Shmoo. You remember the Shmoo? It was a totally boneless and wildy affectionate little animal which, when broiled, came out steak and, when fried, tasted like chicken. It also laid neatly packaged and bottled eggs and milk, all carefully labeled "Grade A." It multiplied without the slightest effort. It loved to be eaten, and would drop dead, out of sheer joy, when you looked at it hungrily. Having created the animal, I let it run wild in the world of my cartoon strip. It was simply a fairy tale and all I had to say was wouldn't it be wonderful if there were such an animal and, if there were, how idiotically some people might behave. Mainly, the response to the Shmoo was delight. But there were also some disturbing letters. Some writers wanted to know what was the idea of kidding big business, by creating the Shmoo (which had *become* big business). Other writers wanted to know what was the idea of criticising labor, by creating the Shmoo, which made labor unnecessary.

It was disturbing, but I didn't let it bother me too much. Then a year later, I created the Kigmy, an animal that loved to be kicked around, thus making it unnecessary for people to kick each other around. This time a lot more letters came. Their tone was angrier, more suspicious. They asked the craziest questions, like: Was I, in creating the Kigmy, trying to create pacifism and thus, secretly, non-resistance to Communism? Were the Kigmy kickers secretly the big bosses kicking the workers around? Were the Kigmy kickers secretly the labor unions kicking capital around? And finally, what in hell was the idea of creating the Kigmy anyhow, because it implied some criticism of some kinds of Americans and any criticism on anything American was (now) un-American? I was astounded to find it had become unpopular to laugh at any fellow Americans. In fact, when

I looked around, I realized that a new kind of humorist had taken over, the humorist who kidded nothing but himself. That was the only thing left. Hollywood had stopped making ain't-America-wonderful-and-ridiculous movies, and was making ain't-America-wonderful - but - anyone - who - says - it's - ridiculous - too - deserves - to - be-picketed movies. Radio, the most instantly obedient to pressure of all media, had sensed the atmosphere, an atmosphere in which Jack Benny is magnificent but in which Will Rogers would have suffocated.

So that was when I decided to go back to fairy tales until the atmosphere is gone. That is the real reason why Li'l Abner married Daisy Mae. At least for the time being, I can't create any more Shmoos, any more Kigmies; and when Senator Phogbound turns up now, I have to explain carefully that, heavens-to-Betsy, goodness-no, he's not typical; nobody like THAT ever holds public office. After a decade and a half of using my characters as merely reasons to swing my searchlight on America, I began all over again to examine them, as people. Frankly, I was delighted with them. (Frankly, I'm delighted with nearly everything I do. The one in the room who laughs loudest at my own jokes or my own comic strip is me.) I became reacquainted with Li'l Abner as a human being, with Daisy Mae as an agonizingly frustrated girl. I began to wonder myself what it would be like if they were ever married. The more I thought about it, the more complicated and disastrous and, therefore, irresistible, the idea became.

Will They Live Happily Ever After?

For instance, Li'l Abner has never willingly kissed any female except his mother and a pig. Well—if he got married, he'd *have* to. Even he couldn't avoid it for more than a month or so. What would happen? Would he approve of kissing? Would he say anything good about it? (And thus make it popular with millions of red-blooded young Americans whose "ideel" he is.) Would he do it again? As a bachelor he is frankly a bum. He just sleeps, eats and goes catfishing. As a married man he would have to support his own household. How would he do it? Is there anybody stupid enough to hire someone as stupid as he is? Is there *any* profession that requires as little intelligence as he has? And how about Mammy Yokum? She has always ruled Abner with an iron fist. Would she continue to after he has his own home? And how would Daisy Mae take this? Sure, she's been sweet and docile with Mammy Yokum all these years, but that might only have been because she needed her help in trapping Abner. Now that he's her'n, will she show her true colors and tangle with

Mammy for the lightweight championship of the new Yokum home? How about babies? Married people frequently have babies. Would *they* have a baby? Will he really be born on the Fourth of July? Is it possible that they'd name him Yankee Doodle Yokum? Babies have uncles. Could I freeze the blood of the entire nation by having Mammy Yokum (who can accomplish anything, even singlehanded) produce a baby of her own, five minutes after Li'l Yankee Doodle Yokum was born? Would this child be known as Oncle Yokum?

And how about Sadie Hawkins Day? It has become a national holiday. It's my responsibility. It doesn't happen on any set day in November; it happens on the day I say it happens. I get tens of thousands of letters from colleges, communities and church groups, starting around July, asking me *what* day, so they can make plans. Well, Sadie Hawkins Day has always revolved around Li'l Abner fearing marriage to Daisy Mae. Now that his worst fears have come hideously true, what will he and Daisy Mae do on Sadie Hawkins Day? Will Lower Slobbovia inaugurate its own "Sadie Huckins Day" and import Li'l Abner and Daisy Mae as technical advisers? In short, once Abner and Daisy Mae are married, do they live happily forever after like other people or is this just the beginning of even more complicated disasters, more unbearable miseries? They are married, all right. But if you think the future is serene for them, you're ("Haw! Haw!") living in a fool's paradise.

Part Seven

THE CRITICISM OF COMEDY

Robert W. Corrigan
ARISTOPHANIC COMEDY: THE CONSCIENCE OF A CONSERVATIVE

C. L. Barber
THE SATURNALIAN PATTERN IN SHAKESPEARE'S COMEDY

Gustave Lanson
MOLIÈRE AND FARCE

L. C. Knights
RESTORATION COMEDY: THE REALITY AND THE MYTH

Reed Whittemore
SHAW'S ABSTRACT CLARITY

Ruby Cohn
A COMIC COMPLEX AND A COMPLEX COMIC

Aristophanic Comedy: The Conscience of a Conservative*

ROBERT W. CORRIGAN

The Greek comic poet Aristophanes (circa 450–387 B.C.) was certainly one of the giants of the classical theatre; but on rereading his plays today, he seems more like an early-day version of a Barry Goldwater, who had the quick and contentious mind of William Buckley and the raucous sense of humor and comic invention of Al Capp, and whose program was, in effect, to urge the Greeks to repeal the second half of the Fifth Century. Actually, because of its central concern with society's need and its ability to maintain and preserve itself, comedy is by nature conservative, and Aristophanes and all other writers of comedy tend more or less to be conservatives. Tragedy has always dealt with that rebellious spirit in man which resists the limitations of being human, including the limits imposed on him by society. It focusses on man's heroic capacity to suffer in his rebellion, and celebrates the essential nobility of the rebellious spirit. But while tragedy celebrates the hero's capacity to suffer, and thereby earn a new and deeper knowledge of himself and his universe, comedy tends to be more concerned with the fact that despite all our individual defeats, life does nonetheless continue on its merry way. Or, as Christopher Fry once put it, "Comedy senses and reaches out to that . . . angle of experience where the dark is distilled into light: . . . where our tragic fate finds itself with perfect pitch, and goes straight to the key which creation was composed in." Comedy, then, celebrates man's capacity to endure; such capacity is ultimately conserving in spirit and quality.

* Robert W. Corrigan, "Aristophanic Comedy: The Conscience of a Conservative," to appear in the Laurel Classical Drama series, Dell Publishing Company.

This in large measure explains why love is always central to comedy. The basic comic plot can be reduced to the following elements: (1) boy meets girl; (2) boy falls in love with girl; (3) there is an obstacle to the fulfilling of that love (this obstacle is usually parental); (4) the obstacle is overcome and there is a reorganization of society. The persisting regularity of this pattern has lead Ben Lehmann to observe, quite correctly I think, in his essay "Comedy and Laughter" that the "obstacles to the hero's desire, then, form the action of comedy, and the overcoming of them the comic resolution." * But it must be noted that the reconciliation at the end of comedy always involves the preserving of the social context. Opposition, frustration, malice, lust, prejudice, and greed can and do inhabit the world of comedy, but these divisive powers are always overcome and then assimilated into the lovers' happy world. Comedy always ends in fusion and with a sense of social union. To quote Lehmann once again: "The vision of comedy fixes its eye on separateness, on diversity, even on oppositions, but it insists at last on togetherness for lovers and on the restored social fabric, on solidarity for the group."

As a satirist, rather than a writer of comedies,[1] Aristophanes has plenty of sex in his plays, but no love. First and foremost, the writer of satire must have the gift of turning our eyes inward in hilarious scorn of ourselves. But his purpose is always corrective. In showing us the immensity of our follies, the satirist is either seeking to restore values and patterns of behavior which he believes have been lost, forgotten, or debased, or he is urging us to discover new ideals and ways of living. Therefore, all of his jibes—no matter how bitter—are ultimately directed at the restoration or preservation of the social order.

In each of his plays, Aristophanes is attacking the manifestations of political, social, and moral corruption which he believed were the direct result of the Athenians' shift away from an agricultural to an artisan and mercantile economy, their adoption of a more imperialist "foreign policy," and their willingness to accept the validity of new forms of thought and art. All his life, Aristophanes shared the attitudes of the rapidly disappearing landed aristocracy, whose religion, morality, ideals, and patterns of social organization were based upon an agricultural economy and a closed, heroic view of society. He re-

---

* [See in this collection, p. 163.]

[1] It should be understood that for the Greeks in the Fifth Century, any play with an invented plot and subject matter drawn from contemporary life was called a comedy, and therefore was presented during the afternoon portion of the Dionysian Festivals.

sisted all that was modern. He condemned innovators or any who would seek to change or reform the traditional ways of doing things because they were old or outmoded. Euripides, Socrates, the Sophists, the orators, the early scientists Empedocles and Pythagoras—all were characterized in Aristophanes' plays as charlatans and subversives who were destroying the national fiber and upsetting the traditional patterns of government, thought, art, and everyday behavior. The Delian League (the classical Greek equivalent to the United Nations) was a striking instance of government waste and a good example of the evils of the new policy of Greek "internationalism." The increased number of people depending upon the government for support was seen by Aristophanes as a maneuver on the part of the central government to gain greater power, as well as another symptom that the old value that each man should earn his own way was rapidly breaking down. One could continue this list of his grievances at some length.

To be sure, Aristophanes had a point and his position was not without justification. He lived and wrote in one of the most turbulent periods in the world's history. It was a time of war, expansion, and rapid, radical change, and the breakdown of the traditional ways of doing things can be seen in every aspect of Greek life, from architecture to the worship of Zeus. As a larger and more centralized government became necessary, it was easier for the demagogues to gain power and widespread graft soon came to be commonplace. New religions from foreign lands, and especially the Orient, were introduced into the country by the merchants, traders, soldiers, and slaves with the result that new moralities did begin to emerge. As the Athenian people began to produce a great deal more than they consumed, the acquiring and accumulating of wealth (not to mention the social problems that the acquisition of capital wealth creates) tended to become the central concern of more and more people. Aristophanes, then, lived in a volatile atmosphere and he was deeply disturbed by the many changes that were taking place and the effects they were having on Athenian life. He was determined, like so many of our Southerners today—although for different reasons—to do all he could to resist this erosion of the time-honored Greek traditions. He would fight till the death for the old order, and he did.

To those who might consider this evaluation of Aristophanes' position to be either erroneous or too harsh, I call attention specifically to the following plays. In *The Birds,* probably the greatest of Aristophanes three "Utopia" plays, the ideal society (Cloud-Cuckoo-Land) will be established by the farmers who will then run their brave new world like a large farm. Certainly, this solution is exaggerated and fanciful, but there is little doubt that Aristophanes did believe that things would be much better in Athens if the old values—as embodied and propounded by Pithetaerus—were restored to their former position of dominance. For all of its delightful (and sometimes scatalogical) grotesquerie, *Peace* celebrates the same values. Only the farmers, of all the people in Greece, are shown to be strong enough and capable of working together long enough to pull Peace out of her underground prison so she can once again rule the earth. Not only do the farmers save Greece from the horrors of war, but Trygaeus—who is clearly Aristophanes' mouthpiece—states explicitly that peace is the opportunity for the farmers to work in their fields. In *The Plutus* the solution to all the misuse of wealth in the world is to give Plutus, the god of wealth, to the honest, hard-working farmers. They will solve all of the problems: no more corruption, no more injustice, no more crime. If only it were so, even in Fourth Century Greece. Finally, behind all the sexual fun of *Lysistrata,* Aristophanes is really trying to solve the question of Pan-hellenic unity and the problems of war. After the women have overcome the old men who were guarding the treasury on the Acropolis, Lysistrata begins the long *agon* (the most significant one in the play) with the Commissioner. As her arguments become increasingly persuasive she finally gets to the central issue: "How can we have peace?" I should like to quote this passage at some length, because I believe it makes my point so clearly.

COMMISSIONER   And how, on the international scale,
    can you straighten out the enormous
confusion among all the states of Greece?

LYSISTRATA   Very easily.

COMMISSIONER   How? Do inform us.

LYSISTRATA   When our skein's in a tangle we take it thus
    on our spindles, or haven't you seen us?—
one on this side and one on the other side,
    and we work out the tangles between us.
And that is the way we'll undo this war,
    by exchanging ambassadors, whether
you like it or not, one from either side,
    and we'll work out the tangles together.

COMMISSIONER   Do you really think that with wools and skeins
    and just being able to spin you
can end these momentous affairs, you fools?

LYSISTRATA   With any intelligence in you
  you statesmen would govern as we work wool,
    and in everything Athens would profit.

COMMISSIONER   How so? Do tell.

LYSISTRATA   First, you take raw fleece
  and you wash the beshittedness off it:
just so, you should first lay the city out
  on a washboard and beat out the rotters
and pluck out the sharpers like burrs, and when
  you find tight knots of schemers and plotters
who are out for key offices, card them loose,
  but best tear off their heads in addition.
Then into one basket together card
  all those of a good disposition
be they citizens, resident aliens, friends,
  an ally or an absolute stranger,
even people in debt to the commonwealth,
  you can mix them all in with no danger.
And the cities which Athens has colonized—
  by Zeus, you should try to conceive them
as so many shreddings and tufts of wool
  that are scattered about and not leave them
to lie around loose, but from all of them
  draw the threads in here, and collect them
into one big ball and then weave a coat
  for the people, to warm and protect them.

COMMISSIONER   Now, isn't this awful? They treat the state
  like wool to be beaten and carded,
who have nothing at all to do with war!

Lysistrata's arguments make such very good sense. She's so logical, and therein lies the play's great appeal. But such a solution to the problems of achieving world peace is too simple; it assumes that the tightly wound and complex strands of world affairs can be worked like a skein of wool. It also assumes that once the skein has been untangled it will stay that way. It is this desire for a simple solution to complex problems, and more important, the belief that the use of time-tested patterns of the past makes such solutions possible, that prompted me to link Aristophanes with Mr. Goldwater at the beginning of this selection.

For better or worse, Aristophanes failed in his attempts to change the patterns of Greek history. Quite predictably, the Greeks did not follow his advice and go back to the good old days. Nor, have his condemnations of Euripides and Socrates held up; as a teacher of literature and philosophy, Aristophanes was a failure. But in one very important area of the history of ideas he has had a profound and lasting influence: namely, the judging of poetry. Quite correctly, Aristophanes can be called the "father" of Greek literary criticism, and his belief that the chief function of poetry is to teach morality is an idea which is still very much with us. Euripides is condemned in nearly all of the plays because Aristophanes believed that the tragedian's poetry corrupted the youth of Athens, poisoned patriotic spirit, and advanced the cause of immorality everywhere. Aeschylus is set up as the model for tragedy in *The Frogs,* not because of his ability with language (even Aristophanes admitted that Euripides was the best versifier of all writers of tragedy), but because his plays—like "all genuine poetry"—helped to make us better human beings. Aristophanes was the first Greek writer to insist that the basic aim of the arts and all culture should be education. This idea was developed more fully by Plato in *The Republic* and *The Laws,* and it was finally expanded in its fullest (although somewhat compromised) form in Horace's *Art of Poetry* in the dictum that art should both delight and teach. The idea was militantly reasserted in the Eighteenth and Nineteenth centuries by Lessing, Herder, and the Schlegels in their criticism of Greek drama; and it is fascinating to note that even Nietzsche's description of the decay of Greek tragedy is nearly identical to the one put forth by Aristophanes better than 2,000 years earlier. And this view has lost none of its virulence today—ranging in scope and significance from the controversy over awarding the Bollingen Prize to Ezra Pound to local obscenity trials.

I have no intention of getting involved in this argument here, but I believe that Aristophanes must finally be seen as a romantic reactionary who refused to give up what was already lost. Instead of welcoming the new, he mourned the loss of the old. History has shown that he (and all like him) was wrong in his moral objections to change. The traditional code is never the *only* morality; there is always the possibility of another sanction. The fact that men oppose traditional values and appeal to other and new authorities does not make them troublemakers, nor immoral. What Aristophanes either did not see or refused to recognize, is the fact that as long as a new idea of what is right is held with conviction and is not just an isolated sentiment, it may be fully as moral as obedience to established laws or customs.

However, thus far I have presented only one side of the case. Aristophanes may have been a reactionary but he was certainly no weepy sentimentalist. As I said earlier, he lived in a volatile atmosphere when life was wide open, and so too are his plays. All of his work has an extravagant power and a quality of over-riding buoyancy and verve. This almost animal exuberance and vitality is probably best seen in the wide-open use of sex in his plays. We sense neither neurotic lust nor puritanical guilt in his use of it, and this probably explains (differences in taste and dramatic conventions notwithstanding) why his blatant sexuality is still so inoffensive when it is read or produced on our stages today. But no matter what he took for his subject, he had the capacity as a writer to take any idea and push it as far as it would go, and then give it one more push. He is probably best compared in our day to such comedians as Mort Sahl, Dick Gregory, Lenny Bruce, or Shelley Berman. (The only writer in the theatre today who even approaches Aristophanes is the Swiss playwright, Friedrich Duerrenmatt, whose grotesque ironies and biting satire in such plays as *The Visit, Romulus The Great,* and *The Physicists* have a certain resemblance to the Athenian's wit.) However, with these modern satirists, unlike Aristophanes, it is difficult to know exactly what they are for—except on the issue of civil rights— but their techniques are much the same.

Actually, a fuller understanding of the Aristophanic techniques is the key to our enjoyment of his plays. Rather than having a comic action, Aristophanes' plays are built upon the comic conceit (the sex strike in *Lysistrata* or Socrates in the balloon in *The Clouds*), which acts like a mousetrap to create the world of the play for us. To be sure, all of the plays share certain structural characteristics which make it possible for us to talk of an Aristophanic structure, and such giants of classical scholarship as Gilbert Murray, F. M. Cornford, and Jane Harrison have shown that his structure originated in the rituals of the Dionysian worship. But such discussions, while undoubtedly true, tend to be misleading for they force upon early Greek comedy a terminology of dramatic criticism which is for the most part either inappropriate or irrelevant. There is really very little plot to most of Aristophanes' plays (certainly not in the sense that there is a plot in the comedies of Shakespeare, Molière, Congreve, or Shaw), only a series of episodes which serve as the occasions for his wit and satiric thrusts. His plays move from moment to moment and have a sense of spontaneity rather than structure. Such an episodic structure (if the term must be used) not only gives freedom to the ranging and wayward movements of Aristophanes' comic mind, but it also sets up the audience for the rapid-fire potshots which he takes at every kind of subject. Like our own late George M. Kaufmann, or more recently Bob Hope, Aristophanes was a master of the phraseology and attitude of the wisecrack. But the basic strategy of the wisecrack is to keep the audience with you. This becomes almost impossible if the audience becomes too involved in the workings of a plot.

Aristophanes was not a subtle writer, and his plays—more than most—are a theatrical rather than a literary experience. He has little interest in the more refined phases of human absurdity, and everything in his comedy is dependent upon the immediacy of the theatrical effect. His satiric wit is, of all forms of wit, the most ephemeral. The basic comic gesture is universal in its appeal but the particularities of the form are based on immediate, topical references—usually the absurdities of current political or social behavior—and almost impossible to translate or pass on to future generations. In tone, Aristophanic comedy is much like the newspaper cartoons of a Herblock, Bill Mauldin, the early Al Capp, or Jules Pfeiffer; in technique, it is like the gridiron dinner show or the topical review.

Almost, that is! But one important ingredient is still missing. Aristophanes wrote in verse, and it is clear that music and dance played an all-important role in the productions of classical Greek comedy. For this reason we will completely miss the essential quality of an Aristophanic play if we do not think of it as a comic musical revue. The two most significant and highly praised recent revivals of his plays were successful because they accented this musical base. The well-known Greek director, Karolos Kouns, won the first prize and world-wide acclaim at the International Theatre Festival in Paris in 1962 with a production of *The Birds*. Not only did he modernize the dialogue, but he had new music composed by Manos Hadjadakis (the composer of "Never On Sunday") and the production was choreographed by the eminent Greek dancer, Zouzou Nicoloudi. More recently (1964), in our own country, Herbert Blau had a similar success with the same play at the Actor's Workshop in San Francisco when he presented it in a jazz version. These two productions provide sufficient proof that Aristophanes can continue to live in the theatre (and not just as a museum piece in the library or the classroom) if we understand the dynamics and techniques of his plays.

But for all of Aristophanes' vitality, what is known as Greek "Old Comedy" went into a decline shortly after the turn of the Fourth Century, and this decline is probably best described as a process of diminution which was finally completed in the drama of Menander. The fact that the decline had begun can easily be seen in Aristophanes' last preserved play, *The Plutus*, which was first performed some time during the years 390–388 B.C. We can still discover traces of the old Aristophanes: his bias toward the farmers, the episodic structure, the open stagecraft and the presentational style of musical comedy, and the too-simple solution. Yet, everything is different. The bite is gone. The comedy is generalized. Instead of dealing with the particular behavior of specific people, we find a gentle mockery of the manners of people in general. The episodes seem unrelated; each of them deals with human foibles, but they lack a cumulative force. The whole play is probably best summed up by Browning in his "Aristophanes' Apology."

> Aristophanes
> Surmounts his rivals now as heretofore,
> Though stinted to mere sober prosy verse—
> "Manners and Men," so squeamish gets the world!
> No more "Step forward, strip for anapaests!"
> No calling naughty people by their names.[2]

The final question to be asked here is "what happened?" Why in less than a century had the scope of comedy been so drastically reduced? Obviously, we cannot know for certain, but it is very likely related to the Greeks' loss of political freedom. This had been coming for some time, and with the fall of Athens to Sparta in 404 B.C., the end was in sight. Then in 338 B.C. Athens was conquered by the Macedonians and all public occasions (including the theatre) were rigidly censored. Comedy has never flourished under a dictatorship. Audiences who do come to the theatre in such times want to escape the problems of life, and more important dictators have never tolerated comedy. S. N. Behrman put it best, when he wrote: "Dictators are terribly afraid of comedy and its laughter. For laughter is the most humanizing—as well as the most critical—agency in the world. The ability to laugh at his own pretensions and shortcomings is the true mark of the civilized nation, as it is of the civilized man." One need only remember what happened to the German theatre under Hitler to see the truth of these remarks. More important, we should realize that in recent times even in our own country there are some things we can no longer make fun of and laugh about. One of the most significant documents on the subject of comedy and freedom that I know of is an essay entitled "It's Hideously True" by the cartoonist Al Capp.* It was published as an article in 1952 in *Life* magazine, and in it Mr. Capp explained why he finally

---

[2] I am indebted to my colleague, Lionel Cassen, for bringing my attention to Browning's poem in his fine book *Masters of Ancient Comedy*.

* [See in this collection p. 343.]

decided to have Li'l Abner marry Daisy Mae. Admittedly, this was at the time when Senator MacCarthy was at the height of his power and an almost hysterical fear was sweeping the nation. But Capp, who had thrived for twenty years kidding hell out of all the lunacies of American life, suddenly discovered that there were some things he no longer had the freedom to kid. (He had noted "the gradual loss of our fifth freedom. Without it, the other four freedoms aren't much fun, because the fifth is the freedom to laugh at each other.") When the comic writer loses this freedom, he invariably turns from broad, topical satire on a national level to the more gentle forms of humor found in domestic life. (It's significant, I think, that "Blondie" is the most popular comic strip in America.) And if this restricting atmosphere continues, the comic must eventually turn in upon himself, and he becomes the butt of his own humor. This is what probably happened to classical comedy, and the decline in Aristophanes' comic power is probably more a matter of political freedom than it is of artistry. Aristophanes was the Will Rogers of the classical Greek theatre; unfortunately, he wasn't able to be its Jack Benny as well.

The Saturnalian Pattern in Shakespeare's Comedy*

C. L. BARBER

> MESSENGER *Your honour's players, hearing your amendment,*
> *Are come to play a pleasant comedy. . . .*
> BEGGAR *. . . Is not a comonty a Christmas gambold or a tumbling*
> *trick?*
> LADY *No, my good lord; it is more pleasing stuff.*
> BEGGAR *What, household stuff?*
> LADY *It is a kind of history.*
> BEGGAR *Well, we'll see it. Come, madam wife, sit by my side and*
> *let the world slip. We shall ne'er be younger.*
> —*Induction to* The Taming of the Shrew

Recent literature has accustomed us to the conscious use of mythical and ritual prototypes as a means of organizing the life of our time in the absence of a self-imposing tradition. *Ulysses* and *The Waste Land* expressed life in a modern city by representing it as recapitulating basic myths and rituals. Such creative ordering of experience by earlier archetypes has involved, in our time, a kind of explicit awareness of analogies not necessary in earlier periods, when traditional symbolic values came to the writer as a matter of course with his themes and materials. Psychology and ethnology have developed a corresponding set of generic names—"the Oedipus complex," "the fertility spirit," "the rebirth archetype." In earlier cultures such pat-

---

* C. L. Barber, "The Saturnalian Pattern in Shakespeare's Comedy," *The Sewanee Review*, Vol. LIX, No. 4 (Autumn, 1951), pp. 593–611. The interpretation outlined in this essay is more fully developed in C. L. Barber's *Shakespeare's Festive Comedy: a Study of Dramatic Form and its Relation to Social Custom*, Princeton, 1959 (Meridian Paperback, 1962). [Footnotes in this selection have been renumbered.]

363

terns were implicit in particular observances and did not need to be named. We have to name them, because for our cosmopolitan and relativistic mentality no particular symbolism is any longer self-evident. Our literary criticism is recognizing and describing in the writing of the past underlying configurations which earlier readers did not need to discriminate consciously. After the Nineteenth Century's preoccupation with the individual in society, with characters in drama, we are recovering, about art at least, an awareness of the creative function of form. To explore patterns which drama has in common with ritual is one way to develop this awareness, to see how the role precedes the character, how the larger rhythm of the whole action shapes and indeed creates the parts:

> O body swayed to music, O brightening glance,
> How can we know the dancer from the dance?

This essay will attempt to describe a major pattern in Shakespeare's gay comedy—the comedy before *Hamlet* and the problem plays. Proof by citation will not be feasible within the limits of an article; and I shall not be able to indicate in detail where my generalities do and do not apply to particular plays. But Shakespeare is so familiar that if I can express a notion of the dominant mode of organization of the comedy, the reader will be able to try it on the plays for himself. Shakespeare's gay comedy is fundamentally saturnalian rather than satiric. It dramatizes pleasure as release from normal limitations, and the judgments implicit in its humor primarily concern the relation between man and nature, not relations between social classes or types. The plays give form to feeling and knowledge by a movement which can be summarized in the formula: *through release to clarification.*

This pattern for organizing experience came to Shakespeare from many sources, both in social and artistic tradition. It appeared, for example, in the theatrical institution of clowning: the clown or Vice, when Shakespeare started to write, was a recognized anarchist who made aberration obvious by carrying release to absurd extremes. The cult of fools and folly, half social and half literary, embodied a similar polarization of experience. One could formulate the saturnalian pattern effectively by referring first to these traditions: indeed, Shakespeare's first completely masterful comic scenes were written for the clowns. I have chosen, however, first to approach the pattern of the gay plays by looking at them in relation to the social rituals of Elizabethan holidays. The festival occasion provides a paradigm for the organization of impulse and awareness not only of those comedies where Shakespeare drew largely and directly on holiday motifs, like

Love's Labour's Lost, A Midsummer Night's Dream, and *Twelfth Night,* but also in plays where there is relatively little direct use of holiday, notably *As You Like It,* and *Henry IV.* The language that described festive occasions, or was used in them, provides a more adequate vocabulary than that of any other tradition for making explicit the "form in mirth" of the plays about pleasure. The attitudes adopted on holiday were archetypes in English Renaissance culture for the attitudes adopted about pleasure whenever people set out to have a good time.

We can get hold of the spirit of Elizabethan holidays because they had form. "Merry England" was merry chiefly by virtue of its community observances of periodic sports and feast days. Mirth took form in morris-dances, sword-dances, wassailings, mock ceremonies of summer kings and queens and of lords of misrule, mummings, disguisings, masques—and a bewildering variety of sports, games, shows and pageants improvised on traditional models. Such pastimes were a regular part of the celebration of a marriage, of the village wake, of Candlemas, Shrove Tuesday, Hocktide, Mayday, Whitsuntide, Midsummer-eve, Harvest-home, Hallow-e'en, and the twelve days of the Christmas season ending with Twelfth Night. Custom prescribed, more or less definitely, some ways of making merry at each occasion. The seasonal feasts were not, as now, rare curiosities to be observed by folklorists in remote villages, but landmarks framing the cycle of the year. Shakespeare's casual references to the holidays always presume that his audience is familiar with them:

> As fit as ten groats is for the hand of an attorney . . .
> as a pancake for Shrove Tuesday, a morris for May Day,
> as the nail to his hole. . . .

The whole society observed the holidays. Elizabeth's court, on occasion, went a-maying; it always had a Midsummer bonfire, and kept the Christmas season with high revels. So did the noble households. In the entertainments tendered Elizabeth during her summer progresses, traditional festive observances were developed in masque, pageant or play.[1]

Study of the historical process by which holiday came to be trans-

---

[1] The most authoritative and complete summary of court festivities is E. K. Chambers, *The Elizabethan Stage,* Oxford, 1923. Folk festivities of the Elizabethan period are treated with equal authority in *The Medieval Stage,* Oxford, 1903. These two books, and especially the latter, contribute more than any other work by recent scholars to enable one who is not a folklorist to look at Shakespeare's drama from that point of view. Chambers himself, when he finally came to write about Shakespeare, did little or nothing with this part of his immense knowledge.

lated into conscious art leads through the occasional literature produced for aristocratic entertainments. But my concern here is to describe the saturnalian pattern as it was finally worked out in dramatic materials. For this purpose, connections of details are less important than the correspondence between the whole comedy and the whole festive occasion. The holiday archetypes provide a way of talking about an underlying movement of feeling and awareness which is not adequately expressed by any one thing in the play, but is the play. At this level, one cannot say just how far the analogies between ritual and art show an influence, and how far they reflect the fact that a holiday occasion and a comedy are parallel manifestations of the same pattern in our culture, of a basic way that we can polarize our human nature, moving through release to clarification.

I. Release and Clarification in the Idyllic Comedies

Release, in the idyllic comedies, is expressed by making the experience of the whole play like that of a revel.

Come, woo me, woo me; for now I am in a holiday humour, and like enough to consent.

Such holiday humour is often abetted by directly staging pastimes: dances, songs, masques, plays extempore, etc. But the fundamental method is to shape the loose narrative so that "events" put its persons in the position of festive celebrants: if they do not seek holiday it happens to them. A tyrant duke forces Rosalind into disguise: but her mock wooing with Orlando amounts to a Disguising, with carnival freedom from the decorum of her identity and her sex. The misrule of Sir Toby is represented as personal idiosyncracy, but it follows the pattern of the Twelfth Night occasion; the flyting match of Benedict and Beatrice, while appropriate to their special characters, suggests the customs of Easter Smacks and Hocktide abuse between the sexes. Much of the poetry and wit, however they may be occasioned by events, is controlled in the economy of the whole play to promote the effect of a merry occasion where Nature reigns.

F. M. Cornford, in *The Origins of Attic Comedy,* points to invocation and abuse as the basic gestures of a nature worship behind Aristophanes' union of poetry and railing. The two gestures were still practiced in the "folly" of Elizabethan Maygame, harvest-home, or winter revel: invocation, for example, in the manifold spring garlanding customs, "gathering for Robin Hood"; abuse, in the customary license to flout and fleer at what on other days commanded respect. The same double way of achieving release appears in Shakespeare's

festive plays. There the poetry about the pleasures of nature and the
naturalness of pleasure serves to evoke beneficent natural impulses;
and much of the wit, mocking the good housewife Fortune from her
wheel, acts to free the spirit as does the ritual abuse of hostile spirits.
A saturnalian attitude, assumed by a clear-cut gesture toward liberty,
brings with it an accession of "wanton" vitality. In the terms of
Freud's analysis of wit, the energy normally occupied in maintaining
inhibition is freed for celebration. The holidays in actual observance
were built around the enjoyment of vital pleasures: in the summer,
love in out-of-door idleness; in the winter, within-doors warmth and
food and drink. But the celebrants also got something for nothing
from festive liberty—the vitality normally locked up in awe and respect. E. K. Chambers found among the visitation articles of Archbishop Grindal for the year 1576 instructions that the bishops determine

whether the ministers and churchwardens have suffered any lord of misrule
or summer lords and ladies, or any disguised persons, or others, in Christmas
or at Maygames, or any morris dancers, or at any other times, to come un-
reverently into the church or churchyard, and there to dance, or play any
unseemly parts, with scoffs, jests, wanton gestures, or ribald talk. . . .[2]

Shakespeare's gay comedy is closer to Aristophanes' than to any other
great comic art because the matrix for its awareness of life is the
form of feeling of such saturnalian occasions as these. Dicaeopolis,
worsting pompous Lamachus in *The Acharnians* by invoking the tangible benefits of Bacchus and Aphrodite, acts the same festive part as
Sir Toby baffling Malvolio's visitation by an appeal to cakes and ale.

The *clarification* achieved by the festive comedies is concomitant to
the release they dramatize: a heightened awareness of the relation
between man and "nature"—the nature celebrated on holiday. The
process of translating festive experience into drama involved extending
the sort of awareness traditionally associated with holiday, and also
becoming conscious of holiday itself in a new way. The plays present
a mockery of what is unnatural which gives scope and point to the
sort of scoffs and jests shouted by dancers in the churchyard or in
"the quaint mazes of the wanton green." And they include another,
complementary mockery of what is merely natural, a humor which puts
holiday in perspective with life as a whole.

The butts in the festive plays consistently exhibit their unnaturalness by being kill-joys. On an occasion "full of warm blood, of mirth,"
they are too preoccupied with perverse satisfactions like pride or greed
to "let the world slip" and join the dance. Figures like Malvolio and

---

[2] *The Medieval Stage,* Vol. I, p. 181, note 2.

Shylock embody the sort of kill-joy qualities which the disguised persons would project on any of Grindal's curates who would not suffer them to enter the churchyard. Craven or inadequate people appear, by virtue of the festive orientation, as would-be-revellers, comically inadequate to hear the chimes at midnight. Pleasure thus becomes the touchstone for judgment of what bars it or is incapable of it. And though in Shakespeare the judgment is usually responsible—valid we feel for everyday as well as holiday—it is the whirligig of impulse that tries the characters. Behind the laughter at the butts there is always a sense of solidarity about pleasure, a communion embracing the merrymakers in the play, and the audience, who have gone on holiday in going to a comedy.

While perverse hostility to pleasure is a subject for aggressive festive abuse, highflown idealism is critized too, by a benevolent ridicule which sees it as a not unnatural attempt to be more than natural. It is unfortunate that Shakespeare's gay plays have come to be known as "the romantic comedies," for they almost always establish a humorous perspective about the vein of hyperbole they borrow from Renaissance romances. Wishful absolutes about love's finality, cultivated without reserve in conventional Arcadia, are made fun of by suggesting that love is not a matter of life and death, but of springtime, the only pretty ring time. The lover's conviction that he will love "for ever and a day" is seen as an illusion born of heady feeling, a symptom of the festive moment:

Say "a day" without the "ever". No, no, Orlando! Men are April when they woo, December when they wed. Maids are May when they are maids, but the sky changes when they are wives.

This sort of clarification about love, a recognition of the seasons, of nature's part in man, need not qualify the intensity of feeling in the festive comedies: Rosalind when she says these lines is riding the full tide of her passionate gayety. Where the conventional romances tried to express intensity by elaborating hyperbole according to a "pretty," pseudo-theological system, the comèdies express the power of love as a compelling rhythm in man and nature. So the term "romantic comedies" is misleading; "festive comedies" would be a better name. Shakespeare, to be sure, does not always transform his romantic plot materials. In the Claudio-Hero business in *Much Ado,* for example, the borrowed plot involved negative behavior on the basis of romantic absolutes. The caskets story in *The Merchant of Venice,* again, is romantic narrative which, though handled gayly and opulently, has not been given a festive orientation: Fortune, not Nature, is the reigning goddess. Normally, however, as in *Twelfth Night,* he radically alters the emphasis when he employs romantic materials. Events which in his source control the mood, and are drawn out to exhibit extremity of devotion, producing now pathos, now anxiety, now sentiment, are felt on the stage, in the rhythm of stage time, as incidents controlled by a prevailing mood of revel. What was sentimental extremity becomes impulsive extravagance. And judgment, not committed to systematic wishful distortion, can observe with Touchstone how

We that are true lovers run into strange capers; but as all is mortal in nature, so is all nature in love mortal in folly.

To turn on passionate experience and identify it with the holiday moment, as Rosalind does in insisting that the sky will change, puts the moment in perspective with life as a whole. Holiday, for the Elizabethan sensibility, implied a contrast with "everyday," when brightness falls from the air. Occasions like May-day and the Winter Revels, with their cult of natural vitality, were maintained within a civilization whose sad-brow view of life focused on the mortality implicit in vitality. The tolerant disillusion of Anglican or Catholic culture allowed nature to have its day, all the more headlong because it was only one day. But the release of that one day was understood to be a temporary license, a "misrule" which implied rule, so that the acceptance of nature was qualified. Holiday affirmations in praise of folly were limited by the underlying assumption that the natural in man is only one part of him, the part that will fade.

"How that a life was but a flower" was a two-sided theme: it was usually a gambit preceding "And therefore take the present time"; but it could also lead to the recognition that

so from hour to hour, we ripe and ripe,
And then, from hour to hour, we rot and rot . . .

The second emphasis was implicit in the first; which attitude toward nature predominated depended, not on alternative "philosophies," but on where you were within a rhythm. And because the rhythm is recognized in the comedies, sentimental falsification is not necessary in expressing the ripening moment. It is indeed the present mirth and laughter of the festive plays—the immediate experience they give of nature's beneficence—which reconciles feeling, without recourse to sentimentality or cynicism, to the knowledge they convey of nature's limitations.

In drawing the parallel between holiday and Shakespeare's comedy, it has been hard to avoid talking as though Shakespeare were a primitive who began with nothing but festival custom and invented a comedy to express it. Actually, of course, he started work with theatrical and literary resources already highly developed. This tradition was complex, and included folk themes and conventions along with the practice of classically trained innovators like Lyly, Kyd, and Marlowe. Shakespeare, though perfectly aware of unsophisticated forms like the morality and the jig, from the outset wrote plays which presented a narrative more or less in the round. In comedy, he began with cultivated models—Plautus for *The Comedy of Errors,* and literary romance for the *Two Gentlemen of Verona;* he worked out a consistently festive pattern for his comedy only after these preliminary experiments.

In his third early comedy, *Love's Labour's Lost,* instead of dramatizing a borrowed plot, he built his slight story around an elegant aristocratic entertainment. In doing so he sketched, in thin and overfanciful lines, the holiday sequence of release and clarification which comes into its own in *A Midsummer Night's Dream.* This much more serious play, his first comic masterpiece, has a crucial place in his development. To make a dramatic epithalamium, he expresses with full imaginative resonance the experience of the traditional summer holidays. He thus finds his way back to a native festival tradition remarkably similar to that behind Aristophanes at the start of the literary tradition of comedy. And in expressing the native holiday, he is in a position to use all the resources of a sophisticated dramatic art.

A combination of participation and detachment was necessary to express holiday pastimes as three-dimensional drama. In *A Midsummer Night's Dream,* the expressive significance of popular cult is kept, while its literal, magical significance is mocked. The lovers, like folk celebrants on the eve of May-day, "run gadding to the wood overnight." In the woods they take leave of judgment, immersed in irrational impulse under the influence of a Summer Lord and Lady who preside over the cleanly wantonness of nature. Oberon and Titania enter the great chamber to bring the blessings of fertility to the bridal couples, as country gods, half English and half Ovid, would bring their powers in tribute when Elizabeth was entertained, and as the group of folk celebrants making their quête would "bring in summer" to the village and manor house. Instead of garlands of flowers, Shakespeare uses poetry about "the rose distill'd" and "field-dew consecrate." The game is translated into dramatic and poetic action, the personifications of pageantry into dramatic personalities. But the magical events of holiday, when they are understood as human experience, are humorously recognized as mental, not actual happenings. The whole action in the magic wood is presented as a release of shaping fantasy which leads to clarification about the tricks of strong imagination. We watch a dream; but we are awake, thanks to a pervasive humor about the delusive tendency to take fancy literally, whether exhibited in love, or in superstition, or in Bottom's mechanical dramatics. It is part of the aristocratic urbanity of Titania, Oberon and their jester Puck to intimate in their own lines that they do not exist. So perfect an expression and understanding of folk cult was only possible in the moment when it was still in the blood but no longer in the brain.

Shakespeare never made another play from pastimes in the same direct fashion. But the pattern for feeling and awareness which he derived from the holiday occasion in *A Midsummer Night's Dream* becomes the dominant mode of organization in subsequent comedies until the period of the problem plays. The relation between his festive comedy and naïve folk games is amusingly reflected in the passage from *The Taming of the Shrew* which I have used as an epigraph. When the bemused tinker Sly is asked with mock ceremony whether he will hear a comedy to "frame your mind to mirth and merriment," his response reflects his ignorant notion that a comedy is some sort of holiday game—"a Christmas gambold or a tumbling trick." He is corrected with: "it is more pleasing stuff . . . a kind of history." Shakespeare is neither primitive nor primitivist; he enjoys making game of the inadequacy of Sly's folk notions of entertainment. But folk attitudes and motifs are still present, as a matter of course, in the dramatist's cultivated work, so that even Sly is not entirely off the mark about comedy. Though it is a kind of history, it is the kind that frames the mind to mirth. So it functions like a Christmas gambol. It often includes gambols, and even, in the case of *As You Like It,* a tumbling trick. Though Sly has never seen a comedy, his holiday mottoes show that he knows in what spirit to take it: "let the world slip;" "we shall ne're be younger." Prince Hal, in his festive youth, "Daff'd the world aside and bid it pass." Feste sings that "Youth's a stuff will not endure."

II. Release and Clarification in the Clowning and in *Henry IV*

The part of Shakespeare's earliest work where his mature patterns of comedy first appear clearly is, as I have suggested, the clowning. Although he did not find a satisfactory comic form for the whole play until *A Midsummer Night's Dream,* the clown's part is satisfactory from the outset. Here the theatrical conventions with which he started writing already provided a congenial saturnalian organization of experience, and Shakespeare at once began working out its larger implications. It was of course a practice, going back as far as the *Second Shepherd's Play*, for the clowns to present a burlesque version of actions performed seriously by their betters. Wagner's conjuring in *Dr. Faustus* is an obvious example. In the drama just before Shakespeare began writing, there are a great many parallels of this sort between the low comedy and the main action.[3] One suspects that they often resulted from the initiative of the clown performer; he was, as Sidney said, thrust in "by head and shoulders to play a part in majestical matters"—and the handiest part to play was a low take-off of what the high people were doing. Though Sidney objected that the procedure was "without deceny or decorum," such burlesque, when properly controlled, had an artistic logic which Shakespeare was quick to develop.

At the simplest level, the clowns were foils, as one of the aristocrats remarks in *Love's Labour's Lost:*

> 'Tis some policy
> To have one show worse than the King's and his company.

But burlesque could also have a positive effect, as a vehicle for expressing aberrant impulse and thought. When the aberration was made relevant to the main action, clowning could provide both release for impulses which run counter to decency and decorum, and the clarification about limits which comes from going beyond the limit. Shakespeare used this movement from release to clarification with masterful control in clown episodes as early as *Henry VI, Part II*. The scenes of the Jack Cade rebellion in that history are an astonishingly consistent expression of anarchy by clowning: the popular rising is presented throughout as a saturnalia, ignorantly undertaken in earnest; Cade's motto is: "then are we in order when we are most out of order." In the early plays, the clown is usually represented as oblivious of what his burlesque implies. When he becomes the court fool, however, he can use his folly as a stalking horse, and his wit can express directly the function of his role as a dramatized commentary on the rest of the action. [4]

In creating Falstaff, Shakespeare fused the clown's part with that of a festive celebrant, a Lord of Misrule, and worked out the saturnalian implications of both traditions more drastically and more

---

[3] William Empson discusses some of the effects achieved by such double plots in *English Pastoral Poetry,* New York, 1938.

[4] See C. L. Barber, "The Use of Comedy in *As You Like It,*" *Philological Quarterly,* Vol. XXI, No. 4 (October, 1942).

complexly than anywhere else. If in the idyllic plays the humor of perspective can be described as a looking outward from a reigning festive moment to the work-a-day world beyond, in the two parts of *Henry IV* the relation of comic and serious action can be described by saying that holiday is balanced against everyday and doomsday. The comedy expresses impulses and awareness excluded by the urgency and decorum of political life, so that the comic and serious strains are contrapuntal, each conveying the ironies limiting the other.

The issue, so far as it concerns Prince Hal, can be summarized quite adequately in our key terms. As the non-historical material came to Shakespeare in *The Famous Victories of Henry the Fifth*, the prince was cast in the traditional role of the prodigal son, while his disreputable companions functioned as tempters in the same general fashion as the Vice of the morality plays. At one level, Shakespeare keeps this pattern; but he shifts the emphasis away from simple moral terms. The issue, in his hands, is not whether Hal will be good or bad, but whether his holiday will become his everyday, whether the interregnum of a Lord of Misrule, delightful in its moment, will develop into the anarchic reign of a favorite dominating a dissolute king. Hal's secret, which he confides early to the audience, is that for him Falstaff is merely a pastime, to be dismissed in due course:

> If all the year were playing holidays
> To sport would be as tedious as to work.

The prince's sports, accordingly, express not dissoluteness but a fine excess of vitality—"as full of spirit as the month of May"—together with a capacity for looking at the world as though it were upside down. His energy is controlled by an inclusive awareness of the rhythm in which he is living: despite appearances, he will not make the mistake which undid Richard II, who lived saturnalia until it caught up with him in earnest and he became

> a mockery king of snow
> Standing before the sun of Bolingbroke. . . .

During the battle of Shrewsbury, when in Hotspur's phrase "Dooms-day is near," Hal dismisses Falstaff with "What, is it a *time* to jest and dally now?"

But of course Falstaff is not so easily dismissed. Hal's prodigal's role can be summarized fairly adequately in terms of the holiday-everyday antithesis. But no formula derived from words current in Shakespeare's work is adequate for the whole effect produced by the dynamic interplay of serious statement and comic counter-statement in the drama as a whole. The more one reads the two *Henry IV* plays, the more one feels that Shakespeare was doing something with Falstaff which he could not summarize, which only the whole resources of his art could convey. His power of dramatic statement, in developing saturnalian comedy, had reached to primitive and fundamental modes of organizing experience for which general terms were not available in his culture.

It is here that our modern command of analogies between cultures can help—by providing a vocabulary to describe the pattern given dramatically by Shakespeare. We can read in Frazer how such figures as the Mardi Gras or Carnival first presided over a revel, then were tried, convicted of sins notorious in the village during the last year, and burned or buried to signify a new start. In other ceremonies described in *The Golden Bough,* mockery kings appear as recognizable substitutes for real kings, stand trial in their stead, and carry away the evils of their realms into exile or death. One such scapegoat figure, as remote as could be in space and time from Shakespeare, is the Tibetan King of the Years, who enjoyed, until very recently at least (if not even now), ten days' misrule during the annual holiday of Buddhist monks at Lhasa. At the climax of his ceremony, after doing what he liked while collecting bad luck by shaking a black yak's tail over the people, he mounted the temple steps and ridiculed the representative of the Grand Lama, proclaiming heresies like "What we perceive through the five senses is no illusion. All you teach is untrue." A few moments later, discredited by a cast of loaded dice, he was chased off to exile and possible death in the mountains.[5] One cannot help thinking of Falstaff's catechism on honor, spoken just before another valuation of honor is expressed in the elevated blank verse of a hero meeting death: "Can honor take away the grief of a wound? no . . . What is honor? a word. What is that word honor? What is that honor? air." And Hal's final expulsion of Falstaff, which so offended humanitarian nineteenth-century critics, appears in the light of these analogies to carry out an impersonal pattern, not merely political but ritual in character. After the guilty reign of Bolingbroke, the prince is making a fresh start as the new king. At a level beneath the moral notions of a personal reform, we can see a non-logical process of purification by sacrifice—the sacrifice of Falstaff. The career of the old king, a successful usurper whose conduct of affairs has been skeptical and opportunistic, has cast doubt on the validity of the whole conception of a divinely ordained and chivalrous kingship to which Shakespeare and his society were

---

[5] See James G. Frazer, *The Scapegoat,* London, 1914, pp. 218–223.

committed. But the skeptical and opportunistic attitude has been projected also in Falstaff, who carries it to comically delightful and degraded extremes. In turning on Falstaff as a scapegoat, in the same way that the villagers turned on their Mardi Gras, the Prince can free himself of the sins, "the bad luck," of his father's reign, to become a king in whom chivalry and the sense of divine ordination are restored.[6]

The use of analogies like the scapegoat rituals can be misleading, or merely amusing, if the pattern is not rigorously related to the imaginative process in the play. Janet Spens, a student of Gilbert Murray's, wrote in 1916 a brief study which attempted to establish the presence of ritual patterns in Shakespeare's work.[7] Although she throws out some brilliant suggestions, her method for the most part consists of leaping intuitively from folklore to the plots of the plays, via the hypothesis of lost intermediary folk plays. But the plots, abstracted from the concrete emphasis of their dramatic realization, can be adjusted to square with an almost unlimited range of analogies. Miss Spens argues, for example, that because Antonio in *The Merchant of Venice* is enigmatically detached from personal concerns, and

---

[6] The old king, about to die, says

> all the soil of the achievement goes
> With me into the earth.

The new king says

> My father hath gone wild into his grave;
> For in his tomb lie my affections. . . .

The image in these two passages of getting rid of sin or appetite by burying it appears again in Hal's final, menacing joke about Falstaff's belly, symbol of the misrule to which he has subscribed:

> Know the grave doth gape
> For thee thrice wider than for other men.

But an extended treatment is necessary to show how the scapegoat pattern is concretely symbolized. Shakespeare's culture did not afford general terms for the sacrificial part of it, so that there are no summary passages for quotation. L. C. Knights, in discussing *Henry IV, Part I* in *Determinations* (ed. F. R. Leavis, London, 1934) [See in this collection p. 186.], acutely explored a number of imaginative connections between Falstaff's counterfeiting and the king's. He concludes that Falstaff, himself corrupt, completely undercuts irrational honor in Hotspur and hollow majesty in Bolingbroke, so that the play is a drastic satire on the institutions of war and government. "Thus ever did rebellion find rebuke" is to be taken with ironic scorn by the audience. This is an anachronistic, philosophical-anarchist interpretation which Shakespeare's heroic lines simply cannot admit. But the only way to avoid it, once one has faced the fact that Falstaff's role acts on the historical part, is to recognize that in the irrational rhythm of the whole action, misrule works to consolidate rule.

[7] *An Essay on Shakespeare's Relation to Tradition*, Oxford, 1916.

because in accepting the prospect of death at Shylock's hands he says "I am the tainted wether of the flock," he "is" the Scapegoat. To be sure, at a very general level there is a partial analogy to scapegoat rituals, since Antonio is undertaking to bear the consequence of Bassanio's extravagance; and perhaps the pound of flesh motif goes back ultimately, through the tangle of legend and story tradition, to some such ceremonial. But there is no controlling such analogies if we go after them by catching at fragments of narrative; and one can understand, on that basis, the impulse to give up the whole approach as hopelessly capricious.

The case is altered, however, if attention is focused, not on this or that group of people in this or that story, but on the roles the persons are given in the play. When we are concerned to describe dramatic form—the rhythm of feeling and awareness in the audience which is focused through complementary roles in the fable and implemented by concrete patterns of language and gesture—then the form of rituals is relevant to the form of the plays as a parallel expression of the same kind of organization of experience. Shakespeare arrived at Falstaff's speech on honor, which has a function so extraordinarily similar to the heretical speech of the King of the Years, by working out the implications of the clown's established role—in the directions suggested by the saturnalian customs and sensibility of his time. The pattern of all clowning involves, moment by moment, the same movement from participation to rejection that appears at large in scapegoat ritual: the clown expresses our aberrant impulses for us; but he undercuts himself, or is undercut from outside, so that we can divert sympathy to laughter. In *Henry IV* Shakespeare developed a scapegoat's role for Falstaff which writes this movement large. In other words, Falstaff's part in the story is a manifestation of the meaning of the saturnalian form itself.

The sort of interpretation I have proposed in outline here does not focus on the way the comedies imitate characteristics of actual men and manners; but this neglect of the social observation in the plays does not imply that the way they handle social materials is unimportant. Comedy is not, obviously enough, the same thing as ritual; if it were, it would not perform its function. To express the underlying rhythm his comedy had in common with holiday, Shakespeare did not simply stage mummings; he found in the social life of his time the stuff for "a kind of history." We can see in the Saint George plays how cryptic and arbitrary action derived from ritual becomes when it is merely a fossil remnant. In a self-conscious culture, the heritage of cult is kept alive by art which makes it relevant as a mode of perception and expression. The artist gives the ritual pattern aesthetic actuality by discovering expressions of it in the fragmentary and incomplete gestures of daily life.[8] He fulfills these gestures by making them moments in the complete action which is the art form. The form gives life meaning.

---

[8] One can watch this process, carried out with a modern consciousness of psychological and historical implications of artistic form, in the Circe episode of *Ulysses*. Joyce uses a version of the saturnalian pattern, though what is released is often so shameful by everyday standards that amusement converts to shock or pathos. He casts Bloom as a clown and dramatizes the aberrant motives latent in his responses during the past day by having him act out a series of scapegoat roles. Exemplars of the pattern taken from contemporary life are syncretized with archetypes as diverse as the hunting of the wren on St. Stephen's Day and the sacrifice of the Messiah. See in particular pages 469 to 499 (Modern Library edition), where Joyce merges an astonishing variety of temporary king ceremonials with modern equivalents, to provide a social correlative for an upsurge in Bloom of libidinal egotism followed by anxiety and counterwishes for punishment.

Molière and Farce*

GUSTAVE LANSON

We are so used to speaking piously of Molière, we pay such respectful attention to his maddest pranks as though they were serious and full of deep meaning, that when one of his contemporaries tells us that he is "the first jester of France," [1] or that he is the heir of Scaramouche, this inadequate praise seems to us to be an insult. We grow angry, we shrug our shoulders with pity, when we read in some obscure satire that our great Molière studied the role of a quack and pleaded for the part, or that his plays drew upon manuscripts that he bought from Prosper, the mountebank Braquette's fool, or from Guillot-Gorju's widow.

We prefer to ascribe these remarks to pure malice and mad envy. It is true that critics quickly set aside the stories of buying manuscripts—an easy way to deny the talent of an author whose success cannot be denied; and it would be imprudent to accept as historical truth the account of the relationship between Molière and the quack-doctor.

But there is some truth in every legend. And if these malicious stories were complete lies, they would be too idiotic to be dangerous. Can Molière be a jester, an author of farce, a monkey at play, a plagiarist in his plays? These malicious rumors would have no effect if the public did not feel an affinity between Molière's character and that of farce; and this affinity is the basis for slander and calumny.

But what do we do, we who scorn the Somaizes and the *Hypochondriac Elomire* (*Elomire hypocondre*) and all such miserable gos-

---

[1] The phrase in French is "le premier farceur de France." It is difficult to translate, meaning at once "the greatest creator of farce in France" and "the greatest farce actor in France."—*Translator's note.*

* Gustave Lanson, "Molière and Farce," Ruby Cohn, tr., *Tulane Drama Review*, Vol. 8, No. 2 (Winter, 1963), pp. 133–154.

sip? Tuesdays at the Comédie-Française there is ice in the air when slaps, blows, and kicks are distributed on the face, back, and other parts of the anatomies of the Sganarelles and Gérontes, when squirts of liquid pursue a frightened clown, when grotesque and outrageous figures deliver themselves of smutty stories that seem "to be picked up in the gutters of les Halles." We show frozen faces, frowns of disdain; it would take very little to make our fashionable audience say, "This Molière is fit for the fair!"

Our critics do their utmost to separate these low and coarse aspects from the delicate and refined parts. They manufacture divisions and definitions—comedy of character, comedy of manners, farce—in order to isolate the profound masterpieces, and to prevent the trivial antics, "through the contagiousness of their image," from soiling the noble and pure conception of comic genius given to us by *The Misanthrope* and *Tartuffe*. They explain to us that blows, pranks, and slapstick are an easily detachable trimming, that Molière descended so low to attract a large audience, to make a living for his company, and to enable himself to write and perform the lofty works that did not make money. We can, of course, prefer to believe that it was in spite of himself, forcing himself, that he created all these little scenes and plays, low and trivial if you like, but spontaneous and bursting with verve.

Have we, who believe ourselves so free in our taste, made much progress since Boileau wrote:

Molière might have won the prize for his writing if he had been less popular in his instructive plays, if he had not made his characters grimace, abandoning the pleasant and refined for the slapstick, combining Tabarin and Terence; I do not recognize the author of *The Misanthrope* in the ridiculous sack enveloping Scapin.

Actually, the poet's friend saw less clearly than his enemies. Molière would not be Molière if he were not "a good jester."

I do not want to enumerate all the farcical effects that fill Molière's comedies, nor to persuade people to take pleasure or delight in them; one does not laugh when one wishes, or take delight through demonstrable proof. Nor do I wish to pause to discover whether it is easy to separate farce from high comedy in Molière, or whether the effects, words, and techniques of farce lie in such scenes as the Miser catching his own arm to stop himself, or pretending to be dead, or obstinately blowing out a candle as obstinately relit by Maître Jacques. In *Learned Ladies* (*Femmes Savants*) Philaminte is played by a man, by that same Hubert who played Mme. Jourdain;

there is that lout of a viscount, in the pure and noble *Misanthrope,*
spitting in a well to make circles in the water, and the frightened
valet seeking a letter in all his pockets; in the serious and tragic
Tartuffe, the husband under the table while the hypocrite courts his
wife. One can scarcely deny that farce is everywhere in Molière, and
a little analysis discovers it even in works where it would seem absurd
to look for it.

I do not say this to denigrate Molière's genius, but to understand
it. The trouble with the disgust of refined people and the distinctions
of critics, is that they cut Molière off from reality, leaving him in
the void, separated from his ancestors and from the popular ground
in which his comedy is rooted.

This comedy is very rich and complex; like all great geniuses,
Molière was a big profiteer, for even in literature, nothing is produced
from nothing. He made use of Latin, French, Italian, and Spanish
comedy, Italian and French farce, Italian and French fiction, and
just about everything in existence in the domain of comic, satiric, and
moral literature, whether in dramatic form or not. But these materials,
which he took from everywhere, slipped into a form and were assimilated into a pattern; where did this form and this pattern come from?
They could come from only two sources, the only kinds of comic
drama that then existed: literary comedy derived from Latin through
Italian Renaissance comedy, and popular comedy or farce.

And between these two, one cannot possibly hesitate. Farce is at
the root of all Molière's comedy, even in its highest forms, the comedy of manners and comedy of character. That is Molière's spring-
board: upon the trunk of farce was grafted everything his superior
genius invented through an original vision of life, every seriousness
and profundity his robust and free mind introduced into these hilarious images of the ridiculous. And it is by the cultivation, by the
transformation—extraordinary, if you like—of farce that Molière came
to those masterpieces that seem furthest from farce.

*   *   *

Let us imagine the dramatic education that Molière might have received in Paris under Louis XIII, where he was born and brought up.
Literary historians scarcely see anything but the literary comedy of the
intellectuals, of the coteries and the Academy—the comedy we still
read. They scarcely mention farce, of which a very few rare and
coarse examples survive. But in the first half of the seventeenth century farce delighted both the masses and the middle classes. It was
everywhere: on makeshift stages on the Pont-Neuf, starring Tabarin,

Descomes (who went under the title "Baron of Scratchfat") and their successors; it was at the Fair of St. Germain; it was at the Hotel de Bourgogne following the main play, a tragedy, tragi-comedy, or comedy. It was farce that guaranteed box-office receipts, attracting to the theatre merchants from Rue St-Denis, clerks, scholars, and lackeys.[2] It was farce that made actors famous; until about 1630, until the time of Bellerose and Mondory, we have no specific information about the talent of any actor, except in farce.

The farces played in Paris under Louis XIII were no longer those of the French tradition that flourished in the fifteenth and sixteenth centuries, although those little plays in a few scenes, with rudimentary or no action, in octosyllabic couplets, had not disappeared. A certain number of them were published in Paris, Lyons, and Troyes between 1610 and 1635; certainly they were published only because they were played. In the provinces this was still a living form, and in 1659 La Fontaine wrote and played in a farce: the circumstances of composition and performance, subject, tone, length, octosyllabic couplets all show that *The Mockers of Handsome Richard* (*Rieurs De Beau Richard*) is a farce, although it was called a ballet.

But in Paris Italian farce had replaced French farce. The success of the *commedia dell'arte* during the reign of Charles IX is well known; the dialogue was governed by a supple, loose plot and by rigid comic types or *masks*,[3] Pantaloon, the Doctor, the Captain, Brighella, Harlequin, etc., whose moods, characteristics, and poses the actors kept in all plays, in every situation. From the time of the success of *Gelosi* (in the reigns of Henri III, Henri IV, and Louis XIII), Italian actors had frequently returned to France, and were always appreciated for their vivacity and inventiveness, and for the expressive originality of their *masks,* which were enriched with new traits from one company to the next, one actor to the next. The valets above all developed into various charming types: Scapin and Trivelin were added to Brighelle and Harlequin, and, finally, the famous Scaramouche. During his lifetime, each actor had exclusive use of the *mask* that he had modified or created.

French players of farce worked on this popular model. This was evident among the performers on the Pont-Neuf about 1620. If the

---

[2] "If comedy were not seasoned with this accessory (farce), it would be a meat without sauce, and a bread without flour." (Guilot-Gorju, *Apology,* 1634).

[3] For convenience, I shall designate as masks stock types of the *commedia dell'arte* and their French counterparts. In italics, *mask* will have this meaning; in Roman type, mask will have its usual meaning of face-covering.

one extant farce of Descombes, *The Hunchbacks* (*les Bossus*) is based
on an old French *fabliau,* it nevertheless follows Italian custom in
that prose replaces verse in the dialogue of Patelin and Cornette. In
the four extant farces of Tabarin, we also find prose and Italian
plots; lovers with designs on the wife or daughter of a neighbor,
tricks and misunderstandings serving or crossing these designs, letters
inadvertently delivered to husbands, disguises—not to mention the
famous sack in which the old man or captain is beaten. In these
plots stock characters figure: old Piphagne and old Lucas, both married
and both libertine, Captain Rodomont, an Isabelle who is a malicious
young wife or maiden, and finally Tabarin, the tricky valet, and his
wife Francisquine.[4] Antoine Girard, brother of the charlatan Mondor,
picked up this Italian stock character of Tabarin, and marked it
with originality. The Tabarin-Francisquine couple is a marriage of
the theatre; they are married by farce. In life, Antoine Girard married
Vittoria Bianca in Rome, and a certain Anne Begot played the *mask*
of Francisquine.

Towards 1630 or 1632, we find similar shows at the Hotel de Bourgogne, prose farces with sketchy plots: the valet who is supposed to
watch his master's daughter, but delivers her lover's messages while
he makes off with his gifts, or the valet helping his amorous master
seduce the wife of an old bourgeois.[5] Their Italian origin is betrayed
by the way in which the valet directs the action.

But what appears most clearly is the way the acting company was
formed to play farce, in the Italian manner: each actor had his *mask,*
his stock type, the same name every time he played. And that is why
the actors of the Hotel de Bourgogne had three names: a real name,
a name for the theatre, and a name for farce: Robert Guérin, also
la Fleur, also *Gros-Guillaume*; Henri Le Grand, also Belleville, also
Turlupin; Hughes Guéru, also Fléchelles, also *Gaultier-Garguille.*
The last name, the name from farce, is the *mask.* The actors use
this name in their roles; it is the name that designates the type.

There are two valets. Gros-Guillaume, "covered with flour, like a
miller," red cap, white blouse, and trousers with broad red stripes,
a huge stomach circled with a hoop and emphasized by two belts
that support it from above and below, underneath the blouse: this
is the drunken, good-natured valet; he has a "visible naïveté," "a

---

[4] In one farce Francisquine is Lucas' wife. She is a vigorous gossip of the
people, but honest.

[5] The Italian provenance is evident in the fact that the old *Parisian* does
business with India, and intends to leave on one of his ships; here we can
recognize the Venetian Pantaloon.

way of talking grandiloquent nonsense," and "a funny face." In contrast is Turlupin, masked, in about the same costume as Brighella, a clever valet, a rogue and wit.

Then there are the old men, husbands or fathers, and ridiculous lovers: Gaultier-Garguille, tall and thin, masked, white-haired with round glasses, black doublet with red sleeves, skull-cap, black shoes and stockings, inkstand,[6] game-pouch and belt, stick in his hand. This is the Italian doctor, Frenchified into a lawyer. He is jealous, greedy and lascivious. His successor was Guillot-Gorju, summoned from a company in the country. This *mask* was the creation of an actor who had studied medicine, and introduced into his role a much-appreciated imitation of the jargon and ridiculous ways of doctors; his specialty was to exaggerate these. Boniface, another old man, was a merchant, sometimes a Doctor or Pedant. Lady Perrine (certainly a man) played the wife of Gaultier-Garguille, who fought with him and was seduced by Horace (*mask* of Bellerose) with the help of Turlupin.

Terrible Captain Fracasse, mixing the rodomontades of the Spaniard from Naples (recalling the country from which he came), with the braggadocio of the Gascon (which was the living model in France); Alison, *mask* of an old nurse or gossip, played by a man; and Florentine, the lady in love, completed the company. About this same time, other less famous types appeared: a Doctor Fabrice, a lady Gigogne, a Gringalet (which seems to be a *mask* played by various actors in the first half of the century), Goguelu, a kind of scrounger, whom a contemporary print shows going to a picnic, carrying in one hand his plate, and behind his back in a basket his whole family, wife, children, dog and cat who will devour much more than he contributes—it has been claimed that he replaced Gros-Guillaume.

As we know it, this company of the Hotel de Bourgogne was the counterpart of Italian companies. But the French tradition did not completely disappear; it was blended with the foreign inspiration. Side by side with the actors masked in the Italian fashion we find the white-face of the French tradition: Turlupin has a mask, but Gros-Guillaume is in white-face.[7] Side by side with Italian plots, we see simple dialogues, without a shadow of plot, such as in the two-

---

[6] In *The Testament* that humorous author makes him write, Gaultier-Garguille wills his dagger with his game-pouch: in the drawing of Guillaumot, it is impossible to see in this "dagger" anything but a writer's inkstand.

[7] Clémont Marot, *Epitaph for Jean de Serres, excellent actor in farce*: ". . . When he came on stage, with a dirty shirt, and his forehead, cheek, and nostril covered with flour . . ."

character farces of Turlupin and Gros-Guillaume—Turlupin the husband arguing with Gros-Guillaume, his wife. In spite of the prose and improvisation, nothing could be more firmly in the French tradition.

Mondory, who founded a rival company in Paris, scorned farce and did not produce any; he wished to dedicate his talent and his theatre to regular and literary plays which the middle classes and ladies could enjoy. Nevertheless, in order to live, he had to introduce farce into his theatre. We know several characters of Marais' farce: Tibaut Garray "with his puffed up mask and pygmy size," trying to compete with Gaultier-Garguille, the valet Filipin, but above all Captain Matamore, the Bellemore's creation who eclipsed Captain Fracasse of the rival company, and Jodelet, "the naïve one in white-face," long, thin, speaking through his nose. For fifty years, in many theatres, without tiring his public, Julien de L'Espy presented this *mask* of a valet who was a foolish and insolent milksop.

This is what the ten- or twelve-year-old Poquelin might have seen if, as tradition has it, his grandfather took him to the theatre.

The vogue of farce, and above all of its *masks,* was such that more than one author introduced the best-known actors of farce into his plays, keeping their names and stock types. Du Ryer put Gros-Guillaume into his *Harvest of Surène;* Alison was the main character in a five-act comedy; Corneille and others put Captain Matamore's swashbuckling into high style; and the *mask* of Jodelet gave its name to several comedies by Scarron and his contemporaries.

Nevertheless, farce tended to disappear by the middle of the century. Literary comedy absorbed it and smothered it. In the long run it probably was the victim of the middle class and the ladies. Mme. de Rambouillet, says Tallemant, who blamed her for it, could not listen to an obscene word; and farce put precious ears to a cruel test. Corneille, Rotrou, and other polite writers introduced, instead of farce, a witty and respectable comedy which, even in the daring plays of Scarron, did not disgust the refined and fashionable world.

Although abolished in Paris (except for Jodelet, who played at the Marais) farce lasted in the provinces, in country companies, and above all in the Béjart company of Molière. When they arrived in Paris in 1658, they resembled the actors who played twenty-five years earlier in farce at the Hotel de Bourgogne. Each actor of the company had his fixed *mask,* name, and character. For old men, there were the Doctor and Gorgibus. For valets, there was first of all Gros-René or the Painted One, meaning the "floured one," with his white face, his big belly, his naïveté (for he is a "big round man in every way"), his drunkenness which resurrected Gros-Guillaume, his philosophical nonsense, his double-talk of doctrine. Besides Gros-René, there were Mascarille and Sganarelle, two masks composed and played successively by the chief of the company.

After playing *Nicomede* before the king at the Louvre on October 24, 1658, Molière requested his Majesty's permission to play "one of these little entertainments which had made his reputation and which amused the provinces"; and he gave *The Amorous Doctor* (*le Docteur amoureux*). This is a *farce,* but since farce was no longer fashionable, Molière dared not use the word, and he employed the more elegant word *entertainment.* "Since for a long time these little comedies were not mentioned, the invention seemed new." [8]

Thus, as author and actor, it is in farce that Molière was first revealed to Louis XIV and the Parisian public. Between the Hotel and the Marais, the originality of his company lay in the resurrection of this genre. He revived the tradition of Gros-Guillaume, Gaultier-Garguille, and Turlupin; isn't this the grain of truth in the absurd accusation that he bought the manuscripts of Guillot-Gorju?

Moreover, when he offered his own inimitable novelty to Paris, it was not high comedy in the manner of *The Fool* (*l'Étourdie*) or *The Liar* (*le Menteur*), but farce. For how else can we designate *The High-Browed Ladies* (*Les Précieuses Ridicules*)? In publishing it, the author called it a comedy, and we reject the word *farce* through respect to him. But never mind the label; let us look at the play. First of all, there are three *masks,* characters straight from the *commedia dell'arte,* already presented to the public with their names and comic faces: Gorgibus, Mascarille, Jodelet. The other characters are nameless; they keep the names of the actors who play them, La Grange, Du Croisy, and also Madelon, Cathos, Marotte; for it is probable that "Madelon" is Madeleine Béjart, "Cathos," Catherine du Rosé (Mlle. de Brie), "Marotte," Marotte Beaupré. Is this the way of literary comedy? No more than prose, which was so rare in seventeenth-century comedy before Molière—and the few exceptions were closely linked to farce.

What is the fundamental comic idea upon which the satire is built, the characters of Mascarille Marquis and Jodelet Viscount? We have already seen Gros-Guillaume as the wife of Turlupin, and the improvised Italian comedy will show Scaramouche as a hermit, Harlequin as a wardrobe-keeper of the Palace, Colombine as a lawyer; can we not then see the quality of Molière's scenario?

[8] La Grange, in his preface to the 1682 edition of Molière. But La Grange was mistaken; there was still Jodelet, but Jodelet alone.

Old Jodelet rushed to join this young company that was reviving the tradition he alone maintained, and Molière rushed to welcome him; is it mere deference to a friend that he allowed him to invent the slapstick climax of being stripped of many jackets? Is Mascarille of a different quality from Jodelet? Like Turlupin before Gros-Guillaume, a masked Mascarille stands before Jodelet with his floured face; and here are the entrance and costume of the character:

Imagine, Madame, his wig was so big that it swept the floor every time he bowed, and his hat was so small, that one could easily see that the marquis carried it much more often in his hand than on his head; his lapel could be called a fair-sized dressing-gown, and his canions seemed to be made only to serve as hiding-places for children playing hide-the-haversack; in truth, Madame, I do not believe that the tents of the young Massagetes could be more spacious than these respectable canions. A torch of elegant sayings came from his pocket as from a horn of plenty, and his shoes were so covered with ribbons that I cannot tell you whether they were made of Russian, English, or Moroccan leather; what I do know is that they were at least six inches high, and I was most anxious to know how such high, fine heels could carry the marquis and his ribbons, his canions, and powder.[9]

Doesn't this quotation indicate the tone of the part? And isn't the character taken right from farce?

Everybody knows how close Molière's acting was to that of Italian farce, how he admired Scaramouche with whom he shared the applause of the Petit-Bourbon. Everybody knows how his enemies condemned his grimaces, contortions, and poses, and that this meant that Molière had adopted the expressive gestures, the vivid mimicry of the Italians. But does it follow that Molière the author had the same teachers as Molière the actor, that his written work had the same source as his acting style?

First of all, it must be said that a certain way of acting imposes a certain style when the author is an actor and is writing what he will play. Before Molière, literary comedy, like tragedy, neither saw nor displayed bodies; it expressed manners by abstract discourse, by fine analysis or lively, stylized images, and it underlined thought only by the accent of the voice, at most supported by an oratorical gesture; before Molière, a comic part was merely the voice of a witty or foolish spirit. In Molière, on the other hand, the inner feeling thrusting itself outward sets the entire man into motion, and his discourse is accompanied by a grimace, a pose, which interprets and complements it. There is no room for literary development, for words

---

[9] Mlle. Desjardins, *Story of the Farce of the Precieuses.* Nor was she an enemy; on the contrary.

that do not include a revealing gesture of character. The impersonal naïveté of Molière's style is closely linked to his acting; because he clung to the greatest economy of words in order to give an animated picture of the original, he had neither the time nor the desire to show off his wit.

Let us look at Molière's development. In the provinces he began with farce: *Gros-René the Scholar* (*Gros-René Écolier*), *The Dowdy One* (*le Fagoteux*), *Gorgibus in the Sack* (*Gorgibus dans le Sac*), *The Amorous Doctor*, *The Jealousy of the Painted One* (*la Jalousie du Barbouillé*): one act in prose, which was still the form in *The High-Browed Ladies*, not to mention the *masks* or stock types. After *The High-Browed Ladies* came *Sganarelle*, also a farce in both subject and tone, and again in one act, but this time in verse. Then Molière tried the unfortunate experiment of *Don Garcie*, a literary comedy in verse in five acts, with Italian plot and witty dialogue; then he went back to one act plays; then he moved on, in verse, to three acts, which was usual in the *commedia dell'arte*: *School for Husbands* (*l'École des Maris*) and *The Angry Ones* (*les Fâcheux*). Again he tried the full form of five acts with *School for Wives* (*l'École des Femmes*). After these attempts, he grew through his talent and craftsmanship, not by mechanical observation of conventions.

Molière followed two paths: that of literary comedy in *The Fool*, *The Chagrin* (*le Dépit*), *Don Garcie*, and that of farce in *The Dowdy One* and, analogously, *The High-Browed Ladies* and *Sganarelle*. In which will we finally find those superior manifestations of Molière's comic genius, comedy of manners and comedy of character? Does *The Fool* promise more than a Rotrou or a Regnard? But is not *The High-Browed Ladies* high comedy? Is it astonishing that the man who created the dialogue for Mascarille and Madelon created that used by the miser or the hypocrite? Is it astonishing that the man who revealed the imagination of Sganarelle created Arnolphe and his terror, or Chrysale and his wrath?

One might raise this objection: "But that is the point, *The High-Browed Ladies* and *Sganarelle* still preserve elements of farce but are already comedy. Molière's growth consists in a double effort, in which he progressively reduced, if he did not entirely eliminate, farce, while he developed the elements of true comedy which are still hidden under farce, even in *The High-Browed Ladies*. He produced his masterpieces when he just about got rid of farce."

But here we must distinguish between two things to avoid confusion: the scenic effects of farce and the esthetic principle of farce. The effects of farce are coarse, and that is explained by the public it seeks. It is certain that these effects are rare in Molière's masterpieces, for he evokes laughter by more subtle methods than blows of the stick and coarse caricature. But that is only the exterior, the envelope of farce. Although the words may seem pretentious, farce is a dramatic genre that has its own esthetic, its method of invention. And it is this esthetic of farce, this method of invention, a certain original fashion of dealing with the stuff of life, that I am claiming to find even in Molière's masterpieces.

*   *   *

If there was one part of his art that Molière neglected or scorned, it was putting together a plot, manipulating its threads to lead the spectator to the dénouement by every sort of detour and surprise. Molière's art was never one to entangle in order to disentangle, to give new impetus to an action whose momentum seems exhausted, to scramble it up the moment it seems clear, and to unscramble it suddenly by a facile trick just when it seems insoluble. He is just a little boy in this domain, compared to Beaumarchais, Scribe, Sardou, or even Corneille. Must we refer to *School for Wives,* clumsily built on an overlong quidproquo and disentangled by a badly prepared recognition; *The Learned Ladies (les Femmes Savantes)* and the naïve and convenient invention of false letters; *Tartuffe* and the miracle of the king's intervention—a deus ex machina whatever one says; *The Miser* and its cascade of recognitions that permits marriages needed by the comedy without sacrificing anything of Harpagon's character; *George Dandin* which has no dénouement, leaving things hanging after the play, as they ran ahead in the play? Even *The Misanthrope* with its minimal action cannot attain its dénouement without the unexpected artifice of letters suddenly discovered.

But that is enough to prove the point; it is not through plot that Molière's comedy rates high. Everybody admits it. But let us examine the implications of this admission. Plot is precisely that characteristic of literary comedy that the Italian Renaissance derived from classical comedy. It is plot that Italy gave to Spain and France for their modern comedy. Invention consists in scrambling and unscrambling a skein of deceptions and errors; the *inganno* is the inexhaustible source of interest and laughter. The principal theatrical agents are valets, messengers, fools of every kind and every costume; they take triumphant possession of the stage because in them are the springs of action.

Moreover, it is plot that characterizes most French comedy before Molière: *The Gallantries of the Duke of Ossone (les Galanteries du duc d'Ossone)* by Mairet and Corneille's *Liar (le Menteur), The*

Sister (*la Soeur*) by Rotrou and *The Invisible Beauty* (*la Belle invisible*) by Boisrobert, *The Foolish Spirit* (*l'Esprit follet*) of d'Ouville and *The Foolish Master* (*le Maître étourdi*) of Quinault. And when young Molière wishes to aspire to authorship, he first handled comedy in his own way; he wrote *The Fool*, a series of deceptions, and *The Chagrin of Love*, a web of error.

But by the time he wrote *The High-Browed Ladies*, and when he offered *The Misanthrope* or *The Forced Marriage* (*le Mariage forcé*), *Tartuffe* or *Pourceaugnac*, *The Learned Ladies* or *The Imaginary Invalid* (*le Malade imaginaire*), then, as in the plays in which Trivelin and Scaramouche acted, the plot is only a thread to link comic situations, a framework for witty scenes. It is only a pretext to control the strings of human puppets whose expressive gestures make the comedy.

I do not even mention *The Angry Ones*: the insignificant plot serves to put on stage a hunter, a musician, a scholar, a gambler, etc. Is this not the resurrection of our ancient theatre's comic monologue? But rather than a single character like the marvelous "Archer of Bagnolet," the masterpiece of the genre, the plot permits a whole series of types to present themselves through their own words.

The Angry Ones is an exception, but all through Molière we find scenes that are scarcely attached to the plot, and yet do not compete with it. The scenes of *Chagrin of Love*, artificially divided into three different plots, can be detached from any of them, and isolated, as the Comédie-Française produces them, make a delightful little farce. Similarly, we find Sganarelle's discussions with his master, and Don Juan getting rid of a creditor in *Don Juan*; in *The Miser* (*l'Avare*), the calculations of the miser who wants to give a dinner and the memorable scene of the flocks that the moneylender wants to lend instead of money; in *Learned Ladies*, the conference of wits and Chrysale's quarrels with his wife; in *The Misanthrope*, the scene of the sonnet, the conversation of the coquette and the prude. There are many more such scenes, whose resonance goes far beyond the plot, and whose effect does not reside in the help or hindrance that they give to the dénouement, to the marriage that is essential to literary comedy. Separated from the plot, they retain their essential value and their full flavor, which lie entirely in the naïve and witty interpretation of manners and character through dialogue. But plotless and expressive dialogue of manner and character is the domain of Italian farce, with its imaginative slapstick, and of French farce, with its coarse platitudes. Molière enlarges the boundaries, multiplies the stock types and the reactions of each type; he does not change the principle, which is always to seek the comic in some relationship with life, not in a relationship to a climax.

It may seem audacious to link farce to the great comedy of character of which Molière alone was capable. Nowhere else was he more truly creative. But where did he get the idea?

Certainly not from literary comedy, dominated by a plot upon which one generalized. From each actor the situation drew feelings adapted to his role in the play. Dialogue was assigned to the characters by a vague classification into humors or tastes, based on age, sex, and profession, and this classification was supported by generalizations from Aristotle and Horace on the four seasons of life, and by the models of Terence. The same situations called for similar feelings in various people, and different situations evoked different feelings in the same person. Facial expressions that could scarcely be distinguished from one another, generally believable moods, but without specific and individual cohesion—that is what literary comedy offered Molière. There were no *characters*.

For Molière a character is a person who is powerfully unified by the domination of a passion or vice that destroys or subdues all other likes and dislikes of his soul, and this quality becomes the motivating force of all his thought and action. Love alone can sometimes resist this tyranny, and the comic springs forth from this resistance, from its partial defeat or its unforeseen compromises.

Nevertheless, there are several works of literary comedy that might have guided Molière in this way. Not *The Liar,* which no one today dreams of playing as a comedy of character, but *The Comic Illusion* (*l'Illusion Comique*) with the startling fantasy of the braggart; *The Pedant Fooled* (*le Pédant joué*), with the caricatures of pedant, captain, and peasant; *The Parasite* (*le Parasite*) by Tristan, with another captain playing with the parasite; *Don Japhet* and *Jodelet* by Scarron, those monstrous caricatures; and above all Gillet de la Tessonnerie's *The Countryman* (*le Compagnard*), in which the conventional character of the captain is almost completely transformed into a country gentleman through real observation. Aren't these works, whose plots contain a marked and burlesque figure, sketches and models for comedy of character? Molière might have started there.

He might have, since almost all these comedies take on a distinctive quality through introducing into the plot a stock type taken from French or foreign farce.[10] He might have, but he did not. Otherwise, why did he not continue Corneille's *Braggart* (*le Matamore*) or Gil-

---

[10] Le Metamore and Jodelet are taken from contemporary French farce. Scarron, Thomas Corneille, and others draw upon the Spanish genre called *commedia de figuron,* and these *figurones* seem to be stock types transplanted

let's *Countryman* in verse comedies? Why in his first effort at character did he turn to the limitations of prose, in the style of farce?

If the comedy of character is sketched in *The High-Browed Ladies* and *Sganarelle,* there is proof that Molière first conceived character in the form of the Italian *mask,* which the French actors of farce had made their own.

Masks of the *commedia dell'arte,* for that matter, are nothing but sketches of general characteristics. Originally, to be sure, the *masks* had local and professional traits that particularized them: Pantaloon was a Venetian merchant; the Doctor was from Bologne, and, as his name indicates, knew his law; Harlequin was a peasant from Bergamo; Scaramouche, a Neapolitan adventurer; and the Captain (also Neapolitan vaguely crossed with Spanish), although not the great lord he claimed to be, was a rich gentleman.

But in France these origins and professions were not noticed, and were transformed into general characteristics. The Captain is no more than vanity and cowardice; Scaramouche, roguery and impudence; Brighella, the insolent tricky valet; Harlequin, the naïve and awkward valet; the Doctor becomes a pedant of philosophy and letters; and Pantaloon is melancholy old age, miserly and foolish. Italian authors in France modified the original types, varying them to bring out their general meaning and thus transforming Trivelin and Harlequin. In spite of dialects and costumes that still continued to reveal the local origin of more than one *mask,* the French spectator saw and could see only general expressions of foolishness and deceit, of lasciviousness and avarice—all humanity gracefully individualized by the imagination and personal observation of the actor.

And that is exactly the principle of *character* as Molière uses it. He knew it so well that he first molded his observation and invention into *masks.*

He began by creating Mascarille and Sganarelle,[11] two *masks* of valets that, in the Italian manner, he submitted to various conditions.

Mascarille, *fourbum imperator,* close relative of Scapin, completely

---

from popular comedy to literary comedy. In the works of Tristan, his parasite, aside from being a personal satire, is merely a mold for tirades, a theme with variations in the manner of farce. I would say the same about Desmarets' *Visionaries;* its characters are mere labels tacked on to several kinds of literary amplification.

[11] Of these two *masks,* only Mascarille is masked. From *School for Husbands* on, Sganarelle is not masked. In various documents of the time, he has exaggerated, pencilled (or perhaps inked) eyebrows and moustache; Ronsard in *The Royal Grove* speaks of "A Janin whose face is marked with flour or ink." This actor without a mask, whose face is made up but not in white-face, belongs more than the masked actor to the French tradition.

Italian in features and costume, helped Molière ridicule *The High-Browed Ladies*. But this valet's mask is narrow. He is only a rascal, he can only *imitate* others by exaggerating their foibles. With him, there could be no true and exact portrayal of French manners; he would remain Mascarille carrying out his duties, Mascarille imitating the marquis, and not what the poet now envisaged, a true marquis lifted from life on to the stage.

Then Molière took up another valet, Sganarelle, from the pageants of his youth. Only his name is still Italian, and if he was masked at first, Molière unmasked him. Valet though he is, he seems to be the heir of Guillot-Gorju; he ridicules doctors. We find him rigged out in doctor's robes three times: in *The Flying Doctor* (*le Médecin Volant*), in *The Doctor in Spite of Himself* (*le Médecin malgré lui*), and in *Don Juan*. But Molière broadens the mask and transforms Sganarelle. In contrast with Mascarille, who is essentially a valet, Sganarelle is only occasionally a valet. In essence, he is of the people, ignorant, selfish, a drunkard and coward, rather simple except when fear or acquisitiveness sharpens his mind. His gift is for coarse common sense rather than brilliant grace and light verve. He may be mature or old, peasant or bourgeois, husband, teacher, or father, but as any of these, he is robbed, deceived, and beaten. Between 1660 and 1666, having rejected Mascarille, Molière gave us Sganarelle in six plays, but we can see the *mask* disintegrate in his hands. These Sganarelles share little more than their name; the permanence of Italian Harlequin and Pantaloon are gone, and under this one name we now find a whole family of spirits and temperaments.

However, Molière got rid of Sganarelle as well. The Italian *masks* helped him to simplify life, to delineate moral aspects in the physical; when he had acquired the method, he rejected the *mask*. The artificial identity created by a name hampered him. If Sganarelle remains in the drunken peasant whose wife's revenge converts him into a doctor, the old amorous bourgeois of *The Forced Marriage* is no longer Sganarelle. There are two men and two lives, no longer a single man in two roles. And Molière broke the last bond that attached him to the comedy of the *commedia dell'arte*. He even strove to wipe out of the public mind the identity of these Sganarelles; he dressed them differently (as the inventory of his wardrobe shows): here in crimson satin, there in "musk-colored" satin, elsewhere in "olive-colored breeches and coat" and "underbreeches of flower yellow." [12]

----

[12] Similarly, in his last years, Molière changed Mascarille from his Italian original; the frontispiece of the 1682 edition shows Mascarille of *The High-Browed Ladies*, recognizable in wig and costume, but without a mask; he no longer has one, but shows his face, that of Molière as 'Sganarelle.

Before 1666, he often liberated himself from Mascarille and Sgana-relle; after 1666, he no longer returned to these *masks*. How much Tartuffe would have lost in being called Mascarille the hypocrite, and Orgon, Sganarelle the pious! In giving each bourgeois or fool his own name, the author revealed no less of their basis in good common sense and fearful credulity, of ingenious wit and audacious mischief. But he did not allow the abstract, general type to dominate. He per-mitted himself to individualize that type, to give it characteristics that renewed it. Thus he came closer to life. Sganarelle shows progress over Mascarille; the disappearance of Sganarelle marks a new step in the true imitation of manners.

To arrive at this point, Molière had to go through half his Parisian career. But although he rejected its appearance, he kept the structure of the *mask*. Arnolphe, Harpagon, Tartuffe, Alceste, are made up no differently from the six Sganarelles, from Pantaloon or Scaramouche. They retain the invariable fixity of character in any situation of Italian *masks*. They are placed before the public, they are allowed to take any positions, to make all gestures relevant to their character. We see the Misanthrope with the flatterer, with the vain wit, the prude, the flirt; with everyone, he says the word, makes the grimace, that characterize him. The *mask*, emphasized by melancholy, contains and makes entertaining the dialogue of the jealous lover;[13] and Alceste, retaining certain speeches from *Don Garcie* and literary comedy, is unique. Everywhere else, the only purpose of the action is not to show a change in feeling, but to bring forth inexhaustibly, by different acts and under different light, that feeling which is the single mainspring of the character. As Harlequin, through all his contortions, invariably expresses his own sly naïveté, so Harpagon is a miser in every syllable of his part—and Tartuffe a hypocrite.

The permanence of their types is dazzling and changeless; for this reason La Bruyère found them coarse and Fénlon forced. For this reason, too, their comedy has no dénouement, because they have to be as they are from start to finish; they cannot say *yes* after having said *no*, a *no* which resides in the necessity of their essence; for such char-acters, dénouements would be artificial. Lapses and repentances are as impossible for them as an act of bravery or decency for Scaramouche.

* * *

But in Molière's comedy, there is an important part that Italian

---

[13] As everyone knows, *The Misanthrope* borrows its strongest scene and its finest lines from *Don Garcie*. But the development of the feeling of jealousy is subordinated to the comic caricature of the man who would speak openly.

farce does not contain, at least for the French spectator: the painting of social conditions and relationships.

Molière shows us all the classes and relationships that composed French society in his time: peasants, bourgeois, squires, wits, great lords, servants, middle-class women, young and older ladies. A large part of his gift lies in spreading vices and ridiculous qualities through these different classes.

Already, under the name of Sganarelle, he had created a figure that was well known in our comic tradition. Sganarelle, valet or master, widower or husband, lover or father, resembles the rascal of our farce more than he does Pantaloon or Harlequin of the *commedia dell 'arte*. Like him, he is always beaten, robbed, and deceived. Saint-Beuve realized it—Sganarelle contains Arnolphe, Dandin, and Orgon; in spite of his Italian name, he is pure French.

And what was distinctive about our own farce, as opposed to the character sketches of the Italian *masks,* was the witty image of social relationships. Our farce shows not libertines or misers or scoundrels, but a gentleman, a priest, a lawyer, an old soldier, a rascal, a cobbler, a tailor, a hosier. It portrays not love but home life, and love as a disturbance in home life, and a worry for the husband. It displays the details of quarrels and mistakes in the home, but the eternal conflict between feminine ruse and masculine brutality results less from opposition of two moral natures than from a conflict between two social conditions. It is the state of marriage that is revealed to us in this conflict of the two sexes' maliciousness.

In that way Molière reflects old French farce. How did he come to know it? Could its spirit and trends still be seen under its Italianized form in the farces at the Pont-Neuf and the Hotel de Bourgogne? Did he see it in the provinces, where it was still being played? Could he envision it through the printed text? Did he come upon booklets like those of Oudot, Rousset, and Barnaby Chaussard that chance has preserved for us? He knew French farce—the fact is certain, since he borrowed from it; the path is uncertain. Although there is a marked difference, due to his ‚poetic genius and the refinement of his classical art, the figures of Arnolphe, Jourdain, Dandin, Pourceaugnac recall the Naudet's, George le Veau's, Colin's of old farce, as well as the draper Guillaume, and the lawyer Patelin. These are the germs that Molière developed, the first use of the comic method of his masterpieces. Although his characters are infinitely richer in substance, far less spare in design, they are constructed by the same method. They have no other way of looking at life than these coarse creatures who so easily amused the subjects of Louis XI and Louis XII.

On the one hand are the great characters with conventional names, Alceste, Tartuffe, Harpagon, who are like *masks* of humanity, on the other hand are characters with real and probable names, Pourceaugnac, Dandin, Jourdain, Arnolphe (or Arnould), deriving from a more purely French tradition. The first are more abstract and moral, the second more localized and social.

What they share, and what unites them in the theatre, is their naïve expression in dialogue. Comedy is *active conversation*; dialogue is all, if we mean that expressive and mimed dialogue of which I have spoken, that copious dialogue spilling over the plot so that the internal originality of a vigorously characterized nature reveals itself without reservation or hesitation, with candid passion.

And finally old French farce, differing from the pure artistry of Italian farce, contains a social moral which is usually low and coarse. The farce evokes a judgment about the character and situation. *The Wash-Tub* (*le Cuvier*) or *The Bridge for Asses* (*le Pont aux ânes*) contains an implicit ideal of what relationships should exist between husband and wife; *Georges le Veau,* a statement about bad matches; *Master Minim the Student* (*Maitre Minim Étudiant*) or *Pernet Who Goes To School* (*Pernet qui va à l'école*), judgments on the practical usefulness of knowledge. *Naudet* applauds the vengeance of the thief over the gentleman; this is the morality of Figaro wishing to serve his master with what he fears to receive from him. Both "The Archer of Bagnolet" and Colin who "goes to Naples and brings back a Turkish prisoner" judge, the brutal, pillaging soldiers by portraying them. In other words, many farces are expressions of popular conscience, of its way of looking at domestic and social relationships. There is an infinite distance between this rudimentary morality and the profound philosophy of Molière's comedies, which contain a seriousness, force, and personal freedom of thought that are unique. Nevertheless, the conception of life of these comedies is also not that of Corneille's *Liar,* nor of Rotrou, nor Scarron, nor Machiavelli, nor Aretino, nor Rojas, nor Moreto; consciously or not, Molière followed in the path of French farce, where what is laughable is what shocks the moral judgment and social prejudice of the public.

No matter how much we pay homage to Molière's genius, to his creative powers, to the suggestions of classical, Italian, French, and Spanish comedy, it is here that we have his true roots. He began with farce, and there he formed his true and expressive style. There he found the principle of *pantomime,* of *active gestures* that freed him from seeking witty words and brilliant dialogue. There he found a tendency that he could develop, and a method that he could use, the principle of concentration on a general character or on the socially ridiculous, there above all he found the habit of situating the source of laughter outside of the plot and entirely in the relationship that his people bear to people in real life.

Let us therefore accept the title thrust upon him by his malicious contemporaries: Molière is "the first jester of France." This is truer than the criticism of his friend Boileau, who reproached him with having been too close to the people. Boileau dreamed of an academic Molière, but the true Molière is seen in a picture of the Comédie-Française, where he stands amid other illustrious actors of farce, both Italian and French. In this picture of *farceurs,* Molière figures in the company of Harlequin and Gros-Guillaume, of Scaramouche and Guillot-Gorju. These are his masters, these are his origins. And he is great enough not to blush at them.

He is the best farceur, and for this reason he is the best creator of comedy. That is why he has not dated in two hundred and fifty years. Whereas Corneille and especially Racine are practically inaccessible except to the educated who are trained to appreciate their intelligence and beauty, mass audiences without instruction or training respond at once to Molière; Molière enters their minds and goes right to their hearts. He appeals to the people, because he springs from the people; because his works, having assimilated all the learned and witty inventions, take their main form and their essential flavor from popular Italian or French comedy; because popular comedy revealed to him that in the "strange enterprise of amusing decent people" and others as well, nothing is more effective than holding "the mirror up to nature."

Restoration Comedy: the Reality and the Myth*

L. C. KNIGHTS

I

Henry James—whose "social comedy" may be allowed to provide a standard of maturity—once remarked that he found Congreve "insufferable," [1] and perhaps the first thing to say of Restoration drama—tragedy as well as comedy—is that the bulk of it is insufferably dull. There are long stretches of boredom to be found in the lower ranges of Elizabethan drama, but there is nothing comparable to the unmitigated fatigue that awaits the reader of Love in a Tub, Sir Martin Mar-all, Mr. Limberham, The Relapse, or The Mourning Bride. And who returns to Dryden's heroic plays with renewed zest? The superiority of the common runs of plays in the first period to that of the second is, at all events, a commonplace. It should be equally commonplace that the strength of the Elizabethan drama lies partly in the kind and scope—the quality and variety—of the interests that the playwrights were able to enlist, partly in the idiom that they had at their command: the drama drew on a vigorous non-dramatic literature, and literature in general was in close relation with non-literary interests and a rich common language. That is not the whole story, but it is an important part of it, and it seems profitable in a discussion of Restoration comedy, to keep these facts in mind for comparison. Ever since Collier published A Short View of the Profaneness

---

[1] Letters, Vol. I, p. 140.

* L. C. Knights, "Restoration Comedy: the Reality and the Myth," in Explorations (New York University Press, 1964). [Footnotes in this selection have been renumbered.]

and Immorality of the English Stage opponents of Restoration comedy
have conducted their case almost entirely in moral terms, and it has
been easy for recent critics, rightly discarding Lamb's obvious subter-
fuge, to turn the moral argument upside down, to find freedom of
manners where Macaulay found licentiousness. "Morals" are, in the
long run, decidedly relevant—but only in the long run: literary criticism has prior claims. If, to start with, we try to see the comedy of
manners in relation to its contemporary non-dramatic literature—to
take its bearings in the general culture of the time—we may at least
make possible a free and critical approach.

During the forty years that followed the Restoration, English literature, English culture, was "upper-class" to an extent that it had
never been before, and was not, after Addison, to be again. "Now if
they ask me," said Dryden, "whence it is that our conversation is so
much refined? I must freely and without flattery, ascribe it to the
court," and his insistence, as a writer, on "the benefit of converse"
with his courtly patrons was not merely dedicatory fulsomeness; the
influence of the current conception of "the gentleman" is shown plainly
enough by the urbane ease of his critical prefaces; and Dryden's non-
dramatic prose is fairly representative of the new age.[2]

It is this that explains why, if one comes to Restoration literature
after some familiarity with the Elizabethans, the first impression made
by the language is likely to be a sense of what has been lost; the
disintegration of the old cultural unity has plainly resulted in impoverishment. The speech of the educated is now remote from the speech
of the people (Bunyan's huge sales were, until the eighteenth century,
outside "the circumference of wit"), and idiomatic vigour and evoca-
tive power seem to have gone out of the literary medium. But there
was gain as well as loss. The common mode of Restoration prose—
for there is now a common mode, a norm—was not evolved merely
in the interests of good form and polite intercourse; it had behind
it a more serious pressure. When, in 1667, Sprat attacked "this vicious
abundance of phrase . . . this volubility of tongue, which makes so
great a noise in the world," he had in mind the needs of scientific
inquiry and rational discussion. "They have therefore," he said of the
Royal Society, "been most rigorous in putting in execution the only
remedy that can be found for this *extravagance,* and that has been
a constant resolution to reject all amplifications, digressions, and swell-

---

[2] On "the last and greatest advantage of our writing, which proceeds from
conversation," see in particular the *Defence of the Epilogue.* And the dialogue
form in which Dryden cast the *Essay of Dramatic Poesy* was not unrecogniz-
ably far from actuality.

ings of style; to return back to the primitive purity and shortness, when men delivered so many *things* almost in an equal number of *words*. They have exacted from all their members a close, naked, natural way of speaking, positive expressions, clear senses, a native easiness, bringing all things as near the mathematical plainness as they can." [3] For the first time the English language was made—and to some extent made consciously—an instrument for rational dissection.

> When once the aversion to bear uneasiness taketh place in a man's mind, it doth so check all the passions, that they are dampt into a kind of indifference; they grow faint and languishing, and come to be subordinate to that fundamental maxim, of not purchasing any thing at the price of a difficulty. This made that he had as little eagerness to oblige, as he had to hurt men; the motive of his giving bounties was rather to make men less uneasy to him, than more easy to themselves; and yet no ill-nature all this while. He would slide from an asking face, and could guess very well. It was throwing a man off from his shoulders, that leaned upon them with his whole weight; so that the party was not gladder to receive, than he was to give.

This is from Halifax's *Character of Charles II,* and the even tone, the sinuous ease of movement and the clarity of the analysis mark the passage as unmistakably post-Restoration. Halifax, of course, is in some ways an unusually handsome representative of his age; he is racy (the apt adjective is supplied by his editor, H. C. Foxcroft) as well as polite. But the achievement represented by his style was far from being a merely individual achievement. The shrewd and subtle portrait of Charles II is unlike anything that had appeared in English before his time, and it could only have appeared when it did.

Now an upper-class culture that produced *Absalom and Achitophel, The Character of a Trimmer,* Dryden's critical prefaces and Locke's *Second Treatise of Government,* may have been limited, but it was not altogether decadent. If the drama is inferior it is not because it represents—by Elizabethan standards—a limited culture, but because it represents contemporary culture so inadequately; it has no significant relation with the best thought of the time. Heroic tragedy is decadent because it is factitious; it substitutes violent emotionalism for emotion, the purple patch for poetry, and its rhetoric, unlike Elizabethan dramatic rhetoric, has no connexion with the congenial non-dramatic modes of the age; it is artificial in a completely damaging sense, *and by contemporary standards.* If we look for an early illustration of the bad mid-eighteenth-century conception of poetry as

---

[3] *The History of the Royal Society of London: Spingarn, Critical Essays of the Seventeenth Century,* Vol. II, pp. 112 ff.

something applied from the outside[4] we find it in Dryden's verse plays, where he adopts canons of style that he would not have dreamed of applying—apart from his Odes—in his non-dramatic verse. Tragedy, he said, "is naturally pompous and magnificent." Nothing in English literature is more surprising—if we stop to consider—than the complete discrepancy between the sinewy ease of Dryden's satires and the stiff opaqueness of his dramatic verse; and "the lofty style," since it cannot modulate, is always coming down with a bump.

> I'm pleased and pained, since first her eyes I saw,
> As I were stung with some tarantula.
> Arms, and the dusty field, I less admire,
> And soften strangely in some new desire;
> Honor burns in me not so fiercely bright,
> But pales as fires when mastered by the light:
> Even while I speak and look, I change yet more,
> And now am nothing that I was before.
> I'm numbed, and fixed, and scarce my eyeballs move;
> I fear it is the lethargy of love![5]

It is only in the easy strength of occasional lines ("A good, luxurious, palatable faith") that we hear his natural voice. In the plays as a whole—each made up of a succession of "great" moments and heroic postures—the "nature" that is "wrought up to a higher pitch"[6] bears little resemblance to the Nature that was to figure so largely in the Augustan code.

This, or a similar account, would probably be accepted by all critics of the Restoration heroic play. What is not commonly recognized (it is, at all events, not said) is that the comedy of manners exhibits a parallel attenuation and enfeeblement of what the age, taken as a whole, had to offer. I am not, for the moment, referring to the moral or social code expressed. The observation to start from is that the prose in which Restoration comedy is written—select which dramatist you like—is poor and inexpressive in comparison with the staple non-dramatic prose.

Congreve is usually accepted as the most brilliant stylist of the

---

[4] ". . . enriching every subject (otherwise dry and barren) with a pomp of diction and luxuriant harmony of numbers."—Gray's note to *The Progress of Poesy*, 1754.

[5] *The Conquest of Granada*, Part I, III, i.

[6] ". . . the nature of a serious play; this last is indeed the representation of nature, but 'tis nature wrought up to a higher pitch."—*Of Dramatic Poesy*. The final paragraph of the Preface to *Religio Laici* has some interesting remarks in this connexion; e.g. "The florid, elevated, and figurative way is for the passions."

five or six comic dramatists who count. But place beside the extract quoted from Halifax a passage or two from *Love for Love* or *The Way of the World* (it makes no difference whether the speaker is Scandal or Mirabell), and Congreve's style shows as nerveless in the comparison:

A mender of reputations! ay, just as he is a keeper of secrets, another virtue that he sets up for in the same manner. For the rogue will speak aloud in the posture of a whisper; and deny a woman's name, while he gives you the marks of her person: he will forswear receiving a letter from her, and at the same time show you her hand in the superscription; and yet perhaps he has counterfeited the hand too, and sworn to a truth; but he hopes not to be believed; and refuses the reputation of a lady's favour, as a doctor says *No* to a bishopric, only that it may be granted him. In short, he is a public professor of secrecy, and makes proclamation that he holds private intelligence. A. To give t'other his due, he has something of good nature, and does not always want wit.
B. Not always: but as often as his memory fails him, and his common-place of comparisons. He is a fool with a good memory, and some few scraps of other folks' wit. He is one whose conversation can never be approved, yet it is now and then to be endured. He had indeed one good quality, he is not exceptious; for he so passionately affects the reputation of understanding raillery, that he will construe an affront into a jest; and call down-right rudeness and ill language, satire and fire.

This reminds me of Arnold's definition of Macaulayese, "The external characteristic being a hard metallic movement with nothing of the soft play of life, and the internal characteristic being a perpetual semblance of hitting the right nail on the head without the reality." Both construction and movement are so far from being expressive *of* anything in particular that the main function of some words is, it seems, to complete an antithesis or to display a riddling wit.[7] The verbal pattern appears at times to be completely unrelated to a mode of perceiving. The passages quoted have an air of preening themselves on their acute discriminations, but the antitheses are mechanical, and the pattern is monotonously repeated: "She has beauty enough to make any man think she has wit; and complaisance enough not to contradict him who should tell her so"—the common form soon loses the sting of surprise. Burnet can write in an antithetical style which also penetrates:

---

[7] *The Old Bachelor* shows the riddles in the process of manufacture. *Bellmour:* He is the drum to his own praise—the only implement of a soldier he resembles; like that, being full of blustering noise and emptiness. *Sharper:* And like that, of no use but to be beaten, etc.

And tho' he desired to become absolute, and to overturn both our religion and our laws, yet he would neither run the risk, nor give himself the trouble, which so great a design required. He had an appearance of gentleness in his outward deportment: but he seemed to have no bowels nor tenderness in his nature: and in the end of his life he became cruel.[8]

The nearest approach to subtlety that Congreve's style allows is represented by such things as this:

FAINALL   You are a gallant man, Mirabell; and though you may have cruelty enough not to satisfy a lady's longing, you have too much generosity not to be tender of her honour. Yet you speak with an indifference which seems to be affected, and confesses you are conscious of a negligence.

MIRABELL   You pursue the argument with a distrust that seems to be un-affected, and confess you are conscious of a concern for which the lady is more indebted to you than is your wife.

It isn't really, very subtle. As for the "wit," when it isn't merely verbal and obvious ("Fruitful, the head fruitful;—that bodes horns; the fruit of the head is horns," etc.) it is hopelessly dependent on convention.

She that marries a fool, Sir Sampson, forfeits the reputation of her honesty or understanding: and she that marries a very witty man is a slave to the severity and insolent conduct of her husband. I should like a man of wit for a lover, because I would have such a man in my power; but I would no more be his wife than his enemy. For his malice is not a more terrible consequence of his aversion than his jealousy is of his love.

An intelligent husband, you see, must be jealous; take away that entertaining assumption and the point is blunted. Halifax is a witty writer, but his wit springs naturally from the situation he is concerned with and illuminates it. "A partner in government is so unnatural a thing that it is a squint-eyed allegiance which must be paid to such a double-bottomed monarchy." [9] Congreve's wit is entirely self-regarding.

If there were space to discuss the manner of Wycherley, Etherege and Vanbrugh, it is a similar account that would have to be given. I am not suggesting that they write in a completely indistinguishable common mode (though they all have passages that might come from any play); but in essentials—in the way in which they use their similes and antitheses, in the conception of "style" and "wit" that they exhibit—they all stand together. Not one of them has achieved a genuinely sensitive and individual mode of expression; and in each the

---

[8] Quote from Professor Nichol Smith's excellent anthology, *Characters from the Histories and Memoirs of the Seventeenth Century* (Clarendon Press).

[9] Also from *The Character of a Trimmer*:—". . . the indecent courtship of some silken divines, who, one would think, did practise to bow at the altar, only to learn to make the better legs at Court."

pattern of the prose inhibits any but the narrowest—and the most devastatingly *expected*—response. That, I should claim, is the judgment to which an analysis of their prose inevitably leads. The trouble is not that the Restoration comic writers deal with a limited number of themes, but that they bring to bear a miserably limited set of attitudes. And these, in turn, are factitious to exactly the same degree as the prose is artificial and non-representative of the current non-dramatic medium.

II

Apart from the presentation of incidental and unrelated "wit" (which soon becomes as tiring as the epigrams of the "good talker"), Restoration comedy has two main interests—the behaviour of the polite and of pretenders to politeness, and some aspects of sexual relationships. Critics have made out a case for finding in one or other of these themes a unifying principle and a serious base for the comedy of manners. According to Miss Lynch, the "thoroughly conventionalized social mode" of the courtly circle "was discovered to have manifestly comic aspects, both when awkwardly misinterpreted, and when completely fulfilled through personalities to which, however, it could not give complete expression," [10] and both these discrepancies were exploited by Etherege and his successors. Bonamy Dobrée, attributing to the comic dramatists "a deep curiosity, and a desire to try new ways of living," finds that "the distinguishing characteristic of Restoration comedy down to Congreve is that it is concerned with the attempt to rationalize sexual relationships. It is this that makes it different from any other comedy that has ever been written. . . . It said in effect, 'Here is life lived upon certain assumptions; see what it becomes.' It also dealt, as no other comedy has ever done, with a subject that arose directly out of this, namely sex-antagonism, a consequence of the experimental freedom allowed to women, which gave matter for some of its most brilliant scenes." [11]

These accounts, as developed, certainly look impressive, and if Restoration comedy really answered to them—if it had something fresh and penetrating to say on sex and social relations—there would be no need to complain, even if one found the "solutions" distasteful. But Miss Lynch's case, at all events, depends on a vigorous reading into the plays of values which are not there, values which could not possibly be expressed, in fact, in the prose of any of the dramatists. (The candid reader can turn up the passages selected by Miss Lynch

[10] K. M. Lynch, *The Social Mode of Restoration Comedy*, p. 216.
[11] Bonamy Dobrée, *Restoration Comedy*, pp. 22–23.

in support of her argument, and see if they are not all in the factitious, superficial mode that I have described.)

We may consider, by way of illustration, Etherege's *The Man of Mode*. When the play opens, Dorimant ("the finest of all fine gentlemen in Restoration comedy") is trying to rid himself of an old mistress, Mrs. Loveit, before taking up with a new, Bellinda, whilst Young Bellair, in love with Emilia, is trying to find some way out of marrying Harriet, an heiress whom his father has brought to town for him. The entertainment is made up of these two sets of complications, together with an exhibition of the would-be modishness of Sir Fopling Flutter. Events move fast. After a night spent in various sociabilities Dorimant keeps an appointment with Bellinda at 5 A.M. Letting her out of his lodgings an hour or so later, and swearing to be discreet "By all the Joys I have had, and those you keep in store," he is surprised by his companions, and in the resulting confusion Bellinda finds herself paying an unwilling visit to Mrs. Loveit. Dorimant appears and is rated by the women before he "flings off." Meanwhile Young Bellair and Emilia have secretly married. Dorimant, his equanimity recovered, turns up for the exposé, followed by his mistresses. The lovers are forgiven, the mistresses are huddled off the stage, and it is decided that Dorimant, who, the previous day, had ingratiated himself with Harriet's mother, and whose "soul has quite given up her liberty," shall be allowed to pay court to the heiress.

It seems to me that what the play provides—apart from the briskly handled intrigue—is a demonstration of the physical stamina of Dorimant. But Miss Lynch sees further. For her, Dorimant is "the fine flowering of Restoration culture." Illustrating her theory of the double standard, she remarks: "We laugh at Sir Fopling Flutter because he so clumsily parodies social fashions which Dorimant interprets with unfailing grace and distinction. We laugh at Dorimant because his assumed affectation admits of so poor and incomplete an expression of an attractive and vigorous personality." [12] The "unfailing grace and distinction" are perhaps not much in evidence in Dorimant's spiteful treatment of Mrs. Loveit; [13] but even if we ignore those brutish scenes we are forced to ask, How do we know that there is this

---

[12] *The Social Mode of Restoration Comedy*, p. 181.

[13] See II, ii, and V, i, where Dorimant, trying to force a quarrel with Mrs. Loveit, attributes to her a fondness for Sir Fopling. The first of these scenes was too much for Etherege, and he makes Bellinda say:

> He's given me the proof which I desired of his love,
> But 'tis a proof of his ill nature too.
> I wish I had not seen him use her so.

But this is soon forgotten, and we are not, of course, called on to register an unfavourable judgment of Dorimant.

"attractive and vigorous personality" beneath the conventional forms? Dorimant's intrigues are of no more human significance than those of a barn-yard cock, and as for what Miss Lynch calls "his really serious affair with Harriet" (I feel this deserves a *sic*), it is purely theatrical, and the "pangs of love" are expressed in nothing but the conventional formulae: "She's gone, but she has left a pleasing Image of herself behind that wanders in my Soul." The answer to the question posed is that Miss Lynch's account is a mere assumption. Nothing that Dorimant actually *says* will warrant it—and nothing in the whole of Restoration comedy—in the words actually spoken—allows us a glimpse of those other "personalities" to which the conventional social modes "could not give complete expression." The "real values" [14] simply are not there.

A minor point can be made in passing. It is just possible to claim that Restoration comedy contains "social criticism" in its handling of "the vulgar." "Come Mr. Sharper," says Congreve's Belinda, "you and I will take a turn, and laugh at the vulgar; both the great vulgar and the small," and Etherege's Lady Townley expresses the common attitude of the polite towards the social nuisances: "We should love wit, but for variety be able to divert ourselves with the extravagancies of those who want it." The butts, unfortunately, are only shown as fools by the discrepancy between their ambitions and their achievements, not because their ambitions are puerile. The subject is hardly worth discussing, since it is obviously nothing but an easily satisfied sense of superiority that is diverted by the "variety" of a constant succession of Dapperwits, Froths and Fopling Flutters. "When a humour takes in London," Tom Brown remarked, "they ride it to death ere they leave it. The primitive Christians were not persecuted with half that variety as the poor unthinking beaus are tormented with upon the theatre . . . A huge great muff, and a gaudy ribbon hanging at a bully's backside, is an excellent jest, and new-invented curses, as, Stap my vitals, damn my diaphragm, slit my wind pipe, sink me ten thousand fathom deep, rig up a new beau, though in the main 'tis but the same everlasting coxcomb." [15]

III

In the matter of sexual relations Restoration comedy is entirely dominated by a narrow set of conventions. The objection that it is only cer-

---

[14] "The love affairs of Courtal and Ariana, Freeman and Gatty [in *She Wou'd if She Cou'd*] are similarly embarrassed by social convention. . . . The conduct of these polite lovers acquires comic vitality through the continually suggested opposition of artificial and real values."—*Op. cit.*, p. 152.

[15] Tom Brown, Works, Vol. III, *Amusements Comical and Serious,* "At the Playhouse," p. 39.

tain characters, not the dramatists themselves, who accept them can be more freely encountered when the assumptions that are expressed most frequently have been briefly illustrated.

The first convention is, of course, that constancy in love, especially in marriage, is a bore. Vanbrugh, who was the most uneasy if not the most honest of the comic dramatists (I think that in *The Provok'd Wife* he shows as unusually honest), unambiguously attributes this attitude to Sir John Brute:

> What cloying meat is love—when matrimony's the sauce to it! Two years marriage has debauch'd my five senses. . . . No boy was ever so weary of his tutor, no girl of her bib, no nun of doing penance, or old maid of being chaste, as I am of being married. Sure there's a secret curse entail'd upon the very name of wife!
>
> The woman's well enough; she has no vice that I know of, but she's a wife, and—damn a wife! [16]

What Vanbrugh saw as a fit sentiment for Sir John had by that time (1697) served the Restoration stage—without change—for thirty years. In *She Wou'd if She Cou'd* Etherege had exhibited Sir Oliver Cockwood in an identical vein: "A pox of this tying man and woman together, for better, for worse." "To have a mistress love thee entirely" is "a damn'd trouble." "There are sots that would think themselves happy in such a Lady; but to a true bred Gentleman all lawful solace is abomination." [17] If Sir Oliver is a fool it is only because he is a trifle gross in his expression. "If you did but know, Madam," says the polite Freeman, "what an odious thing it is to be thought to love a Wife in good Company." [18] And the convention is constantly turning up in Congreve. "There is no creature perfectly civil but a husband," explains Mrs. Frail, "for in a little time he grows only rude to his wife, and that is the highest good breeding, for it begets his civility to other people." [19] "Marry her! Marry her!" Fainall advises Mirabell, "Be half as well acquainted with her charms, as you are with her defects, and my life on't, you are your own man again." [20] And Witwoud: "A wit should not more be sincere than a woman constant; one argues a decay of parts, as t'other of beauty." [21] Appetite, it seems (and this is the second assumption), needs perpetually fresh stimulus. This is the faith of Rhodophil in *Marriage à la Mode* and of Constant in *The Provok'd Wife*, as well as of Wycherley's old procuress, Mrs. Joyner. "If our wives would suffer us but now and then to make

---

[16] *The Provok'd Wife*, I, i, II, i.
[17] *She Wou'd if She Cou'd*, I, i; III, iii.
[18] *Ibid.*, III, iii.
[19] *Love for Love*, I, ii.
[20] *The Way of the World*, I, ii.
[21] *Ibid.*

excursions," Rhodophil explains to Palamede, "the benefit of our variety would be theirs; instead of one continued, lazy, tired love, they would, in their turns, have twenty vigorous, fresh, and active lovers." [22] "Would anything but a madman complain of uncertainty?" asks Congreve's Angelica, for "security is an insipid thing, and the overtaking and possessing of a wish, discovers the folly of the chase." [23] And Fainall, in *The Way of the World,* speaks for a large class when he hints at a liking for sauce—a little gentleman's relish—to his seductions: "I'd no more play with a man that slighted his ill fortune than I'd make love to a woman who under-valued the loss of her reputation." [24] Fainall, of course, is what he is, but the attitude that makes sexual pleasure "the bliss," that makes woman "delicious"— something to be savoured—as well as "damned" and "destructive," demands, for its support, "the pleasure of a chase." [25]

> Would you long preserve your lover?
> Would you still his goddess reign?
> Never let him all discover,
> Never let him much obtain.[26]

Restoration comedy used to be considered outrageously outspoken, but such stuff as this, far from being "outspoken," hovers on the outskirts of sexual relations, and sees nothing but the titillation of appetite (" 'Tis not the success," Collier observed, "but the manner of gaining it which is all in all").[27] Sex is a hook baited with tempting morsels; [28] it is a thirst quencher; [29] it is a cordial; [30] it is a dish

---

[22] *Marriage à la Mode,* II, i, Cf. *The Provok'd Wife,* III, i: *Constant,* "There's a poor sordid slavery in marriage, that turns the flowing tide of honour, and sinks us to the lowest ebb of infamy. 'Tis a corrupted soil: Illnature, sloth, cowardice, and dirt, are all its product."

[23] *Love for Love,* IV, iii.

[24] *The Way of the World,* I, 1.

[25] *The Old Bachelor,* I, i; III, ii ("O thou delicious, damned, dear destructive woman!") ; IV, ii.

[26] *Ibid.,* II, ii.

[27] *A Short View of the Profaneness and Immorality of the English Stage,* Fifth Edition, 1738, p. 116.

[28] " 'Tis true you are so eager in pursuit of the temptation, that you save the devil the trouble of leading you into it: nor is it out of discretion that you don't swallow the very hook yourselves have baited, but . . . what you meant for a whet turns the edge of your puny stomachs."—*The Old Bachelor,* I, i. "Strike Heartwell home, before the bait's worn off the hook. Age will come. He nibbled fairly yesterday, and no doubt will be eager enough to-day to swallow the temptation."—*Ibid.,* III, i.

[29] "What was my pleasure is become my duty: and I have as little stomach to her now as if I were her husband. . . . Pox on't! that a man can't drink without quenching his thirst."—*The Double Dealer,* III, i.

[30] You must get you a mistress, Rhodophil. That, indeed, is living upon cordials; but as fast as one fails, you must supply it with another."—*Marriage à la Mode,* I, i.

to feed on; [31] it is a bunch of grapes; [32] it is anything but sex. (This, of course, explains why some people can combine a delighted approval of Restoration comedy with an unbalanced repugnance for such modern literature as deals sincerely and realistically with sexual relationships.)

Now the objection referred to above was that sentiments such as these are not offered for straightforward acceptance. Many of them are attributed to characters plainly marked as Wicked (Maskwell, for example, is the black-à-vised villain of melodrama), or, more frequently, as trivial, and the dramatist can therefore dissociate himself. He may even be engaged in showing his audience the explicit, logical consequences of the half-conscious premises on which they base their own lives, saying, as Mr. Dobrée has it, "Here is life lived upon certain assumptions; see what it becomes." To this there are several answers. The first is that reflexions of the kind that I have quoted are indistinguishable in tone and style from the general epigrammatic stock-in-trade (the audience was not altogether to be blamed if, as Congreve complained, they could not at first "distinguish betwixt the character of a Witwoud and a Lovewit"); and they are largely "exhibited," just as all the self-conscious witticisms are exhibited, for the sake of their immediate "comic" effect. One has only to note the laughter of a contemporary audience at a revival, and the places where the splutters occur, to realize how much of the fun provides a rather gross example of tendency wit.[33] The same attitudes, moreover, are manipulated again and again, turning up with the state monotony of jokes on postcards, and the play that is made with them demands only the easiest, the most superficial, response. But it is, after all, useless to argue about the degree of detachment, the angle at which these attitudes and assumptions are presented. As soon as one selects

---

[31] "Because our husbands cannot feed on one dish, therefore we must be starved."—*Ibid.*, III, i.

[32] "The only way to keep us new to one another, is never to enjoy, as they keep grapes, by hanging them upon a line; they must touch nothing, if you would preserve them fresh."—*Ibid.*, V, i.

[33] The Freudian "censor" is at times projected in the form of the stage puritan. The plays written soon after the Commonwealth period appealed to Royalist prejudice by satirizing the "seemingly precise"; and even later, when "the bonfires of devotion," "the bellows of zeal," were forgotten, a good deal of the self-conscious swagger of indecency seems to have been directed against "our protestant husbands," city merchants, aldermen and the like; the "daring" effect was intensified by postulating a shockable audience somewhere—not necessarily in the theatre. Not that the really obscene jokes were merely bravado: Collier quite rightly remarked that "the modern poets seem to use smut as the old ones did Machines, to relieve a fainting situation."—*A Short View*, Fifth Edition, p. 4.

a particular comedy for that exercise one realizes that all is equally grist to the mill and that the dramatist (there is no need, here, to make distinctions) has no coherent attitude of his own. A consistent artistic purpose would not be content to express itself in a style that allows so limited, so local an effect.

But it is the triviality that one comes back to. In Dryden's *Marriage à la Mode* the characters accept the usual conventions: constancy is dull, and love only thrives on variety.

PALAMEDE   O, now I have found it! you dislike her for no other reason but because she's your wife.

RHODOPHIL   And is not that enough? All that I know of her perfections now, is only by memory . . . At last we arrived at that point, that there was nothing left in us to make us new to one another . . .

PALAMEDE   The truth is, your disease is very desperate; but, though you cannot be cured, you may be patched up a little; you must get you a mistress, Rhodophil. That, indeed, is living upon cordials; but, as fast as one fails, you must supply it with another.

The mistress that Rhodophil selects is Melanthra, whom Palamede is to marry; Palamede falls in love with Doralice, Rhodophil's wife, and the ensuing complications provide sufficient entertainment (the grotto scene, III, ii, is really funny). Mr. Dobrée, however, regards the play as a witty exposure of the impossibility of rationalizing sex relations, as Palamede and Rhodophil attempt to rationalize them. Dryden "laughs morality back into its rightful place, as the scheme which ultimately makes life most comfortable." [34] But what Dryden actually does is to *use* the conventions for the amusement they afford, not to examine them. The level at which the play works is fairly indicated by the opening song:

> Why should a foolish marriage vow,
>   Which long ago was made,
> Oblige us to each other now,
>   When passion is decayed?
> We loved, and we loved, as long as we could,
>   'Till our love was loved out in us both;
> But our marriage is dead, when the pleasure is fled:
>   'Twas pleasure first made it an oath.
>
> If I have pleasures for a friend
>   And further love in store,
> What wrong has he, whose jobs did end,

---

[34] *Restoration Comedy*, p. 133.

> And who could give no more?
> 'Tis a madness that he should be jealous of me,
>   Or that I should bar him of another:
> For all we can gain, is to give ourselves pain,
>   When neither can hinder the other.

The lovers make no attempt to "rationalize sex" for the simple reason that genuine sexual feelings no more enter into the play as a whole than feelings of any kind enter into the song. (The obviously faked emotions of the heroic plot are, after all, relevant—and betraying.) And according to Mr. Dobrée, "In one sense the whole idea of Restoration comedy is summed up in the opening scene of *Marriage à la Mode*.[35]

In a sense, too, Mr. Dobrée is right. Restoration comedy nowhere provides us with much more of the essential stuff of human experience than we have there. Even Congreve, by common account the best of the comic writers, is no exception. I have said that his verbal pattern often seems to be quite unrelated to an individual mode of perceiving. At best it registers a very limited mode. Restoration prose is all "social" in its tone, implications and general tenor, but Congreve's observation is *merely* of the public surface. And Congreve's, too, relies on the conventional assumptions. In *The Way of the World*, it is true, they are mainly given to the bad and the foolish to express: it is Fainall who discourses on the pleasures of disliking one's wife, and Witwoud who maintains that only old age and ugliness ensure constancy. And Mirabell, who is explicitly opposed to some aspects of contemporary manners, goes through the common forms in a tone of rather weary aloofness: "I wonder, Fainall, that you who are married, and of consequence should be discreet, will suffer your wife to be of such a party." But Congreve himself is not above raising a cheap snigger; [36] and, above all, the characters with some life in them have nothing to fall back on—nothing, that is, except the conventional, and conventionally limited, pleasures of sex. Millamant, who says she loathes the country and hates the town, expects to draw vitality from the excitement of incessant solicitation:

I'll be solicited to the very last, nay, and afterwards . . . I should think I was poor and had nothing to bestow, if I were reduced to an inglorious ease, and freed from the agreeable fatigues of solicitation. . . . Oh, I hate a lover that can dare to think he draws a moment's air, independent of the

---

[35] *Ibid.*, p. 106.
[36]   Ay there's my grief; that's the sad change of life,
          To lose my title, and yet keep my wife.
                              The Way of the World, II, ii.

bounty of his mistress. There is not so impudent a thing in nature, as the saucy look of an assured man, confident of success. The pedantic arrogance of a very husband has not so pragmatical an air.

Everyone seems to have found Millamant intelligent and attractive, but her attitude is not far removed from that expressed in

> Would you long preserve your lover?
> Would you still his goddess reign?

and she shares with characters who are decidedly not attractive a disproportionate belief in "the pleasure of a chase." Which is not surprising in view of her other occupations and resources; visiting, writing and receiving letters, tea-parties and small talk make up a round that is never for a moment enlivened by the play of genuine intelligence.[37] And although Congreve recognizes, at times, the triviality of his characters,[38] it is to the world whose confines were the Court, the drawing-room, the play-house and the park—a world completely lacking the real sophistication and self-knowledge that might, in some measure, have redeemed it—that he limits his appeal.

It is, indeed, hard to resist the conclusion that "society"—the smart town society that sought entertainment at the theatres—was fundamentally bored.[39] In *The Man of Mode* Emilia remarks of Medley, "I love to hear him talk o' the intrigues, let 'em be never so dull in themselves, he'll make 'em pleasant i' the relation," and the idiotic conversation that follows (ii, i), affording us a glimpse of what Miss Lynch calls "the most brilliant society which Restoration comedy has to offer," [40] suggests in more than one way how badly society *needed* to be entertained. It is the boredom—the constant need for titillation —that helps to explain not only the heroic "heightening" of emotion, but the various scenic effects, the devices of staging and costume that became popular at this period. (Charles II "almost died of laughing"

---

[37] As Lady Brute remarks. "After all, a woman's life would be a dull business, if it were not for the men . . . We shou'd never blame Fate for the shortness of our days; our time would hang wretchedly upon our hands."—*The Provok'd Wife*, III, iii.

[38] *Mirabell:* You had the leisure to entertain a herd of fools; things who visit you from their excessive idleness; bestowing on your easiness that time which is the encumbrance of their lives. How can you find delight in such society?—*The Way of the World*, II, i.

[39] The constitution, habits and demands of the theatre audience are admirably illustrated by Alexandre Beljame in that neglected classic of scholarship, *Le Public et les Hommes de Lettres en Angleterre au Dix-Huitième Siècle, 1660-1740.* See also C. V. Deane, *Dramatic Theory and the Rhymed Heroic Play,* Chapter I, Section 6.

[40] *The Social Mode of Restoration Comedy,* p. 177.

at Nell Gwynn's enormous hat.) The conventions—of sexual pursuit, and so on—were an attempt to make life interesting—an impossible job for those who were aware of so limited a range of human potentialities.

The dominating mood of Restoration comedy is, by common account, a cynical one. But one cannot even say that there is here, in contrast to naïve Romantic fervours, the tough strength of disillusion. If—recognizing that there is a place in the educational process for, say, La Rochefoucauld—one finds the "cynicism" of the plays distasteful, it is because it is easy and superficial; the attitudes that we are presented with are based on so meagre an amount of observation and experience. Thus, "Elle retrouvait dans l'adultère toutes les platitudes du mariage" [41] has, superficially, much the same meaning as, "I find now, by sad experience, that a mistress is much more changeable than a wife, and after a little time too, grows full as dull and insignificant." But whereas the first sentence has behind it the whole of *Madame Bovary*, the second comes from *Sir Martin Marall*, which (although Dryden shares the honours with the Duke of Newcastle) is perhaps the stupidest play I have ever read, and the context is imbecility.

But the superficiality is betrayed at every turn—by the obvious rhythms of the interspersed songs, as well as by the artificial elegance of the prose. And the cynicism is closely allied with—merges into—sentimentality. One thinks of the sentimentally conceived Fidelia in the resolutely "tough" *Plain Dealer;* and there is no doubt that the audience was meant to respond sympathetically when, at the end of *Love for Love,* Angelica declared her love for Valentine: "Had I the world to give you, it could not make me worthy of so generous a passion; here's my hand, my heart was always yours, and struggled very hard to make this utmost trial of your virtue." There is, of course, a good deal of loose emotion in the heroic plays, written—it is useful to remember—for the same audience:

> I'm numbed, and fixed, and scarce my eyeballs move;
> I fear it is the lethargy of love!
> 'Tis he; I feel him now in every part:
> Like a new lord he vaunts about my heart;
> Surveys, in state, each corner of my breast,
> While poor fierce I, that was, am dispossessed. [42]

---

[41] [She found in adultery all the platitudes of marriage. From Flaubert's *Madame Bovary*.]

[42] *The Conquest of Granada*, Part I, III, i.

> A secret pleasure trickles through my veins:
> It works about the inlets of my soul,
> To feel thy touch, and pity tempts the pass:
> But the tough metal of my heart resists;
> 'Tis warmed with the soft fire, not melted down.[43]

"Feeling," in Dryden's serious plays, is fairly represented by such passages as these, and Dryden, we know, was not alone in admiring the Fletcherian "pathos." But it is the lyric verse of the period that provides the strongest confirmatory evidence of the kind of bad taste that is in question. It is not merely that in Etherege, Sedley and Dorset the feelings comes from much nearer the surface than in the Metaphysical and the Caroline poets, intellectual "wit" no longer strengthens and controls the feeling. Conventional attitudes are rigged out in a conventional vocabulary and conventional images. (The stock outfit—the "fair eyes" that "wound," the "pleasing pains," the "sighs and tears," the "bleeding hearts" and "flaming darts"—can be studied in any anthology.[44]) There is, in consequence, a pervasive strain of sentimental vulgarity.

> Farewell, ungrateful traitor!
>   Farewell, my perjured swain
> Let never injured creature
>   Believe a man again.
> The pleasure of possessing
> Surpasses all expressing,
> But 'Tis too short a blessing,
>   And love too long a pain.
>
>   . . . . .
>
> The passion you pretended,
>   Was only to obtain;
> But when the charm is ended,
>   The charmer you disdain.
> Your love by ours we measure
> Till we have lost our treasure,
> But dying is a pleasure
>   When living is a pain.

This piece of music-hall sentiment comes from Dryden's *The Spanish Friar,* and it does not stand alone. The mode that was to produce,

---

[43] *Don Sebastian,* III, i.

[44] See, for example, Aphra Behn's "Love in fantastic triumph sate," Buckingham's *To His Mistress* ("Phyllis, though your all powerful charms"), Dryden's "Ask not the cause why sullen spring," and "Ah, how sweet it is to love," and Sedley's *To Chloris*—all in *The Oxford Book of English Verse,* or Ault's *Seventeenth Century Lyrics.*

among other things of equal merit; "When lovely woman stoops to folly," had its origin in the lyrics of the Restoration period. Most of these were written by the group connected with the theatres, and they serve to underline the essential criticism of the plays. The criticism that defenders of Restoration comedy need to answer is not that the comedies are "immoral," but that they are trivial, gross and dull.

Shaw's Abstract Clarity*

REED WHITTEMORE

Those of you who have taken any courses here in English literature—and I believe a number of you have—have surely at one time or another used, and therefore abused, that difficult word, Realism. For we all abuse it, whether we naively rub it, as Aladdin rubbed his lamp, hoping thereby to produce the jinni of Ernest Hemingway, or like grand metaphysicians toy with it by conjuring up the likes of Plato, Berkeley and Dr. Johnson. It seems to be a word made to be abused, and sometimes I think we would be better off if we did not regard it as a word at all but as a lower form of utterance, a noise perhaps, like a pig's grunt or a dog's bark, that we just have to give off with on certain literary occasions. There are of course a number of other words or grunts like it—romanticism, transcendentalism, neoclassicism, even criticism—but no other in our time has quite the carrying power, on a still night, of Realism.

Realism—"the doctrine that universals exist outside the mind."—Or, in literature, "the theory that art or literature should conform to nature or to real life."—Or, again in literature, "representation without idealization." Such definitions give resonance to the original grunt—so we may at least begin with them. You will note that all of them suggest their opposite—that is, "representation without idealization" suggests that there is something (something, presumably, rather ridiculous) that we can call "representation with idealization." Similarly, if there is a theory that art should "conform to real life," there is also, presumably, a theory that art does not need to conform to real life. And, again, if there is a doctrine that universals exist

* Reed Whittemore, "Shaw's Abstract Clarity," *Tulane Drama Review*, Vol. 2, No. 1 (November, 1957), pp. 46–57. (A lecture delivered at Carleton College, February 27, 1957.)

415

outside the mind, then there must be a doctrine that universals exist
inside. And indeed there is. In other words our understanding of the
word "realism," through these definitions, is contingent upon our
understanding of its assumed opposite, just as our understanding of
the word "front" depends upon our knowing, also, "back"; "old" depends upon our knowing, also "young"; and "high" depends upon our
knowing, also, "low."

Now I suspect that any word, and in fact any *thing,* comes into
the world of our understanding through some sort of process of comparison, but the comparisons involved are not always neat. Thus "animal" does not have as its opposite, necessarily, "spiritual"—animal
is also relatable or comparable to bird or reptile, vegetable or mineral;
or to specific animals: bear, bison, behemoth. Only when the word
"animal" is thought of abstractly as the essence of fleshiness do we
conjure up "spiritual" as its opposite.

I am not against the process of abstraction. How could I be?—
I don't understand it. Nor do I propose to discuss that process here.
All I wish to point out is what should be obvious but sometimes
isn't—that much of the neatness, the tidiness of our thinking about
realism and idealism, naturalism and romanticism is very arbitrary,
just as the abstracting of the word "animal" to mean the opposite
of "spiritual" is arbitrary. We *make* the neatness; we *make* the dualism; and having made it we sometimes forget that we have.

And Mr. Shaw? What has he to do with all this? I'm not sure. I
know that he is not frequently labelled as a realist. He is more apt
to be thought of as a playwright of ideas or a playwright of thesis
plays—and everybody knows that ideas and theses are not real. Furthermore I understand from Brooks Atkinson that thesis plays are no
longer fashionable now, which is even worse. At any rate, I suppose
we think of Shaw as a playwright of ideas because his characters are
so infernally talkative and because, also, they insist in talking about big
issues. Such talk is in some quarters regarded as quite the opposite of realism, realism consisting, indeed, of the absence of ideas and
the presence, instead, of young, strong, incoherent bodies who till the
earth and make love in blue jeans under the pines. Thus this familiar
dialogue in *Farewell to Arms* might be called realistic:

> "What's the matter, Catherine?"
> "Nothing. Nothing's the matter."
> "Yes there is."
> "No nothing. Really nothing."
> "I know there is. Tell me, darling. You can tell me."
> "It's nothing."

"Tell me."

"I don't want to. I'm afraid I'll make you unhappy or worry you."

"No it won't."

"You're sure? It doesn't worry me but I'm afraid to worry you."

"It won't if it doesn't worry you."

"I don't want to tell."

"Tell it."

"Do I have to?"

"Yes."

If this is realism, then surely Shaw is mightily unrealistic. And yet I think he would not like to be denied as a realist, and to demonstrate what I mean let me take as a preliminary text a description by Shaw of how he as a child reacted to his elders' religious designs upon him:

I wanted to get at the facts. I was prepared for the facts being unflattering: had I not already faced the fact that instead of being a fallen angel I was first cousin to a monkey.

This is a characteristically flip Shavian statement, and I think it would be a mistake therefore to take it as gospel. Still, the word "fact" is repeated three times in it, and it is used by Shaw as one of those words with an opposite—in this case, "fiction." Fact vs. fiction. Up to this point in his life, he is saying, his elders had provided him with fictions only, and he therefore wanted, in contrast, facts. Nor is the fact vs. fiction dualism the only one in the passage —for he says that one of the facts he had already "gotten at" was the fact that he was not a fallen angel but first cousin to a monkey. This is, as I understand it, merely Shaw's rendering of the animal-spiritual dualism I have already mentioned. So I am inclined to think that even if we take the passage at a discount, assuming that Shaw would have been glad to elaborate upon it and qualify it endlessly, we can still say of it, first, that in it he likes to think of himself as a realist, and, second, that he thinks of realism as a good dualist is apt to, that is, as a force facing its opposite in the universe, namely, illusion. Let me provide some more texts.

In *Major Barbara* the realist, the man who faces the facts is, clearly, Undershaft. Any number of passages in the play demonstrate this, but I will read you just one, where Undershaft is consoling Barbara for having lived by a fiction for so long:

Come, come, my daughter! Don't make too much of your little tinpot tragedy. What do we do here when we spend years of work and thought and thousands of pounds of solid cash on a new gun or an aerial battleship that turns out just a hairsbreadth wrong after all? Scrap it. Scrap it without wasting another hour or another pound on it. Well, you have made for yourself something that you call a morality or a religion or what not. It doesn't fit the facts. Well, scrap it. Scrap it and get one that does fit. That is what is wrong with the world at present. It scraps its obsolete steam engines and dynamos but it won't scrap its old prejudices and its old moralities and its old religions and its old political constitutions.

Now another text, this time from the preface to *St. Joan:*

She . . . was the first practioner of Napoleonic realism in warfare as distinguished from the sporting ransom-gambling chivalry of her time. She was the pioneer of rational dressing for women.

And finally, here is a text from *Don Juan in Hell* with which, doubtless, some of you are very familiar:

Hell is the home of the unreal and of the seekers for happiness. It is the only refuge from heaven, which is, as I tell you, the home of the masters of reality, and from earth, which is the home of the slaves of reality. The earth is a nursery in which men and women play at being heroes and heroines, saints and sinners; but they are dragged down from their fool's paradise by their bodies: hunger and cold and thirst, age and decay and disease, death above all, makes them slaves of reality: thrice a day meals must be eaten and digested: thrice a century a new generation must be engendered: ages of faith, of romance, and of science are all driven at last to have but one prayer: "Make me a healthy animal." But here you escape the tyranny of the flesh; for here you are not an animal at all: you are a ghost, an appearance, an illusion, a convention, deathless, ageless: in a word, bodiless . . . Here you call your appearance beauty, your emotions love, your sentiments heroism, your aspirations virtue, just as you did on earth; but here there are no hard facts to contradict you.

Now I confess that I am less interested in the nature of the dualism than in the fact of it. Still, from these speeches and others, I think I could readily set up two small armies of words that are constantly at war with each other in Shaw's work. One army would consist of, among others: illusion, romance, chivalry, convention, fiction, sentiment, unreason, morality. The other army would consist of, among others: facts, hard facts, actuality, reason, realism. And then if I were to attempt to reduce each one of Shaw's plays to some manifestation of the conflict between these two armies, I could probably do so. I wouldn't be knighted for doing so; I wouldn't be awarded any scholarships, prizes, plaques for doing so; for there would be nothing particularly remarkable about what I had done; I simply would have found a kind of basic formula to which Shaw, like many many other writers, was committed and with which he normally began in the construction of his plays. Some such formula obviously underlies almost any drama, drama being a conflict between forces which are somehow opposed. How, then, is Shaw different from any other playwright?—he is clearly not different if I go only this far in my study of the formula.

I want to go a little farther, though—partly because I still have about two-thirds of a lecture left to enlighten you with, and partly because I feel Shaw's formula, as he employs it, is an interesting and rather special one, one nobody else has used quite as he has, and one he probably would not have used if he had lived in another time.

Let me get into this by talking, in my own ignorant way, about his time. A long time ago I wrote a very scholarly treatise on the Haymarket riot in Chicago. The Haymarket riot took place in 1886, about the time that Shaw was becoming an active, writing Fabian. The riot involved the dropping of a bomb at a public, open-air meeting of workers who were on strike at the McCormick reaper plant. The bomb was directed not at the workers but at a squadron of police who had been sent to break up the meeting. The bomb killed one policeman; the blame for the bomb was placed upon a group of anarchists who had been preaching and printing the virtues of the planting of bombs among policemen. The anarchists were convicted; the case became a great one, and I recommend it to you whether you are historians or poets; but here I am not interested in it but in the statements of some of the anarchists after they had been convicted. These anarchists played their cards wrong from the beginning by denying the justice of the courts in which they were being tried;— by, in short, being anarchists. One of them said, after his conviction, "I do not recognize your law, jumbled together as it is by the nobodies of by-gone centuries." Another said, addressing his convictors, "You, who oppose the natural course of things, you are the real revolutionists." In other words they took a high and mighty line about the whole thing—a line hardly designed to placate court officials. In doing so they were in effect hanging themselves, but they apparently didn't care much, for, in professing to be great realists, in professing that they saw through the shams, the illusions, the falsehoods of the civilization judging them, they became passionately idealistic. They saw the whole problem very clearly in terms of principle; they were right and their opponents—and the whole tradition of law and justice by which their opponents stood—were wrong. Thus you may think of the statement, "I do not recognize your law," as either magnificent or foolhardy, but you cannot deny that it is absolute. The speaker of that statement is throwing out most of Western Culture in one breath, saying in effect that it is false and that he knows what is *not* false—that is, what is true and real.

Now the Haymarket anarchists were first-class extremists, and I certainly don't want you to think that I think they were representative of their time. But the clarity of their thinking on subjects which, I confess, I find not clear at all—the clarity of it is, I think, a characteristic of the age. I don't know whether to blame Darwin or Marx for this clarity—or Hegel or Carlyle or any of the other distinguished nineteenth century clarifiers—but at any rate the clarity was there, ready and waiting for those who needed things cleared up, that is, for those who wanted to face the facts, the hard facts about the world and not be held down by the dead hand of custom, convention, irrational faith or any of those other words in the bad army of Mr. Shaw's war. Not all thinking people, of course, accepted the new clarities, and those who did accepted them in different ways. There were the clarities of the imagists, for example, who discovered, or thought they had discovered, that certain old poetic conventions weren't poetic. There were the clarities of the writers we call naturalists,—who as I understand them thought they had discovered what was wrong with the romanticists. And there was the symbolic clarity of Conrad which did not, for the most part, create novels that a realist would call realistic but nonetheless managed to make the world of his fictions remarkably clean and symmetrical. All these clarities had perhaps, under different guises, been sent forth to illuminate the world before; but to the writers who were busy clarifying, clarity suddenly seemed to be something new under the sun. They had perhaps some of the feelings of one of the wilder of the Haymarket anarchists, T. Lizius, who wrote a letter to an anarchist newspaper as follows:

Dynamite! of all the good stuff, this is the stuff. Stuff several pounds of this sublime stuff into an inch pipe (gas or water pipe), did up both ends, insert a cap with a fuse attached, place this in the immediate neighborhood of a lot of rich loafers who live by the sweat of other people's brows, and light the fuse. A most cheerful and gratifying result will follow.

One didn't need, either, to be annoyed *merely* by rich loafers to share some of T. Lizius's feelings that a good shaking up would do the world some good. Ezra Pound, for example, whose revolutionary activities were hardly related to those of the Marxists or the Fabians or any recognizable group busy, before World War I, at social improvement—Ezra Pound took pot shots at all sizes and shapes of what he regarded as illusion. He took shots at Swinburnian poetry, Stracheyan history, Victorian morality, bourgeois practicality and almost anything else that came into his sights as a manifestation of a civilization living by false values—what he called, later, a botched civilization. He had revolutionary impulses from the beginning; he was, and remained, a kind of literary dynamiter, sharing this characteristic— and almost no other—with Shaw. It was an age for throwing out the old and bringing in the new, for pulling back curtains and exposing things, for cleaning the windows of the world's mind, or, as Shaw has Undershaft say, for scrapping things that didn't fit the facts.

I can't seem to get away from that word "facts." Hard facts. I am reminded, as I hope you are, of the hero in Conrad's novel *Victory*, Axel Heyst. Heyst was described in a number of ways at the beginning of the book, partly to confuse us and partly to indicate the complexity of the man. He was described as a utopist, as a perfect gentleman, as a spider, as a wanderer, as a devil and as a spy. But he was also described, though only in passing, as "hard facts" Heyst. I want to read you the relevant passage:

"Are you interested in . . . ?"
"Facts," broke in Heyst in his courtly voice. "There's nothing worth knowing but facts. Hard facts. Facts alone, Mr. Tesman."

and then Conrad comments:

"I don't know if old Tesman agreed with him or not, but he must have spoken about it because, for a time, our man got the name of 'Hard Facts.' He had the singular good fortune that his sayings stuck to him and became a part of his name. Thereafter he mooned about the Java Sea in some of Tesman's trading schooners, and then vanished on board an Arab ship in the direction of New Guinea."

I have often wondered who the model for Heyst was, if there was a model, for he seems to me to be a fine if trumped-up example of an intelligent pre-war European. He is a realist (if you will pardon my using the word) to the extent that he no longer accepts his world's traditional ideals; he is a utopist to the extent that he thinks he can get away from a world he does not respect. He is thus a kind of walking contradiction, as Conrad well indicates by having this hard-facts man *mooning* about the Java Sea. Now Shaw is not like Heyst at all in many ways; he was no escapist and would, I think, have been shocked to be called a Utopist. One doesn't think of Shaw as mooning about anywhere, the Java Sea or England; his mind always seemed to be facing up to things, whether they were facts or fictions, not mooning about them. Nor was he one to reject the world, even though he found fault with it; on the contrary he was a most active, gregarious man *in* the world, almost the opposite of Heyst. And yet in a way I find these two figures—one fact and one fiction—similar; and I am the more struck by their similarity because the Shaw I am talking about and the mythical Heyst are roughly contemporary (*Victory* was published in 1915, in the late middle of Shaw's career).

How are they similar? Well, both of them had an excessively clear view of what a fact is. Conrad knew this about Heyst; I don't know that Shaw knew this about Shaw. Conrad knew that Heyst was a mooner; Shaw, I am convinced, knew that Shaw was not—and yet he was a mooner, indeed he was, in the sense that he had dreamed up all his clarities; he had *made up* in his own head, with the help of Marx, Hegel, Darwin and the Coles, the neat dualisms of which I spoke earlier. Now this, I think, is what makes him, like Heyst, a walking contradiction; for all the time that he insisted he dealt with hard facts he dealt, on the contrary, with ideas. Hard facts are not clear and simple at all, mostly, as any historian, even any newspaper reporter will tell you. In the first place we never *have* all the facts; in the second place we are too frequently not sure that they *are* facts; and in the third place they are seldom "hard" in the sense of being understandable in only one, clearcut way. Ideas on the other hand may be clear and simple; and the best of them are clear and simple. They are creations of the mind, and the mind is an ordering influence, putting things neatly in cubbyholes, making it possible for an anarchist to reject the whole of western culture in a phrase and for a playwright to scrap a whole religion in a sentence. The culture won't remain rejected; the religion won't remain scrapped—but at least the possibility will have been entertained, pleasantly, *in the mind* which is where Shaw, and Heyst, really lived.

Apparently it was easier to live in the mind in the early 20th Century than it is now. Somewhat earlier I mentioned, rather fliply, Brooks Atkinson's remark that thesis plays are no longer fashionable. I suspect, despite my flipness, that there is some truth in this remark— for though I am very ignorant of our contemporary theater, I can find evidence in my own business of a comparable shift in fashions. Thus contemporary literary criticism does not have much to say about truth, beauty, reality, nature—all those wonderful abstractions that dominated and controlled the paragraphs of my predecessors—it does not, that is, have much to say about them unless it is trying to define them somehow. My own embarrassment, at the beginning of my lecture, in talking about realism at all is a small indication of the state of things. My line was that I don't know what this word means; it is too much for me; I would prefer not to discuss it in general but to get you all off reading some particular text which would perhaps give us an instance of at least *a* meaning of the word. This sounds more modern, doesn't it? It is. Abstractions, at least among literary people, are not in favor now, as some of you who are Freshmen discovered this year when you read George Orwell's piece on the decay of our language in your text, *The Province of Prose*. There, if you remember, he said,

What is above all needed is to let the meaning choose the word, and not the other way about. In prose the worst thing one can do with words is to surrender to them. When you think of a concrete object you think wordlessly, and then, if you want to describe a thing you have been visualizing, you probably hunt about till you find the exact words that seem to fit it. When you think of something abstract you are more inclined to use words from the start, and unless you make a conscious effort to prevent it, the existing dialect will come rushing in and do the job for you, at the expense of blurring or even changing your meaning.

Now I would not go so far as to say the "existing dialect" rushed in for Shaw and did his job for him; nor that he "surrendered" to such words as "realism" without putting up a good verbal fight. My thesis here is at least partly that Shaw was a tremendously clear thinker and writer, not a blurrer of meaning. But while he did not surrender to the words (what Orwell calls the "dialect") he did, I think, surrender to the logical frame in which the big words of his time appeared (what I will call the dialectic). That is, he had a much greater respect for the validity, the reality, the whatever-you-want-to-call-it of an abstract dialectic than Orwell had or, for that matter, than I have. We are a long way now from Shaw, and from Axel Heyst, as well as from the Haymarket Anarchist; our distance from them doesn't perhaps put us ahead of them, but it at least puts us in a position to see them as they could not see themselves. From this distance I confess that I have not a dialectic of my own of which I'm proud, but at least, I say, I see holes in theirs. And particularly Shaw's. Sometimes he appears as a mooner talking about hard facts, sometimes as a hard facts man talking moonshine, but in either role he fails to reconcile his difficulties, his dialetical difficulties, to my satisfaction; and the best explanation I have for him when he gets into these difficulties with me is that his fallacies were not so much his as his world's; he did not seek them; they were, unlike his greatness, thrust upon him. Let me elaborate.

He was most obviously a mooner, a walking contradiction of what he professed, when he was discussing his art. Drama is after all a kind of moonshine, as Shakespeare, Bottom, Pyramus, Thisbe and a number of others have pointed out. Now Shaw professed to be aware of this. He said, for example, at the end of his preface to *Major Barbara:*

> This play of mine, *Major Barbara,* is, I hope, both true and inspired; but whoever says that it all happened, and that faith in it and understanding of it consist in believing that it is a record of an actual occurrence, is, to speak according to Scripture, a fool and a liar, and is hereby solemnly denounced and cursed as such by me, the author, to all posterity.

I would have you note here his conventional distinction between two kinds of truth, one of which he describes as "actual occurrence" and the other of which he does not describe except as truth. From the mouth of almost any playwright except Shaw such a distinction would cause not a ripple on my placid surface. Have we not all been bred up to entertain (though we may not accept) the notion of two kinds of truth or reality, the one we see taking place (or just *being*) around us, and the other posited by dramatists, poets, philosophers, priests— all those creators of some ideal or transcendent reality they would like us to do homage to? But for Shaw to accept the notion I find hard to take. I boggle. For in his plays he does not accept the notion at all. He does not distinguish between *two* realities. He does not, for example, ask as Keats did, "Do I wake or sleep?" Or as Lear did, "Who is it that can tell me who I am?" At all times he seems to know exactly who he is, that is, what reality is really real, and so the other possibility, the opposing force in the Shavian *agon,* is not normally conceivable as a reality of another order; it is *merely* illusion, fantasy, fiction. It is therefore not really deserving of our respect, even though some fairly intelligent Shaw characters are occasionally deluded enough to believe in it. All I am saying here is that most of the time Shaw looks very much like what I suppose I must call a materialist, that is, a person whose image of reality is ultimately singular; and because his dualistic world is, in this sense, not a dualistic world at all but a singular world containing a lot of confused persons who happen to think that it's double, his art, his drama should, I think, to be consistent, *not* be aimed at revealing another order of truth or reality. Why? Because no such other order exists. And yet, in that preface to *Major Barbara,* he said that *Major Barbara* was true and inspired even though it was a fantasy.

Let me put all this differently. You are surely familiar with Aristotle. You can't help being so, even if you would like not to be. You remember then that in drama he wanted everything to be a little more than life-size, like cigarettes these days. The heightening process that he, thus, recommended is in the best tradition of our literature and drama. It is not only intelligently *discussed* by Aristotle and Sir Philip Sidney and people of that kidney, but we find it in the plays and poems themselves. For example, we find it making life eloquent and sensible (even though life isn't) in the plays of Shakespeare. And we find it, also, in Shaw, as Shaw himself says in the preface I have just read from. Thus in *Major Barbara* our great realist, Undershaft, is put at the head of a fantasy of a factory. The factory is described as the kind of factory we will have, come the Millennium, a factory where a symphony orchestra pops up and begins to play when one pushes a button, a factory full of Shinto temples, green fields, and busts of Marx, Ferdinand LaSalle, Wells and Shaw. Similarly, in *St. Joan* and in *Don Juan in Hell*, particularly the latter, the settings are anything but what we might call realistic, even though the talk is constantly of realism. Now how can Shaw constantly *talk* reality and constantly *write* theater? How can he ridicule illusions and at the same time construct illusions with such loving care?

When I was growing up—that is, about fifty years ago, but still a few years after Shaw had produced *Major Barbara*—most of my fellow literary workers at college were materialists like myself, and we faced up to the difficulty of keeping art alive, even though we didn't believe in it, by trying desperately hard *not* to produce "heightening effects." Some of the stories I wrote then I now look upon with horror—they were so real, so actual, so unheightened, so (indeed) flat, that any occasional resemblance between them and the great artistic models that lurked behind, way behind, me was purely accidental, purely an adolescent mistake on my part, for I was trying hard to avoid the models. There is something, as I see it now, faintly ridiculous about throwing away the fundamental premise about the nature of truth in art, and then continuing to try to be artistic—but at the time the humor of this somehow missed me. I was trying to write fiction which was indistinguishable from "actual occurrence" even though it was fiction, and I was ready to stand up on a platform, if asked to do so, and declare that every artist should emulate me. I wanted to carry the burden of art and light even though I thought the burden was chaff.

Ridiculous. But commonplace. Every full-blown materialist—at least the kind I am describing for you—must face this difficulty some time unless he eliminates art from his agenda entirely; for the full-blown materialist is by his convictions prohibited, as it were, from acknowl-

edging that the world of Keats' nightingale (or the world of Mr.
Undershaft) *is* a kind of reality. At best he may say that it is a
projection, an exaggeration, an interesting hypothesis about reality;
at worst he will say that it is a pleasant or unpleasant diversion *from*
reality. For, like it or not, poetry and the drama have their roots
deep in a double, not a singular earth.

Well, Shaw, as I've said, looks remarkably like a materialist, a hard
facts man, *except* in his dedication to his art. There, perversely and
happily, he is a perfectly traditional mooner. I envy him a bit for
his capacity to contradict himself—I have grown somewhat moony
myself since my salad days, but not moony enough yet, wholly to
abandon my doubts about nightingales. And that Shaw was able to
do so with one part of his mind, while holding on, in another part,
firmly to the utter ridiculousness of nightingales is, I think, just one
indication of a difference between his climate of reality and mine. He
and many of his literary contemporaries were great debunkers of old
illusions, but they continued to have faith in illusion, whether they
knew it or not.

We should be thankful for this; without such faith the plays we
have would not have been written; humanity would never have been
so neatly (and in some sense I think truly) divided between the Un-
dershafts and the Lady Britomarts; and we would as a result have
lost one of the astonishingly few English dramatists who have enjoyed
taking the world, and not the drawing room, for raw material. But
all my gratitude to Mr. Shaw and his contradictions (which I hope
you share) cannot, I think, obscure the fact—shall I say the hard
fact?—that the contradictions are there. And particularly, I think, are
the contradictions apparent when that beastly word "reality" crops
up in his plays. Then the very clarity of his distinctions between
illusory and real things points up the illusoriness of the reality he is
discussing. At least this seems to me, at this distance, to be so, though
it may not have seemed so to his contemporaries. I think you too
will find it so in *Major Barbara*, which is a fine play but an archaic
play now, a play that seems *most* unreal—that is, most like a dream
out of the past—just when it is professing to be most real, that is,
just when the great realist Undershaft is talking.

A Comic Complex and a Complex Comic*

RUBY COHN

Something old, something new,
Something borrowed, something blue.

The old wedding jingle may be used to symbolize and summarize
Beckett's work, much as he himself used the round song about the dog
in *Godot,* or Schubert's "Death and the Maiden" in *All That Fall,*
or the duet from *The Merry Widow* in *Happy Days.* At first glance,
a marriage rhyme might seem singularly inappropriate for an author
haunted by man's loneliness and alienation, and yet Beckett conveys
man's essential solitude through various couples, from Belacqua and
his sundry *amours* to Winnie-Willie of *Happy Days,* passing through
several sets of master and servant, friend and friend, Molloy and his
mother, Moran and his son, Krapp and his tape recorder.

Even the first line of the wedding rhyme, "Something old, something new," may be illustrated by a double view of a single characteristic. Thus, the illiberal jest so central to Beckett's work is at
least as old as the *Iliad,* but Beckett plays it for a new metaphysical
resonance. Similarly, man's fate is one of the oldest themes of literature, but Beckett composes in a minor key that is constantly enriched
by fresh comic overtones. Beckett's heroes are old fools in the old
fool tradition of the one who gets slapped, but Beckett inveigles us
to laugh at the slap and the slapper, as well as at the one who
gets slapped.

The Beckett hero incorporates other features of the fool tradition—

* Ruby Cohn, "A Comic Complex and a Complex Comic," in *Samuel
Beckett: The Comic Gamut* (Rutgers University Press, 1962), pp. 283–299.

427

his appearance of physical freak, his inspired idiocy that borders on wisdom, his alienation from a society that is criticized through his comic gift. And again Beckett, with comic astringency, gives new depth to these old traditions. Often a dwarf or cripple, the traditional fool is as splendid as a Greek statue by comparison with Beckett's protagonists in their various stages of disintegration. The wisdom of Beckett's heroes, bolstered by his own considerable learning, is maintained by tenacious ignorance in the face of modern stockpiling of information. Beckett's fools are alienated not only from society but from all the modern world. Beckett's buffoon rejects a social role, and yet by his fierce obsession with himself in a hostile world, he stands for every individual in that world. A sacrificial victim, Beckett's fool no longer achieves anyone's catharsis, least of all his own.

One of the best-educated men of our time, Beckett has undoubtedly read the major philosophers from Aristotle, "qui savait tout," to Sartre, possibly the "agregé de philosophie" of the French *Murphy*. He adheres to no school, denying Existentialist affiliations. Yet he has mingled and published with French Existentialists; his theater has been called a "theater of existence." [1] Like the Existentialists, Beckett is haunted by death, and his ghosts react raucously to this climactic event of human life.

Beckett's first hero, the poet Belacqua Shuah, dies quietly enough on the operating table. His second hero, Murphy, is in a rocking trance when he is burned to death in his garret retreat. Watt seems too busy to have time for death. But Beckett's French heroes long explosively for death while they endure the sentence of their lives. From Molloy, the first of the writing heroes, each of them has to earn his way to death through his works. The process of writing becomes an approach to death; composition takes place during decomposition. In living, we slowly kill ourselves; however agonizing, however farcical, life kills time. It is a cruelly comic Beckett paradox: While we live, we die; we must compose while we decompose. And faced with death, what attitude can we adopt?

Just before his fatal operation, Beckett's Belacqua ponders this question:

At this crucial point the good God came to his assistance with a phrase from a paradox of Donne: *Now among our wise men, I doubt not but many would be found, who would laugh at Heraclitus weeping, none which would*

---

[1] Jacques Guicharnaud, *Modern French Theatre from Giraudoux to Beckett* (New Haven, 1961), p. 219. The analysis of Beckett's theater is remarkably fine in this book.

weep at Democritus laughing. This was a godsend, and no error. . . . Belacqua snatched eagerly at the issue. Was it to be laughter or tears? It came to the same thing in the end, but which was it to be *now?* . . . He [Belacqua] must efface himself altogether and do the little soldier. It was this paramount consideration that made him decide in favour of Bim and Bom, Grock, Democritus, whatever you are pleased to call it. ("Yellow," 235–237)*

Even though tragic and comic "came to the same thing in the end," both Beckett and Belacqua consciously choose laughter some few hours before the latter's death. They ride in the wake of Bim and Bom, who joke about the things that other people would be shot for saying; of Democritus, the laughing philosopher of antiquity; and of Grock, the clown who mimicked human failure—"Nicht möglich."

Later Beckett heroes are less able than Belacqua to make this clear-cut choice between tears and laughter. In *Watt,* the hero's predecessor, Arsene, and his successor, Arthur, are both practiced laughers, but Watt himself alternates between smiles and tears. Moran "at the thought of the punishments Youdi might inflict . . . was seized . . . with mighty silent laughter and [his] features composed in their wonted stillness and calm." Malone, fighting the gravity into which he was born, "plays the clown." The Unnamable wonders whether his constant flow of tears can be tears of mirth at this joke of a life; later, however, he admits to weeping to keep from laughing, and he invokes Democritus as the last proper name in a comedy of namelessness. In *Godot,* it hurts Vladimir to laugh; in *Endgame,* Hamm muses, "You weep, and weep, for nothing, so as not to laugh." In *Embers,* Henry can only laugh a "long horrible laugh." The crawling creature of *Comment c'est* at first wants to laugh all the time, then only sometimes, three times out of ten, four out of fifteen, but he finally settles for "trois quatre rires réussis de ceux qui secouent un instant ressuscitent un instant puis laissent pour plus mort qu'avant" ("three four successful laughs of those that shake one an instant revive one an instant then leave one more dead than before"). Winnie asks Willie after a laugh, "How can one better magnify the Almighty than by sniggering with him at his little jokes, particularly the poorer ones?" At no time is there a hint of catharsis to be achieved through laughter, either for Beckett's characters or for us.

Of all Beckett's characters, the specialist in laughing matters is Arsene, Watt's predecessor and mentor at Mr. Knott's house. Arsene's hierarchy of laughs, "the bitter, the hollow, and the mirthless," suggests the ironic complexity of Beckett's own comic:

---

* [Page references are to "Yellow," in *More Pricks Than Kicks* (London: Chatto and Windus), 1934.]

The bitter laugh laughs at that which is not good, it is the ethical laugh. The hollow laugh laughs at that which is not true, it is the intellectual laugh. . . . But the mirthless laugh is the dianoetic laugh, down the snout— Haw!—so. It is the laugh of laughs, the *risus purus,* the laugh laughing at the laugh, the beholding, saluting of the highest joke, in a word the laugh that laughs—silence please, at that which is unhappy. (48)*

Practitioners of the *risus purus,* Beckett's heroes laugh at suffering. Like the Surrealists, they laugh helplessly at cosmically illiberal jests upon themselves or others, and like the Surrealists, too, they enter into the cruel cosmic spirit by perpetrating sadistic jokes of their own. Responding to cosmic cruelty with "black laughter," the Surrealist hero defied and transcended his fate, triumphantly expelling a laugh with his last lungful of breath. But Beckett's laughter—the laughter he expresses and the laughter he evokes—is a mask for, not a release from, despair. It may start with a bang, but it trails off in a whimper; it is "yellow laughter," often rasped out in spite of the laughter. It defies no one and transcends nothing. Such laughter is as automatic and anguished as a response to tickling.

From Beckett's earliest writing, callousness and cruelty evoke bitter ethical laughter. An execution amuses Belacqua Shuah; the sadistic routines of the Magdalen Mental Mercyseat are itemized for our amusement; and all the heroes of Beckett's French fiction invite our laughter at their savage drives—Moran's towards his son, Molloy's towards his mother, Malone's towards his creations, the Unnamable's towards his creators. Vladimir and Estragon turn their stichomythic humor to suicide and murder. Hamm and Clov engage in verbal torture, to their and our ironic appreciation. In *Comment c'est* all men are paradoxically and statistically revealed as both victim and executioner, and the more one suffers, the more wildly one laughs: "j'ai toute la souffrance de tous les temps je m'en soucie comme d'une guigne et c'est le fou rire dans chaque cellule" ("all suffering of all time is mine but it doesn't phase me and it's the wild laugh in every cell"). Winnie quotes: "laughing wild amid severest woe."

By Arsene's definition, the dianoetic laugh is the obverse of the ethical laugh. The latter is inspired by the executioner, the former by the victim. Beckett's heroes swing from one to the other, from sadism to suffering and back again. Midway between the ethical and dianoetic laughs, Arsene situates the hollow or intellectual laugh, and, in a somewhat broader definition than Arsene allows, the middle range of laughter undergoes the most significant modification through Beckett's successive works.

Intellectual laughter, aroused by deviation from truth, may be

---

* [Page references are to *Watt* (Grove Press), 1959.]

compared to Bergsonian laughter, aroused by mechanical rigidity imposed upon the authentic free flow of life, which is a kind of truth. Beckett's early works exhibit the twists of plot, distortion of character, and tricks of language, much as Bergson analyzed them. Thus, in *More Pricks Than Kicks*, Beckett twists plots for comic effect when Belacqua abandons a damsel in distress, urges his fiancée to take a lover, is himself the object of a lady's lust, and is finally supplanted in the arms of his third wife by his best friend. In *Murphy* the hero consents to take employment so that his prostitute-mistress need not continue hers. After Murphy's death, his ashes, instead of being flushed down the toilet of Dublin's Abbey Theater, are dispersed in a busy London bar—in crooked comic comment on Murphy's teetotaling, solipsistic life.

From *Watt* on, however, Beckett's plots are so unpredictable that they cannot be twisted, since there is no norm from which to twist. One seemingly senseless incident follows another without sequence or motivation. Place, time, and season are described at inappropriate intervals; day and night, land and sea, town and forest, light and dark, cathedral and slaughterhouse figure incongruously in the plots. From volume to volume, these excursions into "reality" are reduced until in *Comment c'est* the narrator's encounters with Pim and Bom are maddeningly and ridiculously rehearsed. Amorphous and non-concatenated, the volumes of the French trilogy mock the well-made novel. Pointed and repetitive, *Comment c'est* mocks the traditional novel by diminishing plot to human situation.

In Beckett's fiction there is an almost straight-line movement to a single human center. The debonair and detached elegance of *More Pricks Than Kicks* is soon perforated by the embryonic philosophical explorations of *Murphy*. In *Watt,* the hero painstakingly attempts to make sense of his world; both his efforts and his failure are conveyed in a comic mode, and yet traditional comic distance is shortened as Beckett moves us closer and closer to his hero's suffering, for his predicament is that of everyman, is our own.

In the French fiction, with increased control and concentration in each successive work, Beckett channels man's absurd fate into anguish at that fate. As fiction follows fiction, Beckett reduces his plots, diminishes his characters, and compresses his language. It is perhaps partly this voluntary impoverishment that caused Beckett to turn from English to French, where the vocabulary is more limited, and where there is a greater divergence than in English between the literary language to which Beckett was habituated and the colloquial discourse his narrators employ.

As early as 1929, Beckett observed in his essay on Joyce, "No lan-

guage is so sophisticated as English. It is abstracted to death." He
compared English to Medieval Latin in order to establish an analogy
between Dante's use of the vulgar tongue and Joyce's creation of one.
Perhaps the all-powerful language of Joyce inhibited Beckett's development in English. Beckett himself contrasted the two: "The more Joyce
knew the more he could. He's tending toward omniscience and omnip-
otence as an artist. I'm working with impotence, ignorance." [2]

The emphasis should be placed on "working." It is a simple fact
that Beckett's erudition compares with that of Joyce. Although they
work differently, they both strive for maximum inclusiveness in their
fiction. Joyce's reach is encyclopedic; he finds a syllable or symbol to
suggest everything, from the most trivially accidental to the most
mythically universal. Omniscient and omnipotent, detached and smiling, he creates a universe of unparalleled linguistic wealth. Beckett,
in contrast (and perhaps in direct reaction), seeks ignorance, impotence, nakedness. He comes as close to them as literature can, but he
cannot achieve them. He may change his language so that he speaks
an alien tongue literally as well as metaphorically, but he cannot do
away with language and still manage to think. And that is his curse,
as it is ours—that man is, as Descartes defined him, "a thing that
thinks."

Thus sentenced, thus cursed, Beckett's protagonists insist upon the
ridiculous details of their physical situations—Murphy in his rocker,
Molloy on his compulsive voyage, Malone in bed, the Unnamable in
limbo, an uprooted Gogo and Didi by their rooted tree, a defenseless
Hamm and Clov in their shelter, the partner of Pim and/or Bom
in the mud, Winnie and Willie on a scorched earth beneath a hellish
blazing sun. Mobile or immobile, in frantic activity or absurd tableau,
they evoke laughter at their physical situations and pity for their
metaphysical situation. Seeking sense and sensibility in an indifferent
cosmos, reflecting the Absurdity of the Macrocosm in the absurd details of his microcosm, the Beckett hero cries out in the frustration of
his humanity, which is our own.

A poet and not a philosopher, Beckett had to work through his
own creations to attain his bleak, comic vision of the human condition.
Thus, the early English fiction is inhabited by caricatures, and only
for the heroes does Beckett modify his attitude between *More Pricks*
and *Murphy*. In the short stories, Belacqua is seen through detached
and mocking eyes, but Beckett tacitly admits his sympathy for Murphy:
"All the puppets in this book whinge sooner or later, except Murphy,

---

[2] Israel Shenker, "Moody Man of Letters," New York *Times,* May 6, 1956,
sec. 2, p. 1.

who is not a puppet." In the Magdalen Mental Mercyseat, Murphy's mind is even vouchsafed a vision of what the French heroes will seek in vain to glimpse: "that rare postnatal treat . . . the Nothing, than which in the guffaw of the Abderite naught is more real." Appropriately enough, Murphy's response—like Belacqua's in the hospital, like that of Democritus the laughing Abderite—is laughter.

Watt, who cannot laugh, is a grotesque throwback to Cooper, a servant in *Murphy,* and a grotesque foreshadowing of the French heroes, who finally cast off servitude. The grotesque has been identified by its assimilation of animal and human worlds, of real and dream worlds.[3] In *Watt,* termites, frogs, rats, dogs, men, are confused. Although Watt's concerns are not with reality, it is nevertheless a kind of reality that he seeks at Mr. Knott's establishment, where events are as illogical and inexplicable as in dreams.

Ungainly and plodding, Watt consecrates his life to trying to understand Mr. Knott's establishment. Sam the narrator pokes fun at Watt's senses and reason, which fail their owner in his time of need, but Sam Beckett's sympathy for Watt (an ironic, ambivalent sympathy, to be sure) peeps through the account of Sam, surname unknown. Not so completely detached from Watt as he would have us believe, Sam-narrator dwells on the same physically disgusting and mentally agonizing details that preoccupy Sam Beckett in his French works, and, through Sam Beckett, his French heroes. Far from Bergson's analysis of the comic as mechanical aberration imposed on the *élan vital,* Beckett's comic heroes are limp rags of life lost in a stone-cold universe.

Beckett neither discovered nor invented the coldness of the cosmos, nor is he alone in finding indifference in the so-called moral as well as the natural order. The hypocrisy of faith, the stupidity of hope, and the brutality of charity are familiar attitudes in the contemporary scene, and contemporary art is riddled with the breakdown of belief, motivation, and communication. As the painter Burri expresses the poignancy of the human situation with his ludicrous sacks and scarlet gashes, Beckett's comic, violent bums become a metaphor for modern man, fallen too low for the contingencies of history or religion.

Unlike the biblical patriarchs who are ironically reflected in Watt, faithful servant of Mr. Knott, Beckett's French heroes have no job. Vagrants, paralytics, beggars, they move compulsively or do not move at all. Molloy is semiparalyzed, Malone is completely paralyzed, and the Unnamable is virtually bodiless except for a possible head and rump. Hilariously incongruous collections of impulse and habit, they

---

[3] Wolfgang Kayser, *Das Groteske* (Oldenburg, 1957).

are sentenced to recount their experience in all its unreconstructed absurdity. In those accounts, events blend into one another, along with places and times; characters change names, pop up and vanish, are invented and expunged; paragraphs disappear, sentences expand and contract, and phrases reflect forwards and backwards, suddenly denied or repeated. But the haphazard, irrational surface is actually a mosaic of extraordinary conceptual and linguistic control.

Trapped between birth and death, Beckett's French heroes fill the interim with stories, "And all funny; not one not funny." In the long interval between birth and death, while yearning for an exit through womb or tomb, these compulsive narrators spawn words as incoherent as the cries of the newborn, as incoherent as the death rattle, but the incoherence is calculated by Beckett.

To arrive at these approximations of the noises of the nascent and moribund, Beckett underwent intensive linguistic discipline. His early characters share with him a penchant for comic verbal elegance that depends upon breadth of vocabulary and reference. The titles of the early works, like the works themselves, contain puns: *Whoroscope, More Pricks Than Kicks,* "Enueg," *Murphy* (where Beckett declares, "In the beginning was the pun"). In these works, an intellectual laugh springs from linguistic techniques that are indifferent or irrelevant to truth: polished paradox, sneering irony, twisted quotation, erudite jargon. Even the heavier humor of misplaced literalism is lightly and elegantly applied. Beckett's wit glitters mainly in parody, where the tone is sometimes riotously, sometimes grotesquely, out of key with its subject. *Watt,* the bulk of whose prose is a heavy-handed parody of the workings of the rational understanding, opens and closes in light social satire, and it is enlivened midway by a caricature of an academic committee. But *Watt* also abounds in verbal repetition, flat contradiction, and ambivalent irony, all later transferred intact into Beckett's French work.

From the first burst into French prose, an incisive and vulgarly colloquial tongue replaces the elegant language of *Murphy* and the laborious logic of *Watt.* The cultivated English smile explodes into a Rabelaisian guffaw when pedantic jawbreakers give way to Basic-French-and-dirty-words, when a Latinate syntax gives way to pygmy phrases and giant sentences. The twisted quotations turn no longer about literature but about biblical or commonplace sayings, and, unlike the polished gems of the English fiction, they are deeply imbedded in the philosophic context. Only incidental in the English work, ingenuous literalism, flat self-contradiction, and hammered repetition become tools for comic creation and epistemological exploration. They are blunt, clumsy instruments, extensions of the hands that hold them, of the heads that conceive them. They do not, finally, discover or construct a universe; we laugh, finally, at the outlandish idea that they ever could, and yet the tension of their effort supports all of Beckett's work, inspiring bitter, hollow, mirthless laughter at their failure, which reflects ours.

In Beckett's latest work, Arsene's three laughs are merged; the ethical laugh is aroused by cruelty, the intellectual laugh by ignorance, but cruelty and ignorance dissolve in suffering. Bitter and hollow laughter are drowned in mirthless, dianoetic laughter—the only possible reaction to the impossible human situation, in which we live.

Cursed with a mind, man cannot be content with his animal body. Cursed with a body, he cannot retire into the life of the spirit. Forever alone, he is immersed in words, married to phenomena, and he spawns reasons before he knows what is happening to him; he spends the rest of his life foisting names on things, and things on names. If he is lucid beyond logic, he attempts to understand raw experience, but the pattern of ready-made things, names, and values intrudes upon his efforts at an intimate and idiosyncratic interpretation. He comes to doubt everything, and even to doubt the interpreting subject; his "I" is a working hypothesis that no longer works, and yet there is no one else he can be. Unable to penetrate into his microcosm, unable to break out into a macrocosm, he agonizes, poised awkwardly between them, and he is aware of his precarious position: "on the one hand the mind, on the other the world, I don't belong to either."

Beckett's extraordinary achievement has been to give dimension to this tightrope-walker, so that we care profoundly about his equilibrium. Beckett's is an intellectual accomplishment, for all the vaunted ignorance of his heroes. Using comic cliché phrases, he farcically deprives us of ready-made concepts. Using ludicrously simple events, he ironically invests them with metaphysical meaning. But he does not deal in philosophical problems; he plunges us into an emotional situation so that we alternate between panic and hilarity, as we anxiously watch the tottering of subject and object, of world and self, of *our* world and *our* self.

In Beckett's work, coherence is jarred at every level—the cosmos, the plot, the person, the sentence. In the "wordy-gurdy" of his protagonists' monologues, we are persuaded by our dizziness of his heroes' authenticity. They know no respect for time or place; they disdain sequence and proportion. But they must not be too readily confused with their creator. Unlike Sartre and Camus, who paint an absurd world in logical language and syntax, Beckett strives for a more mi-

metic art. Cosmic absurdity is reflected by non-concatenation of incidents, as in the fiction of Kafka; personal disintegration is reflected
by syntactical fragmentation, as in the drama of Ionesco. Beckett uses
the words and moods of our time, but he weaves them into a fabric
of impressive design; the surface gibberish is packed with significance,
the surface chaos with symbolism. Beckett's precise workmanship is
readily apparent if we examine his revisions. Successive versions of
his stories contain no modification in the abrupt *non sequiturs,* but
there are many phrasal changes in order to achieve ludicrous incongruity, syntactical ambiguity, symbolic ambivalence, and more intense
rhythms.

By use of a first-person, alogical narration, Beckett links his presentation of cosmic irony with his heroes' consciousness of that irony.
Introspectionists who descend from Descartes, his protagonists show
how miserably the line has deteriorated. Grotesque, ancient, crippled,
hysterically caressing what they scarcely dare call possessions, thinking
tenderly of their hats, clinging frantically to pencil, stick, or sack,
Beckett's French "I's" mock themselves as they suffer. Gradually
stripped of possessions and clothes, they grow larger in meaning as
their silhouettes shrink. In *Comment c'est* the narrator is naked even
of hat, bereft even of pencil, and literally dumb, reduced to voiceless,
sentenceless, significant phrases. In *Happy Days* Winnie is reduced to
a hatted head, thinking staccato thoughts in fewer and older phrases.
As the very number of words is reduced, the tension is tautened between knowledge and ignorance, between sense and non-sense. With
consummate verbal skill, Beckett involves us more deeply in his heroes,
as they become more obsessively involved with themselves. And at the
same time, we are more involved with *our*selves. Beckett's fellow playwright Ionesco speaks for Beckett's heroes too when he writes:
"By expressing my deepest obsessions, I express my deepest humanity." [4]

Instead of laughing in a civilized and detached way at comic figures
whom we do not resemble, instead of reforming after laughing at our
own weakness as seen in another, we come, in Beckett's work, to doubt
ourselves through our laughter. But through the obsessions of Beckett's
heroes, we understand our own deepest humanity. Since names are
interchangeable, perhaps we too are nameless and unnamable. We
laugh at the leg ailments, verbal difficulties, ignorance, and passion
of Beckett's heroes, but our laughter is nervous and anxious. Are *our*
feet solidly grounded, *our* words expressive of *our* meaning, *our* tears

---

[4] Eugène Ionesco, "The Avant-Garde Theatre," *World Theatre VIII,* No. 3
(Autumn, 1959), quoted in Martin Esslin, "The Theatre of the Absurd," *Tulane Drama Review* (May, 1960), 7.

of grief or mirth? What shall we take as fact? We laugh in fear as we realize that there is no fact, only fiction. "Know thyself." What, that fiction? "Connaître, c'est mésurer." What, a fiction?

Beckett has achieved an ambiguously ironic confusion and communion of identity: Beckett, his creation the "I" who creates, his creation the "I" who sees. At this late stage of human history, when man cannot decipher his identity from the comic complexity of fictions and words, he nevertheless is compelled to seek that identity. Life and letters alike become a dianoetic joke of creations feeding upon their creators, with whom they are assimilable and irreconcilable. The artistic condition is no longer a pinnacle of privilege from which one may nod in neighborly fashion at God the Creator. Instead, creator and creature wallow together in dust or mud, whence they came. Or perhaps they never left it.

The modern man of letters who turns against letters was not fathered by Beckett, but no other modern writer—not Proust or Gide or Joyce or Mann—has integrated the act of creation so consistently and ironically into his own creation. Joyce held that the greatest love of a man was for his own lies, and yet the artist-liar is only one of his mythic prototypes. For Beckett, all literature and all life reduce to his portrait of the artist-liar as old bum: "You either lie or hold your peace," says Molloy, and Beckett's heroes do not hold their peace. Do we?

Beckett's art-lies, his fictions, know each other, if they know anything at all. Murphy's mind contains Belacqua, and the voiceless narrator of *Comment c'est,* recounting his life as the penitential task that all Beckett's heroes perform, likens himself to Belacqua, comically turned on his side in the slime. In Beckett's unpublished novel, Mercier speaks to Watt of Murphy, for the one reminds him of the other. Moran refers to Murphy, Watt, Yerk, Mercier. Malone groups himself with other Beckett fictions: "Then it will be all over with the Murphys, Merciers, Molloys, Morans and Malones, unless it goes on beyond the grave." Perhaps it does, since the Unnamable carries on a discourse with Molloy and Malone, Mahood and Worm, and others "from Murphy on"; he insists in vain that he is not they "who told me I was they, who I must have tried to be, under duress, or through fear, or to avoid acknowledging me." The crawling, voiceless creature of *Comment c'est* intermittently encounters and is Pim and Bom, voiced and voiceless aspects of Beckett's earlier fictions. So, all knowledge is a dialogue between man and his fictions; reason and calculation, emotion and imagination—all are taught to man through his fiction, even if the fiction is himself, and the dialogue reduced to a monologue of ready-made phrases, stubbornly, clumsily, ironically, searching for an individual and independent self. But the search itself is paradigmatic of all human endeavor.

Like his fiction, Beckett's drama focuses on man as artist-liar, often in the guise of artist-actor. It is this accent that distinguishes his drama from the comparably comic anti-plays of Ionesco. Although Beckett and Ionesco both have learned from Artaud and Jarry to express serious theatrical concerns in spectacular farcical terms, it is Beckett for whom theater is the more immediate metaphor of the world. The worn-out acts of vaudeville and the threadbare devices of drama emphasize our presence at a spectacle, and symbolize our lives. In *Godot* each of the characters performs for an audience, and conflicting testimonies thread through the play. In *Endgame,* the artist is the hero whose chronicle seems to relate to his life in the penitential fashion that Belacqua's dream relates to his. In *Embers,* Henry's fictions, Bolton and Holloway, are possible doctors to cure him. In *Krapp's Last Tape,* Krapp attempts to fix the flux of himself through a tape recorder, for love has not accomplished this task. In *Happy Days,* Winnie needs the spectacle of Willie, as she needs to feel herself a spectacle in other eyes.

Beckett's heroes are aware of playing a role, as though they had read Epictetus the Stoic: "Remember that you are an actor in a drama, of such a kind as the author pleases to make it. . . . For this is your business, to act well the character assigned to you; to choose it is another's." [5] We are all actors, playing stock parts in the repertoire of the *commedia dell'arte.* Although ad lib dialogue is encouraged, it must be couched in familiar phrases and re-enforced by violent slapstick. If there ever was a script, we cannot know it; much less can we know an author or audience.

Dramatic or fictional, Beckett's work paints an ironic portrait of man, Everyman, as artist-liar. He paints in words—in the words that his heroes revile and unravel, in the words he weaves into one of the masterly prose styles of our time. Superbly controlling his medium, Beckett probes both source and product of language. The succinct redundancy of his dramatic dialogue is in ironic contrast to the logorrhea of his fictional narrators.

Within each literary genre, Beckett undermines that very genre— fictional formulae in the fiction and dramatic conventions in the drama. By mocking the literary form within that form, Beckett questions the boundary between art and life, between fiction and fact.

---

[5] Quoted by Jean-Jacques Mayoux, "The Theatre of Samuel Beckett," *Perspective* (Autumn, 1959), 142.

Such interrogation is part of the traditional stock in trade of the fool, and Beckett plays it for all its farcical, metaphysical worth. He pommels existence with the questions of his characters, or with their frenzied affirmations immediately followed by more frenzied negations. These questions slap at life as well as art; for any interpretation of life is a construction, a game, a work of art, bordering on a reality that is necessarily unknown, unknowable, and frustratingly seductive.

"I'm working with impotence, ignorance," Beckett has explicitly admitted. "My little exploration is that whole zone of being that has always been set aside by artists as something unusable—as something by definition incompatible with art. I think anyone nowadays, who pays the slightest attention to his own experience finds it the experience of a non-knower, a non-can-er." [6]

"A non-knower, a non-can-er" is, however, still another role, that of the old comic Eiron or self-deprecator, the fool of his fictions. Aristotle, "qui savait tout," wrote that comedy paints men as worse than they are, and the Eiron paints himself as worse than he is. Beckett's comic ironist is ugly, small, poor, cruel, ignorant, miserable, and infinitely vulnerable. It is above all in that vulnerability that we recognize ourselves. As long as man remains ugly, small, poor, cruel, ignorant, miserable, and vulnerable, Beckett's ironic works will have lively and deadly relevance for us.

Through the years Beckett has hacked at his plots and characters; he has decimated his sentences and the number of his words, until he is left with a single protagonist in the generalized human situation, an "I" in quest of his "I" through fiction, who is in quest of his "I" through fiction, who, etc. Perhaps the old wedding jingle should be applied with a shotgun, for each "I" conceives another who conceives another who conceives another until we arrive full circle laughing—hysterical perhaps at our plight.

---

[6] Shenker, "Moody Man of Letters."

Part Eight

FROM THE CLASSICS
OF COMIC THEORY

Molière

PREFACE TO TARTUFFE

Charles Baudelaire

ON THE ESSENCE OF LAUGHTER

George Meredith

FROM AN ESSAY ON COMEDY

Henri Bergson

FROM LAUGHTER

Preface to

Tartuffe*

MOLIÈRE

Here is a comedy that has excited a good deal of discussion and
that has been under attack for a long time; and the persons who are
mocked by it have made it plain that they are more powerful in
France than all whom my plays have satirized up to this time. Noble-
men, ladies of fashion, cuckolds, and doctors all kindly consented to
their presentation, which they themselves seemed to enjoy along with
everyone else; but hypocrites do not understand banter: they became
angry at once, and found it strange that I was bold enough to represent their actions and to care to describe a profession shared by so
many good men. This is a crime for which they cannot forgive me,
and they have taken up arms against my comedy in a terrible rage.
They were careful not to attack it at the point that had wounded
them: they are too crafty for that and too clever to reveal their true
character. In keeping with their lofty custom, they have used the cause
of God to mask their private interests; and *Tartuffe*, they say, is a
play that offends piety: it is filled with abominations from beginning
to end, and nowhere is there a line that does not deserve to be
burned. Every syllable is wicked, the very gestures are criminal, and
the slightest glance, turn of the head, or step from right to left conceals mysteries that they are able to explain to my disadvantage. In
vain did I submit the play to the criticism of my friends and the
scrutiny of the public: all the corrections I could make, the judgment
of the king and queen who saw the play, the approval of great
princes and ministers of state who honored it with their presence, the

* Molière, "Preface" to *Tartuffe* [1669], Haskell M. Block, tr. and ed.
(Appleton-Century-Crofts, 1958), pp. 1–7.

443

opinion of good men who found it worthwhile, all this did not help. They will not let go of their prey, and every day of the week they have pious zealots abusing me in public and damning me out of charity.

I would care very little about all they might say except that their devices make enemies of men whom I respect and gain the support of genuinely good men, whose faith they know and who, because of the warmth of their piety, readily accept the impressions that others present to them. And it is this which forces me to defend myself. Especially to the truly devout do I wish to vindicate my play, and I beg of them with all my heart not to condemn it before seeing it, to rid themselves of preconceptions, and not aid the cause of men dishonored by their actions.

If one takes the trouble to examine my comedy in good faith, he will surely see that my intentions are innocent throughout, and tend in no way to make fun of what men revere; that I have presented the subject with all the precautions that its delicacy imposes; and that I have used all the art and skill that I could to distinguish clearly the character of the hypocrite from that of the truly devout man. For that purpose I used two whole acts to prepare the appearance of my scoundrel. Never is there a moment's doubt about his character; he is known at once from the qualities I have given him; and from one end of the play to the other, he does not say a word, he does not perform an action which does not depict to the audience the character of a wicked man, and which does not bring out in sharp relief the character of the truly good man which I oppose to it.

I know full well that by way of reply, these gentlemen try to insinuate that it is not the role of the theater to speak of these matters; but with their permission, I ask them on what do they base this fine doctrine. It is a proposition they advance as no more than a supposition, for which they offer not a shred of proof; and surely it would not be difficult to show them that comedy, for the ancients, had its origin in religion and constituted a part of its ceremonies; that our neighbors, the Spaniards, have hardly a single holiday celebration in which a comedy is not a part; and that even here in France, it owes its birth to the efforts of a religious brotherhood who still own the Hotel de Bourgogne, where the most important mystery plays of our faith were presented; that you can still find comedies printed in gothic letters under the name of a learned doctor of the Sorbonne; and without going so far, in our own day the religious dramas of Pierre Corneille have been performed to the admiration of all France.

If the function of comedy is to correct men's vices, I do not see why any should be exempt. Such a condition in our society would be much more dangerous than the thing itself; and we have seen that the theater is admirably suited to provide correction. The most forceful lines of a serious moral statement are usually less powerful than those of satire; and nothing will reform most men better than the depiction of their faults. It is a vigorous blow to vices to expose them to public laughter. Criticism is taken lightly, but men will not tolerate satire. They are quite willing to be mean, but they never like to be ridiculed.

I have been attacked for having placed words of piety in the mouth of my impostor. Could I avoid doing so in order to represent properly the character of a hypocrite? It seemed to me sufficient to reveal the criminal motives which make him speak as he does, and I have eliminated all ceremonial phrases, which nonetheless he would not have been found using incorrectly. Yet some say that in the fourth act he sets forth a vicious morality; but is not this a morality which everyone has heard again and again? Does my comedy say anything new here? And is there any fear that ideas so thoroughly detested by everyone can make an impression on men's minds; that I make them dangerous by presenting them in the theater; that they acquire authority from the lips of a scoundrel? There is not the slightest suggestion of any of this; and one must either approve the comedy of *Tartuffe* or condemn all comedies in general.

This has indeed been done in a furious way for some time now, and never was the theater so much abused. I cannot deny that there were Church Fathers who condemned comedy; but neither will it be denied me that there were some who looked on it somewhat more favorably. Thus authority, on which censure is supposed to depend, is destroyed by this disagreement; and the only conclusion that can be drawn from this difference of opinion among men enlightened by the same wisdom is that they viewed comedy in different ways, and that some considered it in its purity, while others regarded it in its corruption and confused it with all those wretched performances which have been rightly called performances of filth.

And in fact, since we should talk about things rather than words, and since most misunderstanding comes from including contrary notions in the same word, we need only to remove the veil of ambiguity and look at comedy in itself to see if it warrants condemnation. It will surely be recognized that as it is nothing more than a clever poem which corrects men's faults by means of agreeable lessons, it cannot be condemned without injustice. And if we listened to the voice of ancient times on this matter, it would tell us that its most famous philosophers have praised comedy—they who professed so austere a wisdom and who ceaselessly denounced the vices of their times. It would tell us that Aristotle spent his evenings at the theater and took the trouble to reduce the art of making comedies to rules. It would tell us that some of its greatest and most honored men took pride in writing comedies themselves; and that others did not disdain to recite them in public; that Greece expressed its admiration for this art by means of handsome prizes and magnificent theaters to honor it; and finally, that in Rome this same art also received extraordinary honors; I do not speak of Rome run riot under the license of the emperors, but of disciplined Rome, governed by the wisdom of the consuls, and in the age of the full vigor of Roman dignity.

I admit that there have been times when comedy became corrupt. And what do men not corrupt every day? There is nothing so innocent that men cannot turn it to crime; nothing so beneficial that its values cannot be reversed; nothing so good in itself that it cannot be put to bad uses. Medical knowledge benefits mankind and is revered as one of our most wonderful possessions; and yet there was a time when it fell into discredit, and was often used to poison men. Philosophy is a gift of Heaven; it has been given to us to bring us to the knowledge of a God by contemplating the wonders of nature; and yet we know that often it has been turned away from its function and has been used openly in support of impiety. Even the holiest of things are not immune from human corruption, and every day we see scoundrels who use and abuse piety, and wickedly make it serve the greatest of crimes. But this does not prevent one from making the necessary distinctions. We do not confuse in the same false inference the goodness of things that are corrupted with the wickedness of the corrupt. The function of an art is always distinguished from its misuse; and as medicine is not forbidden because it was banned in Rome, nor philosophy because it was publicly condemned in Athens, we should not suppress comedy simply because it has been condemned at certain times. This censure was justified then for reasons which no longer apply today; it was limited to what was then seen; and we should not seize on these limits, apply them more rigidly than is necessary, and include in our condemnation the innocent along with the guilty. The comedy that this censure attacked is in no way the comedy that we want to defend. We must be careful not to confuse the one with the other. There may be two persons whose morals may be completely different. They may have no resemblance to one another except in their names, and it would be a terrible injustice to want to condemn Olympia, who is a good woman, because there is also an Olympia who is lewd. Such procedures would make for great confusion everywhere. Everything under the sun would be condemned; now since this rigor is not applied to the countless instances of abuse we see every day, the same should hold for comedy, and those plays should be approved in which instruction and virtue reign supreme.

I know there are some so delicate that they cannot tolerate a comedy, who say that the most decent are the most dangerous, that the passions they present are all the more moving because they are virtuous, and that men's feelings are stirred by these presentations. I do not see what great crime it is to be affected by the sight of a generous passion; and this utter insensitivity to which they would lead us is indeed a high degree of virtue! I wonder if so great a perfection resides within the strength of human nature, and I wonder if it is not better to try to correct and moderate men's passions than to try to suppress them altogether. I grant that there are places better to visit than the theater; and if we want to condemn every single thing that does not bear directly on God and our salvation, it is right that comedy be included, and I should willingly grant that it be condemned along with everything else. But if we admit, as is in fact true, that the exercise of piety will permit interruptions, and that men need amusement, I maintain that there is none more innocent than comedy. I have dwelled too long on this matter. Let me finish the words of a great prince on the comedy, *Tartuffe*.

Eight days after it had been banned, a play called *Scaramouche the Hermit* was performed before the court; and the king, on his way out, said to this great prince: "I should really like to know why the persons who make so much noise about Molière's comedy do not say a word about *Scaramouche*." To which the prince replied, "It is because the comedy of *Scaramouche* makes fun of Heaven and religion, which these gentlemen do not care about at all, but that of Molière makes fun of *them*, and that is what they cannot bear."

On the Essence of Laughter, and, in General, on the Comic in the Plastic Arts*[1]

CHARLES BAUDELAIRE

I

I have no intention of writing a treatise on caricature: I simply want to acquaint the reader with certain reflections which have often occurred to me on the subject of this singular genre. These reflections had become a kind of obsession for me, and I wanted to get them off my chest. Nevertheless I have made every effort to impose some order, and thus to make their digestion more easy. This, then, is purely an artist's and a philosopher's article. No doubt a general history of caricature in its references to all the facts by which humanity has been stirred—facts political and religious, weighty or frivolous; facts relative to the disposition of the nation or to fashion—would be a glorious and important work. The task still remains to be done, for the essays which have been published up to the present are hardly more than raw materials. But I thought that this task should be divided. It is clear that a work on caricature, understood in this way, would be a history of facts, an immense gallery of anecdote. In caricature, far more than in the other branches of art, there are two sorts of works which are to be prized and commended for different and

---

[1] Earliest traced publication in *Le Portefeuille,* 8th July 1855; reprinted, with minor variations, in *Le Présent,* 1st Sept. 1857, with the addition of the succeeding articles on French (1st Oct.) and Foreign (15th Oct.) Caricaturists.

* Charles Baudelaire, "On the Essence of Laughter" [1855], in *The Mirror of Art,* Jonathan Mayne, tr. and ed. (Phaidon Press Ltd., 1955), pp. 131–153. [Footnotes in this selection have been renumbered.]

almost contrary reasons. One kind have value only by reason of the *fact* which they represent. No doubt they have a right to the attention of the historian, the archaeologist, and even the philosopher; they deserve to take their place in the national archives, in the biographical registers of human thought. Like the flysheets of journalism, they are swept out of sight by the same tireless breeze which supplies us with fresh ones. But the others—and it is with these that I want to concern myself especially—contain a mysterious, lasting, eternal element, which recommends them to the attention of artists. What a curious thing, and one truly worthy of attention, is the introduction of this indefinable element of beauty, even in works which are intended to represent his proper ugliness—both moral and physical—to man! And what is no less mysterious is that this lamentable spectacle excites in him an undying and incorrigible mirth. Here, then, is the true subject of my article.

A doubt assails me. Should I reply with a formal demonstration to the kind of preliminary question which no doubt will be raised by certain spiteful pundits of solemnity—charlatans of gravity, pedantic corpses which have emerged from the icy vaults of the *Institut* and have come again to the land of the living, like a band of miserly ghosts, to snatch a few coppers from the obliging administration? First of all, they would ask, is Caricature a genre? No, their cronies would reply, Caricature is not a genre. I have heard similar heresies ringing in my ears at academicians' dinners. It was these fine fellows who let the comedy of *Robert Macaire* [2] slip past them without noticing any of its great moral and literary symptoms. If they had been contemporaries of Rabelais, they would have treated him as a base and uncouth buffoon. In truth, then, have we got to show that nothing at all that issues from man is frivolous in the eyes of a philosopher? Surely, at the very least, there will be that obscure and mysterious element which no philosophy has so far analysed to its depths?

We are going to concern ourselves, then, with the essence of laughter and with the component elements of caricature. Later, perhaps, we shall examine some of the most remarkable works produced in this genre.

II

The Sage laughs not save in fear and trembling. From what authority-laden lips, from what completely orthodox pen, did this

---

[2] The character of Robert Macaire (in the play *L'Auberge des Adrets*) had been created by the actor Frédérick Lemaître, in the 1820s. Later (see p. 168 below) Daumier developed the character in a famous series of caricatures.

strange and striking maxim fall?[3] Does it come to us from the
Philosopher-King of Judea? Or should we attribute it to Joseph de
Maistre,[4] that soldier quickened with the Holy Spirit? I have a vague
memory of having read it in one of his books, but given as a quotation, no doubt. Such severity of thought and style suits well with
the majestic saintliness of Bossuet; but the elliptical turn of the
thought and its quintessential refinement would lead me rather to
attribute the honour to Bourdaloue, the relentless Christian psychologist. This singular maxim has kept recurring to my mind ever since
I first conceived the idea of my article, and I wanted to get rid of
it at the very start.

But come, let us analyse this curious proposition—

The Sage, that is to say he who is quickened with the spirit of
Our Lord, he who has the divine formulary at his finger tips, does
not abandon himself to laughter save in fear and trembling. The Sage
trembles at the thought of having laughed; the Sage fears laughter,
just as he fears the lustful shows of this world. He stops short on the
brink of laughter, as on the brink of temptation. There is, then, according to the Sage, a certain secret contradiction between his special
nature as Sage and the primordial nature of laughter. In fact, to do
no more than touch in passing upon memories which are more than
solemn, I would point out—and this perfectly corroborates the officially Christian character of the maxim—that the Sage *par excellence,*
the Word Incarnate, never laughed.[5] In the eyes of One who has all
knowledge and all power, the comic does not exist. And yet the Word
Incarnate knew anger; He even knew tears.

Let us make a note of this, then. In the first place, here is an
author—a Christian, without doubt—who considers it as a certain fact
that the Sage takes a very good look before allowing himself to laugh,
as though some residue of uneasiness and anxiety must still be left
him. And secondly, the comic vanishes altogether from the point of
view of absolute knowledge and power. Now, if we inverted the two
propositions, it would result that laughter is generally the apanage
of madmen, and that it always implies more or less of ignorance and
weakness. I have no wish, however, to embark recklessly upon a theo-

---

[3] Lavater's remark 'Le Sage sourit souvent et rit rarement' (*Souvenirs pour
des voyageurs chéris*) has been suggested by G. T. Clapton; see Gilman p. 237,
n. 32.

[4] On Baudelaire's debt to Joseph de Maistre, see Gilman pp. 63–66.

[5] This suggests a line in a poem by Baudelaire's friend Gustave le Vavasseur,
published in 1843. *Dieux joyeux, je vous hais. Jésus n'a jamais ri.* See also
Gilman p. 237, n. 32.

logical ocean, for which I should without doubt be insufficiently equipped with compass or sails; I am content just to indicate these singular horizons to the reader—to point them out to him with my finger.

If you are prepared, then, to take the point of view of the orthodox mind, it is certain that human laughter is intimately linked with the accident of an ancient Fall, of a debasement both physical and moral. Laughter and grief are expressed by the organs in which the command and the knowledge of good and evil reside—I mean the eyes and the mouth. In the earthly paradise—whether one supposes it as past or to come, a memory or a prophecy, in the sense of the theologians or of the socialists—in the earthly paradise, that is to say in the surroundings in which it seemed to man that all created things were good, joy did not find its dwelling in laughter. As no trouble afflicted him, man's countenance was simple and smooth, and the laughter which now shakes the nations never distorted the features of his face. Laughter and tears cannot make their appearance in the paradise of delights. They are both equally the children of woe, and they came because the body of enfeebled man lacked the strength to restrain them.* From the point of view of my Christian philosopher, the laugh on his lips is a sign of just as great a misery as the tears in his eyes. The Being who sought to multiply his own image has in no wise put the teeth of the lion into the mouth of man— yet man rends with his laughter; nor all the seductive cunning of the serpent into his eyes—yet he beguiles with his tears. Observe also that it is with his tears that man washes the afflictions of man, and that it is with his laughter that sometimes he soothes and charms his heart; for the phenomena engendered by the Fall will become the means of redemption.

May I be permitted a poetic hypothesis in order to help me prove the accuracy of these assertions, which otherwise many people may find tainted with the *a priori* of mysticism? Since the comic is a damnable element, and one of diabolic origin, let us try to imagine before us a soul absolutely pristine and fresh, so to speak, from the hands of Nature. For our example let us take the great and typical figure of Virginie,[6] who perfectly symbolizes absolute purity and naïveté. Virginie arrives in Paris still bathed in sea-mists and gilded by the tropic sun, her eyes full of great primitive images of waves,

---

* Philippe de Chennevières (c.b.), an early friend of Baudelaire's. He wrote a number of books, and had a distinguished career in the official world of art. The exact source of this idea has not been traced among his works.

[6] From Bernardin de Saint-Pierre's *Paul et Virginie*.

mountains and forests. Here she falls into the midst of a turbulent, overflowing and mephitic civilization, all imbued as she is with the pure and rich scents of the East. She is linked to humanity both by her birth and her love, by her mother and her lover, her Paul, who is as angelic as she and whose sex knows no distinction from hers, so to speak, in the unquenched ardours of a love which is unaware of itself. God she has known in the church of *Les Pamplemousses*— a modest and mean little church, and in the vastness of the inde- scribable tropic sky and the immortal music of the forests and the torrents. Certainly Virginie is a noble intelligence; but a few images and a few memories suffice her, just as a few books suffice the Sage. Now one day by chance, in all innocence, at the Palais-Royal, at a glazier's window, on a table, in a public place, Virginie's eye falls upon—a caricature! a caricature all very tempting for us, full-blown with gall and spite, just such as a shrewd and bored civilization knows how to make them. Let us suppose some broad buffoonery of the prizering, some British enormity, full of clotted blood and spiced with a monstrous 'Goddam!' or two: or, if this is more to the taste of your curious imagination, let us suppose before the eye of our virginal Virginie some charming and enticing morsel of lubricity, a Gavarni of her times, and one of the best—some insulting satire against the follies of the court, some plastic diatribe against the Parc-aux-Cerfs,[7] the vile activities of a great favourite, or the nocturnal escapades of the proverbial *Autrichienne*.[8] Caricature is a double thing; it is both drawing and idea—the drawing violent, the idea caustic and veiled. And a network of such elements gives trouble to a simple mind which is accustomed to understand by intuition things as simple as itself. Virginie has glimpsed; now she gazes. Why? She is gazing at the un- known. Nevertheless she hardly understands either what it means or what it is for. And yet, do you observe that sudden folding of the wings, that shudder of a soul that veils herself and wants to draw back? The angel has sensed that there is offence in it. And in truth, I tell you, whether she has understood it or not, she will be left with some strange element of uneasiness—something which resem- bles fear. No doubt, if Virginie remains in Paris and knowledge comes to her, laughter will come too: we shall see why. But for the moment, in our capacity as analysts and critics who would certainly not dare to assert that our intelligence is superior to that of Virginie, let us simply record the fear and the suffering of the immaculate angel brought face to face with caricature.

[7] Louis XV's private brothel at Versailles.
[8] Marie Antoinette.

III

If you wished to demonstrate that the comic is one of the clearest tokens of the Satanic in man, one of the numerous pips contained in the symbolic apple, it would be enough to draw attention to the unanimous agreement of physiologists of laughter on the primary ground of this monstrous phenomenon. Nevertheless their discovery is not very profound and hardly goes very far. Laughter, they say, comes from superiority. I should not be surprised if, on making this discovery, the physiologist had burst out laughing himself at the thought of his own superiority. Therefore he should have said: Laughter comes from the idea of one's *own* superiority. A Satanic idea, if there ever was one! And what pride and delusion! For it is a notorious fact that all the madmen in the asylums have an excessively overdeveloped idea of their own superiority: I hardly know of any who suffer from the madness of humility. Note, too, that laughter is one of the most frequent and numerous expressions of madness. And now, see how everything falls into place. When Virginie, once fallen, has declined by one degree in purity, the idea of her own superiority will begin to dawn upon her; she will be more learned from the point of view of the world; and she will laugh.

I said that laughter contained a symptom of failing; and, in fact, what more striking token of debility could you demand than a nervous convulsion, an involuntary spasm comparable to a sneeze and prompted by the sight of someone else's misfortune? This misfortune is almost always a *mental* failing. And can you imagine a phenomenon more deplorable than one failing taking delight in another? But there is worse to follow. The misfortune is sometimes of a very much lower kind—a failure in the physical order. To take one of the most commonplace examples in life, what is there so delightful in the sight of a man falling on the ice or in the street, or stumbling at the end of a pavement, that the countenance of his brother in Christ should contract in such an intemperate manner, and the muscles of his face should suddenly leap into life like a timepiece at midday or a clockwork toy? The poor devil has disfigured himself, at the very least; he may even have broken an essential member. Nevertheless the laugh has gone forth, sudden and irrepressible. It is certain that if you care to explore this situation, you will find a certain unconscious pride at the core of the laughter's thought. That is the point of departure. 'Look at me! *I* am not falling,' he seems to say. 'Look at me! *I* am walking upright. *I* would never be so silly as to fail to see a gap in the pavement or a cobblestone blocking the way.'

The Romantic school, or, to put it better, the Satanic school, which is one of its subdivisions, had a proper understanding of this primordial law of laughter; or at least, if they did not all understand it, all, even in their grossest extravagances and exaggerations, sensed it and applied it exactly. All the miscreants of melodrama, accursed, damned and fatally marked with a grin which runs from ear to ear, are in the pure orthodoxy of laughter. Furthermore they are almost all the grandchildren, legitimate or illegitimate, of the renowned wanderer Melmoth,[9] that great satanic creation of the Reverend Maturin. What could be greater, what more mighty, relative to poor humanity, than the pale, bored figure of Melmoth? And yet he has a weak and contemptible side to him, which faces against God and against the light. See, therefore, how he laughs; see how he laughs, as he ceaselessly compares himself to the caterpillars of humanity, he so strong, he so intelligent, he for whom a part of the conditional laws of mankind, both physical and intellectual, no longer exist! And this laughter is the perpetual explosion of his rage and his suffering. It is —you must understand—the necessary resultant of his contradictory double nature, which is infinitely great in relation to man, and infinitely vile and base in relation to absolute Truth and Justice. Melmouth is a living contradiction. He has parted company with the fundamental conditions of life; his bodily organs can no longer sustain his thought. And that is why his laughter freezes and wrings his entrails. It is a laugh which never sleeps, like a malady which continues on its way and completes a destined course. And thus the laughter of Melmoth, which is the highest expression of pride, is for ever performing its function as it lacerates and scorches the lips of the laugher for whose sins there can be no remission.[10]

IV

And now let us recapitulate a little and establish more clearly our principal propositions, which amount to a sort of theory of laughter. Laughter is satanic: it is thus profoundly human. It is the consequence

---

[9] *Melmoth the Wanderer* (1820) was the masterpiece of its author, the Rev. C. R. Maturin (1782–1824). It was one of the most influential of all the novels of horror, and Baudelaire's great admiration for it was revealed in his desire to make a new French translation, on the grounds that the existing translation was inadequate. See G. T. Capton, 'Balzac, Baudelaire and Maturin,' *French Quarterly*, June and Sept. 1930; see also Mario Praz, *The Romantic Agony* (O.U.P., 2nd ed., 1951) pp. 116–118.

[10] 'A mirth which is not riot gaiety is often the mask which hides the convulsed and distorted features of agony—and laughter, which never yet was the expression of rapture, has often been the only intelligible language of madness and misery. Ecstasy only smiles—despair laughs . . .' *Melmoth* (2nd ed., 1824), vol. III, p. 302.

in man of the idea of his own superiority. And since laughter is essentially human, it is, in fact, essentially contradictory; that is to say that it is at once a token of an infinite grandeur and an infinite misery—the latter in relation to the absolute Being of whom man has an inkling, the former in relation to the beasts. It is from the perpetual collision of these two infinites that laughter is struck. The comic and the capacity for laughter are situated in the laugher and by no means in the object of his laughter. The man who trips would be the last to laugh at his own fall, unless he happened to be a philosopher, one who had acquired by habit a power of rapid self-division and thus of assisting as a disinterested spectator at the phenomena of his own ego. But such cases are rare. The most comic animals are the most serious—monkeys, for example, and parrots. For that matter, if man were to be banished from creation, there would be no such thing as the comic, for the animals do not hold themselves superior to the vegetables, nor the vegetables to the minerals. While it is a sign of superiority in relation to brute creation (and under this heading I include the numerous pariahs of the *mind*), laughter is a sign of inferiority in relation to the wise, who, through the contemplative innocence of their minds, approach a childlike state. Comparing mankind with man, as we have a right to do, we see that primitive nations, in the same way as Virginie, have no conception of caricature and have no comedy (Holy Books never laugh, to whatever nations they may belong), but that as they advance little by little in the direction of the cloudy peaks of the intellect, or as they pore over the gloomy braziers of metaphysics, the nations of the world begin to laugh diabolically with the laughter of Melmoth; and finally we see that if, in these selfsame ultra-civilized nations, some mind is driven by superior ambition to pass beyond the limits of worldly pride and to make a bold leap towards pure poetry, then the resulting poetry, as limpid and profound as Nature herself, will be as void of laughter as is the soul of the Sage.

As the comic is a sign of superiority, or of a belief in one's own superiority, it is natural to hold that, before they can achieve the absolute purification promised by certain mystical prophets, the nations of the world will see a multiplication of comic themes in proportion as their superiority increases. But the comic changes its nature, too. In this way the angelic and the diabolic elements function in parallel. As humanity uplifts itself, it wins for evil, and for the understanding of evil, a power proportionate to that which it has won for good. And this is why I find nothing surprising in the fact that we, who are the children of a better law than the religious laws of antiquity—

we, the favoured disciples of Jesus—should possess a greater number of comic elements than pagan antiquity. For this very thing is a condition of our general intellectual power. I am quite prepared for sworn dissenters to cite the classic tale of the philosopher who died of laughing when he saw a donkey eating figs, or even the comedies of Aristophanes and those of Plautus. I would reply that, quite apart from the fact that these periods were essentially civilized, and there had already been a considerable shrinkage of belief, their type of the comic is still not quite the same as ours. It even has a touch of barbarity about it, and we can really only adopt it by a backward effort of mind, the result of which is called *pastiche*. As for the grotesque figures which antiquity has bequeathed us—the masks, the bronze figurines, the Hercules (all muscles), the little Priapi, with tongue curled in air and pointed ears (all cranium and phallus); and as for those prodigious phalluses on which the white daughters of Romulus innocently ride astride, those monstrous engines of generation, equipped with wings and bells—I believe that these things are all full of deep seriousness.[11] Venus, Pan and Hercules were in no sense figures of fun. It was not until after the coming of Christ, and with the aid of Plato and Seneca, that men began to laugh at them. I believe that the ancients were full of respect for drum-majors and for doers of mighty deeds of all kinds, and that none of those extravagant fetishes which I instanced a moment ago were anything other than tokens of adoration, or, at all events, symbols of power; in no sense were they intentionally comic emanations of the fancy. Indian and Chinese idols are unaware that they are ridiculous; it is in us, Christians, that their comicality resides.

V

It would be a mistake to suppose that we have got rid of every difficulty. The mind that is least accustomed to these aesthetic subtleties would very quickly be able to counter me with the insidious objection that there are *different varieties of laughter*. It is not always a disaster, a failing or an inferiority in which we take our delight. Many sights which provoke our laughter are perfectly innocent; not only the amusements of childhood, but even many of the things that tickle the palate of artists, have nothing to do with the spirit of Satan.

There is certainly some semblance of truth in that. But first of all we ought to make a proper distinction between laughter and joy. Joy exists in itself, but it has various manifestations. Sometimes it is al-

---

[11] Curious readers will find examples reproduced in Fuchs, *Geschichte der erotischen Kunst*, 1908, vol. I, book 2, 'Das Altertum.'

most invisible; at others, it expresses itself in tears. Laughter is only an expression, a symptom, a diagnostic. Symptom of what? That is the question. Joy is a unity. Laughter is the expression of a double, or contradictory, feeling; and that is the reason why a convulsion occurs. And so, the laughter of children, which I hold for a vain objection, is altogether different, even as a physical expression, even as a form, from the laughter of a man who attends a play, or who looks at a caricature, or from the terrible laughter of Melmoth—of Melmoth, the outcast of society, wandering somewhere between the last boundaries of the territory of mankind and the frontiers of the higher life; of Melmoth, who always believes himself to be on the point of freedom from his infernal pact, and longs without ceasing to barter that superhuman power, which is his disaster, for the pure conscience of a simpleton, which is his envy. For the laughter of children is like the blossoming of a flower. It is the joy of receiving, the joy of breathing, the joy of contemplating, of living, of growing. It is a vegetable joy. And so, in general, it is more like a smile—something analogous to the wagging of a dog's tail, or the purring of a cat. And if there still remains some distinction between the laughter of children and such expressions of animal contentment, I think that we should hold that this is because their laughter is not entirely exempt from ambition, as is only proper to little scraps of men—that is, to budding Satans.

But there is one case where the question is more complicated. It is the laughter of man—but a true and violent laughter—at the sight of an object which is neither a sign of weakness nor of disaster among his fellows. It is easy to guess that I am referring to the laughter caused by the grotesque. Fabulous creations, beings whose authority and *raison d'être* cannot be drawn from the code of common sense, often provoke in us an insane and excessive mirth, which expresses itself in interminable paroxysms and swoons. It is clear that a distinction must be made, and that here we have a higher degree of the phenomenon. From the artistic point of view, the comic is an imitation: the grotesque a creation. The comic is an imitation mixed with a certain creative faculty, that is to say with an artistic *ideality*. Now human pride, which always takes the upper hand and is the natural cause of laughter in the case of the comic, turns out to be the natural cause of laughter in the case of the grotesque too, for this is a creation mixed with a certain imitative faculty—imitative, that is, of elements pre-existing in nature. I mean that in this case laughter is still the expression of an idea of superiority—no longer now of man over man, but of man over nature. Do not retort that this idea is too subtle; that would be no sufficient reason for rejecting it. The difficulty is to find another plausible explanation. If this one seems far-fetched and just a little hard to accept, that is because the laughter caused by the grotesque has about it something profound, primitive and axiomatic, which is much closer to the innocent life and to absolute joy than is the laughter caused by the comic in man's behaviour. Setting aside the question of utility, there is the same difference between these two sorts of laughter as there is between the *implicated* school of writing and the school of art for art's sake. Thus the grotesque dominates the comic from a proportionate height.

From now onwards I shall call the grotesque 'the absolute comic', in antithesis to the ordinary comic, which I shall call 'the significative comic.' The latter is a clearer language, and one easier for the man in the street to understand, and above all easier to analyse, its element being visibly *double*—art and the moral idea. But the absolute comic, which comes much closer to nature, emerges as a *unity* which calls for the intuition to grasp it. There is but one criterion of the grotesque, and that is laughter—immediate laughter. Whereas with the significative comic it is quite permissible to laugh a moment late—that is no argument against its validity; it all depends upon one's quickness of analysis.

I have called it 'the absolute comic.' Nevertheless we should be on our guard. From the point of view of the definitive absolute, all that remains is *joy*. The comic can only be absolute in relation to fallen humanity, and it is in this way that I am understanding it.

VI

In its triple-distilled essence the absolute comic turns out to be the prerogative of those superior artists whose minds are sufficiently open to receive any absolute ideas at all. Thus, the man who until now has been the most sensitive to these ideas, and who set a good part of them in action in his purely aesthetic, as well as his creative work, is Theodore Hoffmann.[12] He always made a proper distinction between the ordinary comic and the type which he called 'the innocent comic.' The learned theories which he had put forth didactically, or thrown out in the form of inspired conversations or critical dialogues, he often sought to boil down into creative works; and it is from these very works that I shall shortly draw my most striking examples when I come to give a series of applications of the above-stated principles, and to pin a sample under each categorical heading.

[12] On Hoffmann, and on the particular stories which Baudelaire cites in this section, see H. W. Hewett-Thayer's *Hoffmann, Author of the Tales* (Princeton and O.U.P., 1948).

Furthermore, within the absolute and significative types of the comic we find species, sub-species and families. The division can take place on different grounds. First of all it can be established according to a pure philosophic law, as I was making a start to do: and then according to the law of artistic creation. The first is brought about by the primary separation of the absolute from the significative comic; the second is based upon the kind of special capacities possessed by each artist. And finally it is also possible to establish a classification of varieties of the comic with regard to climates and various national aptitudes. It should be observed that each term of each classification can be completed and given a *nuance* by the adjunction of a term from one of the others, just as the law of grammar teaches us to modify a noun by an adjective. Thus, any German or English artist is more or less naturally equipped for the absolute comic, and at the same time he is more or less of an idealizer. I wish now to try and give selected examples of the absolute and significative comic, and briefly to characterize the comic spirit proper to one or two eminently artistic nations, before coming on to the section in which I want to discuss and analyse at greater length the talent of those men who have made it their study and their whole existence.

If you exaggerate and push the consequences of the significative comic to their furthest limits, you reach the *savage* variety, just as the synonymous expression of the innocent variety, pushed one degree further, is the *absolute* comic.

In France, the land of lucid thought and demonstration, where the natural and direct aim of art is utility, we generally find the significative type. In this genre Molière is our best expression. But since at the root of our character there is an aversion for all extremes, and since one of the symptoms of every emotion, every science and every art in France is an avoidance of the excessive, the absolute and the profound, there is consequently but little of the savage variety to be found in this country; in the same way our grotesque seldom rises to the absolute.

Rabelais, who is the great French master of the grotesque, preserves an element of utility and reason in the very midst of his most prodigious fantasies. He is directly symbolic. His comedy nearly always possesses the transparence of an allegory. In French caricature, in the *plastic* expression of the comic, we shall find this dominant spirit. It must be admitted that the enormous poetic good humour which is required for the true grotesque is found but rarely among us in level and continuous doses. At long intervals we see the vein reappear; but it is not an essentially national one. In this context I should mention certain interludes of Molière, which are unfortunately too little read or acted—those of the *Malade Imaginaire* and the *Bourgeois Gentilhomme*, for example; and the carnivalesque figures of Callot. As for the essentially French comedy in the *Contes* of Voltaire, its *raison d'être* is always based upon the idea of superiority; it is entirely significative.

Germany, sunk in her dreams, will afford us excellent specimens of the absolute comic. There all is weighty, profound and excessive. To find true comic savagery, however, you have to cross the Channel and visit the foggy realms of spleen. Happy, noisy, carefree Italy abounds in the innocent variety. It was at the very heart of Italy, at the hub of the southern carnival, in the midst of the turbulent Corso, that Theodore Hoffmann discerningly placed his eccentric drama, *The Princess Brambilla*. The Spaniards are very well endowed in this matter. They are quick to arrive at the cruel stage, and their most grotesque fantasies often contain a dark element.

It will be a long time before I forget the first English pantomime that I saw played. It was some years ago, at the *Théâtre des Variétés*.[13] Doubtless only a few people will remember it, for very few seem to have taken to this kind of theatrical diversion, and those poor English mimes had a sad reception from us. The French public does not much like to be taken out of its element. Its taste is not very cosmopolitan, and changes of horizon upset its vision. Speaking for myself, however, I was excessively struck by their way of understanding the comic. It was said—chiefly by the indulgent, in order to explain their lack of success—that these were vulgar, mediocre artists—understudies. But that was not the point. They were English; that was the important thing.

---

[13] It has not proved possible to identify this pantomime beyond doubt, but, according to information kindly supplied by the Bibliothèque de l'Arsénal, it seems more than likely that it was a production entitled 'Arlequin, pantomime anglaise en 3 actes et 11 tableaux,' performed at the Théâtre des Variétés from the 4th until the 13th August, 1842. The newspaper *Le Corsair* (4th August) gives the following cast:—Arlequin: Howell.—Clown: Matthews (presumably the well-known clown, Tom Matthews).—Pantalon: Garders.—Colombine: Miss Maria Frood.—Une fée: Anne Plowman—Reine des fées: Emilie Fitzj (?). A review of this pantomime by Gautier, in *La Presse*, 14th Aug. 1842, has several points of agreement with Baudelaire's description. First, Gautier describes the apathy of the audience; secondly, he gives special praise to the clown's costume; finally, he refers to the incident of the clown's stealing his own head and stuffing it into his pocket (though the guillotine is not mentioned). Champfleury quotes the whole passage in his *Souvenirs des Funambules*, 1859, pp. 256–257, and provides evidence for dating the pantomime to the early 1840s when he ironically assigns the fragment to an article by Baudelaire 'sous presse depuis quinze ans seulement'.

It seemed to me that the distinctive mark of this type of the comic was *violence*. I propose to prove it with a few samples from my memories.

First of all, Pierrot was not the figure to which the late-lamented Deburau had accustomed us—that figure pale as the moon, mysterious as silence, supple and mute as the serpent, long and straight as a gibbet—that artificial man activated by eccentric springs. The English Pierrot swept upon us like a hurricane, fell down like a sack of coals, and when he laughed his laughter made the auditorium quake; his laugh was like a joyful clap of thunder. He was a short, fat man, and to increase his imposingness he wore a beribboned costume which encompassed his jubilant person as birds are encompassed with their down and feathers, or angoras with their fur. Upon his floured face he had stuck, crudely and without transition or gradation, two enormous patches of pure red. A feigned prolongation of the lips, by means of two bands of carmine, brought it about that when he laughed his mouth seemed to run from ear to ear.

As for his moral nature, it was basically the same as that of the Pierrot whom we all know—heedlessness and indifference, and consequently the gratification of every kind of greedy and rapacious whim, now at the expense of Harlequin, now of Cassandre or Léandre. The only difference was that where Deburau would just have moistened the tip of his finger with his tongue, he stuck both fists and both feet into his mouth.

And everything else in this singular piece was expressed in the same way, with passionate gusto; it was the dizzy height of hyperbole.

Pierrot walks past a woman who is scrubbing her doorstep; after rifling her pockets, he makes to stuff into his own her sponge, her mop, her bucket, water and all! As for the way in which he endeavoured to express his love to her, anyone who remembers observing the phanerogamous habits of the monkeys in their famous cage at the Jardin des Plantes can imagine it for himself. Perhaps I ought to add that the woman's role was taken by a very long, very thin man, whose outraged modesty emitted shrill screams. It was truly an intoxication of laughter—something both terrible and irresistible.

For some misdeed or other, Pierrot had in the end to be guillotined. Why the guillotine rather than the gallows, in the land of Albion? . . . I do not know; presumably to lead up to what we were to see next. Anyway, there it was, the engine of death, there, set up on the French boards which were markedly surprised at this romantic novelty. After struggling and bellowing like an ox that scents the slaughter-house, at last Pierrot bowed to his fate. His head was severed from his neck—a great red and white head, which rolled noisily to rest in front of the prompter's box, showing the bleeding disk of the neck, the split vertebrae and all the details of a piece of butcher's meat just dressed for the counter. And then, all of a sudden, the decapitated trunk, moved by its irresistible obsession with theft, jumped to its feet, triumphantly 'lifted' its own head as though it was a ham or a bottle of wine, and, with far more circumspection than the great St. Denis, proceeded to stuff it into its pocket!

Set down in pen and ink, all this is pale and chilly. But how could the pen rival the pantomime? The pantomime is the refinement, the quintessence of comedy; it is the pure comic element, purged and concentrated. Therefore, with the English actors' special talent for hyperbole, all these monstrous buffooneries took on a strangely thrilling reality.

Certainly one of the most remarkable things, in the sense of absolute comedy—or if I may call it so, the metaphysics of absolute comedy—was the beginning of this beautiful piece, a prologue filled with a high aesthetic. The principal characters, Pierrot, Cassandre, Harlequin, Colombine and Léandre are facing the public, gentle and good as gold. They are all but rational beings and do not differ much from the fine fellows in the audience. The miraculous breath which is about to inspire them to such extraordinary antics has not yet touched their brains. A few quips from Pierrot can give no more than a pale idea of what he will be doing shortly. The rivalry between Harlequin and Léandre has just declared itself. A fairy takes Harlequin's side; she is the eternal protectress of mortals who are poor and in love. She promises him her protection, and, to give him immediate proof of it, she waves her wand in the air with a mysterious and authoritative gesture.

At once a dizzy intoxication is abroad; intoxication swims in the air; we breathe intoxication; it is intoxication that fills the lungs and renews the blood in the arteries.

What is this intoxication? It is the absolute comic, and it has taken charge of each one of them. The extraordinary gestures executed by Léandre, Pierrot and Cassandre make it quite clear that they feel themselves forcibly projected into a new existence. They do not seem at all put out. They set about preparing for the great disasters and the tumultuous destiny which awaits them, like a man who spits on his hands and rubs them together before doing some heroic deed. They flourish their arms, like windmills lashed by the tempest. It must be to loosen their joints—and they will certainly need it. All this is carried out to great gusts of laughter, full of a huge contentment. Then they turn to a game of leap-frog, and once their aptitude and their agility have been duly registered, there follows a dazzling volley of kicks, punches and slaps which blaze and crash like a battery of artillery. But all of this is done in the best of spirits. Every gesture, every cry, every look seems to be saying: 'The fairy has willed it, and our fate hurls us on—it doesn't worry *me!* Come, let's get started! Let's get down to business!' And then they *do* get down to business, through the whole fantastic work, which, properly speaking, only starts at this point—that is to say, on the frontier of the marvellous.

Under cover of this hysteria, Harlequin and Colombine have danced away in flight, and with an airy foot they proceed to run the gauntlet of their adventures.

And now another example. This one is taken from a singular author—a man of ranging mind, whatever may be said, who unites to the significative mockery of France the mad, sparkling, lighthearted gaiety of the lands of the sun as well as the profound comic spirit of Germany. I am returning once again to Hoffmann.

In the story entitled *Daucus Carota, the King of the Carrots,* or by some translators *The King's Betrothed,* no sight could be more beautiful than the arrival of the great company of the Carrots in the farm-yard of the betrothed maiden's home. Look at all those little scarlet figures, like a regiment of English soldiers, with enormous green plumes on their heads, like carriage-footmen, going through a series of marvellous tricks and capers on their little horses! The whole thing is carried out with astonishing agility. The adroitness and ease with which they fall on their heads is assisted by their heads being bigger and heavier than the rest of their bodies, like those toy soldiers made of elderpith, which have lead weights in their caps.

The unfortunate young girl, obsessed with dreams of grandeur, is fascinated by this display of military might. But an army on parade is one thing; how different an army in barracks, furbishing its arms, polishing its equipment, or, worse still, ignobly snoring on its dirty, stinking campbeds! That is the reverse of the medal; the rest was but a magic trick, an apparatus of seduction. But her father, who is a wise man and well versed in sorcery, wants to show her the other side of all this magnificence. Thus, at an hour when the vegetables are sleeping their brutish sleep, never suspecting that any spy could catch them unawares, he lifts the flap of one of the tents of this splendid army. Then it is that the poor dreaming girl sees all this mass of red and green soldiery in its appalling undress, wallowing and snoring in the filthy midden from which it first emerged. In its night-cap all that military magnificence is nothing more than a putrid swamp.

There are many other examples of the absolute comic that I might take from the admirable Hoffmann. Anyone who really wants to understand what I have in mind should read with care *Daucus Carota,* *Peregrinus Tyss, The Golden Pot,* and over and above all, *The Princess Brambilla,* which is like a catechism of high aesthetics. What pre-eminently distinguishes Hoffmann in his unintentional—and sometimes very intentional—blending of a certain measure of the significative comic with the most absolute variety. His most supernatural and fugitive comic conceptions, which are often like the visions of a drunken man, have a very conspicuous moral meaning; you might imagine that you had to do with the profoundest type of physiologist or alienist who was amusing himself by clothing his deep wisdom in poetic forms, like a learned man who might speak in parables and allegories.

Take for example, if you will, the character of Giglio Fava, the actor who suffered from a chronic dualism, in *The Princess Brambilla.* This *single* character changes personality from time to time. Under the name of Giglio Fava he swears enmity for the Assyrian prince, Cornelio Chiapperi; but when he is himself the Assyrian prince, he pours forth his deepest and the most regal scorn upon his rival for the hand of the Princess—upon a wretched mummer whose name, they say, is Giglio Fava.

I should perhaps add that one of the most distinctive marks of the absolute comic is that it remains unaware of itself. This is evident not only in certain animals, like monkeys, in whose comicality gravity plays an essential part, nor only in certain antique sculptural caricatures of which I have already spoken, but even in those Chinese monstrosities which delight us so much and whose intentions are far less comic than people generally think. A Chinese idol, although it be an object of veneration, looks very little different from a tumble-toy or a pot-bellied chimney-ornament.

And so, to be finished with all these subtleties and all these definitions, let me point out, once more and for the last time, that the dominant idea of superiority is found in the absolute, no less than in the significative comic, as I have already explained (at too great a length, perhaps): further, that in order to enable a comic emanation, explosion, or, as it were, a chemical separation of the comic to come about, there must be two beings face to face with one another: again, that the special abode of the comic is in the laugher, the spectator: and finally, that an exception must nevertheless be made in connection with the 'law of ignorance' for those men who have made a business of developing in themselves their feeling for the comic, and of dispensing it for the amusement of their fellows. This last phenomenon comes into the class of all artistic phenomena which indicate the existence of a permanent dualism in the human being—that is, the power of being oneself and someone else at one and the same time.

And so, to return to my primary definitions and to express myself more clearly, I would say that when Hoffmann gives birth to the absolute comic it is perfectly true that he knows what he is doing; but he also knows that the essence of this type of the comic is that it should appear to be unaware of itself and that it should produce in the spectator, or rather the reader, a joy in his own superiority and in the superiority of man over nature. Artists create the comic; after collecting and studying its elements, they know that such-and-such a being is comic, and that it is so only on condition of its being unaware of its nature, in the same way that, following an inverse law, an artist is only an artist on condition that he is a double man and that there is not one single phenomenon of his double nature of which he is ignorant.

From

An Essay on Comedy*

GEORGE MEREDITH

There are plain reasons why the comic poet is not a frequent apparition, and why the great comic poet remains without a fellow. A
society of cultivated men and women is required, wherein ideas are
current, and the perceptions quick, that he may be supplied with matter and an audience. The semi-barbarism of merely giddy communities, and feverish emotional periods, repel him; and also a state of
marked social inequality of the sexes; nor can he whose business is
to address the mind be understood where there is not a moderate
degree of intellectual activity.

Moreover, to touch and kindle the mind through laughter demands,
more than sprightliness, a most subtle delicacy. That must be a natal
gift in the comic poet. The substance he deals with will show him
a startling exhibition of the dyer's hand, if he is without it. People
are ready to surrender themselves to witty thumps on the back, breast,
and sides; all except the head—and it is there that he aims. He must
be subtle to penetrate. A corresponding acuteness must exist to welcome him. The necessity for the two conditions will explain how it
is that we count him during centuries in the singular number. . . .
Life, we know too well, is not a comedy, but something strangely
mixed; nor is comedy a vile mask. The corrupted importation from
France was noxious, a noble entertainment spoilt to suit the wretched
taste of a villainous age; and the later imitations of it, partly drained
of its poison and made decorous, became tiresome, notwithstanding

---

* George Meredith, "An Essay on Comedy" [1877], collected works first
published by Chapman & Hall, 1885–1895.

their fun, in the perpetual recurring of the same situations, owing to the absence of original study and vigor of conception. Scene 5, Act 2, of the *Misanthrope*, owing, no doubt, to the fact of our not producing matter for original study, is repeated in succession by Wycherley, Congreve, and Sheridan, and, as it is at second hand, we have it done cynically—or such is the tone—in the manner of "below stairs." Comedy thus treated may be accepted as a version of the ordinary worldly understanding of our social life; at least, in accord with the current dicta concerning it. The epigrams can be made; but it is uninstructive, rather tending to do disservice. Comedy justly treated, as you find it in Molière, whom we so clownishly mishandled—the comedy of Molière throws no infamous reflection upon life. It is deeply conceived, in the first place, and therefore it cannot be impure. Meditate on that statement. Never did man wield so shrieking a scourge upon vice; but his consummate self-mastery is not shaken while administering it. Tartuffe and Harpagon, in fact, are made each to whip himself and his class—the false pietists, and the insanely covetous. Molière has only set them in motion. He strips Folly to the skin, displays the imposture of the creature, and is content to offer her better clothing, with the lesson Chrysale reads to Philaminte and Bélise. He conceives purely, and he writes purely, in the simplest language, the simplest of French verse. The source of his wit is clear reason; it is a fountain of that soil, and it springs to vindicate reason, common sense, rightness, and justice—for no vain purpose ever. The wit is of such pervading spirit that it inspires a pun with meaning and interest. His moral does not hang like a tail, or preach from one character incessantly cocking an eye at the audience, as in recent realistic French plays, but is in the heart of his work, throbbing with every pulsation of an organic structure. If life is likened to the comedy of Molière, there is no scandal in the comparison.

Congreve's *Way of the World* is an exception to our other comedies, his own among them, by virtue of the remarkable brilliancy of the writing, and the figure of Millamant. The comedy has no idea in it, beyond the stale one that so the world goes; and it concludes with the jaded discovery of a document at a convenient season for the descent of the curtain. A plot was an afterthought with Congreve. By the help of a wooden villain (Maskwell), marked gallows to the flattest eye, he gets a sort of plot in *The Double-Dealer*. His *Way of the World* might be called "The Conquest of a Town Coquette"; and Millamant is a perfect portrait of a coquette, both in her resistance to Mirabell and the manner of her surrender, and also in her tongue. The wit here is not so salient as in certain passages of *Love for Love,*

where Valentine feigns madness, or retorts on his father, or Mrs. Frail
rejoices in the harmlessness of wounds to a woman's virtue, if she
keeps them "from air." In *The Way of the World,* it appears less prepared in the smartness, and is more diffused in the more characteristic
style of the speakers. Here, however, as elsewhere, his famous wit is
like a bullyfencer, not ashamed to lay traps for its exhibition, trans-
parently petulant for the train between certain ordinary words and
the powder-magazine of the improprieties to be fired. Contrast the
wit of Congreve with Molière's. That of the first is a Toledo blade,
sharp, and wonderfully supple for steel; cast for dueling, restless in the
scabbard, being so pretty when out of it. To shine, it must have an
adversary. Molière's wit is like a running brook, with innumerable
fresh lights on it at every turn of the wood through which its business is to find a way. It does not run in search of obstructions, to
be noisy over them; but when dead leaves and viler substances are
heaped along the course, its natural song is heightened. Without effort,
and with no dazzling flashes of achievement, it is full of healing, the
wit of good breeding, the wit of wisdom.

"Genuine humor and true wit," says Landor, "require a sound and
capacious mind, which is always a grave one." . . . The life of the
comedy is in the idea. As with the singing of the skylark out of
sight, you must love the bird to be attentive to the song, so in this
highest flight of the comic Muse, you must love pure comedy warmly
to understand the *Misanthrope;* you must be receptive of the idea of
comedy. And to love comedy you must know the real world, and know
men and women well enough not to expect too much of them, though
you may still hope for good. . . .

Now, to look about us in the present time, I think it will be
acknowledged that, in neglecting the cultivation of the comic idea,
we are losing the aid of a powerful auxiliar. You see Folly perpetually
sliding into new shapes in a society possessed of wealth and leisure,
with many whims, many strange ailments and strange doctors. Plenty
of common sense is in the world to thrust her back when she pretends
to empire. But the first-born of common sense, the vigilant Comic,
which is the genius of thoughtful laughter, which would readily extinguish her at the outset, is not serving as a public advocate.

You will have noticed the disposition of common sense, under pressure of some pertinacious piece of light-headedness, to grow impatient
and angry. That is a sign of the absence, or at least of the dor-
mancy, of the comic idea. For Folly is the natural prey of the Comic,
known to it in all her transformations, in every disguise; and it is
with the springing delight of hawk over heron, hound after fox, that

it gives her chase, never fretting, never tiring, sure of having her, allowing her no rest.

Contempt is a sentiment that cannot be entertained by comic intelligence. What is it but an excuse to be idly-minded, or personally lofty, or comfortably narrow, not perfectly humane? If we do not feign when we say that we despise Folly, we shut the brain. There is a disdainful attitude in the presence of Folly, partaking of the foolishness to comic perception; and anger is not much less foolish than disdain. The struggle we have to conduct is essence against essence. Let no one doubt of the sequel when this emanation of what is firmest in us is launched to strike down the daughter of Unreason and Sentimentalism—such being Folly's parentage, when it is respectable.

Our modern system of combating her is too long defensive, and carried on too ploddingly with concrete engines of war in the attack. She has time to get behind entrenchments. She is ready to stand a siege, before the heavily-armed man of science and the writer of the leading article or elaborate essay have primed their big guns. It should be remembered that she has charms for the multitude; and an English multitude, seeing her make a gallant fight of it, will be half in love with her, certainly willing to lend her a cheer. Benevolent subscriptions assist her to hire her own man of science, her own organ in the press. If ultimately she is cast out and overthrown, she can stretch a finger at gaps in our ranks. She can say that she commanded an army, and seduced men, whom we thought sober men and safe, to act as her lieutenants. We learn rather gloomily, after she has flashed her lantern, that we have in our midst able men, and men with minds, for whom there is no pole-star in intellectual navigation. Comedy, or the comic element, is the specific for the poison of delusion while Folly is passing from the state of vapor to substantial form. . . .

The comic poet is in the narrow field, or enclosed square, of the society he depicts; and he addresses the still narrower enclosure of men's intellects, with reference to the operation of the social world upon their characters. He is not concerned with beginnings or endings or surroundings, but with what you are now weaving. To understand his work and value it, you must have a sober liking of your kind, and a sober estimate of our civilized qualities. The aim and business of the comic poet are misunderstood, his meaning is not seized nor his point of view taken, when he is accused of dishonoring our nature and being hostile to sentiment, tending to spitefulness and making an unfair use of laughter. Those who detect irony in comedy do so because they choose to see it in life. Poverty, says the satirist, 'has nothing harder in itself than that it makes men ridiculous.' But poverty is never ridiculous to comic perception until it attempts to make its rags conceal its bareness in a forlorn attempt at decency, or foolishly to rival ostentation. Caleb Balderstone, in his endeavor to keep up the honor of a noble household in a state of beggary, is an exquisitely comic character. In the case of "poor relatives," on the other hand, it is the rich, whom they perplex, that are really comic; and to laugh at the former, not seeing the comedy of the latter, is to betray dulness of vision. Humorist and satirist frequently hunt together as ironists in pursuit of the grotesque, to the exclusion of the comic. That was an affecting moment in the history of the Prince Regent, when the First Gentleman of Europe burst into tears at a sarcastic remark of Beau Brummell's on the cut of his coat. Humor, satire, irony, pounce on it altogether as their common prey. The Comic Spirit eyes, but does not touch, it. Put into action, it would be farcical. It is too gross for comedy.

Incidents of a kind casting ridicule on our unfortunate nature, instead of our conventional life, provoke derisive laughter, which thwarts the comic idea. But derision is foiled by the play of the intellect. Most of doubtful causes in contest are open to comic interpretation, and any intellectual pleading of a doubtful cause contains germs of an idea of comedy.

The laughter of satire is a blow in the back or the face. The laughter of comedy is impersonal and of unrivaled politeness, nearer a smile—often no more than a smile. It laughs through the mind, for the mind directs it; and it might be called the humor of the mind.

One excellent test of the civilization of a country, as I have said, I take to be the flourishing of the comic idea and comedy; and the test of true comedy is that it shall awaken thoughtful laughter.

From
Laughter*

HENRI BERGSON

THE COMIC IN GENERAL—THE COMIC ELEMENT IN FORMS AND MOVEMENTS—EXPANSIVE FORCE OF THE COMIC

What does laughter mean? What is the basal element in the laughable? What common ground can we find between the grimace of a merry-andrew, a play upon words, an equivocal situation in a burlesque and a scene of high comedy? What method of distillation will yield us invariably the same essence from which so many different products borrow either their obtrusive odour or their delicate perfume? The greatest of thinkers, from Aristotle downwards, have tackled this little problem, which has a knack of baffling every effort, of slipping away and escaping only to bob up again, a pert challenge flung at philosophic speculation.

Our excuse for attacking the problem in our turn must lie in the fact that we shall not aim at imprisoning the comic spirit within a definition. We regard it, above all, as a living thing. However trivial it may be, we shall treat it with the respect due to life. We shall confine ourselves to watching it grow and expand. Passing by imperceptible gradations from one form to another, it will be seen to achieve the strangest metamorphoses. We shall disdain nothing we have seen. Maybe we may gain from this prolonged contact, for the matter of that, something more flexible than an abstract definition,— a practical, intimate acquaintance, such as springs from a long companionship. And maybe we may also find that, unintentionally, we

---

* Henri Bergson, from "Laughter" [1900], Fred Rothwell, tr., in *Comedy,* Wylie Sypher, ed. (Doubleday & Company, 1956).

have made an acquaintance that is useful. For the comic spirit has a logic of its own, even in its wildest eccentricities. It has a method in its madness. It dreams, I admit, but it conjures up in its dreams visions that are at once accepted and understood by the whole of a social group. Can it then fail to throw light for us on the way that human imagination works, and more particularly social, collective, and popular imagination? Begotten of real life and akin to art, should it not also have something of its own to tell us about art and life?

At the outset we shall put forward three observations which we look upon as fundamental. They have less bearing on the actually comic than on the field within which it must be sought.

The first point to which attention should be called is that the comic does not exist outside the pale of what is strictly *human*. A landscape may be beautiful, charming and sublime, or insignificant and ugly; it will never be laughable. You may laugh at an animal, but only because you have detected in it some human attitude or expression. You may laugh at a hat, but what you are making fun of, in this case, is not the piece of felt or straw, but the shape that men have given it,—the human caprice whose mould it has assumed. It is strange that so important a fact, and such a simple one too, has not attracted to a greater degree the attention of philosophers. Several have defined man as "an animal which laughs." They might equally well have defined him as an animal which is laughed at; for if any other animal, or some lifeless object, produces the same effect, it is always because of some resemblance to man, of the stamp he gives it or the use he puts it to.

Here I would point out, as a symptom equally worthy of notice, the *absence of feeling* which usually accompanies laughter. It seems as though the comic could not produce its disturbing effect unless it fell, so to say, on the surface of a soul that is thoroughly calm and unruffled. Indifference is its natural environment, for laughter has no greater foe than emotion. I do not mean that we could not laugh at a person who inspires us with pity, for instance, or even with affection, but in such a case we must, for the moment, put our affection out of court and impose silence upon our pity. In a society composed of pure intelligences there would probably be no more tears, though perhaps there would still be laughter; whereas highly emotional souls, in tune and unison with life, in whom every event would be sentimentally prolonged and re-echoed, would neither know nor understand laughter. Try, for a moment, to become interested in everything that

is being said and done; act, in imagination, with those who act, and
feel with those who feel; in a word, give your sympathy its widest
expansion: as though at the touch of a fairy wand you will see the
flimsiest of objects assume importance, and a gloomy hue spread over
everything. Now step aside, look upon life as a disinterested spectator:
many a drama will turn into a comedy. It is enough for us to stop
our ears to the sound of music in a room, where dancing is going
on, for the dancers at once to appear ridiculous. How many human
actions would stand a similar test? Should we not see many of them
suddenly pass from grave to gay, on isolating them from the accompanying music of sentiment? To produce the whole of its effect, then,
the comic demands something like a momentary anesthesia of the
heart. Its appeal is to intelligence, pure and simple.

This intelligence, however, must always remain in touch with other
intelligences. And here is the third fact to which attention should be
drawn. You would hardly appreciate the comic if you felt yourself
isolated from others. Laughter appears to stand in need of an echo.
Listen to it carefully: it is not an articulate, clear, well-defined sound;
it is something which would fain be prolonged by reverberating from
one to another, something beginning with a crash, to continue in
successive rumblings, like thunder in a mountain. Still, this reverber-
ation cannot go on for ever. It can travel within as wide a circle
as you please: the circle remains, none the less, a closed one. Our
laughter is always the laughter of a group. It may, perchance, have
happened to you, when seated in a railway carriage or at *table d'hôte,*
to hear travellers relating to one another stories which must have
been comic to them, for they laughed heartily. Had you been one of
their company, you would have laughed like them, but, as you were
not, you had no desire whatever to do so. A man who was once
asked why he did not weep at a sermon when everybody else was
shedding tears replied: "I don't belong to the parish!" What that
man thought of tears would be still more true of laughter. However spontaneous it seems, laughter always implies a kind of secret freemasonry,
or even complicity, with other laughers, real or imaginary. How often
has it been said that the fuller the theatre, the more uncontrolled
the laughter of the audience! On the other hand, how often has the
remark been made that many comic effects are incapable of translation from one language to another, because they refer to the customs
and ideas of a particular social group! It is through not understanding the importance of this double fact that the comic has been looked
upon as a mere curiosity in which the mind finds amusement, and

laughter itself as a strange, isolated phenomenon, without any bearing on the rest of human activity. Hence those definitions which tend to make the comic into an abstract relation between ideas: "an intellectual contrast," "a patent absurdity," etc., definitions which, even were they really suitable to every form of the comic, would not in the least explain why the comic makes us laugh. How, indeed, should it come about that this particular logical relation, as soon as it is perceived, contracts, expands and shakes our limbs, whilst all other relations leave the body unaffected? It is not from this point of view that we shall approach the problem. To understand laughter, we must put it back into its natural environment, which is society, and above all must we determine the utility of its function, which is a social one. Such, let us say at once, will be the leading idea of all our investigations. Laughter must answer to certain requirements of life in common. It must have a *social* signification.

Let us clearly mark the point towards which our three preliminary observations are converging. The comic will come into being, it appears, whenever a group of men concentrate their attention on one of their number, imposing silence on their emotions and calling into play nothing but their intelligence. . . .

Before going further, let us halt a moment and glance around. As we hinted at the outset of this study, it would be idle to attempt to derive every comic effect from one simple formula. The formula exists well enough in a certain sense, but its development does not follow a straightforward course. What I mean is that the process of deduction ought from time to time to stop and study certain culminating effects, and that these effects each appear as models round which new effects resembling them take their places in a circle. These latter are not deductions from the formula, but are comic through their relationship with those that are. To quote Pascal again, I see no objection, at this stage, to defining the process by the curve which that geometrician studied under the name of *roulette* or cycloid—the curve traced by a point in the circumference of a wheel when the carriage is advancing in a straight line: this point turns like the wheel, though it advances like the carriage. Or else we might think of an immense avenue such as are to be seen in the forest of Fontainebleau, with *crosses* at intervals to indicate the crossways: at each of these we shall walk round the cross, explore for a while the paths that open out before us, and then return to our original course. Now, we have just reached one of these mental crossways. *Something mechanical encrusted on the living* will represent a cross at which we must halt, a central image from which the imagination branches off in different directions. What are these directions? There appear to be three main ones. We will follow them one after the other, and then continue our onward course.

1. In the first place, this view of the mechanical and the living dovetailed into each other makes us incline towards the vaguer image of *some rigidity or other* applied to the mobility of life, in an awkward attempt to follow its lines and counterfeit its suppleness. Here we perceive how easy it is for a garment to become ridiculous. It might almost be said that every fashion is laughable in some respect. Only, when we are dealing with the fashion of the day, we are so accustomed to it that the garment seems, in our mind, to form one with the individual wearing it. We do not separate them in imagination. The idea no longer occurs to us to contrast the inert rigidity of the covering with the living suppleness of the object covered: consequently, the comic here remains in a latent condition. It will only succeed in emerging when the natural incompatibility is so deep-seated between the covering and the covered that even an immemorial association fails to cement this union: a case in point is our head and top hat. Suppose, however, some eccentric individual dresses himself in the fashion of former times our attention is immediately drawn to the clothes themselves; we absolutely distinguish them from the individual, we say that the latter *is disguising himself,*—as though every article of clothing were not a disguise!—and the laughable aspect of fashion comes out of the shadow into the light.

Here we are beginning to catch a faint glimpse of the highly intricate difficulties raised by this problem of the comic. One of the reasons that must have given rise to many erroneous or unsatisfactory theories of laughter is that many things are comic *de jure* without being comic *de facto,* the continuity of custom having deadened within them the comic quality. A sudden dissolution of continuity is needed, a break with fashion, for this quality to revive. Hence the impression that this dissolution of continuity is the parent of the comic, whereas all it does is to bring it to our notice. Hence, again, the explanation of laughter by *surprise, contrast,* etc., definitions which would equally apply to a host of cases in which we have no inclination whatever to laugh. The truth of the matter is far from being so simple. . . .

2. Our starting-point is again "something mechanical encrusted upon the living." Where did the comic come from in this case? It came from the fact that the living body became rigid, like a machine. Accordingly, it seemed to us that the living body ought to be the perfection of suppleness, the ever-alert activity of a principle always at

work. But this activity would really belong to the soul rather than to the body. It would be the very flame of life, kindled within us by a higher principle and perceived through the body, as though through a glass. When we see only gracefulness and suppleness in the living body, it is because we disregard in it the elements of weight, of resistance, and, in a word, of matter; we forget its materiality and think only of its vitality, a vitality which we regard as derived from the very principle of intellectual and moral life. Let us suppose, however, that our attention is drawn to this material side of the body; that, so far from sharing in the lightness and subtlety of the principle with which it is animated, the body is no more in our eyes than a heavy and cumbersome vesture, a kind of irksome ballast which holds down to earth a soul eager to rise aloft. Then the body will become to the soul what, as we have just seen, the garment was to the body itself—inert matter dumped down upon living energy. The impression of the comic will be produced as soon as we have a clear apprehension of this putting the one on the other. And we shall experience it most strongly when we are shown the soul *tantalised* by the needs of the body: on the one hand, the moral personality with its intelligently varied energy, and, on the other, the stupidly monotonous body, perpetually obstructing everything with its machine-like obstinacy. The more paltry and uniformly repeated these claims of the body, the more striking will be the result. But that is only a matter of degree, and the general law of these phenomena may be formulated as follows: *Any incident is comic that calls our attention to the physical in a person, when it is the moral side that is concerned.* . . .

3. Let us then return, for the last time, to our central image—something mechanical encrusted on something living. Here, the living being under discussion was a human being, a person. A mechanical arrangement, on the other hand, is a thing. What, therefore, incited laughter, was the momentary transformation of a person into a thing, if one considers the image from this standpoint. Let us then pass from the exact idea of a machine to the vaguer one of a thing in general. We shall have a fresh series of laughable images which will be obtained by taking a blurred impression, so to speak, of the outlines of the former and will bring us to this new law: *We laugh every time a person gives us the impression of being a thing.* . . . The comic is that side of a person which reveals his likeness to a thing, that aspect of human events which, through its peculiar inelasticity, conveys the impression of pure mechanism, of automatism, of movement without life. Consequently it expresses an individual or collective imperfection which calls for an immediate corrective. This corrective is laughter,

a social gesture that singles out and represses a special kind of absent-mindedness in men and in events. . . .

Hence the equivocal nature of the comic. It belongs neither altogether to art nor altogether to life. On the one hand, characters in real life would never make us laugh were we not capable of watching their vagaries in the same way as we look down at a play from our seat in a box; they are only comic in our eyes because they perform a kind of comedy before us. But, on the other hand, the pleasure caused by laughter, even on the stage, is not an unadulterated enjoyment; it is not a pleasure that is exclusively esthetic or altogether disinterested. It always implies a secret or unconscious intent, if not of each one of us, at all events of society as a whole. In laughter we always find an unavowed intention to humiliate, and consequently to correct our neighbour, if not in his will, at least in his deed. This is the reason a comedy is far more like real life than a drama is. The more sublime the drama, the more profound the analysis to which the poet has had to subject the raw materials of daily life in order to obtain the tragic element in its unadulterated form. On the contrary, it is only in its lower aspects, in light comedy and farce, that comedy is in striking contrast to reality: the higher it rises, the more it approximates to life; in fact, there are scenes in real life so closely bordering on high-class comedy that the stage might adopt them without changing a single word.

Selected Bibliography

There has been no attempt to make this bibliography as inclusive as possible. To do so would require a volume in itself. The books and articles listed here, in addition to the sources used for the text (listed elsewhere), constitute a basic working bibliography for all students interested in the subject of comedy. I have divided the bibliography so that it more or less corresponds to the divisions which I have established in the text. For a more extensive bibliography, the student is advised to check those included in several of the books listed under the heading of "General Books on Comedy," and also Chapter 15 of *Contemporary Literary Scholarship* edited by Lewis Leary.

General Books on Comedy

Cook, Albert S. *The Dark Voyage and the Golden Mean,* Cambridge, Mass., 1949.
Eastman, Max. *The Enjoyment of Laughter,* New York, 1936.
Enck, John J., Elizabeth T. Forter, and Alvin Whitley (Eds.). *The Comic in Theory and Practice,* New York, 1960.
Feibleman, James K. *In Praise of Comedy,* London, 1939.
Kronenberger, Louis. *The Thread of Laughter,* New York, 1952.
Lauter, Paul (Ed.). *Theories of Comedy,* New York, 1964.
Palmer, John. *Comedy,* New York, 1915.
Perry, H. T. E. *Masters of Dramatic Comedy,* Cambridge, Mass., 1939.
Thompson, A. R. *The Anatomy of Drama,* Berkeley, 1942.
Tynan, Kenneth. *Curtains,* New York, 1961.

The Spirit of Comedy

Chapman, John Jay. "The Comic," *Hibbert Journal,* 1909.
Emerson, Ralph Waldo. "The Comic," *Complete Essays,* New York, 1940.
Feibleman, James K. "The Meaning of Comedy," *Aesthetics,* New York, 1949.
Guthrie, William N. "A Theory of the Comic," *The International Quarterly,* 1903.
Huizinga, Johan. *Homo Ludens,* London, 1949.
White, E. B. "Some Remarks on Humor," *The Second Tree from the Corner,* New York, 1954.

The Form of Comedy

Cornford, Francis. *The Origin of Attic Comedy,* Cambridge, 1914.
Frye, Northrop. "The Argument of Comedy," *English Institute Essays: 1948,* New York, 1949.
Harrison, Jane. *Themis,* Cambridge, 1912, 1927.

The Characteristics of Comedy

Beerbohm, Max. *And Even Now,* New York, 1921.
Behrman, S. N. "What Makes Comedy High?" *New York Times,* 1952.
Courtney, W. L. "The Idea of Comedy," *Fortnightly Review,* 1914.
Seward, Samuel S. *The Paradox of the Ludicrous,* London, 1930.
Stoll, E. E. "The Comic Method," *Shakespeare Studies,* New York, 1927.
Vexler, Julius. "The Essence of Comedy," *Sewanee Review,* 1935.

The Nature of Comedy

Duerrenmatt, Friedrich. "Problems of the Theatre," *Tulane Drama Review,* 1958.
Eberhart, Richard. "Tragedy as Limitation: Comedy as Control and Resolution," *Tulane Drama Review,* 1962.
Lipps, Theodor. *The Foundations of Aesthetics,* London, 1903.
Myers, Henry A. "An Analysis of Laughter," *Sewanee Review,* 1938.
Smith, Willard M. *The Nature of Comedy,* New York, 1930.
Thompson, A. R. *The Dry Mock,* Berkeley, 1948.
Welsford, Enid. *The Fool, His Social and Literary History,* London, 1935.

The Psychology of Comedy

Bergler, Edmund. *Laughter and the Sense of Humor,* New York, 1956.
Brody, Morris W. "The Meaning of Laughter," *Psychoanalytic Quarterly,* 1950.
Ferenczi, Sandor. "The Psychoanalysis of Wit and the Comical," *Further Contributions to Psychoanalysis,* London, 1950.
Greig, J. Y. T. *The Psychology of Laughter and Comedy,* London, 1923.
Kris, Ernst. "Ego Development and the Comic," *International Journal of Psycho-Analysis,* 1938.
Kris, Ernst. *Psychoanalytic Explorations in Art,* London, 1952.
Piddington, Ralph. *The Psychology of Laughter,* London, 1933.

On Farce and Satire

Bentley, Eric. "The Psychology of Farce," *Let's Get a Divorce,* New York, 1958.
Cannon, Gilbert. *Satire,* New York, 1915.
Ionesco, Eugène. *Notes and Counternotes,* New York, 1964.
Kernan, Alan. *The Cankered Muse,* New Haven, 1950.
Worcester, David. *The Art of Satire,* Cambridge, Mass., 1940.

The Criticism of Comedy

Bentley, Eric. *Bernard Shaw,* New York, 1957.

Brown, John Russell. *Shakespeare and His Comedies,* London, 1957.

Casson, Lionel. *Masters of Ancient Comedy,* New York, 1960.

Coghill, Nevill. "The Basis of Shakespearian Comedy," *Essays and Studies,* 1950.

Cooper, Lane. *An Aristotelian Theory of Comedy,* New York, 1922.

Corrigan, Robert W. "The Theatre In Search Of A Fix," *Tulane Drama Review,* 1961.

Dean, Leonard F. (Ed.). *Shakespeare: Modern Essays in Criticism,* New York, 1957.

Dobrée, Bonamy. *Restoration Comedy,* Oxford, 1924.

Esslin, Martin. *The Theatre of the Absurd,* New York, 1961.

Fergusson, Francis. *The Idea of a Theater,* Princeton, 1949.

Fernandez, Ramon. *Molière, the Man Seen through the Plays,* New York, 1958.

Fujimura, Thomas H. *The Restoration Comedy of Wit,* Princeton, 1952.

Kronenberger, Louis (Ed.). *George Bernard Shaw: A Critical Survey,* New York, 1953.

Murray, Gilbert. *The Classical Tradition in Poetry,* London, 1927.

Sharp, William. "Getting Married: New Dramaturgy in Comedy," *Educational Theatre Journal,* 1959.

Wilcox, John. *The Relation of Molière to Restoration Comedy,* New York, 1938.

Wimsatt, W. K. (Ed.). "English Stage Comedy," *English Institute Essays: 1954,* New York, 1955.